SIXTEEN TONS

SIXTEEN TONS

THE MERLE TRAVIS STORY

**MERLE TRAVIS
& DEKE DICKERSON**

BMG

Sixteen Tons:
The Merle Travis Story

Book production by Adept Content Solutions.

Cover design by Patrick Crowley.
Cover image courtesy of Deke Dickerson.
All other images courtesy of Merlene Travis-Maggini and Cindy Lee Travis unless otherwise indicated.

Library of Congress Cataloging-in-Publication Data available upon request.

Hardback ISBN: 9781947026582
Ebook ISBN: 9781947026599

First printing
Published by BMG

bmg.com

CONTENTS

PREFACE

Merle Travis was, without a doubt, one of the greatest musical talents this country has ever known. He has never been forgotten. Since his death in 1983, a constant new crop of young fans and musicians have become intimately familiar with his work thanks to regular reissues of his music and guitar enthusiasts' never-ending attempts to master his namesake thumb-picking style.

Yet despite his long career, hit records, fantastic showmanship, and excellent songwriting abilities, there hasn't been a Merle Travis biography. The one attempt, in the booklet accompanying the Merle Travis CD box set released by Bear Family in 1994, was woefully incomplete since it only covered Travis's life and career through 1955. This was a huge injustice, and I felt compelled to rectify the situation. I resolved to undertake the writing of a comprehensive Merle Travis biography. But time had been an enemy, and I feared that it might not be possible to tell Merle's story fully. He died long enough ago that virtually all his contemporaries are deceased. The proper moment to do a biography would have been when he was still alive, his childhood friends were still around, his music industry peers were still active, and his fame was still a recent memory in the hearts of his fanbase. Undaunted, I decided to talk to Merle's surviving daughters, Merlene and Cindy, about my idea. I discovered a wonderful surprise: they were sitting on a gold mine of documentation. They had saved everything after Merle's last wife, Dorothy, passed away in 1991, and it was all in a storage facility in Santa Barbara. Did I want to take a look? Of course I did.

When I met with Merlene and Cindy, they told me something no one else knew: Merle had written quite a lot of autobiographical material before he died. Letters from publishers reveal that there was interest in a Travis autobiography in the late 1970s. He never finished the project, but he'd left a hundred or so pages of (raw, unedited, incomplete, unorganized) writing. I was floored. It was exactly what was needed to fill in the gaps where death and time had swallowed memories.

There were also hundreds of short stories, poems, song lyrics, love letters, family letters, fan letters, and miscellaneous notes. There were literally thousands of photographs. There were scrapbooks full of posters, newspaper articles, and promotional materials. There were reel-to-reel tapes with interviews and unreleased performances. There were vintage Nudie suits and boots and guitars and amps. There was a nine-page list of "life events" that Travis had scribbled down in the 1970s that constituted the most accurate (and honest) accounting of his life's memories. The Merle Travis book was all in there—it just needed to be written. It needed a curator, someone to come in and organize the jumble, to recognize the obscure faces in the old photographs and make sense of it all. That's where I came in.

What had started with a vague worry that there would not be enough to fill a book quickly turned into a very real worry that there was too much great stuff, an overload of information. It was a transformation from famine to feast. When writing a biography of someone who passed away almost forty years ago, there are far worse problems to have.

I can't thank Merlene and Cindy enough for preserving this material. In particular, Cindy spent a great deal of time organizing everything, which made my job infinitely easier. After a book deal was signed through the tireless historian and publisher Scott B. Bomar with BMG Books, I borrowed a literal truckload of material from the Santa Barbara storage unit and got to work.

My regular job as a touring musician allowed me to meet personally with many of those still alive who had known Merle well. Getting to sit down with these octogenarians and nonagenarians brought the story to life. I'm glad I started when I did because at least eight of my interviewees—Jack Rogers, Herb Remington, Claude Travis, Gary Williams, Ray Campi, Jimmy Capps, Bobby Anderson and Rose Lee Maphis—have passed away since I spoke with them. One regret was not interviewing people I had met years earlier—Wesley Tuttle, Hank Penny, Lorrie Collins, among others—who passed away before the book project got underway.

I also discovered that three historians had done much research on Merle Travis and left their archives for unknown future interested parties to access after they had passed on. Although I am unable to thank them in person, I am eternally grateful for the work that Ed Kahn, Archie Green, and Charles K. Wolfe did before me, and to the Southern Folklife Collection at the University of North Carolina, Chapel Hill, and the Center for Popular Music at Middle Tennessee State University for allowing me access to these archives.

The book you hold is, partially, Merle Travis's autobiography. My job has been to finish his life story—to fill in the blanks (which were many), explain why certain things mattered, and put it all in the proper context of its time and place.

My goal throughout has been to demonstrate, to even a contemporary reader with no idea who Merle Travis was, his greatness and rightful spot in music history. After diving into the deep end, becoming engrossed in every scrap of paper, every second of music, and obsessing over the complicated, difficult, and fascinating personal life of Merle Travis, I hope I have done his story justice. I'm honored to be the one to tell it.

—Deke Dickerson
Northridge, California

Merle (right) and his brother John Melvin demonstrate proper
Muhlenberg County thumb-picking technique as young teenagers,
early 1930s.

CHAPTER 1

MUHLENBERG COUNTY, KENTUCKY

The book you hold is the life story of one of America's foremost musical legends, Merle Travis. His story is complex and multilayered. It stretches from the rolling hills of his native Kentucky all the way to Hollywood, California; Nashville, Tennessee; and the Cherokee Nation in Oklahoma. Along the way, Merle wrote several songs that became beloved folk standards, popularized and refined a regional guitar style that now bears his name, recorded an impressive body of work that still astounds listeners today, and entertained people for decades both through live performances and in recordings for radio, television, and motion pictures. Along the way, he befriended and worked with other legends like Johnny Cash, Grandpa

1

Jones, Gene Autry, Johnny Mercer, Lead Belly, Chet Atkins, Tex Ritter, Hank Thompson, Joe and Rose Lee Maphis, B. B. King, the Nitty Gritty Dirt Band, Doc Watson, and Dolly Parton. Merle is a member of the Country Music Hall of Fame, the Songwriters Hall of Fame, the Gibson Guitar Hall of Fame, and the Kentucky Music Hall of Fame. He was a man who did a lot of things very well. It could be said, accurately, that he lived several lifetimes while on this planet. His very interesting life began at the end of the horse-and-buggy era and ended at the dawn of the computer era.

Merle stands alone among other country music stars of the twentieth century in his voracious curiosity and appetite for knowledge. Besides his virtuoso guitar abilities, knack for writing hit songs off the top of his head, and easygoing and likable stage persona, Merle also had a passion for American history, short story writing, cartooning, taxidermy, poetry, watch repair, motorcycling, guitar inventions, and guns, among many other interests. Country music star Marty Stuart, who is always good for such quotes, wrote perhaps the best summary of Merle Travis in his 1999 book *Pilgrims: Sinners, Saints, and Prophets*:

> Merle Travis was a genius. He was a guitar great, prolific song-writer, journalist, teller of tall tales, actor, cartoonist, watch repairman, inventor, jack of all trades, and one of country music's pioneer statesmen.... He was the best at it. He was from the old line of hillbilly royalty. They knew how to shine on the outside even when they were crying on the inside. He had the act mastered.[1]

Merle led a difficult life. The extreme highs of his genius-level abilities and show-business successes were interrupted by staggering lows and lifetime struggles with undiagnosed mental illness, alcoholism, and pill addiction that nearly killed him. In an interview with Merle's daughter Merlene Travis-Maggini for this book, she revealed a conversation she had with her father before he died. The reader should keep this in mind while taking in the story of his life. I certainly remembered this quote every step of the way:

> He said, "Someday, someone's gonna write a book about me. They're gonna say he was a womanizer, and he was married a million times, and he was in insane asylums, and he had the DTs, and he got in fights, and he was not always the nicest person in the world. And it'll all be true. But you've heard it from me first."[2]

Now you, the reader, have heard it from Merle first as well. It was a challenge to write this book, knowing that telling the whole story—not whitewashing the truth, not flinching from the difficult moments—would present a more truthful and complicated picture than many people would find comfortable. Genteel readers may flinch at some of the details. In real life, Merle Travis was a complex man, and his life story was filled with incredible greatness and unbearable sadness. Despite his frailties, his family, friends, and fans loved him and respected him and held the man and his achievements in very high regard. I felt it was important to simply tell the story. This belief was reinforced when I interviewed Bobby Anderson, friend of Merle's, author of *That Muhlenberg Sound* (1993), and himself a lifelong newspaper journalist. Bobby told me, "You've got to tell the whole story when you tell it. You've got to tell it like it is."[3]

To distinguish it from my own prose, Merle's autobiographical writing will appear in *italics*.[4]

"Will you take that job at the mines," my mother asked as I was leaving, "if your Pappy can get them to hire you?"

"I don't reckon so, Mammy," I answered. "I'll write to you ever' now and then and let you know how things are goin'."

She wrapped her hands in her checkered apron as the cold, drizzling rain dampened her face that morning in January 1937. Her youngest son was walking out of the yard, past the storm cellar and up the muddy wagon road to the little crossroads community of Ebenezer, Kentucky. I was determined to make my way to Columbus, Ohio, to join Clayton McMichen and his Georgia Wildcats. I didn't have a penny, but that was not unusual in those days. I had a telegram in my pocket that said a job awaited me, and I was on my way.

I didn't know it then, but I was to never live another day at home with my parents the rest of my life. Fatalists would say this was destined to be the exact time for me to begin my life's work. If this is true, then so be it. I don't know. But like David Copperfield, let me "begin my life with the beginning of my life..."

I was born November 29th, 1917, in Rosewood, Kentucky. Rosewood, by the way, is in Muhlenberg County. If you'd look for it on the map, you wouldn't find it. It's not there. You'd find Greenville, though. It's the county seat. It's in southwestern Kentucky, almost exactly between Nashville, Tennessee, and Evansville, Indiana. I never lived in any other county in Kentucky but Muhlenberg. I want to make this clear for two reasons.

Number one: I'm very proud to have been born in the same county where my father, my sister, and my two brothers were born. My mother was born in neighboring Logan County but spent most of her life in Muhlenberg. Number two: in 1947 I made a record of a song by the title of "Nine Pound Hammer." One of the verses in part has these words:

"It's a long way to Harlan
It's a long way to Hazard..."

It's flattering that so many folks must have heard the old record, for constantly I meet people who got the wrong impression from the song. "I'm from your neck of the woods, Merle," they'll say, "up around Harlan and Hazard." When I explain that I'm from the other end of the state and was never in east Kentucky until I was grown, they look a little confused. "But you sung about it," they'll say, "in that song about the nine-pound hammer!" It's strange that folks would get mixed up about the old hammer song. I've sung about Heaven all my life, and nobody ever thought I was from there. Let me explain to folks from other states that in Kentucky, like in Ireland, a person first mentions the county he's from, and then gets around to the town later.

I was a baby when Dad quit tobacco farming in Rosewood and moved to Browder, in the same county, to spend the rest of his working days as a coal miner—a move that I believe he always regretted. I've heard him tell of the days when he was a young man and would travel all the way to Springfield, Tennessee, about sixty-five miles away, to spend the summer working on a tobacco plantation with a Col. Washington. His light blue eyes would look across the bygone years as he'd tell how he'd go back to Rosewood in fine shape. "I'd have fifteen or twenty dollars in my pocket," he'd reminisce, "an' a new suit o' clothes." As a miner, the dollars were "flickers" or "script" (brass money tokens bearing the name of the coal company they were issued by) and the "suit o' clothes" was a picture in the Sears Roebuck catalog.

Just before the turn of the century, William Robert Travis married a black-eyed, black-haired girl whose name was Laura Etta Latham. A year-and-a-half later my oldest brother, Taylor, came along. Two years from then my only sister, Vada, was born. Thirteen years passed and my brother John Melvin appeared on the scene, and I cropped up a couple of years after that. My sister took care of me while my mother worked as hard as any other field hand in the tobacco patch, alongside Dad.

After we moved to Browder, Vada watched over me as if I were her own child instead of her baby brother. She actually taught me to read, write, and spell before I started school. The only thing I've ever done that I can brag about is that I started school in the first grade. I didn't have to go "through the primmer" as we used to say. Vada was a grand gal and a wonderful sister.

From the time I was old enough to remember, my parents were Uncle Rob and Aunt Etter to most everybody. I like to think they called them that because they liked them and in some way felt a kinship toward them. Let me explain why my mother's name was pronounced Etter instead of Etta. Rural Southerners (and most of the urban ones) sound an "er" on many words that end with "ah" or "o." Banjo is "banjer," hollow is "holler," window is "winder," fellow is "feller," and so on. So my mother's name was Etter in Kentucky. I called my mother Mammy and my father Pappy until I was almost grown. Then I taught myself to call them Mom and Dad.

The first house I remember living in was owned by a good old Negro couple that we called Uncle Rufus and Aunt Rowena Littlepage. They had been slaves before the war between the states and were quite old when we moved to the Old Littlepage place at the top of Browder Hill. Uncle Rufus was a kind and colorful old gentleman. His white hair and black skin, his mild manners and wisdom, were right out of a story by Joel Chandler Harris or a song by Stephen C. Foster. It was at this old pre–Civil War house that I discovered music. Dad traded his brother, Uncle John Travis, out of an old five-string banjo. I was completely fascinated by the instrument and hounded Dad by the hour to play it. Mom remembered him as quite a "banjer picker" in his younger days. "Rob used to could just make the banjer talk," she'd say, "and had the finest kind of a singin' voice." Dad played what college folklore enthusiasts call the "rapping style" of banjo playing. The right hand almost appears to be a fist. The top of the index fingernail hits the strings on the down stroke, while the thumb gaily dances from the fifth, or "thumb-string," to the other four. With the monotone of the thumb-string and the sparkling melodic ring of the others, one can picture long-forgotten ancestors in Scotland and Ireland ages ago who, as pipers, stirred their listeners with music of a defiantly similar effect.

I learned to pick the banjo that way when I was about eight. I'm sure the word "talent" shouldn't enter here. I was merely imitating Dad. I fancied myself exactly like him when I'd rear back with the old five-stringer and yelp in my squeaky little voice the songs I'd heard him sing.

"Ginny Weaver climbed a tree
Hopin' fer her Lord to see
Limb it broke, and she did fall
Never got t' see her Lord a'tall"

I could usually get by with my singin' and pickin', but I'd hear Mom say things to Dad when they didn't know I was listening. "Rob Travis, you ort not to be learnin' that young'un them ol' songs," she'd declare, "that's takin' the name of the Lord in vain!" "Never mind, Etter," he'd chuckle back to her. "I 'spect the Lord enjoys a little fun once in a while."

Dad had a way of telling tales about the days when he was a young man that always held me spellbound. Every boy grows up remembering the things his father told, I suppose, but let me demonstrate one of my favorite stories. Time might have altered some of the facts, but according to a number of old timers who were friends and kinfolks, I'm pretty sure the story is true. Dialect is hard to set down on paper, but I'll try and write it just as I remember him saying it.

Used to, they had a heap of still-houses about th' country. They wuz a feller named Jim Winders that hung aroun' one still-house I knowed of. Jim could jis' spread his se'f when it come to banjer pickin'. He allus had a hick'ry rim banjer hangin' on th' peg, an' all you'd haf' to do to get him t' pick one wuz jis' say, "Jim, knock me off a tune er two," an' he'd commence.

In them days, th' war hadn' been over so awful long, an' in that part o' th' state, people had bad feelin's about both sides. They wuz allus getting' their back up about th' fight b'tween th' North and th' South. Now, one day I walked in to the still-house an' Jim Winders happened to not be thar. I eased over an' picked up Jim's banjer an' commence to pickin' an' sangin'. This here's what I sung:

"Jeff Davis swore when the cruel war begun
He wouldn' be the Union man an' carry the Union gun.
But I 'druther be th' Union man an' carry the Union gun
Than to be th' Rebel, th' Rebel had to run..."

Well Sir, them fellers started to arguin' 'mongst one 'nuther about whuther th' Rebel had t' run er not, an' 'fore long they was th' dad-gummest fist-fight goin' on that ever you seen in yor life!

I've read a book or two about the Travis family (they sure was hard up for something to write about). They always start out by telling about three Travis brothers that came to North Carolina from the "old country" (County Cork, Ireland). The brothers split up and went in all different directions. Two of them supposedly went north to Kentucky and Virginia, while the other one had a famous descendant whose name was Col. William Barrett Travis, the feller who was in command at the Alamo and was killed along with Davy Crockett, Jim Bowie, and all the rest. When Dad would meet a Travis that he couldn't trace back to kinfolks, he'd say, "I 'spect we're all from th' same litter o' pups." Whether we're from the same litter of pups as the Colonel, I don't rightly know. Dad would say of the famous Texas martyr, "He's th' only Travis that ever amounted to much, an' he got shot."

My first remembrance of anything about a guitar was while we lived at the old Littlepage place. Some miners were staying in a tent near the house. One night one of them was playing his guitar and singing. Dad called some of us out to listen. I'm not sure who all in the family came out, but I remember well the sound and the song. To my young ears it was something beautiful floating to me from out of the black, mysterious night:

"Your voice is ringing like silver bells,
Under your spell
I come to tell you of a love that is blooming o'er hill and dell
I love you so, my Silver Bell..."

I couldn't possibly have learned the words by hearing them that one time. It could be that Vada, my sister, had learned them from the old "morning-glory horn" talking machine we *left in Rosewood, and I learned the words from her, but I do remember the melody and the occurrence. She had memorized all the songs from the cylinder records and sang them often. She doesn't realize how closely I listened while she swept and dusted and sang:*

> *"Good night, Mr. Elephant*
> *Mr. Tiger, take your place*
> *Lie down and you're sure to dream*
> *That you're roaming in the jungle far away..."*

My mother never realized how I was listening while she was needling away on a homemade quilt, hanging from the ceiling and stretched between quadrangle frames, and she'd hum or sing. Or how her voice floated away on the wind as she hung out clothes. I'm sure "On Jordan's Stormy Banks I Stand" made her toil a little easier. It certainly made her son a little happier. I must not paint a word picture of my mother as dull and wrapped in backwoods religious beliefs that made her critical and morbid. She was a God-fearing Christian woman and went to church. But that by no means kept her from having a sharp sense of humor, an almost constant smile, and a wit that was quick as the back of her hand, which lashed out to my face when I deserved it. When I would be doing something that I shouldn't be doing, she'd ask me to quit in a calm voice and with somewhat of a smile on her face. After the second time she asked and I didn't pay heed, it happened. Like a flash of lightning, she'd pop me with a blinding whack in the face. It didn't really hurt, but the shock was tremendous. Her black eyes would flash and her lips would tighten. "Merle Robert," she'd snap, "go get me a hickory!"

When she used my middle name, I was in serious trouble. I'm sure she didn't send me after the hickory switch nearly often enough. The wrath would be gone from her as suddenly as it came. Dad never whipped me. I understand this is not necessarily so with John and Taylor. I suppose I had an advantage being the youngest in the family. They were wonderful parents, Rob and Etter. I loved them equally.

When I was about nine we moved again, this time to a farm owned by the coal company where my dad spent the rest of his working years—not as a farmer, but as a miner, working for the Beech Creek Coal Company. The farm was about four miles from the mines and was known as the Old Reed Place. I lived there until I left for good or bad in 1937, as I told you at the beginning of my story. I finished the eighth grade in the little one-room schoolhouse at Ebenezer (the extent of my education). Vada and Taylor married while we lived at the old Littlepage place. This left only John and me with our parents. I didn't know at that age that I was living in what would later be referred to as the Great Depression. The Rob Travis family never lived in a house with electricity or plumbing (inside or out). We never had a radio, and we never had rugs on the floor. Dad never owned a car in his life, we had no horses or mules, our lights were coal-oil (kerosene) lamps, and our drinking water came from a spring. Mom cooked on a coal stove, and the house was heated with a coal fireplace. We raised most of our vegetables and kept the cellar full of food Mom canned. We usually raised a few hogs, chickens were all over the place, and there was always a cow. The cow was my mother's property. She treated it like a pet. The cow always had a name and was milked only by Mom. There was no money, and new clothes, bought on credit at the Beech Creek Company Store, came seldom. When they did, it was new overalls for us menfolk and a few yards of cloth. Mom made our shirts and her own dresses from the cloth. Flour sacks were never thrown away. The cotton material was much too valuable. Our clothes were patched over the patches (this is a fact, not a poor attempt at a joke). But we stayed clean, and always had enough to eat, except a few times during coal mine strikes.

John's middle name is Melvin. We called him by his middle name at home. When he grew up he started using his first name. We grew up fighting each other, yelling insults at each other, stealing from each other, and loving each other as much as two brothers could. Before his teens, John was pretty plump. Kids would call him "fatty" and he'd charge them like an overfed bulldog. In his teens he grew tall and broad shouldered. I grew taller but stayed skinny as a shikepoke. Ol' John would have been a fine athlete under different circumstances. He never finished high school but went to Drakesboro High almost through his senior year. He was an excellent boxer and would run all the way home from Drakesboro—some four miles away—to keep himself in good condition. There was a big rock up by our little corn-crip [corn crib]. He tied a wire around it and spent a good deal of time lifting it to develop his muscles. John's hair was black and wavy, and like most boys with waves in their hair, he didn't like it. He'd try to slick it down with all sorts of goo. But after a while a curl would suddenly pop out like releasing a clock spring.

Like Taylor, John had a lot of different talents. With showing very little interest he learned to play the banjo and the guitar and could sing like a bird. He had a high-pitched voice that was clear and on pitch and could sing better than anyone in the neighborhood if you could get him to. His singing came natural, but about the extent of it was joining in with me to sing a little harmony at home, or to amuse himself sittin' on the front porch with the guitar. He wrote poetry and prose and read every book he could borrow. He loved hunting and dogs above everything else, I believe. He could train his dogs to do any sort of trick you could imagine. Still, they would tree possums, point quail, and run rabbits.

A few years ago I made an album titled "Songs of the Coal Mines." I asked John if he'd write a few words for the back of the album (people in the record business call these "liner notes"). I'd like to quote a phrase from his writing that has been quoted before, but it's a tiny example of his way with words. About the album he said, "Now we older ones can listen with nostalgia for the good old difficult days, and the younger ones can doubt a little, laugh a little, and be a little better informed about their elders and their pitifully happy era." It was from one of his clever and interesting letters to me during World War II that I remembered and later used in part for some of the very phrases in a song called "Sixteen Tons."

When I was about twelve, Taylor, who can bind books, overhaul any kind of engine, repair watches, build radios, draw, cook, play the trombone, or anything else he's ever tried, decided to build a guitar. He built one, and it was, as I remember, an excellent instrument. His wife, May, played it and my hair stood on end. She played the thumb-and-finger style, and every note was perfectly clear. She played a few tunes that I'm still trying to learn. She'd never do more than smile and brush off lightly the praise I'd throw to her. When Taylor left the mines and went to Evansville to work in a factory, he wrote home and at the end of the letter mentioned that I could have the guitar. So you see, my very first guitar was "Taylor made."

I don't remember ever actually sitting down and practicing playing the guitar (you can tell that by listening to me!). But then, I don't remember sitting down to drink a lot of water. The guitar was there, and when I felt like it, I'd grab the thing up and pick around on it, just as I'd pass the water bucket and if I was thirsty, I'd take a drink. I'd feel around on the strings until a chord sounded right, then I'd frail away at the pretty sound I'd discovered. I had no idea what the name of the chord was. I learned to play most of what was on the old wind-up phonograph we had. We had records by Vernon Dalhart, Riley Puckett, Jimmy [sic] Rodgers, and others. I played them constantly.

It seemed that every girl in the neighborhood could sing, especially my cousin, Ama Nell Travis. She could sing for hours without repeating a song. I'd "second after her" with the guitar. On Sunday afternoons we'd all meet at Miss Bunnie Baugh's house at Ebenezer. Everybody would sing and I'd play the guitar. Bunnie Baugh was a wonderful, jolly lady who dearly loved music. I've spent many hours at her house, visiting and playing her player piano. I've always called her Miss Bunnie. In 1956, Miss Bunnie donated a little plot of land across the road from her house, where we used to have our little sing-fests. They mounted a bronze plaque on a native boulder about six feet high with my picture on it and saying a lot of flattering things about me that I'm honored to have said, but certainly don't deserve. On July 15, 1956, they did a dedication as a tribute to me, and about twelve thousand people gathered there that day to watch me unveil the thing. I felt about two inches tall. I would have felt much more at ease across the road sitting on Miss Bunnie's porch playing the guitar with my shoes off. I'll forever be grateful to Miss Bunnie and my lifelong friend Paul Camplin and the state of Kentucky, who for some reason felt that it would be nice to do something for Rob and Etter's boy.

It was on a beautiful, sunny summer afternoon at Miss Bunnie's that something happened that was to inspire me and lead me into a style of guitar playing that I've used, and enjoyed, until this day. She had invited two young men from Drakesboro to drop by and bring their guitars. Their names were Mose Rager and Ike Everly. Mose was a tall, sandy-haired boy and a natural showman. He laughed continuously about everything and at everything. Ike was well built, with blond wavy hair and extremely handsome. They played music like I'd never heard before. I'd heard a good many of the tunes they played, like "River Stay 'Way from My Door," "Love Letters in the Sand," "Tiger Rag," and others, but the way they played! They used celluloid thumb picks, with which they played a bouncy accompaniment *to the melody with the index finger playing at the same time. I didn't know there was such music on earth.*

Mose and Ike were by no means playing for money. They worked in the coal mines at Drakesboro and were Miss Bunnie's friends. It was Sunday, and they had just picked up their guitars and either walked or caught a ride out the road to play for their friend in Ebenezer. From Mose Rager and Ike Everly is exactly where I got my style of playing the guitar. I was getting old enough by then to start going places at night by myself, or with my pals, Fuzzy Gregory, (Earl) Talmadge Dukes, Robbie Hogan, B. W. Johnson, and a good many others. My first choice of where to go would be where Mose and Ike were playing. I'd watch every move they'd make, then go home and try it myself.

We became good friends. The Everly family eventually moved out of the Ebenezer neighborhood. I'd spend evenings at their house. The whole family was musical. All the boys—Ike, Charlie, and Leonard, who was my age (Ike and Mose were a few years older than me, but not a lot)—played guitars and sang harmony trios. Ike's father was a first-rate old-time fiddler, so you can see how I would enjoy going to the Everlys.

Ike married a lovely Muhlenberg County girl and they had two sons. When the boys were still very young, the Ike Everly family moved to Iowa and all of them performed on the radio. I had a letter from Ike while they were in Shenandoah. He said his two boys wanted to be entertainers, but he wasn't sure just how well they would do. In 1956 we had a little get-together in Drakesboro at Mose Rager's house. Ike and his family were there. Ike's boys sang a few songs. He said they were planning to make some records. I thought they sang very well. So did millions of other folks a short time later when their records were played around the world. They used their real names. Don and Phil, the Everly Brothers.

Mose had two brothers, and like the Everly boys, they could sing harmony like nobody's business. Lyman and J. R. were their names. J. R., like Leonard Everly, was my age. The first time I was ever paid for singing was with J. R., along with his nephew Guy Laster. We were in Drakesboro one night after going to a "brush harbor" meeting, and were on our way home. [Called "brush harbor" by Merle here, the correct term is "brush arbor." A brush arbor meeting was an outdoor religious meeting, held under a crude, temporary wooden structure, popular in rural areas of the United States from the 1700s through the mid-1900s.] *We felt like singing and started harmonizing "Shine On Harvest Moon" right in front of Mr. Billy Bridges's big white house. Mr. Bridges was the coal mine operator.* [Billy Bridges was one of the wealthiest individuals in the area and had the first house in Muhlenberg County with running water and a modern, indoor toilet.] *Halfway through the song, on came his front porch lights! We started to run, afraid that he might shoot at us or something. Instead, he called us back and handed us fifty cents! I've picked an' sang all night for less than that, as you'll learn later.*

When I was sixteen, I did what many boys were doing in the 1930s. I joined the CCC (Civilian Conservation Corps). Let me briefly explain to the young folks what the CCC was. It was a government program that young men could join, take the tests you would take to join the Army, and be sent to a military-type camp. There you'd work building parks, roads, and national monuments (such as restoring Civil War battlefields). We were paid about thirty dollars a month. All but five dollars was sent home. Remember, this was in the Depression years, and money was terribly scarce. Boys around Muhlenberg County were joining and being sent to faraway places, like Idaho, Colorado, and California. I passed all the tests and was sent to Fort Knox, Kentucky, to take shots and go through "boot training." From there I was to find out what faraway state I would be sent to. After all the preliminaries, I found out. They sent me to Columbus, Kentucky, only a hundred miles from home. There I lived in a barracks, lived by military rules, and stayed long enough to save up thirty dollars. I hitchhiked to Evansville and spent every penny of it for an arched-top, sunburst-finished Gretsch guitar with fiddle sound holes. I laid aside my "Taylor made" guitar. Many years later I saw a picture in a newspaper that was sent to me from Detroit. A man was holding it, and the caption read: "This is the guitar Merle Travis learned to play on." I have not the faintest idea how my guitar got to Detroit. It was the one Taylor had built, all right. I knew the instrument like I know the back of my hand.

By the time I got out of the CCC camp, I had learned to play the thumb and finger style on the guitar fairly well. Muhlenberg County was full of boys who played that style, but Ike and Mose remained my favorites. As I mentioned earlier, we didn't have a radio, but a few people around Drakesboro and Beech Creek did. I'd get to their radios every chance I had to listen to Clayton McMichen and his Georgia Wildcats. They were great favorites of mine. I liked to hear McMichen talk and play the fiddle, and to hear Slim Bryant play the guitar. Once they came to Drakesboro to play the high school auditorium. They pulled into town in the middle of the afternoon, and I just happened to be there. I got acquainted with a young fiddler who was with them. He was about my age. His name was Carl Cotner. Carl was later to become a dear friend of mine. He was musical director for Gene Autry for many years and was conductor on Gene's Melody Ranch TV show in Hollywood.

I mentioned to Carl that I played the guitar a little. Right away we headed for the bus they were traveling in. He got out his fiddle and I took one of the band's guitars and we started playing. We were entertaining ourselves when Clayton McMichen finished eating and came to the bus. Carl introduced me to Mr. McMichen.

"Let's take him with us, Mac," Carl pleaded. "We could sure use him in the outfit."

"We can't do it right now, Carl," Mac answered, "but we'll get him with us one of these days." He took my address and I was thrilled to death.

At Carl's suggestion, I rode all around the county that afternoon while Mac balla-hooed through a public-address system rigged up on top of the bus. He'd talk away on the microphone and tell about the show at Drakesboro. He'd finish with "Don't you dare miss it!" Then he'd hold the mike down by our instruments. Carl would fiddle away while I would "second after him" on the borrowed guitar. I was in hog heaven! I couldn't imagine that such a glorious thing could be happening to me—to actually meet Clayton McMichen—and I didn't believe he'd ever send for me. But he did, if you remember the first part of my story.

It was during this time that I was doing a lot of bumming around the country, usually with a pal who played some instruments. We thumbed rides on the highways, rode freight trains, and even bummed rides on riverboats. My guitar was always with me. We'd play on street corners at night and ask for donations from people who would gather around to see what was going on. "We're trying to make our way to Texas," I'd lie. "I have a sick sister there. If any of you folks would like to help us, just pitch any loose change you have in your pockets here in front of us." I doubt if anybody believed the "sick sister" story, but usually a few coins would be pitched. We'd gather them up and spend them on pork and beans, Vienna sausage, and bread. I've lived on such food days on end. I've slept in every kind of place imaginable and have met all sorts of weird people in boxcars and hobo jungles.

On one of my frequent visits to Evansville to visit Taylor and his family, my big brother told me about a "marathon dance" that was going on down on Franklin Avenue. He asked if I'd like to go down and see it. You can guess my answer. When we got there, the music was playing and couples were on the floor that had supposedly been there a week. One would be asleep while the partner dragged the limp "dancer" around the floor. These marathons were pretty much a fad in the 1930s. The couple who held out the longest was the winner, of course. A local radio station was broadcasting from the hall. The announcer would describe what was going on, then allow some local singer or musician to play a tune over the radio. Taylor, who has always had more energy than a chipmunk, made his way to the announcer. "Let my little brother here get his guitar and play one on that thing," he said. "He can play better than any of the people you've had on tonight."

The announcer agreed to let me play a tune. Good ol' Taylor! He didn't know what he was kickin' off for me. I played "Tiger Rag" the best I knew how. That was in 1935. The very first time I was ever on the radio. The station was WGBF in Evansville. I was to do a lot of broadcasting on that station later. This broadcast led to a job with a band who played on the same station. This was something to write home about. I was on the radio! The boys in charge of the band were Elgie and Freddie James. There were five of us together. The name of the group was the Knox County Knockabouts. They were talented musicians and singers. I imagine we sounded fairly well. There was no pay for playing on the radio, but we were allowed to announce our engagements. "....nd we'll be looking for all you fine folks around Mount Vernon when we come to your schoolhouse next Friday night," the master of ceremonies would say. "If you'd like to have the Knox County Knockabouts play for your private party or school, just drop a letter or a postcard to us here in care of WGBF." We'd drive to our little engagement and play. After the show, we'd stop at some café and divide the money five ways. There wasn't much to divide, but that was beside the point as far as I was concerned. I can honestly say that I wasn't, and have never been, too concerned about what

I was paid. I'll swear to you that I have never felt that I wasn't paid enough. My burning desire was to play music, not to merely make money.

After a time, the band broke up. I hitchhiked back to Ebenezer and home. A few weeks passed and I got itchy feet again. A few days later I was on top of another boxcar leaving the Drakesboro Depot, heading back to Evansville with my guitar beside me. Another band took me on. They were doing the same thing the Knockabouts did. There was one exception. A combination car salesman and radio announcer by the name of Aud Rhodes was personal manager for the group. We were the Tennessee Tomcats. Aud was something of a super salesman and a smooth talker: "Come on out to the Booneville School House tonight, friends and neighbors," *he'd pitch,* "and see Cackle Bennett play the bull fiddle while wearing boxing gloves!"

We traveled in an ancient sedan with three seats. For the life of me I couldn't tell you what kind of car it was. It was long and boxy with big wood-spoked wheels. Under each window on the outside was painted the name of the feller who rode by that window. Under my window was the name "Slim Travis" in big, bright yellow letters. I fit the name in those days. Aud Rhodes divided the money after the dates. I wouldn't want to question his honesty, but in my scrapbook I have sheets out of a little notebook that showed my income. Some nights there'd be twenty cents, fifty cents other nights, and once or twice I was paid over a dollar! (And we had pretty good crowds when we played.) Not a lot of money, but then I got to travel a hundred and sixty miles, do a two-hour show, and be in the company of the Tennessee Tomcats. Very few people can make that statement.

All joking aside, I was doing exactly what I wanted to do. I was pickin' and singin' over the radio, touring with a group and—by golly—I was in show business! Even though Taylor lived there in Evansville, and I could have stayed with him and May, I felt I should be on my own. He had three small daughters then, but they would have made room for me somehow. I'm sure of that. But another boy and I rented a room near the radio station. The rent was $1.50 a week for the two of us. Our room had one creaky bed and a naked lightbulb that swung from the ceiling. Peddlers pushing homemade carts would pass outside our window yelling, "Coal! Coal! By the peck or by the bushel," *or* "Ragman! Ragman! Give us your raaaaags…" We had a one-unit gas burner to cook on, but it was rusty and unhooked. There was a well-worn linoleum floor, and the door *wouldn't lock. The bathroom was in the hall, but there was no hot water. We were professional radio stars, lolling in the lap of luxury.*

When we left our lovely suite, we waded through a foot of water, carrying our guitar in one hand and our shoes in the other. Water was all over the streets in that part of Evansville. It was the winter of 1936. [Merle's memory here slightly misses the date of the great Ohio River flood—it was January and February of 1937, not 1936.] *The ceaseless rain showed no mercy, and the world seemed waterlogged. The Ohio River was on a rampage. It was out of its banks and still rising. The beautiful Ohio came to town and filled the streets of such towns as Louisville, Cincinnati, and Evansville with silt, mud, and rotten logs. Barns, trees, and dead cows floated past Evansville in the muddy, swirling waters.*

We moved to the Moose Lodge, where hundreds of other victims slept on the floor with an army blanket for cover. The Red Cross brought in huge boxes of stale baloney sandwiches and steel barrels of coffee. I was young. It was all a thrill and a brand-new adventure for me. Now I can imagine how dreadful it must have been to some of the people who sat there day after day wondering if their home and all their belongings were on their watery way to Paducah.

Finally the water receded enough for me to get out to Taylor's house and let them know that I was all right. There was a letter there from Mom. Inside was a telegram. It read:

MEET ME. COLUMBUS OHIO.
JANUARY 10. JOB WAITING.
CLAYTON McMICHEN.

I wrapped my extra shirt in a brown paper bag, picked up my guitar, and headed across the river to Ebenezer to say goodbye to Mom and Dad. By the goodness in the heart of a man who ran a rescue boat, I got across to the Kentucky side. By thumbing rides, I went in a roundabout way, following roads that weren't washed out, spent one night in a car someone had forgotten to lock, and made it to the old Reed place the next day. I told my parents that I'd be leaving.

Now you may reread the first two paragraphs again if you've forgotten them.

In Drakesboro I borrowed the money for a train ticket from Carl T. Davis, a school chum, and went to Columbus. I had no idea where to go when I got there, but I wasn't long in finding out. The whole town was plastered with placards advertising:

THE GREAT NATIONAL FIDDLER'S CONTEST BETWEEN CLAYTON McMICHEN AND NATCHEE THE INDIAN! WITH SPECIAL ADDED ATTRACTION—THE FAMOUS DEL-MORE BROTHERS!

I walked to the auditorium, carrying my paper bag and guitar and wearing a suit I had bought in a secondhand store. That was a great day for me. It was my first meeting with Alton and Rabon Delmore (the famous Delmore Brothers). We later became the closest of friends until the end of their lives. That was the day I met Cowboy Copas. He played guitar for Natchee the Indian and never sang at all. "Hello, son," Clayton McMichen said to me, "I'm proud to have you with us." He walked on over and put his hand on my shoulder. "By grannies, I think I'll just call you Ridgerunner." He called me that from then on, whenever I would see him. Young Carl Cotner rushed up and shook hands. He was grinning from ear to ear. "I'm sure glad you're joining us," he bubbled. "We're going to have lots of fun!"

This little synopsis is meant to try and answer a few of the questions friends I meet along the way sometimes ask. I hope it's held your interest to some degree. It is by no means a life story, but a fingernail sketch of how I became a part of a business that seems to fascinate a great deal of people. I could easily tell you how to become a doctor, a lawyer, or a barber, but those of us in the nomadic life of an entertainer followed a thousand different paths that eventually led to stage center.

As I write this, almost thirty years have passed since I joined Clayton McMichen in Columbus, Ohio, and as Carl said, it has been a lot of fun, but he was only partly right. Happiness is a friend who has usually been around, but heartbreak and sorrow are old acquaintances of mine. I've tasted success and gorged on failure. I've walked on red carpets and waded in mud. Every person I know, as far as I'm concerned, is my friend. If I have an enemy, he's kept it a secret from me.

Music, entertaining, song writing, and show business in general has been my life. I've never worked at another trade. I hope I never will. When your grandchildren are playing a show at the Milky Way Theatre on Venus, and I'm a hundred and five years old, I hope I'm the old feller that watches the stage door. After all, that's still "show biz."

Merle Travis
November 1966

. . .

Merle Robert Travis, as you have already read above, was born on November 29, 1917, in Rosewood, Kentucky. It is worth pointing out that even though this was just a little over a hundred years ago, it was a place and time that barely resembles US society today. As Merle reveals, his family was so poor that his father never owned a car, a horse, or a mule. The family had no running water, no indoor plumbing, and no electricity. Their small wooden house was unpainted. His childhood in Muhlenberg County more closely resembled the lives of rural pioneers in the 1700s and 1800s than our modern world.

Merle's older brother John Melvin Travis wrote about their childhood in a letter to Merle's daughter Pat Travis Eatherly later in life:

Let's all go back awhile in time. Let's go back to 1917. Can you imagine a whole county in any state of America that would have no roads except just narrow, one lane roads that were just plain dirt? Just like your front lawn would be if traffic started using it for a street, or highway.

Can you imagine that you would live in a community where there was not one telephone—where no one had ever seen an automobile—where plumbing was unknown—where there was not and had never been a radio, a T.V., where aeroplanes and dinosaurs were equally rare.

Where, there was such a place, once upon a time, it was Muhlenberg County, Kentucky. Town of Rosewood.[5]

As Merle grew from a boy to a man, and especially as he began to travel as a young musician, he would witness the introduction of many things that we take for granted today: electricity, radio and television, musical amplification, running water, indoor plumbing, automobiles and airplanes, and America's transition from isolated hamlets and villages (each having their own local, regional identity) into a nation homogenized by mass media, standardized fast food chains, and shopping malls.

Muhlenberg County in 1917 certainly qualified as one of those isolated places with its own regional identity. It had been named in 1798 after a Pennsylvania Revolutionary War general, John Peter Gabriel Muhlenberg. The county in Kentucky was so named because many from his regiment had pioneered there. Many settlers of European descent came to Muhlenberg County—mostly Irish, English, Welsh, and the "Scotch-Irish," who found their way to the most remote areas in the rural landscape of the Appalachians. There were also slaves of African descent, but Muhlenberg County had few residents wealthy enough to be slave owners. Today the demographics remain much as they were then: roughly 95 percent Caucasian, 5 percent African American.

The area would never be a great farming region, but by the early 1800s, its most valuable natural resource had been discovered—a resource that would put Muhlenberg County on the map: coal. The county had a rich, seemingly endless supply of coal, and it prospered with the nation's demand for it, through the eras of using coal for heating home fires, for powering factory steam engines and steam locomotives, and eventually fueling the huge power plants that to this day supply more than a third of the nation with electricity (a common sign around Muhlenberg County in the last half-century reads: "If you don't like coal, you can do without electricity").

The first commercial coal mine in Muhlenberg County, the McLean Drift Bank Mine, opened in 1820 in the town of Paradise. Through the nineteenth century, coal production slowly grew in the region, and hundreds of small, temporary mining operations flourished. Coal mining in Muhlenberg County accelerated rapidly in the late 1800s and early 1900s. The combination of railroad access (for transporting the coal) and electrical power (which helped light the mines and power the processing equipment) enabled the coal companies to go from what had previously been little more than a hardscrabble surface vocation into an enormously profitable underground industry.

Merle Travis was born into this coal boom in Muhlenberg County. The county's population rapidly accelerated through the early 1900s until 1930, when it peaked at 37,784, a number that has been slowly declining ever since. The coal industry reached its commercial peak in the 1970s, when Muhlenberg County produced more coal annually than any other place on Earth. The industry is so ubiquitous in the region that it is difficult to find any male resident who has not worked for a coal company at some point in his life. As Merle wrote earlier, his father, William Robert Travis (born 1868), known to all as Rob, and his mother, Laura Etta Latham Travis (born 1882), known as Etta or Etter, were originally a farming family before Rob began working in the coal mines. Earl Talmadge Dukes, Merle's childhood friend, avowed: "Merle had the greatest parents you ever met.... I want the whole world to know that."[6] In a 1961 interview, Merle observed: "My mother's folks was Irish, and my grandmother on my dad's side was second generation of Irish. My mother was a descendent of the North Irish, and my dad's folks was from County Cork, which is down in southern part of Ireland, you know? So my mother had dark eyes and dark hair, and my dad had the real light blue eyes and the jowls and the face of the typical County Cork Irish."[7] The family's first two children were considerably older than those that followed. Andrew Taylor Travis, known as Taylor, was born in 1899, and sister Una Vada Travis, known as Vada, was born in 1902. A third, John Melvin Travis, known as Melvin or John Melvin, was born thirteen years later, in 1915. Merle Robert Travis, the baby of the bunch, was born two years later, in 1917, when his father was forty-nine years old.

Merle (misspelled "Murrell" by the county recorder on his birth certificate) and the Travis family lived in several locations in Muhlenberg County, as he tells above. They lived in Rosewood when he was a baby, on a farm known as the Old Frack Place, and Rob was a farmer, sharecropping tobacco. The few existing photos from this time show the entire family working in the tobacco fields, with young John Melvin and Merle at their feet. In those times, as it is today, getting ahead was difficult in a place as remote as Rosewood. Merle recalled the family's situation at a jam session in his later years:

> I didn't know we was poor. We had as much as everybody else did. We had one pair of overalls, and patch 'em. If that patch wore out, put a patch over that patch. Sounds funny, putting a patch over a patch, but that's the way it was. Dad, to have a shoe last, he'd have to [re]sole his shoes. And we'd pick blackberries, gather hickory nuts and walnuts, raise chickens, and feed all the scraps to a couple old hogs, and kill one of them and that's where your money come from, and maybe order something from Sears and Roebuck.[8]

The lure of better pay in the mines prompted the family to move twice more in search of work during Merle's Kentucky childhood. Merle noted in the same 1961 interview:

They raised tobacco up there. My dad raised tobacco. My brother, my oldest brother Taylor, he moved… and got a job in the mines, so he went back to Rosewood and told Dad, he said, "Pappy, you're crazy raisin' this tobacco." He said, "You can go down to the mines and really make some money." So Dad spent the rest of his days out there going to the mines in Browder, Kentucky, and then… Beech Creek, he worked sixteen years. Dad always said, "I wished I would have stayed on the farm."[9]

John Melvin Travis recalled:

Dad had sharecropped for [a man named] Sile Rust for 18 to 20 years. But big brother Taylor had refused to work on the farm and had found work at the coal mines away off down in the other end of the county about 8 miles away. Beech Creek, Kentucky. Why sometimes he [Taylor] would make as much in a week as a sharecropper would earn in two months, maybe $20.00. Big brother worked on Mom. He couldn't budge Dad, quit farming and come to the mines. Learn how to live. Taylor couldn't budge Dad but Mom could. We were going to move to Beech Creek if Dad could get a job and find a house to rent.[10]

The family moved from Rosewood in 1920 to the "Old Littlepage Place," near Browder and Beech Creek, so that Rob Travis could join his oldest son, Taylor, working in the Browder mine. "Uncle Rufus" Littlepage, a former slave who had been left the property by his former owner, owned the house. Merle later recalled:

Now, the first memories that I have is of Uncle Rufus and Aunt Rowena.… They lived down under the hill by an old country coal mine, you know. And my dad rented from them, so our landlord and landlady was formerly slaves.[11]

The Browder mine was a large operation that began in 1903. It was owned by the Wickliffe family and was often referred to as the Wickliffe mine. In 1910, when the mine was briefly owned by the Elk Valley Coal Company, there was a large explosion that killed thirty-four men, roughly one-third of the workforce (many decades later, in 1963, Merle would record an original song about the event, "The Browder Explosion," as one of the tracks on his *Songs of the Coal Mines* album for Capitol). This was the dangerous work environment that Merle's father, Rob, and brother Taylor walked into at the Browder mine.

When Merle's father began working for the coal company, the family's finances changed from a cash-based system to a system where credit would be given to employees' families at a "company store" owned by the coal company. Money was replaced by metal tokens created by each coal company, known as "flickers" or "scrip." Often, families would stay in debt to the coal company, never seeing a profit even after a year's work in the mines. It was this culture that would eventually spawn lyrical imagery of indentured servitude in Merle's most famous song, "Sixteen Tons."

Five years later the family moved again, this time to a small community called Ebenezer, where they rented a home known as the Old Reed Place. The new home was owned by the Beech Creek mining company, where Rob Travis began working in 1925 at Beech Creek Mine Number Five. Rob Travis wouldn't go underground, so he worked as a sulfur picker on the surface. As Merle writes above, his father would work at the Beech Creek mine until he retired at the age of seventy. Though Rob spent some time in Cincinnati, living with Merle after Etta's death, both would die in Muhlenberg County—Etta in 1939 and Rob in 1942. Eventually his older brothers, Taylor and John Melvin, would relocate to Evansville, Indiana, for work. His sister Vada remained in Muhlenberg County until her death in 2004 at the age of 101.

Music was a huge part of daily life for rural families in the era of Merle's upbringing. The Travis family was no exception. Author Bobby Anderson describes these pre-phonograph, pre-radio, pre-television times quite well in the introduction to his book *That Muhlenberg Sound* (1993):

> In the long summer evenings after dark in Muhlenberg County, Kentucky, as in every other county across the nation and in every borough throughout the world, folks have gathered wherever space permitted—on front porches, in their yards, or in their living rooms—to entertain and be entertained with music. On any one of those summer nights, it was not uncommon for the sound to be carried in the air from hill to hill, providing enjoyment for many who were not in actual attendance. Some actually preferred to enjoy such entertainment from afar in the comfort and privacy of their own living rooms or on their front porches.
>
> Every conceivable instrument was used: guitar, banjo, fiddle, upright piano, foot-pumped organ, harmonica, or a set of kitchen spoons. Tuned in harmony, they were used by self-taught musicians who accompanied the singing voices as the family circle gathered. There always seemed to

be an abundance of singing voices, traits, and talents passed from generation to generation. Every such talented family had its share of those who could sing and join their harmony with others, adding tenor and alto voices to the sometimes gruff, coarse lead and the deep bass; one always seems to appear in each family.

Gospel and folk songs were the favorites. That which was learned in church was often sung at home. Songs that were sung or played by an earlier generation were handed down.... Many of these were well-worn by the time they reached the next generation. They were sung and re-sung, with the lyrics often undergoing changes to suit specific localities.[12]

The Travis family, like almost every other family in those days, had music in the house. They all sang together, the men all played instruments, and during Merle's early years in Rosewood, they had a hand-cranked cylinder phonograph. The problem with nailing down the exact history one hundred years after the fact is that several stories exist concerning what instruments were in the Travis home and how they got there. It's difficult to say with certainty which stories are true. Merle spoke in several interviews about making a handmade banjo when he was around five years old using a can from a carbide lamp, a board from a picket fence, and wires from a screen door for strings. The first real instrument in the house, however, was a five-string banjo that his father acquired. Merle's brother John Melvin remembered the story of the family banjo quite well in a 1987 interview with Eddie Pennington:

Uncle John [Rob's brother] lived down near Beechmont and Browder. We went over there to stay all day Sunday with him. One of Uncle John's sons, named Earl, had this old banjo there, a frame. Didn't have anything but a frame and a neck. But Dad felt it, and he knew enough about banjos to know that it was a really good neck. So he asked Earl what he'd take for it. Well, Earl knew we didn't have any money, 'cause nobody had any in those days. Depression, you know.

So he said if Dad would trade him five of those big black chickens that Mom raised, why, he'd trade him for it.... Monday morning, Dad went out and caught five chickens. Put two of them in one sack. Put three in the other one. I had the sack with three in it [*laughs*]. Took them down to Earl to get the banjo, and he told me before we left, said now, don't you let Merle have that because he's too little. He's liable to break it before he gets home. Well, I had to fight Merle all the way home. He wanted to play with it too, you know.

But we got home, and doggone it, Dad wouldn't let us fool with it, he put it up. We couldn't fool with it while he ordered a head, and strings, and a bridge, some patten [patent] keys. They called them patten keys because you had to drill a hole in there and drive them in, you know.

Well, it seemed like the doggone stuff would never come. Finally, we lived on a Star Route, finally Miss Sorrows that drove the mail wagon, she come by and left it. Man, we thought, we'll have music tonight. Got in and Dad said no boys, got to soak that head 'cause you can't put it on dry. And he said I've got to take the banjo down, and get wood smacked to put them keys on, 'cause Dad didn't have anything to drill a hole with it, or anything.

So he took it down to [his friend] Lewis, and Lewis took a week or so before he ever brought it back. And then had to put that head in the water, and let it soak all night. Must have been a Saturday night, 'cause he was home the next day and he worked—it had to be. So, Sunday morning, and he got it and stretched the head on it. Well, we still had to wait for the head to dry.

Finally he got the doggone strings on it and started playing for us. And man, we just ate that up. And I wanted—he let me have it, and I couldn't do nothing with it. He let Merle have it, he showed Merle, and Merle could do it! Well, just in a little while, Merle was playing the heck out of it. Playing it better than Dad could. Played it as good as Uncle Dave Macon on the *Grand Ole Opry!*

Well, if anybody would come in, Dad couldn't wait to get them to sit down and get the banjo and let Merle play for them. Man, I was jealous.[13]

Merle recalled the fiddle played into his musical childhood, as well:

I used to try and play a fiddle, too. There was an old man named "Uncle" Merrit Addison who lived up on the road—we lived way down in the woods—in Ebenezer. And Uncle Merrit played the fiddle. I'd heard him play a couple of times—maybe I was ten years old. He was an old man. I'd go up there and say, "Uncle Merrit, play me one on the fiddle." I liked that fiddle—putting the rosin on the bow, and the fiddle smelled so good when he opened the case. I thought, "When I grow up I'll be a fiddler, just like Uncle Merrit."[14]

Merle's father would entertain his family and friends with well-known folk songs. He would also teach Merle risqué lyrics to many of those songs, much to Etta's consternation. Merle would inherit his father's sense of humor and eventually injected much of that homespun humor and mischievousness into his own original songs and musical presentation. His father, he remembered, "knowed a thousand little songs that he would sing... songs that I've never, never heard anybody else sing. Songs like 'Moonlight on the Lake' and 'Jenny [Ginny] Weaver.' He had a song called 'Jeff Davis,' a song about the Civil War."[15]

It is significant that the first instrument in the Travis household was a five-string banjo, played in the old "rapping style," as Merle writes in the first part of this chapter. By the 1920s, the old five-string banjo style—played with a constantly moving thumb with finger accompaniment—had almost died out, replaced by the four-string tenor banjo, which was played chord-melody style in jazz and Dixieland bands, with a flat plectrum, also known as a pick. The five-string banjo at this time was a rural relic, a throwback to the Civil War era (it wasn't until Earl Scruggs appeared in the 1940s with Bill Monroe's Bluegrass Boys that the five-string banjo began its comeback from obscurity that has continued to this day). Merle's first exposure to thumb style was here, watching Rob Travis's banjo playing. This is where Merle learned the basics of what later became his signature thumbpicking style for the guitar.

The story of the first guitar in the Travis household has a few different variations on the same basic theme. As Merle writes, his first exposure to hearing guitar music was when some local miners, bunking in tents, performed near his house. The sound captivated the youngster and sparked his interest in the instrument that he would make world famous. Merle often told the story of his first guitar, the "Taylor-made" he claimed was made by his oldest brother. He told it so often, usually as part of his stage patter, that it became the official story even though there is quite a bit of evidence that the "Taylor-made" story wasn't exactly the way it happened. For one thing, in those days, making a flat-top acoustic guitar good enough to play was quite difficult, and certainly beyond the abilities of the average rural woodworker with limited tools. In addition, the few photos that exist of Merle playing guitar during this early moment show him with what appears to be a fairly standard-issue budget "catalog" guitar, made by a manufacturer like Regal or Harmony. These cheap, beginner instruments were called such because they could be mail-ordered through catalogs from Sears and Roebuck or Montgomery Ward. "Catalog" guitars were common in those days, especially in rural areas where there were no music stores to speak of.

Merle's brother John Melvin always insisted, privately, that the "Taylor-made" story was just that, a story that delivered a good punchline at a show:

> The way the first guitar come in the family.... My brother [Taylor] and his wife [May] came home, and she could pick a little. The Gregorys

had lived up the road from us, about a quarter of a mile. They had an old guitar. The head was busted on it, the back was busted on it, and everything, but it had strings on it. This little ol' boy that played with Merle, called Fuzzy [Gregory], well, Merle and Fuzzy went up there to get that guitar, brought it down. And May played those two pieces. Now, she couldn't hardly play anything else, but them two pieces, she could just play the fool out of them.[16]

Eddie Pennington recalled: "Taylor's wife, I think her name was May, she could play about four tunes. 'Rose Time,' 'Aunt Dinah,' and I think a couple more. She could just play those fast and just wear 'em out, but that's all she played."[17]

John Melvin Travis notes:

And that set Merle on fire for the guitar. Okay, there was another chicken trade. Traded five chickens for that. That's his first guitar, and he learned a whole lot on that. That's the one he had when he got to following Mose and Ike around. Now this "Taylor-made" guitar that you've heard about, read about, I don't remember a bit more about that. I don't actually believe it ever happened. I never did see it. I never did hear tell of it. And I know Taylor couldn't make a guitar to start with. But maybe that's a publicity story, you know. But I think Merle told it so long he believed it.[18]

Both John Melvin and Merle were interested in the guitar, and John Melvin became a proficient thumbpicker in his own right. A photo from the early 1930s shows the two of them playing guitars, both teenagers equipped not only with the required thumb picks, but also with their left thumbs wrapped firmly and deliberately over the top of the neck, another hallmark of the Muhlenberg style. One interesting detail about Merle's first guitar, evident in the same photo, is an inlaid heart symbol on the third fret. Whether this came stock on the guitar or was part of the "Taylor-made" story, it would influence the design of his famous Bigsby solidbody guitar two decades later. One evening when Merle was just learning, Merrit Addison's son Coley showed him how to play the old standard "Tuck Me to Sleep in My Old Kentucky Home." John Melvin recalled, "Coley was good, but by the time we left that evening, Merle could play it as well as Coley could."[19]

The Muhlenberg County thumbpicking guitar style was (and still is) a wholly unique regional American musical achievement. An entire book could be devoted to the subject, and it certainly deserves more attention than the space available in this biography. The simplest way to describe it is to explain that most styles of guitar feature the right hand of the player either strumming chords or playing single-note lead parts holding a flat pick, or plectrum. In simple terms, usually a guitarist either plays a rhythm part, a strum to back up the other instruments, or a lead part, a solo that occupies the focus of attention. The style that became prevalent in Muhlenberg County was neither of these; it was unique. It was both rhythm *and* lead, played at the same time. The thumb plays a bass part, often in tandem with the player's left-hand thumb reaching over the fretboard to play bass notes—an unusual and technically improper way to hold the left hand, the antithesis of classical guitar left-hand technique. Merle described it thus: "Mostly I grab a guitar neck like a hoe handle."[20] The first finger of the right hand, and in some cases the other fingers as well, play the melody (lead) parts, fretted on the left hand by the available fingers. The bass/rhythm parts and the lead parts are often syncopated, similar to the ragtime piano style. For many of the advanced Muhlenberg-style players, in addition to the bass notes and the melody (lead) parts, there is an accompanying rhythm strum being played at the same time, in syncopation with the bass notes. The resulting sound, in the hands of an accomplished player, is nothing short of astonishing—a rhythm and lead part, played simultaneously, often described as sounding like an entire band played by one musician. As Merle put it, "Well, they done the thumb and finger pickin', you know, where as you play the accompaniment with your thumb, sort of an oompah-oompah bass, you know, then you play the melody with... one finger."[21]

The physical part of thumb-style guitar was not by any means unique to Muhlenberg County. There were African American players playing with their thumb and fingers during this time, and it is safe to assume that the earliest recording artists popularizing finger-style guitar in the 1920s—Blind Blake, Mississippi John Hurt, Blind Lemon Jefferson, Reverend Gary Davis, and Kentucky's own Sylvester Weaver—did not invent their finger-style methods, but learned it from earlier generations playing both banjo and guitar. It was not exclusive to African American players, either. Mother Maybelle Carter of the Virginia-based Carter Family played with a thumb pick and her fingers in a style known as the "Carter scratch." In Tennessee, Sam McGee played thumb-style guitar as one of the first performers on the radio broadcast of the *Grand Ole Opry*. Roy Harvey, from West Virginia, was another white guitarist who played in this style, recording several brilliant guitar instrumentals in the late 1920s with Leonard Copeland and Jess Johnson in addition to being a member of Charlie Poole's North Carolina Ramblers. What was unique about the Muhlenberg style, as opposed to other regional thumb-picking styles such as the Piedmont style or the styles of the Delta bluesmen, was a level of chordal complexity, the use of the entire fretboard, and a mixture of genres and styles—hillbilly, blues, pop, Dixieland, jazz, ragtime, big band, gospel—that gave it a sophisticated perch in the hierarchy of rural music of that era.

When the guitar became more popular at the beginning of the twentieth century, a loose network of musicians around Muhlenberg County would often get together and play music. Sometimes it was in private homes. Sometimes it was on the porch of the coal company general store, or at informal gathering places, like Cleaton Crossing, a popular Saturday-night gathering place in Cleaton where the railroad tracks came through the small mining community between Drakesboro and Central City. The guitarists all knew one another and taught each other licks and songs. Sometimes white guitarists would interact with African American guitarists; they often worked together in the mines during the day. In the case of Muhlenberg County, a very special distillation of guitar playing styles came into being during the first part of the twentieth century.

Kennedy Jones (1900–1990) is credited as the man who started the Muhlenberg County thumbpicking guitar style. Kennedy was also quick to give credit to his mother, Alice, as the one he'd learned it from. Local historians credit Alice DeArmond Jones as the true originator of the style. Kennedy made the claim that he was the first standard ("Spanish" guitar, to use the proper terminology) guitarist to use a thumb pick. The metal thumb pick had been around for some time, since the latter part of the 1800s, but was designed for and exclusively used with banjo or the Hawaiian guitar. The earliest known mention of a celluloid plastic thumb pick was the 1907–8 Lyon and Healy dealer catalog, and it was also introduced for the same purpose—banjo or Hawaiian guitar. Spanish-style guitarists either used their bare fingers or a flat pick. They did not use a thumb pick.

It's difficult to know exactly who was the first Spanish-style guitarist to try using a celluloid thumb pick, but Kennedy Jones insisted he was the first in an interview with researcher Bill Lightfoot:

I'm the first man ever picked six-string guitar with a thumb pick. I didn't make the pick, nor have it made. I got out one night, and I played for a dance. And I wore a blister on my thumb, and boy, it was really sore. I was sleeping with it out from under the covers, it burnt so bad. And I went down to Central City, just below where I was raised. And I went in the music store down there. And they had the picks just sitting out on the counter. I said to the man that owned the place, "How much you get for the picks?"

He said, "I'll sell you three for a quarter, or I'll sell you a whole box for $1.35."

I said, "Well, let me see one of your guitars up there."

He said, "No, no. A pick wasn't made to play a six-string guitar."

I said, "I know, I know. I'm gonna try something. Hand me down your guitar, I'm not gonna run off with it."

So he handed it down to me. And I started picking with it. Just finger and thumb, that's all I used, right there. Couldn't do a good job to start with, but it gave me a good idea, 'cause I could. So I bought the whole box. Turned the box up and filled my pockets full of them. I started picking, and oh, about a week, two weeks, I was really rockin'. Oh, I could just do it and talk to you.

I guess I was about eighteen years old. I was eighteen years old when I started picking with a thumb pick. And everybody down there saw me playing with a thumb pick, used to follow me around, saying, "I'm gonna get me a thumb pick, play like Kennedy Jones."[22]

Over the years, musicologists have given much attention to an African American musician named Arnold Shultz (1886–1931), who was born in nearby Ohio County, Kentucky. Assorted researchers have attempted to crown Schultz as the originator of the thumbpicking style that took root in Muhlenberg County. Shultz, known locally as Shultzy or Shootz, was by all accounts a great musician. He played guitar, fiddle, mandolin, banjo, and piano. Kentucky Bluegrass legend Bill Monroe interacted with Shultz quite a bit as he was growing up and often spoke of him as an important influence on the bluesy side of bluegrass music's creation. Another fiddler from the same county (Ohio County, Kentucky) as Bill Monroe, Tex Atchison (who also played later with Merle), also claimed Arnold Shultz as an influence.

Shultz was different than other musicians in Kentucky during that time in that he traveled extensively. Some referred to him as a hobo, but like many itinerant musicians, he followed work and found himself going to places like Louisville, Evansville, and St. Louis, and in the winter months heading south to New Orleans on the steamboats that cruised down the Ohio River. Shultz was said to be a huge follower of early jazz pioneer Jelly Roll Morton, and another legend says that he played with W. C. Handy, the father of the blues, in Henderson, Kentucky.

It would be a mistake to say that Shultz invented the Muhlenberg County thumbpicking style. Kennedy Jones was always adamant that he had learned the style from his mother and was already quite advanced by the time he met Shultz:

I was about nineteen or twenty. I'd say that. I can't remember, it's too far back. Anyway, I went in, and he [Arnold Shultz] had his guitar. Big, flat guitar, just like, made like that. And he played a tune with a knife. He tuned that guitar, E tuning. And he put it there in his lap, he took his knife, and made a bar out of it. And boy, he could really play. Yeah, I loved to hear him play. He was a fine guitar player. As far as me ever learning anything from him... I done played a guitar, but I never did see him before.[23]

Jones describes Shultz as playing Hawaiian-style guitar on his lap in an open tuning, but Shultz did also play thumb-and-finger-style standard guitar. However, Jones's point is that he had already been playing thumb-style guitar for at least twelve years before he saw Shultz for the first time. Certainly the thing that differentiates the Muhlenberg County thumbpicking style from other regional guitar styles is the sophisticated use of chords, in particular "passing" chords, or connecting chords inserted between the main chords of a song. Passing chords are a hallmark of New Orleans jazz, so the notion that Shultz brought this chordal knowledge to Muhlenberg County after seeing Jelly Roll Morton in New Orleans is quite possible.

Shultz died in 1931 at the age of forty-five. There are only a handful of photos of the man, most of which show him playing the fiddle. He never recorded, so it's difficult to say with certainty what he sounded like and how he played and impossible to evaluate his true contributions to the Muhlenberg sound. The best educated guess would be that Shultz is the individual who brought the sophisticated chord knowledge into Muhlenberg County. The subject of Shultz still inspires spirited debate among thumbpickers, however. Thom Bresh notes: "Chet Atkins would say, 'I'd never heard of Arnold Shultz before those suspenders-wearing goddamn college professors started bringing him up.'"[24]

Jones, with or without the exact known influence from Shultz, became the best known and most admired guitarist in Muhlenberg County during the 1920s, and his thumbpicking style became widely copied in the area. Jones also wrote what became the best-known song in the entire thumbpicking songbook, "Cannonball Rag." Jones told the story that he wrote it as a young man and performed it often but that it was unnamed for many years. As local legend has it, Jones would often pick guitar near Cleaton Crossing. Mose Rager recounted the origin of the song's name in an interview with Bill Lightfoot:

> Ol' Jones told me about that—Kennedy was the one told me that. The one he told me... that him and a feller by the name of Frock Lewis was up on Cleaton ball diamond, that run down kindly on the railroad; it was on down a big hill, you know, by the railroad track. There was two mines down there, Lam's and Crescent. The railroad track goes through there, goes through Drakesboro, goes through Central City, it's an L&N Railroad.
>
> So Frock and Kennedy was up in Cleaton ball diamond one night, and they's both a-drinkin', you see. Ol' Kennedy run down on that

chord—he was sittin' right in the middle of the ball diamond with a guitar—and he run down on that ol' "Cannonball Rag" chord. And Frock said, about that time, he said, "Listen to that cannonball!" [Eddie Pennington cites another Muhlenberg County legend that a man named Roy Casey was the one who actually uttered this line.] There's a railroad engine come through there and that's what he meant—it was blowin', you know, the whistle was—and Frock said, "Listen to that cannonball!"

So Kennedy named that ol' tune "Cannonball Rag." That's the way he told it to me.[25]

From that night forward, Jones's composition was known as "Cannonball Rag," and it became one of Merle Travis's most performed and oft-imitated numbers.

Other guitar players in the area used the thumbpicking style. Recall that Merle's friend Colie Addison showed him how to play the tune "Tuck Me to Sleep in My Old Kentucky Home." His friend Fuzzy Gregory played several instruments, including the guitar. Amos Johnson, another African American guitarist from the area, is generally credited with writing the song "Guitar Rag" that Merle would later record. And African American guitarist James Mason, born in 1899, claimed to have taught Mose Rager much of his "neck-choking" style while the two worked together in the mines around Drakesboro. Lester "Plucker" English did not play finger style like Kennedy Jones but was known in the area for his extensive chord knowledge and excellent rhythm guitar skills. Merle later remembered: "Lester was the first rhythm man I ever knew. He would use his thumb pick but he'd play rhythm on a guitar. You know, with a thumb pick, just as we say now, like a powerhouse, like a pile driver."[26]

None of these players, however, had the impact on young Merle Travis that a pair of local musicians did: Mose Rager and Ike Everly. According to Merle, "Mose Rager and Ike Everly and, I might say, Lester English was the guys that I just idolized. They were my heroes. Not baseball players, not boxers, [but] Mose Rager, Ike Everly... and Lester English."[27] Moses "Mose" Rager (1911–1986) was a guitar player whose influence was felt far beyond the small region where he spent the majority of his life. He came from a large musical family and began playing guitar at a young age. When he was fourteen, around the year 1925 or 1926, a friend told him about a local guitarist who played all up and down the neck, and he was intrigued. The guitarist his friend mentioned was Kennedy Jones, who often performed at Cleaton Crossing on Saturday nights. Hitching a ride in a mule-driven log wagon to see Jones, Rager tried to sleep on the way to Cleaton but was too excited about meeting Jones (the many bumps in the road didn't help). When they arrived, Jones was in the middle of a date with a girl, but Rager convinced him to play for him. Jones interrupted his date to play a tune for Rager, and the young lad immediately became an ardent disciple, striving to learn everything he could from the man:

> I didn't know a guitar could be played like Kennedy Jones played it. He went all up and down the neck, played good tunes and used pretty chords. He was the first good guitar player I ever heard. We got him over on my brother-in-law's porch. He sat right down there and played that guitar like I had never seen one played before—"My Old Kentucky Home," and he came on down there. It was really something for me, just run me crazy as a lunatic. I didn't have a bit of sense after that. Every time I got around Kennedy Jones I'd follow him around. We'd play together. I'd go down to Kennedy's house and stay out two or three days and nights picking.[28]

By all accounts, Rager took what he learned from Jones and further refined it. Rager loved the blues he heard from local African American musicians and added a layer of blues to the local thumbpicking repertoire. Jones's daughter Lee remembered, "Everybody socialized. Nobody thought anything about the mixing of races or social classes."[29] Merle later recalled his own fascination with Rager's style of playing:

> Mose did not strum his instrument, but had developed the technique of using his thumb pick and fingers. With his thumb he played his accompaniment, while his fingers fell to the melodies he desired. By so doing, the guitar was two instruments in one. Without effort he would play tunes that scolded, lilted, caressed or moaned—like a laugh hiding a cry—these were the blues, at which Mose sings as well as he plays.[30]

Unable to purchase any commercially available celluloid thumb picks, Rager made his first one by heating up a toothbrush, bending it around his thumb, and whittling the end into a point.

Like most other men in Muhlenberg County, Rager worked in the mines. From 1927 to 1943 he was employed by the Black Diamond Coal Company in Cleaton and Madisonville, Kentucky. During that time Mose picked guitar, hanging around the mines with white and African American mine workers: "If there was no work for that day, [we would] pass a guitar around. [Our] songs and tunes had humor, and each of the more accomplished players developed show-off items."[31] As his reputation as a local "hot" guitarist grew, the lure of a professional career beckoned. Rager quit the mines and left in the summer of 1942 to join Kennedy Jones in Chicago, playing in the clubs for displaced Southerners who liked hillbilly music. He briefly toured with Grandpa Jones, a star of the *Grand*

Ole Opry (who knew Merle Travis well, as later chapters will discuss). Jones introduced Rager to the reality of a professional music career—traveling long hours in cramped cars for little pay. Rager also worked tours with Zeke Clements, Ernest Tubb, and Curly Fox, along with Fox's wife and singing partner, Texas Ruby. Touring with the latter group in the 1940s, he recorded a few performances with them, most notably a short but hot electric thumbpicked solo on their recording of "Black Mountain Rag" for King Records.

Blistered by the grueling pace of the road and concerned about the abundant alcohol and bad behavior he witnessed in the music business (he was a deeply religious man), Rager quit the Curly Fox and Texas Ruby band in late 1947 or early 1948. For several years he played around the region with Les Smithhart and a few other artists, but on a limited basis. With the exception of some later folk concerts in his later years—as well as the two times he was coaxed out of Muhlenberg County in 1973 and 1976 to perform with Merle at the Festival of American Folklife in Washington, DC—that was the sum total of his professional career. But although Rager didn't like being on the road, he still loved music and continued to play the guitar. He opened a barbershop in Drakesboro, and for the remainder of his life he hosted thumbpicker jam sessions either there or at his home. Rager died in Greenville, Kentucky, in 1986.

Whenever Merle was back home in Muhlenberg County, he would sneak off and find Mose and the two would disappear for hours, picking together in private. A letter Merle wrote to Rager in 1979 sums up his influence: "I won't ever get to believing the stuff they write about me, when it should be about you. I ain't forgot where I learned about all I know about pickin' the guitar. It was from a feller by the name of Mose Rager. I tell that every chance I get. I hope you know that. If it hadn't been for you, a lot of us would be pickin' up cans along the highway to sell."[32]

Another local Muhlenberg County man, Ike Everly, was almost certainly Merle's second-greatest influence. Isaac Milford "Ike" Everly Jr. (1908–1975) is best known today as the father of the world-famous Everly Brothers, Don and Phil. Certainly the Everly Brothers are giants in Muhlenberg County history, as they are far and away the most commercially successful musical act to come from the area. But long before Don and Phil began their careers, Ike and his brothers Charlie and Leonard performed as the original Everly Brothers around Kentucky and Chicago in the 1930s.

Ike Everly had nine brothers and sisters. They were another musically inclined family, and by the time Ike, Charlie, and Leonard were in their teens, all three were proficient guitar players and singers. (Interestingly, while Charlie was in Chicago playing, he played briefly with the Xavier Cugat Latin orchestra. When

Cugat discovered that Charlie Everly could not read sheet music and was also functionally illiterate, he was let go.) Leonard Everly played a multitude of instruments, according to his son Darris: "He played lead guitar with a straight pick, like Les Paul. He played some thumbstyle, especially on rhythm and blues numbers. He also played the banjo. He could play a French harp and would play the strings on a piano like someone plucking a harp."[33] Ike Everly distinguished himself from his brothers as one of the great thumbpicking legends of Muhlenberg County. Like Mose Rager, Ike spent time around Kennedy Jones since the family lived near Cleaton, where Jones resided. One story told by Jones's daughter Lee Jones is that Ike idolized Jones so much, he began using a cane despite not needing one simply because he had seen Kennedy Jones walking with the assistance of a cane.

Before long, teenage Mose Rager and Ike Everly met in the coal mines and started talking about music and guitars. From that moment on, they became almost inseparable. Many people (including Merle Travis) would often speak of Mose and Ike as a pair. Ike was known as a gentle, kind man with a big sense of humor. During the early 1930s, he played with his brothers around western Kentucky and picked guitar with his friend Mose. In the late 1930s, the original Everly Brothers decided to move to Chicago to get work (Leonard refused to work in the mines). They performed there until Charlie Everly's untimely death right after Christmas in 1945 at the age of thirty-one. Leonard stayed in Chicago, but Ike took his family (which by this time consisted of his wife, Margaret, and their two young sons, Don and Phil) to Waterloo, Iowa, to perform hillbilly music as a family band on a radio station there.

The Everly family performed on the radio in various locations in Iowa, Chicago, Knoxville, Nashville, and Peoria. When the music business waned, Ike studied to be a barber, like Mose, in the hopes of retiring from music. Those plans were disrupted when their sons Don and Phil began writing songs and singing in harmony. Ike called in a few favors and asked Chet Atkins to get the boys an audition in Nashville, marketing his teenage sons as the Everly Brothers. Outside of Muhlenberg County and a few honky-tonks in Chicago, few people remembered that there had been another act by the same name two decades before. Atkins didn't sign the Everly Brothers to RCA Records, where he worked as an A&R man, but the Nashville audition opened some doors. The pair got signed and had a flop country single on Columbia Records in 1956, but they were quickly snapped up by Cadence Records in 1957 as a rock 'n' roll act after Elvis Presley's fame exploded.

Don and Phil became huge stars with their breakout hit, "Bye Bye, Love," and Ike and Margaret became show-business parents to one of the most successful acts in the country. One of their first albums, which didn't sell particularly well at the time, was a collection of older songs called *Songs Our Daddy Taught Us*, a thoughtful tribute to their father's music and their Kentucky upbringing. In the late 1960s the Everly Brothers again revisited their country heritage, releasing an album of country-rock songs called *Roots* in 1968. Soon after that they appeared on *The Johnny Cash Show* on ABC-TV, where they brought out their father to demonstrate where they had learned their craft. It is from these brief TV appearances that we are able to hear Ike's thumbpicking style—firmly rooted in the Muhlenberg tradition but with distinct differences from Mose Rager and Merle Travis. The only other recorded legacy of Ike consists of six songs taped live at a guitar workshop at the Newport Folk Festival in 1969. These were released decades later on a compilation called *Nashville at Newport*. While the recording is somewhat noisy at times, it is enough to hear what a master guitarist Ike was. Ike Everly never released any recordings under his own name, which explains why he isn't well known to guitar enthusiasts today. The Everly estate apparently has many radio transcriptions from the 1940s and 1950s that feature guitar instrumentals played by Ike, but with the exception of one or two that have been posted to YouTube, these remain unheard. Don and Phil produced an Ike Everly solo album in 1969, following the critical success of their album *Roots*, but it was never released, and the master tapes have mysteriously been removed from the Warner Bros. archive.

When Mose Rager and Ike Everly wanted to play together during the 1930s, there were no commercial venues in Muhlenberg County such as nightclubs or theaters. In those days, musical performances took place in people's homes, on the porch of the coal company store, or at informal lawn gatherings like the one at the baseball diamond at Cleaton Crossing. It was at one of these informal functions that young Merle Travis first heard Mose Rager and Ike Everly play, namely at Mrs. Bunnie Baugh's house across the road from the church in Ebenezer. Merle describes the meeting in his own words earlier in this chapter. He uses reverential tones, and in typical fashion, he doesn't brag on himself.

Mose Rager recalled meeting Merle: "We played there a long time, and finally he took ahold of the guitar and made a few chords on it and done pretty good! And that's the first time I met Merle. And from then on, old Merle, he'd try and make the rounds. Anywhere I'd go play around, he'd try and be there. Maybe I'd be comin' in somewhere—I'd have my old guitar under my arm, and Travis'd be right behind me."[34] Even though Merle describes his discovery of Mose Rager and Ike Everly in his own words above, another quote sheds further light on how much of an impact these two slightly older pickers had on him:

I felt I was listening to an angel's harp. I had never heard anything so beautiful in my life as the way these two boys played their guitars. I would sit and watch every move they made. I would think, "My God, if I could ever learn to play like that, I would give anything in the world." Whenever I heard that Ike Everly or Mose Rager were playing anywhere in the county, I would walk, start at four o'clock in the afternoon, be on the road to be there. I would sit with open eyes and listen to them play. I would go home and do my very best to imitate them in every way I could.[35]

Earl Talmadge Dukes recalled: "Merle, he was a little younger than Ike and Mose. And all he had to do—he got so good in what he was doing at an early age—was just watch them, and listen at them. He didn't have to ask any questions; no one heard him ask any. But he could go home and grab that guitar and sit down and do the same thing. And he just kept going like that until he got to where he could do his own thing. It's just one of them deals where you can't hold a good man back, and that's what you had."[36]

Recall that Merle was born in 1917. The electronic vacuum tube had been commercially introduced only two years earlier, enabling the production of radios and other electrical amplification. After the end of World War I in 1919, radio broadcasting began in earnest and would eventually carry its signal deep into the US heartland. Merle's family had no electricity in their home, like many rural families, so when they did eventually get a cylinder record player, they relied on hand cranking, not electricity. Merle remembered the family "talking machine" in an interview with Mark Humphrey:

The first records I remember hearing were Edison cylinders. Then we traded the Edison machine for a Westrola phonograph. We didn't have the money to buy records, [so] Taylor, who was twenty years older than me, must've drug in most of them. But when we'd order a new pair of overalls from Sears and Roebuck in the fall, my dad would put in and get a new record. Sometimes it would be a Hawaiian record, Hawaiian chants, and sometimes it would be a comedy record. My uncle had a whole bunch of records—Carson Robison, Vernon Dalhart, and all that. We had a guitar solo record by Nick Lucas. One side was called "Pickin' the Guitar" and the other side was called "Teasing the Frets." And boy, we'd say, "Can't that feller play! Wow!"[37]

Merle was born before the term "country music" was invented. Certainly, rural folk music existed throughout the country, with oral traditions passed down through families from their roots in European folk music (and African folk music, among the African American communities). But while the Travises were certainly country people, perhaps "hillbillies" in the eyes of city dwellers of the era, like a great many rural families, they were interested in many different types of music. Music was not so carefully corralled into genres then, and in a region like Muhlenberg County, the influences came from North, South, East, and West (and the Sears and Roebuck mail-order catalog). Merle variously recalled later:

> We had Hawaiian music and of course Gid Tanner and His Skillet Lickers and a lot of Clayton McMichen records.... And then Taylor got hold of some brass band records and some popular records of the day, which we call Dixieland bands now. That was the "talking machine."[38]
>
> You see, I listened to everything. We had Paul Whiteman and His Ambassador Orchestra playing "Stars and Stripes Forever" and "Under the Double Eagle," and all sorts of Strauss waltzes. We didn't know that there was a name called country music or a name called popular music. It was all just music if we knew it and played it. We probably played some of it wrong and some of it right.[39]
>
> I had records by Chris Bouchillon, the old talkin' blues boy. If you don't pay attention to the jokes he's tellin', you're gonna hear some mighty fine guitar pickin'. I'd listen to the pop records, too, along with the "country," and I'd learn a tune from the Skillet Lickers one day and maybe Paul Whiteman's Orchestra the next.[40]

By the early 1930s, radio crept into the area, which widened Merle's musical horizons even further:

> Frank Travis, he lived up across the field there from us, and his son-in-law, Bewley Shutt, he had a battery radio and a great big high poplar pole out there with an arrow on it. Now, we used to, the way Dad would say it, "Let's go up to Frank's tonight and radio." So we'd go up there and listen to the radio, and we'd hear the *Grand Ole Opry*. The Fruit Jar Drinkers and them people down in Nashville them days and Robert Lunn, doing the talking blues, every Saturday night. And then Del Rio, Texas, and Eagle Pass. There was a guy down there named the Lonesome Cowboy.
>
> Now, at the age of about thirteen or fourteen, Bewley Shutt moved up on top of the hill towards Beech Creek. And I used to make it a point to go up there every day I could at noon to hear Gene Autry and Clayton McMichen and the Log Cabin Boys. And Cousin Emmy. Especially Clayton McMichen and Gene Autry. I liked to hear them on the radio. And that was when I got real conscious of the radio.[41]

Merle also remembered the diversity of radio programming in those days and the effect it had on his heroes, Mose Rager and Ike Everly: "They played the black man's blues, they played 'Tiger Rag,' they played the tunes they heard Ferde Grofe and Hugo Winterhalter do, they played the tunes they heard from Chicago on their battery [radio] sets. They played the songs they heard Bing Crosby sing in the pictures."[42]

Merle had a very active mind and was often described by those who knew him as highly intelligent. One of his school report cards from 1927–28 survives, and it shows that he was a good student, receiving mostly A marks, with a few Bs. Regardless of his abilities, school was an unaffordable luxury for many Depression-era families, who needed their children to begin working manual-labor jobs as soon as they were able. Merle quit public school after the eighth grade—shocking today, but quite common then in rural communities. But whereas most kids who quit school did so to begin working jobs, Merle had no plans for the future except avoiding manual labor: "I started out playin' at play parties and dances. I quit school after the eighth grade. It was during the Depression, and I figured I had to start makin' my own way. My folks weren't none too happy about that, but by 1935 I was out hoppin' freight trains and playing on street corners to make some money."[43]

In 1947, when Merle returned as a conquering hero to raise money for a local baseball field, his history teacher Wallace Ward remembered his former student's attitude toward academia and habit of bringing his guitar into the classroom: "I'd protest and tell him to leave the thing outside. Merle would say, 'Professor Ward, I ain't going to make my living like you do. I'm going to make it with my guitar.'"[44]

Merle was always curious to learn new things. In the liner notes to his 1963 album *Songs from the Coal Mines*, his brother John Melvin recalled: "One could almost see his brain storing up data of all kinds when he was a dirty-faced kid. Nobody ever asked so many questions, made as many observations, experimented as much, or made such a nuisance of himself, or had as many friends. Young people, old people, white or colored, all knew this fellow and marveled at his capacity to understand them. He made them laugh and cry with his music. He made them furious with his practical jokes."

Merle found other things to pique his interest—dismantling and rebuilding wristwatches, guns and hunting, taxidermy, cartooning. He would remain keen on all of these hobbies for his entire life. In the words of Earl Talmadge Dukes:

> When he was just a boy, he was always doing something. I don't care what. He was either working on a watch, out in the woods trying to find a squirrel to stuff, just anything. Merle stayed busy. He could draw like

crazy. He used to be a pretty good shot with a rifle. In fact maybe he was real good—I thought at least, anyway. And one Sunday morning we went behind my brother's house, and my brother said, "I don't know, but I believe you boys are crazy." [Merle] was shooting fire out, off a cigarette in my mouth. My brother said, "One of these days, you're gonna kill one another if you don't quit doing these crazy things." But we lived through it. He didn't make no bad shots. But I've let him do that several times. He was real good with a rifle… and he'd usually get that fire.[45]

Like most budding musicians, Merle found himself no longer in school, trying to figure out what he was going to do with the rest of his life. The mines beckoned, but they brought the unwelcome prospect of manual labor. Dukes further recalled:

One time, Merle and myself was gonna clear some ground for my dad. We wanted a pair of Big Mac overalls and they cost a dollar. Dad said he'd give us thirty-five cents a day, so it was fine. We're gonna clear ground for three days. Well, first day, done pretty good. Second day, I seen Merle, he was shaking his hands and looking at them. I'd kinda been used to working a little bit and I said—now, of course Merle had corns on the end of his fingers from his guitar—and I says, that axe handle kind of getting to you, digging holes? He just stuck his hands out. He had blisters all over his hands; he couldn't slide his hands up and down the guitar neck, I don't think, [and it] had him squalling a little bit. I said, if I was you, I would stop right where you're at. And he said no, I can't do that. I said, well why can't you, if I could play a guitar like you, I sure would. And he said, well, I just don't want to be a quitter. And I said, well, it's up to you, but I don't see how the hell you're gonna stand it.[46]

Unsure of what to do next, Merle did what many rural teenage boys and young men did in the Great Depression: he joined the Civilian Conservation Corps. He devotes a few words to his experience there in his own section of this first chapter, but a little background on the CCC brings perspective.

The CCC, as Merle describes, was a government program enacted during the Depression. Franklin D. Roosevelt started it in 1933 as one of the more ambitious parts of his New Deal legislation. The CCC was a way to take government money and pay unemployed and unmarried young men to do necessary improvement and maintenance work on public lands, national monuments, battlefields, and the like. It was socialism, pure and simple, but it was a lifesaver for many young men like Merle who had no job skills and no way to make a living wage. The young men (aged eighteen to twenty-five when the project first started, widened to seventeen to twenty-eight by the time the program ended in 1942) lived in camps, worked on the projects, and received pay of about thirty dollars a month in addition to free meals, housing, medical care, and work clothes while they were enrolled. Merle remembers that although he dreamed of going to an exotic location on his CCC adventure, he was assigned to Columbus, Kentucky, near the Missouri border, where he worked on a Civil War battlefield memorial: "The next big money—big tycoon that I became—was when I joined the CCC camp. I was fifteen, I guess. Fifteen or sixteen." His tenure in the CCC only lasted a short time: "I stayed in there about a month or two and then I caught a freight train and went home and went back and everything. I wasn't a very good CCC boy, I tell ya."[47]

According to recently discovered military records from 1944, Merle told the aptitude board at the Marine boot camp at Parris Island, South Carolina, that during his time at the CCC, he was placed in the Fort Knox hospital for his nerves. It is unknown what nervous condition Merle suffered from, but it meant an early dismissal from the CCC camp. His lifelong friend Grandpa Jones recalled in a 1993 interview: "He [Merle] told me he had nerve problems when he was... fifteen or sixteen years old."[48] If Merle's memory is accurate, he would have joined the program around 1934 (a date that matches the year that the Columbus-Belmont battlefield memorial park was created, according to the Parks Service). Since that would have made him sixteen at the time, he had to have lied about his age to get accepted, a common practice in those days before computer ID databases:

There wasn't any work, period. It was during the Depression. And if a person made a dollar a day, you was doing well. If you went to CCC camp, the price that you was paid was thirty dollars a month, and you got to keep five and send the twenty-five home, and golly, that helped your folks out tremendously. The mines wasn't working well at all. People didn't walk around with a dollar bill in their pocket. A dollar bill—[a person] looked like a rich man if he reached in his pocket and pulled out a dollar bill.

It was at Columbus, Kentucky. About a hundred miles from home. And what they done there was rebuild the old Columbus-Belmont battlefield. That's where they put the big chain across the Mississippi River to keep the Lincoln gunboats from going south. I think the first boat to come down blewed [sic] up the chain and went on down. But they dug up the anchor and now it's on a big concrete block, and it's a pretty popular park now in Columbus, Kentucky. If you're ever down there, you can say, "There's the park that Travis built."[49]

His brief flirtation with manual work inspired only one idea in Merle's mind: getting a better-quality guitar:

> I learned a lot of things at the CCC camp. I learned that I got paid enough money that when I got out, I bought me a Gretsch guitar. I caught a freight train when I got home, so much money was sent home and then the boy got the rest, and I told my folks all I wanted was a guitar. I caught the L&N train to Owensboro down on the Ohio River, and then I caught a train out of there to Evansville, Indiana, to the Howell Railroad yard. And my brother, he lived there—Taylor, you know—so I went up to Taylor's and went down to the music store, a few days and I bought this fine Gretsch guitar. I think it must have cost about twenty dollars. And boy, was I happy![50]

Also around this same time, Merle became experienced in the teenage hobo's art. His first musical traveling experiences centered on hopping freight trains and steamboats with friends, surviving any way he could, and playing music:

> There was a feller, his name was Raymond McClellan.... He knows a thousand songs, and he was a funny lookin' little feller, you know, he had crossed eyes, little and short and had a nasal-y way of speakin', you know?... Well, me and Raymond would go on hobo trips and we'd play on the street corners and people would give us nickels and dimes. We'd go to faraway places like Springfield, Tennessee, and Paducah, Kentucky, and Fulton, Tennessee, and Indiana and them places, you know.
>
> I used to ride steamboats a lot with a fella named Junior Rose. Now, Junior was a mandolin player. He played the mandolin and lived over at Powderly, Kentucky. That's between Central City and Greenville. Well, me and him was about the same age, about fifteen or sixteen, and we used to go on the trips. We would go, we would catch the L&N out of Drakesboro, Louisville, and Nashville. We'd catch what they called a local, and we'd go up to Central City and catch the I.C. We'd find an empty boxcar.... We'd ask a brakeman, you know, in the yard which one is makin' up to go to Paducah. He'd show us and then we'd catch the I.C., the Illinois Central. And we'd go to Paducah and then get off and go uptown Paducah and play around on the street corners and pick up collections, you know. Pennies and nickels. Once in a while a dime.
>
> Then we would catch a boat called the *Cordella*, a little sternwheeler that went up the Cumberland River to Dycusburg, Kentucky, up the

Ohio to where the Cumberland runs into it.... And the crew would let us ride because they liked to hear us play, they said, you know....

One night we's playing on the streets of Dycusburg, Kentucky, and picking up collection to buy Coca-Cola and cheese and crackers, you know, and pork and beans, and figured we're a million miles from home. Then we'd get on the boat and climb up and get in the pilot house, you know, and count our money. One night the moon was shinin' real bright and we went up there, and it was an awful good night! We just had lots of money in our pockets, you know. And I was counting my part over there and Junior was countin' his and in the moonlight he'd say, "Here's a penny and there's six, seven, eight, nine," and directly he started saying, "Come here, come here," and I thought maybe the boat was sinkin' or something, and I said, "What is it?" and he said, "Here's a quarter!" And gee whiz, I was proud of that. I guess about four or five summers we'd go and ride the steamboats.[51]

It was during this aimless period that Merle discovered something else that would figure heavily in his future: alcoholic beverages. By most accounts, it was Merle's oldest brother, Taylor, who introduced Merle to alcohol. Earl Talmadge Dukes recalls:

Merle's brother Taylor, he'd made some home brew, and he didn't sell it or anything like that, he was a fine fellow, but he just decided he'd like to have a taste of a good old home brew. And he made him some, and he'd taken it home with him. Mr. and Mrs. Travis never really approved of it, but they didn't mind that much; he was a good fellow, and he didn't drink or get drunk to amount to anything, or didn't get drunk, period.

So, he had a quart of it left. He had it sitting in a back room, and Merle was there. So Merle said, "Let's go back in this room a minute." So we went back there. It was one Sunday morning. It was about ten or eleven o'clock. He said, "Looka there, Taylor's got a quart of home brew." He said, "You wanna drink of it?" And I said we'll liable to get killed, and he said no, I don't think so. So he had a puller in his pocket and he pulled that thing [removed the cork stopper], we sat there and drank that quart of home brew. Nobody came back there to see what we was doing. Of course we was drunk, or thought we was, anyway. So when we got done drinking that home brew, there was a gallon of vinegar, real vinegar sitting there, and Merle filled that quart bottle up about as full as Taylor had it of home brew, and then we capped it back up. So we just sat it back down.

John [Melvin] probably don't even remember this, it's been so long, but he went ahead and told a story. He said Taylor said, "Dad [Rob], I want you to watch the blue smoke roll when I pull this top on this bottle" ["Blue smoke" refers to a faint puff of gas that would appear when opening a capped or corked jug of moonshine—it also later became the title of one of Merle's best-known guitar instrumentals]. Taylor went over there and he yanked the top off of it, of course it just sat there, naturally.... So he just turned it up and was gonna get a little taste of it, and when he did, I think he spit vinegar all over the table. So, I guess that was enough to make him want to kill us.[52]

From an early age, Merle drank to excess. It was common among coal miners and omnipresent among musicians. As Merle would learn over the rest of his life, there was often a steep divide between rollicking, laughing-drunk times and a medical condition with severe life consequences: alcoholism, or as it is properly known today in medical and psychiatric terminology, alcohol use disorder. Sleepy Marlin remembered:

See, Merle was a real, real alcoholic at the age of about fourteen. Before he ever got into broadcasting, any form or shape. When he was still at home in Ebenezer. I don't know how or where they were, but he was letting alcohol get to him. He had an older brother in Evansville; Taylor was his first name. All this was going on and Merle's lapping up the Kentucky moonshine, and its returning part [alcoholism]. Soon as Taylor got ahold of that information he brought Merle to Evansville and put him in the hospital. Got him back on his feet.[53]

Merle had problems with alcohol his entire life. Looking at the progression of his disease through the years, everything followed a textbook pattern of alcoholism. There are genetic markers for it—it runs in a family's DNA. Merle's DNA was Irish, and although some of Ireland's alcoholic reputation is certainly due to social drinking and family history, it is true that Ireland has almost double the alcohol abuse cases per capita than other Western European countries. Another factor that has been suggested as a gene trigger is childhood drinking. As we can see from Sleepy Marlin's story above, Merle was already drinking and suffering from alcohol-related withdrawal symptoms, such as delirium tremens (the so-called DTs) and involuntary shaking, by the time he was a teenager. Such early excessive drinking seems to create more serious problems down the road as the disease progresses. Alcohol and its related problems would play a large role in Merle's life.

Merle suffered from anxiety and nervousness as a child, and drinking may have been a way to cope. It is unknown what his condition really was, as he was never properly diagnosed. The abovementioned recently discovered 1944 military records state that Merle suffered from "psychoneurosis, anxiety type," and that he had told the Marine aptitude board that when he was seventeen, "he had a nervous breakdown which kept him away from his work for a year."[54] This may be the hospitalization that Marlin remembered in his earlier quote.

Merle often recounted the story in the earlier part of this chapter about meeting Clayton McMichen for the first time, giving him his address, and waiting to hear about the possibility of a job. But like many of Merle's stories, it was a shortened version of a series of events that transpired over a longer time—in this case, three meetings over two years.

Merle began his professional music career sometime in between the first, second, and third times he approached McMichen about a job, although what he was doing was really just a slight notch above playing on the street and sleeping on steamboats. As Merle writes above, after purchasing a new Gretsch archtop guitar with the money he earned from the CCC, he made his way to Evansville to visit his brother Taylor. Taylor and Merle found themselves at a dance marathon. Again, Merle streamlined the story in his own autobiographical chapter, but revealed more detail in an interview with Ed Kahn:

> One night, why, Taylor said they're having a walk-a-thon, you know, a marathon down on Franklin Street, so me and Taylor went down there and they was broadcastin'. These people, you know, the girl would be asleep and the boy would be walkin' around dancin', they was supposed to be music playin', you know. But they would broadcast from there, over radio station WGBF, and they had some entertainers and everything.
>
> Well, Taylor, he's quite a boy, you know, so he flogged up there and said, "My little brother here, he's got a guitar," and said, "He can really pick it." He's a liar too, you know. So they decided to put me on the next night to do a tune. So I went down the next night with that Gretsch guitar and I got up and played "Tiger Rag" just as much like Mose Rager as I could. That's the first lick I ever hit on the radio.[55]

As Merle writes above, the dance marathon radio appearance on WGBF led to his first professional job as a musician. A search of old newspaper archives nails down the timeline: a series of ads from June 1935 advertises the Knox County Knockabouts performing around the Evansville area, and a similar newspaper archive search finds numerous references to the Tennessee Tomcats performing on radio station WGBF from September 1936 through the end of that year. The

Knox County Knockabouts era for Merle was mid-1935, followed by his stint with the Tennessee Tomcats beginning in the fall of 1936.

Another major event of 1936 that Merle failed to mention in his own writing: he began seriously dating Mary Johnson, a seventeen-year-old Ebenezer girl who was the daughter of a local preacher and coal miner, "Preacher Will" Johnson, and sister of one of his musician buddies, Paul "B. W." Johnson. In Merle's daughter Pat Travis Eatherly's photo memoir *A Scrapbook of My Daddy* (2000), she refers to her parents, Merle and Mary, as "childhood sweethearts." In an interview with the Drifting Pioneers' Sleepy Marlin, Marlin refers to Mary as Merle's "high school sweetheart," but since Merle dropped out of school in the eighth grade, it's more likely that they met through an Ebenezer church or some other local social gathering. Mary and Merle were a couple by 1936 and would continue to date when he was home in Kentucky, interrupted by his many trips to Evansville and the surrounding region.

After his experience working with both the Knox County Knockabouts and the Tennessee Tomcats, Merle met a group then working in Evansville who would later figure greatly in his professional career: the Drifting Pioneers. In his words, "Then there was three boys from Southern Illinois. Walt and Bill Brown from Springerton, Illinois, Southern Illinois, and Sleepy Marlin. Well, these three boys come to Evansville there, and they call themselves the Drifting Pioneers. Well, I finally got a job with them."[56] In Marlin's recollection:

> At another station in the same city of Evansville, there was a band called the Tennessee Tomcats, and in that band was this young "Slim" Travis. We [the Drifting Pioneers] were attracted to his guitar playing because he was pretty good.... We got to talking to him, and he showed great interest in joining our band, because he saw the success we were having....
>
> We made arrangements on a certain day that he would come and join our group. Meanwhile, in past years or months sometime or other, Merle had talked to Clayton McMichen and had some kind of a partial commitment or something. Mac had told him, "Yeah, someday, son, I want you in my band." That's the way he had talked.... On the very day that Merle was to join us, he got a phone call from Clayton McMichen [as Merle tells the story, it was a telegram, not a phone call], who was at that time working at WLW, Cincinnati....
>
> Well, he came to us with his head down, he felt so sad about it. He didn't know what to say. He said he felt like it'd be a bad thing to do to walk out on his promise that he'd come and join us. Very quickly we told

him, don't be bothered about that. We wasn't going to stand in his way from something like that, you know.[57]

Merle describes in great detail earlier in this chapter the tale of how he came to join Clayton McMichen's band. He received a letter in Evansville at his brother's house with a telegram inside from McMichen (sometimes he would vary the story slightly, saying that he received a letter from his mother in Evansville, then went home to Kentucky to retrieve the telegram). Finding his way across the waters during the great Ohio River flood of 1937, he finally got to his parents' house in Kentucky, where he bade his parents adieu, borrowed some money, and went off to join McMichen in Columbus, Ohio.

A minor point, but in Merle's autobiographical telling above, he says that McMichen told him to meet in Columbus, Ohio, on January 10; in other interviews, Merle told the same story but cited either February 4 or March 1. The flood of 1937 happened over the last two weeks of January and the first week of February. It still ranks as one of the worst natural disasters in US history. In Merle's words: "The Ohio River went uptown in Evansville and Louisville and Paducah and all them places that made itself at home, by washing dead cattle and things right up on Main Street.... It was a terrible place then."[58] But it is impossible that Merle would have crossed floodwaters to go home to Kentucky with a telegram instructing him to arrive January 10 in Ohio because the flood hadn't happened yet. Flood levels were reached around January 18. An interview Merle did with Mark Humphrey reveals more detail, and more accurate dates: "The 1937 flood came. I was over in Evansville on the radio at the time. Wow, it was bad. The town was covered with water. When the water went down, there was a letter from my mother saying that I had a telegram at Ebenezer. So I bummed a ride on a rescue boat and got across this flood waters, and got home. It was a telegram from Clayton McMichen saying, 'Meet me in Columbus, Ohio'—the date was a month away."[59]

Newspaper archives contain a few references to a show in Columbus that probably nails down the date Merle joined McMichen's band. No ads mention McMichen by name, but there are a few references to an "Old Time Fiddler's Contest," an angle that McMichen often used, scheduled to appear at the Columbus Auditorium on Sunday, February 7, 1937. This, in all likelihood, was the gig in question. It was the beginning of Merle Travis's serious professional music career, and also the date he moved away from his boyhood home in Muhlenberg County, Kentucky. He would return to visit numerous times but would never again reside in the state. At nineteen, Merle was on his way, and there was no looking back.

Merle on stage with The Drifting Pioneers, Cincinnati, 1939.

CHAPTER 2

CINCINNATI: WLW, THE GALLOPIN' GOOSE, AND THE "KING OF THEM ALL"

I went downstairs to have breakfast with Hugh Gross, Red Phillips, and Donnie Hall. This was in the early '40s. World War II was raisin' hell in Europe, but the Japs hadn't demolished Pearl Harbor yet, so we could still play our radio shows and tour abroad. "The Gallopin' Goose," as somebody had labeled the old Studebaker bus that had never heard of a spring or shock absorber. The Goose had all the riding comforts that a good healthy earthquake would have. I'll tell you more about the Gallopin' Goose later.

Now, back to the breakfast with Hugh, who looked like Oliver Springs Tennessee's Mister America. Red Phillips, who looked somewhat like a tiger. His wavy hair was about the reddest I'd ever seen. He loved fishing and hunting and was an absolute master at profanity. One of the girls on the show, Ramona Riggins (who later became Mrs. Grandpa Jones) remarked one day, "I just love to hear Red cuss!" She would have shocked the whole crew if she'd said such a lowly exclamation as "dog-gone!" Red's favorite hobby was to get into a good knock-down, drag-out fistfight. Sometimes he'd win, and then there were other times. I've been present at both.

I'll never forget one night when Red and I went out on a cold Cincinnati night with the sole purpose of having a few drinks and seeing if we could promote a nice fight. After a couple or three double shots of Seagram's, we were feeling just right. The cold wind hit our faces as we turned the corner to see what we could get going at the Walnut Café. The Walnut always had a goodly group of idiots with the same thing in mind that we did. Some ten feet from the door of the smoke-filled joint that reeked of stale beer, we were walking right toward two men in overcoats that had the appearance of just what we were looking for.

"I'll take the big one, and you get the shorter one," Red said. I glanced at Red Phillips, dressed to the teeth and wearing an expensive camelhair overcoat. I was warm in my combination of Seagram's and a black leather jacket. "I'm with you, pal," I said bravely.

As we started to pass the two young men (none of us was over thirty years old), Red purposely bumped the larger of the two as if the guy was a swinging door.

"Watchit, Buddy," said the bumped one. "I don't like being walked into."

"I don't give a damn what you like, you sonofabitch," said Red in his best combat voice. "When you see me comin', get the hell out of the way."

"If you're lookin' for a fight, you red-headed bastard, you don't have to go another step," said the stranger in the overcoat.

We'd struck pay dirt. Here's where we'd have some fun. We'd have a nice little battle, and when we'd showed these two to be a little more particular with such people as Red Phillips and Merle Travis, we'd stroll into the Walnut Café and have ourselves a victory drink.

"Let's me and you see who has the most teeth when this little fracas is over," said my friend, looking a little more like a tiger than ever as he pulled off his camelhair coat and handed it to me. "Hold this coat, Travis," said the Alabama battler who'd found him a good fight, his favorite hobby. "If that other bastard tries to join in, beat the hell out of the sonofabitch."

I took the coat, feeling sure I'd get to drop it and try my luck on the number two of the trio. Red's man just stood there with his overcoat buttoned.

"Take off that Goddamn overcoat," Red growled. "I don't want any excuses when I've beat the hell out of you."

"Don't worry about me, you red-headed sonofabitch," the guy said with a little too much calmness.

The man I was to beat to a pulp sort of yawned and looked toward the Ohio River as if he was dreaming of sunny days aboard the Island Queen.

But the battle began as Red said, "OK, bastard, you asked for it…" The freckled hand of Red Phillips shot out like a striking rattlesnake. There was a loud thud… but the stranger's nose was safe. He leaned a little to the left and bent his arm. Red had landed a killing blow on the forearm of the man's overcoat. Red followed with a left, which had something like the sad ending of his first blow. Red moved in closer and tried for a body shot, but was only playing hell with the man's overcoat buttons. He tried a few more jabs at the man's face, which seemed to always be somewhere else.

Then it happened. The man's overcoated arm zipped through the cold Ohio night and landed in the tough-looking face of Red Phillips. Blood squirted from Red's nose. His white shirt had more blood on it now than starch. A few more hefty blows landed on Red's face. He was doing his best to block some of the blows, but one Sunday punch caused Red to reel and go down on the cold sidewalk.

"Stay out of it, Travis!" he was mumbling through lips that were beginning to swell. "Don't try the other one… pitch me my coat."

I walked over and handed him his coat as he wobbled to his feet. The two others glanced around at the crowd that had gathered from out of the Walnut Café, and strolled away. Then we heard the sound of police sirens. They whizzed up to the sidewalk, got out, and in loud, authoritative voices gave out with the usual "Alright, let's break it up… inside or go home… break it up!"

A hefty lady kept yelling to the policemen, "That red-headed one started it! He's the one to take to jail… He started it!" Her loud voice kept repeating her verdict while the policemen were questioning us.

"Oh, it was just a little misunderstanding, Officer," Red said with his swelled lips and bloody nose.

"That red-headed one started the whole thing, Officer… I seen it all…" Red obviously had had enough for one night. He looked over at the lady, who must have weighed over two hundred pounds, and shouted in his loudest voice, "AW, SHUT UP FATTY!"

The police advised that we clear the neighborhood of the Walnut Café, which we were glad to do. As we walked away, Red said more or less to himself, "I believe that sonofabitch was a pro… I couldn't touch him."

"You can't win 'em all, Red," I said. "What we need is a drink."

Red agreed heartily, suggesting we find a bar as soon as possible. A couple of blocks from the battle ground, we saw the welcome sign flashing its neon lights, "Whiskey, Wine and Beer." We lost no time in getting there… into a gin mill and out of the cold wind that was starting to chill us, what with our Seagram's Seven Crown wearing off. The place was empty. Only the bartender was there. A stocky little man with a walrus moustache and an accent you could cut with a knife. We seated ourselves at the bar, me and my black leather jacket, Red and his camelhair overcoat. The little bartender came over and we made our order. The bartender also placed his order. He took a look at Red's face and glanced at the blood on his starched shirt.

"I'll have a double shot of Seagram's Seven Crown," said Red, looking at the man through the eye that hadn't quite swollen shut yet, and speaking through lips that had obviously been well mistreated. The blood on his shirt didn't impress the stocky Greek bartender to any great extent.

"Gimme the same with a little water chaser," was my order. The Greek's order was a stubby finger pointing to the door.

"Get out my place of business," he demanded. "You're all nothing but trouble makers… GET OUT!"

"Now Hell, Mister, we ain't started no trouble," Red let him know. "We're just stopping in your place of business to get a drink. Now by God, serve your customers or I might just come back there and raise some trouble!"

The bartender reached under the bar and came out with a big black billy club, which I learned later must have been filled with lead. Around the bar he came like a charging bull. Red jumped to his feet and managed to deliver a few choice cuss words before the bartender made a believer out of him. He made a swing like Mickey Mantle that hit Red's coat. Red had a sudden change of mind. He headed for the door.

I figured a plan of attack. If I could get a hold of that stick, I could get in a few licks on the little Greek and have him a swelled eye or busted lip to go home and show his wife. So I waded in. As I was making grabs for the stick—if I could only grab it—I'd have it made.

With every swing, I'd grab and miss. His black stick was hitting my black leather jacket, sounding like a 32 caliber with every connection. In a twilight sort of zone, I could hear Red Phillips yelling, "Give it up, Travis! That sonofabitch will kill you!" But I kept dreaming of getting a good grab on the stick. But the pops seemed to get louder, and I started feeling like an elephant was doing a tap dance, making my leather coat pop with every tap. There just wasn't any way to grab the stick! So I hurried out the door where Red had been watching the painful pop-corn popping.

"Did he hurt you any, Travis?"

"No, I'm fine. I just couldn't get a hold on that stick."

Red doubled over laughing.

"That was one of the funniest things I've ever seen!" roared Red. "That Goddamn little Greek flailin' away, you grabbin' at that billy club and that coat poppin' like an automatic shotgun…" I joined in the laughing. We both agreed this just wasn't our night.

At the Top of the Morning broadcast next morning, Red's eye was almost swollen shut, but his lips were in good enough shape to tell the whole cast about my battle with the Greek bartender. The whole night wasn't so bad, without one exception. Joe Maphis had to help *me on with my shirt and coat. One of the girls tied my tie, and one of the Drifting Pioneers, bless 'em, gently lifted my guitar over my shoulder.*

Red Phillips may have had a black eye and smashed lip, but I had more bruised spots than he had freckles.

. . .

It's odd that in his autobiographical writing, Merle devotes the entire period of 1937 to 1944 to a few tales of he and his friends getting in fights. While his memories of youthful scuffling seem genuinely nostalgic, it is strange that he gives such short shrift to a very eventful period. The seven years that Merle spent in Cincinnati gave him his first taste of fame, his first recording session, the death of his parents, his first marriage, and his first child.

When Merle joined Clayton McMichen's band in Columbus, Ohio, sometime in the early spring of 1937, he joined a show business world that he had previously only dreamed about. McMichen toured with a traveling show caravan. It included not only his own band, the Georgia Wildcats, but also Natchee the Indian (real name Lester Vernon Storer), a young Cowboy Copas, the Delmore Brothers, and a cast of dancers and other musicians and female singers. It was a musical version of running off and joining the circus. Merle later recalled in various interviews:

> I went to Columbus, Ohio, and played my first job with Clayton McMi-chen, and it was a fiddler's contest between Clayton McMichen and Natchee the Indian. In Natchee's band, he had a boy who played rhythm guitar for him named Cowboy Copas, and the bass player was Rusty Gabbard. The thing in them days, a fella named Les [Larry] Sunbrock would buy time on two different radio stations, and each group—McMi-chen would brag about how he's going to beat that Indian fiddler, or he'd just fiddle on the stage, and they'd do the same thing on the other station. And you talk about country music drawing big crowds now. Well, that was 1937, and it was one of the biggest auditoriums in Columbus, Ohio, and people was lined up for blocks and blocks, couldn't get in.[60]
>
> [Larry] Sunbrock would go out and hold his hand over his head. Said, the one who gets the most applause, it'll be obvious, he's the winner. They'd point at McMichen and say, "All you who thinks he's the world champion fiddler," you know, they'd put their hand over there, and all this applause. "Now, here's Natchee the Indian. Who all thinks…" And they like to tore the place apart. He [McMichen] opened his fiddle case,

and he had him a half a pint of Cream of Kentucky whiskey, he took him a big drink... he'd walk out on the middle of that stage, and half the people are hollerin' "Booooo!" and the other half of the people are applaudin', and he held his hand up, and got 'em quieted down, and he said, "Ladies and Gentlemen, all of you that applauded for me, much obliged. And the rest of you can just go to hell!" Me and Carl Cotner was standing there, and Carl said, "I bet we got the only boss in the world that'd go out there and tell that many people to go to hell."[61]

In one 1961 interview with Ed Kahn, Merle remembers playing on McMichen's 1937 recording session for a song called "Farewell Blues." But in a number of subsequent interviews, he notes that he never entered a recording studio until much later, in 1943. Based on the fact that Georgia Wildcats guitarist Slim Bryant said that he played on the "Farewell Blues" session, and the fact that the guitar part sounds like Slim Bryant's style and not Merle's, it is reasonable to assume that Merle did not play on the session, but was perhaps in the room as a bystander. A few more recollections from Merle:

If you would take just one song of Clayton McMichen's, maybe "Farewell Blues," you'd say, "See there, McMichen's playing Western swing." But then, how about taking "Ida Red," when Clayton McMichen and Riley Puckett did it, or how about taking some of the tunes that McMichen did with Gid Tanner and the Skillet Lickers? Or take "Arkansas Traveler," "Hog Trough Reel," "McMichen's Breakdown," a bunch of old stuff he played—that certainly wasn't Western swing. "Dreamy Georgiana Moon" was a beautiful, harmonious waltz. Complicated—well, not complicated, but not three-chord things that campfire girls could play. Clayton McMichen could play whatever he wanted to play. He wasn't just one style—not McMichen. You could say "Hey, you know 'Darktown Strutters Ball'?" He'd say, "What key?" And he could play it there. And then you'd say "Hell Among the Yearlings." "Let's play it," and he'd play it South Georgia style just as good as you please. Well now, how about "Over the Waves"? Okay, he'd play it, and his theme song was "Sweet Bunch of Daisies."[62]

[McMichen] and Carl Cotner played two fiddles. They played, it wasn't scratchy, corny, out of tune or anything, or McMichen would run his head through the wall, and Carl Cotner would have bit his tongue off because it had to be pretty, you know. Once I read an article that referred to him [McMichen] as a "reluctant hillbilly." McMichen liked good music, and he liked it played right and everything.[63]

[McMichen] called me "Ridgerunner" and always gave me a featured tune on the show, something like "Tiger Rag" or "I'll See You in My Dreams." When Riley Puckett came out with us for a show, it was my job to sort of be his lead man, and I'd help him get around. That was okay with me since here was another guitar man I'd listened to on records for years, and now I got to see and pick with him in person.[64]

Riley was the most helpless blind man I've ever seen. I've seen sightless people could do everything that you and I do. Now, Riley Puckett, playing the guitar, played with two steel finger picks and he played as if his fingers were walking on the strings like that.... Riley was a very famous musician and "Put My Little Shoes Away" and "Rock All Our Babies to Sleep" and things like that. He sold many, many records.[65]

Merle saved a series of notes that he wrote, probably in the last few years of his life. It would seem at first glance that these might be proposed chapter titles for his autobiography, but a good majority of them are ribald, off-color, personal, and obviously meant only for Merle's eyes. His daughter Merlene Travis-Maggini observes: "I don't know if those were chapter titles. I think those were just memory joggers. I think that he would just write them down, he's going, 'Okay, I've gotta remember this, I've gotta remember this, I've gotta remember this.'"[66] Likely these were indeed Merle's own notes to himself, remembering the events of his life as they came back to him in his later years. "Merle's memories," as they shall be called in this biography, offer probably the most accurate and honest accounting of his life events that he ever committed to paper. Unfortunately, he passed away without adding details to many of these jotted memories. Although some of the stories are lost to time, others reveal truths and can be verified by comparing interviews from several sources.

"McMichen said, 'The Rest Can Go to Hell'" is one of Merle's memories that we have the story for. Merle's story quoted above about watching McMichen telling those who didn't vote for him in the fiddler's contest to "go to hell" was obviously a memorable incident in his early career.

"McMichen Fiddled for the Railroad Man" is another memory we've got the story for. Merle wrote a long story about the incident, too long to reproduce here. In a nutshell, the band's car was stopped at a railroad track waiting for a long freight train to pass. Clayton McMichen's name was painted on the side of the vehicle, and the railroad man in charge of flagging cars down and stopping traffic came over and asked to meet Clayton McMichen. McMichen obliged the fan, asked Merle to grab his guitar and McMichen's fiddle from the top of the vehicle, and the two gave a concert for the signal man in the dark moonlight, illuminated only by the railroad man's lantern and the long freight train passing by. Hopefully someday this story and many other short stories that Merle wrote can be published in a separate book.

We'll probably never know the full stories behind the memories **"Riley Puckett wouldn't 'look' at his lunch,"** or **"McMichen 'Let's get a half pint and drink it,'"** but we do know the story behind **"McMichen was my father"** and **"Bert Lane [Layne] was my father-in-law."** Shortly after joining McMichen, Merle and Mary Johnson planned to marry, probably under the misguided belief that the McMichen gig would be a long and profitable one. They were both very young, and Merle was convinced he could never get Mary's father's consent. In Pat Travis Eatherly's photo memoir *A Scrapbook of My Daddy*, she tells the story she heard growing up about her parents getting married:

> Merle was nineteen and Mary only seventeen, but they were in love and wanted to get married. After all, Merle now had a "steady" job with the World Champion Fiddler, Clayton McMichen and his Georgia Wildcats! Clayton noticed how sad Merle was acting and he asked what the trouble was. Merle admitted he was lovesick and wanted to get married, but said that he and Mary were legally too young and he just knew that Mary's father, "Preacher Will," would never give his consent. Clayton said, "Son, I'll be your pappy and stand up with you and we'll get ol' Bert Layne [one of the fiddlers in the Georgia Wildcats; also McMichen's brother-in-law and one of the founding members of the Skillet Lickers] to be her daddy!"
>
> So with a little help from their "stand-in fathers," Merle and Mary were married on April 12, 1937, in Covington, Kentucky. When Merle's and Mary's parents learned of this marriage, Merle's father told Mary's mother, "Sister Bivie, I don't know how in the world my son will ever earn a living for your girl. All in the world he knows how to do is pick that guitar!"[67]

Merle's job with McMichen also landed him on a radio station that would figure heavily in his future career: WLW in Cincinnati. WLW was the brainchild of millionaire entrepreneur Powel Crosley Jr., who made the first affordable radio sets and decided he also needed to own a radio station to provide content for those radios. (Crosley also made automobiles, airplanes, automobile accessories, refrigerators, vibrating exercise belts, and baby carriages, and owned the Cincinnati Reds baseball team, among other things.) The FCC had formed in 1927 and begun issuing permits for more and more powerful stations, as electrical and technological advances permitted. Crosley, flush with money and eager to dominate the market, quickly went from twenty to fifty to five hundred watts. After the FCC approved WLW's "clear channel" broadcast frequency of 700 kHz on the radio dial in 1927, the station went to fifty thousand watts in 1928, and soon became known as "The Nation's Station."

Crosley applied to become the country's first five-hundred-thousand-watt radio station in 1932, and spent two years constructing a half-million-dollar transmitter, a behemoth built by RCA, GE, and Westinghouse, with several buildings to house the electronic apparatus and a 3,600-square-foot water cooling pond. When WLW began to broadcast at a half-million watts in 1934, suddenly the station could be heard in all four corners of the United States. There were side effects, of course: nearby farmers heard it coming from their barbed-wire fences, milking machines, and water faucets; electric lights and neon signs near the transmitter wouldn't turn off; and metal items like gutters and weather vanes vibrated and rattled loose from houses. (Their experimental five-hundred-thousand-watt license, unique in the United States, was revoked in 1939, and the station dropped to the now-standard fifty-thousand-watt maximum.)

WLW produced its own programming, which was of high caliber and very popular. They made a point of playing no prerecorded music or programs—everything was live on the air, happening in the WLW studio. The station was instrumental in making national stars out of Rosemary Clooney, the Mills Brothers, Andy Williams, and Doris Day (whom, incidentally, Merle said he briefly dated in Cincinnati when Day was still known by her real name, Doris Mary Kappelhoff). WLW developed the first soap opera radio drama programs, which became hugely successful. WLW also realized that rural listeners were important, with their signal covering so many square miles of farmland and small towns, and developed programming that would appeal to these audiences, including farm reports (the station had its own 750-acre parcel, known as "Everybody's Farm," for developing agricultural techniques) and hillbilly music programming that ran on their *Top of the Morning* show (which Merle mentions above), as well as other fifteen- and thirty-minute specialty programs by various hillbilly acts.

Hillbilly music proved very profitable for WLW, and Merle would spend the next seven years in Cincinnati broadcasting from the station with McMichen, the Drifting Pioneers, and on his own. Before WSM's *Grand Ole Opry* became established as the country music radio powerhouse, WLW and its country programming dominated. For a while they broadcast the *Renfro Valley Barn Dance,* then established their own *Boone County Jamboree* show, which would employ Merle for the next phase of his life. By fate or by luck, Merle had managed to drop into Cincinnati radio at a unique time and place in history. He had literally been plucked from obscurity as an unknown nineteen-year-old from rural Kentucky, and through McMichen was suddenly on the most powerful radio station in the nation.

Mary Johnson, now Mary Travis, and the Johnson family back home must have been thrilled at his prospects. But the McMichen gig proved to be short-lived. Alton Delmore of the Delmore Brothers recalled, "Clayton McMichen was a high-tempered person when anybody tried to put something over on him, and he didn't mind fighting for what was right. If you fooled around with him, he would knock the hell out of you with his bare hands."[68] Sleepy Marlin noted of Merle at this time:

> He was very unhappy, oh yeah. Yeah, very unhappy. See, at that time I had never met Clayton McMichen. He's a fiddler, and I'm a fiddler. I had never met him. Years later I got well acquainted with the man, worked some with him. Mac [McMichen] was like many, many musicians that I've known in my life. He liked the bottle. We began to monitor the radio station up there just to hear Merle and hear the band. We wanted to keep up with what he was doing. Spring passed, and summer came along. About July it would have been, I guess [1937]. We decided to take a few days off and run up to Cincinnati to visit Merle. It'd be a treat to visit the station. We'd never been there. Which we did. We got to Cincinnati to find that Merle was anything but happy with the job. He had, on the strength of it all, gone out and gotten married to his high school sweetheart, Mary Johnson. Newlyweds and all that, things just weren't going as they should financially with him. We eventually got around to saying, "Would you have any interest in coming back to us?" Right away, just that quick, he seemed to be waiting for the question.[69]

Merle, for his part, said the following: "A lot has been made of me working with Mac, but actually I didn't stay with him very long, only a few months and by late summer I was back in Evansville with the Drifting Pioneers. I think the reason so much has been made of my time with Mac is because of that real good band picture we had taken with my old Gretsch Model-30 guitar in it [Merle's Gretsch was actually a Model-35]. That photo has been in more picture books and magazine articles than you could shake a stick at."[70] And, in another interview, "I got tired of driving around, touring so much and everything, and I liked the other guys and liked picking with them. McMichen and me were good friends until his passing. He was like a big brother to me."[71]

Almost as quickly as it began, Merle's time on McMichen's payroll was over. McMichen broke up the Georgia Wildcats in 1939. In the following years, he formed another string band, then a Dixieland band in Louisville. He retired from performing in 1955 but was persuaded to appear at several folk festivals in the 1960s before he died in 1970. Late in life, Merle and Mac Wiseman recorded a double tribute album, *The Clayton McMichen Story*, which was eventually released by CMH Records in 1988. With McMichen's employment behind him, Merle returned to Evansville to rejoin the Drifting Pioneers, but almost right away, the group set their sights on Chicago. In Merle's words, the Drifting Pioneers

> had a beautiful blend, singing trios. And Sleepy played the fiddle, and Bill Brown played the guitar, and Walt [Brown] played the mandolin. Well, there wasn't much room for me in there, playing another guitar, so they put me on bass fiddle. They bought a bass fiddle, a dollar down and a dollar a week, and we'd tie it on top of the cars and play schoolhouses. And I'd play the bass fiddle, and that's about all. But I worked my way up to playing the guitar, and Bill started playing the bass fiddle and never even touched the guitar. So I become the guitar player and we sung quartets and trios, and they had a lot of novelty songs. In fact it was just a lot of talent in that act, excluding me, the rest of them.
>
> And so we worked around, and one day we got in the car and went to Chicago. We met all the guys at the *National Barn Dance*. First time I ever met Doc Hopkins was then. We auditioned; but we never heard from them, because I guess we had the same instrumentation as the Prairie Ramblers. Remember the Prairie Ramblers? They was there, and they had a mandolin and a guitar and a bass fiddle and a fiddle. So that was Tex Atchison, and Chick Hurt, and Taylor, what's his name? His last name is Taylor, and he played the bass. Anyhow, they had the same instrumentation. We met a bunch of them, they was all real nice to us, and we just felt wonderful. Well, then we went back to Evansville.[72]

Though the group didn't get accepted for a permanent job in Chicago, they continued to play on WGBF in Evansville and tour around the area. The exact details have been lost to time, but it would appear that Western singer Bob Atcher (who made records for Okeh and Columbia, in addition to appearing nationally on WBBM out of Chicago) was the one who assisted in the Drifting Pioneers' next career move by helping the group get an audition with WLW in Cincinnati. They were accepted, and by the fall of 1937 the Drifting Pioneers, along with Merle and his new wife, left Evansville and moved to Cincinnati. A newspaper article dated September 26, 1937, states that the group "recently joined 'The Nation's Station' (and) are featured in their own program of frontier music from 6 to 6:30 am, EST, over WLW."[73]

In Merle's words: "Well, the Drifting Pioneers first tried to get it goin' in Chicago... we just never seemed to get beyond the guest shot stage in that city, but Bob Atcher, who we got to know pretty well, phoned George Biggar at WLW in Cincinnati, Ohio, and they were settin' up a new barn dance show named after the Kentucky county across the Ohio River from Cincinnati and that's how we got on the *Boone County Jamboree*."[74] His memory here is spotty, because the Drifting Pioneers joined WLW in the fall of 1937, a full year before George Biggar came on at WLW to start the *Boone County Jamboree*, but the best guess is that Bob Atcher was directly or indirectly responsible for getting the Drifting Pioneers hired at the station. In another interview Merle remembered:

> With the Drifting Pioneers, we just did everything. We played what today would absolutely be called bluegrass music. We had a mandolin, guitar, fiddle, and bass, and I played five-string banjo now and then. I was with them quite a while, at radio station WLW in Cincinnati. They were heard all over the United States, and we got a lot of mail. We sang gospel quartets, we sang duos, trios, solos, guitar solos, fiddle tunes. We did comedy, we had a girl singer named Judy Dell. We would go out and do a two-hour show easy as you please.
>
> In those days you didn't just walk up and say, "I sing," and not play anything. They'd say, "Well, that's great. Feller out there plowing can also sing. Why do you want on radio? Can you play anything? We can't just hire a guy to sing." In those days, you had to know how to play the fiddle a little bit, how to be a straight man, how to be a comedian, you had to know all the jokes, you had to know how to present yourself, you had to know how to [take a] bow, how to get on, how to get off, and play two or three instruments, sing any part of harmony.
>
> At that time we'd back up other acts and we had a comedian named Denny Slofoot, he'd come out and do a great comedy routine; a girl singer, we'd back her up. [Merle also did a comedy routine at WLW, using the name Possum Gossett. Grandpa and Ramona Jones remembered the character as hilarious and brilliant in a later interview.[75]] I'd do guitar solos, Sleepy would do a fiddle specialty. We had a half-hour program every day of gospel songs—the Drifting Pioneers Gospel Quartet.[76]

The Drifting Pioneers joined a group of other singers and musicians at WLW that included "Lazy" Jim Day, Bradley Kincaid, Helen Diller, Lafe Harkness (the harmonica wizard), Tillie Q. Smith, Dolly Good, the Delmore Brothers (whom Merle had met touring with Clayton McMichen), guitarist Harold Maus and his group the Novelty Aces, Hugh Cross with Shug Fisher, Pa and Ma McCormick, and

Fiddlin' Charlie Linville, who at the time played with Harry C. Adams in a group called Eldon Baker and the Brown City Revelers. During these years at the station, he would also meet several men and women who would become lifelong friends: Louis Marshall "Grandpa" Jones and Jones's future wife, Ramona Riggins, cowboy singer Jack Rogers and his tap-dancing wife, Marge, singer-bassist (and future Western character actor) Shug Fisher, guitarist Joe Maphis, guitarist Roy Lanham, singer-comedian Hank Penny, and Western singer and preacher Wesley Tuttle.

Tuttle was from Colorado originally but had lived in Southern California since the age of five. He sang with Stuart Hamblen, a popular radio star on the West Coast, and lent his yodel to the "Silly Song" in the 1937 Disney film *Snow White and the Seven Dwarfs*. Tuttle worked with several groups during the 1930s, including the original Sons of the Pioneers. He took a job at WING in Dayton in 1939 and met Merle through the many live performances that the WLW *Boone County Jamboree* cast did in the southern Ohio area. Tuttle eventually auditioned for WLW and joined a group called the Sunset Rangers. He moved back to California in mid-1941 but would be pivotal in Merle's eventual path to stardom. Wesley Tuttle remembers: "That's where I met Merle, because he was a member of the old *Boone County Jamboree*, and I had never heard anything like that in my life. When I first heard Merle play that guitar, I was absolutely dumbfounded, and I didn't, I just didn't see how it could be true."[77]

Cincinnati was for many decades a fertile breeding ground for American music. White culture interacted with African American culture there; the town was physically and culturally where the Southern part of the United States met the Northern part. Steamboats headed up and down the river carrying jazz bands. From the Northern and Southern influence to the mixing of white and African American cultures and the vast array of live music and sheer culture that Queen City offered, Merle was exposed to many new things. For a young entertainer in his early twenties, moving to Cincinnati was the equivalent of going off to college.

The Drifting Pioneers photos in Merle's personal archive show how the group quickly evolved from simple stage clothes to fancy, matching suits after being accepted at WLW. The group wore buckskin jackets and coonskin caps as part of their "pioneer" persona. "We dressed like Daniel Boone," Merle said, "and called ourselves the Drifting Pioneers."[78] Besides the coonskin caps, the Pioneers also wore cowboy hats and cowboy boots, something novel and exotic for the Midwest in the 1930s. They were copying the look from Western movies. This would be Merle's introduction to Western tailoring, which would be a major part of his stage persona for the rest of his life.

Most of the backstories have vanished into the ether, but some of the other "Merle's memories" make clear that the WLW years were full of good times:

"Lazy Jim—'If you screws like you talk'"

"Lazy Jim—wrecks Buick 'Walt, I thought he was dead'"

"Lazy Jim—describes drinks and hamburgers"

"Lazy Jim—sings 'Oxen Snot'"

"Lazy Jim—takes Gene's whiskey—twice"

"Lazy Jim—sings news—interviews freckled boy"

"Alton picks songs out of air"

"Rabon sits in closet all night"

"Alton hears things that go yoooop"

(This memory's origin was revealed in an interview that Grandpa Jones did with researcher Charles K. Wolfe. According to Jones: "It was in Cincinnati, he [Alton Delmore] said, 'I got me a new apartment, it's over by the zoo. But I don't like it.' He said, 'Just about the time you get asleep, one of those old African birds'll go 'Yooooop!' He never did have nothing right, everything was always wrong. Me and Merle just used to laugh at him.")[79]

"Grandpa—'That Dam Nellie'"

"Grandpa comes home to a cold Nellie"

"Harold Maus loses '17 pound sonofabitch'"

"Harold Maus and I get tattooed—sweet sour"

Merle did not often display them, but he had two bluebird tattoos, one on each forearm. Tattoos are commonplace now, but in the 1930s they were quite taboo. Later in life, Merle would refer to his tattoos as "The bluebirds of happiness."[80]

"I ride up on orchestra pit—Hank Penny's idea"

"Jack Abrams furnishes spirits for WLW"

"Dolly Good gets sick in Akron—I get in jail"

"Rufe Davis drives while I cook a rabbit"

"Harry C Adams says he can outpick anybody"

"Harry C Adams drinks plenty"

"Harry C Adams bugs me, I slap him—sorry"

"Donnie Hall 'collects silver coffee pots'"

"Bradley Kincaid and I raise a crop"

"Bradley give me and Red Phillips a keg of wine"

"Red Phillips is refused apartment for poodle"

"Red Phillips and I get beat up by Greek"

Since Merle devoted nearly an entire chapter of his autobiography to the "Red Phillips and I get beat up by Greek" tale, one can only imagine that every one of these memories could have been turned into a lengthy story. Unfortunately, all the people involved have now passed on. But the titles are enough to imagine the lively stories behind them, experienced by a young man in the full sprint of living.

The Drifting Pioneers became a popular act on WLW, and were featured on the original, short-lived Cincinnati-based version of the *Renfro Valley Barn Dance* radio show, broadcast live from Cincinnati Music Hall. The debut of John Lair's *Renfro Valley Barn Dance* was in the fall of 1937, right around the time Merle and the Drifting Pioneers arrived at the station. (Merle and the Pioneers would also be one of the first acts featured on the *Renfro Valley Barn Dance* when it switched its broadcast to station WHAS in Louisville in 1939 and were also one of the first to perform at the newly constructed *Renfro Valley Barn Dance* performance venue near Mount Vernon, Kentucky, which still exists today as the permanent home of the *Renfro Valley Barn Dance*.) By fall 1938, still broadcasting as the only five-hundred-thousand-watt station in the United States (there was another just over the border in Mexico, XERA in Ciudad Acuña), WLW expanded on its hillbilly music programming. Jim Shouse of the Crosley Corporation hired George Biggar from WLS in Chicago with the intent of creating a show at WLW similar to *Renfro Valley Barn Dance* or Chicago's *National Barn Dance*. The resulting *Boone County Jamboree* became hugely popular, and until the FCC reduced the station's wattage the following year, it was by leaps and bounds the most powerful hillbilly music program on the air, covering all of North America and beyond.

The Drifting Pioneers were part of the *Boone County Jamboree* from the beginning (as well as their participation in the *Renfro Valley Barn Dance* and other programs), broadcasting every Friday night from the Emery Auditorium in Cincinnati, where the *Jamboree* was performed live to a paying audience. Merle remembered:

> Well, in them days, "show" is the right word. You didn't just go out and do your latest record and then go offstage or something like that. You was expected to entertain. You didn't play beer joints and things. We played the biggest theaters. There was four of us and a girl singer named Judy Dell... and we had a comedian.... We'd go out and play theaters in them days. Had singers, songs, quartets, duets, trios; pull gags and all sorts of jokes; a girl singer; and it was sort of show business-like. There was a stage and curtains, and the curtain would open with the spotlight.[81]

The group performed on the radio production of *Boone County Jamboree* and the cast was also farmed out to play *Boone County Jamboree* events and shows in the region. There was little downtime—Merle was playing for hours with the Drifting Pioneers every single day of the week. He played bass when he first joined, then switched to guitar. His command of the instrument must have been apparent to everybody, especially Bill Brown, the guitarist. The earliest Drifting Pioneers photos that include Merle show him playing a small-bodied L-30 Gibson archtop guitar, not the budget Gretsch archtop he had bought with his CCC camp money. Merle was only photographed with the small Gibson on two occasions, and it is likely that he borrowed the guitar for the photo sessions.

Within a year of the Drifting Pioneers establishing themselves on WLW, the group had achieved moderate success. In additional to several stage outfits, they invested in promotional photos and postcards, and their fan club published a mimeographed Drifting Pioneers newsletter. In 1939 the American Music Publishing Company published a song folio to add to the items they could sell at shows. "The Drifting Pioneers Song Folio No. 1" (there never was a "No. 2") contained photos of the group, a brief biography, and sheet music for many of their most popular numbers. It is notable for featuring Merle's first published song: "The Dust on Mother's Old Bible." That tune was not a hit; in fact, Merle never recorded it, save for a transcription recording he did with his wife and singing partner Tex Ann Nation several years later (Merle's song from 1939 should not be confused with a song with a near-identical title written and recorded by Buck Owens in the 1960s). However, "The Dust on Mother's Old Bible" was significant for one reason—Merle Travis was now a published songwriter, in addition to being a singer and guitar player.

When Merle and his new wife first moved to Cincinnati, they lived at a cheap boarding house at 3227 Colerain Avenue, just a few blocks from the WLW studios. It was directly across the street from the Cincinnati City Workhouse, an ominous-looking nineteenth-century stone prison full of dangerous characters. This arrangement must have seemed transient, at best. It was at this boarding house that Mary Travis became pregnant, and on March 25, 1939, the couple welcomed a daughter, Patricia Adeline Travis. Merle's mother passed away on February 21 of that year, just a few days short of her fifty-seventh birthday, and a month before she would have become a grandmother to Merle and Mary's new baby. Merle wrote a letter to his father, letting him know of the new grandchild:

Dear Dad-and-all,

This leaves us all well, and doing fine. I guess you know by now about the stork fetching me a little gal. She's a dandy and has black hair about an inch long. She's fat as any one of Johnny's pigs—and can squeal as loud as all of them put together.[82]

Pat Travis Eatherly remembered in *A Scrapbook of My Daddy* that sometime after Etta's death and her birth, Merle's father came from Ebenezer to live with the family.

Several months after Patty was born, Merle made the newspapers, but it was in the arrest and courts section, not the entertainment page. On June 3, the *Cincinnati Enquirer* reported that Merle had been fined three dollars and given ten days' suspended license on a reckless driving charge. It would be the first of many newspaper appearances Merle would make over the years for running afoul of the law.

In 1939, feeling a bit of success from the Drifting Pioneers, Merle took a huge leap for a poor kid from Kentucky who played for pennies and slept on steamboats, and invested in his future. During his stay at WLW, he purchased two new professional instruments, both of which he would use to further his career over the next decade and beyond. The first was a lightly used 1936 Gibson L-10 archtop guitar, not quite as fancy as the L-5 he had admired Slim Bryant playing with Clayton McMichen back in Kentucky, but one of Gibson's top professional models. The L-10 was a full-fledged, advanced, seventeen-inch archtop with most of the same design features (X bracing, carved top, fancy binding, and ornate headstock inlay) of the more expensive L-5. The model was produced from 1931 to 1939, mainly as a Depression-era lower-cost alternative to the L-5, which is exactly why it appealed to Merle. It was fancy and professional, but still affordable. The new guitar would undoubtedly take many months or a year to pay off, but Merle used the L-10 until Paul Bigsby made him a solidbody electric guitar in 1948, and he valued the old Gibson hollowbody so much that he kept it until he died.

At first, Merle played the L-10 as a stock acoustic guitar. Photos of the Drifting Pioneers from this time show him crowding the microphone with it in an attempt to be heard. Electric instruments were creeping into the mainstream by the late 1930s. The first commercially available electric lap steels and electric Spanish guitars were made in 1932 by the Ro-Pat-In company, which eventually became Rickenbacker; by 1936 and 1937 almost all instrument brands offered some version of an electric guitar. Merle must have seen bands come through Cincinnati that used electric instruments. Bud Dooley of the Novelty Aces played electric lap steel on WLW as early as 1940. For years before electric Spanish guitars became common, it was not unusual to see hillbilly acts with electric Hawaiian lap steels. It was only a matter of time before Merle, fascinated with gadgets and inventions, would get around to electrifying his guitar. In his words: "It was a Gibson L-10 with a DeArmond pickup. The first time I used it on radio was on a show called *Plantation Party*, a network show. This would've been in 1939 or 1940."[83]

The second item Merle obtained was on the cutting edge of technology at the time: one of the earliest DeArmond "Guitar Microphone" FHC floating pickups. It was the first commercially available electric guitar pickup, introduced in 1939. Merle mounted the pickup on his Gibson L-10, and then bought the best amplifier then on the market, a Gibson EH-185. Merle recalled that at first, the WLW brass didn't like his electric instrument and told him not to use it. But it would have been easier to stop a tsunami that had already hit shore. Merle had gone electric, with consequences that would eventually reverberate around the world. It wasn't long before newspaper reviews of the *Boone County Jamboree* shows took notice: "Versatile Merle Travis, an electric guitar expert, is often the center of attention. The rest of the performers maintain their usual radio standards."[84]

A few years later, Merle upped his game and bought a slightly used 1941 Martin D-28 flat-top acoustic guitar from West Virginia singer Jimmy Walker, who guested on the *Boone County Jamboree*. The Martin D-28 was the "it" guitar for hillbilly string bands at the time; if you could afford one, you had truly achieved success. Only the rich singing cowboys in the movies could afford the higher-priced Martin D-45; the D-28 was the working professional's choice. Merle would use this Martin D-28 as his primary acoustic instrument for the rest of his life; a new neck was installed by Paul Bigsby in the late 1940s. (It should be noted that there is some difference of opinion about the manufacture year of Merle's D-28. When the guitar was sold at a Christie's auction in 2007, the Martin guitar company dated it to 1941 through its serial number, but Merle had always stated that it was a 1938 instrument. Paperwork from the Martin Guitar archives shows that Merle's D-28 was indeed manufactured in March 1941.)

With the birth of his first daughter, a fancy new Gibson archtop, and a breakthrough in commercial success, 1939 seemed like a banner year for Merle, with the sad exception of his mother passing away. Sometime in 1939, the four members of the Travis clan moved to a new home in a residential neighborhood at 14 Kessler Avenue.

In the spring of 1940, there was a major shift in the dynamic of the Drifting Pioneers. The group had begun in the mid-1930s, several years before Merle met them. But within two years of Merle joining the band, his exceptional abilities were hard to deny. His guitar playing, singing, comedy, and entertainment mastery had propelled him to become the most popular band member among the WLW listening audience. To reuse a quote from Merle's childhood friend Earl Talmadge Dukes: "It's just one of them deals where you can't hold a good man back, and that's what you had."[85] The edict came down from George Biggar's office at WLW, issued on a Crosley Corporation internal memo dated April 24, 1940:

> In referring to The Drifting Pioneers in writing scripts or ad libbing—
> always call them "Merle Travis and the Drifting Pioneers." We will also
> feature Merle in a vocal as well as a guitar solo. It is very important that

this be followed out, as we wish to develop Merle as a personality and thus make the Pioneers set of more value to this station.[86]

From that day forward, Merle Travis was a featured performer—a *personality*—and no longer merely a background member. People would know and remember his name. We don't know how the rest of the Drifting Pioneers felt about the change. Bill and Walt Brown never gave an interview; Sleepy Marlin speaks in glowing terms about Merle in his only known interview. It is doubtful that the salary of anyone involved was much affected. They were struggling to make ends meet, even though the station sent them around constantly for personal appearances. One of the reasons for their financial shortcomings, the hillbilly musicians discovered, was an arrangement with the musicians' union that cheated them financially. As Grandpa Jones put it: "WLW had a union for musicians that we all had to join. But there were separate unions for the hillbilly performers and the regular performers because a lot of the regular musicians' unions didn't want to accept country pickers and singers in those days; they felt that unless you could read music, you couldn't play. And it didn't take us long to figure out that the scale in the hillbilly union was a lot lower."[87] The group continued to play on WLW and tour around the tri-state area—Ohio, Indiana, and Illinois.

The newspaper ads now read "Merle Travis and the Drifting Pioneers," but little else changed in their world until the United States joined World War II in December 1941. All men between the ages of twenty-one and forty-five had had to register for the draft in September 1940, and after Pearl Harbor, all eligible men entered a draft lottery. Merle, Sleepy, and Walt Brown all volunteered to enter the armed forces; Bill Brown did not. All waited to hear from their local draft board over the next few years to find out if they would have to go and fight.

The lineup of the *Boone County Jamboree* changed regularly. Some musicians were full-fledged cast members and lived in Cincinnati. Some were merely featured guests for a short period. Some only appeared as guests on road shows and not the radio broadcast. There were a number of other hillbilly music programs on the station as well, including *Top of the Morning*, *Boone County Jamboree*, *The Renfro Valley Barn Dance*, and *Plantation Party*. There were always a great number of musicians coming and going. And as the war began to take cast members away, 1942 became a pivotal moment for the show. Hank Penny arrived at WLW from Atlanta, bringing along his band, the Plantation Boys. Penny was a comedian, singer, and excellent "sock rhythm" guitar player. His lead guitarist, Roy Lanham, was a Kentucky native who had come up from Florida to join Hank's band. Penny and Merle fell in like long-lost cousins when they met. They shared a sense of humor and a rebellious streak.

Roy Lanham was an exceptional lead guitarist—indeed, one of the best country and jazz guitarists of all time. He played sophisticated chord-melody style alternating with a fast single-note style. During his time at WLW, Lanham also learned how to play the thumbpicking style after watching Merle. Lanham followed Hank Penny and Merle out to the West Coast at Merle's behest after a few years of working with his group The Whippoorwills in Dayton, Ohio, and Springfield, Missouri. Merle described meeting Roy Lanham for the first time in a piece called "Ramblin' Roy Lanham" for *Guitar World* magazine in 1981:

> Roy Lanham, as he [bandleader Gene Austin] called him, with a little confused expression, would look at his fingers, his eyebrows tilted in a sad slant, like Fred Lasswell's mountaineer cartoon, Snuffy Smith. His guitar would whine, grumble, complain and snort as Roy would push the B string halfway under the A bass string to get a bluesy effect. Then he'd stick his flat pick between his teeth, start playin' four string chords with his thumb and three fingers. There were four boys at the radio station where I worked at the time called the Four Modernaires, who later went with a bandleader named Glenn Miller. Roy's four string chords sounded like their four-way singing. I stayed until closing time. I wanted to meet that boy.[88]

Otis "Joe" Maphis was another exceptional guitarist and multi-instrumentalist who came to WLW in 1942. Maphis had been working on WRVA in Richmond, Virginia, playing acoustic flat-top guitar and doing comedy with a group known as Sunshine Sue and the Rock Creek Rangers. Merle later recalled: "I first heard Joe Maphis when he was with Sunshine Sue Workman at WRVA in Richmond, Virginia. I'd listen to him every opportunity I got. When he came to WLW in 1943 or so [actually August 1942], I found out he'd been listening to me on WLW. We struck up a friendship right away."[89] In another written piece, Merle describes hearing Joe play guitar for the first time, on the radio with Sunshine Sue: "I'd hear guitar pickin', the likes of which I'd never heard before. It was, of course, on a flat-top acoustic guitar. He'd pick something like the old fiddle tune, 'Fire on the Mountain.' Every note would be as clear as the mid-winter sky in January in Southern Ohio. I couldn't imagine such guitar pickin'. So you can imagine how thrilled I was when I learned that Sunshine Sue was bringing her group to Cincinnati."[90] Merle and Joe discovered immediately that their guitar styles worked well together. Maphis played blazingly fast fiddle-inspired leads, and Merle's rhythm-based thumb-picking style meshed naturally and effortlessly. Maphis, along with his wife, Rose Lee, would also move to Southern California at Merle's behest in 1951.

There were other performers at WLW during 1942 and 1943 who became good friends with Merle: Fiddlin' Charlie Linville, Rome Johnson, Jack and Margie Rogers, Western movie actor Shug Fisher, and Gene Autry's movie sidekick Smiley Burnette. All of them would head west to California during or after the war, a great migration of talent from the Midwest to the West Coast. Alton and Rabon Delmore, professionally known as the Delmore Brothers, had been part of Clayton McMichen's touring group when Merle toured with McMichen in spring 1937. Several years later, they signed on with WLW. The Delmores were already seasoned professionals by this time, having spent most of the 1930s recording for Columbia and Bluebird Records, and as popular performing members of the *Grand Ole Opry* in Nashville. When they arrived at WLW, the pair reignited their friendship with Merle from the McMichen days. Their shared love of guitar-based hillbilly music, drinking, and fighting united them into an unholy trinity.

Grandpa Jones, another Kentucky musician who sang and played banjo and guitar, came to WLW in early 1942 after honing his act on radio stations in Akron, Ohio, and Wheeling, West Virginia. Though he was only in his early twenties, he had adopted a humorous "Grandpa" stage persona, complete with whisker mustache and makeup to make him appear older. His act was so popular that Jones kept wearing the makeup and mustache until he was old enough to simply look the part, and remained a beloved character in country music for the remainder of his life. Merle and Jones hit it off immediately. They shared many things—a similar Kentucky upbringing, a similar catalog of "old songs," and a similar sense of humor. They were completely different, though, when it came to their proclivities. Jones preferred to avoid trouble and nightclub carousing, whereas Merle would drink and raise hell. It was an odd juxtaposition of temperaments, but the pair got along famously. Daughter Merlene Travis-Maggini remembered: "I gotta tell you, some of the times I saw him [Merle] laugh the hardest, I mean the real belly laughs, was with Grandpa Jones. 'Cause they go back to almost day one. They would crack each other up beyond belief, and Dad would act just like a kid.... I think Grandpa was almost like a sibling for Dad."[91]

Jones recounts in his 1984 book *Everybody's Grandpa* that Merle's street-fighting stories were genuine, and not a tall tale:

Merle already had a reputation as one of the best guitar pickers in the business, even though he was barely into his twenties. Merle had learned his thumb-and-finger-style picking down in Muhlenberg County, Kentucky, where they take their guitar playing seriously, and had worked with Clayton McMichen and the Georgia Wildcats before coming to WLW with a popular band called the Drifting Pioneers. Merle was a rough-and-tumble boy in those days, and he and Red Phillips used to go out and get in fights just for the exercise of it. Sometimes they'd come in pretty banged up, but they would be able to do their show and pick as clean as ever.... Merle and I got along fine and began singing together as early as 1943; he had a nickname for me that I can't print here, but he said it had to do with my ability to ride for hours without getting up and stretching or reaching for a cushion.[92]

Ramona Riggins was another performer on the show who came to WLW as a member of Sunshine Sue's band, alongside Joe Maphis. After Grandpa Jones's first marriage ended, Grandpa and Ramona began dating, and they married in 1946. Grandpa and Ramona would remain close, personal friends with Merle for the rest of their lives.

WLW's still-powerful signal of fifty thousand watts in 1939 was enough to carry the station's signal over much of the United States, and even more so at night. One of its listeners during the war was a young Tennessee lad who was then living with his father near Columbus, Georgia. His name was Chester Burton Atkins, a determined kid who had built himself a homemade crystal set to hear music over the radio. Chester would eventually become famous as guitar virtuoso and record producer Chet Atkins, and in a 1976 *Rolling Stone* interview, he remembered tuning in to WLW around 1942 and hearing Merle Travis for the first time: "I didn't know what in the hell he was doing, but I knew he was fingerpickin'. I started trying to play like I thought Merle would play and I was playing with a thumb and three fingers. I didn't know he was doing it with a thumb and one finger. And that was luck, see, because if I'd been in Cincinnati and seen him I'd-a wound up playing exactly like him."[93]

Atkins would eventually become the other great star of country music finger-style guitar. In fact, today's country finger-style guitarists can be divided into two camps: Chet-style players and Travis-style players. (There is another camp that came along later, Jerry Reed style; Jerry came from the Atkins school and developed his own style from there.) Atkins's commercial success eclipsed Merle's thanks to a series of instrumental albums from the 1950s through the 1970s that sold by the truckload. But both had immeasurable influence on generations of finger-style players who followed them, and Atkins always reminded anyone paying attention that his greatest influence and hero was Merle Travis. The two wouldn't meet face-to-face until after the war, but when they did, they became very close friends. Atkins was known to be a no-nonsense businessman, and he became a very successful producer and A&R man for RCA Records. Some have described his persona as cold or impersonal. Merle Travis, however, seemed to be his kryptonite, as the letters between them are full of warmth and mutual respect, with Atkins showing a softer, emotional side he rarely revealed in public.

Merle and his family moved to a new duplex at 598 DeVotie Avenue in Cincinnati sometime in the latter part of 1942. Unlike their other residences in the city, this one was on a quiet, dead-end street butted up against a hillside. Photos from that time show what appears to be a happy period—Merle showing off fish he's caught, the well-dressed family posing with the family car, Merle and Mary in a photo booth from a county fair. A sad moment came, however, when Merle's father passed away at age seventy-three in Drakesboro, Kentucky, on December 20, 1942, five days before Christmas. He had been sick and returned to Kentucky to be cared for. He was buried in the Ebenezer church cemetery, where his wife, Etta, had been laid to rest three years earlier. With both of his parents gone and his two older brothers working in Evansville, his sister Vada became Merle's only immediate family tie to Kentucky. For a young man of twenty-five to suddenly live in a world without his parents must have seemed like being set adrift without an anchor. It undoubtedly influenced his decisions over the next few tumultuous years.

The Drifting Pioneers moved for a time to radio station WHAS in Louisville, Kentucky, to perform on the *Renfro Valley Barn Dance*. It is unknown whether the group left WLW to do the *Barn Dance* or were on both stations for a time. They remained at WLW through most of World War II.[94] Their repertoire had always featured religious songs in addition to hillbilly numbers, guitar and fiddle solos, and comedy. Merle, Walt Brown, and Bill Brown often sang gospel quartet numbers with WLW staff musician Buddy Ross, who played accordion with Hugh Cross and Shug Fisher on the station. The gospel quartet numbers proved so popular that they got their own thirty-minute program every morning. Grandpa Jones noted of the group:

> They had to sing really early in the morning, and they found themselves reading hymns that they didn't know too well out of old books. Early one particular morning, Bill had a tenor solo with the words "way down in my soul." He got a little mixed up and started to say "heart" instead of "soul," then realized his mistake and tried to catch himself. But what came out in his nice tenor voice was "way down in my HOLE." There was no tape at the time; it was all live, and out it went over the air. Everybody in the studio broke up, including the quartet, who got to laughing so bad they had to stop singing. The announcer, between gasps of breath himself, finally got a record on the turntable to take up the dead air. Later on, Merle and I would be getting involved in gospel music at WLW with slightly better results.[95]

In 1943, Bill Brown from the Drifting Pioneers was drafted into the Army. Sleepy Marlin decided to enlist in the Air Force to avoid being sent to the front lines. The war effectively broke up the Drifting Pioneers, although the Brown brothers would revive the name for a brief period in the late 1940s, playing gospel music back home in their native Illinois. Merle recalled:

> The war talk come about, and Walt and Bill Brown were concerned about the draft, so they quit singing on the radio and took a job in a factory. And Sleepy Marlin was a flyer, so he started teaching soldiers how to fly combat planes. And I thought, "Well, if it gets bad enough I'm going to join the Marines." So I just stayed on at the station there, and Grandpa Jones was there, and Alton and Rabon, the Delmore Brothers. The Drifting Pioneers had a half-hour spot every day singing gospel songs, and also spirituals and hymns.... When we left, the program director, Mr. George Biggers [Biggar], said, "We could sure use a good down-to-earth, country gospel quartet in that spot." And Alton Delmore said, "Well, I used to teach gospel singing, shape notes." He had taught me how to read shape notes, which is the best style in the world of reading music. It makes all the sense in the world. It doesn't matter what key you're singing in them, you can sing in any key.[96]

A couple of "Merle memories" that date from this time period:

"Browns Ferry Four is born in hallway"
"Browns Ferry Four smells like cheap wine"

In Grandpa Jones's recollection:

> The Drifting Pioneers had sort of drifted away as the war heated up, and since they had a daily half-hour show featuring old-time gospel singing, George Biggar (the program director) had told Alton Delmore that he would like to come up with a good country gospel group to fill that spot. Alton had learned to read shape notes and do real gospel singing as a boy in Alabama, so he went and got his brother Rabon, Merle Travis (who was about the only one of the Drifting Pioneers left), and me, and we marched up to the studio and stood out in the hall and tried out a couple of songs. They sounded okay, and we told Mr. Biggar that he had his country gospel group. "Good," he said, "start in the morning."[97]

Merle picks up the story:

Well, out in the hall, we said, "What in the world will we call ourself?" And we couldn't think of anything to save our life.... I seem to remember kidding about it, but I said, joking, "We should call ourselves the Brown's Ferry Four." One of the first songs Alton Delmore wrote was "Brown's Ferry Blues," which is a bawdy sort of a song. We all had a good laugh about that. I think it was Alton, he kind of got serious, and said, "You know, that's not a bad name." And we said, "Yeah, but what are we going to use 'Brown's Ferry Blues' for a theme song?" And we laughed about it again. But Alton said, "Wait a minute. You think about it. Brown's Ferry Four, it's got a good ring to it." So we went on and called ourselves the Brown's Ferry Four, and nobody ever connected it to Alton's bawdy "Two old maids layin' in the sand" song.[98]

The Brown's Ferry Four, formed in a hallway and according to Merle's memory smelling like cheap wine, would continue performing on WLW for another six months. It was the beginning of a fruitful gospel career under the Brown's Ferry Four name, and even though Merle would only briefly be associated with the group, it proved a lucrative commercial success for the Delmore Brothers and Grandpa Jones. Many decades later, the Brown's Ferry Four would be the inspiration for Grandpa's highly successful Hee Haw Gospel Quartet on the syndicated *Hee Haw* television show. Alton Delmore noted:

Merle Travis, Grandpa Jones, Rabon, and myself formed a quartet and Merle named it The Brown's Ferry Four after the song I had written by that title. We worked together fine and I taught some of them how to read music. Grandpa and Rabon learned to read pretty well and neither of them could pick out a song, but Merle used to come over to my house and we would talk nothing but music and how it was written, and so forth, till away past midnight. He was determined to read and also write music, and he did. It took him about two weeks to learn to read and about that long to learn how to write it. And when he learned to write, he could beat me, and I had been writing music since I was about eleven years old. About one month after I taught Merle Travis how to write music, I told him about the Williams boys [a family act on WLW featuring future pop singing star Andy Williams], and in no time at all he was doing some writing and arranging for them and they all liked it very much. So that is the kind of talent that Merle Travis possesses. I don't believe I have ever seen one person with so much talent. But he worked hard to gain it from the start. Unless he had listened to what I taught him about music, he couldn't have possibly have done it.[99]

Unfortunately, Merle never made a record with the Drifting Pioneers or the Brown's Ferry Four during the time he lived in Cincinnati. Part of that was due to a ban on outside recording by WLW. Recall that one of the station's advertising gimmicks was that they played no prerecorded music, and that ban extended to all their salaried employees. Reinforcing that was the blasé attitude toward making records shared by the WLW performers at the time. According to Merle:

> At the time we were on the radio... just before the war, records meant nothing in the world. Lulu Belle and Scotty were on the station there, and Alton came up to us one day, said, "Hey, we had a new release yesterday." We all looked at each other—"You had what?" "Had a release—a new release yesterday." We said, "Well, I guess that's good. What do you mean, a release?" He said, "A record. Columbia Records had a new release." We all said, "Oh. Well, we'll have to listen to that sometime. What else do you know?" It didn't mean nothing.... The thing to do was to see if you could get on a big radio show; that was the best. And of course, to top it all off would be to get on the network. That's the place where the millionaires were made.[100]

During the middle of World War II, American Federation of Musicians union president Joseph C. Petrillo instigated a strike against the record labels over royalty payments. All union musicians throughout the country were banned from making records from August 1, 1942, until September 1943. It remains the longest union strike in entertainment industry history. Alton Delmore recalled it later:

> Rabon and me had been under contract with Decca Records but Boss Petrillo called a musician's strike and no one was allowed to play any music on a record.... We tried saving our records and tried to keep one of each and every one we made, but somebody would come and borrow it and never bring it back. So I got in touch with a young man who was a distributor for Decca in Cincinnati. I thought he might have some way of getting the [Delmore Brothers] records for me, but he tried and they had gone out of print.... One day, he [Paul Cohen, the Decca distributor at the time, and later the Decca A&R man in Nashville] snapped his finger and said: "Alton, I know where you can go and maybe pick up those old records you need for your folio. Go over to Syd's record shop. He handles only old and used records, and he has a lot of them. He is located down in the Negro section of town. But you might do some good there."
>
> When I first found the place, it looked like a dump. It was old and when I went inside, I found that the floors were littered and dusty and

filthy. I thought I had come to the wrong place because no one answered when I called out. I waited for a moment, and then I saw the old records stacked in a rack along the wall. He didn't have as many as Paul thought he had, but I began looking and found exactly the ones I needed to send to the publisher. I knew there was someone around somewhere, so I called out again and then Syd Nathan came out.

He was all stained with the dyes of different colors of the pictures that he had been developing. He had on double lens glasses. He was fat and short and with all that coloring he looked like someone from another planet. His hands were held up to keep the color from getting on his clothes, and he really looked like a groundhog, just emerging from the ground. I told him and he began shaking his head. "I don't want any money for these records. I used to use your records on my juke box route down in Florida and you have made me plenty of money, so I guess it's about time for me to pay back some of those things you did for me while I was working for a living."

He was very jolly and he began to talk about forming a record company. He was smart and up to date.... I had been approached by many phonies before but I didn't recognize this guy as one. He seemed like the real thing to me.... He wanted some of the talent on WLW and he thought I could pull the deal for him....

He wanted Grandpa Jones, Cowboy Copas, and the Carlisles, Bill and Cliff to start with and then he said we could get along nicely. All of them were real close friends of mine, and I knew I could get them and they would believe me if I told them that Syd was on the level. I promised to talk with them and then I left with the records he had given me. It seemed incredible to me that a guy like that could start a record company, but I respected his intelligence and knowledge, but I thought it just as impossible as the verse in the Bible about turning a mustard seed into a mountain, or turning a mountain into a mole hill.[101]

Over the course of Merle's long career, he often found himself at important crossroads of the twentieth century. He was born into a world without electricity or automobiles, and as a young man he watched these things become an indispensable part of daily life. He came of age as the older vaudeville theater acts gained national audiences over high-powered radio stations, and then found himself right in the middle of that transformation at WLW. He electrified his guitar at a time when it was a novelty, but would bear witness to the electric guitar's explosion in popularity. Merle would witness further vast changes in society as World War II came to an end.

With that postwar boom, making records would supplant radio as, to paraphrase Merle, "the thing to do." Many times in his life, Merle found himself just slightly ahead of the curve, and at the right place at the right time:

> Singing these gospel songs on these early-morning shows, we'd always throw in a spiritual, a Negro spiritual. We liked to sing them, and I knew quite a bunch of them. But not enough. So, me and Grandpa Jones, we found a place down on Fourteenth and Central Avenue in Cincinnati, and the man who run it was a fellow named Syd Nathan. Syd was a short, fat, cigar-smoking little fellow that wore real thick glasses. And we liked Syd, and Syd liked us, and he got used to us coming in and saying, "You got any more good spirituals, by colored singers?" And we'd buy blues songs as well as spirituals. We'd buy these quartets and then learn them and sing them ourself.[102]

> I started to hang around Syd Nathan's Record Shop on Central Avenue, particularly after the Brown's Ferry Four got started. I was looking for those old black gospel quartets on record so we could steal stuff for our group.[103]

> Finally, Syd one day said, "Why don't you boys make some records of your own?" And Grandpa Jones said, "Ain't nobody asked us." And Syd said, "Well, I'm going to make some records." He said, "I'm going to start pressing them." He said, "Why don't you boys record for me?"[104]

Grandpa Jones remembered:

> Though I had wanted to record throughout the 1930s, there were only three big record companies operating then, and it was tough to get an audition with any of them. I had pretty well given up—everyone said that you couldn't make much money at records, anyway, and that radio work was what counted—until one afternoon in the fall of 1943. There was a man named Syd Nathan who owned a record shop down the street from WLW. Syd was quite a character; he was a Cincinnati native, about forty when I met him—a short, round man with thick, thick glasses and a case of asthma. He had been a jazz band drummer as a teenager, and then had done everything from promoting wrestling to running a chain of shooting galleries. He didn't really know much about country music, or care, but one day he bought out a radio store owned by Max Frank and found that most of the stock was what they then called "hillbilly" records, and that most of his customers wanted that kind of music.

A lot of people from Kentucky and West Virginia were working in the war factories around Cincinnati then, and there was quite a market. One of the problems was that in 1943 there was a recording ban on, and it was hard to get records of any sort. Syd got all hot to start his own record label, one that would feature hillbilly music, and he came up to WLW and talked to some of us about it…. He didn't have much money, we knew, but finally Merle Travis and I said we would try to make some records for him.[105]

Merle continues:

We said, "All right, but we're under contract to this radio station here. It's a fifty-thousand-watt station—that's as big as you get unless you go network—and they don't allow us to work anywhere else. They pay us a weekly salary, and if they found out we were making records for you, they'd kick us off." He said, "Well, why don't we slip out of town and go up to Dayton, Ohio, and make 'em?" I said, "Well, what do you think?" And Grandpa said, "I will if you will." And we did.[106]

Here's another Merle memory:

"Grandpa and I make first King Record"

Merle continues:

So he said that he had everything fixed one day, and me and Grandpa Jones and Syd Nathan slipped out of Cincinnati and went to Dayton to cut records. Now on the way up there, we got to deciding what we would cut. And Syd said, "Why don't you boys write some songs?" So we started throwing songs together, and we wrote four songs to record. [One of them, "When Mussolini Laid His Pistol Down," was written by WLW singer Roy Starkey.] Now, we stopped by a cornfield, and Grandpa wanted to take a look at the cornfield [a country way of saying that he needed to urinate] and me and Syd was waiting in the car, and I do believe that the first time that Syd Nathan ever said "King Records" was at that time, because he was sitting there trying to think of something to call his records. And the name this and that come up, and finally he said "King," something about a king. He said, "That would be a good name, King Records." And then, being the smart businessman that he's proved to be, he said, "King Records, that's it." He said, "I'll call it King Records," and said, "only it'll say King, the King of them all."[107]

Grandpa Jones:

It turned out that there wasn't a suitable studio anywhere in Cincinnati, so we all three got into Syd's old DeSoto sedan and drove down to Dayton. There was a little studio there, a room over the Wurlitzer Piano Company, and that's where Merle and I made our first records. For one of them, we sang duets on "The Steppin' Out Kind" and "You'll Be Lonesome Too." On the other, Merle sang "Two-Time Annie" and "When Mussolini Laid His Pistol Down." Syd asked us what we wanted to be called on the records; we thought awhile. Merle and I both liked to draw cartoons in those days, and one of my favorite characters was a little old man in long underwear with a kerosene lamp in his hand and a pipe in his mouth. I called him Mr. Sheppard because of the old man I had known as a boy. So Merle said, "Why don't we call ourselves The Sheppard Brothers?" I started laughing, but Syd said, "That's as good a name as any." Merle chose the name "Bob McCarthy" to cover his dirty work. I don't know where that one came from, but it got us on the label.[108]

Back to Merle:

So we went to Dayton and cut four sides for King Records. That was the Sheppard Brothers, and that was the first King Record that was ever made. Finally it was released, and I took home a copy and I put it on the machine. I had a Wilcox-Gay home recording outfit, but also a playback. And it turned around and around and around, I don't know how many grooves, and finally here come a distant voice of me and Grandpa. Sounded like it was off in the barn.[109]

It was a terrible record. But King Records got to be a pretty big outfit.[110]

And, finally, from Grandpa:

Syd had trouble getting the records pressed because back in 1943, there weren't too many independent record companies and it was hard to find someone to do custom pressing, especially someone to do it well. Some of the early King Records came out warped so badly you could use them for bowls or ashtrays; as Merle said, watching a needle go around one was like watching a stock car on a banked race track. On November 15, 1943, our first two records were released; the Sheppard Brothers was King 500, and McCarthy was King 501. It was the start of a new company that was to become one of the country's biggest in the 1940s, but at the time we weren't too worried about that. The records weren't exactly best sellers; in fact, for years I wondered if the Sheppard Brothers had ever been released to the public, because no one I knew had a copy. Finally, a few years ago, a fan found one and sent it to me in a special mahogany box, and that's the only copy I've seen.[111]

"I guess they came out," Merle likewise noted, "but I don't ever remember seeing one in a store anywhere."[112] The Sheppard Brothers disc featured two guitars—neither player using Merle's signature thumbpicking style. Listening to it (the tracks were mastered from Grandpa Jones's copy and included on the Bear Family Records Merle Travis box set), it would appear that Merle and Grandpa were trying to make the Sheppard Brothers sound like the Delmore Brothers, their friends at WLW. The "Bob McCarthy" disc features Merle playing and singing, and is the recording debut of his distinctive Muhlenberg County thumbpicking guitar style. The A side, "When Mussolini Laid His Pistol Down," was a reference to the Italian dictator's removal from power in July 1943. The song itself, with its chorus about laying pistols down, was obviously stolen almost directly from the popular song "Pistol Packin' Mama," a hit for Al Dexter in 1942 and then Bing Crosby in September 1943, just before the first King sessions.

Both Merle and Grandpa Jones were beginning their long recording careers that day in Dayton, Ohio. As Merle states, the recordings were of poor quality, and the songs themselves just average. But what makes the story exceptional are not the records themselves. First, the Sheppard Brothers and Bob McCarthy 78 rpm discs were the recording debuts of two major country music stars, and they are today some of the rarest records in existence. Only one copy of the Sheppard Brothers 78 is definitively known to exist (there are rumors of a second), turned up by bluegrass historian Pete Kuykendall in a record hunt in the 1970s. There are rumored to be two or three known copies of the Bob McCarthy 78. Merle once told an interviewer that he backed a chair over his only copy and cracked it.[113] It is difficult to say what they'd be worth today because there has never been a copy of either disc offered for sale on the collector's market in the seventy-five years since they were manufactured. For two country music stars who would both go on to sell millions of records, these first two King discs were humble beginnings, indeed.

Researcher Ed Kahn wrote to Syd Nathan about the matter in 1964. Nathan, who by that point had sold millions and millions of King releases, did not remember that the two recordings had been commercially released: "To the best of my knowledge, number 500 and number 501 were never released because at that time we were very green in the business. We found that the studio in Dayton did not put any volume at all on the original acetates."[114] But the few surviving copies of

King 500 and 501 prove that they *were* released. Their scarcity indicates that the original pressing must have been incredibly small, perhaps fifty or one hundred copies of each disc.

The second thing that makes these first two King discs so remarkable is that from this tiny beginning, Syd Nathan built King Records into one of the most successful independent labels of the 1940s, 1950s, and 1960s. The man who ran the dirty, crowded record store became a mogul, eventually running not only King but a slew of subsidiaries: Queen, DeLuxe, Federal, Bethlehem. The label had its own recording studio, mastering studio, pressing plant, and distribution center all under one roof in a large industrial building in Cincinnati. The label had hits, both national and regional.

Years later, Merle and Grandpa Jones would still get a chuckle out of the fact that they had made the first two King Records—that they had played a part in the birth of one of America's most famous and important independent record labels.

Just a few weeks after the records' release in November 1943, Merle received a letter from his local draft board, dated December 7, to report for induction into the armed services on December 11. When he showed up, he was given a choice of military branches, and he opted to enlist in the Marines, the most rigorous one. The details surrounding Merle's time in the military are among the murkiest of his entire life. In interviews, he would occasionally reference going to Parris Island, the South Carolina boot camp for the Marines, for basic training. His lone photo in Marine uniform was reproduced in several publications throughout his career as evidence of military service. But beyond that, Merle never spoke in public about that time. Many fans and friends thought that he had fought overseas. The reality was much different. Military records obtained recently through the National Archives reveal that Merle enlisted December 29, 1943, and was released February 12, 1944. Slightly less than six weeks after he left Cincinnati for Parris Island, he was sent back home.

Merle's "qualification card" that he filled out as he entered the service showed optimism that the Marines might use him for entertaining, stating that he "played violin, guitar, banjo, mandolin, string bass, harmonica on radio programs and dances, wrote some of own music, made own arrangements." In addition, he listed his second-best occupation as "stage and radio actor, took character and comedy parts in radio and stage plays, acted as master of ceremonies [for the] Crosley Radio Corporation." Finally, he listed additional occupations as "watchmaker, cartoon drawing."[115]

Michael Robinson, who was Merle's stepson for twenty years, offers this take on the situation:

I think his fantasy was that he was going to be the singing Marine. But they started holding him to higher standards there, and he just wasn't ready for that intense Marine boot camp experience. He was a little bit too easygoing of a guy. He thought this whole thing was going to be duck soup. A drill instructor will look for your weak point, and then he will ride that weak point and try and break you. They found his weak point, and I think they found a crack in there that was unacceptable or something.[116]

Many people who knew Merle have tried to guess why the military sent him home. The only one who ever spoke on the record about it was Drifting Pioneers fiddler Sleepy Marlin:

Merle was sort of a rough and tough guy, right, he liked to get down and scrap around, had a few fights. And you know Marine Corps boot camp is really tough. That's the last place for a sissy to be. Well, he went in the Marines, and was in the Marines two weeks [actually closer to six]. While we were working the whole time at WLW it wasn't all that uncommon... see, he never did get over the shakes that goes on with the alcoholism. He tried, he tried his best to get off of it. I could never understand why he picked the Marines, because that's the most rugged outfit... in the world. I don't know where he got the ambition for that, but I never would have thought that he could pass the physical to get in there in the first place, but he did. In two weeks' time they gave him a medical discharge because he'd wake up in the middle of the night and shout, "hit the deck," things of that sort. Wasn't no place when the barracks was trying to sleep. They gave him a medical discharge.... He never completely recovered from that addiction as a teenager.... When he'd have these nightmares, there was no alcohol involved in that. That was just a hangover from the health problem he had gotten into from his alcoholism. The thing about this: telling a story about any one entertainer and alcohol is telling a story about a lot of them.[117]

The only surviving record of Merle's take on the military is a letter to WLW's Jane Allen, a member of the Happy Valley Girls act, and kept in the possession of Ramona Riggins, who was also a member of the Happy Valley Girls and another recipient of Merle's letters. On Marine barracks stationery from Parris Island, Merle wrote a pleasant letter that reveals many intriguing details:

I liked it when I was training, and I liked it in Cincinnati, but this in-between which is known as the Casual Company—I don't like.... Shucks, I ain't helpin' the war effort, myself, or nobody else out here! My Saturday night will be quite different [than yours]. No show—no radio—no nothing... not even a recreation hall—the only books to read are *Superman* or through a miracle one might uncap a *Life* or *Click* magazine... but they're not common. So I'll amuse myself by twiddling my little thumbs until 7:30—then I'm allowed to shave and shower—then I'll go to bed!

I'm anxious for Sunday morning to come, because 10 of us gets to march over to the big shots offices, and mop-sweep-and clean them up.... We only get to do this every day.... I really shouldn't say "we," for I'm the boss... big ole me. I just hand the brooms and mops to the guys. Some life I'm leadin' Jane, some life.[118]

Merle closed the letter with some revealing cartoons—showing himself rudely awakened at half past four in the morning, getting his hair cut by a barber who threatens cutting "half of that flap off" Merle's big ears, painfully receiving shots in the arm while joking, "I took a few double shots since I've come here, but I ain't seen a saloon." Lastly, Merle drew himself marching in a regiment of soldiers, but heading in the opposite direction of all the others, with the caption "Although being assistant National Champion Buck Dancer, I've learned lots of new steps." He also relates that he will be released from the military soon: "I was all set, and planning on leaving here Wednesday, Feb. 9th but I'm afraid that's been knocked in the head, somehow. I may leave the 12th... I hope, I hope."

Merle's aptitude board review, recently released by the National Archives, reveals details about his personal history and his discharge that have never been known until now:

Personal History: Since grade school he has been nervous apprehensive and fearful. In 1935 while a member of the CCC he was placed in the Fort Knox hospital for his nerves. A year later he had a nervous breakdown which kept him away from his work for a year.

Psychologist's Report: This man has normal adult intelligence with a GCT [General Classification Test] score of 107. His job and emotional adjustments have been seriously interfered with by his emotional unstability [*sic*]. He feels insecure and apprehensive and his feelings of anxiety have produced functional symptoms which prevent him from operating efficiently. His marital adjustments have been poor and several separations have resulted from his drinking.

Board's Impression: This man has normal intelligence, has worked as a radio entertainer, and since childhood has had trouble with his nerves. On one occasion, he stayed away from work because of his fears, apprehensiveness, etc. for a year. He denied his nervousness at induction and took 14 days of training here, but his nerves have gotten the best of him. His psychoneurosis, anxiety type, renders him unfit for the Marine Corps.[119]

Merle returned to a wintry Cincinnati on February 12, 1944, feeling like a failure. Undoubtedly his family and friends were glad that he hadn't been shipped off to the front lines, but the guilt and shame of being rejected by the Marines would haunt Merle for the rest of his life. He saved his draft card, induction letter, Marine photo, and metal dog tags for his scrapbook, but destroyed his discharge papers so no one could see what had really happened. Wesley Tuttle was asked in a 1995 interview about his knowledge of Merle's military experience:

You know Travis, you know what he was. He was a flake... in settling down. He was just a genius, but he couldn't settle down to anything. He was irresponsible. And so he decided he was going to quit his job and join the Marines. He was going to be a hero... so he enlisted in the Marines, but he didn't last.... He was discharged on a Section 8.... He was just Travis and when he got in there he couldn't be handled, he was insubordinate and he couldn't take it and they discharged him on a Section 8. Well, he was so embarrassed by this, because he was very vain... most humble on the outward, but he was very vain, as anybody would have been.[120]

Merle was actually discharged honorably, not dishonorably as Tuttle theorized, with the reason for discharge listed as "unsuitability." Grandpa Jones's future wife Ramona Riggins remembered Merle's state of mind at the time: "He [Merle] wanted so much to do his part. He was patriotic. He wanted to be in the Marines. It was sad that he couldn't stay there. He said, 'Well now, what'll I tell my grandchildren someday? I was in the Marines and I couldn't take it.' He hated that."[121] Grandpa Jones additionally remembered a humorous anecdote that may or may not be true, but makes for a good story: "He wondered, while he was in there, he said, 'I didn't know where the musicians were.' There was no musicians in there [the Marines]. And finally they put him in the—I don't guess it's a hoosegow [stockade, military jail], but there they all were."[122]

Upon returning to Cincinnati, Merle did one more session with Grandpa Jones for King Records that resulted in Grandpa's first record under his own name and his first modest hit, "It's Raining Here This Morning." Unlike the great majority of Jones's banjo-dominated records, this is a guitar duet, with Merle playing lead acoustic guitar and Grandpa playing rhythm guitar. Merle's two blazing solos show why he was so highly regarded on the *Boone County Jamboree*. During this session Merle recorded a total of eight songs with Grandpa and another two of his own. For unknown reasons, the songs Merle recorded remained in the vaults for decades. One of them, "What Will I Do," appeared (with added reverb) on a strange various-artists collection in 1963, after Merle had achieved mainstream success. The second, "So Long, Farewell, Goodbye," remained in the vaults until Bear Family released its Merle Travis box set in 1994. Merle rejoined the WLW *Boone County Jamboree* and continued where he had left off before his experience in the Marines.

Shortly after the February recording session, Grandpa Jones was drafted into the Army. World War II changed a lot of people's lives in the United States. Merle's life was about to change as well.

Merle in a publicity still for the 1946 western film *Galloping Thunder*, starring Smiley Burnette (wearing black hat).

CHAPTER 3

HOLLYWOOD TEETH

Walking on the ice-covered sidewalk from the Albee Theatre in Cincinnati to the nearby restaurant wasn't easy. One slip and you could bust your bottom. What's more, the wind chilled me to the bone. But it wasn't every day that I had a chance to have a bite with Smiley Burnett [sic]. He was playing on the bill with Bill "Bojangles" Robinson at the theatre, and I had gone backstage to talk with him. He asked me to go have a bite to eat with him. "I'd rather live in California and live on lettuce," said the famous screen comic and Gene Autry's side-kick, "than live in Cincinnati and eat caviar."

I was fresh out of the United States Marine Corps and had been where it was warm. I didn't like the cold either. What's more, my marriage to Mary wasn't going too smoothly.

Nevertheless, I'd come back to my old job at radio station WLW and was doing early morning programs and a Saturday night show called Boone County Jamboree. Smiley's words was ringing in my head when I went to the early morning broadcast the next morning. I decided to do something a little drastic.

I went from friend to friend to borrow ten dollars. Ramona Riggins (Mrs. Grandpa Jones now), Jane Allen, Rabon Delmore, Roy Lanham, Lula Belle and Scotty, Curly Fox and Texas Ruby, Captain Stubby and all the Buccaneers and a few more. Not only did I borrow ten from Hank Penny, but I asked him to drive me to the railroad depot. I didn't tell anybody where I was going, or why. Hank drove me to the station, said his goodbye, and left without asking me a single question. Years later he told me he had a pretty good idea what I was up to.

I rode a crowded day-coach to Los Angeles. It took several days. I lived on stale sandwiches and slept sitting up. Finally we reached Los Angeles.

Places to live in March 1944 was almost impossible to find. I walked up the street from the depot and found a room for seventy-five cents a night. I rented it and laid across the ancient, filthy bed. I fell asleep and slept like a baby for about twelve hours.

I knew two people in Los Angeles County: Fiddlin' Charlie Linville and Wesley Tuttle. I went to a pay phone and looked in the book. There was the name of a dear friend. So I called Wesley Tuttle.

"I'll be right down to get you," said the voice on the phone. In a short time Wesley pulled up.

"I'll help you carry your suitcase," he offered.

"I didn't bring one," I told him.

"Well, what did you bring?" he asked, puzzled.

"Just my guitar," I answered.

Wesley lived far, far out in the country. As we drove west on a boulevard with the late evening sun blinding both of us, he said, "You can see why they named this Sunset Boulevard." We drove over a winding, narrow road north of Hollywood. Wesley said the stretch of crooked road was called Cahuenga Pass.

The pass led us into a wide-open country called the San Fernando Valley. Ranch houses and small farms were scattered here and there. Sagebrush gave a wonderful scent in the warm breeze. The mountains in the background looked like you could reach out and touch them. The sky was blue, the sun was bright, and the air was clean and clear. There were sleepy little towns with names like Van Nuys, Burbank, Encino, Glendale, and Tarzana. Far across the spaces was a larger, older town where the early Californians had built one of their many beautiful missions. It was called San Fernando. Wesley lived out in that spacious part of the valley.

Wesley got in touch with my other friend, Charlie Linville. Charlie introduced me to a friend of his who was a singer and guitar player. He was a very tall, slim young man. His wife was extremely pretty. I liked them both from the minute I met them. Their names were Dorothy and Johnny Bond.

I don't believe anybody could ride a horse better than big Wesley Tuttle in those days. Charlie could ride like an expert, too. I hadn't done much of that, but I had fun going out on Riverside Drive, renting horses, and riding them at night up in the Griffith Park hills. We'd play hide-and-seek on horseback. Wesley would charge out of a clump of bushes in the moonlight, fly by me on his horse, tap me on the shoulder with his hat, and yell, "You're it!" That meant that I had to try and do the same to him or Charlie. I remained "it" most of the time.

I transferred from Local 1 in the Cincinnati Musicians Union to Local 47 in Hollywood. Mr. Phil Fischer was president of the Union at that time. I was informed that I could not work a steady job until I'd been there three months. I could work casual jobs, but nothing steady. I had an offer from two different people: Spade Cooley and Foreman Phillips. Somehow the Union got word and let me know again that I could work for neither of them. Charlie Linville, along with a couple of musicians whose names I cannot recall, were playing in a little cubby-hole on Hollywood Boulevard and McCadden Place. Charlie's wife, Margie, played fiddle, and the two of them were doing a lot of recording sessions. Charlie told his friend Tex Ritter about me. Tex came by one night and flattered me by asking if I'd do a recording session with him.

To me, Tex Ritter was not human, by any means. He was a movie star. And movie stars ain't human, I thought. I learned, after meeting dozens of them, that they're very much human. Fame and photographs has nothing to do with your blood and bones.

The first recording I did in Hollywood was for a brand-new company Tex was recording for called Capitol Records. He sang a Jennie Lou Carson song called "Jealous Heart." Paul Sells played the accordion, Cliffie Stone played bass, Wesley Tuttle played rhythm guitar, the Linvilles played fiddles, and I played electric guitar.

I played one or two nights a week down on Hollywood Boulevard with Charlie and Margie. The old fellow who wrote "The Music Goes 'Round and 'Round" was playing with a band next to us. Once in a while his whole crew would come marching through our place playing horns, drums, and clarinets and singing such songs as "When the Saints Go Marching In." I wish I could recall his name, but it's been a long time [the song was written by big band musicians Eddie Farley and Mike Riley, so it must have been one of the two co-authors].

One night Tex Ritter came by to talk with me. "I've heard about the Union crackin' down on you," he boomed. "Well, I've got a plan. Me and Slim Andrews are goin' on the road to play some theatres. We'll take you along. When you come back to town, your three months period will be up and you can go to work with Foreman and Spade."

I have no idea how, but the Union found this out and let me know quite definitely that if I went on the road with Tex Ritter, I'd have to start my three months all over again when

*I came back. Charlie told Tex, and he was in the club that night. "I'm awful sorry, Merle,"
he said. "But that's the Union for you. If they've ever done anything in my favor, I'd just
like to know what it is."*

*"Tex Ritter told me to give you this envelope after him and Slim Andrews got out of
town," Charlie said one night shortly after I'd talked with Tex. I figured it was mighty nice
of Tex to follow up with a little note. I opened the white envelope. There was a note inside,
but there was something more. A one hundred dollar bill. The note said:*

> *This is not a loan, it's a gift. Don't try to pay it back.*
> *I hope it helps and I wish you were with us.*
> *A mi amigo, Tex*

*Tex would not like for me to tell that story. But after we were friends for some thirty
years, I found it to be characteristic of him. I know why Rex Allen was told when he first
came to Hollywood, "If anybody says anything against Tex Williams or Tex Ritter, watch
out for them. They're no good."*

*Somehow with the help of such friends as Wesley, Charlie, and Tex, I got past the three
months period and could work steady. A big jolly bass player who played on Stuart Hamblen's afternoon radio broadcasts had begun doing a few things on his own. Stuart called him
Cliffie Stonehead, but he called himself Cliffie Stone. We always seemed to find something
to laugh about. Nobody has a greater sense of humor than Cliffie Stone. We first worked
together on a noon show which was ram-rodded by a Cherokee Indian girl from Oklahoma
who called herself "Dixie Darling." Her husband, Hal Hart, would ride up and down
Hollywood Boulevard in the afternoons on a beautiful white horse. He dressed in the finest
western clothes, wore a big white hat, and sat astride a silver-mounted saddle. Servicemen
from all over America would know they'd seen somebody, but wasn't exactly sure who. But
they could write home about colorful Hollywood.*

*After Dixie Darling left the noon show, Cliffie took it over. He was kind enough to
ask me to be on it, as well as a left-handed fiddler who had just got out of the Navy and
was well known as Tex Atchison and a girl singer from Chanute, Kansas, who called herself
Tex Ann. Cliffie's father, who was also on the Stuart Hamblen broadcasts, came over to
play whatever you handed him. He'd grown a big bushy black beard for a movie and liked
it so well he never shaved it off. Cliffie called his father by the same show name that Stuart
did: Herman the Hermit.*

*A complete book should be written about Cliffie Stone and his career. We broadcasted
from a studio over a coffee shop on Hollywood Boulevard, from a record and music store
at the corner of Sunset and Vine, from the KXLA studios in Pasadena, and from the El
Monte Legion Stadium, to name a few. There was Cliffie Stone's Dinner-Bell Roundup,
Cliffie Stone's radio shows on two radio stations other than KXLA, and, of course, Cliffie
Stone's Hometown Jamboree.*

To name some of the people that I had the pleasure of knowing from Cliffie's shows: Terry Preston, who confided in me one day that his real name was Ferlin Husky; Molly Beechboard, who Cliffie hired before she was a teenager and changed her name to Molly Bee; a Los Angeles fireman's beautiful red-haired daughter whom Hedda Hopper once called Hollywood's Cinderella girl because of her extraordinarily beautiful voice and went on to do such things as the leading lady in "The Alamo," starring John Wayne... her name, Joannie O'Brien; [and] my former wife and mother of our two wonderful daughters, Merlene and Cindy, June Hayden. Cliffie called her Judy. Then there was the violet-eyed brunette with a striking smile that I suggested to Cliffie as a girl singer when Judy wanted to quit the show. Polly Bergen was the girl's name; great musicians like Speedy West, Jimmy Bryant, Harold Hensley, Charlie Aldrich, and on and on who played for Cliffie. Petite little Bucky Tibbs sang with him. So did Colleen Summers. She later married Les Paul, and Les changed her name to Mary Ford. The two made recording history.

I could go on and on, but I must mention the black-haired, dark young man who had been a radio announcer up in San Bernardino, California, since his discharge from the Air Force. He came to KXLA in Pasadena as an announcer. He had a fine speaking voice on the air, but off, and at our rehearsals, we found him to be a real down-to-earth country boy. He loved to sing. When we'd rehearse a song, he'd step in and sing any part that was needed. He loved to sing bass when we rehearsed our spirituals and gospel songs. His eyes would twinkle and a little grin would curve just below his black moustache as he sang. He was our announcer. Two or three times a week, Harold Hensley, Speedy West, or I would say to Cliffie, "You ought to let that announcer sing on the program. He knows all the songs and has a fine singing voice."

"Now, come on," Cliffie would joke. "Do you boys want to do his announcing?"

Cliffie would usually come in just before the program went on the air. He hadn't had a chance to hear the young fellow with the moustache sing. One day he came in in time to hear him, and had him sing a song on the show. This young radio announcer was doing an early morning disc-jockey show over at the station. He'd talk in a high nasal countrified voice. Then when it was time for a commercial, he'd change to his deep, resonate [sic] radio announcer voice. Very few people knew they were two and the same. He became extremely popular at the Saturday night Hometown Jamboree as well as on the daily shows. He even made some records for Capitol before he used his last name, Ford.

Otherwise, everybody knew and loved just plain ol' Tennessee Ernie.

After I got into the Musicians Union, I didn't have much trouble finding work. The war was still on and factories, as well as entertainment, went on twenty-four hours a day. Spade Cooley was going strong.... Red Murrell formed a dance band, so did T. Texas Tyler and Olie [Ole] Rassmussen. Bob Wills owned a place near Sacramento, California, called Wills Point. He played the Los Angeles area often. Once Roy Acuff came out as a guest at a pier where Foreman Phillips was having a dance. So many people tried to get on the pier, the fire department had to stop them, lest a few thousand factory workers and Roy Acuff fall in the Pacific Ocean!

Al Dexter's "Pistol Packin' Mama" had made him even more famous, and he had a band that played for dances. I played with him about six months. Movie actor, songwriter-singer-musician Rudy Sooter formed a band. I played with him a while. Other than Cliffie Stone, I played more dances with Ray Whitley than with anyone else. With Ray Whitley, we'd play a dance in Baldwin Park until midnight. Then we'd head for the "Plantation" out by MGM in Culver City, a big white building that, I was told, Fatty Arbuckle, the silent screen star, had built. We'd play there until daylight. Other dance bands around Los Angeles were rotating likewise. Some of the people that played the dance music with these "front men" were Porky Freeman, Tex Atchison, Noel Boggs, Charlie Morgan, Jesse Ashlock, George Bamby, and a few thousand others.

One of the better bands came from the Spade Cooley organization. When Tex Williams (who had sung "Shame on You" with Spade's band on record) decided to try it on his own, almost all of Spade's band went with him. There was Earl "Joaquin" Murphey, Smokey Rogers, Deuce Spriggens, Ossie Godson, Cactus Soldi, Larry "Pedro" De Paul, Dean Ecker, and a few others. Tex played for Marty Landeau [Landau] at the Riverside Rancho, where Spade and a lot of other bands had been.

When Tex signed with Capitol Records, he made some very nice records, but somehow they didn't seem to hit the way they should have. I'd always enjoyed hearing Tex, with his deep voice, perform the old Bert Williams recitation "Darktown Poker Club." So I threw together a set of words along the same line, and Tex Williams and the Western Caravan recorded it. It was titled "Smoke, Smoke, Smoke That Cigarette." We were lucky enough to have had Capitol's first million-dollar seller.

Let me say here and now that I had a line in the song that would have no doubt kept it off of all radio stations, as well as possibly being offensive to some people. But Tex changed the line and saved the song, I'm sure. You'll see both of our names as the writers of the song.

During the dancing days in Los Angeles County and thereabouts, Ted Daffan, Texas Jim Lewis, Curly Williams, and Adolph Hoffner [Hofner] had bands playing. I tried my hand at it for a while. I made some dandy tours later, playing for dances through the southwest. In my band of the early fifties were Rose Lee and Joe Maphis, Margie Warren (known as Fiddlin' Kate), Homer Escamilla, Dick Stubbs, and Dale Warren, who's now head man of the Sons of the Pioneers.

Every Saturday night, down by Sunset and Gower in Hollywood, Cottonseed Clark held forth with the old Hollywood Barn Dance. This went on from the mid-forties until the early fifties. This was before Cliffie Stone sprouted such fabulous wings. He, along with Johnny Bond, did the comedy on the show. The Hollywood Barn Dance was an hour radio show broadcast over KNX, at the CBS studio. Cottonseed and Johnny Bond wrote it. Cliffie played bass, [and] Andy Parker and the Plainsmen (Clem Smith, Hank Caldwell, Charlie

Morgan, and Joaquin Murphey) were there some of the time. Other times, Foy Willing and the Riders of the Purple Sage (Foy Willing, Scotty Harrell, and Al Sloey) sang some mighty pretty harmony. The cast of the Hollywood Barn Dance changed from time to time. In fact, I was the M.C. of the show for a year or so. But I always think of it as Cottonseed's brain child.

Before Colleen Summers became Mary Ford, she sang with June Widener and Vivian Earles. They called themselves "The Sunshine Girls." (Later, Colleen's sister, Eva, sang with June and Vivian as "The Three Rays" on the Jimmy Wakely Show on CBS.) Dusty King, who worked as one of the Three Musketeers in the movies, along with Crash Corrigan and Max Terrhune (and dozens of other cowboy actors), came down and sang for a few months. So did Sally Foster, who was very popular when she was on the Brush Creek Follies, the show Pappy Cheshire had for many years in the late thirties and early forties in St. Louis over KMOX radio. [Merle's memory is slightly off here: Pappy Cheshire was in St. Louis, and the *Brush Creek Follies* show was based out of Kansas City.] *Pappy also ended up in Hollywood, playing dignified old white-haired judges, doctors, etc. in pictures.*

I worked on a series of transcriptions that he made in Hollywood in the forties. Once I had supper with a police lieutenant and his wife. After supper, I explained that I hated to eat and run, but Pappy Cheshire was waiting down in Hollywood for me and my lady friend, Tex Ann, who I mentioned as a girl singer. We were far out on Ventura Boulevard. I was driving. I was also late. I was stopped for speeding and drunk driving. They had our pictures on the front page of the Los Angeles paper. I hired an attorney and fought it in court. I lost.

Once I was sitting in Brittinghams, a restaurant next to CBS, having a sandwich with Colleen Summers. Cottonseed had been to the hospital for a minor hernia operation. Now, I wouldn't attempt to paint Colleen as a "dumb blonde," but she'd bite on almost any joke, or believe almost anything you'd tell her. Let's say she was "colorful." As we were sitting there, in walked Cottonseed. Colleen's eyes lit up as she saw someone she liked back on their feet after a bout in the hospital.

"Did the operation hurt much, Cottonseed?" she asked, wide eyed.

"No, not at all." Cottonseed told her. "But from now on I'm not supposed to make love to anybody except my wife."

"Gee, that's awful!" Colleen said tenderly.

The year I went to Hollywood, 1944, was the year Monogram Pictures signed up a new singing star named Jimmy Wakely. There was a little theatre on Hollywood Boulevard called The Hitching Post. Every time one of our gang (us Hollywood Hillbillies) would be showing in a picture, we'd all gather to see it. We watched Monte Hale striking a match on his teeth as he told Ted French, "I'm warnin' you, Slade, don't try to cut out none of my heifers." We'd go down and watch Lash LaRue yank a six gun out of Cactus Mack's hand with a bull whip. Lash had a slight resemblance to Humphrey Bogart. "They call me 'Little Bogie' down on the set," he'd say over a cold glass of buttermilk at Brittinghams.

When Eddie Dean started making feature-length musical westerns down at PRC, we'd all sit in The Hitching Post and listen to his well-controlled voice sing as he rode along smiling.

Gene Autry was in the service, and would drop in to a country show every now and then when he was in the United States. Tex Ritter's pictures were an absolute must. The first movie set I ever saw was when Shug Fisher took me out to watch Roy Rogers and the Sons of the Pioneers do some location shoots in Chatsworth. I remember how bright and warm the sun was. Big Bob Nolan was lying on his back on a rock with his shirt off getting some sun. Shug introduced me to everybody, but I doubt very much if they'd remember a skinny kid in his twenties with a crew cut coming out where they were working. Some light man ordered a tin foil reflector to be a little "hotter" on Roy's face. Roy grinned and said, "O.K., keep getting it bright if you want to film a Chinese cowboy." Roy's eyes were laughing little slits in his boyish face.

Back to Jimmy Wakely. If I possibly could, I'd go see the Wakely films two or three times. Jimmy Wakely would no more sing a song out of tune, or allow a bad note in his music, than Rembrandt would paint with a toothbrush. He's a perfectionist. I consider the Wakely family as some of my closest friends. I used to look forward to being a guest on Jimmy's CBS radio show. I had no idea that many years later, he'd take the old tapes from the show and release an album of me singing and pickin' on his own Shasta record label. I've got a good many Jimmy Wakely albums. I could never tire of hearing the Sons of the Pioneers, Les Paul and Mary Ford, Chet Atkins, or Jimmy Wakely.

Every country entertainer that hangs around Hollywood is bound to find himself in front of a motion picture or TV camera now and then. My first experience was when Ray Whitley asked in his subtle way if I'd "mind comin' out and being in a picture with me and Rod Cameron." I didn't mind, and went out. Ray explained to me that if I said one line, I could get in the Screen Actors Guild. He promoted one line for me. A bunch of us were supposed to play act like we were digging a ditch, when a tough-looking hombre rides up and spiels off something that I was too scared to hear. All I know is, I was to answer back, "Let's see what Nevada's got to say." That's it. The rest of the time, I sat around a phony camp fire while Ray sang and yodeled. Rather, he'd lip-sync what he recorded on tape [in 1944, this would have actually been recorded to disc, as it predated tape] *before they started shooting the picture. But good ol' Ray, I got the SAG card.*

President Roosevelt's son, I forget which one, and a couple of other gents came up with an idea that if you'd film the people that sing on the juke box, folks would gladly pay a quarter to see them rather than just hear them. So about 1947, Spade Cooley's girl singer, Carolina Cotton, and I made about twenty of the little films. We pre-recorded the music with Spade's musicians. When the film was shot, all the musicians were girls. There was a cheap hotel called the Regent Hotel on Hollywood Boulevard. I lived there at the time. They had one of the machines in the lounge with some of our R.C.M. Soundies on it. One day some customers were putting quarters in and watching the pictures.

"I don't think much of that blonde bouncin' around singin'… and I don't like that skinny kid with his guitar, but them girls has got a helluva band."

I made about eight or ten of them the following year. Carolina was doing fine in pictures and couldn't do them with me, so I started looking for another girl. I took every pretty girl I knew down to the producers, but they kept saying, "Don't you know of a pretty girl anywhere in Hollywood?" I had brought them some pretty celebrated (later) beauties, if they had known it. But finally I said, "I know a girl in Salinas. She's beautiful. If you'll pay my expenses, I'll go ask her if she wants to make the films." They agreed, and away I went.

Up in Salinas, when I told Betty Devere what I was up to, she threw her pretty head back and laughed loud and long. "If the other girls wasn't pretty enough," she said, "why on earth do you think I'd be?" I didn't really have an answer, but I was relieved when she said she was game to give it a try. When I walked in with Betty, the men in charge took one look and almost shouted at me. "Why in the world didn't you bring her in the first place?!"

We had fun making the films. At the time, she had a grown son and her husband, Bill Liebert, [years later] played accordion with the Sons of the Pioneers.

A few years later, Mr. Snader had about the same notion the people who made the "soundies" had. He figured, now that television's here, folks will want to see the people who make records as well as hear them. He reasoned that a day would come when there'd be some sort of "jockey" on TV playing music, but they wouldn't call him a disc jockey. He'd probably be a film jockey. For years transcriptions were played on the radio, so why not do the same thing with film. So that is how Snader Telescriptions came about.

I made a good many of them. I've done some alone, wherein I'd walk on the scene and spout off a little about what I was going to pick and sing, then go to it. I also made a few with Judy Hayden. They were fun. I still have a few of them. When I see the films, I wonder if I was ever really that young and foolish. The strange thing is neither the R.C.M. Soundies nor the Snader Telescriptions were successful. It seems to me that it could have been. An awful lot of talented people made them, excluding me, of course.

Bobbie Bennett was a wonderful gal. She was Spade Cooley's manager, as well as Carolina Cotton's and mine. She also got a starring role at Columbia for a handsome young singer named Ken Curtis. Years later he was to become famous as the bewhiskered ol' squinty-eyed deputy that rode his mule right along by Matthew Dillon in a series called "Gunsmoke." He was playing "Festus." I worked in one of Ken's pictures. I have no idea what the title of it was. But there was a scene where he was the Master of Ceremonies at some sort of shindig. We were on the set, which was a theatre stage with curtains. He was to walk out and announce me. Then I was to come on and perform, as best I could. Ken and I were always kidding, so when we were all set to do the scene, I said, "Ken, be sure and say MISTER Merle Travis." He grinned and said that he wouldn't think of saying anything else.

The director hollered "ACTION!" and Ken walked out.

"And now Ladies and Gentlemen," he spoke very loudly, "it gives me great pleasure to introduce MISTER Merle Travis."

"CUT!" shouted the director. "For Heaven's sake, Ken, don't say 'Mister,' whoever he is! He's not that important!"

For days after that, Ken would say to me in his "Festus" voice (which I always called his Fred voice), "you ain't very im-portent, air y'Fraid?"

In the summer of 1945, my friends Lula Belle and Scotty Wiseman came to Hollywood to make a movie. We had a nice visit. I got Scotty to sing a lot of songs like only he can do them. One was "Ol' Mountain Dew." Scotty looks happy when he sings. His eyes have a mischievous little sparkle.

"I don't do 'Old Mountain Dew' much now," he told me. "Since President Roosevelt died last April, I have cut out the verse that said he told them just how he felt when he saw the dry law was through. I had him saying you'd better stick to that good ol' mountain dew. Now the song's a little too short."

"In time," I reasoned, "folks will get over the shock of his death. Then you can go back to singing 'Ol' Mountain Dew.'"

"In the meantime," Scotty said, "I'd like to be singing it. Do you suppose you could make up a couple of verses?"

"I can try," I said.

The next day I threw together a verse that I thought up that said my Uncle Nort was sawed off and explained that he only measured about five feet and two. But he feels like a giant when he gets him a pint of that good ol' mountain dew. I made up another one about my Uncle Bill. The verse said he had a still where he'd run off his mountain dew and the buzzards would get drunk just by smelling it.

I showed them to Scotty. He chuckled, Lula Belle giggled, and I was proud. He didn't put my name on the song, and I certainly didn't expect him to. I'm pleased when I hear the verses sung. "There's my brain-child," I'll think to myself.

Of course, Grandpa Jones put a verse about his Aunt June buying some perfume that smelled like good ol' mountain dew. My verses about Uncle Bill and Uncle Nort, plus Grandpa's Aunt June addition, along with Scotty's Old Holler Tree and the thirsty preacher ridin' by, make "Good Ol' Mountain Dew" an interesting tale of the mountain moonshiner.

I went to Southern California with two recording sessions under my belt. The Sheppard Brothers and Bob McCarthy didn't amount to much. But Syd Nathan's King Records became a major label. Syd was kind enough to ask me to be the West Coast A&R man. Today they call A&R men "Producers." But this was the forties. Everybody that could strike a tune, I put them on King Records. Charlie and Margie, the Fiddlin' Linvilles, Jimmie Widener, and Leon Rusk did just fair. Syd was pleased, but I didn't feel like I earned my pay.

Once Leon Rusk came in with a song he'd started. He called it "A Petal from a Wilted Rose." Just for fun, I started making up juicy lyrics and trying to imitate the sincere style of Gene Autry. I sang about holding one part near my aching heart then sang the title, "Just a Petal from a Faded Rose."

"You've got the wrong thing wrong with the rose," Leon laughed. "It's supposed to be wilted, not faded!"

"Well, I'll make up another juicy verse," I said, "and wilt the rose instead of fade it."

"Put some more verses to it and I'll sing it," Leon said, half joking.

When I got through fooling with it, I was having the singer promising to live with the roses, but to keep the petal near his poor aching heart. Leon sang it. It sounded sort of nice when he did it. So he recorded it. So did Wesley Tuttle. So did Johnny Bond. So did Rex Allen. Red Foley sang it with tears in his eyes. Hank Snow, Eddy Arnold, and, yes, Gene Autry sang it. A couple of weeks before this writing, I was watching Marty Robbins' show on T.V. He sang a song Leon Rusk and I joked about in 1946. His voice fairly dripped as he sang "Just a Petal from a Faded Rose."

I recorded in the forties under the name of Dusty Ward for Globe Records. I did some stuff for another label or two which I'd have to concentrate very hard to remember. All the while, I was doing A&R work for Syd Nathan's King Records.

Two or three people helped me to get on Capitol Records in 1946.

Wesley Tuttle was signed to record for them. Wesley had everything. He was big and extremely handsome. He could sing like a dream. He was approached constantly to do leads in pictures. Only one thing kept him from being a major picture star, I'm sure. When he was a child, his father ran a meat market. Little Wesley got his left hand in the meat cutter. He ended up with only his little finger and thumb on his left hand. He plays guitar very well. Left handed. I suppose to shoot movies and have to constantly dodge the star's left hand would be a little awkward. However, Wesley did very well on records.

His first Capitol record was an old Alton Delmore song, "Rainin' on the Mountain." I sang it with him. We wrote the flip side together, a railroad song about an engineer's child, "I Dreamed That My Daddy Came Home." When Wesley recorded a song that was to become a standard, "Detour." I sang it with him. I was happy for Wesley. I love him like a brother.

At the time, Lee Gillette was in charge of who recorded and who didn't. I learned that Tex Ritter put in an awful lot of good words for me, so did Ray Whitley, who went to the company and almost demanded that they sign me up. Once in the parking lot at CBS, Jimmy Wakely mentioned me recording as a single.

"Why don't you make some records on your own, Trav," he asked, calling me what a lot of people do.

"Because in the first place, nobody's asked me," I told Jimmy. "In the second place, I'm not much as a solo singer. If I sing anything, it's harmony."

"I'll bet Lee Gillette records you pretty soon," Jimmy said, smiled that million dollar smile of his and walked away. Jimmy Wakely was on the Decca label at the time. I never did understand what he meant. Since, I've heard that he too put in some good words for me. Be that as it may, Capitol signed me. I had a streak of good luck, but never took recording seriously. All of my records sounded very much alike. I just had fun making them.

It was Cliffie Stone who got after me to make an album of "folk songs." I made up a bunch of stuff, rearranged some old stuff, and threw together an old 78 RPM album called "Folk Songs of the Hills." In the album was such stuff as "Mus'rat," "Nine Pound Hammer," "I Am a Pilgrim," "Dark as a Dungeon" (a song I made up under a street light on the way to Hollywood after a date with a girl in Redondo Beach), and "Sixteen Tons."

. . .

Merle's own writing about 1944 to 1947 barely scratches the surface of all the events that transpired in his life during those years. This period would ultimately be the most eventful of his entire professional career. He traveled westward as a broke but moderately successful regional radio performer, and over the next three years would take the Southern California country music world by storm with his guitar playing, songwriting, and entertaining abilities. He would appear in a great many Western films. He would lead dance bands around Southern California and play guitar behind just about every other Western bandleader in town. He would make records under pseudonyms; he would record transcriptions (noncommercial recordings for radio play); he would play on sessions for other artists; and he would get signed to a fledgling new label called Capitol Records. He would get married for the second time, and quickly divorce. He would father the first of two out-of-wedlock sons. In the midst of all of this, Merle Travis would become a country music star.

Los Angeles, California, barely existed at the turn of the twentieth century. The dusty, dry intersection of a few horse paths and mission trails had little growth potential until William Mulholland brought water from the high desert via the Los Angeles Aqueduct. When the aqueduct was completed in 1913, it was hailed as the second-greatest engineering accomplishment in history, behind the Panama Canal. It turned Southern California into a place where industry and population could flourish with unfettered acceleration. Los Angeles had a population of 102,479 in the 1900 census; by 1940 the city was home to 1.5 million people. It became a center of industry, producing airplanes, automobiles, motorcycles, ships, steel, aluminum, and all manner of goods, from appliances to guitars. Oil was discovered and became a big business, with refineries to turn the crude oil into gasoline. The film industry took over the Hollywood area, with its year-round good weather and plentiful space for filming. With these industries came a never-ending supply of jobs. Migration from other areas, especially those affected by the Dust Bowl in the 1930s, became the stuff of legend, with trucks and cars and buses and trains full of "Okies" and "Arkies" migrating west in search of a better life.

When Merle arrived in California, World War II was still raging on both the European and the Pacific fronts, and Los Angeles had become a major producer of defense industry essentials. For a time it was the world's largest manufacturer of ships, and it made one-third of the airplanes used in the war effort. Private industry, taken over by government contracts, ramped up to a level never surpassed in the years since; manufacturing plants ran three consecutive eight-hour shifts. With the incredible war effort and its associated influx of rural people to work in those industry jobs, live entertainment was particularly in demand. Dance bands provided welcome relief for the workers, and the most popular acts, like Spade Cooley and His Western Dance Gang and Bob Wills and His Texas Playboys, played as many shows as they could cram into their schedules—often two or three per night.

Merle describes above his meeting with film star Smiley Burnette (Merle misspells his stage name "Smiley Burnett," but the actor's given name was actually Lester Alvin Burnett, something Merle may have known) on a frozen night at the Albee Theater in Cincinnati. Newspaper records indicate that Burnette appeared with William "Bojangles" Robinson for a stint that lasted from February 25 through March 2, 1944. If Merle's memory is correct, he would have attended Burnette's show on February 28, where Burnette spoke his now-famous line that he would "rather live in California and live on lettuce than live in Cincinnati and eat caviar." In a 1961 interview with researcher Ed Kahn, Merle remembered more details about that night:

> Smiley was playing the theater there and I went down backstage to meet him.... I had just met him slightly before, but this time I had a visit with him, you know, and he got his guitar out and I played some on it and he complimented me, you know. [Smiley said,] "Wait a minute, I want Bill Robinson (to hear this)."... Remember "Bojangles"... he was on the bill too. So old Bill Robinson, the colored tap dancer, he come in and I played some and Bill Robinson got between the door and the hallway where the marble wasn't carpeted and done a little dance, while I played a tune, "Buckdance Tune," I learned from Mose Rager. Smiley said to old Bojangles, he said, "That boy could go to Hollywood and stand on the corner of Hollywood and Vine and make a fortune playing that guitar." Well, I'd had a few compliments before that and I got to thinkin' it would be nice out there.[123]

Merle woke up the next day and decided it was time for a change of scenery:

On March 1st, 1944, I borrowed $10 from about six WLW musicians
and just took off. I started off to visit Joe [Maphis] in Chicago and told
him I was going to California to seek my fortune, and that's just what I
did. Joe loaned me an extra $25 to get me on my way. I never forgot all
those folks who loaned me money. I paid every one of them back and
I hope I've shown them all how proud I am to have them as friends. I
took the train to L.A.—ate sandwiches, slept sitting up, got into town,
and crashed at a flophouse across from the station. The next day I called
Wesley Tuttle, and he came and got me and took me out to his house in
the San Fernando Valley. The next day he called the Linvilles and took
me down to Stuart Hamblen's radio show where I appeared as a guest.
He also took me over to a movie set where I met Tex Ritter.[124]

When Merle landed in Los Angeles in March 1944, there was literally no more
employable human being than a good hillbilly singer and guitar player. Through
luck or good timing, he was in exactly the right place at the right time. But it
wasn't as though he had completely thought things through. He had abruptly left
his wife, Mary, and daughter, Patty, behind, with only the clothes on his back
and his Martin acoustic guitar. Sleepy Marlin explained their split thus: "Mary
was a sweet woman, boy she was sweet as a doll. They divorced when he came
out of service and he went back and don't want to live with her."[125] Wesley Tuttle
recalled: "Mary did not want to mix in. He didn't abuse her. She did the laundry
and was the mother of his child. [She] was a plain country girl who didn't want
anything to do with show-business people."[126]

Leaving Cincinnati for California was like many major decisions over the
course of Merle's life: whenever he failed, as he had done in the military and with
his home life in Cincinnati, he would pack up and start from scratch in a fresh
location. California was a land of opportunity in the spring of 1944, but he arrived
with no game plan and only the names of two musicians he had known in Cincinnati: Wesley Tuttle and Charlie Linville. Merle's memories from this time include:

"Smiley Burnett had 'rather live on lettuce'"
"I come to Hollywood after borrowing money"
"Wesley Tuttle picks me up"

Wesley Tuttle continued in that same interview:

All he brought with him was his Martin guitar and a paper bag with some
extra socks in it. And he hit Los Angeles. The Greyhound bus station

was down there at Fifth and Main, and right across the street was an old cheap brick hotel, a two-story hotel. My telephone rang: "Hello Wes, this is Trav." I said, "Merle, where in the heck are you at?" He says, "I'm down here in Los Angeles, let me look out the window." He says, "I'm across the street from the Greyhound bus station." I says, "I know where that's at." He says, "Can you come and get me?"

I supposed if he was here, he had plans, you know.... I said, "Okay, I'll be down, take me about an hour to get there." And I drove to Fifth and Main and saw this shabby hotel and I went in and had to walk up a flight of stairs... the ceilings were like twelve feet high in those days. I got in that room and of course we did our hugs and handshakes and everything and it was a dark, dark, dingy room, and I look up and there's this big fixture hanging from the ceiling, which was a gas light fixture for lights. Hangin' off the arms of that thing was his underwear and socks. He'd washed them out and hung them up there to dry.... I got him and brought him home with me.

I took him the next night to the radio program with me, and of course Stuart [Hamblen], anytime anybody came in with any talent, he'd put 'em on as a guest. Well, of course, he played the "Bugle Call Rag" and "Cannonball Rag" and a couple of things, and everybody just went out of their gourd, you know. Nobody'd ever heard a guitar player like that.

He stayed with me for several weeks at our house until he got on his feet. In the meantime, he got a job with Foreman Phillips frontin' one of his bands.... Then he was crazy to meet the Sons of the Pioneers and Roy Rogers, and they were shootin' out here in Newhall at the old Iverson Ranch, so I got in the car and we drove out to the location. And of course we were all old friends and buddies, and we went in there and I says, "This is Merle Travis, a friend of mine from WLW in Cincinnati." And he got to meet 'em all and they treated him nice and he had his guitar with him so during a couple of breaks, why, he played the guitar.

So now all of a sudden Travis is in town and everybody knows it. They'd say, "Have you heard this great guitar player?" They didn't know then the other talents he had as far as his artwork and his composing abilities, and it wasn't long 'til he was really on his own and goin'. But in the meantime 1944 rolls around and he is busy.[127]

Tuttle introduced Merle to the fertile farm region north of Los Angeles known as the San Fernando Valley, where Tuttle was living at the time. The place was experiencing rapid population growth following the walled-in, cemented river channel construction that came after the great flood of 1938 brought federal flood control money. When the large swath of Valley land was free from flood worries, housing tracts were built as quickly as they could be thrown up, and the Valley became a place where hillbillies who migrated from other rural places could feel at home. In 1944 it was a mixture of Western movie sets, orange groves, and suburban housing set on grassy lots, with small towns popping up every few miles along gravel roads. It was a far cry from the urban landscape of downtown Los Angeles or Hollywood. The San Fernando Valley became the place where Merle would put down roots for more than twenty years. Housing in Los Angeles was at a premium during the 1940s, with more people moving into the city than there were places to live. Many hillbilly music performers lived in rented trailers during this time. Merle recalled: "I went out and stayed a few weeks at his [Wesley Tuttle's] house and then I rented a trailer and lived up on Ventura [Boulevard] behind a house in a trailer.... It was then mostly open fields."[128]

Merle lucked out connecting with Wesley Tuttle, who at the time was involved with just about every important mover and shaker in the LA hillbilly music scene. Tuttle bringing Merle to Stuart Hamblen's widely heard radio show the day after he arrived in Los Angeles was akin to throwing up a Bat Signal in the sky that read "Amazing guitarist, new in town, available for hire." Betsy Gay, a veteran of the *Our Gang* 1930s child film shorts who began yodeling with Stuart Hamblen's group in the early 1940s, recalled: "I first met Merle when I was fifteen, on the Stuart Hamblen show. There was a show out there in the Valley somewhere, and he was on it. It was his first appearance in California, and nobody'd ever seen anything like that, the way he played the guitar. It was a big hit."[129]

Merle describes in the first part of this chapter having to wait three months for his musicians' union membership to be transferred over from Cincinnati. During that time, he lived with Wesley Tuttle and Tuttle's first wife, Marie, at their house at 7457 Troost in North Hollywood, a suburb in the Valley over the hill from the "real" Hollywood. A letter from singer Jimmy Walker to Merle's last wife, Dorothy, indicates that Merle also lived at Walker's house in the San Fernando Valley for a short time in the first year he was in California.[130] In a letter to Ramona Riggins (Grandpa Jones's future wife) dated May 11, 1944, Merle talked about his plans once the three-month waiting period ended:

Well partner, I guess you wonder what I'm doin'—I *ain't* yet, but the union is all that holds me down... gotta be here 3 months 'fore you can do any good. Not boastin' 'er nothing, but I've had some good offers put up to me, but I ain't got the say-so. I'm under the management of Don

Rose, and Smiley Burnett... of course they're gonna make a great star outen me... but you know what a star is.

I cut some records last night with Smiley Burnett. We had the following instruments. Clarinet, piano, bass, vibro-phones ([like] the guy who played for the Merry Macs) and me with my humble ax. Smiley liked "Step It Up and Go" so he wrote some war-time words to it, and it's a dilly if there ever was one—wait 'till you hear it (if you do), goes thus. "Gotta Figure There's a War."[131]

Although Merle mentions recording with Smiley Burnette in May 1944, the song he refers to, "Gotta Figure There's a War," was never released. It was published by Burnette's music publishing company, but presumably remains unissued.

During his union probation period, Merle worked informal gigs and radio appearances, making friends with many of the local working hillbilly musicians. The camaraderie among them helped keep him on his feet during this lean period. Singer and future Capitol recording artist Larry Cassidy gave Merle a car he could use, an essential part of living in Southern California. Three of Merle's memories:

"Larry Cassidy gives me 37 Ford"
"Larry Cassidy shoots chicken"
"Larry Cassidy meets prostitute friend in bank"

Merle described Cassidy in a press release for Capitol Americana: "Next is a big ol' husky, raw-boned boy from Texas by the name of Larry Cassidy. This feller never made a livin' playin' music in his life. He just sings because he likes to sing. He's a Los Angeles policeman... and one of the best, says the force."[132] There was no mention of Cassidy's banking practices.

There was a very important distinction in the 1940s between the West Coast hillbilly music scene and the scene back East. The West Coast scene was all about dancing. While the shows back East like *Boone County Jamboree* and the *Grand Ole Opry* performed theater shows to sit-down audiences, on the West Coast, groups like Spade Cooley's Barn Dance Boys and Bob Wills and His Texas Playboys, among many others, had brought the 1930s Western dance band sound from Texas and Oklahoma to large ballrooms holding thousands of dancing patrons. Up and down the West Coast, big bands and swing bands were hugely popular during the late 1930s and early 1940s. What happened in Southern California was a combination of the popularity of these big bands and the influx of many people from rural areas to Los Angeles thanks to the migration of Dust Bowl refugees. Thus, although the music originated in other locations, the result would become known as Western swing, a term coined in the early 1940s to denote a combination of big-band dance orchestras and cowboy music. According to Wesley Tuttle: "When Gene Autry first came out, before he moved out, 1935 or '6, was the first time 'Appalachian-type' music came out here. 'Appalachian' music was not popular out here [in California]."[133]

Bob Wills and His Texas Playboys came to California for the first time in 1940 to appear in a Western movie with Tex Ritter. Wills's type of Western-flavored, jazz-infused countrified big-band music (not yet called Western swing) appealed to West Coast dance audiences and became immensely popular in California. Wills would move to California in 1943 and lived on the West Coast through his peak years of popularity in the 1940s. The other "cowboy" singers who ruled the live music venues and radio airwaves during this time included Ray Whitley, a Georgia-born vocalist who had found fame on the radio in New York and then moved to Hollywood to star in Western B movies. In 1937 Whitley designed a new jumbo acoustic guitar, the SJ-200, for Gibson, and also wrote the classic Western song "Back in the Saddle Again," which Gene Autry would adopt as his signature number. Merle remembered:

> Tex Ritter gave me $100 to see me through these hard times and I promised him I'd give him some gig time in the studio or on the road or wherever. During that time I was working in the honky tonks, mostly with Charlie and Margie Linville, and sometimes with Texas Jim Lewis and his brother Jack Rivers [Rivers was in the service until 1945]. The first thing I did when the probation ended was a dance date with the "Pistol Packin' Mama" man Al Dexter and did some radio stuff with [Wesley] Tuttle.
>
> Smiley Burnette introduced me to Ray Whitley and I became a part of his Rhythm Wranglers. At that time they were one of the top Western swing groups on the L.A. ballroom circuit. There were lots of good folks in that band. While I was with them Joaquin Murphey, Herb Remington, and Noel Boggs all played steel; fiddlers included Tex Atchison and Jesse Ashlock, and a co-lead guitar man by the name of Charlie Morgan. The hours this band worked were incredible. It was wartime and everyone was working and musicians had to entertain around the clock. We worked for Foreman Phillips, who operated a chain of ballrooms and nightclubs in the L.A. area.... I stayed with Ray for a year or so until I went back to Cincinnati for a bit in 1945.[134]

More of Merle's memories:

Ray Whitley says "Get Out of the house"
Ray Whitley says "Drape your balls"
Ray Whitley says "Can you stand it 15 minutes"

The first appearance of Merle Travis's name in any Los Angeles newspaper was in late May 1944 as a member of Ray Whitley's band (although his name was misspelled in the ad as "Merle Travers"). It was an ad for the group's appearance at the Riverside Rancho club in the Los Feliz section of Hollywood, and it listed the guest performers. Besides Merle, these included some very talented musicians, for instance guitarist Charlie Morgan, left-handed fiddler Tex Atchison (an ex-member of the Chicago-based Prairie Ramblers), ex–Bob Wills fiddler Jesse Ashlock, and a revolving door of great LA-based steel guitarists, including Noel Boggs, Joaquin Murphey, and Herb Remington. Remington told me: "I was with Ray Whitley's band. I was at Riverside Rancho. Merle Travis was on the bandstand with me, playing with Ray Whitley's band, there in California. And then the army got me, so I wasn't there long, but Merle was not 'Merle' at that time. He got big after that."[135] In Merle's words:

I was in my twenties when I worked for Ray Whitley. I was skinny as a summer 'possum and had a weak chin, narrow shoulders, and big eyes. I have no idea why, but young gals would gather around the bandstand when Ray would let me sing or play a solo. I've never fancied myself a fantastic guitar player, I've never found a handsome feature about me, and heaven knows I'm no singer. But I am lazy. And thereby hangs a tale... or sits a stool.

There was a high stool that I would take advantage of when I had the chance. I'd leave one foot on the floor and put the other one on a rung. This way I was in a semi-sitting position during the all-night jobs. When Ray would call me up late at night, I'd bring the stool right up front and use it. If you think Ray Whitley frowned on this, you're dead wrong. He encouraged it.

"When I call you up to do a tune, Trav," he told me on the way to a job one night, "bring up the stool. I think it adds to the act. The girls like to see you sittin' on the stool playin' your guitar."

I couldn't imagine what he meant. But he was the boss and the stool was comfortable. That night I was daydreaming and playing the guitar when a tune the whole band was playing was about finished. Whitley turned around to me, glanced at the stool, and boomed, "Alright, Trav, get ready to drape your balls!"[136]

Whitley's band had two bass players, one of whom was an attractive female singer with cowgirl attire and curly blonde hair named "Tex Ann" Nation—born Sidna J. Nation in Chanute, Kansas, in 1905. She was the great-niece of Carrie Nation, the alcohol prohibitionist who rose to fame thanks to her violent, destructive raids on establishments selling liquor. Sidna aka Tex Ann was involved in show business for more than two decades and married at least five times. She married Ernest Fritz in Durango, Colorado, when she was eighteen and had a son, Ernest Junior, a year later. Unhappy in her marriage, she then left her husband and son to pursue a radio job in Kansas City, where she sang popular music for a brief time, then received an offer to audition for a job in Detroit at WJR. While in Detroit at the station singing with a forty-eight-piece big band, she overheard a cowboy band rehearsing down the hall. The band was known as the Cowboy Caravan and featured a lead singer named Rex Kelley, whom Sidna had heard performing on a Mexican border radio station in the early 1930s.

Tex Ann loved hillbilly music and decided to take a job traveling with Kelley and his group to New York, where they appeared regularly on station WOR. She and Kelley became romantically involved. In New York, Tex Ann met visiting singing cowboy stars like Tex Ritter, Gene Autry, and Ray Whitley. The boss of their job there at the World Championship Rodeo, Colonel Johnson, decided that "Rex Kelley" sounded too Irish, so he christened Kelley "Buck Nation," giving him Tex Ann's last name. From there, Buck Nation and Tex Ann and the Cowboy Caravan began a successful career on the East Coast, appearing on the radio in Bangor, Maine; Boston, Massachusetts; and Reading, Pennsylvania. In Pennsylvania, they established a successful cowboy park and put on shows and events with traveling recording artists.

When World War II took many of the Cowboy Caravan band members into the armed forces, Buck and Tex Ann decided to move to Oregon and then California, where they got radio work through their friendships with Tex Ritter and Ray Whitley, who by that time had both relocated to the West Coast. Buck Nation managed to get himself songwriting credit on several of the earliest Capitol country record releases in 1943 and 1944, mostly with Tex Ritter. Even though information is scant about Buck and Tex Ann's activities in California at this time, they were obviously part of the active country and Western swing scene, and knew all the right people.

Tex Ann married Buck Nation in December 1943, after years of living together. She explained in her unpublished autobiography that most people thought the couple had married already because Rex Kelley had taken her last name. Their legal wedding may have been in response to Buck getting drafted in November 1943, as he left to serve in World War II shortly after their wedding date (this was common in wartime, to ensure that if the husband was killed in action, the widow would receive compensation from the government).

In Hollywood and living by herself, Tex Ann began working with Ray Whitley's band, where she met Merle Travis. It is unknown at exactly what point the two became romantically linked, but Tex Ann would be Merle's off-and-on girlfriend (and briefly his wife) for the next three years. They would play together in Whitley's band, tour with Smiley Burnette's roadshow, appear on CBS Radio together, cut numerous Capitol Records transcriptions as a singing duo, and work side by side on Cliffie Stone's many radio shows. Though she was twelve years older than Merle and had a son only seven years younger than Merle, Tex Ann was a new kind of woman for him—a sassy show-business type who could sing, play bass and guitar, and entertain an audience. She could hold her own with the boys. She may have lied to Merle about her age, as she reduced it by eleven years in a 1942 "Tex Ann and Oklahoma Buck Nation" printed song folio. It's also possible that after his first marriage to an innocent country girl, Merle enjoyed being with an older woman.

Given the aforementioned consecutive eight-hour shifts at defense plants, musicians likewise worked constantly during World War II. As Merle recounts in his own words above, bands might play a typical gig until midnight, then drive somewhere else and play another show until the sun came up. These all-night gigs were called swing-shift dances. Singer Johnny Western remembers:

It was perfect, the mid-1940s. The war was just ending, and you've got all the influx of people coming back from the military; you've got all those people out there making airplanes and stuff for the war. And your basic country music and Western music audience in the world was right there. I mean, those people were there. They'd come up from Texas, Arkansas, Oklahoma.... It was a hotbed for country music. They were working three shifts, and they had to have entertainment after an eight-hour shift. Where are you going to go? Well, you're going to get a drink, at least have a beer before you go to bed. And there was pickers [musicians], you bet. You realize everything was radio; there was no TV at that time.[137]

There were bars, there were nightclubs, and there were ballrooms, all featuring live music around the clock. A showman named Bert "Foreman" Phillips became the biggest promoter in Los Angeles for Western music, seizing on the demand and unlimited booking possibilities. During the World War II years, Foreman Phillips booked three large venues around Los Angeles, calling the group of shows the *County Barn Dance*. He booked Spade Cooley and his band at the Venice Pier, Texas Jim Lewis and his band at a club between Hollywood and Glendale called the Riverside Rancho, and Happy Perryman, brother of Lloyd Perryman from the Sons of the Pioneers, at a ballroom in the working-class enclave of Wilmington called Wilmington Hall. He booked special touring acts like Bob Wills and His Texas Playboys at his venues when they came through the area.

As Merle recounts, during this time, he played with other bandleaders around Southern California. These included Al Dexter, who had a big hit in 1943 with "Pistol Packin' Mama"; Quilla Hugh "Porky" Freeman, an electric guitarist who had a hit in 1945 with a guitar instrumental titled "Boogie Woogie on the Strings"; his old friend from Cincinnati, Smiley Burnette, who according to the letter Merle sent to Jane Allen in May 1944 managed Merle when he first hit Hollywood;[138] "Texas" Jim Lewis, a singer and bandleader who recorded for Decca and played a novelty noisemaking instrument called the "Hoot-Nanny" at his shows; and Spade Cooley, the temperamental bandleader who would later become infamous for killing his wife.

Merle's memories:

> **"Al Dexter thinks 'I'm on the weed' row with J.K."**
> **"Al Dexter says 'If I want guitar solo I'll ask'"**
> **"Al Dexter says 'Bobbie run off with a tinker'"**
> **"Al Dexter says 'I'm not gonna ruin a 3,000 car'"** [Merle retained a telegram he had received July 28, 1944: "Call me immediately upon arrival very important Hollywood 5469—Al Dexter"]
> **"Smiley Burnett throws 'non-drinkin' party"**
> **"Smiley tells how to catch croppie"**
> **"Porky Freeman's amp picks up KFI"**
> **"Spade would never let me court the girls"**

By June 1945, Foreman Phillips had put Merle in charge of the band at Wilmington Hall, taking over what had been Happy Perryman's band. The new group, dubbed Merle Travis and the Mountaineers, was the first band Merle would lead in California. Merle Travis and the Mountaineers was an eight-piece Western swing band that featured electric guitars, fiddle, accordion, banjo, bass, and drums. The band worked consistently through 1945, but as the war ended, it was difficult to meet the payroll on such a large group, and the Mountaineers disbanded.

A letter from Merle to Ramona Riggins (not yet Ramona Jones) in August 1944 reveals the status of the situation with his wife back in Cincinnati: "My ol' lady is suein' for divorce (thank th' lord)."[139] Merle no longer had to wonder about his marital status—he was now a single man.

In addition to a breakneck schedule of live shows, Merle began working on the radio during the day. It was a pace he was accustomed to from his days at WLW in Cincinnati. Wesley Tuttle was responsible for getting Merle his first job on the radio in Los Angeles. At the time, LA radio had a varied range of programming, and the popularity of hillbillies and cowboys ensured their place on the airwaves. Artists like the aforementioned Stuart Hamblen, and Ezra Paulette with the original Beverly Hillbillies, were popular radio stars in the area. Singing cowboy and film star Gene Autry had a popular radio show called *Melody Ranch*, but when Autry was drafted into the military, a new show, *Hollywood Barn Dance*, took its place.

CBS Radio executive Tom Hargis wrote a brief history of the show at the end of the 1945 book *Cottonseed Clark's Brushwood Poetry and Philosophy*. The book also featured illustrations and cartoons throughout by Merle Travis, one of his first professional illustrating jobs. Hargis recalled: "It was the latter part of November, 1943, that CBS program officials handed the title of *Hollywood Barn Dance* to Cottonseed Clark and said, 'build us a western show.' Ten days later on December 4, the new *Hollywood Barn Dance* took to the air lanes with a new idea in western entertainment that was destined to make the peoples of the west coast western-minded."[140]

Marilyn Tuttle noted: "At that time [mid-1944], Foy Willing and the Riders of the Purple Sage had a daytime slot on CBS Radio [station KNX in Los Angeles, which carried the CBS Radio Network]. Foy wanted to take a vacation, so Wesley put together a group with Merle and Jimmie Dean, the brother of Eddie Dean."[141] Calling themselves the Trailriders, the trio with Wesley Tuttle and Jimmie Dean (not the sausage magnate and country singer who had a hit with "Big Bad John," this Jimmie Dean was a singer and an original member of Foy Willing's Riders of the Purple Sage. As Marilyn Tuttle points out above, he was also the brother of Western actor and singer Eddie Dean) was only supposed to last for the duration of Foy Willing's vacation, but the temporary trio was so well received that they remained on the *Hollywood Barn Dance* show as regular performers on and off for the next two years.

Merle had told Wesley Tuttle when they first met back in Cincinnati that he was a fan of the Sons of the Pioneers recordings (Tuttle had worked with the Sons of the Pioneers as a temporary replacement for Tim Spencer in 1936). But the Trailriders Trio on the *Hollywood Barn Dance* radio show may have been the first time that Merle actually played "Western" music. Like many southern transplants to the West Coast, he soon learned to love the sagebrush-infused Spanish melodies of Western music as well as the swinging, jazzy hybrid called Western swing that had become hugely popular. By all accounts, Merle was a quick study. Transcriptions of some of these 1940s radio performances offer aural proof that he learned these new styles readily.

Many of the same musicians who performed at night in the clubs and ball-rooms around Southern California also wound up on the *Hollywood Barn Dance*. Merle reunited with several ex-WLW friends he had known back in Ohio, including fiddler Charlie Linville and singer and slap bassist Shug Fisher, who also became a member of the Sons of the Pioneers. Tex Atchison, the left-handed Kentucky fiddler who had been with the Prairie Ramblers in Chicago at WLS, likewise found himself in California, and he and Merle became fast friends and musical partners. A female singing group called the Sunshine Girls featured a young singer named Colleen Summers, who became one of Merle's first girlfriends in Hollywood. Years later, as Merle writes in his own words, Summers would marry guitarist Les Paul and change her name to Mary Ford. Johnny Bond was an Oklahoma singer who came west with Jimmy Wakely and then became an integral part of the Gene Autry organization in addition to recording hundreds of titles under his own name. Eddie Kirk, known as the "Hillbilly Sinatra," was a good-looking, slender singer who led the *Hollywood Barn Dance* choir on the show. Tex Ann, the singer and bass player Merle had met through the Ray Whitley gigs at the Riverside Rancho, was also on the *Hollywood Barn Dance*.

Many of these personalities became key figures in Merle's career and the trajectory of country music in Southern California over the next few decades, but none would be as important as Stuart Hamblen's portly bass player, who possessed seemingly unlimited ambition and creative impetus: Clifford Snyder, who was dubbed Cliffie Stonehead by Hamblen, and known from the mid-1940s onward as simply Cliffie Stone. (In Cliffie's words: "I got the name of 'Cliffie Stonehead' and down through the years, like I say, I lost my head and became Cliffie Stone."[142]) Cliffie was the same age as Merle but was born in Stockton, California, and raised in Burbank. He was the son of famous character actor and comedic musician C. Herman Snyder, aka Herman the Hermit, who grew his beard long for a Western movie part in the 1930s and never shaved afterward, hence the "hermit" stage name. The elder Snyder had a one-man-band apparatus made of tin cans, horns, metal pots, and all matter of junkyard detritus, and became a radio personality on Hamblen's show. Cliffie, eager to follow in his father's footsteps, became a bass player and joined the Hamblen show in 1935 after graduating from Burbank High School.

By 1944, Cliffie was already molding himself into the chief mover and shaker in Los Angeles's Western music scene. He played bass with a great, swinging feel; he sang; he promoted shows. He appeared not only on the *Hollywood Barn Dance* but also on several other stations, hosting other country music radio shows. He later remembered: "*Hollywood Barn Dance* was a show on CBS Radio for five years, and we did it in Hollywood, emceed by Cottonseed Clark. You ever hear of Cotton? Cotton wrote wonderful country poems. And it was on for five years and never was sponsored, which didn't seem to make any difference in those days. It was a Saturday night jamboree. We all had local shows. This was the CBS Radio network up and down the coast. I did comedy on the show and played bass."[143]

From the mid-1940s through the advent of television around 1950, Cliffie had a cornucopia of country showcase radio shows, with dozens of different names. A 1951 newspaper column wrote: "After 10 years of rising at 5 a.m., Cliffie is experimenting with some Rube Goldberg contrivances that he says will enable him to broadcast right from his bed. He figures it will give him an extra 300 hours of sleep over a year's period."[144]

Cliffie promoted shows and concert events. He understood the audience for country recordings and began producing a multitude of cowboy, Western swing, and hillbilly records for small LA-based labels. He took note when a new Hollywood record label began in 1942, bankrolled by ex–Paramount Pictures producer Buddy DeSylva, and partnered with record store owner Glenn Wallichs and Tin Pan Alley songsmith Johnny Mercer. The new label was called Capitol, and despite its humble offices, it had a very successful early hit release with "Cow Cow Boogie," a 78 rpm disc by Freddie Slack with Ella Mae Morse on vocals.

Capitol was then still small, but it was determined to compete with bigger, more established East Coast labels like RCA Victor, Decca, and Columbia. It went from being a start-up to a legitimate major label within a few short years. Its first records were by Johnny Mercer, big-band leader Paul Whiteman, and boogie-woogie pianist Freddie Slack. But with the growing popularity of hillbilly music, it didn't take long for Capitol's executives to realize that they needed "folk"-type acts, and Tex Ritter became the first such to sign with the label. The second was Foy Willing and the Riders of the Purple Sage from the *Hollywood Barn Dance*.

In September 1944, Tex Ritter entered the C. P. MacGregor transcription studio (Capitol did not have its own studio yet), with both Merle and Cliffie Stone hired as musicians, to cut his sixth release for Capitol: "Jealous Heart" backed with "We Live in Two Different Worlds." It was Merle's first appearance on Capitol, a label that he would have an association with for the next twenty-five years. It was also at this session, Merle recalled, that he met Cliffie Stone: "On September 20, 1944, I did that first Capitol session to pay back Tex, and that's where I met Cliffie. He was calling himself 'Cliffie Stonehead' in those days and he was all over the Los Angeles radio scene as an MC, comedian, and long-time studio bassist. Cliffie was a mover at Capitol and had been an L.A. radio personality since the mid-1930s. He was just the guy I needed to meet to get me goin' on the L.A. scene."[145]

Wesley Tuttle was the next country artist signed to the label. In his recollection, "Tex Ritter was the first Capitol [country] artist, and I was the second.
[Tuttle's memory is slightly off; Foy Willing and the Riders of the Purple Sage
were actually the second.] And it's a strange story. Merle was out here, and I
went in to meet Lee Gillette [Capitol's country music A&R man], and I took
Merle with me. And we talked, and he auditioned us, and he signed me because
he thought Wesley Tuttle was a more commercial-sounding country name than
Merle Travis. If only he could have seen into the future."[146]

Just a few weeks after the Tex Ritter session, Merle was back in the Capitol
studio on October 6 and 11, backing up Tuttle for his first Capitol releases. Merle
sang harmony vocals with Tuttle and played in a style that alternated between fast
bluegrass-style flat picking (listen to his solo on Tuttle's cover of Alton Delmore's
"Rainin' on the Mountain") and his Kentucky thumbpicking style. Charlie Linville rounded out the trio with his fiddle. Billed as Wesley Tuttle and the Coonhunters, the sessions were pure hillbilly music, bordering on bluegrass, a style that
had little audience on the West Coast, which most likely means that the records
were intended for audiences back East.

Merle would continue his sideman work on Capitol country recordings
through 1945, appearing on sides by Shug Fisher as well as more recordings by
Tex Ritter and Wesley Tuttle. On March 3, 1945, he appeared on Shug Fisher
and the Ranchmen Trio's Capitol recording of Johnny Bond's song "Ridin' Down
to Santa Fe." His guitar solo jumps out of the speakers like a young tiger thirsty
for blood; this was a man who was trying to show everyone what he was capable
of. It remains one of Merle's most memorable solos from his session sideman era.
Though the song was not released as a single, it came out as part of a 78 rpm
"album" called Cowboy Hit Parade and today can easily be found on YouTube. It's
worth seeking out.

Merle's studio encounters with Cliffie Stone set the ball rolling for Stone to
hire Merle for one of his daytime radio shows. Eventually Travis would become
a regular guest on almost every show of Cliffie's. Merle recalled: "By the time I
met Cliffie he had his own show with a gal named Dixie Darling, and he invited
me on that show along with a fellow Kentuckian named Tex Atchison, who could
play one heck of a fiddle."[147]

In late March 1945, Merle wrote a letter to Jane Allen and Ramona Riggins
at WLW chronicling his activities: "I've had lots of fun out here, done a lot of
radio work, stage work, transcriptions, records, soundies, dances, camp shows,
rodeos, and spent a few lovely hours sweeping the streets, but all in all it's been lots
of fun."[148] In the same letter he also revealed that his marriage to Mary Johnson
had ended:

I reckon you know I ain't married no more. It ain't that I'm proud of it, so much, but it ain't no fun livin' with somebody that you don't care for... even if she is the mother of your daughter. I miss my kid worse than I would my right arm, but somehow I've stuck it out. Sunday was her birthday. She was six. I sent her a few little things, along with a letter. Golly, I'd like to have watched that kid grow up. I can't help feeling that someday I'll run smack dab into some pitiful halfwitted old homely gal that is a match for me, and we'll hit 'er off together and be happy. I'm sure with a halfway chance I could make a success out of a marriage. I know it ain't the truth, but I like to imagine that I'm a purty good ol' boy, and ain't too reprobatic (as Alton says).

Merle mentions in the same letter that he'd had a few small parts in Western movies. Through his association with Smiley Burnette and the core group of Los Angeles–based Western singers who also starred or acted in films, he found himself drawn into the film world, although his roles would never be major ones. His first such role was as an accordion player for the 1944 PRC Pictures film *I'm from Arkansas*, miming prerecorded parts behind featured performers Jimmy Wakely, the Sunshine Girls (featuring a young Colleen Summers, before she became Mary Ford), yodeler Carolina Cotton, and the vocal group the Pied Pipers: "I worked a picture called *I'm from Arkansas*, and I was an accordion player. All I knew is just how to hold it. I don't know one note on the accordion. A guy who worked with Spade Cooley, Pedro DePaul, made the soundtrack. And I've done the picture playing the accordion."[149] Merle also had a few lines, though he seemed to forget that when he repeated his oft-told story of how he got his Screen Actors Guild union card, which actually involved the second film he appeared in.

In November 1944 Merle appeared in *The Old Texas Trail*, a Universal Pictures film starring Rod Cameron. Ray Whitley and his Bar-6 Cowboys were the featured musical group in it, and Ray brought Merle in on the production as the guitar and banjo player. Merle often told the story about Ray bringing him in and ensuring that he would have a spoken line so he could qualify for SAG. His spoken line was itself the punch line when Merle told the story, alluding to the second-rate nature of his acting career:

Ray [Whitley] never referred to anyone he employed as working "for" him. He always said, "When we were working together," even when he paid a salary to them. He had the same attitude when he employed someone. For instance, one day he said, "Trav, I wish you'd do me a favor." When I asked what I could do, he replied, "Well, me and Rod Cameron are makin' some feature pictures out at Universal and I wondered if you'd drop out and appear in one of them."

I gladly did Ray the "favor." It was the first time I was ever photographed by a real live movie camera.

"If you speak just one line, we can get you in the Screen Actors Guild," Ray told me. He went and talked with the director and came back with some dialogue for me, then he told me what I was to say. It sort of taxed my brain, but I memorized it somehow. With us movie actors the show's the thing, no matter how rough things get. Me and John Wayne... we're about the same caliber of men. Action movie actors, me and the Duke, here is how I got in the Guild.

As the picture was being filmed, there were a bunch of us cowboys working on a road. I had a pick and was supposed to be digging when up rides a tough hombre asking something. I was so engrossed in my own line I didn't listen to him. When he delivered his line I went into action. I said, "Let's see what Nevada's got to say." I did it in one take. Seven whole words of dialogue in a western movie. Merle Travis, brilliant actor of the cinema, they call me.[150]

From 1944 to 1946 Merle appeared in quite a few Western films and shorts. From 1944's *Montana Plains* to *Beyond the Pecos*, the short *I'll Tell the World* in 1945, and finally in 1946 *Roaring Rangers*, *Galloping Thunder*, *Lone Star Moonlight*, and the shorts *Silver Spurs* and *The Old Chisholm Trail*. All were formulaic budget Western movies, with Merle mostly playing the part of a background guitarist but sometimes with a few lines or a featured song. He also appeared without credit in other Western films, such as *Buckaroo from Powder River* in 1947, and undoubtedly there were many more uncredited film appearances. A few of Merle's memories:

"We record picture on spot at PRC"
"I make my only top billing picture—swollen"
"We ride off mountain in a movie"

He recalled his film career in an interview with Mark Humphrey:

When I first went out there, I'd say to someone, "Hey, you want to go fishing tomorrow?" "Oh, I can't, I'm working a picture tomorrow." You'd say, "Who with?" "Oh, Robert Taylor, or Rod Cameron, Jimmy Wakely or Van Johnson." Somebody would call you up and ask you to come out for a little part in a picture, or a musical thing. It wasn't any big deal. It was sort of like going to Nashville and calling someone to go fishing and they'd say, "Sorry, I've got a recording session."

In the case of most of the movies I made, a lady named Bobbie Bennett, who was Spade Cooley's manager, got me in dozens of pictures. She'd call up and say, "Hey, do you want to do a little thing in a picture?" I'd say, "What?" "Oh, a musical thing." We'd always wind up riding along on horses singing or sitting around the campfire singing. And we were always hanging around the leading man, whether it was sitting around a barroom or out on the range. We'd say, "Okay, boss, it'll be done when you get back." And that might be the only line.[151]

Merle's memory:

"Hezzie catches me with my teeth filed"

Merle's brother John Melvin Travis remembered in an interview with Ed Kahn that Merle had had to fix his teeth to appear in the movies: "When Merle went to Hollywood, they wanted him to have his front fangs filed off [crowns put on] so he could be a leading man in the films. Merle complained that it cost him $1,200."[152]

Through his group of Western movie friends, Merle also met the biggest Western movie star of them all: Gene Autry. Merle and Gene would become fast friends and remained so for the rest of their lives. They also became drinking buddies. Carl Cotner, who had helped Merle get his first job with Clayton McMichen back in 1937, was now another transplant to the West Coast, working as Gene Autry's musical director. Autry would employ Merle for many years on the road as a featured act in his touring troupe, but before that, Merle cowrote a song that Autry recorded for Columbia in late 1945, "I Want to Be Sure." In John Melvin Travis's words, "It didn't do very well. Merle thought at the time that he would have a hit because everything that Autry recorded was a hit. The first check he got, he bought a Plymouth fluid-drive automobile. He did get enough out of it for that."[153]

Around this time, Merle was approached by a company with the novel idea to produce short music films called Soundies, to be played on a special film-projector-equipped jukebox called a Panoram. Merle's memories:

"I make Soundies with all girl band—2 lesbians"
"We make Soundies and transcriptions"
"Betty DeVere is only girl I can find"

Soundies are an interesting footnote in music history. These were professionally directed music "videos" shot on film, a concept that preceded MTV by about thirty-five years. The company must have had a decent budget because the music was prerecorded with the actors miming the instruments while the vocalist sang live on camera. Between 1940 and 1947, there were 1,800 Soundie films produced, with artists from all genres—popular big-band music from the likes of Jimmy Dorsey and Lawrence Welk, rhythm and blues and boogie-woogie from Louis Jordan and Harry "The Hipster" Gibson, novelty music from Spike Jones and the Hoosier Hot Shots, and hundreds more. Merle was brought in to film cowboy-themed Soundies along with other California-based Western artists like Jimmy Wakely, Smokey Rogers, and Spade Cooley. According to research done by historian and musicologist Mark Cantor, the Soundies that Merle filmed in 1945 and 1946 featured a combination of the performers seen in the films and studio musicians (mostly from the Spade Cooley band) performing the prerecorded music. Merle played on all the tracks, of course, being the featured performer, but in several Soundies he was shown with an all-female band. Based on union contracts, audible evidence, and interviews, it would appear that a few of the women shown in the film, including Glee Gates on violin, Lucille Blake on accordion, and Boots Wayne on upright bass, did participate in the music recording session as well as the film shoot, while a couple of unidentified women (one of whom was Bonnie Dodd, who played on Tex Ritter sessions) mimed prerecorded parts. For instance, Art Wenzel, who played frequently with Merle, recorded the accordion parts that were mimed by Lucille Blake on camera.

Merle appeared playing guitar in several Jimmy Wakely Soundie films as early as fall 1944, and then in April 1945 he was hired to star in his own films alongside Spade Cooley female singer and yodeler Carolina Cotton (real name Helen Hagstrom). It would be the first of many occasions that Merle and Cotton worked together over the years. Three Soundies were recorded on April 25, 1945, and then filmed in mid-May, including "Why Did I Fall For Abner?, " "Texas Home," and "When The Bloom Is on the Sage." To make things even more confusing, the director switched the women around on their instruments at the film shoot, so that they appeared to be playing instruments they didn't really play to accommodate the look the director was going for. Despite how confusing this may sound, Merle fronting the all-female band made for a good visual impact on film.

Merle wrote to Ramona Riggins on May 11, 1945, between the recording of the soundtracks and the filming: "You know what Soundies are... you put a dime in a juke box of a thing and a little picture comes on a screen, and lasts a few minutes. Well, I'm making a batch of them. They're under my name. 'Merle Travis and his Cowgirls.'... It'll be me and six trim little crafts. We've already made the records, and will shoot the pictures starting May 16th. It's so hard to refrain from conceit when I think that I am a big movie star playing lead in my own series of three minute features."[154]

Merle detailed in his own words above how the next batch of Soundies came about. In his search for an attractive female singer, as requested by the director, he recruited Betty DeVere to star in four more Soundie films alongside a band featuring left-handed fiddler Tex Atchison, pianist Ozzie Godson, steel guitarist Eddie Martin, and accordionist Hi Busse. Cliffie Stone's father, Herman the Hermit, made an appearance in a couple of them as an actor and banjo player. Betty DeVere was later married to Billy Liebert, who played accordion and piano and soon became integral to Merle's orbit of musicians in Los Angeles. Liebert played on almost all of the first ten years of Capitol country recordings, from Merle's discs to records by Tennessee Ernie Ford, Cliffie Stone, Speedy West and Jimmy Bryant, Wesley and Marilyn Tuttle, and countless more. DeVere was also part of an act with her sister, Margie, the DeVere Sisters, who were part of the Stuart Hamblen band for a time in the late 1930s before going off on their own. Margie DeVere later married fiddler Dale Warren and became "Fiddlin' Kate," known for her signature tune, "Katie Warren Breakdown," and her many appearances on the *Town Hall Party* television show.

Filmed in September 1946, the second batch of Soundie films were released under the name Merle Travis, Betty DeVere with the Bronco Busters. Songs included "Silver Spurs," "Old Chisholm Trail," "Catalogue Cowboy," and "No Vacancy."

After World War II ended, there was a great boom in the phonograph and record industry. People were eager to buy records, and country and hillbilly music was very popular, even more than pop or jazz, in many regions of the United States. In Los Angeles, in addition to Capitol Records' serious push to become one of the nation's major labels, there were also hundreds of small labels releasing everything from boogie-woogie and jazz to hillbilly and Western swing. Cliffie Stone was intent on capitalizing on the growing record market, and Merle would be in the mix as well. Merle made a group of 78 rpm records on small labels in the summer and fall of 1945.

The first was released on Atlas, a label co-owned by Art Rupe, who would later run Specialty Records, the influential rhythm and blues label that launched the careers of Little Richard, Lloyd Price, and Larry Williams. Atlas released records by white and black artists, including future stars Nat King Cole and his trio and Frankie Laine. Merle cowrote a song and probably performed on a Red Murrell release called "Texas Home" for Atlas in July 1945. Immediately following this was the first record to bear Merle Travis's name as an artist: Red Murrell sang one side and Merle did "That's All" on the other. Merle would perform "That's All" throughout the rest of his career (and would rerecord the number several times). It was an odd choice to begin his West Coast recording career. It's an electric guitar blues number with single-string solos, with none of the Muhlenberg County style of thumbpicking that would become his trademark. On the other hand, it fit in well with the label's other bluesy releases by the King Cole Trio, Luke Jones, and Johnny Moore's Three Blazers. It may have been suggested by label owner Art Rupe, given his penchant for blues. The disc, like many released on these small labels of the day, sold poorly, disappeared quickly, and today is quite rare. Merle and Red Murrell would work together often through Cliffie Stone's radio shows and other live work, and Murrell would continue to record for Atlas for another year, including recording other songs written by Merle.

Merle entered the studio with Porky Freeman in September 1945 and cut a side on vocal and guitar with Freeman's trio for ARA Records, "Boogie Woogie Boy." ARA is another fascinating slice of mid-1940s Los Angeles history. It was formed as a cover for label owner Boris Morros (a naturalized US citizen originally from Russia) to engage in Soviet spy activities. It's doubtful that Merle or any of the other artists who recorded for ARA (including Smiley Burnette, Stuart Hamblen, jazz pianist Art Tatum, and Hoagy Carmichael) had any idea about Morros's secret activities, but such was the colorful world of LA during this era. An alternate take of this cut was licensed to another fledgling Los Angeles label, Four Star Records.

Cliffie Stone, then still known as Cliffie Stonehead, began producing records for another small Los Angeles label called Bel-Tone in summer 1945. Mostly centered on Western music in the style of the Sons of the Pioneers (the first release on Bel-Tone was Cliffie's cover of the Pioneers' "Cool Water"), the label also released pop by Frankie Laine and jazz and blues recordings by Slim Gaillard. Cliffie Stone recalled:

> Darol Rice and I had $300 apiece, $600. I was doing this *Wake Up Ranch* show and I needed records real bad. So we had a record date. We started a label called Lariat Records. On that record date, I played bass, Darol played clarinet, and I recorded Merle Travis on "Hominy Grits," Wesley Tuttle and the Sunshine Girls with "Cool Water," [and] Stan Freberg with a thing called "Maggie."...
>
> Darol Rice and I would go—we'd pick up fifty records at the pressing plant in our car and go sell them to the record store and come back and get fifty more, because we didn't have any money. We got an order in for ten thousand records out of Chicago for "Cool Water," and we couldn't do it. We couldn't finance it. So I went to the bank, and in those days the music business was a very bad investment according to everybody. So two guys called Dick Elliot and Jack Elwell were vocal

coaches at Republic Studios.... They had started a little label called Bel-Tone Records, and they heard about me, and bought my masters—"Cool Water," and a Freberg thing, and the Merle Travis things. They hired me to become a producer at Bel-Tone Records.... So while at Bel-Tone, I produced Frankie Laine, Dale Evans, Smiley Burnette, Eddie Dean, and Monte Hale.[155]

Merle's first appearance on one of Cliffie's Bel-Tone productions was a spoken-word recitation on "Tomorrow Never Comes," the B side of a disc by Scotty Harrell with the Cliffie Stonehead band. The next record on Bel-Tone featured a Merle Travis performance on the B side of the disc, "Hominy Grits," released under the pseudonym Tem Martin. The same record was licensed again and released on the Gold Seal label a few years later, during the recording ban of 1948, with Merle's pseudonym now changed to Tex Travers. Merle recalled:

Now one day I was playing guitar on a recording session for Bel-Tone Records, which I don't think is in existence now. And the man recording was Smiley Burnette, and three girls were singing with him, and they were called the Sunshine Girls. [Smiley recorded for ARA Records, so this may be a mistaken detail in Merle's memory.] That was Vivian Earles, and June Widener, and Colleen Summers... [aka Mary Ford]. So they were the girl trio, and Smiley Burnette, it was his session. He recorded "It's My Lazy Day." A few things like that.

I was there, and they had a song called "Hominy Grits." And Smiley said, "Why don't you sing this?" Because I like to sing stuff like this, and I said, "Oh, no, you go ahead." And he said, "No, you sing it." So I sung "Hominy Grits," and Smiley said, "We'll release that on the record." And I said, "Well, don't put my name on it." Actually, it didn't sound that bad to me.... So, I don't know who made up the name, but they released it under the name Tem Martin. "Hominy Grits" by Tem Martin.[156]

Merle confuses two memories in this story, as he recorded "Hominy Grits" twice, once with Smiley Burnette (with Merle singing background parts) for ARA, and then singing the song on his own for Bel-Tone. Presumably both sessions happened around the same time. If the hokey pseudonyms weren't enough, Cliffie continued with two more Bel-Tone discs featuring Merle singing and playing with Tex Atchison under a new nom de plume, Tin Ear Tanner and His Backroom Boys (Tex Atchison was Tin Ear Tanner). One of these discs featured Atchison on vocals, and the other featured Merle trading verses with Smokey Rogers on "I Used to Work in Chicago." One of the songs, "Cincinnati Lou," was credited as a Travis original on the label, but Merle worked a deal, common in those days, to swap out the rights for half of the song in exchange for half of the song rights to a Shug Fisher composition called "I'm All Through Trusting You." Today both men share the songwriting credits on both songs.

The last of Merle's pseudonym records was released as Dusty Ward and His Arizona Waddies on the tiny Globe label, another LA-based "bucket lid" label (a derogatory period term for a no-budget independent label). Globe released records by bluesmen like Jimmy McCracklin and Memphis Eddie Pee, as well as Western swing from acts like Jerry Irby and Elmer Christian and His Bar X Cowboys.

The next record release on the tiny Globe label was by an unknown singer from Waco, Texas, named Hank Thompson. Though the release was recorded in Dallas and released by Globe in Los Angeles, Thompson's and Merle's lives would become intricately intertwined in the following decades.

Sometime in 1945, Merle traveled back to Cincinnati: "Mostly it was to visit family, check in with some old friends at the Jamboree, and meet this new young talent they were talkin' about named Chester Atkins. I asked him how he come to get that style, which involved using the thumb and two fingers, and he said he thought that's what I was doing. I also checked in with Syd Nathan at King Records."[157] Merle and Chester "Chet" Atkins began a friendship that would last the rest of their lives. The two shared similar upbringings, similar musical backgrounds, and somewhat similar thumbpicking techniques, yet their styles and personal tastes were different enough that neither represented a threat to the other. As mentioned in a previous chapter, Chet had a serious, businesslike approach to music and the music industry, but the subject of Merle Travis would always be his soft spot, so great was his indebtedness to Merle. Atkins would sign with Nashville independent label Bullet Records in 1946 and then to RCA Victor in 1947. Originally Chet was signed as a vocalist who played guitar, which inspired one of Merle's most oft-told stage jokes:

> Back in the forties, I was making records, and still am, with Capitol Records out in Hollywood. I was lucky enough to be selling some records. My records was all on the jukeboxes everywhere. The boss man at RCA Victor was named Steve Sholes. He said, "We got to get somebody to compete with this, whoever he is, Merle Travis, because if we can find somebody can pick that way and sing, why, we'll have somebody to compete with him." RCA is a bigger company than Capitol, so he started looking.
>
> One day he heard a fellow named Chet Atkins play a tune called "White Heat" on what they used to call transcriptions for radio, with

Red Foley. He said, "There is the guy." Chet Atkins, he wrote it down. Steve Sholes was going all over the country looking for Chet Atkins. He finally found him at Chet's brother's house, who was program director of radio station KOA in Denver, Jimmy Atkins. And so Steve Sholes found Chet Atkins. He said, "You're the man I've looked for all over the country." He said, "How would you like to make records?"

Chet said, "Oh, I'd like that. I'd love to make talking machine records."

He said, 'Well," he said, "you're the guy that we've been looking for.... We want you to make some records for RCA Victor."

Chet said, "Well, I sure would love to."

Steve Sholes said, "Do you sing?"

Chet said, "No."

He said, "You don't sing?"

"No," he said, "I can't sing a bit."

He said, "Oh, don't you sing just a little?"

He said, "No, I can't sing none. I can't sing. I talk. The one thing I can't do is sing."

Steve Sholes said, "Well, that's too bad... we wanted somebody that could play a guitar and sing like Merle Travis."

Chet said, "Oh, I can sing *that* good."[158]

By late 1947, after several vocal releases, RCA Victor realized that Chet's unmatched talent was his guitar mastery and began releasing instrumentals that showed his prowess, like "Dizzy Strings" and "Galloping on the Guitar." These were successful, especially as intros and segues for radio disc jockeys. And just as Capitol noted Chet's instrumentals gaining in popularity, they began to realize Merle's value as an instrumentalist. Back in California, Merle began producing recordings for King. He later recalled:

When I come to Hollywood, why, I got acquainted after so long a time with just about everybody around town, the country musicians around Southern California here. And my old friend Syd Nathan, he called me one day on the phone, and he said, "I'd like for you to be an A&R [artists and repertoire] man for King Records." And I said, "What's an A&R man?" He said, "You find anybody you want to out there, if you think they've got talent, and you set up a studio and you get the musicians you want or that they want, however many, and the songs that they want to do, and record it." He said, "You sit in the control room," and I said, "Oh yeah, sure." Because I'd been in on a lot of recording sessions. They didn't use the word "A&R man" then as much, but Syd Nathan said it first, as far as I was concerned.

So I was the A&R man for King Records, and I recorded Leon Rusk, and the Fiddling Linvilles, and Tex Atchison, Jimmie Widener, oh I don't know, a whole bunch of people. I never did have a hit, but I had some songs on the King Records that later become pretty big. So I was A&R man for King Records, and it was a pretty good little thing.[159]

In addition to the artists Merle talks about, he also produced records by his WLW friend Jack Rogers, who had recently relocated to California at Merle's behest. Merle also produced King releases for Hank Penny, his friend who had taken him to the train station when he was leaving Cincinnati. Penny had relocated to Southern California and led a Western swing band at local clubs (a few years later, in 1949, while working at a honky-tonk in North Hollywood called The Mule Kick, Penny renamed the place "The Palomino Club," which would go on to be the most famous West Coast country music venue). Penny recorded several tracks with Merle in Hollywood at Radio Recorders. One was a guitar instrumental called "Merle's Buck Dance," a fabulous feature of his electric guitar style. It was the first commercial release of a Merle Travis guitar instrumental, even though it was issued as a Hank Penny disc. Penny described it: "Gracious sakes alive, it was like a piledriver! These were some of the most commercial things I ever recorded. Everything on those twelve songs had a real good, strong beat, mainly because of Travis and his ability to give it a good whack!"[160] One of the Hank Penny King discs that Merle produced and played on, "Steel Guitar Stomp," became a hit, although it didn't feature Merle's playing like "Merle's Buck Dance."

Merle also brought out Grandpa Jones and the Delmore Brothers from Cincinnati, with Syd Nathan in tow, to do some recording in California. He recalled: "Now, after the war, when I was living in California, Grandpa come out to see me. He said, 'Why don't we get ahold of Alton and Rabon [Delmore] and record some gospel songs.' We both thought that'd be a lot of fun. So we got ahold of Syd Nathan. He said, 'Yeah,' said, 'The Commercials, we sell a lot of gospel songs.' So we got ahold of Alton and Rabon and they flew out to California, and Syd Nathan come out, and we went in the studio and we recorded—I don't know, I guess maybe 150 on King Records. All gospel songs."[161]

Merle's memories:

"Grandpa comes to California to visit me"
"Grandpa records 'Eight More Miles' and drinks"
"Browns Ferry Four records with wrong A&R man"
"Alton makes Hollywood Hotel Multitude of Frog"

"Grandpa Jones meets Hamblin who has a banjo"

The exact details vary with memory, but Grandpa Jones and the Delmore Brothers came to California twice to record with Merle for King, once in early 1946 and again in the fall of 1946. They recorded new releases for Grandpa Jones, the Delmore Brothers, and the Brown's Ferry Four, all with Merle playing electric guitar, and in the case of the Brown's Ferry Four, singing harmony vocals. It was a large group of songs, many of which became seminal recordings for each artist and regional sales successes, if not smash hits. The industry in the 1940s was vastly different than it is today—a disc that sold ten thousand records was considered a success in the country music field, and several of these hit that mark.

Moreover, for fans of each of these artists, in many cases the recordings made with Merle in Hollywood became favorites. Grandpa's electric guitar rendition of "Eight More Miles" became his theme song; for the Delmore Brothers, their hillbilly boogie numbers with Merle on guitar such as "Hillbilly Boogie," "Stop That Boogie," and "Barnyard Boogie" started a movement of fast hillbilly boogie-woogie numbers with electric guitars (noted by many as an early influence on rock 'n' roll); and the Brown's Ferry Four recordings with Merle became some of the most cherished and beloved country gospel recordings of all time. In Grandpa Jones's words:

> All of these things came together in March of 1946, when Syd bundled the Delmores and me on a plane and took us to Hollywood to record with Merle, who had already moved to the coast. The ride was long and bumpy; we were on an old C-47, and after a really rough series of bumps, I said, "Tell that pilot if he sees a hole in the fence to get back on the road." The boys laughed, but Syd said, "That would make a great song title. Why don't you write a song about that?" I realized he was serious, and began thinking; before the flight was finished, I had the best part of a gospel song called "Get Back on the Glory Road." And before long we had recorded it.
>
> Syd was wanting another hit record from me, something that would go as well as "It's Raining Here This Morning," and he thought "Eight More Miles" was it. Looking back on it, I can see he was right; it did become one of my big hits, and eventually became so associated with me that I use it as my theme song yet today. But we had quite a time making that original recording. Merle was to play his electric guitar behind me, and he had to capo it up pretty high, and the strings were ringing a lot. Electric guitars were still pretty new back then, but Merle's picking style—it was an old western Kentucky style where you picked rhythm

with the thumb and did melody with the fingers—was so suited to the song that we really wanted it. I would do a clean take of the song, but Syd wasn't happy, and he'd shout from the control booth, "Pa, put some life into it!" And I'd do another one, and he'd say, "We need more life!" I finally got mad and stormed out of the studio.

Pretty soon Merle came after me. "That Syd makes me so mad," I said. "Yeah, he does kind of get you, doesn't he?" said Merle. We talked for a while, and then he said, "Come on back in and take a drink of this stuff." He had asked one of the studio men to go across the street for a bottle of whiskey. "I'm not much of a drinkin' man," I said. "How much should I drink?" Merle got a paper cup from the water cooler and filled it half full of whiskey. I drink it all down at once. "It stinks like the splatterboard of a gut-wagon," I said. Everyone laughed, but pretty soon I was feeling more ambitious. "All right, Syd," I shouted, "see if this has enough life," and Merle and I ripped into "Eight More Miles." When Merle started his solo, I shouted, "Play it, Merle!" Syd left the comment in, and Merle said later that he got more reaction and people commenting on that record than any other record he played on.

Later on at that session, we did record "Get Things Ready for Me, Ma, I'm Coming Home," and the first two sides by the Browns Ferry Four, but nothing caused as much stir as "Eight More Miles." Before long I was recording a session every five or six months for King, both under my own name and with the quartet. In fact, that first record by the Brown's Ferry Four was successful enough that later the same year Syd flew us to Hollywood to do a whole session, twelve tunes, of gospels. But he almost caused the whole thing to fall through. Syd was wanting to do something else in Los Angeles the day of the session, so he brought the local bald-headed guy who had worked a lot with pop music and dance bands but didn't know beans about country music. We didn't know him and he didn't know us, but we started recording, and regardless of how we did on a take—we could tell at times that we had made a mistake—he would gloss over it and say, "Okay, let's go on to the next one." Alton and I were getting madder and madder—I had sort of a reputation for having a short fuse in those days—and we finally called a halt and took off for the hall. Alton said, "That guy won't even look at us. He doesn't care a thing about our music." We all agreed, and finally Merle went and phoned Syd and told him he'd better get over to the studio.

Syd arrived and went into the control room. The four of us and the bald-headed producer stood in the studio. "Let's all take a vote on this," came Syd's voice over the intercom. "Rabon, what do you say about this guy?" Rabon always held his head at a little angle and had a habit of grunting before he spoke. "Mmmm, well," he said. "I don't think he understands our music." The bald-headed man just stared at us. "What about you, Merle?" said Syd. Merle walked up to the microphone and said, "Syd, he's not paying attention to anything we're doing, and he doesn't know anything about gospel music." "What about you, 'Pa?" Syd asked me. Merle said later that when I was this mad I looked like the devil on a lye can. I walked up to the mike: "Well, I just don't like the poor so-and-so." This time the bald-headed man really flinched, but the best was yet to come. "Alton?" said Syd. Alton had a nasal voice, and took little quick steps across the studio to the mike. "Well, I tell you, Syd, he acts like a man with all the pores of his skin stopped up." This finally did it; the bald headed producer left, and Syd took over the session himself. We started in on "I'll Fly Away," and the Brown's Ferry Four stayed in business.[162]

While Merle was recording small-label records under pseudonyms and working as an A&R man for King Records, he also kept his foot in the door at Capitol. Although he had not been signed on as an official Capitol recording artist, Cliffie Stone, now working at Capitol in their transcriptions department, employed Merle on a great number of transcription recording sessions between late 1944 and early 1946. Transcriptions were large, sixteen-inch records that ran at 33 1/3 rpm, and were given to radio stations to fill up time on the air. During the 1940s there were a great number of transcription companies that provided "content" for radio stations, paid for by a subscription fee. Capitol was one of those, running the transcription service in a separate business than the official Capitol label, and for a few years in the 1940s, they produced hundreds of transcription discs for radio airplay by artists as varied as Peggy Lee, the King Cole Trio, Duke Ellington, The Jordanaires, and country acts like Tex Ritter. These were not commercial records; you could not go into a record store and buy a transcription. But because so many radio stations across the country played them, they were heard by a great number of people.

Merle was called in to Capitol with Wesley Tuttle, Charlie Linville, and Tex Ann Nation as a group called The Coonhunters (a name also used on Tuttle's records as his backing band). The Coonhunters recorded an enormous amount of material for the Capitol Transcription Service during this time. There were nearly thirty duets with Merle and Tex Ann singing (including Merle's first published composition, "Dust on Mother's Old Bible"). There were nearly thirty songs with

Merle and Wesley Tuttle taking turns singing. There were numerous fiddle show-case tunes by Charlie Linville. There was also a batch of incredible solo acoustic guitar performances by Merle. Years later, Merle would remember these sessions: "They had such a thing as 'fillers,' and I went in to do some transcriptions, and Cliffie Stone was the producer. He'd say, 'Play something that lasts thirty seconds.' Okay, when the clock went straight up I'd just begin pickin' something, and when the thirty seconds was up I'd quit. 'Now play one that lasts forty-five seconds.' And so forth and so on. So I played one—'Keep playing 'till you get tired'—so I played 'Ike Everly's Rag,' one that Ike Everly used to play. But some of those transcriptions only lasted fifteen seconds."[163]

Even though Merle's words would indicate a certain apathy about the pro-ceedings, to listen to those solo guitar performances is to hear him at his peak ability as a guitarist. The performances are flawless, cleanly picked, and the fast numbers are breathtaking in their speed. More importantly, Merle was now expos-ing the Muhlenberg County style of thumbpicking to vast numbers of people over the radio airwaves. Ultimately these Capitol transcriptions were among the first, if not *the* first, instrumental guitar "albums" ever released (transcriptions were not technically "albums" as the term is understood now, but effectively they were the same as long-playing albums, which came along a few years later). Usually guitar instrumentals were reserved for one song on an album, as a chaser or a filler song. Merle's instrumental guitar transcriptions were groundbreaking in their singular focus.

Cliffie Stone had been playing bass on recording sessions at Capitol since the label's inception, and produced country sides for their transcription service. Eventually the head of the Capitol country division, Lee Gillette, decided to bring him on in a more official capacity. In Cliffie's recollection:

There was a guy over at Capitol Records called Lee Gillette, who was head of country, and I played some bass with him. I played bass on "Jin-gle, Jangle, Jingle," Tex Ritter's first record.... I played—I'll never for-get—I played their record "This Lonely World" by Eddie Dean [released earlier on Cliffie's Bel-Tone label] on my show, and Lee Gillette called me. Now, he was the guy at Capitol who was head of country. He said, "Can I talk to you?"

I said, "Sure." So I went up to Capitol. He said, "Who produced 'This Lonely World?'" I said, "Well, I did." He said, "Would you like to come to work here?"

Well, you know, it was like asking me to go to heaven. He said, "We need somebody to head up the country music department." He said, "Would you like to do it? Seventy-five a week." I would have *paid* seventy-five to do it.... That's how I got in the record business.

So I ended up at Capitol. I went over there, I signed Merle Travis.... I brought him in to Capitol.[164]

Cliffie signed Merle to Capitol Records in March 1946. At the time, the offices were a few small rooms in a building at Sunset and Vine. Merle was the sixth country act signed to the label, joining a small roster that included Tex Ritter, Foy Willing and the Riders of the Purple Sage, Wally Fowler and the Clodhoppers, Jack Guthrie (Woody Guthrie's cousin), and Wesley Tuttle. Merle later recalled:

Finally, I got signed by Capitol Records on March 18, 1946, and we kinda all got together to decide on how the Travis package was gonna work. That was the time, you know, when each country artist had a pre-packaged sound, so you'd know who the performer was going to be. Gene Autry, Ernest Tubb, and all the rest had a backup band. Cliffie and Lee sort of decided on a sound for me that was kind of like Gene's sound but a little bit peppier. The band would have a sharp muted trumpet, along with accordion, fiddle, steel guitar, and my guitar to keep the beat and take a break or two. I guess it worked okay as we kept that beat for the next five years or so. The first session I did used Joaquin Murphey and Pedro DePaul from Spade Cooley's band, this trumpet guy Jack McTaggart, who had worked with Stuart Hamblen, and Tex Atchison on the fiddle. We did four songs. Two of them, "No Vacancy" and "Cincinnati Lou," became my first singles. The first got up to number two on the [*Billboard* magazine] country charts and the second got up to number three. On the second session we did "Divorce Me C.O.D.," which got to number one, and "Missouri," which got to number five. I guess we had arrived.[165]

Cliffie Stone remembered: "We figured that country people would absorb that kind of a [muted] trumpet where they wouldn't absorb just a big blaring thing. We wanted to give Travis a different sound than just the same old stuff and it seemed to work."[166]

Merle is correct in his statement that his first three releases were successful out of the gate. With Capitol's distribution and promotion, his initial ascent to the top of the music charts was effortless. His first hit, "No Vacancy," was inspired by a vacation that Cliffie Stone and American Music song publisher Sylvester Cross had made to Palm Springs. Merle later remembered: "Cliffie said, 'I'll tell you a good song to write... you ought to write one called 'No Vacancy.' [He] said, 'That's all we saw all the way up there [to Palm Springs]."[167] Merle's second release, "Divorce Me C.O.D.," was also a success, but he had to push for its release. Cliffie Stone, who always erred on the conservative side of executive decisions, was leery of a song about the then-taboo subject of divorce. Merle's humorous wordplay was so clever, however, that he eventually allowed it. In a letter to a fan in 1980, Merle remembered: "On the original record of "Divorce Me, C.O.D.".... I used an L-10 Gibson with a Rickenbacker pick-up, which I'd took off a steel guitar and put in it."[168]

Capitol News, the in-house Capitol Records magazine, wrote about the new-comer's success in early 1947: "Although he has had but two records released, Merle Travis easily was named one of the three most popular folk artists on discs in the recent poll conducted nationally by 'Billboard' Magazine. Merle's own tune, "Divorce Me C.O.D." also won honors, being tagged as one of the three biggest hits of 1946."[169] In those days, the charts were determined not only by sales and radio plays, but also through jukebox plays in restaurants, bars, and nightclubs. Merle did so well in the jukebox market that he was given the title "King of the Jukebox" in his promotional materials and advertising.

Within a few short months, Cliffie Stone approached Merle with an unusual idea: he wanted Merle to record an album for Capitol of original folk songs. Capitol had been toying with the genre since the war's end, releasing 78 rpm singles by African American artists such as T-Bone Walker and Lead Belly in 1945 and 1946. In fact, it was Tex Ritter who brought Huddie Ledbetter, aka Lead Belly, to the label in 1944; the pair had worked together in New York when Ritter was on radio station WINS. Merle and Lead Belly even had an informal jam session together, according to the book *The Life and Legend of Lead Belly* (1992). The pair reportedly also both performed at a benefit show in Hollywood around the same time. Seeing Lead Belly play his unusual twelve-string guitar may have influenced Merle to have his own twelve-string guitar built a few years later, another of his many passing fancies. Lead Belly's biographers tell how it happened:

> In the summer of 1944, shortly after Lead Belly had arrived [in Hollywood], he met an old friend on the streets of downtown Los Angeles: cowboy singer Tex Ritter.... Now Ritter emerged as a radio, film, and recording star, and had recently signed with Capitol. He urged Lead Belly to sign with the new label, and mentioned the singer to Lee Gillette, one of the Capitol executives. "One night at my house," Ritter recalled, "I had Merle Travis... Lee Gillette, my A&R man that I loved so much, and I said, "Instead of auditioning at your office, Lee, why don't you just

come back to the house tonight?" And Lee helped sign him and they made an album at Capitol at that time.[170]

Albums in the 1940s were literally albums—book-style compilations of individual 78 rpm singles. Few today realize that this is where the term "record album" originated. In the mid-1940s it was virtually unheard of for a new artist like Merle to be asked to record an album; they were usually reserved for established names with proven track records. But Capitol was generously experimenting in the market. Cliffie Stone, however, had something else on his mind besides promoting Merle's career. He wanted a product to go head to head against the competition back East. Folk music was selling well and drawing well in concert tours in the major cities and college campuses. Artists like Carl Sandburg, Burl Ives, Josh White, Susan Reed, and others were creating a popular niche, and Capitol wanted in. The executives in the other offices grumbled to Cliffie that they needed an artist to compete with Burl Ives. It made perfect sense to approach Merle, their Kentucky wunderkind, the best example of a real down-home "folk artist" they had on the label. Merle was also an artist proving himself adept at quickly writing songs on demand. Merle recalled:

> Cliffie Stone was the A&R man then. He said, "We're gonna put out an album on you." In them days, of course, they was 78 [rpm] albums, four records in an album. And he said, "We need an album on you."
>
> And I said, "Well, what sort of album? Guitar picking?" He said, "No, no." [He] said, "We want folk songs."
>
> I said, "Well, Bradley Kincaid and Burl Ives have sung all the folk songs. I don't remember what they even sung." And he said, "Make up. Write some."
>
> I said, "You don't *write* folk songs."
>
> He said, "Well, write them that sounds like folk songs."
>
> So I said, "Well, I'll try."
>
> And I got to thinking about a song that Josh White sung. And I was messing around with that in a minor key, and I got to thinking about a saying around the coal mines, "I owe my soul to the company store." And so I made up a song called "Sixteen Tons." "Load sixteen tons and what do you get? Another day older." So I wrote "Sixteen Tons," just messing around. I thought, "Well, there's one."
>
> And then I had a date with a girl down at Redondo Beach. To show you what inspiration will do, a lot of people think you're inspired to write a song, and I was inspired because I had to write them. So I drove the girl home, and on the way home, it was about two o'clock in the morning,

and I thought, "Boy, I've got to write them songs. What'll I write?" And it was dark, and I thought, "Well, it's dark." Thoughts go through your mind, and I thought, well, it's dark in the mines. I thought, it's something around that, I thought, "Dark as a Dungeon." "There's a good title," I thought. "Dark as a Dungeon."

So I pulled up under a streetlight and looked in the glove compartment and found some old piece of paper. And I sat under that streetlight and wrote a little song called "Dark as a Dungeon." And people said to me, said, "You must have been really inspired." I was inspired because I had an album to make, and I had to get it done pretty quick.[171]

Merle told the story of his auspicious debut as a folk songwriter so many times in his life that the details fluctuated, although the basic facts stayed the same. In another retelling at a jam session later in his life, some of the details were slightly different, with the name of his female companion earlier in that evening finally revealed:

I had a date with a girl, and I rode a motorcycle all the time, and I had a date with a girl named Fern Judge [Merle also used Fern's name in a similar retelling to researcher Archie Green.[172] Fern's name pops up in several other "Merle's memories."]. Pretty little ol' girl. She lived down in Redondo Beach. And on the way home, I's ridin' along on my motorcycle, and I was thinking, and doggone, I don't know what the heck to write, that'd sound like a folk song. Cliffie had said, "Well, write a song about the coal miners, you're always talking about the coal mines." And I was riding along and I said, "What in the heck am I gonna write. Johnny Mercer, I can't write a song about just anything." You can tell him write a song about... [anything], and he'd come up with a classic. And I was riding along on that motorcycle, and it was dark, and I thought dark... dark as a dungeon. Somehow or another that title came to mind. Dark as a dungeon. I said, that's it. Dark as a dungeon way down in the mine. I stopped at a streetlight, reached in my saddlebag, got a piece of paper, I wrote "Come all ye young fellers," like an Irish... they call them "Come All Ye" songs. That's why I wrote a "Come All Ye" song, under that street light. I was on my way back from Fern's house, going back to the Regent Hotel. Me and Tex Atchison was rooming together... Regent Hotel on Hollywood Boulevard.[173]

Merle may have confused details in his various retellings of the story decades after the fact. For one thing, Merle appears to have purchased his Indian motorcycle in 1947, which would make it impossible for him to have been riding it in 1946 when he wrote his two most famous songs. Similarly, according to research found on Ancestry.com, Fern Judge and her family lived in Ocean Park, a suburb of Santa Monica, so Merle may have taken his oft-repeated "Redondo Beach" reference from another one of his amorous escapades, Virginia "Ginny" Cushman, who became his cornet player in 1947, as Cushman did live in Redondo Beach. We can only surmise three-quarters of a century later that although some of the details fluctuated, the basic facts remained the same in Merle's many retellings of the story. On "Sixteen Tons" Merle also later remembered:

> Ernie Pyle was a war correspondent; he'd do human interest stories about the soldiers. He wasn't up there with the generals; he went down to the front and talked to the men. He would write about individual soldiers— where they were from, their interests and hobbies. They named a ship the USS *Ernie Pyle*. He got killed right at the end of the war. My brother [John Melvin] wrote me a letter and said, "That's a damn shame about Ernie Pyle. He went through the whole war and then got killed right at the end of it. It's just like working in the coal mines. You load sixteen tons and what do you get? You get another day older and deeper in debt." And I said, "Hey, that's a good line for a song."...
>
> I actually copied it from a Josh White song that had the line "I've got a head like a rock and a heart like a marble stone." It's sort of like "Fly around My Pretty Little Pink": "Coffee grows on white oak trees and the river flows with brandy / Rocks on the hillside big as the moon and the girls all sweeter than candy / Fly around my pretty little pink." The verses have nothing to do with "Fly around My Pretty Little Pink." The verses on "Sixteen Tons" are fun verses, the chorus was just thrown in.[174]

On a side note, there has always been a rumor that on its original release, "Sixteen Tons" was blacklisted for being a "communist" song. There is no official record of this, but Capitol Records producer Ken Nelson recalled that at his pre-Capitol job at WJJD in Chicago, the FBI approached the station and told them not to play Merle Travis records because of what they viewed as "communistic" lyrics. Whether or not this affected sales of Merle's *Folk Songs of the Hills* is speculation.

In the same vein as "Sixteen Tons," the complex narrative that Merle imagined in "Dark as a Dungeon" proves his incredible skill as a songwriter. In just a few rhyming lines, those who had never ventured out of the big cities could imagine themselves working alongside the coal miner, far below the ground, "where the danger is double and the pleasures are few." Merle often joked about how he wrote songs, a style he either copied or refined after watching Capitol Records songsmith Johnny Mercer writing songs. Like Mercer, Merle wrote his songs "backward": "Write a good strong last line. It's like you have to lay a foundation for your house before you can build it. If you start at the top it gets kind of rough—you can't lay much concrete when you get to the bottom of it. That's the whole idea. But that was Johnny Mercer's idea, and he's written some four hundred hits. He said, 'It's always easier to write your last line first and build from there. Otherwise, you're likely to write yourself off into a hole.'"[175]

Merle would also tell of how he attempted to make "Dark as a Dungeon" sound like an authentic Irish folk song. Thom Bresh recalled: "He said, 'All the great folk songs come from Ireland.' 'Listen Ye Fellers' and that sort of thing. So I started it that way: 'Listen ye fellers so young and so fine, and seek not your fortune...' See, it's backwards in folk songs—'seek not your fortune in the dark dreary mine.'"[176] Merle's brother John Melvin always objected to the lyrical content of "Dark as a Dungeon," insisting that coal miners were happy to have their jobs and didn't mind their subterranean environs.

Having gathered his first group of four new folk songs, Merle entered the studio on August 6, 1946, and recorded "Sixteen Tons," "Dark as a Dungeon," "Nine Pound Hammer," and "Over by Number Nine." Taking a cue from folk singer Carl Sandburg, he gave a spoken-word introduction to each and sang with only his guitar as accompaniment. A week later, he returned to the Capitol studio to cut four more folk songs for the album, bringing along Cliffie Stone and Tex Ann as accompanying musicians. This batch was a hodgepodge. Merle recut "That's All," the blues song he had recorded for Atlas the year before. He recorded a version of the folk standard "John Henry." There was a number that he learned from fiddler Harold Hensley, "Mus'rat," that Hensley had taught him while the two were relaxing on the beach a few days before the session. This first version of "Mus'rat" must not have been to Capitol's liking, as Merle would recut it before the album was released. Finally, there were two traditional gospel numbers, "I Am a Pilgrim," and "This World Is Not My Home." Merle is often credited with writing "I Am a Pilgrim," but in his own words, he recalled: "I first heard a version of this song from Lyman Rager [Mose Rager's younger brother], who had learned it while he was in the Elkton, Kentucky, jail. I rewrote it, rearranged it, and added to it."[177] When the album was released, "This World Is Not My Home" didn't make the cut, and remained shelved for decades.

As gung-ho as the Capitol executives had been about Merle recording a folk song album, once the songs were in the can, they seemed less enthused about releasing it. One of the reasons may have been "Mus'rat," which was recut in April 1947. The rest of the album sat in the vaults for eleven months before Capitol finally released the album in May 1947. As Merle put it later: "Then Capitol let them sit on it for two years [actually one year] before they issued them and by that time the folk fad had passed and the album went nowhere."[178] Indeed, it was a commercial failure. Since none of the songs were honky-tonk or Western swing, which dominated the country music charts of the era, an acoustic folk album couldn't have been expected to sell as well as Merle's singles. It did find an audience in the folk music crowd, where Merle's authentic portrayal of life in the Kentucky coal mines endeared him to collegiate, educated music cognoscenti. These folkies, college professors, and beatniks would repay their debt in Merle's later years when he was hired to play many folk festivals and college campuses. Merle always took the folk crowd's attention with a grain of salt; he insisted that his folk songs were written on deadline and meant to be fun attempts at copying "real" folk songs. But he couldn't hide the sheer excellence of his compositions, and these songs would follow him for the rest of his career. Both "Sixteen Tons" and "Dark as a Dungeon" would be included in Alan Lomax's influential 1960 book *Folk Songs of North America*. *Folk Songs of the Hills* also entered into the National Recording Registry at the Library of Congress, an honor reserved for recordings vital to the history of America, cementing its importance regardless of sales. Despite his protestations, after *Folk Songs of the Hills*, the folk crowd always treated Merle like a hero.

A press release that Capitol Records issued had Merle pitching the album with a self-penned bit of advertising prose:

Hello there, it seems to me like every day I run into somebody that says to me, "Why don't you make some records where you just sing and pick your guitar like you do over the radio?"

I talked this over with my boss down at CAPITOL RECORDS and he thought it was a good idea.... So here's a picture of the results.

Yes sir, I had a big time makin' these records. I tuned up the ol' box and got me a good easy chair and just picked and sang and told stories about when I was a young'un at home in Kentucky 'till I filled up eight sides of records.

I tried to do a little bit of ever'thing on these records. I sung some old spirituals, some coal miner songs, some blues songs and even a couple of songs for the kids.

I hope you'll ask your music store man for one of these MERLE TRAVIS FOLK SONGS OF THE HILLS albums. If he ain't got one, get him down and [w]ring his sassy neck till he orders you one from CAPITOL RECORDS in Hollywood.

Be sure and let me hear from you.

Your friend, Merle Travis.[179]

When the album sold below expectations, Merle returned to his honky-tonk and Western swing styles on his next few rounds of Capitol single releases.

Merle's personal life during this time remained as busy as his professional one. He had been popular with the women in Cincinnati, and when he hit Hollywood, the cute, young guitar wizard from Kentucky had a reputation in town of being a ladies' man. A few of Merle's memories:

"I visit Laverne in Orange Grove"
"I visit girl whose brother had hijacked truck"
"Dusty give me clap"
"Atchison's girl gives me clap"
"I get far to [sic] friendly with trucker's wife"

At some point in early 1945, Merle had a brief relationship with a female Western singer named Jeanne Jackson, who went by the name Jeannie—a young, petite, seventeen-year-old Nebraskan who had recently relocated to Santa Monica. More Merle's memories:

"I get good looker pregnant in Santa Monica"
"Good looker has baby—never tells"

Jackson became pregnant with Merle's child, and little is known about the pact they made. Possibly because Merle's divorce in Cincinnati wasn't finalized, or because Merle was already in a public relationship with Tex Ann Nation, the secret remained a secret. Jackson gave birth to a son, Richard, in October 1945. Either shortly before or after the child was born, Jackson married a man named Franklin Lesher Sr., and Merle's first biological son was given the name Richard Lee Lesher. He lived a short and turbulent life. He performed music and played guitar, sometimes using the stage name Dick Travis, which reveals that he was aware of who his famous father was. He grew up around San Jose and Palo Alto in Northern California. It is not known if he ever attempted to see Merle or contact him. Richard died of chronic alcoholism in 1979 at the young age of thirty-three.

In the late 1970s, there were two letters written to the Travis family that alerted them to Richard Lesher's existence. One was from Richard's mother-in-law, Bernice Hinkley, who sent a copy of Richard's obituary to Merle, noting that Richard was his out-of-wedlock son. Merle sent the letter to his daughter Merlene with a blithe denial: "Hi Sugar, this is a new one on me. I'm sorry the young feller checked in, but I'm even sorrier that I'll have to admit I never ever heard of anybody named

Lesher—ask your mother about 'Elvira!'"[180] (Elvira was a fan/stalker who claimed she was married to Merle in the 1950s.) Later, there was also a random letter from a Merle Travis fan named Robert Puckett in Lodi, California, sent to Merle's first daughter, Pat Travis Eatherly, mentioning "Merle's son Dick Travis" playing music in Northern California.[181] The letter enclosed a photo of Richard Lesher at a live show (curiously, playing a Bigsby solidbody guitar built in 1954 for Jim Webb, a Western swing guitarist in the area). Pat sent copies of the letter to the rest of the family, but at the time, the family assumed that the familial claim was a fabrication. Decades later, Merlene submitted her DNA to the 23andMe national database and received an unexpected match in Northern California—with Richard Lesher's daughters, Sherry and Sandra Gehrung (Gehrung being Jeanne Jackson's final married name. Richard's third daughter, Gina Lesher, hadn't submitted her DNA). Sherry and Sandra Gehrung also matched to another Travis relative, John Melvin's son Dave Travis, who had also put his DNA in 23andMe. When Merlene contacted the Gehrungs, they revealed that they had suspected from overheard conversations Merle was Richard's birth father. But they were discouraged from asking questions, which prompted their DNA submission. Jeanne Jackson aka Jeanne Gehrung died in 2014 and never told her side of the story.

Recall that Merle and Tex Ann Nation were in constant contact from 1944 to 1946 between working together in Ray Whitley's band, touring together with Smiley Burnette, and joining Cliffie Stone's radio show, and that at some point the unlikely pair became a couple. Tex Ann's husband, Buck Nation, came back from the war and found that his wife was now involved with Merle. In her unpublished autobiography, Tex Ann only mentions that Buck had suffered an injury overseas and "was ill in both mind and spirit."[182] Interview notes with Joe Allison, who worked in the country department at Capitol Records at the time, revealed that he was present "when Buck delivered Tex Ann to Merle, with tears in his eyes."[183] It made for an awkward situation. Buck Nation remained in the country music community in Los Angeles, and even cowrote songs that Merle recorded. It was not the last awkward love triangle to arise in Merle's life.

Merle and Tex Ann were a show-business couple. They worked together on the radio and on tour. They sang duets together on Capitol transcriptions. They also apparently shared a passion for alcoholic beverages. They made the front page of the *Los Angeles Examiner* for a drunk driving arrest that occurred on September 4, 1946. Merle's memory:

"Texann an [*sic*] I get jailed for drunk driving"

Merle mentions the incident in his own writing earlier in this chapter. His telling, however, omits several details the newspaper report filled in:

DRIVER DENIES DRUNK CHARGE—Radio musician Merle Travis, 29 [actually 28], insisted in Van Nuys court today he was NOT driving while drunk when Motorcycle Officer C.R. Ericson stopped him on Ventura Boulevard.

But Ericson wanted to know "If you weren't drunk, DO YOU ALWAYS TEAR UP THE CITATION BOOK OF A POLICEMAN WHO STOPS YOU AND HIT HIM OVER THE HEAD WITH IT?" If not, then he was drunk, Ericson told Judge Joseph Call.

Travis will face trial next Thursday. A woman companion, Sidna Kelly, also 29 [actually 41], and also a "radio entertainer," faces a drunk charge with him. She was riding with Travis, police said.[184]

Merle's alcoholism was still in the "fun" phase at this time. High times and career success combined with the celebratory postwar years in Hollywood made drinking a joyful pastime. But Merle's first arrest, as comical as it may have seemed to the average newspaper reader, foreshadowed more serious consequences down the road. Merle's memory:

"Jailor offers to let me out for fee to record"

One of the men guarding Merle at the jail was a police lieutenant and country music fan named Steve Stebbins. Cliffie Stone knew Stebbins, and was able to get Merle out of jail at 1:30 am to do a late-night session with a group of Capitol's all-stars including Johnny Mercer, Wesley Tuttle, and Italian comic Jerry Colonna, then spirit him back to jail before anyone discovered his absence. Shortly after this session took place, Stebbins became an important country music booking agent, forming a company called Americana Booking, which represented many country music stars, including Lefty Frizzell, Johnny Bond, and Tennessee Ernie Ford.

A few months later, Merle and Tex Ann hosted many of their fellow Capitol stars and radio cohorts at their home for a raucous celebration of Merle's twenty-ninth birthday. Merle's memory:

"Texann throws drunken birthday party"

Dozens of photos from this night still exist, from the lens of a professional photographer who was there to document it. Cliffie Stone and his father, Herman the Hermit, were there, as were fiddlers Charlie Linville, Tex Atchison, and Harold Hensley, singer-guitarist Red Murrell, and Capitol Records' Lee Gillette, along with their wives. Capitol recording artist Eddie Kirk, who also played excellent rhythm guitar on many of Merle's recordings, was there that night with his wife, June Hayden, whom Cliffie Stone had branded "Judy" for his daytime radio shows. The photos show the revelers playing banjo, guzzling booze, and pretending to fight each other. Several show Merle and Tex Ann posing with a giant, oversize bottle. We see Merle opening birthday presents. In one group shot, a virtual who's who of California country artists pose around a couch with Merle drunkenly putting his arm around Tex Ann. Standing almost directly above them are Eddie Kirk and Judy Hayden, the latter looking extremely unhappy. This picture is an interesting lens into Merle's future, as the personal web around Eddie, Judy, and Merle would become intensely complicated within the next few years.

There was a huge country music scene in San Diego during this time, based around the Bostonia Ballroom in El Cajon. Thousands of sailors were stationed in the area at the naval base (where the US government housed their Pacific fleet), and those sailors flocked to Western dances. Merle would often head down to San Diego for a gig. At some point, he discovered the border town of Tijuana, Mexico, just a few miles south of San Diego, and the new-to-him concept of a "Mexican marriage." In the 1940s, Tijuana was as much of a vacation destination for Southern Californians as Las Vegas is today. The city was not as dangerous as it has become in recent years, and there were plenty of thrills to be had: drinking, gambling, and cheap shopping for mainstream tourists, as well as drugs, prostitution, and all manner of other illicit things. The city also offered an easy way for couples to get married, usually only requiring signatures and a small cash fee, whereas most US states at that time required blood tests and a waiting period, as well as parental consent if under a certain age. It goes without saying that in the more socially conservative 1940s, many women would not have sexual relations unless they were married. When Merle discovered that marriages in Tijuana were convenient, cheap, and not legally recognized in the United States, it was as if he had found a magic loophole in the rules that society had imposed on his libido. Merle's memories:

"Texann and I are Mexican married one year"
"Wesley Tuttle is at our marriage"

By 1946, Wesley Tuttle had divorced his first wife and begun dating a pretty secretary and song plugger who worked at the CBS Radio headquarters in Hollywood. Her name was Marilyn Myers. She was also a singer, and went on tour with Wesley as part of his troupe in late 1946. Being part of Wesley's life meant having Merle Travis in their orbit. Marilyn Tuttle would recall: "Merle was going with Tex Ann, and Merle said, 'Wesley, we're going down to Mexico and get married, you guys wanna go with us?' And we thought, 'Yeah, we'll go with ya.' So we went down to Mexico and Merle says 'While you're down here, why don't you guys get married?' So we did. All four of us were married at the same time,

February 9, 1947."[185] Wesley and Marilyn Tuttle would remain married for fifty-six years, until Wesley passed away in 2003. Merle and Tex Ann, however, were on a rocky path. Their Mexican marriage barely lasted a year. Merle's memories:

"I buy house in Van Nuys"
"Texann moves in—and out"
"Harold Hensley moves in"

After living in an apartment in Hollywood for two years, Merle purchased a small tract house at 14927 Victory Boulevard in Van Nuys in the San Fernando Valley. Houses were cheap and plentiful in the Valley in the 1940s, with newly developed suburbs opening at a rapid pace, replacing the orange groves that once occupied the entire region. Merlene told this author: "As Dad always told me, Tex Ritter convinced him to move to the Valley, where you could be surrounded by ranches and farms and smell orange blossoms in springtime and still be close to Hollywood. It was more country and more relaxing."[186]

There is no specific record of why Merle and Tex Ann split up, other than Merle's memory that she "moved in—and out." She went back to her ex-husband, Buck Nation, for a short time, then led an all-female touring band for a few years, remarried several more times, and disappeared from public view. But an educated guess regarding her breakup from Merle can be found in her unpublished autobiography, which only mentions him in one brief passage as her "singing partner." One can only surmise by the omission that the marriage ended badly. She never even revealed to her Kansas family that she had been married to Merle, although they found out years later after the internet made such secrets impossible to hide. Sidna Joquetta "Tex Ann" Nation Fritz Kelley Travis DeShago Clements lived out her later years in an apartment in Fullerton, California, before finally returning to Coffeyville, Kansas, where she died on May 4, 1989.

Undeterred, Merle, the ladies' man, would continue to make friends wherever he went. One such was a woman named Ruth Johnson, who had recently relocated to Southern California from Indiana. Ruth's son Thom Bresh remembers the timeline:

Mom had a grocery store in Washington, Indiana. [Everett] "Bud" Bresh [who worked as a traveling salesman for Good Humor Ice Cream] came in with a trailer, and he found out Ruth was quitting the job and moving to California. They came out together. She brought her two kids from her first marriage. When they landed in California they wound up at Pickwick Trailer Park in Burbank because that's where the musicians wound up at out there. Spade Cooley's whole band was around there;

Tex Williams's bunch was around the pool, drinking beer, suntanning, and all that.

Bud came out there to see Ruth, and he would shoot pictures of them. Ruth's friend was dating Leon McAulliffe, and Ruth and [Merle] Travis had a one-night stand. She got pregnant. As mom was getting bigger, Travis was worried it would ruin his career, but Ruth said not to worry about it. "I can handle myself."[187]

Thom grew up thinking that Bud Bresh was his father. Bud moved into the trailer, and after that they got a house. But they never lost track of Travis.

Tom Bresh was born February 23, 1948, in Hollywood (he changed the spelling of his name to Thom in the 1970s for career purposes). His parents were listed as Bud Bresh and Ruth Johnson on the official birth certificate. Merle had now impregnated two women with out-of-wedlock sons in the space of three years. Unlike the note he made regarding Jeanne Jackson's son, Richard Lesher ("Good looker has baby—never tells"), Merle made no such mention of Ruth Johnson or her son Thom Bresh in his notes. Merle's former stepson Michael Robinson says: "I wouldn't put anything past... you know, these guys, man, they were rounders. They were getting around."[188] But unlike the situation with Richard Lesher, Merle and Thom Bresh would interact often, both when the latter was young and then as professionals when Thom began his own music career, working for Merle's close friend Hank Penny. Bud Bresh, who raised Thom as his own, was a photographer who befriended all of the country music stars around Los Angeles, including Merle and his closest friends. It is thought that Bud Bresh went through his life believing that Thom was his biological son. All parties involved are deceased now. We do know from Thom: "I wasn't old enough to know anything, but my dad was nuts about Travis. I don't know what I thought he was, but [when] I was five or six years old, he [Merle] showed up and rolled out a blueprint of his new Super 400, showed it to my mom and dad."[189]

Merle's memory:

"Ginnie Cushman sends picture"

Virginia "Ginny" Cushman was a petite, attractive woman from Santa Barbara, a cornet prodigy who had gone to music school and toured professionally with orchestras and big bands all over the globe beginning in her teens. She was a year older than Merle, well traveled, and wise to the ways of the world. Merle's Capitol singles prominently featured muted trumpet. The man playing on the records was Jack McTaggart, an older musician who had previously played with Stuart Hamblen. Cushman heard Merle on Cliffie Stone's radio shows and figured she might be a good candidate for Merle's new trumpet player (even though she played cornet, the two instruments are very similar). She sent a letter offering her services and a photo of her holding her cornet to Merle, care of Capitol Records. Merle was no dummy. He got in contact with her immediately. Cushman would later comment, on various occasions:

> I used to listen to Merle when he was working with Cliffie Stone over the radio. I think it was coming from KXLA in Pasadena, California in 1946. At that time, I was living in Redondo Beach, California. I decided to write a letter to Merle and told him I played the trumpet and had bought all of his records and could play the trumpet parts on all of those records. It wasn't very long before I heard from Merle, and he soon came down to Redondo Beach to meet me. I guess he liked my musical ability because he came back to see me several times and finally wanted to drive me up to Van Nuys to meet some of his musician friends as he was interested in recording more records.[190]

> Those were such wonderful days for me. I was so happy! Instead of someone telling me I had to go home and play… I got the job with Merle.[191]

Cushman also provided inspiration for one of Merle's most successful original songs:

> Well, that night he drove me home to Redondo Beach with the understanding that I would drive up the next day to rehearse some of those tunes. On that drive home he stopped several times for me to look at the lights, moon, etc. Well, he really was a stranger to me and I right away lighted up a cigarette. I forget how many I smoked before I got home. To make a long story short, I went back the next morning in my car, and he was out in his back yard painting his fence. He told me he was thinking of a new song that might be good for Tex Williams. Well, it turned out to be "Smoke! Smoke! Smoke!" I often think back to that night, if I had been more interested in the moon, instead of the cigarette, that tune might never have been written.[192]

In a later interview, Merle remembered the story with slightly different details, but the same end result:

> I was out painting a fence and Tex Williams came by. He said, "I'm doing a session tomorrow night. Have you got anything?" I said, "No, Tex, I don't." He said, "I sure wish you did. I need another song; I'm not

really pleased with the four I'm going to do. If you think of something, let me know." I said, "Okay, buddy, I will." I was thinking, man, I sure wish I had something for Tex. He's the best guy—everybody loves Tex Williams. So I got to thinking—what the heck could I write? And then I remembered my dad, who worked around the coal mines. He didn't smoke, and he said, "If I was a boss on the coal mines I'd never hire a fellow who smokes, because every time you ask him to do something, he'll say, 'Wait a minute 'till I roll another cigarette.' It would take him half an hour to get that tobacco out and roll that cigarette." I thought, maybe there's a song in that somewhere.

So I thought, "Well, I'll write a talking thing about rolling cigarettes." So in about ten minutes I throwed those little old verses together. I had one line in there at the time, it said:

"The other night I had a date,
With the cutest gal in 48 states,
A high-bred, uptown, fancy little dame.
So friend of mine, if you're a man,
You know mighty well what I had planned,
So hand in hand we strolled down lovers' lane."

Tex, in his kind way, he said, "Now that's pretty good, but I don't hardly believe that they would play that line on the radio. If it's alright with you, why don't we change that one little line?" I said, "To what?" He looked around, and came up with

"She said she loved me and it seemed to me,
That things were like they ought to be."

He said, "That other one's a little risqué." I said, "Okay, you wrote part of the song, now put your name on it." He said, "Oh, no." I said, "Look, this song is by Merle Travis and Tex Williams." Well, he is the guy who saved the song. If I'd left that line in there, they never would've played it on radio. Not in those days.[193]

Ginny Cushman was the "high-bred, uptown, fancy little dame" that Merle was referring to in the lyrics. In her later years, she seemed to delight in the fact that she had inspired them: "'Smoke! Smoke! Smoke!' would never have been written if it hadn't been for me."[194]

There was something that would keep Cushman from joining Merle's band immediately—she was pregnant and about to become an unwed mother. When she had her first child, Helen, aka Tillie, in April 1947, she arranged to have her aunt and uncle adopt the child and raise her. (During the writing of this book, there was some speculation that Tillie may have been another of Merle's out-of-wedlock children, but a DNA test revealed that that was not the case, despite the timeline.) Once she recovered from childbirth, Cushman joined Merle's band. "Smoke! Smoke! Smoke! (That Cigarette)" became a monster hit in the summer of 1947. Merle and others have made claims that it was Capitol's first big hit, or its first million seller, but neither of those claims are exactly true; Freddie Slack's "Cow Cow Boogie" with Ella Mae Morse on vocals was the label's first mega-hit, in 1942. But Tex Williams's hit record of Merle Travis's song was the label's biggest country hit up to that time. Merle's claim above that the song was Capitol's first "million-dollar seller" may also be true. Although it is difficult to prove decades later, it may have been the first Capitol record to sell one million dollars' worth of singles.

Capitol Records in 1947 was not an established label with a guaranteed cash flow, but its country division enjoyed a constant profit margin. Billy Liebert, an accordion and piano player on hundreds of Capitol recording sessions in the 1940s and 1950s, recalled a conversation with Lee Gillette, who headed the division:

> Capitol overextended themselves. They were a new company, they were growing, spending all this money in the pop field and they were having success and all of a sudden that dried up. And the only people that were selling any records—Merle had 3 or 4 songs on the charts at one time, and it didn't cost anything to do a country date.... I think Union Scale was $33 to do a record date for four songs. And the Country Music department at Capitol saved their ass. That was about '46–'47. And I did hundreds of sides for Lee Gillette. The guy that was hot was Merle and he saved Capitol's ass.[195]

Executives were often reminded that the cowboys on the label were hot, especially when confronted with pop or jazz snobs who considered country music beneath them. A press clipping from August 1947 reveals its popularity: "Ever hear of a black market in disks? Blame it on Tex Williams and the furor his "Smoke! Smoke! Smoke!" is causing down Florida way. Music ops sorely pressed for the platter are offering $1.25 for the wax—and can't get it. It's nice to note that Tex's rendition has hit the peak, and is now among the nation's top tunes."[196]

"Smoke!" firmly established Merle as a writer of hit songs (recall that upon its initial release, the album containing "Sixteen Tons" and "Dark as a Dungeon" had sold marginally). Several major artists also recorded the song, including Phil Harris and the Lawrence Welk Orchestra. After "Smoke!" Merle became an in-demand songwriter, something that could have made him a rich man if he had the burning desire to become the next Johnny Mercer: "Inspired songs ain't worth a dime. I heard that from Johnny Mercer. Some songwriters are inspired by their sick mother or their girlfriend that's left them. But a songsmith like Harlan Howard or Cindy Walker, Dallas Frazier—you say 'I need a song next Tuesday,' they don't have to be inspired; they're songsmiths."[197]

Merle continued to put out successful singles for Capitol, maintaining a string of hit records that kept his name in the headlines. "So Round, So Firm, So Fully Packed" was a hit in early 1947, not only for Merle on Capitol, but for several other artists who recorded it, including Johnny Bond on Columbia Records and Ernest Tubb on Decca. The flip side, "Sweet Temptation," found its inspiration in Merle's drunk driving arrest in September 1946:

> I was in Hollywood, and there's a boulevard there called Belvedere Boulevard. [This is an incorrect memory, as Merle was pulled over on Ventura Boulevard in the San Fernando Valley, not Hollywood, according to the newspaper report as well as Merle's own writing about the incident earlier in this chapter.] One night I mistook that for the Indianapolis Speedway, and the police took kind of a dim view of that, as they did of the half-pint bottle of Seagram's Seven laying up in the front seat. They said, "You'd better come downtown with us for a few days." So on our way we picked up some more prisoners. We stopped in Santa Monica and picked up a black fellow, and he was laughing and saying, "Man, a woman ain't nothin' but sweet temptation." So I said to myself, there's a pretty good song title. So when I got out of jail I wrote the song.[198]

For another release, Merle wrote a set of clever lyrics to "Steel Guitar Rag," a popular instrumental number that had its origins in the blues song "Guitar Rag" by Sylvester Weaver. The song became a steel guitar standard when recorded by Leon McAuliffe with Bob Wills as "Steel Guitar Rag" in 1936. Merle gave himself cowriting credit for putting lyrics to it, a practice that was common at the time but is no longer allowed in the business of music writing and publishing. Merle's vocal interpretation of "Steel Guitar Rag" was another successful release in the spring of 1947.

Capitol Records started a new subsidiary in May 1947 called the Capitol Americana Series, designated for its folk releases. Tex Williams's version of "Smoke! Smoke! Smoke!" was the second release on the new imprint. For a year and a half, until the Americana subsidiary ended in June 1948, all of Merle's releases were on the Americana label instead of the regular Capitol label. Several of these were clever compositions but failed to achieve much in jukebox plays, radio airplay, or sales. "I'm Sick and Tired of You, Little Darling" was inspired by Cliffie Stone, who drove by Merle one day and yelled out, "Why don't you write a song called 'I'm Sick and Tired of You, Little Darling'! They're wearing that out in every song I hear!"[199] The song was originally written for Cliffie, who sang it on a Bel-Tone release in 1945. It was also cut by Red Murrell on Atlas Records before Merle recorded it for Capitol.

"Fat Gal" was another of Merle's odes to shapely women, a theme that he revisited several times after "So Round, So Firm, So Fully Packed" became a hit. "Fat Gal" featured another catchy chorus rhyme: "Warm in the winter, shady in the summertime, that's what I like about that fat gal of mine." It became a moderate chart success, as did another ode to larger women, "I Like My Chicken Fryin' Size." The flip side of "Fat Gal" was one of Merle's greatest recording achievements. It was a simple country boogie, but it featured an impressive, pioneering use of multiple overdubbing.

Merle had owned a Wilcox-Gay disc recording machine since his Cincinnati days. It was a crude recording lathe that cut low-fidelity 78 rpm discs made of cardboard. He found, through experimentation, "that I could take one of the old home recording machines and remove a part of the roller that turned the turntable, making it turn slower. Recording on the slow turning acetate discs, then playing it back, got a high pitched mandolin-like sound from a regular guitar. Then, to record with the high pitched instrument it sounded as if someone was playing extremely difficult passages with a normal guitar accompaniment."[200] After four years spent in various recording studios and recording cardboard records at home, Merle's fertile mind spawned an idea. He suggested that the engineer record the band and his vocal at normal speed (these were the days before recording tape became standard, so the master recordings were done direct to disc on lathes running at 78 rpm). Then Merle had him record a guitar overdub with the recording slowed down substantially, enabling him to capture intricate lead guitar parts while the original track played slowly. When the original band recording and the slow-speed guitar overdub were brought up to the final 78 rpm speed, the result sounded like it had been recorded at superhuman speed and had a mandolin-like tone. The song was actually written on several Capitol ledgers as "Merle's Mandolin Boogie" before the title was changed to simply "Merle's Boogie Woogie." The speed manipulation was a trick, and the multiple guitar overdubbing was a gimmick, but it was technically groundbreaking.

The concept of overdubbing and even speed manipulation was not new. In the landmark 1939 film *The Wizard of Oz*, a similar technique of speeding up prerecorded voices created the Munchkins' cries of "Follow the yellow brick road!" Several cartoon voices used the technique as well, including Daffy Duck and Sylvester the Cat, which were essentially the same voice played back at different speeds. Sidney Bechet had released a jazz disc in 1941 that featured him overdubbing all the multiple instruments, released under the moniker Sidney Bechet's One Man Band.

Merle's sharp mind was the first to realize that slowing down an original music recording to do a guitar overdub, resulting in a speeded-up final product, would be an exciting sound for the guitar. He gave credit to fellow Capitol artist Lead Belly for teaching him one of the verses in "Merle's Boogie Woogie": "Lead Belly taught me a verse I use on one of my old records, one of the first multitrack recordings I guess was ever made. It went, 'Got a little gal with great big legs, walks like she's walkin' on soft-boiled eggs.' He was interesting to talk to."[201] "Merle's Boogie Woogie" was a mild hit on its own, but not as much as the flip side, "Fat Gal." The fact that it was released as a B side of Merle's latest single on Capitol Americana meant that he would never receive the full credit for the debut of multitracked guitar recording. Merle was also soon eclipsed by another Capitol guitar wizard who was quick to take credit for the technique, Les Paul.

Paul released his first disc for Capitol, "Lover," in February 1948. The guitar multitracking instrumental came out six months after "Merle's Boogie Woogie" and became a big hit. Paul quickly credited himself as the creator of what Capitol termed "the new sound." Paul, along with his new wife, Mary Ford (who had dated Merle when she was still Colleen Summers), had hit after hit in the late 1940s and early 1950s using guitar multitracking techniques and vocal double-tracking techniques. In the ensuing years, recording and engineering groups lauded Paul for his groundbreaking work in multitrack recording. Guitar magazines often referred to him as the man who had invented the technique. He never corrected them; in later life, he often told colorful stories that interwove his real accomplishments with invented ones admirers had bestowed upon him. He always claimed that he had been engaging in guitar multiple recordings and speed manipulation since the 1930s, but as none of these early experiments were ever released, it may or may not be true.

In late 1947, Merle assembled a band that included Ginny Cushman, Jack Rogers, Tex Atchison, and steel guitarist Phil Marx to embark on a cross-country US tour, with a stop in Kentucky for a special homecoming event. The Booster Club in Drakesboro, Kentucky, tracked down Merle's home phone number through his ex-wife, Mary, who still lived in the area, and asked him to play a benefit show to raise money for a school playground, equipment, and a baseball field at Drakesboro High School. When the Booster Club had asked Merle's manager, they were told Merle was too busy. But when they corralled Merle himself on the phone, he agreed to do the benefit show.

By this time, he had purchased a used DeSoto Suburban from fellow Capitol artist Pee Wee Hunt, an extended length vehicle that held eight passengers. To make it roadworthy for a touring band, he took out the back seats and installed a mattress there for sleeping. Jack Rogers's upright bass was strapped to the luggage rack on the top. The DeSoto was christened "The Boat," and the five-piece band took off on a national tour that brought them to many cities and small towns. According to Ginny Cushman: "Merle had bought a big green DeSoto automobile, and he called it 'the boat.' Anyone caught calling it a car had to pay a fine of 25 cents. I was the treasurer, and I collected enough money on the trip to Drakesboro so that when Christmas came around, I bought a tree and little gifts for all the band members." Cushman continued:

> Merle did most of the driving, and on the way to Kentucky we stopped in several small towns to play short publicity gigs. Since I was the only girl in the band, I had a motel room to myself while Merle and the others shared a room. One morning while Merle was brushing his teeth, a cap popped off a tooth and down the drain it went. The tooth, of course, was sensitive and Merle was really upset. He called for a plumber to remove the pipes, but even after much work by the plumber, the cap was never found. I think he finally put a little wax on the tooth so we could go on.[202]

Jack Rogers had a different memory regarding the sleeping arrangements: "She [Ginny] was always with Merle. They were together all the time. Shacked up together…. I can understand that. I liked Ginny. She was a good kid."[203] Merle's memories:

"Ginnie could blow water in bath tub"
"Ginnie stays undressed during room service"

On tour, Merle worked on a new song he planned on recording, undoubtedly inspired by the Kentucky homecoming festivities, called "Kentucky Means Paradise." Jack Rogers remembered an unusual moment on tour:

> It was in Kansas City, Missouri, and we were playing Kansas City, Kansas, the one across the river. I went to the room to see Merle, and I walked in and he was sitting on the bed with his guitar, dressed in women's clothes, like partly, half naked, playing and writing a song. I said, "What are you doing? I thought you might want to get out and walk around a little." He said, "I'm writing a song for my recording later for Capitol, for them." It was "Kentucky Means Paradise."[204]

Rogers took a candid photo of Merle songwriting while wearing women's clothing, which he kept for decades until it was destroyed in a fire at his house. The memory of the event brought raucous laughter during the interview by this author; Rogers recalled many good times he and Merle shared on the road.

The band also traveled with several guns in the vehicle, which they used for hunting along the way. Cushman says: "The guys would all shoot at crows along the road, but since I was a bird lover, I didn't approve of this and I told them so. During the trip, the steel player, Phil Marx, complained about an earache that would not go away. We stopped at a grocery store where I bought a clove of garlic. I put a small piece in his ear, and in a short time, it really seemed to help the pain."[205] The group arrived in Drakesboro in mid-November, and the *Louisville Courier-Journal* published a large feature entitled "The Home Town Smokes Travis Out." Muhlenberg County turned out in droves to celebrate the return of their local boy made good. Merle had arranged for two of his film actor friends, Western movie villain Terry Frost and Monogram Pictures' femme fatale Teala Loring (sister of Debra Paget), to meet the band in Drakesboro to add some Hollywood pizazz to the affair. Merle was seated in a Jeep convertible, wearing his Western suit, and paraded down the tiny main street in a marching band procession. Finally, in a ceremony on the steps of Drakesboro High School, the mayor presented him with a key to the city.

While in town, Merle reunited with his oldest brother, Taylor, his daughter Patty, Miss Bunnie Baugh (then known as Bunnie Mullens), and his old guitar-picking buddy Mose Rager, among numerous other friends. Cushman notes: "When we were in Merle's hometown, Patty, a little girl appeared back stage. I thought she was real sweet. I hugged her and gave her a kiss and gave her my 'Mascot Dog' I had carried for several years all over the country, including Canada and Mexico. I also gave her my necklace. I don't know if she remembered that, but Merle was so busy, I thought she needed some love."[206]

When the group left Drakesboro, they headed to Nashville, where Merle appeared on the *Grand Ole Opry* and did a recording session with Grandpa Jones and the Brown's Ferry Four. Cushman again: "After leaving Drakesboro for our return trip to California, we stopped to visit Grandpa and Ramona Jones at their home in the country outside Nashville. Merle and Grandpa were shooting and hunting enthusiasts, so a little target practice was in order. They let me shoot one of the guns that was so powerful it knocked me down. Ramona was concerned that it had really hurt me."[207]

Merle performed at the *Grand Ole Opry* on December 6, 1947, immediately following the band's visit with the Joneses. The broadcast was carried coast to coast via network radio affiliates in addition to the regular signal on WSM. According to Cushman: "Since horns were not permitted on the *Opry* back then, I couldn't play with Merle. So I sat on the stage while he performed. But I met Minnie Pearl and so many of the *Opry* stars."[208] After the *Grand Ole Opry*, Merle and the band traveled back to Los Angeles. Ginny recalled that the band drove nonstop, in anticipation of recording more songs for future Capitol releases. Following the ban on recording that Musicians Union president James Petrillo had ordered in 1942–43, Petrillo had announced another imminent ban that would begin on January 1, 1948, and Merle wanted to get home and get a batch of recordings in the vaults before it went into effect. They recorded demos of his new songs on Merle's Wilcox-Gay home disc recorder in advance of the recording sessions, which are among the few Merle Travis recordings that still remain unissued. Cushman kept the cardboard records for decades and eventually gave them to Dave Stewart, publisher of the Merle Travis *Cannonball Rag* newsletter. Most of them were professionally rerecorded for Capitol, but at least one never went beyond the demo stage, a novelty called "Whoa Back Buck."

Starting November 21, for five days Merle and his band, featuring Ginny Cushman and augmented by Billy Liebert on accordion, Eddie Kirk on rhythm guitar, and Vic Davis on piano, did three sessions, cutting twelve songs in anticipation of the ban. These would make up Merle's next batch of Capitol releases, including "My Baby Double Talks to Me," a clever number with advanced wordplay featuring lyrics in pig Latin, "Kentucky Means Paradise," "Crazy Boogie," "Dapper Dan," "The Devil to Pay," "Information, Please," and a song Merle wrote that Tex Atchison had recorded a year earlier for King, "I'm a Natural Born Gamblin' Man." Cushman recalled, "They had me stand on an apple box so I could reach the microphone."[209] And according to Wesley Tuttle, "That was a first. There were no girl musicians, period, some girl singers, but no musicians, especially a trumpet player. That was a whole new innovation."[210]

The studios were all busy in anticipation of the January 1 deadline. Some of the sessions that Merle did at the end of 1947 were recorded in a hastily constructed temporary studio in the Capitol Records company lounge. Also at the tail end of 1947, Merle, Cushman, and Tex Atchison recorded several sides with Jack Rogers singing for two 78 rpm releases on the tiny Crystal label. Merle's command of the Spanish vaquero-style guitar on Rogers's "Stars Over Old Santa Fe" is impressive, since he would have only been introduced to the unique style in the few years since he'd moved to California. Spanish guitar style is as far from the Muhlenberg County guitar style as one can get, but Merle adapted and excelled at it.

As 1948 rolled around, Merle had accomplished most of the major feats of his career. He had moved to Hollywood, appeared in Western movies, starred on the radio, signed to Capitol Records, established himself as a guitar-playing and go-to songwriting man, and written the three defining songs of his professional career, "Dark as a Dungeon," "Sixteen Tons," and "Smoke! Smoke! Smoke! (That Cigarette)." He appeared on the cover of *Billboard* magazine on March 6, 1948, an honor for anyone in the music business. He had hit records, and was now a star in the country music community. Merle Travis was on top of the world. It would be a difficult act to follow.

Merle, holding his new Bigsby solidbody electric guitar, poses with Paul
Bigsby, who is playing the 1948 pedal steel he built for Speedy West.
The photo was taken in Merle's backyard by future Fender guitar shop
foreman Forrest White on his first trip to Los Angeles in early 1949.
(Photo by Forrest White, courtesy of Thomas Sims Archives.)

CHAPTER 4

THE BIGSBY SOLIDBODY ELECTRIC GUITAR

In 1947, I wouldn't go twenty feet unless I was on my motorcycle.[211] *That's when I met a
man who was the announcer at the motorcycle races out around Lincoln Park in Los Angeles
County. His name was Paul A. Bigsby. We all called him "P.A." P.A. had built Joaquin
Murphey a steel guitar that was a work of art. It had a beautiful sound. I kept wondering
why steel guitars would sustain the sound so long, when a hollow body electric guitar like mine
would fade out real quick. I came to the conclusion it was all because the steel guitar was solid.*

The dust was thick and the noise was deafening as the last lap of the motorcycle race saw half a dozen riders still leaning forward over the handlebars, breathing the foul smell of burnt gasoline and alcohol, which added up to the best mixture for racing fuel available that night in 1947. Here they came around the last turn. It was hard to see much with naked light bulbs swinging in the cool Southern California night air, except the spray of sparks from the metal heels on their left boots. Any motorcycle racer knows the best way to turn left is to set your left heel on the track, lean to the left, and pour on the coal. The rear wheel will shoot you right on down the stretch and down will come the checkered flag (if you're lucky).

The crowd was on its feet, screaming. Car horns in the parking lot were blasting away. The man on the microphone was yelling something. The two dusty, greasy, leather helmeted riders roared across the finish. From where most of us were it was impossible to tell who the winner was. But from the announcer's booth it would be easy to tell. So the crowd noise wilted down to a steady murmur. Then came the voice over the loudspeakers.

"That was a close one, folks," came the amplified voice. "I'll tell you who the winner was… in a minute or two, but right now I've got to have another cigarette!" Half the crowd laughed while other portions of the gathering moaned an "Oh no!" along with "Hey, who won it?"

Again the announcer. "Pardon me, folks," he blasted. "For a minute I thought I was Tex Williams. The winner was… Lammy Lamareaux!"

"At least the ol' boy's heard the efforts of Tex and myself, with a little help from Capitol Records," I thought. At the time we had a song called "Smoke, Smoke, Smoke" that was kicking up a little fuss.

The next morning I was at the CBS studios on Sunset Boulevard in Hollywood to do our daily deed of sending out live pickin', singin', and talkin' to whom-so-ever would listen to the likes of Andy Parker and the Plainsmen, Sally [Foster], Jimmy Wakely, and me. The show started at 5:00 am and lasted until 8.

I told my friend Joaquin Murphey (yep, the fantastic steel player), who was working with Andy Parker at the time, about my "night at the races."

"The guy that announces the races is a good friend of mine," Joaquin said, pointing at an inlaid name on his steel guitar, which read BIGSBY.

"Does he have a factory?" I asked.

Murphey answered in a statement that I found to be oh, so true! "He don't have a factory. He's a factory worker. Mostly just a crazy sort of character."

Joaquin phoned him, told him how I loved motorcycles and guitars. He left word with Murphey for me to feel free to come up to the announcer's booth any time he (Bigsby) was at the Lincoln Heights motorcycle race track.

The next time I went to the motorcycle races I made my way up to the announcer's booth and introduced myself. "I'm Merle Travis," I explained, "a friend of Joaquin Murphey's."

"Anybody that's a friend of Murphey's," he bawled, "oughta be shot!" He laughed loud and long at his own joke. I was afraid not to. Then I saw what Joaquin meant by referring to Paul A. Bigsby as a character. His feet were big and he took long steps. His voice was not deep, but loud. I wondered why he didn't just stick his head out of the booth and merely talk loud, instead of using a public address system. His hair was a brownish gray and stuck in all directions. In all the years I was to know him, not once did I see his hair combed.

I called him "Mr. Bigsby," which brought another big laugh. If a nuclear bomb had have hit, that also would have brought a laugh from the big man.

"Call me 'P.A.,'" he boomed.

I never called Paul A. Bigsby anything else. I don't know of anybody who was a close friend that called him anything other than "P.A." I was never around to see what happened when he was called "Paul." I sort of imagine he laughed for 15 minutes.

P.A. Bigsby, possibly 15 years my senior, became a good friend. I learned that he'd helped design the Crocker motorcycle. At his home in Downey, another L.A. suburb, he had dozens of trophies that he'd won as a racer when he was younger. He told me what a pattern maker was in a factory: actually, the man who makes precision molds with special square sand (round sand from the beach won't work). He showed me pictures of a battleship he'd made the pattern for. It took three weeks to cool the metal that was poured in his pattern.

I was on Cliffie Stone's Hometown Jamboree in the late 1940s. We'd do a daily broadcast from the Huntington Hotel in Pasadena. On Saturday nights we'd do a show and dance with Cliffie at a hall in a little hamlet nestled among the orange groves called Placentia. It was four miles from Fullerton, California. P.A. would come over to the noon broadcasts in Pasadena when he could.

I had a gadget called a Vibrola. Mine was secondhand and worked fine, except that it would pull the strings out of tune. One day I said to P.A. Bigsby, "You're a hot shot pattern maker and you built Joaquin Murphey's guitar, do you think you could fix this thing so it won't pull the strings out of tune?"

Without hesitating a second P.A. roared, "I can fix anything!"

In about a week he brought it back. With a flourish he pitched the thing to me and said, "Now, see how it works."

It was as bad as ever. We all kidded P.A. He turned a little red around the ears. His only comment was, "The damn thing's made wrong in the first place."

"You're just a big blowhard," I kidded him. "Let me see you build a vibrato contraption that works."

"By God, I'll do it," Bigsby said, and had a hearty laugh.

P.A. had built Joaquin Murphey a fine steel guitar, but he possibly topped his own work when he made one for Speedy West. Played through an amplifier, they had a beautiful sound and about twice the sustainability as a hollow-body guitar. I found myself wishing

I had a steel guitar with a regular neck on it. Changing strings on my Gibson L-10 and my D-28 Martin was a pain in the neck. The fourth, fifth, and sixth wasn't too bad. But reaching down under to change the first, second, and third bugged me. I wished somebody would build a guitar with all the tuning pegs on the top. How much more simple it would make changing strings, or tuning. In my mind's eye I could see the guitar I'd like to have, but there just wasn't any such animal.

One day P.A. Bigsby blustered into the studio in Pasadena. He watched Cliffie Stone's radio broadcast, which he seemed to enjoy. After the show I had a brainstorm. I called Bigsby aside. "You say you can make anything, right?" I asked.

"Any damn thing," was his loud, typical reply.

Now, since I was knee high I've admired cartoonists (it hasn't stopped), and I taught myself to draw fairly well. So I had a question for P.A. "Can you build me a guitar like I draw the picture of?"

"Sure! Draw it!"

I took a piece of KXLA program sheet paper and sketched off a pretty crude combination of lines. Then I explained it to Paul A. Bigsby, a man who could make "any damn thing." "Here you are," I told the big man. "I want the body thin and solid. That way it'll keep ringing like a steel. I want all the keys (tuning pegs) lined up in a row on top."

"What's this fiddle-looking tailpiece for," he asked, "and the arm rest!"

"They're to make it pretty," I joked, "like the heart, diamond, spade, and club for position dots."

"Wait until you see it. It'll be as pretty as a brand new James A. Prescott!"

That's the kind of motorcycles they were racing when I met P.A. The racers called them by their initials. The J.A.P., like P.A. Bigsby, was very noisy, but got the job done.

In about a month P.A. called. The phone vibrated a little as he roared his message. "I've got that thing that you wanted all finished," said he. "Wanna come over and pick it up?"

"I don't think so, P.A.," I said, not looking forward to driving a car all the way from Van Nuys to Downey, long before the freeways. I'd have been on my way if I could have done it by way of my motorcycle. I finished by asking how it looked.

"Fantastic!" he yelped.

Bigsby was right. The thing was perfection. He had made it out of birds-eye maple, the cosmetic tailpiece and armrest were walnut, as was the pickguard, which had my name inlayed in mother of pearl. At the scroll on the top of the neck my friend P.A., pattern maker and motorcycle announcer, had inlaid his name that was to become famous among musicians around the world: "BIGSBY."

I didn't use it much on radio programs, but every Saturday night when Cliffie Stone's group did a combination show and dance at Placentia, I'd play the odd-looking instrument. One night a friend from four miles away, Fullerton, the town I mentioned earlier, came in. He was an easygoing, quiet-spoken man. His name was Leo Fender. During a break Leo asked me how I liked that newfangled guitar I was playing. I told him all the good points I could think of. He wondered if I'd mind if he borrowed it a week. Being a great craftsman himself, as we all knew, he wanted to build one like it. I had no use for it during the week, so I handed Leo Fender the guitar.

The following Saturday night he brought it back, along with one almost like it, except he'd obviously built his instrument in a rush in order to get mine back to me. I examined his instrument. He asked for an opinion. I told him that I thought it was great. Leo asked me if I'd mind playing his instrument a while. He wanted to see how it sounded. It was flawless, as far as I was concerned. The electric pickup was definitely better than the one P.A. Bigsby had built. This is not saying Bigsby's pickup was bad, not at all. Leo had not gone to the trouble of using birds-eye maple and inlaying a lot of things.

My Bigsby neck was so perfect that I had him take the neck off my D-28 Martin and build a neck for it (I still use that guitar). A number of other friends had their acoustic guitars renecked by Bigsby.

One by one they saw my "funny lookin'" guitar and ended up ordering one from Paul A. Bigsby. P.A. found himself backed into a corner. The wood-working tools in his garage in no way made an assembly line operation. He didn't have enough time to spend with his soft-spoken lovely wife and young daughter, both named Mary. Big Mary and Little Mary, he called them.

I cannot tell you how many "Bigsby" guitars were "manufactured" in P.A.'s garage. I can only tell you that there were not very many. A dozen, maybe. But I can tell you how it ended. Paul A. Bigsby told me. He said something like this.

"Another bastard came in yesterday wanting one of them stupid looking things like I built you. I told him, 'Hell no! Go out to Fullerton and look up Leo Fender. He'll build you one.'"

One man went to Leo Fender. Two men went to Leo Fender. Two thousand men went to Fender. Leo Fender put up a factory. They built Fender guitars. They built Fender bass instruments (which he developed). They built Fender steel guitars, they built great Fender amplifiers. They sold Fender strings of all kinds. Years later, Fender sold out to CBS for something like thirteen million dollars, the papers said. Leo Fender retired.

It all started back in the forties. Many years later I was to see some young man with a beautiful Fender guitar.

"How do you like your Fender guitar?" I'd ask.

"It's the greatest," says the young man.

"I designed that guitar," I'd say. The young man would look at me a little strange and walk away. I can just hear him saying, "I saw this ol' dude. He questioned me about my Fender, then went off his rocker. Said he designed it... some nut!"

Once Chet Flippo, with Rolling Stone magazine in New York, interviewed me in California. I took a chance and told him the story. His piece came out that I was a little dingy, more or less. I imagined I'd designed the Fender guitar, that he'd gone to the factory and they told him I never used solid-body guitar in my life. Mr. Forrest White, who was with the Fender company for years as a vice president, heard about Flippo's write-up and sent me some pictures of P.A. Bigsby and me in my back yard where I hadn't lived since 1949. I put it with my collection of a few more hundred pictures of me playing my Bigsby before a Fender solid-body was built.

I'm happy to say that Leo Fender is still a very good friend. So is Forrest White, the man who built the Music-Man amps before retiring. They're both ace high in my books.

. . .

Merle's memories:

"Bigsby 'fixes' my Vibrola—then builds one"
"Bigsby builds me a guitar"

Merle Travis was a gearhead. He loved all the details on his electric and acoustic guitars and amplifier. He purchased an Indian Chief motorcycle in early 1947 and became almost as obsessed with the motorcycle world as he was with guitars. Indian motorcycles evoked freedom, open roads, independence, and rebellion. Many of the same things appealed to guitarists and professional musicians, so it was easy to see the appeal for a freethinker like Merle. Wesley Tuttle remembers:

> Merle and I both got on a motorcycle craze in 1947. He bought an Indian
> and I bought a Harley…. He loved his bikes. We used to ride together all
> the time. Merle, Ginny Cushman, my wife Marilyn and I, we'd get on
> our bikes and ride up to Santa Barbara.[212]

Tens of thousands of young men purchased motorcycles after World War II. Motorcycling became a lifestyle. Los Angeles gave birth to motorcycle gangs like the Hells Angels, and the year Merle purchased his Indian was the same year that the Boozefighters Motorcycle Club terrorized the town of Hollister, California, an event later made famous in the movie *The Wild One* (1953). Motorcycle racing became a bit of an obsession for many of these speed-crazed young men, and Los Angeles had several venues for it. The motorcycle racetrack in Lincoln Park, near downtown Los Angeles, was the closest one to where Merle lived. The announcer there just happened to be Paul A. Bigsby. Merle gives Bigsby a fitting introduction in his own words above, but leaves out a large chunk of Bigsby's backstory and what made their meeting so consequential.

Paul Adelbert "P.A." Bigsby was born in 1899 and spent the first half of his life working as a machinist, pattern maker, and motorcycle enthusiast. From the beginning of motorcycle racing in California, Bigsby was there. He himself raced in the 1920s and 1930s, then retired from the grueling sport in the mid-1930s to concentrate on promoting races and working for Standard Patterns, who manufactured parts for the Crocker brand of racing motorcycles. Crockers were custom-built machines that dominated motorcycle racing in the 1930s, with their unmatched horsepower and speed. Many of the parts were handmade, sand-cast aluminum parts made by Bigsby himself.

When World War II began, metal and other resources were restricted, and Crocker folded. Bigsby continued to promote motorcycle races, and during the war he began to devote spare time to another hobby of his, country music. He decided he was going to learn how to play the electric steel guitar, and set about using the aluminum casting techniques he had learned working for Crocker to manufacture his own copy of a Rickenbacker "Frying Pan" steel guitar, which he completed sometime around 1944. The first prototype instrument was labeled "P.A." on the headstock. Bigsby took his instrument to various wartime Western swing dances to show it to professional steel guitarists and get their opinions. One of them, Earl "Joaquin" Murphey, who played for Spade Cooley at the time, asked Bigsby to make him an instrument.

The first Bigsby steel guitar was made for Murphey in 1945. It was a combination of cast-aluminum parts and bird's-eye maple, a pretty, decorative wood that was plentiful in Los Angeles after the war. Bigsby made everything by hand except for the tuning machines and volume and tone controls. The necessary skills—aluminum casting, pickup winding, scale length computations with machinist's accuracy, fine woodworking—were far beyond the grasp of the average hobbyist. But Bigsby had been working with metal and wood for decades and had a considerable skill set.

Brilliant and eccentric Joaquin Murphey was widely acknowledged as the best and most creative steel guitarist of the 1940s non-pedal era. To other steel guitarists, Murphey carried the lofty title of "genius." Marilyn Tuttle called him a "good steel player... [but] strange. He lived in a garage. He was quiet and—I don't know, he was just strange."[213] When Murphey played his instrument, he made it sound so exceptional that other players wanted to copy him. As he began playing his Bigsby steel guitar with groups like Spade Cooley, Andy Parker and the Plainsmen, and Tex Williams and His Western Caravan, other steel guitarists began approaching Bigsby about getting their own Bigsby steel guitar. But Bigsby, as Merle recalls, did not have the capability to mass-produce instruments. He was a garage tinkerer who worked mostly with hand tools. All Bigsby instruments were made one at a time, on a custom-order basis.

Merle tells in his own words about meeting and befriending Bigsby. What he leaves out is that for a time in 1946 and 1947, Merle taught himself how to play steel guitar. Already proficient on guitar, bass, harmonica, fiddle, mandolin, banjo, and piano, he took on the steel guitar as a side project, occasionally playing it on Cliffie Stone's various morning radio programs. All those who remember Merle's brief fling with the steel guitar note that he was a good player, taking naturally to the difficult instrument. He was capable of playing licks on the standard guitar that mimicked the slide effects of the steel guitar, so presumably the new instrument came easier to him than to most. An article on Merle in a 1947 fan magazine is the lone mention in print of his short-lived flirtation: "Then comes the steel guitar.... Merle purchased one of the sweetest soundin' steels in Hollywood and proceeded, alone and unaided, to conduct the singing strings. That was a little over ten months ago today, March 27, 1947, nine p.m. Pacific Coast Time.... Now the ole Kentucky boy is a pretty accomplished steel guitar player, addin' one more instrument to the many he has already mastered."[214]

Merle ordered a Bigsby steel guitar in 1947. A metal plaque on its top says "Custom Made for Merle Travis by Paul A. Bigsby." It was essentially an eight-string lap steel, but Bigsby created a unique case that folded out into a stand for it, complete with an apron panel with Merle's name inlaid in the bird's-eye maple front. When the lap steel was placed on top of the case/stand, it was a fully professional steel guitar console unit. Merle may have received the steel guitar before he received the folding case/stand, as the handful of on-stage photos from 1947 show him playing with the steel guitar perched on top of a folding metal stand.

Although Merle never mentioned owning the Bigsby steel guitar in any interviews, his daughters, Merlene and Cindy, still own the instrument. The internal components are date stamped to the sixteenth week of 1947, which means it was put together after that, most likely in the summer of 1947. The Merle Travis Bigsby steel guitar is highly significant because of its 1947 manufacture date. It was one of the first five Bigsby instruments made, and an obvious starting point for the Bigsby electric Spanish guitar that followed.

At this time, Merle was putting a lot of thought into the difference between his electric hollowbody archtop Gibson L-10 and his electric Bigsby solidbody steel guitar. The hollowbody was prone to feedback if the amplifier was turned up too loud. The steel guitar was made from a piece of solid wood, and had a lot of sustain. As he writes above, he began wondering why a standard (Spanish-style) guitar couldn't be made with a solid wood body—the same construction method that steel guitars utilized. In a later interview, he recalled: "I'd seen Spade Cooley's steel player, Joaquin Murphey, play with an electric pickup; it sounded loud and pretty! There was a guy named P.A. Bigsby, a handy guy, a patternmaker, also an announcer at the races where I used to ride my motorcycle. One day I asked him if he could make me one that you held up 'this way.'"[215]

Merle wasn't the first to think along these lines. Since the mid-1930s there had been a few short-lived, unsuccessful attempts at making a solidbody electric Spanish guitar, including the 1936 Rickenbacker Bakelite Spanish solidbody and the 1938 wood-bodied Slingerland Songster. However, these guitars were the same small size as their lap steel counterparts—uncomfortable to hold and not ergonomic to play—and failed to make any significant impact. Though Rickenbacker tried marketing their Spanish solidbody electric guitars, professional musicians treated them as a novelty or a toy. These early attempts looked like a ukulele body with a guitar neck on it. No one had yet marketed a truly professional solidbody electric Spanish guitar. The idea germinated in Merle's mind.

In February 1948, Bigsby made a triple-neck steel guitar for Merle's friend Wesley "Speedy" West. Speedy's instrument was different than the other Bigsby steel guitars in that it had pedals attached to it that would raise or lower strings. While the pedal steel guitar had been introduced by a few companies since the 1930s, these early pedal steels were built like large pieces of unmovable furniture. Paul A. Bigsby was the first one to figure out a way to make a console pedal steel with removable legs and a removable pedal linkage so that the user could disassemble it and transport it easily. It was another one of Bigsby's monumental achievements, and every pedal steel guitar that has been made since that date copied the basic design he used on Speedy West's pedal steel. Speedy's Bigsby pedal steel guitar attracted a lot of interest from other players. As Merle writes in his own words above, he was paying attention to Speedy's steel guitar, and his inventive mind was thinking of how its construction might work on a regular, Spanish-style guitar.

One hobby that Merle actively pursued after moving to Los Angeles was cartooning. Although he had always drawn cartoons, in California he became quite serious about drawing and pursued it as a possible side profession. Indeed, if Merle hadn't been a successful guitarist, singer, and songwriter, he could have been a professional illustrator. Between 1946 and 1947, he contributed humorous cartoons to the independent country music pulp magazine *Tophand*, where he was listed as "staff cartoonist." He illustrated Cottonseed Clark's self-published booklet "Brushwood Poetry." He pursued paid commercial art projects, too. He wrote about his cartoon work in a letter to his brother John Melvin: "Well sir, if you'll excuse the expression, I'm a half-assed professional cartoonist. I don't think 'half' is quite condenced [sic] enough, but it's the current word, and I used the 'professional' just to satisfy my own ego, but I am gettin' paid off for some of my stuff now. I'm drawin' a comic book in color for the same people I went to N.Y.

for, and for th' same purpose. Me an' ol' man Columbia University is sure gonna stomp out venereal disease!"[216]

The reference is to a public service project from around this time devoted to the prevention of venereal disease, sponsored by Columbia University. According to John Melvin Travis:

> During World War Two [actually several years after the war], for Columbia University, he drew that picture about stamp out venereal disease. He drew the picture of a big foot comin' down—nothin' but a big foot like a farm work shoe, or something, comin' down like that, says "Stamp Out Venereal Disease." It was adopted and put in restrooms and everything else all over the United States."[217]

There is mention in letters found in Merle's archives that he did the "Stamp Out Venereal Disease" poster, a full-length anti-VD comic book, and music recordings and voice-overs for radio promotional spots produced by Columbia University as part of the same anti-venereal-disease public service project. Merle traveled to New York City in March 1949 to record at the RCA Building in Radio City Music Hall with Alan Lomax, the famed ethnomusicologist, producing.

Merle also began a friendship with one of his neighbors in Van Nuys, Murat "Chic" Young, who drew the nation's most popular daily comic strip at the time, *Blondie*. Young was a Midwesterner (born in Chicago, raised in St. Louis) who had birthed the *Blondie* strip while living in New York, then relocated to California in 1939 as the *Blondie* franchise began making movies in Hollywood. In a 1948 newspaper article Young remarked: "We like it here in the [San Fernando] Valley for the same reason most people do. It means pleasant living and for that reason I have a feeling we'll stay around."[218] Merle wrote to his brother John Melvin about meeting Chic Young, and spoke in wonderment about watching the nation's most popular cartoonist work with simple and crude drawing tools.

Merle continued to perform on Cliffie Stone's morning radio shows. By 1947, Cliffie's main show was *Dinner Bell Round-Up*, broadcast on KXLA radio from the ornate Huntington Hotel in Pasadena. The cast included Cliffie and his father, Herman the Hermit, as well as hillbilly duo act the Armstrong Twins, accordion player and pianist Billy Liebert, and Merle's housemate at the time, fiddler Harold Hensley. The show also featured Cliffie's new discovery, a disc jockey from San Bernardino named Ernest Ford, who had a hilarious hillbilly alter ego character he called "Tennessee Ernie." Finally, the *Dinner Bell Round Up* featured a husband-and-wife team, singer and rhythm guitarist Eddie Kirk and his wife, singer June "Judy" Hayden. (Although she always used the name June in her personal life, and genealogical paperwork shows her family name was spelled Hayden, she was christened "Judy Hayden"—sometimes spelled "Haydn"—by Cliffie Stone. For ease of reference in the remainder of this biography, she shall be referred to as Judy Hayden.) At some point, a spark of romance ignited between Merle and Judy. It is unclear when it began, but Merle came between Eddie and Judy, splitting up their marriage. Judy Hayden would soon become Merle's third wife. But in 1947 and 1948, during the *Dinner Bell Round Up* era, the pair were still in the early stages of flirtation.

Paul Bigsby would occasionally come to the show's live broadcast, which took place in a large studio room that held twenty or thirty audience members as well as an engineering booth, where the audio mixing was done before sending the program over the air. At one of the performances that Bigsby attended in person, Merle decided on impulse to ask him about the concept he'd been mulling over. In Merle's telling, he mentions grabbing some radio station stationery and sketching a vision of a solidbody electric guitar, which he gave to Bigsby. Merle told the story many times. What he consistently failed to mention was that he saved these historic drawings. Perhaps the most amazing discovery in the writing of this book were the original drawings from early 1948 on the back of two sheets of *Dinner Bell Round Up* stationery, just as Merle described, with his vision of a solidbody electric guitar depicted as a series of cartoons. Merle told interviewer Doug Green in 1975: "I thought, why not build a guitar solid like a steel, and it would have sustainability like a steel. So I drawed a picture of a guitar with all the keys on one side and I said, 'I want it about an inch thick, an inch and a half thick, solid body, and with all the keys on one side,' and everything I'd wrote."[219]

The primary feat of Merle's spur-of-the-moment decision to have Bigsby build him a guitar was taking the concept he'd been dreaming of—a solidbody electric Spanish guitar that sustained like a steel guitar—and applying that abstract idea to what a country music star might actually use. Yet the drawings also reveal how much Bigsby had to do with the final look of the Bigsby electric solidbody guitar. Merle gave Bigsby a couple of pages of what were essentially abstract cartoons, a Dalí-esque surrealist vision, largely because at that time no such instrument existed on the market. Bigsby took Merle's drawings back to his Downey garage shop and made a professional instrument out of them. So, it was a combination of Merle's creative mind and Bigsby's machinist's mind that led to the first modern electric solidbody guitar. The instrument still draws attention today. It is at once old-fashioned in its handcrafted, homemade appearance, and futuristic, especially when viewed in comparison to other hollowbody electric guitars of the era. It was entirely revolutionary.

When Merle took delivery of his Bigsby in May 1948, despite what he writes above, it was not perfect—at least not at first. For one thing, the single pickup situated by the bridge created problems that he had not encountered with his electrified Gibson L-10. As of May 1948, all production electrified guitars put their single pickup either near the neck for a mellow sound, or by the bridge for a brighter sound (the concept of a two-pickup electric guitar was only being experimented with by players like Alvino Rey and Junior Barnard at this time; Bigsby would make his electric guitars with two pickups starting with his third one, in early 1949). The solidbody guitar was a whole new world, and the sound of the bridge-mounted pickup on the new Bigsby was brighter than Merle had anticipated. Thom Bresh remembered: "He didn't like the way the Bigsby electric sounded. He said it was 'tinny.'"[220] Within a month or two, he had it modified with a selector switch and an extra volume control. This allowed a setting for "rhythm" guitar at a lower volume, and "take-off" (lead) guitar at a higher volume. While doing these modifications, Bigsby also gave the non-cutaway solidbody instrument a cutaway, so Merle could more easily reach the high notes on the fretboard.

The Bigsby's original configuration had an elongated headstock to accommodate Merle's vision of the tuning keys all along the top edge, six in a row. But it looked weird—like something a wizard or an elf might play—not exactly the right look for a country musician. Thom Bresh again: "Originally, Travis wanted the Bigsby headstock to look like [the head of] a fiddle. Then when that didn't work, he turned it facing down."[221] The original Bigsby headstock looked like the side profile of a violin's scroll head. There are only two photographs that show it in this original configuration, one a candid shot with Merle and his cornet-playing bandmate and girlfriend, Ginny Cushman, and a rare mid-1948 group shot of the *Dinner Bell Round Up* radio show cast. So, within a month or two, at the same time that Merle returned the Bigsby guitar to have the pickup rhythm/lead switch added, he asked that Bigsby redesign the headstock shape so as to reduce its overall length. Bigsby used a bit of ingenuity to fit six Kluson tuners into a smaller area: He clipped the edges of each so that seven screws could be used instead of twelve to attach the tuners to the back of the headstock. At the time, there were no commercial tuner sets made for six-on-a-side headstocks, so Bigsby had to modify existing three-on-a-side tuners to work.

Merle met another new Capitol recording artist in 1948, a Texan who would become one of the label's biggest stars: Hank Thompson. The pair became good friends, and Thompson would become a true Travis acolyte, often copying Merle in his choice of guitars, amplifiers, stage clothes, and automobiles. Thompson later remembered: "On the radio show he was playin' that Bigsby, and he had that when I first knew him. Merle said, 'I've never known a guitar that there wasn't somewhere on [the neck] that the thing didn't note just right. I cannot find any dischord on this guitar whatever. The neck on it is perfect.'"[222] Future Fender manager

Forrest White took pictures of Paul Bigsby, Speedy West, and Merle posing with their new instruments in Merle's backyard sometime in late 1948 or early 1949. In the photos, the three men beam with pride, their gleaming new instruments shining in the California sun. They knew what they had accomplished.

Despite the instrument's revolutionary nature, this was an era where even hollowbody electric guitars were slow to be accepted by the general public, so the idea of a futuristic solidbody electric guitar was too outlandish for most people to process. In Johnny Western's words: "At that time, when he created that guitar, the solidbody, it was just a 'dream thing' because there were no solidbody guitars. It just wasn't there."[223] In the pre-rock 'n' roll era of the late 1940s, not many people could foresee a need for such a thing. Merle and Paul Bigsby went about promoting it to change minds. Merle took promotional photos with his new guitar, and it was featured in several magazine articles. The October 1949 issue of *Folk Hillbilly Jamboree* magazine contained an article titled "Merle Travis—His Dream Came True," which described Merle dreaming up the design. But the author, unable to grasp the importance of the solidbody construction, noted the "odd shape and the location of the keys" and made the emphasis of the article the fact that Bigsby, after making Merle's initial guitar, "has sold several like it for more than $500 each!"[224]

Despite Merle's recollection that Bigsby didn't want to go into the business of making electric guitars, for a short while between 1948 and 1950 Bigsby took out advertisements in local hillbilly music magazines like *Tex Williams' Western Life* and *Jamboree*. A May 1949 ad in *Jamboree* shows a photo of the new Bigsby solidbody electric guitar, with this blurb:

NAMES COUNT… TOP NAMES IN THE WESTERN AND FOLK MUSIC FIELD USE BIGSBY ELECTRIC GUITARS… MERLE TRAVIS AND BUTTERBALL PAIGE PLAY THE BIGSBY ELEC-TRIC STANDARD, MANUFACTURED AND SOLD BY BIGSBY ELECTRIC GUITARS, 8114 EAST PHLOX STREET, DOWNEY, CALIFORNIA.[225]

A Bigsby flyer from the early 1950s advertised the instrument in the same vein:

THE ORIGINAL SUPER-THIN ELECTRIC STANDARD GUI-TAR WITH ALL TUNING KEYS IN LINE CREATED FOR THE ELECTRIC STANDARD PLAYER WHO WANTS THE UTMOST IN ACCURACY AND PERFORMANCE.

The head is a revolutionary design with all tuning keys on the same side. Merle Travis is responsible for this design and it has many advantages.[226]

Bigsby would go on to make solidbody electric guitars for other top names in the country field, including Ernest Tubb guitarists "Butterball" Paige and Billy Byrd and Nashville studio musicians Grady Martin and Hank Garland.

Bigsby also began re-necking stock guitars with his comfortable necks that intonated perfectly. Merle had Bigsby re-neck his Martin D-28, and also put a twelve-string neck on an old Gibson archtop from the 1930s (the twelve-string may have been influenced by the time Merle spent with Lead Belly, who played a twelve-string Stella guitar from the 1920s). Soon, other country stars ordered their own Bigsby re-necked acoustic guitars, including Hank Thompson, Joe and Rose Lee Maphis, "Little" Jimmy Dickens, Zeke Clements, Carl Smith, and Lefty Frizzell.

As revolutionary as Bigsby's guitar was, making them by hand in a garage one at a time and advertising them in local hillbilly magazines was not going to start a revolution. The revolution would instead be led by a man named Leo Fender.

Fender was a country music fan. When asked by *Guitar Player* magazine's Tom Wheeler in the 1970s if he had ever met Jimi Hendrix, Fender's answer was "No, but I met *Bob Wills!*"[227] At the moment in question in the late 1940s, Fender was manufacturing steel guitars and amplifiers, and supplementing his business by supplying PA systems to local country music dances. Fender's first steel guitars had been cheap, student-level instruments for local players, but he'd developed his products into fine-sounding steels used by many professionals. His amplifiers varied from tiny practice amplifiers to loud, professional amps with big, fifteen-inch speakers. He supplied his amplifiers to bands like Bob Wills and His Texas Playboys and Spade Cooley, who played them at sold-out ballroom dances in front of thousands of people. In 1947 Fender installed a steel guitar pickup with volume and tone controls on Junior Barnard's Epiphone hollowbody archtop guitar, which Barnard played with Bob Wills. Fender was already thinking about making electric Spanish guitars in addition to his line of steel guitars. (He had made a prototype that looked like a lap steel but was meant to be played like a standard Spanish-style guitar, but it was small and uncomfortable to play.) He had a mind for business, and was seeking new avenues for expansion.

Merle's story about Fender borrowing the Bigsby electric guitar at a dance in Placentia, California, has been repeated many times, and the basic elements have been confirmed. Cliffie Stone was promoting a regular show and dance in 1948 and 1949 in Placentia, then a small town in the middle of orange groves in sleepy Orange County. Fender borrowed the instrument and noted its basic elements—solid body, thin neck, string-through-the-body tailpiece (for sustain), and six-on-a-side headstock. His copy mimicked Bigsby's unique method of trimming down the edges of three-on-a-side Kluson tuning keys to make them fit into a smaller area with fewer screws on the back of the headstock. He ignored the Bigsby's deluxe features like neck-through construction, playing-card-suit inlays on the fingerboard, armrest, fancy pickguard, and decorative bird's-eye maple and walnut finishes, and instead crafted a much simpler pair of prototype guitars with pine bodies and maple necks. Fender's prototypes were utilitarian and worked exceedingly well. More importantly, Fender's simple solidbody guitar, copied from Merle's ornate Bigsby, could be knocked out with a band saw and a belt sander in a matter of minutes or hours, not weeks or months. It was made for mass production.

Fender debuted the new Esquire single- and double-pickup solidbody electric guitars in 1950. When first offered, they failed to make much of a dent in the marketplace. Just as Bigsby had discovered, Fender found that the weird, unorthodox solid "plank" instrument was difficult to sell because customers didn't yet understand its advantages. He renamed the Esquire as the Broadcaster, and then the Telecaster one year later, and secured some celebrity endorsements from top guitar stars of the day like Jimmy Bryant, Arthur "Guitar Boogie" Smith, Jimmy Wyble, and even Oscar Moore from the Nat "King" Cole Trio. This, combined with an aggressive team of salespeople and distributors, shoved the new solidbody instrument down people's throats. Fender also came out with an equally revolutionary solidbody electric bass, the Precision Bass, in 1951. Ultimately it took a huge staff, a factory equipped for mass production, and several years, but Fender won over the public with his workhorse, plain-Jane version of Merle Travis's Bigsby solidbody electric guitar. The Telecaster began to sell in large quantities by 1953 and 1954. Also in 1954, Fender introduced his next model, the wildly popular Stratocaster, an instrument that closely copied Bigsby's iconic headstock shape. (Bigsby and Fender would ultimately go to court over Fender's use of the headstock design, but Bigsby lost the lawsuit when Fender showed examples of Eastern European instruments from the 1800s with similar design features. In addition, inexpensive archtops sold in the 1930s by the Harlin Brothers Company, manufactured by Regal, also featured a six-on-a-side headstock, though with a much less refined tuner system.) When rock 'n' roll became popular in 1955 and after, Fender was in position to supply the nation's army of young rockers with electric solidbody instruments, and they became a dominant force in the marketplace—a position they still hold today, decades later.

Another element of the Bigsby guitar story that Merle never spoke about relates to electric guitar wizard Les Paul and the Gibson model guitar that bore his name. Lester William Polsfuss, aka Les Paul, was a Wisconsin guitarist and tinkerer who had been one of the pioneers of electric guitar in the 1930s and 1940s, playing with big-band leaders like Fred Waring and Bing Crosby as well as his own Les Paul Trio, which specialized in hot guitar numbers. After professional stints in Chicago and New York, Paul nearly electrocuted himself in 1941 doing home electric guitar experiments and moved to Los Angeles to recuperate. In LA he befriended Bigsby and installed one of Bigsby's early steel guitar pickups in an Epiphone hollowbody guitar that he had modified for recording. He also began dating Colleen Summers, aka Mary Ford, whom Merle had worked with (and also dated) on the *Hollywood Barn Dance* radio show. (Les Paul and Merle knew each other, but since Merle had dated Mary briefly, Les was apprehensive about having Merle, the "ladies' man," around his wife.)

When Paul shattered his arm in a car accident in 1949, Bigsby made him a small-bodied solidbody electric guitar to play while recuperating. Paul eventually got rid of this instrument, despite the fact that he was an instrument hoarder with hundreds in his collection, presumably because the existence of a Bigsby solidbody guitar made for Les Paul in 1949 would disrupt his own version of the history of solidbody electric guitars. The Bigsby made for Paul surfaced at a garage sale in New Jersey in the 1980s and eventually Paul admitted that Bigsby had made it for him.

The Gibson guitar company approached Les Paul in 1951 with the idea of marketing a solidbody electric guitar with his name on it. Gibson wanted to compete with Fender, whose solidbody electrics were starting to make a dent in the marketplace. Gibson had already designed their own solidbody, and wanted Paul to sign an agreement that would let them put his name on the instrument. When the Gibson Les Paul model solidbody electric guitar debuted in 1952, it featured an attractive gold metallic finish, an odd wraparound tailpiece (the only part on the guitar designed by Paul), and two Gibson P-90 pickups. The body shape was exactly like Merle's 1948 Bigsby electric guitar, with the exception of the six-on-a-side headstock. The similarity was undeniable. It was as if the Gibson people had traced a photo of Merle's guitar.

Like Fender, Gibson sold their solidbody electric guitars, based on Merle's Bigsby guitar design, in fairly limited quantities for the first few years. But when rock 'n' roll hit, sales went through the roof, and when the Beatles emerged a few years later, sales were so massive that Fender and Gibson (along with other makers of electric guitars like Gretsch and Rickenbacker) built enormous new factories to handle the accelerated volume. What had begun as a garage-built hillbilly experiment in 1948 had turned into an industry in less than twenty years. In every music store in countries all over the world were rows and rows of electric guitars that could all be traced back to Merle's groundbreaking Bigsby electric solidbody.

Merle played his Bigsby guitar quite a bit from 1948 to 1950, but not exclusively. According to Jimmy Lee Fautheree of the hillbilly duo Jimmy and Johnny, "I saw Merle play in Dallas at Bob Wills's place [the Bob Wills Ranch House, later called the Longhorn Ballroom]. He rode his motorcycle all the way from California for the gig, and he had that Bigsby guitar strapped to his back."[228] Merle knew that his solidbody guitar was a significant invention, especially when Fender started selling their version by the truckload. But he never fully committed to the solidbody. In a 1980 letter to a fan, he wrote: "A few songs which I did use the Bigsby on were 'Deep South' (original cut), 'Trouble, Trouble,' 'Too Much Sugar for a Dime,' and 'Spoonin' Moon.'"[229] So there is evidence that he played it off and on for a couple of years, but by 1951, he was looking for something new.

Bigsby built Merle a second electric guitar in 1951. It was designed to resemble a hollow archtop, but the top was thick, like a solidbody. It had two pickups, unlike the original solidbody's single pickup. Bigsby made the body from the back and sides of an old Kay archtop, but on Merle's instructions made the top flat, out of thick, solid maple. Bigsby also added one of his own necks with the six-on-a-side headstock. Merle's second Bigsby electric guitar was essentially a solidbody instrument made to resemble a hollowbody. He took delivery at the end of October 1951. He played it some, including in several Snader "Telescription" films. Unlike the original solidbody, there seem to have been no articles or publicity to announce this new guitar. Merle never took any promotional photos with it. And within eight months of its arrival, it was gone. Merle returned the second Bigsby to Paul Bigsby. Bigsby then sold it to a friend, Jack Parsons. Parsons had his name inlaid on the body and kept it until the 1990s, when he sold it to Bob November, owner of McKenzie River Music in Eugene, Oregon. It was only through detective work and research underway for a book about Bigsby's instruments that Merle's second Bigsby was researched and fully identified as the same guitar with Jack Parsons's name on it. There is still no written record to indicate why Merle got rid of it so quickly and began playing a new instrument, a customized Gibson Super 400 archtop electric guitar.

For years, the historic 1948 Bigsby solidbody was on display at Merle's home. Sometimes it hung on the wall. Other times it leaned in a corner. No one in Merle's immediate surroundings had any idea of the instrument's real significance. Michael Robinson remembered his experience with it: "I snuck that Bigsby guitar out of the house many times when I was a teenager. I had a band with some guys and used to bring that guitar to try and play Beatles songs on it. It's a miracle that thing made it through the crisis point."[230] And he wasn't the only one who manhandled the historic instrument over the years, as Joe Maphis's son Jody recalled: "I found that Bigsby guitar. Merle put it in the closet, and I just dragged it around, didn't have a case or nothing.... It got dragged around by me in diapers. It had no case, no sheet, no nothing around it. You open the closet door, there's a pile of *National Geographics* and that guitar."[231]

For years, the subject of Fender guitars was a sore spot with Merle. Johnny Western relates:

I interviewed Roy Rogers and Dale Evans. He had a backup group that featured Jimmy Bryant on lead guitar, and he had the first Fender that I'd ever seen in my life. I talked to Jimmy Bryant, who was very young at that time, but he was all over that guitar and it was called a Fender Broadcaster. Wasn't a Telecaster; it was a Broadcaster. I said, "I've never seen anything like this in person." He said, "Well, Fender, Leo Fender, a guy in California, is making these." And so I mentioned to Travis, I said, "Trav, I talked to Jimmy Bryant, he had a Fender..." But the minute I said "Fender" he got upset. He said, "Well, hell." He said, "I invented that. Paul Bigsby made that exactly the way I wanted him to in his garage." He said, "I wanted that one-side tuning head, so the next thing I know, Leo Fender establishes Fender guitars and what's he got? The one-sided tuning head. Nobody ever offered me a nickel for what I created and invented in that thing." He was kind of ticked about it, and still ticked about it after that time because this was 1956 and the Roy Rogers thing was like 1950.[232]

Merle and Leo Fender quietly feuded for years, but eventually reconciled at the 1965 Nashville disc jockey convention. Forrest White had a hand in brokering the truce. Merle would continue to disparage Fender solidbody guitars when he saw musicians playing them (in several letters to his wife Bettie in 1966, he refers to seeing other musicians playing "cheap" and "tinny" Fender guitars), but he used Leo Fender's new amplifiers in the 1970s, when Leo launched the Music Man brand. In 1973 Merle brought his first Bigsby to be displayed at the Country Music Hall of Fame and Museum in Nashville, which had only been open for a few years and did not yet have a large collection of original artifacts. It was put on prominent display, and has remained so ever since, through a building change in 2001 and many exhibit changes along the way.

Through the decades of the guitar being on display, the realization of its singular importance in guitar history has grown. It was brought to reality thanks to Merle's fertile mind, cartoonist's eye, and love of motorcycles, combined with Paul "P.A." Bigsby's machinist's ability to give Merle's abstract ideas form. The pair of country-music-loving motorcycle buffs produced the world's first modern electric solidbody guitar—an astounding achievement, one that changed the landscape of the electric guitar world and still reverberates globally today.

In 1979, Merle put his contribution to electric guitar history into context, with his typical self-deprecating humor:

He [Leo Fender] revolutionized the guitar. Naturally, somebody had to design it, even if it was an idiot like me.[233]

In the early 1950s, Merle and Judy Hayden starred on several television programs in Los Angeles, including this one, *Merle Travis and Company.*

CHAPTER 5

FAME AND FORTUNE: MARRIAGES, YOUNG'UNS, AND THE GIBSON SUPER 400

When television hit the scene in Southern California, things changed drastically. Just about all of us Country Entertainers was before their cameras with their little red light shining to let us know who was taking the picture.

The first TV show I did was with Cottonseed Clark. Maureen O'Connor, Tex Williams, and I went with Cottonseed down to a factory-type building on Melrose Avenue. Upstairs they had a little western set fixed up for us. The Musician's Union had warned us that we were not allowed to play an instrument on TV, so we took along one of our records, and as the sound was played back, we'd move our mouth as if we were singing. They'd done that in the movies many years, so there we were doing it on television.

My next bout with television is seldom believed by the young folks of today, but it's very true. We were once on a television show that ran six hours a day and one hour on Sunday. We had Saturday off. It was called the Foreman Phillips Show. Channel seven was located at Prospect and Talmadge in Hollywood. Foreman Phillips, who'd promoted all the dances during World War II, was still at it.

Foreman rounded up a gang of us. It took a lot of people to fill three hours in the morning, from nine to twelve noon. Then after an hour off, we were back to perform from one o'clock until four in the afternoon. Six hours!

There was Johnny Bond, Wesley and Marilyn Tuttle, Jack Tucker, Mary Lou Brunell, Betsy Gay, Crazy George Tracy, Hank Caldwell and his trio, Jimmy [sic] Widener, and a few others who slip my mind just now. Foreman came to me and said, "Do you know of any country acts back east that might be interested in coming out here to do this show?"

I told him I sure did. "I know just the couple you need," I said. "The boy plays any string instrument you hand him. He's a great comedian, and a first class M.C. We were together on WLW in Cincinnati before the war. After that, we worked together for Sunshine Sue at the Old Dominion Barndance in Richmond, Virginia. His name is Joe Maphis." Then I sang all the praises I could about Rose Lee. I truthfully told Foreman that she knew hundreds and hundreds of songs, she could sing any part harmony, she's experienced, a real professional, and the sweetest person you'll ever meet. Foreman sent for Rose Lee and Joe Maphis.

Singing songs on the radio is simple enough. You just write the words, put them on a music stand before you, and read them off. On stage it's easy to sing the favorites that you've memorized. But with TV, we came up against a problem. It's impossible to memorize everything you say or sing, especially if you're on six hours a day, five days a week. We figured out an answer.

Rose Lee and I'd go to a stationery store and buy big books of blank paper about the size of a newspaper. Then we'd load up with black crayon pencils and head for the Foreman Phillips TV show at Prospect and Talmadge. If Jack Tucker wanted to sing a song and didn't have it memorized, Rose Lee or I'd print the words in bold black letters on the paper.

"And now folks," Foreman would say to the TV camera as he rolled a cigarette, "let's go down to the stump and listen to Jack Tucker sing his song." Whoever was not working in that scene would grab the printed lyrics and stand beside the camera, holding it so Jack could read the words and sing the song. On television sets he appeared to be singing off-hand.

"You crazy hillbillies," the TV crews would kid us, "you don't even know your own songs. I thought 'idiot sheets' went out when John Barrymore had to have them to remember his lines in the films he made."

Strange as it may seem, today, with our modern color telecasts, a very special man is behind the scenes. When you hear your favorite TV star singing or talking, chances are the "cue-card man" is right there in front of the star, holding up every word that is muttered. Someone has even invented a "tele-prompter." A newscaster sits looking at the words he says as the printed page rolls just above the lens of the camera.

I believe Jack Rogers is the first country singer to go on television in Los Angeles. They had hardly soldered the last wire to complete their studio when Jack was before the camera singing.

Doye O'Dell's afternoon TV show was so popular he could hardly go to the store without signing autographs. Both Doye and Jack Rogers looked fine on the tiny screens when television was an infant.

Mr. Walter A. "Hank" Richards, who produced, wrote, and directed our Boone County Jamboree in Cincinnati, put together a show with some brilliant country-western talent, but the star was a pretty poor choice. It was me. We televised our show, All American Jubilee, over channel seven. It was a one-hour show, and was on only once a week.

The All American Jubilee cast was as follows: Abigail and Buddy, Joe Maphis and Rose Lee, Homer Escamilla, Dale Warren, Margie Warren (Hank named her "Fiddlin" Kate), Sally Foster, Fred Howard, Jack Rogers, Buddy Ray, Billy Liebert, Dick Stubbs, Judy Hayden, Bob Osgood and his Square Dancers, and me. I'm sure I've left out someone, but I'm writing this from memory, not notes and research.

Back in Cincinnati, Hank Richards had me doing a comic character on stage. I was young and thought it was all a lot of fun. I thought up a name for myself. I was "Possum Gossett." I did the same thing on All American Jubilee, except this time, I tried to do a sissy cowboy, with an oversized white hat and an exaggerated smile. I thought up a funny name for my comic cowboy. Today, a prominent, famous comedian in New York uses the exact same name. I have no idea how we both could have come up with a name like Rodney Dangerfield.

In the early fifties, I fronted a band and did a lot of touring with Tex Ritter. He was the most amazing man I ever knew. He was completely versed on any subject you could think of. His mind was unbelievable. We'd be riding along in just about any state when Tex would say, "Slow down, there's a historical marker up there a half a mile I want you to see." There would be the marker, telling about some little thing about something, or somebody. Tex would know the whole story. He'd tell it in such an interesting way you'd hate for it to come to an end.

Another thing was his amazing way with friends. Once we started on a tour late in the afternoon. We figured we might drive as far as Phoenix, rest a while, and go on. Tex never liked to drive. There was only the two of us and I was driving my car. We crossed the Colorado River and entered the state of Arizona during a gully-washing downpour of rain. I took my time and plowed on through the rainy night as Tex discussed just about everything on earth, and some things that are elsewhere. Suddenly, about one o'clock in the black rainy morning, a right rear tire blew out.

"Now, Tex," I started in, "there's not a bit of use in us both getting wet. You sit here in the car and I'll change the tire as fast as I can."

"You'll do nothin' of the sort!" rumbled the big Texan. "We're here in the middle of nowhere together. We'll change the tire together."

There was no way I could persuade him to stay in out of the pouring rain. I got out and opened the trunk, where guitars, amplifiers, satchels, and whatever else could be edged in was packed. As I'd move one, Tex was there to take it. I griped to high heavens about such luck on such a lousy night.

"May I tell you something?" Tex kept saying. "It's all a part of touring."

Just before I started to tighten the last lug bolt, Tex's feet slipped and he fell flat on his back in the mud. He rolled over, picked up a muddy, very wet Stetson and put it on his head, with his straight hair hanging down each side. Mud was all over his powder-blue suit. You could hardly make out what his boots were. I mentioned that his slip was a bad streak of luck too. "It's all a part of tourin'," said Tex Ritter.

Up the highway thirty minutes away we came to sight of the lights of an all-night restaurant near Salome, Arizona. "There it is!" roared Tex. "There's where you'll meet some of the dearest friends I have in this world. Pull in, Piss-ant, and let's have a cup of coffee with my friends."

I appreciated him calling me Piss-ant. That's what he called just about everybody he liked that were men, and not in earshot of a lady, but I held back. "Good Lord, Tex," I whined, "you'r a mess! "You'r hat's ruined, you'r suit's all caked with mud, and it'll take a week to get you'r boots clean. Let me go in and get you a cup of coffee. They won't know me."

"They will in a little while," Tex assured me. "I'm gonna introduce you to some fine people. Friends of mine from 'way back. Pull right on in there."

I'd heard that before. Tex knew everybody. He loved everybody and they loved him. They were his "dear friends." What could I do? I pulled up and parked by the café.

Tex never combed his hair, it still hung down in front of his ears. His appearance was a disaster! But he walked in the brightly lit room.

"My God, it's Tex Ritter!" shouted one of the waitresses as she ran to his open arms.

"Hello, Mamasita!" Tex said to the waitress, calling her "Little mama" in Spanish, which he did very often. What's more, he called her by name and asked about her husband and children.

"Well, I'm a son-of-a-gun!" yelped a man behind the counter who appeared to be a fry cook. "It's ol' Tex, shore as th' world. How y'doin', Tex?"

Out came the owner, a flunky of some sort, and two or three truck drivers that were there getting coffee. I was introduced all around.

We had a hot sandwich and Tex had coffee. I had milk. You'd have thought a long-lost uncle had dropped down in a parachute or something, the way they greeted and visited with my mud-caked friend with the hat completely out of shape and hanging down all around.

After a while, we were back in the car rolling along an endless desert road in the night. Suddenly it came to me that no one mentioned the mud on Tex, or seemed to even see that he had mud on him. I decided to ask Tex about this strange sequence.

"Tex," I eased to him, "about the people back there where we stopped…"

"Ol' Tex didn't lie to you, did he Piss-ant?" he said, using his own name, as he often did. "They're fine people, aren't they?"

"They sure are, Tex. They sure are," I said and drove on toward Phoenix.

Once my little band and I played for a dance at a place Bob Wills had fixed up. It was said to be the biggest dance hall in the Southwest, and I believe it. It seemed to go on for a mile. The posts to hold the ceiling up were made to look like big green cactus. There were thousands of silver dollars inlaid in the bar, and if I wasn't so afraid of high places, I might have tried a parachute jump from the bandstand to the hardwood floor. They called it the Bob Wills Ranch House. It was in Dallas, Texas.

The night I played there, we'd let them dance a reasonable length of time, then I'd make with the tired old line, "And now, friends, here's the man you've all come to see! Gather around the bandstand and let's all make welcome America's Most Beloved Cowboy, TEX RITTER!"

We were booked there for two nights. The first night, which was a Friday, there was enough people there to fill four normal-sized dance halls. Ritter, as usual, was fantastic. He went through his general routine of joking with the audience, and they loved it.

"Why don't you shut up, Catfish, and let Ol' Tex do the talkin?" he'd bawl, pointing his finger at some gent in the crowd who was hollerin' up to him. "I hope you know why I call you 'Catfish.' You've got a big mouth and very little brains!"

"I'm proud to be here in Dallas, m' friends," he'd say. "I believe Dallas has the prettiest girls in the world!" (Folks would applaud vigorously.)

"But Dallas has the poorest crop of ol' boys I've ever seen in my life!" (Folks would laugh at themselves.)

After the first night the man in charge of the hall came backstage, and I was a little scared. John Hitt, who'd booked us in there, had told Tex, "Whatever you do, don't cross the man that runs that place. He's dangerous. He's a mean little 'hood' from Chicago. He carries a pistol under his coat and would just as soon shoot you as to look at you."

Now… here was Tex Ritter talking with him.

"I don't know what happened, Tex," the little man said, sounding like a movie gangster, "but the crowd was pretty bad. There weren't more than a thousand people here."

"Now, you just back up a little, m' friend, " Tex blasted at him. "I've been estimatin' crowds from th' stage for many years. If your count's that far off, you're either lying or you're bad in need of a pair of glasses."

After giving Tex a steely glance, he followed up with a cold shoulder. The little manager in the dark suit turned and walked away.

That night in the Adolphus Hotel where we were staying, Tex came over to the room where Gene Crownover (steel guitar man for Bob Wills for years after then) and I were staying. He walked the floor, he fretted and fumed. Gene and I tried to console him, but it didn't work. Tex Ritter was not a foolish man. Therefore he didn't like to be treated like a fool.

"It's not the money, boys," he'd say to Gene and me, "it's the principle of the thing. I just can't imagine what he's trying to prove."

Our next night was a dandy. From on stage, you could look out and see acres and acres of human beings, milling around, visiting and dancing to our music. Tex outdid himself. He joked with the crowd, threw good-humored insults to conspicuous customers, and finished with his great rendition of "Rye Whiskey." After the playing and singing and visiting was over, we met backstage. Enters the little manager to pay Tex Ritter a certain percent of all the tickets that were sold.

"It's the same old story, Tex," the manager said. "The crowd was far less than I expected. There were only about fifteen hundred people here tonight."

"YOU'RE A LIAR!" Tex loudly informed the short dark-suited man. "Don't come to me with such bull! There was at least four thousand people here! I've seen your kind before… and it makes me sick. If you wasn't such a runty, helpless looking little sonofabitch, I'd break your jaw!"

There stood Tex Ritter with his booming voice and flashing little blue eyes talking to a dangerous ex-gangster who had a real loaded pistol under his coat. This time he wasn't emoting before a movie camera. And he wasn't telling Charlie King that he was caught red-handed. This was for real! I thought of John Hitt's warning, "He'd just as soon kill you as to look at you," when I saw the little man's hand go beneath his dark coat.

Out came his pale hand. In it was a huge roll of money. He threw it on the table, looked at Tex Ritter, whose gaze didn't falter at all. "There's all the money we took in, Tex," he whimpered. "On my dead mother's grave, I'd swear to it."

Years later the little man was to do a deed that will "go down in infamy," to quote President Franklin D. Roosevelt. Millions of Americans saw him shoot Lee Harvey Oswald as the television cameras rolled. His name: Jack Ruby.

Someday someone will write a book about the old Town Hall Party show. We broadcast from a barn-like building in Compton, California. It went on for a good many years. Here's some of the cast: Tex Ritter, Jimmy Pruett, Freddie Hart, Mary Lou Brunell, Billy Hill, Texas Tiny, Fiddlin' Kate, Wesley and Marilyn Tuttle, Abigail and Buddy, the Collins Kids, Quincy Snodgrass, Skeets McDonald, Bobby Charles, Bob Luman,

Johnny Bond, Carrot Top Anderson, Tex Carmen, Mary Jane Johnson, Marion Hall, Jay Stuart, and me.

It seems that most everybody in Los Angeles county turned on Town Hall Party each Saturday night, and just let the TV play away with country music while they went about their card playing, cocktail drinking, or what have you.

When I got a tiny little part in an award-winning picture, "From Here to Eternity," I was floored when Deborah Kerr seemed happy to meet me. She turned the tables when she burst out with, "Oh, I'm a big fan of yours. I watch you every Saturday night on Town Hall Party!"

What on earth is a beautiful English girl, who happens to be a movie star, living in Beverly Hills, doing watching Town Hall Party? I supposed the biggest TV sets will pick up the smallest shows.

I could go on and on forever, I guess, about the times after I got to Hollywood until the middle fifties. They were the good old days, alright. But then, so is today. Once I wrote a silly little song that nobody would ever record. It said what I'm trying to say, more or less, but in the language of a romance between a boy and girl:

> *"Baby, let's you and me*
> *build a few sweet memories*
> *and these will be tomorrow's*
> *Good ol' Days."*

. . .

Merle spends a lot of time in the text above talking about his early television days and touring on the road, but the years 1948 to 1955 were also full of many other significant events in his life and career. Merle would marry his third wife, June "Judy" Hayden, and the couple would have two daughters, Merlene and Cindy. When that marriage ended, he met and married his fourth wife, Bettie, who had two sons, Dennis and Michael, from a previous marriage (Merle and Bettie would stay married, off and on, for more than twenty years). Merle would find his recording career stalled, but took up the slack with work in the new medium of television. He would tour with Western movie stars Tex Ritter and Gene Autry and begin a long friendship and working partnership with another Capitol Records artist, Hank Thompson. As discussed in the last chapter, he would have another Bigsby guitar custom made, only to reject it a short time later for a highly personalized Gibson Super 400 archtop electric. He would field test the prototype of Paul Bigsby's new vibrato invention, which would become a universal standard guitar accessory, used to this day. He obtained a state-of-the-art custom-made

Standel amplifier, the finest built at the time. He also began slowly working on instrumental tunes for what would be his first instrumental album, *The Merle Travis Guitar.*

As 1948 rolled around, Merle's career was riding high. His releases on Capitol had all been successful, charting well and garnering tons of jukebox plays. He toured the country with his band. He made the cover of *Billboard* magazine, invented a revolutionary new solidbody guitar, and was respected in the country music community as an entertainer, songwriter, and virtuoso guitarist. Unfortunately, whenever success entered Merle's life, he seemed unable to deal with the accompanying pressures and responsibilities. Probably because of his own insecurities and fears, his drinking got worse, and his problems got bigger. Although the parlance of the times referred to his condition as "nerves" and his condition was never formally diagnosed, he probably suffered from manic depression, now commonly called bipolar disorder. Unfortunately, in those days, mental health treatment was misunderstood and looked down upon as a sign of weakness. And without proper treatment, Merle turned to the bottle and prescription drugs, with dire consequences.

Fiddler Harold Hensley (Merle's roommate in the late 1940s) remembered an incident en route to Spade Cooley's popular *Hoffman Hayride* television show, broadcast on KTLA-TV from the Santa Monica Ballroom: "I got him in the car, got all his instruments, got all his clothes, started over Sepulveda Pass. He says 'Turn around, we're goin' back, I'm not gonna do it.' I said, 'Merle, the show must go on, you know. That's the old axiom in show business. You gotta do the show.' And he said 'No, I'm not gonna do it.' Nothing I could do or say would convince him to do it. He didn't show up. It would have been a good shot for him." According to Hensley, Merle had insecurities about performing for a live audience: "He had a fetish and it was the strangest thing. We'd be doing Cliffie's show and have a live audience there, and we'd get out of the show, and he'd say, 'Those beady eyes, those people with those little beady eyes, watchin' me all the time. It makes my flesh crawl.' And I thought, 'My lord, you're gonna have people watchin' you all your life if you're gonna be a performer!' That's part of the game, and I'd tell him that. But it bothered him in some ways. He was a fine performer, but boy, he went through the throes doin' it."[234]

Hank Penny remembered Merle's constant self-deprecation: "The one thing that fascinated me about Travis was his lack of confidence in Travis. I never heard him make a positive statement about himself. I've heard him say marvelous things about other people. I used to tell him, 'Merle, don't down yourself.' He'd say, 'Oh heck, I can't even play. Aw shucks, that's terrible. Oh lord, what a li'l ol' ticky guitar player I am.'"[235]

Joe Maphis remembered a similar attitude throughout the time that they worked together:

> Merle had a problem of not thinking he was as good as he was, a com-
> plex. He'd say "Aw, them people don't like what I do." Merle had so
> much talent and yet he didn't think he did. Merle knew he had a style
> that was his own, wherever it come from. He took that style and made it
> into something, but yet I don't think he ever had faith in the style. He'd
> say "Aw, this old thumbpick thing I do, that ain't nothin'." Or he'd see
> somebody like Roy Lanham and he'd say "Oh, well, this stuff I do ain't
> nothin'." But yet all the time it was just settin' the world on fire.[236]

Merle's behavior and mindset followed the classic downward trajectory of
alcoholism. Wesley Tuttle recalled: "When he drank, he was just out of control....
Old Travis, everybody [felt] he could do no wrong, and if he did do wrong? Well,
that's just poor old Travis, we'll overlook it. Anybody else, they'd get fired and be
ostracized."[237] Merle fell into a trap common to many "troubled geniuses." His
skills were so great that when he was able to play guitar, sing, entertain, or write
a song, it was at a genius level of ability. He excelled at what he did, and people
marveled at what he was able to achieve. And when Merle was drunk and unable
to perform, because of his abilities and his likability when sober, he was generally
given a pass. Excuses were made, the bad behavior covered up. Most of the time
Merle showed up, got along with everybody, and did a great job. When he didn't,
people just assumed he'd be back next week to do something great again. As a
result, his alcoholism continued, untreated and ignored.

The Petrillo ban of 1948 discussed in an earlier chapter kept Merle out of the
studio save for one (possibly secret) session in March, when he recorded a cover
of T. Texas Tyler's "Deck of Cards." The "song" was just a recitation with no
musical accompaniment, which apparently allowed a bypass of the recording ban,
but it wasn't released until the Bear Family box set was issued in the 1990s. Capitol
released songs from the November and December sessions the previous year, but
none were as successful as the ones that came out in 1946 and 1947. Merle's luster
as a hit maker was slowly beginning to fade. *Jamboree* magazine summed it up in
plain words in a monthly article about their "Top Ten" artists. Merle came in
at number six: "Yep—we were a little surprised to see this old 'Geetar-plucker'
from Kain-tuck invade the top ten. Couldn't be his current Disc releases. They're
mighty good—but not 'Red-hot.'"[238]

Merle and cornet player Ginny Cushman continued a working and romantic
relationship, but it wouldn't last much longer. Merle's memory:

"Ginnie and I are Mexican married one day"

Official records no longer exist to tell us when Merle and Ginny Cushman were "Mexican married" for a day. Cushman accompanied Merle on another cross-country tour in February 1948. Ads run in small-town newspapers advertised "Virginia Cushman, hill-billie trumpet player" as well as "Tex Atchison, left handed fiddler." In the days before television, such novelty ticket items would draw a crowd. Cushman was originally from Santa Barbara, and a few photos survive showing her and Merle having fun on weekend trips to see her parents. On at least one of them, Merle brought his brand-new Bigsby electric solidbody guitar. The couple beam at the camera, holding their respective instruments, posing like lovebirds. But it was a temporary state of bliss. Cushman later noted: "After spending two years with Merle, and knowing Judy Hayden when I was with Merle and she was married, or had been, to Eddie Kirk at that time, well anyway she was married, and then later married to Merle—I didn't want to get involved." And regarding Merle and his daughter Patty's sometimes-strained relationship, she wrote about feeling unsafe when Merle was drinking: "If their relationship [Merle and Patty] was sometimes difficult, that is why I left in a hurry back to Santa Barbara, while the 'gettin' was safe."[239] We can infer that there was some kind of incident that ended their relationship, probably involving Merle and alcohol.

Cushman's return to Santa Barbara in the fall of 1948 effectively ended her career as a professional musician. She married restaurateur Harry Davis in the early 1950s, and the couple had two daughters, Lynne and Lorelei. Davis was a jealous husband and destroyed most of the photos of Ginny and Merle together. Like Merle, Ginny had her own problems with alcoholism, and she would struggle the rest of her life with her addiction. When she passed away in 2002, her daughter Lynne placed a carton of Salem 100's cigarettes and a bottle of vodka in her coffin—a fitting send-off to one of country music's forgotten female trailblazers.

Cushman's breakup with Merle marked the effective departure, for the time being, of the muted trumpet on his records. There would be only one more Capitol session, in 1950, which attempted to revive the muted trumpet sound with a different session musician. The trumpet (and the accordion) had given Merle a unique, trademark sound on some of his first releases for Capitol, but by 1949, the sound had run its course as Western swing gave way on the charts to the harder edge of honky-tonk country.

Capitol tried marketing Merle as a guitar soloist in mid-1949 with a commercial release of three songs that had been recorded several years earlier for the Capitol Transcription service. All three were performed on acoustic guitar, but were masterful, commanding performances: "Blue Smoke," "Fuller Blues," and "Walking the Strings." These were the first commercial Capitol releases of Merle

Travis guitar instrumentals. It would not be the last time that Capitol dug into its vaults to release material from the mid-1940s Capitol transcriptions.

Several of Merle's recordings in 1949 were blues oriented. This may have been a throwback to the folk recordings, or they may have been done as a whim at Merle's direction. The first such was a recut of the bluesy "That's All" that he had previously recorded in 1945 for the Atlas label. There was also an "all-star" group recording of "Blues Stay Away from Me," a Delmore Brothers classic, featuring group singing by Merle, Eddie Kirk, and Tennessee Ernie Ford.

Recall that after Merle had Paul Bigsby make his historic electric solidbody guitar in the summer of 1948, he asked Bigsby to put a new neck on his Martin D-28 acoustic and a twelve-string neck on an old Gibson L-4 archtop guitar (Bigsby had stripped the L-4's fretboard to use on the famous 1948 Bigsby solidbody guitar, so it may have been a "junker" that either Merle or Bigsby owned). At first, Bigsby made a twelve-string neck with a typical six-on-a-side headstock. This first version of Merle's twelve-string only lasted long enough for a couple of photos to be taken. Bigsby then redid the neck with a unique Bigsby headstock configuration with six tuners on each side, for a total of twelve. It is the only known Bigsby twelve-string instrument. Merle used the twelve-string in two different configurations to record two solo blues numbers, "I Got a Mean Old Woman" and "Start Even." The sound was unusual enough that Capitol noted on the record's label, "Vocal with Twelve-String Guitar" for "I Got a Mean Old Woman," and "Vocal with Eight-String Guitar" for "Start Even." There is no record of Merle owning an eight-string guitar, and tonally it sounds identical to the flip side of the record, so the best guess is that it was the Bigsby twelve-string with four strings removed. Although the record was not a commercial success, it was another innovative moment: the first time a country artist recorded with a twelve-string guitar. Merle wouldn't own the guitar long; in the early 1950s he gifted it to his friend Hank Thompson, who kept the prized Bigsby twelve-string for the rest of his life.

When Merle began making money, he invested in some stage costumes. In the mid-1940s, Hollywood hillbillies had their clothing made by a tailor named Nathan Turk, who made several of Merle's early outfits. Turk's outfits were classy, sedate, and finely crafted, with muted Western flair. The whole concept of "hillbilly flash" went to another level, however, when a Ukrainian-born Jewish immigrant named Nuta Kotlyarenko—who Americanized his name to Nudie Cohn—opened his Nudie's Rodeo Tailors shop in North Hollywood in the late 1940s. Nudie had been making clothes since the 1910s, when he first immigrated to Brooklyn. During stints in Minnesota and Los Angeles through the 1930s, Nudie and his wife, Bobbie, made elaborate stage costumes for burlesque dancers and strippers. When Western music became the most popular genre in Southern California in the mid-1940s, Nudie took notice—not only of the great character imagery and style that the Western stars exuded, but also that these Western stars were flush with cash. Nudie had been a fan of cowboy actor Tom Mix since his days in Kiev (today Kyiv), and his original ideas flowed like a fountain that could not be turned off.

After making his first set of Western stage outfits for Tex Williams and his band, the Western Caravan, Nudie began soliciting business from other Los Angeles entertainers. His suits featured fine chain-stitch embroidery designs that were limited only to the customer's imagination, plus something Nathan Turk did not offer, namely the bling of over-the-top decorative top-stitching and, later, rhinestones. Nudie became as much a part of Southern California hillbilly culture as the entertainers themselves. He played a Bigsby-customized mandolin at jam sessions. Nudie also attended country music shows, and people knew that he loved country music. Nudie's customized cars—Nudiemobiles, of which there were many over the years—were rolling billboards, Cadillacs and Pontiacs adorned with silver-plated horses, guns, and silver dollars, bull's horns on the front bumper, and hand-tooled leather interiors, complete with a saddle seat for kids.

From the 1940s through the 1980s Merle commissioned many Nudie suits with guitars, records, and wildlife embroidered on them. The two began a great friendship, on both a professional and a personal basis, that would last the rest of their lives. Merle may have been from Kentucky and Nudie may have been from Ukraine, but they shared a similar sense of humor and hillbilly style. Today many Nudie suits are important, revered objects in museums and special exhibits across the country, and these include several of Merle's. Merle's memories:

> **"Nudie says to the nurse 'It's a pain in the ass'"**
> **"Nudie says of English Girl 'Look like a good P.O.A.'"**
> **"Nudie say of Bamby's wife "The lady wants to T.A.P.'"**

Merle worked as a session man with many artists in his early years with Capitol, including Tex Ritter, Shug Fisher, Wesley Tuttle, Red Murrell, and Cliffie Stone. In 1949 he played guitar on Tennessee Ernie Ford's first recording sessions. Ford signed with Capitol in early 1949 and started his recording career with a series of successful country boogie records. His first two Capitol releases, "I've Got the Milk 'Em in the Mornin' Blues" and "Country Junction," were fine efforts, but the country boogie formula really took off after his third release, "Smokey Mountain Boogie." Its success was in no small part thanks to Merle and Speedy West, who played hot and exciting lead parts. Merle in particular played a de-tuned, overdriven guitar that stands out for its mixture of country and blues. It bears no connection with the Muhlenberg thumbpicking style, but instead is a wild, free-association blues-based solo that he plucked out of thin air. Though rock 'n' roll would not spring forth for another five or six years, Merle's electric guitar solo on "Smokey Mountain Boogie" is pure proto–rock 'n' roll.

Merle played on several more Tennessee Ernie Ford records in 1949 and early 1950, including "Anticipation Blues," "Mule Train" (where he not only played guitar, but also provided the whip sound effects through pursed lips), and "Tailor Made Woman." Around this time, Cliffie Stone hired Jimmy Bryant, a hot up-and-coming lead guitar player who paired with Speedy West in the *Hometown Jamboree* show band. Bryant and West immediately clicked, and became a legendary instrumental combination. After Bryant joined Stone's band, Bryant and West were the lead soloists on Tennessee Ernie Ford's recordings over the next few years, though Ernie and Merle continued to work together on television, radio, and personal appearances.

In 1949, Merle was asked by the Encyclopedia Britannica Company to narrate, sing, and play guitar in a film the company was producing, *Ballad of the West*, a fourteen-minute short meant for "junior and senior high school classes in American literature, social studies, and music appreciation," according to the company's publicity.[240] Letters that Merle kept show a back-and-forth conversation with producer Frank Cellier between May and December of 1949 in anticipation of his flight to the company's headquarters in Wilmette, Illinois, to record his segments in a weeklong marathon. *Ballad of the West* was released in 1950, and although impossible to find today in any form, it was indeed used for years in classrooms across the country. In doing the film, Merle showed that he could work professionally with the film industry, and create and record music on demand.

Meanwhile, as he continued to perform with Cliffie Stone's band both at live performances and on the *Dinner Bell Round Up* radio show, a relationship began to blossom between Merle and Judy Hayden, wife of Capitol Records singer and rhythm guitarist Eddie Kirk. Merle's memory:

"Judy Kuk [Kirk] takes me home with her"

Hayden had been born Beatrice June Hayden on June 10, 1925. She spent her younger years in Kirkwood, Missouri, then through a series of family hardships moved to Las Vegas when her father got a job working for the railroad at the newly completed Hoover Dam. She moved to East Los Angeles in the 1930s to live with her mother, sisters, and brother, who by that time were all in Southern California. Her daughter with Merle, Merlene Travis-Maggini, told this author:

According to her siblings, she was always a singer. She always sang, and she was real outgoing and a tomboy, kind of a tough little girl. And in high school I think she sang, and then she got married very young. His name was Ollie, I want to say Ollie Lipnisky. And the way it was told to me, it was World War II and everybody was going off to war, and she was I think fifteen or sixteen, and her story was Ollie really loved her, but she loved Ollie's best friend, but Ollie said, before he was shipping out, "Will you marry me?" Because that's what you did. You married somebody, and they went off overseas.

So then Ollie went off to war, and money was tough. She moved up to Oregon and lived [with Ollie's family] for three years. It's almost like the lost years. When Ollie came back from the war three years later, she said—this was what she told me—"I don't know you, I don't love you, and I wanna be a singer." She went back to Hollywood to pursue her singing career.

And then she was the elevator operator for CBS. They didn't have Muzak in elevators in those days. So she would hum in between floors, taking people to their floors, you know, when elevator operators had a job. This woman got out of the elevator and said, "I'm Mary Astor [an actress known for both her appearance in *The Maltese Falcon* and the 1930s "purple diary" scandal, the first big sex scandal in Hollywood], and I'm running a singing contest right now, and you have a beautiful voice so I suggest you go over to Wallichs Music City, come down and submit it." And she did. She cut "As Time Goes By," and she won a recording contract for CBS.

She did radio shows. She was on a radio show called *Sunrise Salute*. She always said that she was a "legit" singer before she sang hillbilly music. And she had a beautiful voice. I've got cassette tapes of her radio shows, and they're with full orchestras. They'd go, "Here's little Junie Hayden," and she'd come out and go, "Hello!" in this little Shirley Temple voice, and then sing these amazing songs.

[Cindy Travis interjects: "And it's so high, she sang that high."]

Incredible! Yes, just a beautiful, beautiful voice. Judy was her country name.[241]

A brief blurb in the December 1948 issue of *Jamboree* magazine summarizes how June Hayden the "legit" singer transformed into Judy Hayden the hillbilly singer: "While filling in on the CBS *Hollywood Barn Dance*—Judy became an overnight sensation—which led to her being signed by CBS, and as Cliffie Stone's leading girl vocalist."[242] When Hayden joined Stone's radio cast, she met two men who would play big roles in the next few years of her life: Eddie Kirk and Merle Travis. The three would work closely for many years to come. Kirk and Hayden became romantically involved, and were married on April 23, 1947. Details of their relationship remain cloudy because Hayden never revealed to her two daughters that she had been briefly, previously married to Kirk. Jack Rogers recalled a bit of the dynamic between Kirk and Hayden that may have led to their breakup: "I said to Eddie, 'What about Judy?' He said, 'She does her thing, I do mine. That's the end of that.' Eddie didn't care one way or another with Judy, so everybody just played with each other. I said, 'Don't you feel strange about it, Eddie?' He said, 'She does her thing. If she wants to do that, that's her business.' I felt sorry for Eddie."[243]

Hayden appeared on the *Dinner Bell Round Up* show and various live performances with Cliffie Stone's band. She also sang lead on some of Stone's Capitol records, including "He's a Real Gone Oakie." Merle was in close proximity the whole time. And at some point, their flirtation turned into something more serious, and Kirk and Hayden divorced. Merlene surmises: "They must have fallen in love and couldn't be without each other. And probably she wasn't divorced from Eddie yet because it used to take a long time. Not like today, you can get it done in a few weeks. You had to file, you had to wait six months, then you had to have the finalization, then you had to wait a year."[244] Despite the awkwardness of the situation, Merle and Kirk remained friends and continued to play side by side for years to come. There is no record of how Kirk felt about what transpired. He moved to the San Jose area in the mid-1950s, and had his own battles with alcoholism. He died in 1997. Merle's memories:

"I marry June Hayden—she won't live on Victory"
"She finally does, and Merlene is born"
"Judy Kuk [Kirk] tells mother 'It's a trial marriage'"
"I leave when being asked about Judy, my wife"

Merle and Judy were married in Tijuana on December 17, 1948. As with Tex Ann Nation and Ginny Cushman, the prospect of a "Mexican marriage" must have seemed appealing, especially since Judy's divorce from Kirk was probably not yet final. Her name is listed as Anne Hayden on the Mexican paperwork, though it is not known if she intentionally gave them the wrong name or if there was a language barrier while dictating their names to the Mexican justice of the peace. The magazine *Record Roundup* announced that "Merle and Judy eloped a week before Christmas."[245] Merlene Travis-Maggini noted: "I asked her once, 'What was your wedding anniversary with Dad?' and she said, 'It's not important, why do you need to know that?' She never said they had a Mexican marriage, you know? She never really said anything, and you don't ask. There's things you don't ask your parents."[246]

By spring 1949, Judy was pregnant, and Merle's second daughter, Merlene Travis, was born October 8, 1949, at Hollywood Presbyterian Hospital, the same hospital where Merle's out-of-wedlock son Thom Bresh was delivered the year before. Merlene recalled:

> I think they hoped for a boy because dad already had a girl. I always asked her. I knew my name was after my dad. He's Merle Robert, I'm Merlene Roberta, so I said to Dad one time, "I think you really wanted a boy, and that's okay. I understand it." Dad wanted a son. He said, "That's not true." He said, "I love you." He said, "I love a gal young'un." I said, "But you didn't have a name picked out for me." He said, "What do you mean?" I said, "You always said, if I was a boy, I'd be John Henry." I was a girl, and he didn't expect that, so he had to come up with something quick. He said, "Honey, that's not true." He said, "We had a name picked out for you," but the reason I got my name is he bought a doll for Patty when he was on the road and she named it Merlene, and so my mother said to him, "I really like that name, Merlene. Patty made it up for her baby doll. If we have a girl, maybe we ought to name her after you." He said, "Okay." I said, "Yeah, but Dad, last minute, right?" He said, "No, we had a name picked out for you." I asked, "What was it?" He goes, "We was going to call you Annie Lou." I never complained about my name again.[247]

Likely seeking legitimacy for their daughter, Hayden persisted with Merle until they had an official wedding in the United States. The couple wed for the second time on December 15, 1949, at the Superior Court in Fresno, California. Her prompting to have an official US wedding may have also been as a result of a public embarrassment. On December 2, Merle had made the newspapers again for an arrest that must have been humiliating to him and all those close to him. Splashed across the front page of the *Los Angeles Times*, accompanied by a photo showing Merle disheveled, shoeless, and sitting on a chair at the police station, was this headline: "Wife Chased Him Out, Barefoot Singer Wails—Merle Travis, Complaining Spouse Wielded Pistol, Faces Court Trial on Drunk Charge." The article continued with more details of the incident:

> Cowboy singer Merle Travis drawled "Not Guilty," when he appeared
> in the Van Nuys courtroom yesterday to answer a charge of plain drunk.
> Municipal Judge Walter C. Allen released him on $20 bail and set Dec.

15 for a court trial. The Kentucky-born singer was arrested in front of his home, 14927 Victory Blvd, Van Nuys, early yesterday barefoot and clad in pajama tops and dress trousers. He told Officers Pat Murphy and H. E. Cunningham his wife had shot five times in the air with a .38-caliber pistol and she said the next one would be for him.

Travis complained he called for police help seven times before the officers arrived.

Police said they asked Travis if he wanted to go to jail, and the singer mumbled, "Sure," and walked to the police car.

Later, the 32-year old singer sang a different tune. He said he had been taking sedatives for the past three months under doctor's prescription because he was on the verge of a nervous breakdown.

"I don't remember what I told the police," he added.[248]

One oft-told quote from this incident involved Merle asking the police officers "What took you so long?" when they showed up, unaware that the officers were about to arrest him. A follow-up article on December 14, "Cowboy Crooner Changes Mind on Drunk Charge," read:

Merle Travis, cowboy crooner, changed his mind about the drunk charge pending in the Municipal Court in Van Nuys.

He appeared before Municipal Judge John A. Shidler yesterday and asked that the date of trial, based on a plea of not guilty, be moved up to yesterday from the original date, Dec. 15.

His petition was granted and the singer promptly forfeited the $20 bail. He waived a trial. Travis was arrested Dec. 1 clad in pajama tops and dress pants, appeal [sic] for police to help prevent his wife from shooting him.

The following morning, sitting in the Van Nuys jail, Travis said he didn't remember the story.[249]

A few weeks after Merle's arrest, Cliffie Stone changed the name of the *Dinner Bell Round Up* radio program to *Hometown Jamboree* and relocated his dances to the El Monte Legion Stadium, about an hour east of downtown Los Angeles. *Hometown Jamboree* also began broadcasting live on television shortly before Christmas 1949. Stone explained:

I began to feel we needed a group name, like the *Grand Ole Opry* [or] *Renfro Valley* [*Barn Dance*]. We were sitting around, Ernie, Merle Travis, myself and a couple other people tryin' to come up with names. Somebody came up with "Hometown" and then "Jamboree." When I was with Stuart Hamblen, we worked the Texas State Picnic in Long Beach. Any Texan in California could come. There was an Oklahoma picnic and one for Missouri, so I was aware that everybody in California was from some other state. You rarely met a native Californian. I was aware of the importance to people of their hometown. This could only happen in Southern California at this time in history.[250]

Hometown Jamboree gave Merle another platform for great exposure in the new world of television. As evidenced by his enthusiasm in the first part of this chapter, television became a saving grace to his waning career as a maker of hit records. Already comfortable in front of the camera, he adapted easily to the new medium. Wesley Tuttle remembered Merle's prowess at writing songs on command in a television interview with Gene Bear: "When Cliffie Stone first started his *Hometown Jamboree*, Cliffie and I were members of that show at the time.... 'Cliffie,' he says, 'well, we need a theme song. Merle, can you write one?' And he says, 'Yeah.' And he got his pad out and I'm not lying to you—within five minutes he had the theme song written. The same thing happened when we started *Town Hall Party*. Within five minutes, he wrote a theme song right from scratch for our *Town Hall Party*."[251]

The pace of touring, recording, and appearing on Cliffie's radio and television broadcasts may have worsened Merle's nervous condition. And the 1949 arrest and public humiliation, not to mention the pressures of having a new baby daughter, didn't help his marriage to Judy. In April 1950, Merle moved to Washington, DC, to join Grandpa Jones and his wife, Ramona Riggins, at radio station WARL, but he came back in less than a month. He was actively seeking a way out of his current situation in Los Angeles.

Back in California, Merle welcomed one of his old WLW guitar buddies, Roy Lanham, who'd moved out West with a powerhouse group he had been working with in Springfield, Missouri, for a few years. The group was called the Whip-poorwills, and they came to join Smiley Burnette's radio show cast. The group at that time included another of Merle's old girlfriends, Juanita Vastine, who went by the stage name Sweet Georgia Brown. Merle's memories:

"Georgia Brown comes to California with me"
"Georgia Brown squeezes my hand as we sing

It is unknown exactly what their relationship was, but Merle kept in his possession an autographed cheesecake photo of Vastine in a reclining, pinup-style pose, signed "To Merle, with love, 'Nita." Friend and fellow musician Johnny Western would recall:

I was twenty-two years old, and I guess my eyes must have been as big as silver dollars hearing these names of people that Travis had been to bed with and dated, like Sweet Georgia Brown and da-da-la, da-da-la-la. Well, he dated a lot of women. Because early on in his career, in between wives or on top of wives or whatever, he had dated Doris Day when she was still known as Doris Kappelhoff. He dated June Christy, who was a great jazz singer with Stan Kenton's band. He dated people you wouldn't think Merle Travis would even be associated with. He dated some big pop stars. There were women all the time in Travis's life.[252]

Whippoorwills guitarist Roy Lanham remains one of the most underrated musicians of the twentieth century. He could play blistering, jazzy, single-string leads like a hillbilly Django Reinhardt, and complex chord-melody jazz that rivaled George Van Eps or Joe Pass. He and Merle were great friends, with unlimited mutual respect. They also shared a mutual passion: drinking. Merle's memories:

"Roy Lanham feels better after near beer"
"Roy Lanham tells border patrol 'I'm from Corbin'"
"Roy Lanham busts his Irish Whiskey"

Merle and the Whippoorwills began working together in California, and would record frequently over the next five years. The arrangements they came up with were complex, sublime, and groundbreaking—jazzy, uptown Western swing with a pop edge in an era when honky-tonk ruled. One of the numbers recorded in July 1950 was a duet featuring Merle and Hayden, "Too Much Sugar for a Dime." (Eddie Pennington recalls in a conversation with producer-manager Dee Kilpatrick that for promotion of "Too Much Sugar for A Dime," Kilpatrick went to the Old Dominion Sugar Company and had little tiny sacks of sugar made to attach to promotional postcards. The postcards, which also contained a dime taped to it, were sent to radio disc jockeys to promote the new release.) Although Merle and Roy Lanham and the Whippoorwills recorded many excellent records, none were successful commercially.

In August 1950 Merle got an offer to come to Richmond, Virginia, and join the *Old Dominion Barn Dance* cast, which featured many of his old friends from WLW, including Joe Maphis (and his new wife, Rose Lee), Grandpa Jones and Ramona, and Sunshine Sue Workman. He figured a change of pace might be a good thing. Joe Maphis recalled that Merle told him: "'I want to come back to Richmond and just join that show for a while and be with you and Rosie, Grandpa and Ramona and Sue and just kind of cool it for a while.' Merle got tired. He just decided he wanted to get away, get back with old friends and just pick."[253]

Merle accepted the offer and went to Richmond to join the show and do live performances around the area with the cast. The September 2 issue of *Billboard* announced: "Merle Travis has become permanent emcee for the *Old Dominion Barn Dance* on WRVA, Richmond, Virginia."[254] Merle was serious about the move, as he brought his family and switched his musicians' union affiliation from Hollywood to Richmond. Around this time, he wrote a piece of unpublished prose that summed up his feelings about Southern California entitled "Good Morning Hollywood." It is by far the most brutal writing that Merle ever committed to paper. It is too long to include here in its entirety, but it sums up his mental state at the time. A sample quote:

> Yes, I've come to know you, Hollywood. You've learned me so much. I've found you infested with fruit of sweet taste, but of poisonous effect. I've learned that there's men who would destroy my faith in this, our human race. Men of broad smiles, and forked tongues. Men within a shell. By this I mean persons appearing to be a gentleman, who has squired a fear of competition, and with such a complex that he would literally strew the guts of his colleagues along your boulevards and satisfactorily smile triumphantly with a neurotic satisfaction that he'd stepped another step up the slimy ladder of temporary success.[255]

When Merle arrived in Richmond he met Rose Lee Maphis, who had married Joe Maphis in the time since Merle and Joe had first met at WLW in Cincinnati. Rose Lee's talent—she was both an excellent rhythm guitarist and a superb vocalist—impressed him. Unfortunately, the *Old Dominion Barn Dance* job didn't last long thanks to a drunken incident so egregious that Judy Hayden quickly returned to Los Angeles. Judy took baby Merlene with her, and the couple split up for a time. The only surviving documentation is a letter dated September 10, 1950, to Merle in Richmond from a pair of family friends who took in his wife and daughter:

> Dear Merle,
>
> I'm truly sorry that you and June have decided on separate roads but if it means both your happiness then I think it is best. She is here with John and me and be sure we will take the best care of her and Merlene and any time that you are in town please feel at ease in coming to the house to see Merlene.... If you intend to remain in Richmond, it would be rather silly for you to keep the house here especially vacant...
>
> Ever sincerely,
> Dot and John[256]

Merle did not stay in Richmond very long thereafter. Ramona Jones recalled: "He was there a short time. In fact, they lived with us, a few weeks. He was married to June, Judy Hayden then. He didn't stay long. They were having trouble. June left him, June walked out and went back to California. So, therefore, Merle wasn't happy staying around there. He stayed a few days and then left."[257] He wrote a farewell letter to his old WLW friends:

Look Gang,

It's rough to leave you. This is the set-up I work for, but, let's face it, I'm evidently not capable.

There not a one of you that I don't sincerely love. And I will carry with me wheresoever I may go, the memories of the pleasant days we spent here together.

I feel that in honor of Sunshine Sue, John and myself, I may say that I was not asked to leave. You may check with Sue and John and find these quotations true:

"We feel that we have been richer having had you, not only as having you as talent on the show, but as knowing you as a person a little better."

Stick with it, guys and gals, you're the best, and my best to you.

Merle Travis[258]

Back in Los Angeles, Merle patched up his relationship with Judy and went back to work. One of the first things he did was a series of short music films produced and distributed by Snader Telescriptions. These were similar to the Soundies he had made in the mid-1940s, but unlike the Soundies concept of showing the films on video jukeboxes, the Snader company leased their Telescriptions (a trade name that combined the old "transcription" recording with the new concept of televised video) for TV airplay. Produced by namesake Louis D. Snader, a theater owner and businessman, Snader Telescriptions launched Liberace's career and released films by acts like Lionel Hampton, Korla Pandit, Nat "King" Cole, Duke Ellington, Peggy Lee, and many others.

Merle produced ten film shorts for Snader in 1950 and 1951. In November 1950, five were shot with just him and his Martin acoustic guitar with the Bigsby neck, which show him in great form and at the height of his abilities. His playing is superb, and we can see the engaging personality that enabled him to captivate audiences at live performances and on television. Three of the five films show him in casual wear—a plaid wool shirt and denim jeans. "Nine Pound Hammer" was filmed in a bunkhouse set that would also be used for the films of him with a band. "Dark as a Dungeon" was also filmed in the bunkhouse set, but Merle's costume and makeup were changed to resemble a coal miner, with overalls and coal-black makeup on his face and arms. Then, on a set that resembled a rural front porch, while sitting on a rocking chair he sang and played guitar on "Lost John" and "John Henry," demonstrating his "freight train whistle" sound effect. "Mus'rat" shows Merle demonstrating his gimmick of making his guitar "talk," a great Vaudeville-style trick of mind control and musical talent.

The following year, five more film shorts were made, these featuring Merle and a band—called "The Westerners" in the credits—made up of his closest Los Angeles musician friends: Speedy West on steel guitar, Eddie Kirk on rhythm guitar, Jack Rogers on bass, Harold Hensley on fiddle, and Bob Wills/T. Texas Tyler band alumnus Danny Alguire on muted cornet. Merle hadn't featured trumpet or cornet on his recordings for two years, but the Snader films resurrected the sound of his 1940s hits. The songs in this group of films were "Petticoat Fever," "Sweet Temptation," "I'm a Natural Born Gamblin' Man" (which featured Hank Thompson and his then-wife Dorothy as actors playing cards), "Spoonin' Moon," and "Too Much Sugar for a Dime," those last two duets featuring Merle and Judy Hayden. Despite their lack of success at the time, the Snader films survive and provide remarkable evidence of Merle's talent and showmanship both as a solo artist and with a band. Today you can find nearly all of the Snader Telescriptions on YouTube, where they inspire many who type in the name "Merle Travis" for the first time.

Merlene notes: "In 'Too Much Sugar,' they're bantering, and now all I can see when I watch 'Too Much Sugar' is that Mom's mad at him, and I can tell she's *really* mad at him because we know her mad face, especially when she looks at him and she says, 'Would you buy the London Bridge?' Like that? She's pissed. You look at Eddie's face in the background, and you're kinda like 'Oh, poor Eddie.'" Cindy Travis adds: "Mom could be intense. She's staring at you and your skin would start falling off."[259]

Merle had made his name in Los Angeles performing on the radio, but it was obvious to many that television was poised to replace radio as the dominant form of entertainment. By 1951, Merle was consistently looking to television for employment. Foreman Phillips, who'd made a name for himself booking shows all over Los Angeles during the war, saw the medium's potential. He began with a live broadcast from the dances he promoted at Town Hall in Compton. (Sometimes Phillips is credited with starting the *Town Hall Party* television show, but that was a different show from the same location. Phillips's show was *The B-K Ranch Show* or *The Foreman Phillips Show*, and *Town Hall Party* was a separate entity, even though they were both filmed at Town Hall in Compton.) Phillips wanted his own daytime show and hired Merle, Johnny Bond, Wesley and Marilyn Tuttle, Betsy Gay, and several others for his new program. Television was so new at the time that

TV sets were sold at auto repair shops, hardware stores, and music studios. Phillips noted the public interest, and soon was hosting special events at these very places, featuring hillbilly music and prize giveaways. Merle's memories:

"Foreman Phillips has to allow me to drink beer"
"Foreman Phillips ask about eastern talent—Joe and Rose"

The official name of Phillips's new show was *The B-K Ranch Show*, combining his own first initial (his real name was Bert) and that of his wife, Kay. But Phillips was so well known in the Los Angeles area that the newspaper television listings called it what everybody else called it: *The Foreman Phillips Show*. Merle would recall: "In the early 1950s I started to work with Foreman Phillips on a show he called *The B-K Jamboree* [sic]. It ran six hours every day in two three-hour shifts. Phillips was always looking for new talent and I suggested Joe and Rose Lee Maphis, who came out and joined the show. So I was doing the *B-K Ranch* and also Cliffie's *Hometown Jamboree*. It got so I was more on TV than off."[260] As Merle recalls above, he jumped at the chance to bring Joe and Rose Lee Maphis into the Southern California circle of talent. Rose Lee remembered that it was a combination of both Johnny Bond and Merle that got them the gig:

> Johnny Bond had stopped in Richmond, and Joe and I—I think it was the first of the week starting a new week when Johnny would come back to start to get back on the show in California, same show that Merle was on. He [Foreman Phillips] said he would like to have somebody that could play all instruments, and sing, and Merle spoke up and said, "I know just the guy you want, but he'll never leave Richmond. And Johnny Bond was there and he says, "He's available," because he had just stopped in Richmond. We had plans to go to Knoxville—that's where Mother Maybelle and the Carter Sisters went, and that's where we were going to go—but instead we went to California.[261]

When the Maphises arrived in California in the fall of 1951, they lived for several months with Merle and Judy at their house on Victory Boulevard in Van Nuys. Merle drew them a cartoon representing their long trip from the East Coast: the couple is riding in an old jalopy with "Custom Made by P.A. Bigsby" on its front. Instruments are strapped to the top, and stage clothes take up the entirety of the back seat. Rose Lee is depicted holding a folder labeled "Cornie songs." Strapped to the running board is a box labeled "Marijuana Cigarette Co." and inside the box are bottles labeled "Hadacol," "Skimed [sic] Bourbon," and "Just Plain Beer." Pictured in front of the car is the character of Mr. Sheppard, upon whom Merle and Grandpa Jones had based their name the Sheppard Brothers, holding a lantern in one hand and a "Movie Contrack [*sic*]" in the other. The cartoon, saved by Grandpa Jones, shows the warped, sharp sense of humor that Merle and his close friends shared. Grandpa remembered another humorous detail of Merle's cartoon in an interview with researcher Charles K. Wolfe:

> He drew a picture of Joe and Rose Lee a–goin' to California. And I swear, he put everything on there that you could think of. It's just so interesting. For instance, on top of the car... he's got a bass fiddle, up there on top of the car, and he's got a little door on it and a dog a–lookin' out of it. Well, you know, they call them a "Doghouse Bass."[262]

Foreman Phillips's *B-K Ranch Show* lasted a little over a year, from September 1950 until early December 1951. Joe and Rose Lee Maphis had moved out in the fall of 1951 to join the cast, and when the show ended, the couple's future seemed in doubt. But promoter William "Bill" Wagnon stepped in and began a radio broadcast on KFI from the ballroom where Phillips had last operated, the Town Hall in Compton. He gathered a new group of musicians that included Merle and the Maphises and most of the Foreman Phillips TV show cast, and called this show *Town Hall Party*. The first radio broadcast was on December 29, 1951. Rose Lee Maphis told this author: "We left California and came back to Richmond for a Saturday night show during Christmas. When we came back we went to Tijuana and got married. I think it was in February that we did that."[263] When the couple returned to Southern California, in addition to performing on *Town Hall Party*, they joined a new road band that Merle put together, Merle Travis and the Travelers, which also included Dick Stubbs on steel guitar, Margie "Fiddlin' Kate" Warren on fiddle, her husband, Dale Warren, on bass, and Homer Escamilla on drums. Rose Lee Maphis recalled: "That was 1952. We toured. In Texas, we played the bar at [Bob] Wills Ranch House. The guy gave me silver dollars at the bar. It was fun. It was just mainly Texas, Oklahoma, because we would play dance places all summer, just that summer tour."[264]

Merle toured extensively in the first half of 1952 with both his band and as a featured artist with Tex Ritter. In June he appeared on the *Grand Ole Opry*. And despite not having a regular television show during this time, he still found himself on TV regularly as a special guest on various Los Angeles daytime shows.

Merle played on Tex Ritter's Capitol sessions beginning in 1944. Through his film and radio appearances, Ritter had maintained his star status and had a series of moderate hit records. Then in 1952 he had a huge hit with "High Noon," a Capitol disc that Merle played guitar on. This brought increased live performance demands, and Ritter brought Merle along for several years as his right-hand man and guitarist. Merle's memories:

"Tex Ritter helps me fix a tire"
"Tex Ritter tells man to keep his hands off"
"Tex Ritter talks politics with looking glass"

A couple of "Merle's memories" coincide with the stories he writes about in his own words earlier in this chapter; a few of them we can only imagine. This period was a good one for Merle, with few problems. Hank Thompson was just getting to know him at this time, but he remembered it as mostly happy and peaceful: "He was really straight. He didn't pull some of those deals, and get drunk and get thrown in jail, and some of that stuff. He was really on the ball and he had a band, they were workin' a lot, he was quite industrious. It was during that time that he had the band."[265] Merle's memory:

"We move to Alcott [Allott], near Ritter—Cindy is born"

In early 1952 Merle and Judy moved to a residential home at 6303 Allot in Van Nuys. According to Merle's memory, it was because it was near Tex Ritter's home. The move may have also been precipitated by a stalker fan who introduced a bizarre distraction in Merle's life at this moment. According to Merlene: "There was a crazy fan who said that she was my mother, and that my mom and dad weren't married, and that they stole me from her. My dad used to call her 'Old Beady Eyes' because she used to sit in the audience and stare at him. My mom said, 'That's why we have your birth certificate, to prove you're ours.'"[266] Merle's archives contain a curious letter from a woman named Elvira dated February 15, 1953. The old home address used (it was forwarded to Merle's new home), the postmark, and the tone of the letter seem to indicate that Elvira was the infamous "Old Beady Eyes":

> Dear Merle,
>
> I love you. I feel very blue, tho. It's going to be difficult to get any-where to see you. I'm certainly glad I can see your TV show. It didn't do any good to go to the Riverside Rancho, but, at least I saw you once in awhile. No telling when I'll see you again, except on TV.
>
> I don't know how a person, man or woman, turns to someone else when they are lonesome for the one that isn't around. When I get lone-some, it's for you. No one else is going to do....
>
> I love my husband.
>
> Your wife,
>
> Elvira

Merle and Judy welcomed their second daughter, Cindy, on April 26, 1952. She was named after one of Merle's good friends, the songwriter Cindy Walker. Merle and Walker became friends in the mid-1940s, when both of them were living in apartments in Hollywood and working in the close-knit community of Hollywood hillbillies. Merlene and Cindy related to this author:

> [Merlene] We obviously know I'm named for Dad, but Cindy was named for Cindy Walker. Her name is not Cynthia.

> [Cindy] People still insist my name's Cynthia. You know, passports and stuff. "Well, what's your real name?" "Cindy." " Is it Cynthia?" "No."

> [Merlene] I did talk to Cindy Walker quite a few times when I worked at [the music publishing company] Warner Chappell, and I was so excited to talk to her because I felt like it was part of my past. She would tell me stories about Dad. I said, "You know my sister's named for you," and she said, "I do know that." She just really liked to talk about Dad. She said, "Out of all my friends, my mother just loved your father." She said, "You know your dad was kind of a hell raiser," and I said, "I know." She said, "He'd come over, we were going to do something one day, or he'd come over to the house," and she said he was always smiling and always happy but he'd be hung over.

> She said, "My mother would want to go feed him immediately and go make him some food." She said, she'd say, "Well, Merle, come in here and eat something." And he'd sit down at the piano, I can just see him doing it, and he'd just bang out, he'd go, "Oh, I hate myself for the things I do." Then he'd sing that little ditty and go in and eat, but she said, he'd just have a grin on his face and you'd think to yourself, wonder what he just did? He was always up to something, she said.

> [Cindy] They thought I was going to be a boy. I was going to be Travis Travis.

> [Merlene] She was. She was going to be Travis Travis.

> [Cindy] I was going to be Travis Travis, which is completely stupid, or else it was going to be April Dawn because I was born in April at dawn. Which is a stripper name. I'm glad I got to be named Cindy Lee.[267]

Merle's first daughter, Patty, came to stay with the family in the summer of 1952. Other than letters and phone calls and the 1947 trip back to Kentucky, Merle had spent little time with Patty. The relationship with Merle's ex-wife Mary was quite contentious. Stories surfaced later in life that Mary would do things to psychologically torture Merle and deny him a relationship with Patty. But now that she was old enough to fly on her own, Patty began making regular summertime trips to visit Merle and Judy and her two new half-sisters. She recalled:

> Flying to Dad's house in California from Kentucky was the highlight of my summers. In 1952 [actually 1953] Dad was the star of his own television show, the *Merle Travis & Company* TV Show. (My stepmother, June, used to kid that her name must be "And Company.") Imagine how thrilled I was when June read a letter from a fan who described himself. Dad would draw a caricature from the self description on a giant easel. After much persuasion and a few quick lessons in cartoon drawing from Dad, I was convinced to do the drawing. However, under the pressure of hot lights and rolling cameras, I nervously completed the drawing before June had completed reading the letter! Oh well, that's show biz![268]

In summer 1952, Merle ordered a customized Gibson Super 400, the top-of-the-line model in the Gibson catalog. By July, he had received a stock model to use while waiting for his custom guitar to be finished. But the interim Super 400 wasn't entirely stock: it was accessorized with the first production Bigsby vibrato unit. The only commercial vibrato unit made before 1952 was a flimsy bent-metal device called a Kauffman Vibrola. As Merle told in the preceding chapter, he had a Vibrola installed on his Gibson L-10, but it wouldn't stay in tune. The first thing he asked Bigsby to do was to make his Vibrola work better, but even Bigsby couldn't make the fragile unit function properly. In addition, the Kauffman vibrato arm awkwardly worked with a side-by-side motion instead of a more natural up-and-down motion. Chet Atkins and several other prominent players used the Kauffman Vibrola in the late 1940s and early 1950s, and all had the same complaint: no one manufactured a vibrato unit that would stay in tune.

It took four years, but eventually Bigsby invented his own sturdy, cast-aluminum vibrato. As Merle remembered in 1979:

> I had the first one ever built, but now a good friend of mine in Los Angeles, Thom Bresh, has it.... He [Bigsby] said, "I could build one that would never pull the strings out of tune." I said, "You can't do it." He said, "By George, I'll show you." Well, in about a week he came up with the one Thom Bresh has now. And it does not pull the strings out of tune. He said he sets the strings on a needle valve in there. They sit on the thing the size of a needle inside there. This one on my Super 400

is probably one of the last ones ever built. He only built three of these with the long handles—two for me and one for Hank Thompson. This one was all dolled up (there's some fancy engraving on it) by a gunsmith, Dick Allen.[269]

For a few years Bigsby made his vibratos on a very small scale, as a custom order accessory. Then when Gretsch and Gibson began offering Bigsby vibratos as an accessory option, the business took off and Bigsby quit making guitars and went full-time into making vibratos. It became his bread and butter, and he manufactured the vibrato unit until he retired in 1965. It became world famous and is still made today—the name "Bigsby" is more or less synonymous with the device. And the very first Bigsby vibrato was made for Merle Travis.

Photos taken by fan Henry Van Wormer at the Riverside Rancho club in July and August 1952 show Merle with his Super 400 and the first Bigsby vibrato, which sported a fixed handle that extended directly underneath the bridge pickup. Merle quickly decided that he wanted a longer, looped handle like the one he had used with his Kauffman Vibrola on his L-10. Bigsby obliged, and made Merle a long vibrato arm with a loop at the end of it, which Merle would use to great effect, playing chimes and harmonics up the neck with the little finger on his right hand looped around the end of the vibrato handle. It resembled sound effects made by an organ or a celeste. Originally, Paul Bigsby only made three of the long arms, but eventually it was put into limited production as a special accessory. Today, one can still order the long looped handle, referred to as the "Merle Travis arm" in the company literature, from the Bigsby company.

By late 1952, Merle's custom Gibson Super 400 had arrived. The new instrument had "MERLE TRAVIS" inlaid on the fingerboard, a fancy headstock cap inlaid with "THE GIBSON SPECIAL SUPER 400," a custom-made armrest, and a special neck built to Merle's specifications—slightly narrower at the nut (1 5/8 inch) and contoured to facilitate the left thumb wrapping over the top of the neck. An article from 1952 spoke of its lofty price tag:

"Most Expensive" Produced by Gibson for Merle Travis

The most expensive guitar ever produced by Gibson, Inc. was built this summer for Capitol record star, Merle Travis. The guitar, a cutaway Super 400 in a sunburst finish, is valued at $1070.

Special detailing, which followed Travis' specifications, includes an elaborately designed fingerboard, head veneer and an inlaid bridge and saddle. The neck, rim and back are curly maple and Travis' name is inlaid in pearl script on the fingerboard.

The order for the guitar was submitted by Fife and Nichols of Los Angeles last May. When delivery was made to them in October, Gibson workmen declared the instrument to be the finest ever produced in Kalamazoo.[270]

The article states that Merle's guitar was the most expensive ever produced *by Gibson*, but in fact it was the most expensive guitar *ever made* up to that point in time—of any type, for any artist. No other even came close. Jimmie Rodgers's widow used to promote Rodgers's custom Martin guitar at exhibits in the 1950s, proclaiming it "Jimmie's $1500 guitar," but Rodgers only paid $168.75 for the instrument in 1928, and the $1,500 figure was merely a guess at what it might be worth. Merle's $1,070 guitar in 1952 was the equivalent of a new car, or a down payment on a nice house. Equipped with its new Bigsby vibrato arm, it was the finest electric guitar money could buy in 1952.

A year later, it would be supplemented by an equally revolutionary amplifier. The Gibson EH-185 Merle had been using since the Drifting Pioneers days in Cincinnati was still a great amp, but traveling had taken a toll on its appearance; it looked dated and heavily used. The Standel amplifier company was originally bankrolled by Paul Bigsby, who wanted to market a Bigsby line of amplifiers. After Bigsby decided against an amplifier line, Standel Amplifiers were ultimately put into production by founder Bob Crooks in fall 1953. The Standel 25L15 was a groundbreaking amplifier when it debuted, with features such as a cast-frame JBL speaker, separate preamp and power amp chassis, separate bass and treble controls, and a sharp-looking colored-Naugahyde padded covering. The Standel was also the loudest amplifier made in 1953.

Speedy West received the first Standel 25L15 amp on October 1, 1953, and Merle received the second. Joe Maphis would also purchase a Standel 25L15 and take delivery of the fourth one a few weeks later. West's amplifier was covered in white Naugahyde. Merle's was bright red, and Maphis's was green. Between the custom Gibson Super 400 guitar and his new Standel amp, Merle now had the best of the best available equipment of the era.

His recordings during this time were good but still failed to make much of a dent on the charts. Singles included "Kinfolks in Carolina" (recorded with Joe Maphis doubling on guitar), "Trouble Trouble," "Dry Bread," and "Lost John Boogie." These were all great efforts with excellent backing but made little or no sales impact when released.

By the fall of 1952, Chet Atkins's instrumental records on RCA were starting to achieve popularity. Capitol's own instrumental duo, Speedy West and Jimmy Bryant, were releasing records that radio disc jockeys loved to use as theme songs or musical segues. Merle's new producer at Capitol, Ken Nelson, decided that Merle should record some new electric guitar instrumentals as well. On September 3, 1952, he entered Capitol's studios with Dale Warren on bass and recorded two masterpieces of thumbpicking guitar, "I'll See You in My Dreams" and "Cannonball Rag." The former was a Gus Kahn pop standard, and the latter was the song Kennedy Jones had written decades earlier, bearing the title given to him at Cleaton Crossing. The results were excellent, with Merle picking hard and clean and fast, and the two songs became standards among thumbpickers. To this day, if you attend any thumbpicking guitar event, you will hear both of these numbers performed by multiple guitarists. "Cannonball Rag" was even the name of the Merle Travis newsletter published by Dave Stewart in the 1990s.

Merle's sessions were engineered by John Kraus, who worked on many of the other Capitol country sessions. Kraus had a good relationship with the country artists, and Merle always spoke very highly of his abilities. The guitar sound that Kraus captured on Merle's instrumentals came from a unique method of direct input to the mixing console instead of using a microphone in front of an amplifier. Les Paul had also used a direct input recording method, but with special low-impedance pickups and his own custom-built direct boxes to plug directly into the mixing board to get his signature sound. The extremely simple yet effective sound of Merle's Gibson Super 400 plugged directly into the Capitol Records mixing console must go down in history as one of the greatest guitar tones ever committed to tape. Merle recalled in a 1980 letter to a fan:

> An engineer at Capitol Records in Hollywood plugged the old 400 directly into the tape and done something else to record the *Merle Travis Guitar* album. I've never really got that tone again. The engineer's name was Johnny Kraus. I tried for that tone in Nashville… but the engineer couldn't come up with it…. I hate to sound "ol' timey," but engineers ain't got the time to mess with stuff like that these days![271]

The results of the session were good enough that Ken Nelson kept insisting Merle record instrumentals at his sessions. Over the course of the next year or two, Nelson began amassing more instrumentals, including "Guitar Rag," "The Waltz You Saved for Me," and "Dance of the Goldenrod." He was determined to eventually release a full guitar album. It would take three years.

In late 1952, another regular TV show opportunity presented itself—a variety show featuring Merle and his wife, Judy Hayden, called *All-American Jubilee*. Merle told an interviewer later: "I also did a show for a short time called the *All-American Jamboree* [*sic*]. I sang and did comedy as a character called Rodney Dangerfield."[272] Merle's memory:

"We have TV shows 'All American Jubilee and Co'"

All-American Jubilee debuted November 5, 1952, on KECA-TV, channel 7 in Los Angeles. The bulk of the program featured Merle and Hayden, with special guest appearances by other artists. Newspaper ads featured Merle and Hayden together and promoted the program as wholesome family entertainment with a country flavor. The show ran for a few months in early 1953, and one of its memorable characters was the "cowboy sissy" character that Merle named Rodney Dangerfield. (Where that name came from is somewhat in dispute. Jack Benny is said to have used it in a December 1941 radio broadcast. It was used in an episode of *Ozzie and Harriet* in the late 1950s, and by a gay comedian on the Camp Records label in the early 1960s. In the 1970s, comedian Jack Roy began using the name in his stand-up comedy act and took it to national prominence.) In April, a newspaper article on Hank Richards announced that he had produced a kinescope (a form of video recording that predated videotape) to try and sell *All-American Jubilee* to a national sponsor.

As soon as *All-American Jubilee* ended in April 1953, Richards hired Merle to host another television show for KECA-TV, called *Merle Travis and Company*. The new show featured Merle and Hayden hosting an intimate program that included solo performances, guest artists, and even a segment featuring Merle drawing cartoons live on air. The *Glendale News Press* had good things to say about *Merle Travis and Company*: "His versatility is of such nature that it has prompted at least one wag to suggest that 'Merle is in violation of the Sherman Anti-Trust Law, because he has a monopoly on talent!'"[273] *Merle Travis and Company* stayed on the air until September 1953. Around this time, a *Los Angeles Times* article announced an exciting bit of news that unfortunately never went any further: "Merle Travis closes his KECA (7) series at 3 this afternoon. He leaves for New York next week to confer with producer Walter (Hank) Richards about the expected network debut of the *All-American Jubilee* show."[274]

Decades later, Richards wrote a card to Merle with thoughts about their work together:

> We had a great little show in *All-American Jubilee*. If they hadn't scheduled it opposite Liberace and the Blue Ribbon Fights, we might, like Lawrence Welk, still be performing the Ether. *Merle Travis and Company* was way ahead of its time. Oh well, what the hell. TV is the grand consumer of youth and talent. It was fun while it lasted.[275]

Even though Merle's national show with Richards never panned out, he kept busy with appearances on *Town Hall Party*, which had begun as a radio broadcast on KFI and then added a live television broadcast on KTTV-TV in December 1952. The TV broadcast of *Town Hall Party* was not immediately successful until producer Bill Wagnon extended the live show to three hours, from 10 p.m. to 1 a.m. every Saturday night. *Town Hall Party* became hugely popular, the closest thing the West Coast had to the *Grand Ole Opry*. Merle would be one of the main cast members from its inception until the show went off the air in 1961. His appearances took place over bits of time between other TV shows, touring, and personal problems, but *Town Hall Party* would be his most visible TV exposure for the rest of the 1950s. *Town Hall Party* performer Larry Collins (of the Collins Kids brother-and-sister act) remembers the atmosphere of the show, and the hot guitar numbers he would often play with Merle and Joe Maphis, using Larry's doubleneck Mosrite guitar as a prop:

> When we were going to pick a song together, the three of us would go into that downstairs, right by the stage. We'd run through it. Joe would do most of the talking. Then we'd rehearse it while the show was going, about two songs before we were going to pick. They didn't give me no slack, not once. So Joe just talked to us, said, "Merle, let's just do that 'Wildwood Flower.'" He says, "I'll start it and then I'll get Larry to just come in, do his part, then you. Then I'll play with him on the top neck, and we'll do it together, and then you walk in and we'll ask you to pick with us, and the three of us will play on the guitar at one time." Joe said, "Well, I'll go down here and Merle go over here," and whatever. We never even did a run-through, we just did it. That's the God's truth. No room for error on live television. I look back at that, I still don't know how I did that. Hell, I couldn't do it now. But then, I did it.[276]

In spring 1953, Merle got what was probably his biggest break in Hollywood—he was approached by his ex-manager Bobbie Bennett about the possibility of acting in a film, and not one of the grade-Z Westerns he had worked in the past. It was *From Here to Eternity*, an adaptation of James Jones's 1951 best-selling novel, and starred Frank Sinatra, Montgomery Clift, and Burt Lancaster. The movie was produced by Columbia Pictures. *From Here to Eternity* is a gritty film about the adventures of several soldiers in Hawaii before, during, and after the Pearl Harbor attack. In Jones's novel, a character named Sal Anderson sings a song called "Re-Enlistment Blues," and Merle seemed perfect for the part when the film's director saw him on television. Merle remembered the sequence of events in a letter to his brother John Melvin, including a humorous encounter with the notorious president of Columbia Pictures, Harry Cohn:

I've signed off for a part in a picture, and some of the scenes call for shots around the barracks in Hawaii. I'm pretty thrilled about this deal, for it's a big production, here they call 'em "A" pictures, and I've never been in one.

It's a movie version of a best seller book called *From Here to Eternity*. Columbia Studios is making it, and the leads are Montgomery Clift and Burt Lancaster (we talked about him once). Deborah Kerr and Frank Sinatra are top billers in it too. I didn't read the book, but they gave me a movie script and I read that. It's a tale about a bunch of soldiers and their antics.

They tried out a Godly number of guys for the part, but I, in an offhanded sort of way knew the director, Fred Zinnemann (who won an Oscar for *High Noon*) and the part called for a Kentucky boy who could play blues on the guitar and sing 'em.... So he contacted an old agent of mine, Bobbie Bennett, and she called me and thereby hangs a tale.

She called me and asked if I'd like to do it, and I told her I was not completely nuts, so we went down to Columbia and I saw just about what is the picture version of how Hollywood wheels turn. It was fun.

Miss Bennett said that first we'd have to talk to Mr. Murtz, Assistant Musical Director. In his office we talked about everything and finally he said, "This part is sure for you. I've known you a long time and I know you can do it. When can you go see Mr. Stoloff, the Musical Director?" I told him anytime, so we set up a date a couple of days later. A couple of days later I went to see Mr. Stoloff.

He said, "Mertz says this part is for you. Well, I'm familiar with your work and I know you can do it. When can you go see Mr. Arnow, the Casting Director?" I told him anytime and we set up a date a couple of days later. I went in to see the casting director.

He said, Mr. Mertz and Mr. Stoloff says, "This part is for you. I've seen you on television and I know you can do it. When can you see Mr. Adler, the Producer?" I told him anytime. A couple of days later I went to see the Producer.

Yep, the producer said what you think I'm going to write. But wondered when I could meet the fellows who wrote the song I was to sing. A couple of days later I did, and even ended up going back to see Fred Zinnemann. He wondered when I could go see the President of Columbia Pictures, Mr. Cohn. We made the date. I'd gone the circle of each man depending on the other, and now to the office of the Great-I-am!

To cap it all off, who should go with me to see Mr. Cohn but Miss Bennett, Fred and Bob Wells, the song writers, Mr. Adler, the producer, Mr. Arnow, the casting director, Mr. Mertz and Mr. Stoloff from music, and Fred Zinnemann, the director. Well, all these fellers acted like real human beings in their offices, but when we got to Mr. Cohn's place they all paled a little and Zinnemann swallered and asked the girl if Mr. Cohn was ready to see us. He was, and we tiptoed in. Cohn was in the very businesslike chore of getting a shave while sitting behind a desk, with a barber scraping away.

Without speaking to the barber, he pushed him away and ordered one of the men to take off his hat in his office, saying, "By God I'm President of this company, when you get to be President I'll take off my hat when I walk in your office." The feller took off his hat. Cohn asked me to sing. I got out my box [guitar] and started on the song the fellers had wrote:

"I woke up this morning, ain't a dog soldier no more
From now on call me mister, ain't goin' back any more
I'm goin' out to lose, Re-Enlistment Blues…"

Cohn pushed the barber away and shouted through the suds…. "That stinks! That's terrible…" I then swallered. Zinnemann asked what stinks, and he said the lyrics to the song. Said if a feller was just out of the army why should he be trying to lose the Re-enlistment Blues? Wells spoke up, "We'll re-write it, Mr. Cohn…"

"See that you do, then let me hear it."

After I'd finally got through the blues and God had shaved, he pointed his finger at me and said, "Fred, do you want that man?" Zinnemann said he did, and Cohn said, "Well, get him, get him, but be damn sure you turn me out a good picture. I don't want no flops at my studio. I won't have no flops at my studio!"

He pointed to (I counted 'em) fifteen Oscars and barked, "I didn't get those with flops. Now get out of here and let me go to work!" Everybody said, "Yes, Mr. Cohn," and exited.

Outside his office every man expressed his affection for Mr. Cohn. As best I remember they referred to him in this way. "Why that ol' son-of-a-bitch has had more flops in Hollywood than anybody."

I go to work the 27th of this month. How much will be cut of what I do, I don't know. I only know how much money I'll make and that I'm playing the part of Sal Anderson. That's in the contract.[277]

Merle's memory:

"I make 'Eternity'—Monte gets loaded"

Merle worked on the film in March and April 1953, including a trip to Hawaii, where several scenes were filmed. He received quite a bit of screen time, including his performance of "Re-Enlistment Blues." The song was used several other times during the film as a recurring theme. The "Sal Anderson" character was changed in the credits to "Hillbilly." Merle was surprised during the filming when the lead actress, Deborah Kerr, mentioned to him that she watched him every week on *Town Hall Party*.

Merle sang and played his Martin/Bigsby D-28 acoustic guitar in the film, with his name on the pickguard blacked out. At some point during the filming, as seen in several still photographs, the pickguard was removed. The guitar would be photographed with the pickguard variously on or off until Merle had a replacement pickguard made for it in the 1960s.

Merle wrote to his brother John Melvin several months after the film was released in August 1953:

> Did you see the picture *From Here to Eternity*? I worked about 3 weeks in the thing, but most of my stuff was cut. The picture ran a-way too long, and they had to trim it down. I think I had 12th billing (Big Stuff).
>
> Anyway, the picture is a big fat success. It's up for 13 awards. (It won't get but maybe three.) Outside of maybe *The Robe* it was Hollywood's biggest picture last year. Frank Sinatra is a cinch for an Oscar, and maybe Burt Lancaster—and Zinnemann, the Director. It was fun, and to spend 12 hours a day for three weeks with people you get pretty well acquainted. This guy, Montgomery Clift is the cream of the crop—and one of our greatest actors.[278]

When *From Here to Eternity* was released, it was, as Merle mused, a "big fat success." Harry Cohn's worry that it might be a flop proved unfounded; it was in fact an enormous commercial and critical achievement for Columbia Pictures. It was number one at the box office for four weeks straight in September, and went on to gross $30.5 million, equivalent to $277 million today, making it one of the year's highest grossing pictures and one of the top ten grossing films of the decade. It won eight Oscars out of thirteen nominations, including Best Picture, Best Director, Best Screenplay, Best Supporting Actor, and Best Supporting Actress. The movie still appears in many "Best of" lists compiled by movie critics.

Appearing in the movie was a huge feather in Merle's cap. For a star who hadn't had a big chart hit since the late 1940s, it was a great opportunity to keep his name in the minds of his fans. As great as the visibility was, however, Merle would never again be offered a similar acting role. It had been a once-in-a-lifetime opportunity. His next film appearance was in a low-budget production called *Festival of Nations* (also released under the title *The World Dances*). It was certainly a lofty concept—to present music and culture from many different nations across the globe. Merle and Carolina Cotton represented America, performing "folk tunes." The director was Boris Petroff, known for such grade-Z fare as *Shotgun Wedding* and *Anatomy of a Psycho*. *Festival of Nations* was a commercial flop, though it was released under both of its names at various times, usually as a second feature at drive-in theaters.

Merle wrote about taking his wife and some family friends to see the film in a letter to his brother John Melvin:

> Speakin' of pictures, if you see June, she'll split if you mention a flicker called *Festival of Nations*. It was in Technicolor, and me and Carolina Cotton had top billing (th' stars??)—Well, we took neighbors (forementioned Kleins) down to see the preview the other night. June had one thing to say—quote: "That was without a doubt, the lousiest, most tiresome mess I've ever sweated out."
> —No Oscar—
> It was about folk songs and dances in a couple of dozen countries. We were the only Americans, so we're th' stars (?). I must admit it was pretty weird.[279]

The year 1953 proved a busy one professionally for both Merle and Hayden. For his part, there were personal appearances, recording sessions, *From Here to Eternity* film work, and television show appearances. One of the recording sessions was with a fellow Capitol Records star named Hank Thompson. Recall that the two had known each other since 1948, when Thompson first traveled to California. In June 1953, Thompson asked Merle to join him in the studio for the first of many recording sessions.

One of the biggest hits of the early 1950s was a song called "Goodnight, Irene." It was originally recorded by Lead Belly in the 1930s, and the folk group The Weavers (one of the acts Cliffie Stone had wanted to compete with when Merle recorded his *Folk Songs of the Hills*) released their version in 1950, which became the number one song of that year. It was so popular that cover versions likewise sold in large quantities. Frank Sinatra, Ernest Tubb and Red Foley, Moon Mullican, Jo Stafford, and Paul Gayten all had hits with "Goodnight, Irene" on the pop, country, and rhythm and blues charts.

Hank Thompson had mostly recorded in a Western swing style since signing with Capitol in 1948. By 1953, he observed the popularity of a West Coast hillbilly act called the Maddox Brothers and Rose, who played up-tempo numbers with wild abandon. Thompson brought Merle into the Capitol studio to record a bouncy number written as an "answer" song, "Wake Up, Irene." The result, with Merle playing guitar, was a giant step toward a style of music that would eventually be known as rockabilly. Thompson remembered the session and Merle's ability to come up with ideas on the spot:

I wanted to use that Mother Maybelle type guitar thing and that's what I was tellin' Merle, I said: "That's the kind of sound I'd like to have" so Merle picked up that guitar, and said "Oh, you mean this right here?" And he started playin' it, and I said "yeah." I said, "Would you come down and do that deal on 'Wake Up Irene' for me when I cut it?" So Merle came down and did that session and from that point on he stayed and helped with some of the other things.

He was so much help on sessions. He was such a good musician and had such good ideas, for turnarounds and fills and things like that if he didn't even play a guitar he would have been handy to have on a session. He could do so many things and had so many good ideas.

So from that point on I used Merle on all my sessions and always planned it around to be sure he was gonna be available. He played on nearly everything I did on Capitol except when I did the Christmas album and he had gone to Alaska. He would be out of the country and I used Joe Maphis. That was the only time I ever did anything where I didn't use Merle. I used Travis even on up into [my post-Capitol Records on] Warner Brothers and some of the Dot Records.

He was just invaluable. He'd come up with all kinds of little things. The little garnishments that he would think of, maybe a little different chord change, or saying, "Why don't you let so and so do this right in here, or tell the bass player to play this particular deal in there?" Just little old things he'd come up with. They weren't all that complicated but nobody thought of them. But he did. He was that creative and he worked so well with [Thompson's bandleader] Billy Gray and with me. The three of us kind of complemented one another and what one didn't think of the other one would.[280]

Thompson used Merle on hundreds of recordings after "Wake Up, Irene"—for instance, a year after this first session, on an updated instrumental version of the

Carter Family standard "Wildwood Flower," which was essentially a Merle Travis instrumental released under Thompson's name. "Wildwood Flower" became a huge hit when it was released in 1955, going to number five on the country charts. It was the biggest instrumental hit featuring Merle's guitar playing that he would have for the rest of his career. Merle and Thompson became so close that Merle began calling Hank his brother. Thompson's wife, Dorothy Ray Thompson, also became Merle's close friend. Hank and Dorothy would often stay at the Travis house with Merle and Judy when visiting Los Angeles for recording sessions or personal appearances.

Shortly after "Wake Up, Irene," at the end of June 1953, Merle again recorded for Capitol. The resulting single, "Gambler's Guitar" backed with "Shut Up and Drink Your Beer," was excellent, although both titles were written by other songwriters. "Gambler's Guitar" didn't sell, though it did spawn a cover version by Rusty Draper. Merle's effort was memorable, with excellent studio production, but in the era of hard-core 1950s honky-tonk, it was simply too sophisticated. Eight months later, Merle returned to the studio and cut another single in the same vein, "Jolie Fille" backed with "I Can't Afford the Coffee (I'm Tired of Drinking Weak Tea Blues)." These 1953 and 1954 sessions were great efforts, but in retrospect, the style was out of step with what was popular at the time.

In spring 1954, Merle hit the road on a package tour with Bob Wills's ex-lead singer Tommy Duncan and fellow Capitol Recording artist Skeets McDonald. Ads for these dates show that the trio of stars started on their trek toward the Pacific Northwest in April. It must have been a memorable tour. Merle's memories:

"Tommy Duncan hates salads"
"Tommy refuses drinks in a peculiar way"
"Tommy Duncan 'dreads to get drunk'"
"Tommy Duncan, Skeets McDonald and I tour"
"Skeets asks stranger for guinea eggs"
"Skeets asks Steve Stebbins for rubber"

During this time, Judy Hayden took a job in San Francisco doing Cottonseed Clark's *Hoffman Hayride* show on KPIX-TV once a week. In a letter to Merle's first daughter, Pat, in December 1953, she described their busy lives:

Dearest Pat,

Don't faint, I'm finally writing. No sense making excuses I know, but just to keep you up on things I'll tell you what keeps me so busy. For one thing I fly to San Francisco every week to do a TV show there. Wednesday is shot getting ready to go, Thursday I go, do the show, and come back Friday, beat! Saturday Dad and I work together at the dance in Compton which includes an hour radio show and a two hour TV show. Getting in so late (or should I say early) messes up what Sunday is left and Monday and Tuesday I try to catch up on what I got behind in.... Of course Dad is on the go as usual and the ride from here to Compton on Saturdays is almost our only time together.[281]

Merle's memories:

"Move to Woodland Hills—Little Peyton Place"
"We fight—divorce—I move to Hollywood"

Life in the Travis household could be idyllic and peaceful. It could also be full of drama and upheaval. Merle and Judy moved from Van Nuys to a new house at 23014 Ostronic Drive in Woodland Hills at some point in the second half of 1953. Woodland Hills sits at the far west end of the San Fernando Valley. Today it is quite densely populated, but back in the early 1950s, it was isolated and rural. Merlene Travis-Maggini recalled: "What Mom always told me was that they moved to Ostronic because Van Nuys was getting too 'citified.' Dad wanted wide, open spaces and we know Dad was always looking for the impossible for him—to relax. So maybe that was why they moved to Woodland Hills. I know Van Nuys wasn't a huge city in 1950–51, but Woodland Hills was the boonies!"[282] But if the family hoped a new home would be peaceful and relaxing, sadly, it would not be the case. Marital troubles had been brewing for a long time. Judy wrote a song-poem called "He Loves Ginny" that she kept with her private papers. The words to "He Loves Ginny" indicate that Judy thought that Merle was still in love with Ginny Cushman and not with her.[283] Things eventually came to a head. Merlene recalled:

I do remember Mom saying she left Dad shortly after Cindy was born because he was physical with her. I trusted my Dad wholly even though he squeezed me once until I passed out. Mom told me that. Cindy was newborn, and she wanted to leave and he said, "Let me hug my baby one more time and I'll let you go." He then started "hugging" and wouldn't let me go. He said, "I'd rather she's dead than not be with me." Mom screamed at him to let me go, and he wouldn't until she promised to stay, which she did; he let me go. Apparently I was passed out while newborn Cindy was screaming. When she went for me, he let her have it. Not pretty.[284]

Merlene recalled more details of the situation at the time:

It was usually Dad that was drunk, and for days. He wouldn't come home and they worked a lot. I remember that. Mom wasn't an innocent because I know she had an affair. There was a boy named Buster—I think it was his dad, the next-door neighbor—and another guy. I know she did have an affair with the next-door neighbor because she told me. She just said, "I had a little affair. It was no big deal." I think they were very much in love and very young. Mom was young. Dad should have known better, but he just got married every other week.[285]

Between Merle's drinking and learning of Judy's affair with the next-door neighbor, the couple fought. Merlene continues:

I just remember being in the backyard by myself and feeling so frustrated that you can't make the screaming stop. They went at each other like wild animals. Mom was screaming and Dad was screaming at her, and Cindy was screaming because Judy was holding her. It was just so cruel. She was just a little baby. That's a very fragmented memory, but I do remember that in my little head because I was just maybe five, maybe four, because Cindy was a baby. Mom was holding her, and it was just like there was no filter, just—it was mean. They were mean, and then he could get violent. I never knew what the fights were about. Just fighting. They just went after it.[286]

Merlene believes that both Merle and Judy may have struggled with mental illness:

To me, he was always so sweet and kind and funny and maybe sad once in a while but not very, very sad. Nothing like what he and Mom went through. Mom had it, too. I think they both had bipolar, manic-depressive tendencies because their highs were high and their lows were low. It was in that middle part. I never saw that with Dad, by the way, but being with Mom, she was either way up here or way down there. If you got that middle part, you'd have a good time. The rest of the time, we were always watching our step. Imagine the two of them together.[287]

Things came to a head in the summer of 1954, prompting a violent incident that tore the marriage apart. Merlene again:

I don't remember the date, but I remember the chaos. I remember being passed through a window. I remember him pounding on the door. Mom was frantic and I'm just thinking, if you open the door and let Dad in, everything will be fine. I remember being passed through windows. My mom just saying, "Take them, take them."

Mom hid us because she was making her escape. She found somebody who took us in. It seemed like a long time. It was a pretty nice lady, but I remember, I had a toothache and I was crying, and she said, "You have to be brave and take care of your little sister and be good for your mom because she's going to need your help." I'm a little girl but I was like, "Okay, I have a job. That must be very important." When we got home, when she came and picked us up finally, we lived in an apartment now.

I remember walking in and she said, "This is our new home." I was like, "Where's my dad?" She goes, "Your dad is on the road for a while. He's got some shows to do." That was the story for a while, but we didn't have any of our stuff. All the furniture was different.

She had a different job. We went to school. Then one day, Dad picked us up. He took us to the store and we could pick out any candy bar we wanted. I got a Milky Way. I remember sitting in the car, and he was crying and saying, "Ask your mom if I can come back and I'll try to be better." I'm like, "Come back from where?" He said, "I don't have anywhere to live. I don't have any food, and I miss my girls and please, tell your mom to give me another chance." I went in. My mother said she never saw me so mad in her life. I was eating a Milky Way. I'll never forget that. I didn't finish it and I still, to this day, cannot stand a Milky Way bar. I went in the house, and she said I was angry with her. Then she told me the truth: "These are my reasons why he should not raise you. He's your father and I know you love him and he can be a very good man, but he's got a lot of demons. He should not be the person that should raise you."[288]

A few weeks later, the couple appeared in court and the local newspapers. The *Los Angeles Times* reported on July 23, 1954:

TV ACTRESS TURNS DOWN RECONCILIATION

Judy Hayden, television comedy actress, yesterday appeared to be on quite friendly terms with her estranged husband, Merle Travis, western folk singer, as they sat together in Domestic Relations Court.

However, she firmly declined his offer to try to reconcile. Superior Judge Elmer D. Doyle held half-an-hour's conference with the pair, discussing their problems, but was unable to shake Miss Hayden's determination to divorce her husband.

The couple, married for five years, had separated less than two weeks ago, when the comedienne moved out of their home at 23014 Ostronic Drive, Woodland Hills, they said....

Atty. Donovan W. Ballinger for Miss Hayden and Jerome Rolston for Travis, agreed to mutual restraining orders under which neither spouse will molest or annoy the other.[289]

Merle and Judy had an acrimonious split, much as it had been with Mary, his first wife. Although the divorce and property settlement were signed in February 1955, the legal battles continued into 1958. After the time where Merlene and Cindy were hidden at a home in Los Virgenes Canyon with a family friend, Judy brought the girls to a new duplex-type apartment in the North Hollywood area. Merlene remembered: "That's where Mom bought steak for us to celebrate our 'new life without Dad' and Cindy choked on it and Mom was screaming as she ran out into the courtyard area for help. It was awful."[290] Also: "We don't have any pictures, hardly, of Mom and Dad together because when she divorced him, she cut him out of everything."[291]

Judy married John Wesner in 1959, and eventually the family settled in the Valley, living in Van Nuys and later in Woodland Hills. Merlene was told that her new name was "Marlene," and her mother refused to talk about past events. She raised the two girls with infrequent visitation and nonexistent child support from Merle. Merlene told this author: "During those times, we would get things in the mail. Presents from Dad, like Eskimo dolls when he was in Alaska. She would never let us play with them, either. She put them up: 'Those aren't for playing with.' 'Your father likes something to show off,' was her thing."[292]

June Wesner, aka Judy Hayden, died on October 20, 1986, three years to the day after Merle's passing. Regarding the circumstances, Merlene recalls: "Mom was in a car accident in Gilroy on her way to my husband's parents' house in Hollister for dinner. She was hit head-on by a car driven by an elderly woman who shouldn't have been driving."[293]

After the divorce in 1954, Merle moved into a motel room in Hollywood and continued his hectic pace of touring, television, and recording. In a blink of an eye, he would be in another relationship—ultimately the longest one of his life. Merle's memory:

"I meet Bettie at Town Hall—She makes fun of suit"

Everyone who ever met Bettie Lou Robinson (née Morgan) described her as an extraordinarily beautiful woman. Born April 1, 1924, she was seven years younger than Merle, but already divorced with two young sons when she met

Merle at the Town Hall in Compton one Saturday night for a *Town Hall Party* dance and television broadcast. At the time she was still going by Robinson, the name of her recent ex-husband. According to Merle's memory, when they met, she made fun of his Western suit. Their relationship began in the summer of 1954, when things were falling apart with Judy (a note Bettie Travis left behind after her death indicated that their relationship began in July of that year).[294] According to Bettie's son, Michael Robinson, the couple started seeing each other when Merle would stop at a roadside café in Banning, California, near Palm Springs, the city where Bettie was working at the time.

Merle was smitten, again. Johnny Western remembered Bettie warmly: "She was pretty, she was smart, she was a great person to be around. A lot of fun, she had a big smile all the time. She probably was about five-foot four, maybe five-five, and weighed no more than 120 pounds. She had a good little figure and she kept it. She was kind of ideal. Travis with his moods, depending on where he was with the drinking and pills and stuff, could be one way or the other. But they hung in there quite a while."[295] Bettie Travis, for her part, noted, "We got along very well because we were both quite childlike. 'You wanna go, let's go play.' That was the way that we were. And that was fun."[296] Bettie lived in Eagle Rock, near Pasadena, keeping things afloat as a single mother of two young sons. She worked as a policy writer for an insurance company. By the end of 1954, according to a receipt saved in his archives, Merle was living out of the Travelodge in Eagle Rock so he could stay close to his new flame. Merle's memory:

"I babysit Mike and live on Scotch"

Michael Robinson recalled to this author that once, "I was sick and staying home for a day and she said she had to go downtown to do something, probably legal things. They sent me down there [to Merle's] and I spent the day in pajamas lying in bed watching television, dropping quarters into the cash box of the vibrating bed. Me and Travis were just lying there, him on one bed and me on the other, dropping quarters in the thing. It was actually a compatibility check. I think that's what it was. To see if Travis and I could get along."[297] Michael and his older brother, Dennis, wound up spending a lot of time around Merle, who suddenly found himself a father figure to two young, rowdy boys. Michael recalled:

Travis hit both ends of the spectrum throughout life. He could be the best guy; he could build you up to where your chest swelled and you felt real good. And then it was almost like a bipolar type thing. You could hit the bottom with him, and there was no soft bottom to it, you know? The depression could be tremendously low, and this happened to him personally and he transmitted that out into the world around him. He could make you feel great, and then you'd be slam-dunked into a complete depression. It was amazing, the mood swings. His fingers were very interesting. He had these little pointy-fingered "yimmy yammies" that could do all this really light work. That's why he was something of a watch tinkerer. His fingers weren't extraordinarily long, but they had the artistic points to them. Little, light, like a raccoon without claws.[298] ·

In late 1954 Merle entered the studio to record more songs for the guitar album Ken Nelson wanted him to complete. Over the course of three sessions on December 20, 21, and 28, he recorded many of his most iconic guitar instrumentals: "Blue Bell," "The Sheik of Araby," "On a Bicycle Built for Two," "Memphis Blues," "Walking the Strings," "Saturday Night Shuffle," and "Blue Smoke."

"Blue Bell" was a reworking of a Civil War–era song originally titled "Goodbye My Blue Bell" and sometimes known as "Farewell My Blue Bell." Merle had learned the number from Pa McCormick, a harmonica player on the *Boone County Jamboree* on WLW in Cincinnati. "On a Bicycle Built for Two" was written in 1892 under its original title, "Daisy Bell." "The Sheik of Araby" was a Tin Pan Alley song from the 1920s that would become a jazz standard. Merle's version is one of the only country adaptations, though several Western swing acts also recorded it. "Memphis Blues" was a W. C. Handy blues number written in 1912. "Saturday Night Shuffle" was an adaptation of the Kennedy Jones song "Buck and Wing." Mose Rager and Ike Everly also performed it, and it was a Muhlenberg County jam-session song before Merle ever went to Hollywood. Merle had recorded a version as "Merle's Buck Dance" with Hank Penny almost ten years earlier for King Records, and he had recorded the song with his acoustic guitar for Capitol Transcriptions around the same time, where the title "Saturday Night Shuffle" first appeared. This time with his electric guitar in late 1954, he played it slightly slower, but with more intricate parts. "Blue Smoke" was a Merle original that he had already recorded with his acoustic guitar for Capitol Transcriptions in the mid-1940s. It was named after the puff of gas that comes off a freshly uncorked jug of moonshine. The electric version of "Blue Smoke" recorded in late 1954 would prove to be the version to beat. To this day, "Blue Smoke" is considered by many the most difficult Merle Travis instrumental to re-create.

These recordings were incredible, some of the best of Merle's career. The final versions that made it to the record, however, were the result of much labor-intensive tape splicing and editing of recording sessions that began as a disorganized mess. In Ken Nelson's words:

Merle had a playing style that was unique. He was the idol of country guitarists and many tried to emulate his style.... Merle had a pleasant, easy-going personality, but unfortunately he took to substance abuse.... The one time he really upset me was when he didn't show up for a session. Thinking he might have forgot about it, we sent someone to get him. When he came to the session it was quite obvious that he was in no condition to play, so we had somebody to take him home. The next day he phoned me and said, "Gee, Ken, I'm sorry I didn't make the session yesterday."[299]

On another occasion Nelson recalled:

I made an album with him and it took me over three months to make it because we had to do it almost measure by measure. I know we had an awful time. It was just a shame that this great talent was loused up like this. I made this album with Merle in Hollywood, he was the sweetest guy in the world when he was okay.... It just used to break my heart that this great talent was under the influence of drugs. Merle couldn't drink. He'd take one drink and he was practically drunk. It was just a crime.[300]

Unfortunately for those of us who would love to reconstruct *how* the splicing and editing of multiple takes came to create each master take, most, if not all, of the original tapes were destroyed in the 2008 fire at Universal Studios in Los Angeles. The only clues are in the final masters themselves. For instance, astute guitarists will point to "Blue Smoke," which ends with a lick that culminates in a low, de-tuned D note on the guitar's low E string. The song cannot be played in its entirety with the de-tuned note, proving that the original recording was made of at least two spliced sections.

There was a four-month break in recording between December and April. In the interim, Merle and Judy's divorce was finalized on February 24, 1955. The divorce was a huge financial burden on him. Money should have been coming in on a regular basis from his songwriting and publishing royalty payments, but Merle's publisher, Sylvester Cross of American Music, failed to make regular payments, even when they owed substantial sums. Merle's lawyer, Jerry Rolston, saved a file of letters to Cross that spanned ten years. They are a strange mixture of old-school formal congeniality, veiled threats, and outright begging. The first is dated February 10, 1955, from Jerry Rolston to BMI (Broadcast Music Inc.), asking why Cross had been ignoring his requests for payment:

The undersigned is the attorney for Merle Travis, who at the present time, is in the throes of a very difficult financial situation, to say nothing of the fact that he is in a domestic situation. Both of these situations would be relieved if he could clear up his obligations that have piled up due to these disturbances. All of us who know Merle know that he has a great talent, both as a performer and as a composer, but he has written practically nothing recently due to his mental disturbances.... I am therefore requesting that you make an advance of $3500 at this time against his BMI royalties, which advance can be recouped by you as rapidly as earned by Merle....

I fully realize that Merle owes more than $3500.00, but this amount will pay the creditors who are now beginning to attach. If we don't raise at least $2000.00 within the next two weeks, the whole house of cards may come down.

Your cooperation will be appreciated,
Sincerely yours, Jerry Rolston[301]

Shortly after his divorce became final, Merle entered a new phase of his career when Gene Autry asked him to replace longtime sideman Johnny Bond on his package tours. In early March 1955, Travis joined Autry's troupe of thirty-five performers (including his old friend Carl Cotner from the Clayton McMichen days, the Cass County Boys, Pat Buttram, "Happy" Kellum the clown, cycling act The Villanaves, trampoline act The Rudells, and Gail Davis, better known as her television character "Annie Oakley"). Merle's memories:

"Gene Autry, Herb and I go to different cities"
"Gene Autry tours—Carl Strongs nose roped"
"Pat Buttram says 'you'r back on the mints'"
"Gene scares Gail Davis flying over frozen lake"
"Gene Autry tells 'chain letter story'"
"Gene, Cotner and I am too drunk—Buttram comes to aid"

The Autry gig would provide Merle with steady employment, as he remembered later in life: "We toured there six years in a row. We'd go out about three months, and make all the state fairs, all up to Canada... all the way from one end to the other."[302] As friend and fellow Autry troupe member Johnny Western remembered, Autry was the sort of benefactor, friend, and sympathetic fellow hard drinker that Travis needed during this dark period in his life: "When he wasn't drinking, Autry was the greatest guy in the world. I mean, for all the millions he would give you the shirt off his back. He was the richest guy in Hollywood, you know. Travis was always needing money. He was short on cash, even though Gene had paid him the amount, whatever they had agreed on."[303] Merle's memory:

"Gene Autry tells 'Mr Agent' story"

Johnny Western elaborates:

It was a joke between them, and the main tag of the joke was a guy named "Mr. Agent." Which turned out to be the guy that sold the tickets for the bus between Yuma, Arizona, and El Centro. You know the time changes there, so when you leave Yuma at seven o'clock in the morning, you get to El Centro at seven o'clock in the morning. You get that picture? They loved that joke, and so Travis's nickname for Gene was "Mr. Agent."

He walked up to him, I was standing maybe three feet away, and said "Mr. Agent, I don't think I'm going to have enough money to make this Alaskan thing." Gene said, "Well, hell, how much do you need?" He said, "Probably about five hundred would cover it. I'll get it back to you. I always do." Gene said, "Don't worry about it," so he reaches in his pocket. Gene had money in both pockets. In his right-hand pocket, he had one-hundred-dollar bills, nice crisp hundred-dollar bills, folded up in a money clip that was given to him by the head of the Texas Rangers. And he popped that money clip over, peeled off five new one-hundred-dollar bills, and stuck them in Travis's shirt pocket.

So, Travis got that five hundred dollars from Gene and, like he said, once he got paid after the last week, he got the money back to him. But that's how close they were. They had that type of relationship.[304]

When Merle returned from his first tour with Autry, he was in bad shape. His drinking was out of control, his personal life was out of control, and his finances were in shambles. It was not the ideal backdrop for going into the studio, but Ken Nelson was determined to complete the guitar instrumental album. On April 14, Merle went to the Capitol studios with the intent of recording several songs, but the session only produced one, "Sleepy Time Gal," another Tin Pan Alley song from the 1920s that Bing Crosby had turned into a hit in 1954. Merle's version was beautifully played, with lush chords, but for unknown reasons, "Sleepy Time Gal" did not meet the standards for release at the time (it eventually was released on the Merle Travis Bear Family box set in 1994). Undeterred, Nelson kept after Merle to come back and finish the album. In his own quaint way, he sent Merle a letter every day for a week, trying to prod him into preparing for the next session. The letters were addressed to a hotel room in Hollywood where Merle was living out of a suitcase, post-divorce. The letters are amusing, and one wonders how effective they were. It's certainly difficult to imagine a modern-day record executive writing similar letters to an artist:

April 14, 1955
Mr. Merle Travis
7665 Hollywood Blvd. Apt. 9
Hollywood 28, Calif.
Dear Merle:
DON'T FORGET TO PRACTICE OR YOU WON'T GET YOUR
BUBBLE-GUM FOR TODAY!
With love and kisses,
Uncle Ken

April 16, 1955
Dear Merle:
THERE IS A BOY AND HIS GUITAR,
HE IS OUR FAVORITE WESTERN STAR.
HE SHOULD PRACTICE DAY AND NIGHT
TO MAKE HIS RECORDS COME OUT RIGHT
OR
HIS UNCLE KEN IS GOING TO BE REAL UNHAPPY.
Uncle Ken

April 17, 1955
Dear Merle:
HONOR BRIGHT—DID YOU PRACTICE TODAY?
LOVE,
Uncle Ken

April 19, 1955
Dear Merle:
EVERY DOG HAS HIS DAY AND THIS IS YOUR LAST DAY TO
PRACTICE!
With all my love to my favorite nephew,
Uncle Ken[305]

The session on April 21, 1955, produced two instrumentals. "Tuck Me to
Sleep in My Old 'Tucky Home," the old standard that Merle had learned from his
friend Colie Addison in his earliest days of thumbpicking. "Rockabye Rag" was
a blisteringly fast original number, created by having Merle lay down a rhythm
part first, then overdubbing the lead guitar part. Six days later, on April 27, Merle
returned to the studio and recorded "Bugle Call Rag," a big-band orchestra

standard that he updated into a solo guitar tour de force. Though the effort had been laborious for both Merle and Nelson (not to mention the splicing and editing abilities of Capitol engineer John Kraus), Nelson finally had enough tracks for the album of guitar instrumentals he had been planning for three years.

Merle and Bettie hadn't been publicly dating very long, and Merle's behavior had already been erratic, marked by drunkenness and mental breakdowns. Nonetheless, Bettie wanted Merle to marry her. She had also been seeing a semiprofessional baseball player when she met Merle, and she gave Merle an ultimatum—she was going to marry either the baseball player or him, but she was going to get married. So on May 4, 1955, Merle and Bettie went to Tijuana and got married, just as he had done with Tex Ann Nation, Ginny Cushman, and Judy Hayden.

Bettie had grown up with an alcoholic father, and her father's drinking was the cause of her parents' divorce. When she and Merle were dating, she didn't know the extent of his problem until she discovered, too late, that it was out of control:

So finally, you know, I said, my daddy was an alcoholic... but I do know that I'm getting very, very serious about you and I said, "If you are an alcoholic, if you can't quit the drinking... then we can't have any life together because I know what it did to my mother... I don't want that and so I don't think we better see each other." And he said, "I can quit," he said, "I swear, I can quit," and I said, "If you can quit then we'll see what we can do." And so he went over there, it was in Eagle Rock to that hospital off of Colorado Boulevard... he was there and he got straightened out and he was really great and he was that way for like two months... and I thought that anybody that can quit for two months is not an alcoholic, and we're okay, and so then we're gonna go Wednesday, we're gonna go get married.

Then we moved over on Chandler, and he said, "Now, I've gotta go see the doctor over there." I said, "Well, whatta you have to see the doctor for?" He said, "Well, he gives me some medicine." I said, "He does? What is it?" And he said, "Oh, it's just some pills, but it helps me not to drink." And I thought, well, that's okay, you know. What's wrong with that?

So he went to the doctor and then he came out and his face was long and he was mad and he said, "He wouldn't give me any of the medication." And I thought, well, what in the world's wrong with that dang, dumb doctor that he wouldn't give him any of the medication? Well, what I found out was that the medication was sleeping pills, it was Tuinol... it's a downer.

So then he started drinking. We were married about two months. He was two months before, two months after, and then he went back to it, you know. And I was very disappointed. But I was in it and I dearly loved him, I did, I mean, I wasn't kiddin'. So I thought, well, like all dumb and stupid women, I can change him, I can fix this, I can be so great to him that I'm gonna make him well. You dummy!

Merle never did say, as far as I know, to his dying day, "I am an alcoholic." I don't think he ever thought he was one, he always just had a nervous condition that nobody in the world understood.[306]

Shortly after getting married, Merle and Bettie and her two sons, Dennis and Michael, moved into a house at 12046 Chandler Boulevard in North Hollywood. The house was a rental located on the back part of a lot, with the landlord, a man named Mr. Artino, in the front house. Merle's memory:

"Mr. Artino gives me wine, and learns my name is Bill"

Michael Robinson remembered:

We rented that place from a guy by the name of Mr. Artino, who didn't even speak English although he'd been in the country for twenty years. He used to grow grapes, and he would press his own wine. I think he was taking up our garage, and that didn't come with the deal because he had all his wine-making stuff in there. Travis would be sitting, lying out there in his chaise lounge. He was out there when we first moved in, reading a *Billboard* magazine. Mr. Artino came up. What Mr. Artino was saying was "What is your name?" Travis didn't understand. He looks down and looked at Mr. Artino and he says, "Oh, this magazine is called *Billboard*." He became "Mr. Bill" to Mr. Artino. It's like *Saturday Night Live* or something, but he was actually the original "Mr. Bill" to me.[307]

Bettie Travis's recollections of when she and Merle got married: "He had just finished recording *The Merle Travis Guitar*. He was very proud of that. He did four sides when we lived on Chandler and worked them out in the living room. Then he bought his own Berlants [two Berlant Concertone reel-to-reel tape recorders] and I learned how to record. He would lay down his own bass line and such. [Author's note: Although there are several photographs from this time that show Merle with the Berlant tape recorders and dozens of reel-to-reel tapes on a shelf underneath the machines, the only home recordings that have surfaced from this time period are a couple of unreleased instrumental Christmas songs on a small reel of tape. Presumably there were many more, but as of this writing, they are lost.] But he was having a lot of problems at that time [drinking]. He did like to record."[308]

Life seemed good for the new family, at least in the public eye. Merle's publisher put out a song folio in 1955 featuring a photo spread of their family life that resembled *Leave It to Beaver*: Merle and Bettie cooking in the kitchen, watering the lawn, relaxing in patio chairs, and a picture of the entire family, along with Merlene and Cindy, sitting in a row on a long couch. Michael Robinson notes: "Cindy and Merlene, they had very little time with him. When they did get there, he was on his best behavior because their mother would not tolerate what was going on. Their mothers were trying to protect them from something that just totally destroyed them."[309]

Pat Travis Eatherly remembered: "Dad married Bettie when I was already a teenager. I always thought it was funny when Dad called his petite wife 'Minnie Mouse.' Bettie was full of energy and a tireless traveler. She was a real trooper."[310] Merlene calls Bettie "such a nice woman. I mean, really, she really was nice. Of course, as a little girl, you go over there and to me she was very glamorous." Cindy Travis uses the same words: "I just remember her being very glamorous." Regarding the photo of the entire family together on the couch, Merlene notes that this was not a common occurrence: "That was a photo shoot."[311]

Merle returned to the studio for another session in June 1955, this time with a band featuring Eddie Kirk, Dusty Rhodes, and Thomas Mills to back him on two more instrumental sides, "Beer Barrel Polka" and "Cuddle Up a Little Closer, Lovey Mine." He was back two days later to do overdubs. These instrumentals were released as a single, to little fanfare.

Merle's last 1955 session was on August 19. This time he brought in Roy Lanham and some of the Whippoorwills to back him, along with Dusty Rhodes on steel guitar and Bakersfield fiddler Jelly Sanders. The four songs that resulted were excellent, with tight arrangements and superb playing. "Turn My Picture Upside Down," "If You Want It, I've Got It," and "Hunky Dory" were all recorded in the pop-meets-Western-swing vein of the Whippoorwills, which Merle obviously liked, but were unsellable in the hard honky-tonk era of the mid-1950s. Merle also laid down another instrumental, a version of the pop standard "Up a Lazy River." Although the results of this session were musically excellent, this would be his last session under his own name for Capitol for six years. He would record with other people as a session man many times between 1955 and 1961, but refused to record anything under his own name. The reasons were many, from the fact that his alcoholism worsened and his mental illness kept his mind in a dark place, to the fact that he was busy doing other things, including performing on *Town Hall Party* and touring with Gene Autry. Bettie Travis noted: "The kind of things he wrote weren't selling in the mid-'50s.... It was as if he had just dried up. He was more concerned with his nerves than anything else, and that's what he always blamed it on—that he had this nervous condition and the only thing that helped was the drink. It certainly did cause him many, many problems.... It caused me many, many problems, too."[312]

Part of the problem, Merle told his last wife, Dorothy Travis, in later years, was Ken Nelson's attitude toward him in the studio. Eddie Pennington recalls: "Merle told Dorothy that he hated that guy with the glasses [Ken Nelson] who would look through the glass at him and say, 'Is that the best you can do?' Merle said it just killed his desire to record."[313]

In the meantime, Ken Nelson began to assemble the guitar instrumental album. He correctly calculated that there were many fans of Merle's playing who would buy a collection of solo electric guitar performances. Despite the fact that Merle had been a mess for most of this time and that the final versions of many of the songs had been pieced together from multiple takes, the album was a tour de force—a guitar masterpiece. *The Merle Travis Guitar* was released in March 1956. Referred to as the "yellow album" by Merle and his fans, it is the record by which thumbpicking-style guitar is judged. It gave birth to the term "Travis picking," as Merle so thoroughly owns the Muhlenberg County guitar style on these recordings. It sold well, beyond expectations, and was kept in print over the years, with repressings in the 1960s, 1970s, and 1980s. There were foreign pressings and even a ten-inch vinyl version released in Australia. It was reissued on cassette in the 1980s. CD reissues began in the 1990s, and one can still purchase it today as an MP3 download. It is difficult to say how many aspiring guitarists have been influenced by *The Merle Travis Guitar*, but the number must be in the tens of thousands. Merle set the bar impossibly high—few players have ever managed to replicate its fire and passion, even as the "yellow album" served as a template for a master class in "Travis picking" that many guitarists followed over the next decades.

The liner notes to *The Merle Travis Guitar* speak of Merle's style and technique

To begin with, there's the tone Merle gets. It is rich and expressive, reflecting a great reverence for the instrument, as does the music of all great folk instrumentalists. When Merle Travis was a youngster, playing tent and medicine shows back in Boone County, Kentucky [they got that wrong, it was Muhlenberg County], he was deeply influenced by the so-called "natural" or "unschooled" musicians. They inherited their style of playing from the frontier and backwoods people who made music back in the days when musical instruments were rare and prized possessions.

In those early days, the few simple songs the people knew were played over and over. In making the tunes "sound better," folk musicians developed full and often very distinctive tones on their instruments. As Merle demonstrates in this recording, tone by itself can impart strength and poignancy to the humblest of harmonies, the simplest of melodies.

The importance of Merle Travis as a guitarist has been obscured by his fame as a vocalist, and as composer of such country and western favorites as "Smoke! Smoke! Smoke!" "No Vacancy," "Cincinnati Lou," and "So Round, So Firm, So Fully Packed." Actually, his technique alone makes him outstanding among guitarists on the American scene. When Merle plays, every phrase is fluent, every note is clean.

The notes bend the truth a bit, skirting the fact that the record was spliced and edited together "almost measure by measure," as Nelson put it, and that several of the songs featured Merle overdubbing lead guitar over his own rhythm guitar tracks:

Even though the music in this album sometimes sounds as though several guitarists were playing at the same time, no recording tricks of any sort were used.

The Merle Travis Guitar was a milestone for Merle. It was his first full-length album (not counting the four-disc, eight-song 78 rpm album *Folk Songs of the Hills* from 1947). It made his name a household word among fans of guitar music. It sold well and kept Capitol Records satisfied while his vocal releases struggled to find a place on the country charts. It was a difficult time in his life, but through the trials and tribulations Merle had created a masterpiece.

On the bottom-right corner of the back cover of *The Merle Travis Guitar* is a tiny sentence that looks a bit like it was added to the graphic design at the last minute. Next to Merle's photo, it states: "The composer of 'Sixteen Tons.'" Fellow musician Jack Rogers told this author:

I went back to California in '55. When I got there Merle said, "That tune we cut five years ago [speaking of "Sixteen Tons"], Ernie made a big hit of that. Capitol thinks it's a smash." He said, "Can you loan me twenty dollars?" I said, "What?" He said, "I can't get any money." I said, "Well, I'll loan you twenty dollars. You're going to be a big star now."[314]

On January 4, 1956, Merle's home troubles were blasted on the front
pages of newspapers across the country.

CHAPTER 6

SIXTEEN TONS— AND THE "SHOOTOUT"

Merle's autobiographical writing stopped with the events of the year 1955. He
produced most of that text later in his life, when he was living in Nashville and
writing for several country music magazines and fan publications. There appear
to have been several attempts to get Merle to complete an autobiography in the

1970s and early 1980s, but it never happened. During a period of sobriety in the 1960s, when his creative juices were flowing, Merle wrote all the time—about people he liked, old memories, funny things that happened to him along the way. There are too many of these short pieces to include in this book, but hopefully the pieces will be collected in another volume at a later date. Thus, the rest of this book you hold now will be a biography, but with as many direct quotes from Merle as possible, so the events can be heard through his voice.

By 1955, Tennessee Ernie Ford had become a full-fledged star. He reprised his early hick persona to play Cousin Ernie on the *I Love Lucy* television show, and he took on the host role in the summer of 1954 for the NBC television game show *Kollege of Musical Knowledge*. No longer known only for his country boogie records, Ford cut pop orchestra records and by early 1955 began to host the *Tennessee Ernie Ford Show*, a national NBC television broadcast from the El Capitan Theatre in Hollywood.

The show featured an orchestra bandleader that Ford had heard on the *Kukla, Fran and Ollie* TV puppet show named Jack Fascinato. Although he was a pop orchestra leader, Fascinato hailed from Bevier, Missouri, and connected on a country-boy-in-Hollywood level with Ford. Ford had made several pop records in 1954 using Billy May's orchestra, and recorded several Davy Crockett–themed songs for the Walt Disney Productions' *Disneyland* television show in early 1955. In May 1955, Ford recorded the first of many gospel sessions for Capitol (Ford included a gospel song every week on his NBC television show). One of the gospel songs that Ford laid down was the Merle Travis updated version of the old gospel number "I Am a Pilgrim." According to Tennessee Ernie's son J. Buck Ford, "Sixteen Tons" was brought up for possible use in June 1955, when Ford and Fascinato were looking for new material:

> Dad and Jack Fascinato dusted it off during a search for material for the daily NBC series. Taking Merle's straight guitar melody, Jack brought the Travis-picking tempo down, and built a spare, jazz instrumentation around it that completely altered the feel and mood of the song; transforming it musically and theatrically, allowing Dad's vocal to bring a sense of drama to the arrangement that was only hinted at in Travis' original version. Backed by Jack's small seven-piece band, the song generated far more response than anticipated.[315]

In Fascinato's recollection: "When we were doing a daytime show in the early 1950s, we were trying to build a library of tunes, and I would pick up my list of tunes to arrange, and one day there was this song, 'Sixteen Tons.' And strangely enough, from the first time we rehearsed in the NBC studio, once we got into that thing, the crew would stop talking and there was a silence as everyone listened. And we knew we had something then."[316] Tennessee Ernie Ford told the *Saturday Evening Post*: "I'd sung 'Sixteen Tons' years before, but it hadn't been any blockbuster, and Merle Travis, who'd written it, had put it on an album of his songs called *Folk Songs of the Hills*. Nothing happened there either. Then we decided to do some of Merle's things with modern instrumentation. When Merle did them, he'd used a straight guitar-music background. When we did them we used a flute, a bass clarinet, a trumpet, a clarinet, drums, a guitar, vibes and a piano. They gave it a real wonderful sound."[317]

When Ford performed the new arrangement of "Sixteen Tons" on his television show, NBC received twelve hundred letters the first week asking him to reprise it. By the second week, NBC had received two thousand more letters. J. Buck Ford picks up the story:

> Pleased with the response, Dad and Jack added it to the road repertoire and performed it for the second time at the Indiana State Fair later that summer. The crowd of thirty thousand was at capacity for the first night's show, and by the fade of the last four notes of "Sixteen Tons," the crowd's decibels had risen to capacity. The response to the song was nothing short of deafening. [Capitol Records producer] Lee Gillette was aware that the song had scored nicely on the morning show, and Cliffie Stone padded his pitch appropriately by bringing in boxes of mail and recounting the reaction it had received in Indianapolis. But Gillette was not impressed enough to make it the A-side of the upcoming session. Moreover, the failure of the album that the song had originally been a part of was—ten years after the fact—still fresh in his mind. "You Don't Have to Be a Baby to Cry" was the A-side. Period. He'd cut "the Travis thing" as the B-side, but he had no hopes for it.[318]

Accordingly, on September 20, 1955, Ford and Fascinato and their seven-piece orchestra recorded "You Don't Have to Be a Baby to Cry" first, then subsequently turned to "Sixteen Tons." They did three takes, eventually choosing the second one for release. Ford noted:

> It had a good solid beat to begin with. In addition, I snapped my fingers all through it. Sometimes I set my own tempo during rehearsal by doing that. The orchestra leader asks me, "What tempo do you want, Ernie?" I say, "About like this," and I begin to snap my third finger and thumb together. After I was through rehearing that song, Lee Gillette, who was in charge of the recording session for Capitol Records, screamed through

the telephone from the control room, "Tell Ernie to leave that finger snapping in when you do the final waxing." It certainly added to that song.... It gave an effect I hadn't heard before.[319]

J. Buck Ford tells what happened then:

On October 17, Capitol shipped the new single to distributors nationwide and to deejays around the country, confident that "Baby" would be a hit. But inexplicably, radio stations coast-to-coast began "flipping" the single and playing the B-side.... In the eleven days following its release, four hundred thousand singles were sold. Demand for the song was so great, Capitol geared all its pressing plants nationwide to meet the deluge of orders. In twenty-four days, more than one million records were sold, and "Sixteen Tons" became the fastest-selling single in Capitol's history. By November it had captured the top spot on every major record chart in the country, and by December 15 (less than two months after its release) more than two million copies had been sold, making it the most successful single ever recorded. Merle Travis was nothing short of immortalized by the song. In later years, whenever he performed the song himself, he'd change the last line, and sing, "I owe my soul... to Tennessee Ernie Ford."[320]

Fellow musician Johnny Western mused to this author: "What's the famous old saying? You're just two and a half minutes away from being a superstar."[321]

"Sixteen Tons" was not only a huge hit, but it also became something else—something rare and difficult to achieve. It got into the nation's consciousness. It was a *phenomenon*. It resonated with people in a way that Merle would never have dreamed when he wrote it back in 1946. Arguably, Merle could have never sold the song the way Tennessee Ernie Ford did. There was something about the combination—Merle's song, Ford's voice, Fascinato's arrangement, the finger snapping, and the exact right moment for the release.

It was rare—if not unheard-of—to hear a song about the trials and tribulations of the blue-collar worker in a hit-parade-topping popular song in the mid-1950s. Yet within weeks, the song had become a smash hit and Merle a folk hero, a writer of important songs of social consciousness. He was profiled in the *United Mine Workers Journal* and the subject of a long feature story in the Owensboro, Kentucky, newspaper celebrating their hometown boy who'd made good. Gene Autry even modified his show to "honor Merle Travis, who wrote the words and music to 'Sixteen Tons.'"[322] Countless folk music musicians and fans who came of age in the folk music boom of the 1960s cited hearing "Sixteen Tons" as children in the mid-1950s as a formative influence on their later musical tastes.

In many ways, Merle's joke about owing his soul to Ford was no joke at all. When "Sixteen Tons" was released and became a hit, his finances were in shambles. The song should have meant an influx of cash for Merle, one that would solve all of his financial woes. As discussed in the last chapter, not only was there substantial debt from his divorce with Judy Hayden, but his lawyer, Jerry Rolston, was having trouble convincing Merle's publisher, Sylvester Cross of American Music Publishing, to pay the money he was due. Bettie Travis, Merle's new wife, recalled later: "Merle was proud of the song becoming a hit. Merle got money out of 'Sixteen Tons.' I don't know which set of books Sylvester Cross... paid from. Up until that time, we were really strapped. We were so poor that we didn't have a bank account. We would get the money and put it into envelopes and pay everybody. 'Sixteen Tons' put the icing on the cake."[323]

In 1956, songwriting royalties on a million-selling single were about $10,000, which meant that Merle would receive somewhere between $30,000 and $40,000. In today's money, that barely registers, but in 1956, when the average working man's yearly salary was around $3,800 (and the average working woman's was $1,100), that was big money. Unfortunately, the troubles with Cross continued. Rolston began sending letters such as this one, dated February 3, 1956, urgently requesting advances on royalty payments:

Dear Mr. Cross:

Several weeks ago we had a conversation wherein I advised you that I might call upon you for a further advance on behalf of Merle Travis, and you at that time advised me that if I absolutely had to have same you could accommodate me to the extent of approximately $1500. With Mr. Travis on the road and many, many things to take care of, it became apparent that I would need the advance on Monday, and since Monday I have been phoning you; but either you have not received my messages or have overlooked them.

It would be sincerely appreciated if you would immediately mail me a check payable to Merle Travis in the sum of $1500 as an advance. You know that I would not ask for the advance if it were not absolutely necessary to properly manage Merle's affairs. Obviously I am managing Merle's affairs so that he will have a clear mind to devote to his performing and composing talents. He cannot have a clear mind if pressures are put upon him. Without a doubt Merle will have earned any and all advances that may give him as soon as you receive the check from Capitol which is due February 15th.[324]

Despite the behind-the-scenes money worries, the beginning of 1956 seemed to mark an incredible second chance for Merle. He hadn't had a real hit since the late 1940s, and the swell of publicity and admiration surrounding "Sixteen Tons" brought him back into the limelight in a way that none of his own records had been able to achieve. In addition, Capitol scheduled the release of *The Merle Travis Guitar* for March 1956. The album was a brilliant work of art and was poised to bring Merle a great deal of respect. Although Capitol must have had limited expectations for an instrumental guitar album, it was a blue-ribbon artistic achievement for both Merle and the label.

Sadly, and somewhat predictably, Merle managed to screw things up. Newspaper headlines on January 4, 1956, all over the country, from Des Moines to Shreveport, Maine to Montana, large and small papers alike, blared in huge capital letters the chaos that had occurred at the Travis house on Chandler Boulevard in North Hollywood:

"16 TONS WRITER AMOK"

"VALLEY COMPOSER DEFIES POLICE IN TEAR-GAS SIEGE"

"POLICE QUELL A '16 TON RAGE' BY BELLIGERENT SONG WRITER"

"COMPOSER LEAVES BARRICADED HOME"

"JAIL '16 TONS' COMPOSER IN WILD BATTLE WITH WIFE"

"WIFE BEATEN BY COMPOSER MERLE TRAVIS"

Merle's memory:

"I shoot up clock—make headlines—go to jail"

According to Bettie Travis:

"Tons" was hot when that happened, so the press paid a lot of attention to it.... We had only been married a short time. I had always told him that I would not live with anyone who had a drinking problem like that. I didn't want it for myself or the kids. There was a party at the house and I knew it would lead to drinking. His friends thought I was a bad influence who didn't want Merle to have any fun. He couldn't be around it and not drink. All night long, I got madder and madder and finally went to bed. [The next morning] I started letting him have it, and he bopped me. I went out the window with my kids and to the neighbor's house.[325]

Michael Robinson, Bettie's son from her previous marriage who was living in the house at the time, remembered: "Our mom came and said, 'Go out the window and go to the neighbor's house.' There was a chain-link fence with a gate in it over to the neighbor's house. I [went over there and was] looking out the curtains to see what was happening."[326]

Merle was no stranger to the front page of the *Los Angeles Times*. He was already known for drunkenness and unpredictable behavior. This time, however, things were different. As Jody Maphis put it: "The headline wasn't 'Merle Travis arrested,' it was 'Writer of 16 Tons Arrested.'"[327] During the altercation, Merle hit Bettie with his pistol, and he would carry the scarlet letter of "wife beater" with him for the rest of his life. Merle had shot at the clock on the fireplace mantel, and in his drunken reasoning, figured that the incident was over. With Bettie and her sons Dennis and Michael safely at the next-door neighbor's house, he passed out on his couch. Unbeknownst to him, the police showed up and surrounded the house, preparing for a gun battle with a berserk, out-of-control madman. Press photographers showed up on the scene, too. The next day, the news headlines and photos across the country made it seem as though a major shootout had occurred:

VAN NUYS, CALIF: Police, armed, cautiously approach the home of western songwriter Merle Travis after his wife reported he had threatened to shoot anyone trying to enter. Earlier he reportedly injured his wife during a drinking spree at home with a friend. Mrs. Travis called police from a neighbor's home.[328]

VAN NUYS, CALIF: Detective Sgt. Charles Stewart talks with Mrs. Bettie Travis, wife of songwriter and guitarist Merle Travis, after she sought refuge at a friend's home. Mrs. Travis reported that Travis, drunk, struck her with a pistol and threatened to shoot anyone who tried to enter their San Fernando Valley home. Police, after a cautious approach, found the "Sixteen Tons" writer in a drunken stupor.[329]

As police surrounded the house with squad cars and tear gas, reporter Sid Hughes from the *Los Angeles Mirror-News* called Merle on the telephone, waking him.

Hughes kept the singer on the telephone for 10 minutes to keep him from shooting anyone. Hughes also tried to persuade Travis to give himself up peacefully.

"Just tell them to let me go to sleep," Travis told Hughes. "I haven't had more than an hour's sleep in five days. Just tell them to let me sleep."

Hughes asked the singer to "go out on the front porch and wave a white handkerchief and they will let you sleep."

"I just want to go to sleep," Travis repeated. "Besides, if I go out it will get in the papers. I feel like Dillinger."

"It will get in the papers if you shoot someone," Hughes argued.

At that point, Police Sgt. Charles Russell and the singer's friend, Joe Maphias [sic], a guitar player in western costume, entered the house and grabbed the singer.

They said Travis did not have a gun in his hands when they entered, and that he had suffered no harm.[330]

Maphis was there because Bettie asked the sheriff to call him while the police were surrounding the home. Joe and Rose Lee Maphis were their close friends from the *Town Hall Party* television show and lived close by, so Joe drove to the scene with the police. Larry Collins recalled that Joe also tried to recruit him to come along:

We lived just down the street from Merle. One day in the afternoon, late afternoon, I think. All these policemen.... We lived on a corner. All these police cars gathered around our house. About twenty people came in our backyard, along with Joe [Maphis]. They went to Joe's house, I guess Bettie told them, "Go get Joe." Then Joe's idea was that he'd come get me, and he and I would walk up and get Merle out of this. I was going to help. Dad came out and asked, "You're going to take the boy up there and Merle's drunk, with guns? Why would you do that?" Joe said to him, this is a quote: "Well, he ain't going to kill no kid." Needless to say, I didn't go.[331]

Jody Maphis recalled later:

The Sheriff calls him [my father], said, "We've got your buddy surrounded. Can you come down and help talk him out?" I guess at the time there had been some shots fired, and they didn't know how Bettie was. The sheriff was going, "Hey Merle, I got your buddy. Joe Maphis is up here." When Merle comes out, he'd done taken a shower and put on a suit and everything. When they run the picture in the paper the next day, Daddy said *he* was the one that looked like the criminal.[332]

While Maphis and the police sergeant entered the house through the front door, a half dozen heavily armed officers entered through the back. The *Los Angeles Times* reported what happened next:

They found Travis sitting at his desk in the bedroom, unarmed, profoundly puzzled and dressed in pajamas. He regarded the raiding party meekly.

"What's this all about?" he asked Johnson. "I'm in my own house."

Lt. Johnson said Travis appeared to him to be "very intoxicated" at the moment.

He was taken to Van Nuys jail and booked on suspicion of wife beating, a felony. He seemed a bit rubbery on his legs, officers said, so he was shown to a cell for a snooze before going through the fingerprinting routine.

"I love everybody!" the chubby tunesmith insisted as he was led away. "You don't do such things as shoot people! I'm the happiest guy in the world!"[333]

Immediately, all parties involved in Merle's personal and professional life realized that drunkenness and shooting guns inside the house might be written off as "good ol' boy" tomfoolery, but the felony charge of spousal battery posed a serious matter legally, as well as for Merle's public image—especially since Merle was now at a different level in show business, having written the number one song in the nation the previous year.

The next day's *Los Angeles Times* showed a photo of Bettie Travis with a gleeful expression on her face, embracing Merle, captioned: "MAKING UP— Merle Travis is greeted warmly by wife at front door of North Hollywood home after his release from jail. He was jailed after spree in home." The accompanying article was a classic example of publicity spin. Bettie refused to press charges, and both she and Merle began to deny that anything bad had really happened: "Travis couldn't remember anything like hitting his wife. And, as a matter of fact, Mrs. Travis told detectives she was unable to remember the clock shooting incident."[334] (The clock-shooting incident was thereafter a perennial punch line among friends and visitors to the house. In country music culture, a line like "I was just killing time" to reference shooting a clock made the uncomfortable public incident a comedic matter.)

Three days after the event, newspapers reported that radio station KITI in Chehalis-Centralia, Washington, was banning airplay of Merle Travis records due to the event. The news had gone national, and was gossip fodder throughout the area where the Travis family lived. Things got so bad that Merle and Bettie pulled Bettie's sons out of public school and enrolled them in a private military school in the San Fernando Valley.[335] Merlene told this author: "It made me sad for both of them. With the guns all drawn on the front page of the newspaper. My God. I think in those days, they always said yes to celebrities. They just let them get away with murder."[336] Larry Collins remembers, "Hell, it was like O.J. [Simpson]!"[337] Three weeks after the event, Merle left for a tour around the country with Gene Autry. There was no mention of the incident. In the grand publicity machine tradition, those in charge of making money from Merle Travis swept the whole thing under the rug. Merle's friend Gary Williams, a young performer on the *Town Hall Party* show at the time, remembered:

> Once he had been let out of jail, Merle showed up a couple weeks later at *Town Hall*, where he was welcomed enthusiastically by the audience (country music fans are very forgiving. Anything you do is a-okay—just so long as you keep on a-pickin' and a-grinnin' fer 'em). On the way home that night, Merle off-handedly commented—
>
> "Well, Gary, I had a few too many drinks the other night and got my name in the papers." THEE [sic] understatement of the season!
>
> "We don't have to talk about it, if you don't want to," I answered.
>
> "No, I wanta talk about it," he insisted. "I'm sure you read what the papers had to say, but I want to tell you what really happened." He then related how he had got to drinking at his house, then, getting out his revolver, he said to Betty [sic]—his 13th wife, by last inventory—"Watch me hit that old clock on the wall!"
>
> He plugged the clock with six shots. Poor Betty, who had gone through this same thing before with him, headed for "sanctuary" in a neighbor's house. Merle, so he said, then went to bed and was soundly sleeping, when the phone rang.
>
> "I answered it and the voice said he was a news reporter. The guy asked me, 'Are you ready to surrender?' 'Surrender what?' I asked. He then told me to look out the window. The yard was full of police, with their guns drawn, and there were spectators and news cameras and searchlights flooding the yard. It looked like a three-ring circus was being held on my front lawn! After awhile, Joe Maphis... came in and we walked out the front door together."

That was Merle's version of this little news sensation, which was carried in papers across the country. Knowing cops, and knowing leeching news hounds, and knowing Trav, it sounds about right.[338]

In March, Sylvester Cross at American Music ran a full-page ad in *Billboard* listing all of Merle's hits going back to 1946. There was no mention of his brush with the law. Merle was never charged with any crime for the January 1956 incident, as Bettie refused to press charges. Anyone who has followed Merle's career knows about the infamous story of the 1956 "police shootout." Various untruths have persisted—many people still believe that Merle shot at the police, for example. What might have once passed for barely acceptable drunken behavior for a Kentucky hillbilly musician was now clearly unacceptable for a Hollywood hillbilly who had written the nation's number one song. For many mainstream Americans, it was a horrific incident that they would remember and associate with the name Merle Travis for decades.

As Jody Maphis put it: "Yeah, well, when you're running around with '16 TONS' on your license plate and you've got the biggest song on the planet, you're gonna attract some attention. The hillbillies took over Hollywood for a while, but they didn't realize what they were doing. They were creating this stuff that took the world by storm. That period of time, all of a sudden you're handing a whole bunch of hillbillies fame and fortune, shit's gonna happen. They're gonna come up with some brilliant stuff, but there's gonna be some dumb shit going on, too."[339]

Gordon Terry (left), Johnny Cash (center), and Merle in a candid photo
from a country music magazine from 1965. Although this is not a great
photo, it is the best image representation of the pill-popping,
all-night antics that nearly killed Merle in the early 1960s.
(*Country Music Review* magazine, May/June 1965.)

CHAPTER 7

THE LOST YEARS: ONE PILL IS TOO MANY AND A THOUSAND AIN'T ENOUGH

The years spanning 1956 to 1966 are in a sense "the lost years" in Merle Travis's life and career. He stayed active, kept performing, and was still a country music celebrity. In the public eye, he was the great folk hero who had written the beloved hit "Sixteen Tons." Though no new material was released from 1955 to 1961, during that hiatus, Capitol released two great albums of previously recorded material. Then in 1961, he went back to the studio and rerecorded many of his 1940s hits for a new album release. In 1962 he recorded a hot guitar duet album with his friend Joe Maphis. In 1963 he recorded a fantastic album of new original folk songs, *Songs of the Coal Mines*. The Guild Guitar Company made an ornate Merle Travis signature model guitar, and Merle was invited to become a member of the Grand Ole Opry in Nashville, though he failed to show up. His drinking and drugging spiraled out of control as he battled his internal demons. He stayed drunk most of the time, was involved in a child custody battle, became roaring buddies with Johnny Cash, developed an addiction to pills, almost died from a pill-induced stomach hemorrhage, bought a large estate and lost it, almost died in a fire he accidentally set in a Hollywood motel room, was committed to the Camarillo Mental Hospital and the Saugus Work Farm to dry out, and was temporarily divorced from his wife, Bettie.

Three months after the 1956 "shootout" incident, Merle appeared in court to plead innocent on a four-year-old drunk charge. The paperwork had been misplaced and had only come up again because of the new national headlines. There was a trial in April and Merle was acquitted because the judge refused to indict on four-year-old charges.

Also in the early months of 1956, Merle toured with Hank Thompson as a special guest and resumed his radio show on KFI in Los Angeles. That summer, he was invited to go on his first international trip, a package tour called "Hollywood Parade" that was a benefit for United Cerebral Palsy. The tour was headlined by movie stars Zsa Zsa Gabor, Pat O'Brien, and Tex Ritter, and also featured Merle, "Yodeling Blonde Bombshell" Carolina Cotton, Metropolitan Opera star Felix Knight, comedians Don DeFore and Bob Hopkins, singer Martha Tilton, actress Shirley Thomas, the dance team of Raalf and Lorraine, and Roy Martin's twenty-piece orchestra. The group arranged plane tickets to Johannesburg, South Africa, with stops thereafter in Nice, Rome, Paris, and London. This was Merle's first time flying across the Atlantic Ocean. At the first stop in New York City, he sent his daughter Patty a postcard:

> Hi, Queen:
> Good to have talked with you last night from N.Y. This is our first stop. Talked to Zsa Zsa about you, she, as well as all the troup [*sic*] is tops.
> Love you, Dad[340]

The "Hollywood Parade" began a week's worth of shows at the Olympia Ice Rink in Johannesburg on May 28, 1956. Newspaper ads hyped the arrival of the American celebrities: "We've taken the Cold out of the Ice and now present the Hottest Show in Town!"[341] Country music was a novelty to the audience of mostly British expats. Although middle-of-the-road artists like Jim Reeves and Slim Whitman enjoyed popularity with British and South African audiences, the rural hillbilly and Western swing varieties of country music were new. The *Johannesburg Star*'s Oliver Walker reported the day after the debut performance: "Carolina Cotton, a yodeler, would have been more effective if there had been some band-parts to support her, while Merle Travis, in a sequined cowboy suit, twanged that popular monstrosity of the age—an electric guitar."[342] Another daily newspaper reported on Merle's debut performance, with a particular giveaway (Merle never toured with a banjo) regarding the locals' lack of knowledge about country music or Merle's background: "Merle ('Sixteen Tons') Travis, in a salmon pink cowboy suit and a great burst of candour, told us 'When I don't sing, I sound better, particularly with this little cold I got,' and thereupon did some engaging gymnastics on his banjo. By the time he got around to 'Sixteen Tons,' he had found his voice again, or most of it."[343]

By the end of the run in Johannesburg, the reviews were less than glowing: "Let's take these visiting Hollywood stars with a grain of sodium pentothal. The truth is that flesh-and-blood Hollywood does not transplant.... The great stars are fine in their celluloid medium, but, shorn of their script-writers, directors, lighting men and all the techniques of dubbing and re-taking, they are naked to the winter wind, which Johannesburg audiences tempereth not."[344] After the Johannesburg shows were over, one newspaper reported that the "'Hollywood' Show Profit or Loss Still Uncertain."[345]

Despite the lukewarm reception, Merle seemed to enjoy his travels to a new and strange land. He sent several postcards to his daughter Patty. One read:

Hello Pats:
> Here I am back in the very heart of Africa. And whew it's hot.
> I'll write you again from Italy.
> My love, Dad[346]

When Merle returned to the United States after the European dates, he prepared for another trip, this time back home to Kentucky. Bobby Anderson, a local journalist and radio announcer on WMTA in Central City, Kentucky, had met Merle before, when Merle was there to play a show on top of a drive-in. Anderson told this author: "I was working at the newspaper, and the editor of the paper asked me, 'You think you could get Merle to come in? Find out what he would take to come.' So I called his manager. She said he would come. It'd be $1,000. That was when you could buy any star for $1,000. Of course, 'Sixteen Tons' was a big song then. They gave me a check to give to Merle. [The day of the show] he took the check, turned it over to the back and put his name on it, handed it back to me, and said, 'This don't cost you anything.'"[347]

Beginning in 1956, Anderson led a campaign to erect a monument to Merle and his song "Sixteen Tons" in Muhlenberg County. Through the efforts of Paul Camplin, along with many others in the community, including Bobby Anderson, Jess Lovelace, and Raymond Fitzpatrick, a Merle Travis Memorial Fund was established.

Despite the fact that Merle had made national headlines at the beginning of the year for his ill-fated police standoff, the folks back home in Kentucky were willing to consider the incident water under the bridge. They were proud of the awareness that "Sixteen Tons" had brought to the coal mining region, and they wanted to honor their hometown hero. Anderson noted: "Merle and his run-in with the law out there? Very little came to us [in Kentucky] about it."[348]

Merle's memory:

"Gene Autry flies back to my home coming"

Merle agreed to come back to Kentucky for the monument dedication in June 1956. Through Merle, Bobby Anderson, and Merle's agent, Bobbie Bennett, other stars were lined up to appear, including Gene Autry, Chet Atkins, Ken Nelson (Merle's producer at Capitol Records), George Vaught and the Dreamers, and Ike Everly's sons Don and Phil, who were now performing under the name the Everly Brothers (the same name Ike had used with his own brothers in the 1930s). The site of the monument's placement was briefly up for debate until Merle's old friend Bunnie Baugh Mullens—hostess of the "pickin' parties" where a teenaged Merle used to watch Mose Rager and Ike Everly play—agreed to donate a plot of land opposite her home in Ebenezer. It was right next to Ebenezer church and the church's cemetery, where Merle's parents were buried.

Merle, Bettie, and her two sons, Dennis and Michael, drove the yellow 1954 Cadillac Eldorado they called "Yeller Eller" across the country to make the event. Merle's daughter Patty made arrangements to be there, and she was put in charge of unveiling the monument. Gene Autry planned to come in his private plane.

When June 29 rolled around, it was one of the hottest days of the year. Tents were erected on the plot of land behind the new monument in an attempt to shield the dignitaries from direct sun. The monument was covered with a cloth, waiting for the grand unveiling. There was no infrastructure in Muhlenberg County to accommodate such large crowds. The throng dwarfed the size of the one that had attended Merle's first homecoming event back in 1947. People were parked along the side of the county's two-lane roads as far as the eye could see. Anderson remembers: "There was—goodness, I don't know how many dignitaries were there. The intersection was blocked for miles. The *Courier-Journal* said there was twelve to fifteen thousand. That's amazing. That's the largest crowd that had ever assembled in Muhlenberg County as far as I know. Nobody was going anywhere. They just left the cars on the side of the road, and some of them parked in the middle of the road."[349]

At the site of the event, guest speakers and performers entertained the folks while Merle, his family, and the visiting dignitaries sat in the hot tent. Although it was sweltering, Merle wore one of his best Nudie Western suits, and smiled and acted like the returned conquering hero that he was. Many locals who'd grown up with Merle and knew his family could hardly believe that his star power was sufficient to bring Autry, one of the biggest movie stars in the world, all the way to tiny Ebenezer, Kentucky. Lynn Wells, a local man who was a child at the time, recalled: "I remember Merle Travis Day in Ebenezer, 1956. We were watching from across the street, and my dad told me to look off to the left. Here come this big white Cadillac, and there was Gene Autry! He was wearing a suit and waving his white cowboy hat at the crowd. I'll never forget it."[350]

When all the speeches and musical performances concluded, the monument was unveiled. Merle's daughter Patty was tasked with pulling back the sheet and revealing it to the crowd for the first time. She remembers that day in her *A Scrapbook of My Daddy*:

> What an honor it was to unveil the monument for Dad on that hot summer day in 1956. I drove the short distance from Owensboro to Ebenezer, Kentucky to participate in the "Merle Travis Day" celebration. And what a celebration it was! Ebenezer swelled from a population of 75 to a crowd of 15,000.... Of course I was a little nervous, but Dad made me laugh when he looked at his image on the bronze plaque and quipped, "Look, Patty, they got the ears right!"
>
> Hollywood's favorite cowboy movie star, Gene Autry was there. He honored Dad with this statement: "I consider Merle Travis to be one of the greatest writers of American music in the world today, and I am glad to count him among my closest friends."
>
> Chet Atkins and his wife, Leona came for the celebration and the folks enjoyed some fine "Chester pickin."... Two young handsome boys who were the sons of Dad's good friend Ike Everly played their guitars

and harmonized a beautiful song. Their names were Don and Phil (later to be known as "The Everly Brothers"). It was a day to remember.

When it was finally time for Dad to speak, the crowd hushed to strain to hear his words. He humbly smiled and reminded the crowd, "I didn't write 'Sixteen Tons'... you did. Some of you lived it." He went on to say, "I hope that I will never bring dishonor to this county, community, this group of people. I left here many years ago, a poor boy, hoping only to find a job. I knew what I wanted, but didn't know if I'd get it. I have had some success and am happy. But the happiest part of all is that I can return and know that all of you are my friends. Otherwise you would not be here."

When Dad sat down, the crowd broke loose with a long and loud applause. Dad buried his head in his hands, not crying, but apparently embarrassed by all this to-do.[351]

Once the marker was unveiled, the crowd quickly dispersed, seeking relief from the heat. Newspapers the next day offered the sort of glowing reviews usually reserved for presidential visits: "Emotions expressed by the several thousand people crowding about a speakers' tent at Ebenezer ranged from the longing of small fry for a look at Gene Autry, to the tears shed by an elderly man with a handlebar mustache. Master of Ceremonies for the day was Bobby Anderson of Radio Station WMTA, Central City. He was executive chairman of the committee which made 'Merle Travis Day' possible."[352]

Capitol Records' A&R man and producer Ken Nelson attended Merle's homecoming celebration. With the success of "Sixteen Tons," it made sense to have Merle record a new album of folk songs in the same style as a response to the song's massive success.

One of the revelations that came to light just as this book was going to print was that Merle recorded an album's worth of unreleased folk material at Gold Star Studios in Los Angeles in 1957. A one-of-a-kind acetate record turned up from the collection of a guitarist named Sonny Richter, one of Merle's old friends. Richter's son Randy Layton sold the acetate on eBay, unaware of its status as a one-of-a-kind rarity. The unreleased album, containing twelve songs ("Comin' Home from the Wake," "The Wise Old Owl," "Green Gravel," and "The Barber of the Hair," among others), sound like demos more than master takes, but it's obvious that these songs were meant for a folk-oriented follow-up to capitalize on the "Sixteen Tons" success. It is unknown why the project never went any further than the acetate demos, except perhaps Travis's continued problems with alcohol and anxiety about recording sessions under Nelson's supervision.

It was obvious that Ken Nelson loved Merle and thought he was a super talent. Unfortunately, he must have realized that Merle's drinking and nerve problems were going to prevent him from making new records in the foreseeable future. Nelson looked to the Capitol vaults to see what old tracks he could repackage and release. It was a no-brainer to take the eight songs from the 1947 *Folk Songs of the Hills* album and rerelease them. With the popularity of Tennessee Ernie Ford's recording of "Sixteen Tons," Capitol would then have a new release with Merle's original recording of "Sixteen Tons" on it. Nelson dipped into the vaults again for four more tracks recorded for the Capitol Transcription service in the mid-1940s: "Possum up a 'Simmon Tree," "John Bolin," "Barbara Allen," and "Lost John." These would sit well thematically with the other eight.

Nelson brought the ten-year-old recordings into the Capitol studios and added reverb to them in an attempt to make them sound slightly more updated and modern. The resulting album, *Back Home*, was marketed as a current product. No one in the Capitol publicity department made overt mention that the recordings were a decade old. The cover was a simple color photograph of the iconic water-powered mill at Mabry Mill, Virginia. The album's title referenced the 1956 homecoming in Ebenezer, and the liner notes on the back cover described the "Merle Travis Day" event, even quoting the inscription on the plaque of the newly dedicated monument. *Back Home* wasn't intended to compete with whatever country artist was storming the charts at the time, but the album still sold beyond expectations. In particular, it was well received in certain music circles of New York and other Northeastern cities where young college students and intellectuals were studying authentic folk music.

Merle spent the rest of the year touring with Gene Autry, keeping up his weekly appearances on the *Town Hall Party* television show whenever possible, and playing his own shows. This was a schedule he would maintain for the next few years. The demands from Autry and *Town Hall Party* were minimal, and he could coast through the appearances while he (and Autry) were drinking.

Merle's memory:

"Gene Autry loans me money for house"

Autry loved Merle, and the feeling was mutual. Merle was a valuable right-hand man on Autry's package tours, and the fact that he had written a beloved song like "Sixteen Tons" made him even more valuable to the Autry organization. Autry was Merle's chief benefactor in the second half of the 1950s, and without his financial help, it is unlikely that Merle would have made it. Even though "Sixteen Tons" had been a multimillion-selling hit, it would take years for his publisher to issue the full royalty payments, only then after a series of bitter legal actions. Autry's generosity bridged the gap:

> Dear "Mr. Agent":
>
> I feel that you were a great addition to our show and know how much value your name and hit tune have now. For that reason and for the fact you always do a fine job, I am enclosing a bonus of $1,000.00 which I feel you deserve.
>
> Most sincerely yours, Gene [353]

Autry also helped Merle and Bettie with a down payment when they found a large, secluded estate in Van Nuys that they wanted to purchase. Located at 5731 Ranchito in a neighborhood filled with large San Fernando Valley estates built in the 1930s, the Ranchito house would be Merle's residence for close to ten years. It had originally been built in 1938 for actress Penny Singleton, known for her film portrayal of Blondie, the popular female comic strip character. Merle was good friends with Chic Young, the creator of the *Blondie* comic strip, and so it may have been through this association that Merle and Bettie discovered the house for sale. It was set back from the street, down a long driveway, and occupied a triple-size lot along with a guesthouse, a smokehouse, several other small buildings, and many fruit trees. There was a large cinderblock wall around the property. It offered the seclusion and privacy Merle so greatly desired.

The Ranchito house was not just another San Fernando Valley tract home. It was an estate, the sort of residence a proper star would own. Many people thought Merle had become rich after "Sixteen Tons." He and Bettie often hosted parties and get-togethers at the Ranchito estate, and those who attended thought that Merle had joined the ranks of LA's well-to-do. Few outside his inner circle knew the grim truth: that he was living there only thanks to Autry's loan while waiting on his lawyer to extract royalties from his music publisher.

Merle had upgraded his Standel 25L15 amplifier to a newer model when he returned from his South Africa, Europe and Kentucky trips. One day when he brought his original red Standel amp to Bob Crooks's garage shop in Temple City, California, for an upgrade to a newer-model Standel, someone was waiting there for him to arrive. Dick "R. C." Allen was a young, aspiring guitar maker from nearby El Monte who idolized Merle. He'd met Merle at several local shows and at *Town Hall Party*, and when he found out that Merle's amplifiers were made in his hometown of El Monte, he made it a point to be there when Merle visited. Merle took a liking to the young, guitar-obsessed fan. When he took delivery of a new Standel in 1956, he gave Allen both his original Standel 25L15 and the Gibson EH-185 amplifier he had used since 1940 (Allen kept both amps until he died, two of his most prized possessions). In the mid-1960s, Allen would make a pair of custom guitars for Merle, and he occasionally did repair work on Merle's other instruments. The pair remained friends for the rest of their lives.

The year 1956 also, of course, marked a sea change in music, as Elvis Presley and rock 'n' roll broke into the mainstream. While the Nashville music establishment and the *Grand Ole Opry* shunned the new music, the West Coast's *Town Hall Party* encouraged it, booking a host of touring rockabilly stars like Carl Perkins, Gene Vincent, and Eddie Cochran. The show also had their own young rockabilly cast members, including Larry and Lorrie Collins, known as the Collins Kids, and teenage singer Gary Williams, who was enamored with Merle and remained a close friend for the rest of his life. In his self-published memoir, Williams recalled:

> We were out at Merle Travis' house in the San Fernando Valley. In those days, before the freeway complex came into being, if you wanted to get anywhere in the West End of Los Angeles from the San Fernando Valley, you had to negotiate the twisting roads of either Laurel Canyon or Coldwater Canyon. Now, these were—and are—winding mountain roads, and you had better do heads-up driving. And you positively shouldn't attempt this while heavily under the influence—unless you've got a death wish.
>
> This didn't bother Merle any, as he climbed behind the wheel of his Cadillac.... So, off we went, on the most hair-raising drive imaginable, one usually experienced only in one's wildest nightmares. Snaking up Coldwater Canyon, traveling at what seemed to be Grand Prix speeds, we zigged and zagged to the edges of sheer drop-offs, screeching over to one side of the road, then back to the other, in a deadly game of dodge ball with oncoming cars. Other drivers made for the ditches, to avoid colliding with this Sixteen Tons of a juggernaut death machine. Jimmie [Rodgers Snow, Hank Snow's son, whom Merle was driving to the Los Angeles airport] and I grabbed each other in death-like grips and I begged Merle to let one of us take over the wheel. But no dice. Quietly but firmly, he would say, "I'm drivin'."
>
> Up, up and over we went, then down the other side of the mountain, with the same literal "cliff hangers" happening all the while. Merle would veer over into the oncoming lane and a car coming towards us would have to swerve over into our lane, in order to avoid a sure-fatal impact. I thought this suicide run would never end, but miraculously, we eventually made it to the canyon floor with no hits, no runs, but plenty of death-defying errors. They say God protects fools and children—and

we weren't no chillin's (Merle once told me, "I've had seventeen drunk driving arrests. So Betty—his wife—does the driving now, 'cause they took away my license." Really? I wonder why?)

Even after we landed at the airport, the Merle melodrama went on. Trav' got miffed at the gateman because he wouldn't let us accompany Jimmie all the way into the plane and he tried to start a fistfight with this official. I succeeded in wrestling him out of it. While we were walking through the parking lot, heading back to the car, Merle quite offhandedly said, "Gary, would you mind doing me a favor and driving us home. I'm tired."

That was ol' Trav... always the gentleman—even when bombed outta his gourd and terrorizing the neighborhood, firing off his six-shooter, or chauffeuring a couple of petrified fellows into the yawning mouth of a fiery holocaust.[354]

Michael Robinson recalled Merle's drinking: "I've never seen anybody drink so much, so quick. He had a gullet like a—I mean, he could take a pitcher of beer and down it in one gulp."[355] Rose Lee Maphis recalled in an interview with the author the role that alcohol played in that era: "[Drinking was] a big part of Joe Maphis's life, too. If he was going to meet somebody for a meeting of sorts, whatever it might be, they always did that in a club, to have a beer, or a drink, whatever; it was always, always in a bar. Joe was susceptible, and I'm sure Merle was, too."[356] Merle's memories:

> **"I get loaded then sober—quick at Bostonia"**
> **"I get loaded then sober—quick at Malimute"**
> **"Hank Penny is in love with Marion—me + Joe drink"**
> **"Buck Sartin brings tubs of booze"**
> **"Gene, Cotner and I am too drunk—Buttram comes to aid"**

Larry Collins of the Collins Kids remembered that it wasn't just Merle and Joe Maphis. In his experience, *all* the male entertainers of the era that drank to excess:

> Everything was good until somebody took a drink, and then everything would go to hell. Everybody back then, from Lefty Frizzell to Joe Maphis to Merle to my dad, to everybody—not the women, but the men drank. They'd drink, get drunk. And strange, it's like Lefty Frizzell, my dearest friend. When he was drunk, he was just drunk, *bad*. They would all come talk to me when they were drunk, like the Bob Wills deal. [Larry is referencing a famous story where Bob Wills, highly inebriated, refused to leave his Cadillac, which was parked behind the venue, to perform on

Town Hall Party. Larry was sent to try and convince Wills to appear on the show, and Wills vomited all over Larry's cowboy boots in the back of the car.] I don't know why. I wasn't a threat and I was just a kid and I'd listen to them and listen to the things they'd say and why they were drunk. The classic line from Bob Wills was, "One day *you'll know why*." I hate to dwell on that. But I'll tell you this. When Merle drank, he got *mean*, and so did Joe, and so did my dad. Usually it took me to calm them down. The women certainly couldn't. They'd send me in, just like me in the back seat of Bob Wills's Cadillac. The women would disappear until it was over. Yeah, they raised some hell. But they got away with it easily. No, maybe they didn't. They paid for it in life. That kind of shit always comes back to you. Hell, I'm seventy-five years old. I look back at these guys. They were talented, the sons of a bitches. And great men in some things, and assholes in others. Just like me today.[357]

Merle, like his friend Joe Maphis and some of the other musicians on *Town Hall Party*, were from an earlier era of music but accommodated the new rockabilly artists who came on the show. Michael Robinson remembered: "Merle hated rock music. But if it still had a lot of the 'billy' in it, the hillbilly element, he liked it. He could relate to that."[358] Merle worked as a session guitarist on several rockabilly recordings at this time. He recorded with *Town Hall Party* member Gary Williams on his "Traveling Blues Boy," on teenage rocker Jackie Lee Cochran's "Mama Don't You Think I Know" and "Ruby Pearl," and on country singer Freddie Hart's forays into rockabilly, "Dig Boy Dig" and "Snatch It and Grab It," among others. Merle and his friend Chet Atkins were highly influential on the guitarists of rock 'n' roll's first generation. Elvis's guitarist, Scotty Moore, played in the thumbpicking style of Merle and Chet, and Scotty's guitar was heard through every AM radio in the country. Both Carl Perkins and Eddie Cochran named Merle among their biggest influences.

Merle, however, would never claim rock 'n' roll as something he had inspired. In a 1973 phone interview, Ray Campi asked him about his thoughts on rockabilly guitar and Scotty Moore. He replied, without a hint of irony, "Scotty Moore—I wouldn't, you know, I'm not familiar with him at all."[359] The rockabilly recordings that he played on during the latter part of the 1950s, however, show that while he would never consider himself a rock 'n' roll guitarist, he was excellent and highly adept at playing rockabilly guitar. There was only a hairbreadth's difference between rockabilly and the hillbilly boogie he had pioneered with the Delmore Brothers in the 1940s, both being hopped-up boogie-woogie variants of hillbilly and Western swing.

One of the touring acts tagged with the rockabilly label who came to California to appear on *Town Hall Party* was Johnny Cash, a singer who had recently achieved great success with a series of highly original country music hits on the Sun Records label out of Memphis. Cash had not yet become a household name, but his huge personality and stage charisma were already evident when he first appeared on *Town Hall Party*. And while others were enamored with Cash, Cash was enamored with "Sixteen Tons." Bob Hilburn relates the story of Cash's obsession with the song in his book *Johnny Cash: The Life* (2013):

> Nothing could stop Cash from listening to music. One song that fascinated him was Tennessee Ernie Ford's recording of "Sixteen Tons," a folk-country tale about a coal miner who works through intense pain only to get "another day older and deeper in debt." The song was played on the radio so often during the winter of 1955 that Marshall [Grant, Cash's bass player] got to the point where he'd turn it off on their long car drives, only to have Johnny turn the knob back to the station.... Initially Cash thought "Sixteen Tons" was an old folk song, but he noticed one day in a music magazine that the writer was Merle Travis and the song first appeared in the late 1940s on Travis's concept album *Folk Songs of the Hills*. Cash was familiar with Travis's lively hits, including "So Round, So Firm, So Fully Packed," but he knew him primarily as a brilliant guitar player, not a songwriter. "Sixteen Tons" made him look at Travis in an entirely different light. From then on, Travis was another of his heroes; he had little further interest in the Ernie Ford record.[360]

It just so happened that the man who wrote one of his favorite songs was also appearing on *Town Hall Party* when Cash was first a guest on the show in late 1956. The two became instant friends—they fell in with each other like peas in a pod. Both were complex men with similar interests and a similar restless, deep inner turmoil.

Merle toured as an added attraction with Johnny Cash and Carl Perkins in December 1957. Cash relocated to Southern California in 1958, first living in Johnny Carson's old house in Encino in the San Fernando Valley, then moving three years later to a ranch home in Casitas Springs, near Ventura, an hour up the coast. Now residing in the same neighborhood, Cash and Merle became roaring buddies and frequent troublemakers.

As much as they were united by music, the pair also bonded over a new mutual interest: pills. Cash had found himself locked into a pill-addicted existence that many country stars of the era also followed: uppers like amphetamines to stay up, and downers like barbiturates to come down. Merle, constantly nervous and manic, was always seeking ways to come down. Gordon Terry, a fiddle player on the *Town Hall Party* show and another of Cash's inner circle of friends, first turned Cash on to amphetamines during a tour in 1957. He gave Cash one pill. Within a few days Cash asked for more. When Terry gave Cash what should have been several weeks' supply, Cash came back a few days later, wondering if the pills were legal and asking how he could obtain more. Cash's friend James Keach is quoted in Hilburn's biography on the subject: "John said one pill was too many and a thousand wasn't enough. And so it was like once he got into it, he couldn't stop."[361] Merle's memories:

> **"Gordon Terry carried 'hillbillie bennies'"**
> **"Johnny Cash gets me a thousand pills"**
> **"Johnny Cash asks 'Who's a Star?'"**
> **"Johnny Cash hides from cops in Canada"**
> **"Johnny and Bettie take fast camper ride"**

Tuinal, a popular downer in the barbiturate family, became Merle's pill of choice. An oft-prescribed and oft-abused sedative, it was popular among celebrities in the 1950s and 1960s. It is no longer produced because of its highly addictive properties, but back then, doctors prescribed it freely as a sleeping pill, and it was easily found (along with amphetamines and all manner of prescription drugs) in large quantities just over the border in Mexico. Michael Robinson told this author:

> I learned about drugs from him [Merle] because I knew that he was taking massive amounts of drugs. Well, when I was in the eighth grade, one weekend, I busted into his pills. He was stashing these pills all over the house, he was a pill stasher. So, I found these things. I took a couple of them. I remember riding around on the bicycle, dizzy in the backyard, laughing and giggling. Well, I went back the next day and took two more pills and guess what? They didn't work. I said, oh, there it is. Now I got to do more. That's the story of his life, right there. I says, no, don't chase it. Leave it alone right there, you know? And I never went back. That was pretty good of me, I thought. Because I looked at him and said, that's where you'll wind up at. And not only that, this stuff probably costs a fortune, and I ain't got twenty-five cents to my name. So it's like, just leave it alone and don't bring it out. Don't do anything with it. Just forget it.[362]

Pills stashed around the house were dangerous for all the members of the family. Whether by accident or out of habitual use, Bettie Travis had her own experience with sleeping pills, making headlines in the newspaper. On August 19, 1956, the *Los Angeles Times* ran a headline that pointed to a troubled household:

PILLS HOSPITALIZE COWBOY SINGER'S WIFE

Mrs. Bettie Travis, 32, wife of Cowboy Singer Merle Travis, was rushed to North Hollywood Receiving Hospital yesterday to be treated for what police termed "a possible overdose of pills."

Travis told officers he had gone to the airport with his stepsons, Michael, 8, and Denny, 10, to ship some hunting gear to Alaska. When they returned to the Travis home... Travis gave his wife some steaks and asked her to fix them for dinner.

He said that as he was preparing to sit down to dinner he noticed that Mrs. Travis was acting strangely and apparently was unable to keep her eyes open. A few minutes later she collapsed.

A fire department rescue unit was summoned and worked on the unconscious woman for an hour. She then was taken to the hospital where her condition was listed last night as satisfactory. She had not regained consciousness.

Travis told the police the only pills of any kind he knew of Mrs. Travis having were some "tranquilizers."[363]

Bettie came out of her pill coma and recovered fully. But between Merle's January "police shootout" incident and her August pill overdose, her ex-husband, Ward Robinson, felt his sons' safety might be in jeopardy and decided to fight for custody of Dennis and Michael. The *Los Angeles Times* ran another lurid story about the Travis household on October 25:

WIFE OF SINGER FIGHTS EX-MATE TO KEEP SON
FORMER HUSBAND SAYS BOYS NOT GIVEN PROPER
REARING IN MERLE TRAVIS HOME

Merle Travis, 37, composer and singer of Western-type music, and his wife, Bettie, 32, were in Domestic Relations Court yesterday contesting for custody of her two sons by a former marriage.

Ward W. Robinson, 38, welding company owner, former husband of Mrs. Travis, averred through Atty. E. Loyd [sic] Saunders, that his sons Dennis, 10, and Michael, 8, are not being reared in a proper atmosphere in the Travis home.

He asked that he be given custody. She divorced Robinson in 1953 and was given custody of the children and $75 a month support at that time.

As proof that the two sons are not being exposed to peace and serenity, Robinson set forth that last January the Travises received public attention when the singer and composer of "16 Tons of Coal" [sic] became intoxicated and allegedly "pistol-whipped" his wife, then barricaded himself in his home, with threats to kill anyone who interfered.

Saunders pointed out that Travis, "drinking again last Aug. 18, had a fight with his wife," and she and the children fled from the house. As a result, Saunders said, Mrs. Travis was taken to North Hollywood Hospital unconscious. Notes of a nurse, Marie Yensen, were read into the record:

"Patient said she took sleeping pills because her husband said he was in love with another woman, and was going to leave her."...

Jerry Rolston, attorney for Mrs. Travis, labeled the incident of last January "ancient history" and the August hospital event as "unimport-ant." Mrs. Travis said she went to the hospital only because she was "tired."

Mrs. Travis said her husband had never intentionally "hit her" but had accidentally scratched her as she tried to disarm him while he was firing his gun at the clock. His marksmanship display was only to "kill time," she suggested.[364]

One of the details in Robinson's custody suit was the assertion that at the time Merle and Bettie were married in 1955 in Tijuana, Merle was still legally married to Judy Hayden. To assuage any doubt about their marriage, Merle and Bettie decided to marry again in November 1956, this time in the United States. The newspapers once again had a field day, with headlines such as "SINGER MERLE TRAVIS WEDS WIFE AGAIN."[365]

Musician Johnny Western told this author: "Travis spent a lot of money with lawyers and so forth backing Bettie up, trying to get custody. Anyway, I know he worked very hard on that adoption thing, or custody deal, I should say."[366] In December, Merle and Bettie won the contest and retained custody of Dennis and Michael. The *Los Angeles Times* painted a picture of redemption:

MERLE TRAVIS AND WIFE WIN CUSTODY OF 2 BOYS

Merle Travis, 38, and his wife Bettie, 32, yesterday won their court contest for custody of her two sons by a former marriage....

Travis on the witness stand admitted he had become intoxicated and had fired six shots from his .22 target pistol into the base of a living room clock, but he said it was only to show his wife he wasn't so drunk as she thought.

He had not had a drink for three months and had not been intoxicated since that incident, he told Commissioner Victor J. Hayek. A parade
of witnesses were questioned by his wife's lawyer, Jerry Rolston, to show
he was a model husband, stepfather, neighbor and friend....

"This court certainly holds no brief for the type of activity participated in by Mr. Travis last January," Hayek declared. "However, tes-
timony showed that Mrs. Travis is a splendid mother and the children
are happy and well cared for. It is for their best interests that they stay
there."[367]

"These guys were wonderful spin doctors" notes Michael Robinson. "They
were really good at keeping up appearances like that."[368]

The reality was that Merle was getting worse. Over the next few years, his
drinking and pill consumption increased while his mental state declined. Having
enablers like Johnny Cash and Gordon Terry (and other members of the *Town
Hall Party* cast who indulged in similar behaviors) constantly in the picture didn't
help. Johnny Western notes: "Travis and Cash were pill buddies. Not drinking
buddies, Cash did not drink. Every time I hear somebody say, 'Yeah, I got drunk
with Johnny Cash; he was drinking that whiskey like you can't believe,' I say to
them myself, 'You don't know what you're talking about. You were never drunk
with Johnny Cash.' Because Cash would have an occasional beer. His thing was
amphetamines, uppers and downers. So consequentially, they [Cash and Travis]
were pill buddies."[369]

At the new house on Ranchito, Merle would stay up all night with his roaring
buddies, often getting into more and more dangerous behaviors thanks to pill and
alcohol consumption. All manner of country music royalty passed through, either
staying in the guesthouse while in town for local appearances or stopping by for
all-night parties after a *Town Hall Party* appearance. Gary Williams said he once
discovered singer Webb Pierce in the pink Cinderella bathtub, fully clothed in his
Nudie Western suit, with a broken ankle from a drunken fall.[370] Hank Thompson
would stay at the house for extended periods when he came to Los Angeles for
album recording sessions or to have his band outfitted with new Nudie suits. Joe
Maphis and his family lived a couple of miles away. Johnny Cash was a constant
presence. Michael Robinson recalled: "I'd get up in the morning, Saturday morning, and I'd walk out into the kitchen and see Bob Wills in there cooking stew at
dawn. That was really something. Some people I tell this to are very impressed,
and other people are not. But how many people have seen Bob Wills with a bottle
of scotch, cooking up stew in the kitchen at eight o'clock in the morning? Merle
liked Scotch. Vat 69. So did Bob Wills. I hated that stuff."[371]

Even though Van Nuys was a suburban area, that didn't stop Merle and Cash from breaking out their guns when they got high. According to Michael Robinson:

These guys, they get out there with [Johnny] Cash at dawn and start doing target practice without waking me up first. They would be shooting in the house. They'd been up all night drinking and come down and they'd decide it was time to start target practice with Colt government models. Travis and Cash would be shooting down through here. If you go over to the back side of the property, you can see some bullet holes, exit holes, at the base of the middle of the stretch of the wall from his 300 Magnum Weatherby. He just had no idea; he probably thought it was a solid wall, but it was just a [hollow] concrete block wall there.[372]

(Author's note: The bullet holes are still there in the wall. The current owners have no idea who or what caused them.)

Working off his manic, restless energy was often an impossible task for Merle, and whatever undiagnosed mental affliction he suffered from, the combination of pills and alcohol didn't help. Sometimes it led him to drastic and eccentric measures. Michael Robinson told this author: "The bowling alley that's in *The Big Lebowski*, that's Hollywood Legion Lanes. Before they had automatic pinsetters, he used to set pins in that place to get exercise. He went down there and explained the deal to the manager, who said, like, 'Okay, yeah, I can have you, I guess you can be a pinsetter here.'"[373]

There were also many good days that balanced the bad ones. Michael Robinson remembered Merle's passion for cooking:

He liked making stews and things like that, and he liked eating steaks. There on Ranchito we had a secondary fireplace in the dining room, which was behind the fireplace in the living room so the flue would go up and join in with the main flue going out of the top of the house. We had a little grill on there, and we'd have grilled steaks; he'd grill the steaks right there in the dining room. We would have ribs. Some of the food over there was incredibly good. Then we got a cast iron pot that he would do a stew in. That thing would always get burnt. We had a hell of a time scrubbing it out.[374]

In July 1957, almost exactly a year after "Merle Travis Day" in Ebenezer, Merle returned to Kentucky to play the Muhlenberg County Fair. The show drew three thousand people. The program also featured Ike Everly and Mose Rager as guests of Merle's, as well as a mule-pulling contest. That same year also found Merle filming the *Western Ranch Party* television show, a syndicated, prerecorded version of *Town Hall Party* that had a national audience. Merle, Joe Maphis, and Larry Collins dazzled with hot guitar instrumentals, just as they did every week to a live audience on *Town Hall Party*. The TV appearances kept Merle in the spotlight even as his Capitol recordings had completely dried up.

Despite the fact that Merle had no new records to promote, the publicity behind "Sixteen Tons" and the influential *Merle Travis Guitar* album were enough to catch the interest of Alfred Dronge, president of the Guild Guitar Company. Dronge pursued Merle to try and convince him to switch brand allegiance from Gibson to Guild. Guild was relatively new, having launched at the beginning of the 1950s, when Epiphone was moving its production out of New York City, and Dronge hired several of its Italian employees who wanted to stay in the Little Italy neighborhood. By the mid-1950s, Guild was producing electric archtops of a very high quality, and Dronge was pursuing celebrity endorsements to advance the brand's cachet. He was astute enough to know that he needed a big country-western name to fill out his roster of celebrity endorsees. Merle recalled his association with Guild in a 1979 interview with Mark Humphrey:

> Same story with Guild. They said, "What can we get you to do to play a Guild?" [Author's note: in the original interview, Merle said "Gretsch" here, but he was talking about Guild.] I said, "I'll do it if you'll build one exactly as I draw it." I had some ideas, and it's not bad. I said, "I want you to carve the top out of a one-inch piece of wood, but leave the inside uncarved. Leave it flat inside." So that guitar is arched on top but it's an inch thick under the bridge. And the back, too. I drew the whole thing—the red checkers around, I got that idea from a guitar Gene Autry used in pictures years ago. The sound hole is copied from an old-time Gibson—the oval sound hole. And I designed that top up there, the curlicue. I wanted it to sound like a solidbody but look otherwise.[375]

Dronge agreed that Guild would make a Merle Travis signature artist model based on Merle's ideas—something that Gibson had never offered, despite Merle's custom Super 400 being the most expensive guitar the Gibson company had ever produced. The Guild Merle Travis Model (originally called the "Kentucky Colonel" model in Merle's first drawings) was going to be a completely new, radically designed, high-end instrument. The company provided Merle with a stock 1958 Guild X-500 with his name on the pickguard to use until the custom signature model was completed. Dronge initially thought that Guild could manufacture the Merle Travis model in less than a year. But in March 1959, he wrote a letter to Merle detailing the delays:

Dear Merle,

Although this is somewhat belated, I do want you to know that we are both happy and proud to have you become a member of the GUILD guitar family....

I am sorry, Merle, that at this time, I can't tell you that we have an instrument anywhere near ready for you. First, a model that is as important as this model is to our line, I wanted to supervise its production personally. Secondly, I have run into delay after delay in getting suitable parts. I am sure that it is not news to you that this model is a radical departure from anything we have made in the past. This means that we have to tool up entirely different and also establish many sources of supply, such as, for the unique style of trimming, etc.

Once we get all these parts assembled, it won't be too difficult to get going on this special instrument, but of course, we will have to wait until we get everything needed to actually go into production. We are very enthusiastic about it and believe that it will make a very fine musical instrument in addition to being a "thing" of beauty.[376]

In the interim, Merle played the stock Guild X-500 at shows, appeared in Guild Guitar magazine ads, and was listed as a Guild endorsee in company literature. When he was on the East Coast, he toured Guild's new production factory in Hoboken, New Jersey. Merle and the Guild X-500 the company had given him never really bonded, however. Within a couple of years, he was back to playing his Gibson Super 400 and using the Guild as an occasional backup. Merle would eventually give the Guild X-500 to his brother John.

The year 1959 would also be the first time Merle crossed over into a new domain—the East Coast folk music college circuit. The folk boom was just getting started, with acts like the Kingston Trio starting to achieve mainstream success; their "Tom Dooley" had been a breakout hit the year before. What began as a small group of fans on New England college campuses and New York's Lower East Side was turning into a full-blown movement—and an important new revenue stream for Merle. In September 1959 he appeared at the prestigious Jordan Hall in Boston to do a "folk concert." Instead of playing with a band, as he did on his tours of honky-tonk nightclubs and fair engagements, the Jordan Hall gig was a solo performance, featuring just Merle—now regarded on the East Coast as a folk legend—and his acoustic guitar.

The show was recorded, and in 2003 the concert was released by Rounder Records as *Merle Travis—Live in Boston*. It shows Merle in fine form, entertaining the crowd, telling jokes, and playing his guitar like the seasoned pro he was. The

liner notes were written by Mitch Greenhill, who as a fifteen-year-old had been
tasked by the promoter with keeping Merle sober before the show. In his notes
he recounted the story:

> I knock on the door with some trepidation. For one thing, hotels are
> unfamiliar to me, even hotels in Boston. For another, I am about to meet
> Merle Travis, an idol since my first attempts, not that long ago, at learning
> to fingerpick the guitar....
>
> Noises come from behind the door, perhaps the creak of bedsprings,
> the shuffle of slippered feet, the rustle of clothing. Then the door opens
> and here he is, smaller than I had imagined. I am surprised to find him
> in pajamas and robe, and wonder if my father has told him to expect me.
>
> I am fresh from sixth period at Boston Latin School, a few blocks
> away. Around the corner stands Jordan Hall, high temple of chamber
> music, where Travis is scheduled to perform a few hours later. The pre-
> senter is Folklore Productions, which has grown into a regular presenter
> of concerts, and a manager and booker of artists.... The Merle Travis
> concert features a guitar virtuoso, so should appeal to the growing army
> of pickers that is becoming a substantial presence on each of the area's
> many campuses.
>
> I'm not sure whether my dad fully believes rumors that Travis may be
> too friendly with the bottle, or if he just wants to channel my hero-wor-
> ship into a useful direction. Whatever the reason, I have been dispatched
> as Folklore Productions emissary, assigned to keep the guitar legend
> company and to deliver him sober before show time.
>
> Invited in, I nervously stumble across the threshold, and am soon
> face-to-face with Merle Travis. He too seems nervous, but possesses the
> skill of southern manners, which he uses to put both of us, if not at ease,
> at least in the middle of a conversation....
>
> When Merle Travis suggests that we share a few beers, I find myself
> in a deep moral dilemma. Do my loyalties lie with family, sobriety and
> the upcoming concert? Or with my new friend and long-time hero, who
> is even now rendering my doubts irrelevant as he negotiates on the phone
> with room service (room service!) for a couple of six packs?
>
> As in Travis Picking, even the most carefully mapped passages
> can at times be navigated only with the aid of improvisation. "Sure," I
> improvise.
>
> After the phone call and an awkward wait, there is a knock on
> the door, and the dangerous beverages arrive, courtesy of an elderly,

ramrod-straight gentleman wearing a red tuxedo. With a flourish, he unfurls a white napkin, carefully places the bottle on a table, accepts a gratuity, and is gone. Merle Travis and I are again alone, except for the new alcoholic presence that now seems to dominate the room. My host makes quick use of a bottle opener, pours a couple of glasses, and resumes conversing, now with a bit more energy. I'm trying to hold my own in that department, partly to justify my place in a suddenly adult world, and partly to keep Merle Travis from over-indulging. Did he just now start to drink a second beer, or maybe a third? I'm still on my first, I think....

My thoughts turn to Jordan Hall, where I imagine the crew is just now arriving, in preparation for the evening concert. What sort of shape will Travis be in, I wonder? Will the audience be angry? Will my dad? I start my second beer. Tastes pretty good, and it's too late now. May as well enjoy the ride.

The rest of the afternoon passes comfortably, or so I later surmise. Travis untaps a font of anecdotes that continue through the darkening hours. That night he plays brilliantly, gently banking rich caroms of acoustic guitar tone off Jordan Hall's hallowed walls, and is in total command of both his faculties and his audience. I, on the other hand, wobble a bit and go to bed with a bad headache.

At school the next morning my Latin grammar lacks the precision of Travis's bass lines.... But in my mind I can hear and see Travis Picking with new clarity, and that helps get me through the day, and ultimately through high school.

Later that afternoon I pick up my guitar and try my best to make it sound like Merle's—clean, dynamic and clearly conjugating the present tense. My fingers still have a long way to travel, but my mind has a better grasp of the goal.[377]

Also in 1959, Merle became a regular guest on a new national ABC-TV country music television show, *Country America*. Merle was hired for the show by its producer and emcee, Joe Allison, who worked for Capitol Records. Allison was a good friend of Merle's who also worked as a disc jockey on Los Angeles-area country radio stations. (Allison would later sign Willie Nelson to Liberty Records, write the song "He'll Have to Go" for Jim Reeves, and in the 1970s head up Capitol's country music division.) During the time *Country America* was on the air, Allison pitched an idea to Ken Nelson at Capitol. He saw what Capitol had done for Merle with the *Back Home* album, repackaging old material from the vaults, and suggested to Nelson that the label should repackage the acoustic guitar instrumentals that Merle had recorded for Capitol Transcriptions in the mid-1940s. Spurred by the success of *Back Home*, Nelson agreed. Again, he added reverb to make the old recordings sound slightly more modern. *Walkin' the Strings* was released on Capitol in 1960 and contained all twenty-two of Merle's instrumental guitar recordings from the mid-1940s Capitol Transcriptions.

It wasn't difficult to package twenty-two songs onto one album, since many of them were only thirty to ninety seconds in length. The brief recordings were never intended for commercial release, but their outstanding quality was impossible to deny—Merle was at the top of his game, playing with fire and precision. Chet Atkins, writing about *Walkin' the Strings* in 1996, stated that he thought these recordings were Merle's finest guitar performances. The album's liner notes by Cliffie Stone made no mention of the fact that the recordings were almost fifteen years old. Merle would later remember:

> A fellow named Joe Allison went to Capitol Records and said, "You should release all those transcriptions on an album by Travis," and they did. And they made up names to the tunes—one was called "Louisville Clog," and one was called "Pigmeat Stomp." This was in the forties when I recorded it, I'm not sure when they released it.... [Anyway,] I didn't know this thing was released, and I was somewhere playing a show, and somebody came in, saying, "Play 'Pigmeat Stomp.'" And I said, "You got me there, I don't believe I've ever heard of it." He said, "Well, you should, you recorded it!" I said, "Well, you're thinking of someone else. Maybe Chet Atkins, although I've never heard Chet play it, and I'm sure I never recorded 'Pigmeat Stomp.'" He said, "You sure did!" And I said, "Well, now buddy, I'd like to see a record of it." He said, "I've got it out in the car." He brought in this album, and on it was a tune called "Pigmeat Stomp." And if it was to save my life, I had no idea what it was.[378]

Merle also joked about the fact that Capitol had chosen to use a current color photograph of him holding his (electric) Gibson Super 400 for the cover when the entire contents of the album featured him playing acoustic guitar:

> The boys down at Capitol Records always seemed to get all screwed up in what they tried to do with me. Not one single tune on the *Walkin' the Strings* album had an electric guitar note on it. And on the cover was me sitting there just as big as life with an electric guitar. Now then, one time I got Curly Chalker and Carl Cotner and Harold Hensley and Jimmy Pruett and a bunch of good musicians there in Hollywood and I went down to recut some of the old stuff I'd done in the 1940s. This was in

the 1960s. The title of the album was *Travis*. I didn't pick one note of acoustic guitar. There they put a picture of me with an acoustic flat-top round hole guitar leaning up against a rock. I declare, I believe that if I'd made an album with me playing the clarinet, they'd have had me on the cover with a dulcimer…. Maybe they should release one of mine and put Johnny Cash's picture on it.[379]

The joke may have hinged on the lack of care Capitol Records devoted to him as an artist, but the reality is that Nelson had had a fairly impossible task in resurrecting fifteen-year-old recordings and making them sound like a current release. The fact that Merle was holding the wrong guitar may not have even occurred to Nelson or his staff as they gamely tried to create salable product for one of the most unreliable artists on their roster.

Despite these obstacles, *Walkin' the Strings* was and is another guitar masterpiece. The title track, "Walkin' the Strings," went back to Kennedy Jones, who called the number "Kansas City Rag." The earlier, acoustic versions of Travis standards like "Blue Smoke," "On a Bicycle Built for Two," "Good Bye My Blue Bell," and "Saturday Night Shuffle" are different and interesting interpretations, masterfully played, with slightly modified arrangements and progressions than the better-known electric versions on the *Merle Travis Guitar* album. Despite the fact that the record was essentially a cash-in by Capitol to get product on the shelves, it stands on its own as a masterful representation of the Travis picking style.

Travis kept up a fairly active touring schedule between 1957 and 1960 despite his drinking, pill taking, and mental state. He continued to tour as a featured guest with Gene Autry, Hank Thompson, and Johnny Cash, perform his own headlining shows at nightclubs, and make regular appearances on *Town Hall Party* when he was well enough. (One live recording from 1959 showcases James Burton, who at the time was Ricky Nelson's guitarist, playing Merle's song "Cannonball Rag" after emcee Johnny Bond announces over the microphone, "Merle couldn't make it tonight—he's not feeling too well.")[380] A young man named Bob Kingsley was managing Merle's career at the moment. Kingsley was a fairly unknown disc jockey on Los Angeles country radio station KGBS who dabbled in promotion, which in Merle's case meant driving him around and getting him sober enough to play shows. Many years later, Kingsley would become famous as the host of the nationally syndicated radio shows *American Country Countdown* and *Bob Kingsley's Country Top 40*. Johnny Western remembers of this time in the late 1950s:

We were in Toronto, and I was rooming with Merle, and there comes a knock on the door. Johnny Cash had been booked at the Casino Theater in downtown Toronto, where they would play a movie and he would do a show. This would start around noon, and the last show would be like nine o'clock, ten o'clock at night. It's a long haul for the whole week. His opening act was the Louvin Brothers, and they had a great guitar player with them—Paul Yandell, a skinny kid about nineteen years old. And during that particular time, Travis was in his shorts, his boxer shorts, that little pot belly hanging out, and he had a glass of whiskey that was about half gone.

They all came in, Ira and Charlie Louvin and Paul Yandell because Paul Yandell idolized Merle Travis. He told me that day before he left, he said, "You know, I love Merle Travis. I know Chet Atkins is great [Yandell would eventually go on to be Chet Atkins's right-hand man for many decades] but if Travis gets a bad cold, I worry about it." That's how much he loved Merle Travis. People gravitated toward him, you know? He had a magnetism, people wanted to be around him. I did. We kind of had a forced issue when I was rooming with him, but I loved every second I was there.

Travis never bothered to put on a robe or anything else, just had his shorts and half glass of whiskey. Well, the whiskey kind of dwindled down—he was drinking Crown Royal, very expensive Canadian whiskey—and he poured another glassful on top of the half a glass that he'd already had. While they were sitting there he poured another glassful. He's sitting on the couch, everybody that could sit someplace, on the edge of the bed or whatever, was just listening to Travis holding court and talking about country music and all these things that they were all interested in.

And then Travis all of a sudden put down that glass that had been full, it was now down to about half full. He didn't say "excuse me" or anything. He just put his hand over his mouth. Now, this was a hotel room, so the toilet was not that far away, with an open bathroom door. And he leaned over that bathroom door and he just yorked. I mean he puked his guts out. Got rid of that whiskey that was downed before they got there and the whiskey that was downed while they were there. Ira and Charlie just looked at each other. They couldn't believe that the legendary Merle Travis was puking ten feet away from them in a hotel room in Toronto. And of course Yandell was beside himself because he thought Travis was sick and might die.[381]

Johnny Western recalled Johnny Cash helping Travis obtain pills on the same trip:

On that Canadian tour, we were up there for twenty-one days, and Travis had that stomach thing going. And Travis had not brought enough pills; he didn't think we were going to be that long up there before he went to Alaska and got some refills. But he was taking these pills that were really terrible for his stomach. He was bleeding out of his rear end and stuff, things were so bad.

Travis had run out of pills, and Cash was extremely well known in Canada. He took him to a doctor, we were in Nova Scotia, we were going to play Halifax. It was the biggest city out there. And he took him to a doctor and convinced the doctor to give Travis a prescription for thirty days, which would, we thought, keep him until we got to Alaska and could do some good with some friends over there.

The doctor would not give him a prescription for more than thirty pills, and he was supposed to take one pill a day. Well, the doctor had no idea Travis was taking five or six pills a day. The doctor said while they were there at the office, I remember Johnny telling me what the doctor had said. He said if he took three or four of those it would knock an elephant to his knees. And Travis was taking five and six of those pills a day, so that whole bottle of thirty pills only lasted a few days.

We didn't know what we were going to do. Travis could not stay up there. He had the jitters, and he absolutely thought as an addict did, like Cash did. He thought he had to have those pills, absolutely thought he had to have them. Cash laid his reputation on the line—he had problems of his own, but the doctor didn't know that—and more or less vouched for him. "Doctor, give him a prescription for thirty pills, and we'll be in your debt forever." So the doctor did, but that's all, he didn't give him any hundred pills. Some of these doctors today will write you a scrip for anything as long as the money's there.

So Travis was in bad shape. He and Cash went through some, I guess, hangovers or so forth to pull them together. But they were very, very close.[382]

Michael Robinson was attending military school during this time and not living at home. When he did see Merle at home, though, things had gone from bad to worse:

I was off in military school. I got the story from my brother's first wife who was staying out there in the guesthouse for a period. Merle was in a straightjacket. They had these, these nurses, they would put him—I don't know how you can even get away with this type of stuff. You certainly couldn't get away with it now, putting somebody in a straightjacket in their own house.

Sometimes they were male nurses, sometimes there were some pretty tough female nurses there too. They had put him in a straightjacket back in that bedroom, and he had done one of these Houdini numbers and got out of this thing somehow. So they're out there and he just walks in like nothing's going on, out into the dining room from the back bedroom, sits down, and lights a cigarette. He just busted out of a straightjacket.[383]

Michael's memory is corroborated by a letter from Merle's attorney, Jerry Rolston, to song publisher Sylvester Cross:

March 17, 1960
    Dear Mr. Cross:
    As you know, Merle's illness has continued to linger on requiring nurses in constant attendance. So far his nursing has cost over $3000.00, to say nothing of the hospital bill and doctor's bill. Next week we will not have sufficient funds to pay the nurses, and therefore on behalf of Mr. Travis I am requesting as large an advance as you can possibly give him at this time....
    I know that the Travis family join me in expressing their appreciation for anything you can do in this regard.
    Sincerely yours,
    Jerry Rolston[384]

Merle had planned on going to Nashville with Johnny Cash to play guitar on a concept album Cash was recording called *Ride This Train*, loosely based on Merle's *Folk Songs of the Hills*, including the spoken-word introductions to each song. With his mental state worsening, Merle ultimately stayed home but loaned his Martin D-28 with the Bigsby neck to Johnny Western and instructed him on how to play "Travis style" on the numbers he had been scheduled to play. Cash recorded a song Merle had written, "Loading Coal," with Johnny Western playing the guitar accompaniment. "Loading Coal" was obviously meant to quell Cash's obsession with "Sixteen Tons," but even though the song had clever wordplay, it had little hit potential. Cash's obsession with folk music, historical events, and songwriting authenticity kept him enamored with Merle and Merle's "magnetism." Years later, when Cash revisited the *Ride This Train* concept on his ABC television show, he hired Merle to write the spoken-word monologues.

One of the things that had brought Cash to California was his own belief that he could be a movie star. He was good-looking, charismatic, and cocksure.

His manager, Bob Neal, pursued roles in film and television, only to come up empty-handed—all Neal managed to book was a guest appearance on the Western television show *The Rebel Johnny Yuma* and a starring role in a grade-Z drama by tiny Sutton Pictures called *Five Minutes to Live*. The latter was destined for obscurity, but it did star Donald Woods, Victor Tayback (later famous as surly cook Mel Sharples on the TV show *Alice*), and a young Ron Howard in one of his earliest roles (before he became famous as Opie on *The Andy Griffith Show*). Merle was cast in a small role, thanks to Cash. It was his first movie appearance since *From Here to Eternity* and *Festival of Nations* in the early 1950s. Unfortunately, *Five Minutes to Live* is a jumbled mess, with low production standards and a meandering plot. It was a commercial flop when released in 1961 (and again in 1966, when it was rereleased as *Door to Door Maniac*).

Almost immediately after the failure of *Five Minutes to Live*, Cash threw himself into *The Night Rider*, a twenty-two-minute color Western. It was originally meant to be a pilot for a proposed television series called *Gallaway House*, but when it didn't sell, Cash pitched it as a short to be screened before feature films. Merle again got a small part, playing a sidekick named Kentucky. It was just as well that Merle's role in both films was small, considering his physical condition at the time. In Michael Robinson's words:

> He would always say that his back hurt, and I would be there with my older brother. He was a little bit heavier than me, and Merle wanted somebody to crack his back, so he would say, "I'm going to lay down here on the floor," and then he would have my brother jump up and down on his back. And this is when we were living on Ranchito, so like '59 or '60. My brother would jump up and down on his back, trying to get this back pain to leave, and Merle would say, "Now, I don't want you to—don't be nice about this, jump! Slam up and down on my back!" He didn't understand that it was the back of his stomach that was giving him trouble.[385]

Merle's increasing dependence on pills, washed down by the handful with booze, had eaten away the lining of his stomach, giving him bleeding ulcers. The resulting pain was unbearable.

In May 1960, Ira and Charlie Louvin, the Louvin Brothers, were scheduled to record a tribute album to the Delmore Brothers in Nashville for Capitol Records. Merle, who had played on many of the Delmore Brothers' most famous recordings, was asked to be present at the sessions for advice and guidance on how the Delmores had arranged and recorded the songs back in the 1940s (Merle also wrote liner notes for the release, recalling his early days with the Delmores). Johnny Western notes:

Cash took real good care of Travis. I mean, he loved him dearly; as a matter of fact he went through this thing with him. He'd been asked by Ken Nelson at Capitol Records to produce the Louvin Brothers in Nashville for Capitol Records and of course, that brightened Travis's pocket because he worked for the Delmore Brothers when he was a kid, before he ever came to the West Coast. He knew Alton and Rabon very, very well. The biggest song they ever had was "Blues Stay Away from Me."

Cash gave me a hundred dollars a day to drive a camper that Merle had down to Nashville to stay down there for the better part of a week while he produced that album with the Louvin Brothers and then make sure to help Travis drive back. He didn't want him on the road by himself. Travis was going to do it by himself. We were offered the cash, and Johnny said, "I want you to go with him and make sure that he gets there and help him drive," and so forth. "He can't perform, but he can darn sure produce that record."[386]

When Merle and Johnny Western got to Nashville for the recording sessions on May 12 and 13, 1960, Merle offered advice and experience but was too weak to perform. Johnny Western notes: "Merle just laid up in the bed all the way, 'cause he was so weak he couldn't hardly stand up. At the session, he would watch Jimmy [Capps, the Louvin Brothers' guitarist at the time] and then say, 'That's good Jimmy, but let me have the guitar and I'll show you the way I did it originally.' He didn't mean to make anybody mad, but he wanted to be certain it was done authentic."[387] Jimmy Capps told this author:

When we did the Delmore thing he came in with Ken Nelson, because he was so close to the Delmores that Ken asked him to come in and produce it. But he would not play on it at all, which was kind of disappointing. I played all the guitar on it, and he helped Ken produce. He was just one of the boys. I think that comes from probably the way he was raised. He had always been headed toward stardom, but I think first and foremost he was a musician. He was a super nice guy. I can't say enough nice things about Travis.[388]

Merle's old friends Chet Atkins and Grandpa Jones dropped in to the recording sessions to visit with Merle. They must have noticed that he didn't look well, but they probably had no idea how close they were to losing him. After Johnny Western drove Merle back from Nashville, Merle's physical pain from the bleeding ulcers got so bad that he worked only sporadically the rest of 1960 and most of 1961.

He traveled at the end of February 1961 to Bristol, Tennessee, to accompany Tennessee Ernie Ford for a homecoming and gospel recording session. The resulting album, *Hymns at Home*, was a moderately successful collection of religious songs recorded in Tennessee Ernie's home church with many of his family and friends in the accompanying choir. Merle wrote the liner notes, where he talks about inviting himself along for the sessions by offering to write the words for the album's back cover.

On that same trip, Merle performed at the *Grand Ole Opry* in Nashville, where his popularity among the other members and the audience put him in consideration for becoming a member. Plans were discussed regarding a possible move to Nashville. Grandpa and Ramona Jones remembered Merle's appearance on the *Opry* around this time in an interview with researcher Charles K. Wolfe:

> [Grandpa:] I remember once he came to the *Opry*, they put him on the *Opry*, and he didn't even have a guitar. He run around and borrowed a guitar.

> [Ramona:] I think that was kind of an act. I'm not saying that to put him down, because we loved him dearly, but I think he enjoyed saying, "Hey, I can do it, with all the odds against me," or something.[389]

Merle's condition was not completely debilitating. He had periods of clarity in between episodes of pain. A case in point is the superb ninety-minute interview he did in July 1961 with folk music researchers Ed Kahn and Archie Green at his home in Van Nuys. Kahn used a portable reel-to-reel tape recorder. Merle was in good spirits and told story after story of his early years and the first part of his career. The interview was made under the auspices of Kahn writing the liner notes to Merle's next album, but it was also the beginning of Kahn's effort to write a Merle Travis biography, which he worked on for three decades but never completed. (Many of his notes and interviews were used in the writing of this book, through the generosity of the Southern Folklife Collection at the Wilson Library, University of North Carolina, Chapel Hill, where his research and collection were archived after his death in 2004.)

Merle's memory:

"I join the *Grand Ole Opry*—and don't show up"

At the beginning of August 1961, newspapers reported that Merle was joining the cast of the *Grand Ole Opry* and would be moving to Nashville in October. Simultaneously, on August 4, Merle's first daughter, Patty (now going by Pat), and her fiancé, Gene Eatherly, got married. Pat had come to Los Angeles a few years earlier, in 1958, after she'd been named the Kentucky Derby Queen and was considering a career in modeling. That didn't pan out, but within a short time she was a working as a flight attendant and met Gene, a native Tennessean living in Southern California who worked for the US Rubber Company. They began dating and quickly became serious and engaged. The marriage took place at a chapel in Inglewood. Merle gave away his daughter, and Wesley Tuttle sang. After their honeymoon, the newlyweds moved into Merle and Bettie's guesthouse.

Less than two weeks after the wedding, Merle entered the studio to make his first new recordings for Capitol in six years. It was not entirely a new record—the idea was to rerecord his 1940s hits for an album of repackaged "favorites." Merle noted at the time:

> My first few records went pretty good, and today I was talking with Ken Nelson, I'm to rerecord them August 14th, 15th, 16th and 17th… all twelve of the first records I made for Capitol. It'll be sort of the same sound, with a trumpet. I used a trumpet. And a clipped rhythm on the first records I made, to try and be a little different…. And it'll be for an album, and if Capitol Records are as smart as I think they are, they'll call it "Merle Travis, America's Worst Singer… and most overrated guitar player."[390]

Ed Kahn would use the biographical material he gleaned from his July interview with Merle to write the liner notes to this new album of re-recordings. The sessions in mid-August went well, and Merle turned in satisfactory performances of his earliest Capitol hits—"No Vacancy," "Divorce Me C.O.D.," "So Round, So Firm, So Fully Packed," "Cincinnati Lou," "Fat Gal," "I Like My Chicken Fryin' Size," and half a dozen others. The album, called *Travis!* (subtitled "Favorite songs written, sung, and played by the great Merle Travis") was slated to be released the following year. Merle took photos for the cover in Griffith Park in Los Angeles, wearing a smart white denim outfit with red boots. Strangely, especially given the earlier confusing cover photo used on *Walkin' the Strings*, he posed with an acoustic flat-top guitar even though the album featured electric guitar exclusively.

Unfortunately, with the prospect of joining the *Grand Ole Opry* and a new Capitol album set for release, Merle once again managed to blow a valuable opportunity to revitalize his sagging career. A few months after their wedding, with the newlyweds living in the guesthouse on his property, Merle severely alienated Pat and Gene. Michael Robinson recalls: "Patty, she was living in the guesthouse on Ranchito in Van Nuys. They ended up running for their lives when he got out of hand and started breaking out the guns one night. I mean, he was in his shorts, T-shirt, and flip-flops, and they hopped in the car and left because they were that scared of him."[391] It was a harrowing incident that Pat wrote about in her book *In Search of My Father*, in a chapter titled "Suddenly Strangers":

> Gene and I enjoyed the guesthouse Dad generously allowed us to move into behind his home.... However, late one evening, only a few months after moving in, something happened that cut an indelible scar into my memory. Gene and I were cuddled up on the sofa after supper watching television like a couple of lovebirds. Since there was no air conditioning, the door was open to allow the cool breezes in.
>
> Suddenly, the screen door flew open, and we were startled to see Dad stagger in. We'd become acutely aware of and sometimes involved in problems that surfaced due to his excessive drinking. Tonight his speech was blurred, and his eyes were glassy. He wanted our full attention and demanded we turn off the television. Gene quietly tried to persuade him to leave when Dad lashed out incoherently, "Who da ya think ya are tryin' to tell me wha' I can do?" His speech was thick and alarming as he waved his bottle of beer in the air.... I insisted, "Let us help you back to your house." Gene reacted immediately to my desperate look for assistance.
>
> Together we determinedly guided him through our door into the dark. The back porch light of the main house cast a dim glow on Dad's distorted face. He seemed agreeable for a moment, then jerked loose and smashed his unfinished beer bottle against the sharp edge of the house. We both dodged the flying, broken glass and stared in disbelief. He began making serious threats. "Dad!" I heard my voice rise and tremble, "Do you know who you're talking to? I'm your daughter!"
>
> My rationale didn't faze him. The curve of his lips snarled like a trapped animal, and he slurred, "I could kill ya and I would kill ya, and don'cha forget it!" Suddenly my own father seemed like a stranger. Fear stung my heart, and my knees went limp. With an unexpected surge of strength, Dad pushed open his back door and rushed in.
>
> Terrified I turned to Gene, "Do you suppose he's going to get a gun?"
>
> "We're not waiting to find out, we're getting out of here!"
>
> Gene ran into our house, grabbed the car keys, we raced barefoot to our car, and sped out the driveway. The logical place to go for help was the police station. But after reporting our experience we were told there was nothing they could do. They explained to us that "the man," as they called Dad, was on his own property and had not broken any

laws. Stunned by this information, we then drove to counsel with Dad's doctor, Dr. Wendell Starr, who was also a family friend and had attended our wedding only a short time before. Dr. Starr sympathetically listened, then advised us not to go back right away. "In Merle's intoxicated state," the doctor stated, "he doesn't realize anything he is saying or doing." Then as kindly, but as straightforwardly as possible, he added, "In his condition, he could harm the ones he loves most.".…

Since Gene's mother lived only an hour away, we decided to go there to spend the night. After a sleepless night, we concluded that we would have to move from the guesthouse into an apartment. We returned the next afternoon to pack our belongings, only to find Dad hurt and insulted.… Our reasoning seemed irrational to him, and he accused us of deserting a sick man.

The sickness of alcohol had overcome Dad. As much as Gene and I wished we could help him, we had to be concerned for our own safety.[392]

For years, Merle told the story that he was so busy with his touring schedule he simply forgot to show up to join the *Grand Ole Opry*. It made for a good laugh. He told interviewer Doug Green in 1975:

Well, I can't name you the year, but it hasn't been too awfully long ago. In fact, I was out here for some reason, maybe to do the *Opry*. But I was staying out with Grandpa Jones, and Grandpa said, "I've got to go down and take pictures today for the yearly *Grand Ole Opry* book." [He] said, "Go down with me."

I said, "All right." So we went down and Grandpa put on his outfit. In them days, he hadn't growed his own mustache.…

Ott Devine was there, and Ott said, "Why don't you come back and join the *Opry*." [He] said, "Why don't you let us take a picture of you today, and we'll put it in the book, and come on back and join us."

And I said, "Ott, you've said that to me so many times. I'll tell you what I'm going to do. I'll call my wife in California, and if she wants to move to Nashville and join the *Grand Ole Opry*, well, I'll do it.".…

And I went in and I called Bettie, my wife. I said, "How'd you like to move to Nashville?".…

She said, "Whatever you think. If you want to move back there, it's all right with me.".…

I hung up the phone. I went back and I told Ott Devine. I said, "Well, you got you a new member. I'll join the *Opry*."

He said, "Good."

I said, "I'll have to have something to take a picture in." So I went across the street, and I got a black shirt and a white scarf and put it on, the western style. And I had my picture took that way. And they put it in the book. I told Ott, "Now, I've got a few dates and a few ends to tie up out on the West Coast before I come back.".…

He said, "I can understand. You take your time. We're just proud to have you with us."

So I went up on the all-night show and done an interview. And they said, "Well, here's the newest member of the *Grand Ole Opry*, just signed up today." I didn't sign anything. "He just signed up today to be a new member of the *Grand Ole Opry*." And they put it in the paper and all, "Merle Travis coming to the *Grand Ole Opry*," and they put my picture in the book, "Newest member of the *Grand Ole Opry*. Merle Travis's hobbies is so and so" and all this stuff.…

I went back to the Coast, and I had a date to play, and I played it, and I had this to do, and I had some little old picture or something to make; and a week went by, and a month went by, and I said, "Hey, we'd better start thinking about moving to Nashville." And another month went by. I'd sort of forgot about it. And six months went by and I said, "You know, I was supposed to have went and joined the *Grand Ole Opry*." And about eight months went by.

I called Ott Devine and I said, "I haven't come back yet to join the *Grand Ole Opry*."

He said, "Well we kind of forgot about you back here." He said, "You might as well stay out there." And I said, "All right."

I come back and Tex Ritter and Ralph Emery was doing an all-night show. And I went on the show and Tex Ritter said, "Ladies and Gentlemen," you know that deep voice he had, he said, "we've got a guy here, the only man in the world that ever joined the *Grand Ole Opry* and never showed up."[393]

Merle's humorous story was actually a cover-up for something that wasn't funny at all: he'd come very close to dying. It was kept out of the papers, so the exact date remains unknown, but a life-threatening event nearly killed him in the latter part of 1961.

Merle played a show at the Ash Grove in Los Angeles in November of that year and then didn't work again for six months. Although there are no official records, the best guess is that it was after the Ash Grove appearance that the tragic event occurred. The pills had taken a terrible toll on his stomach. His bleeding ulcers were painful, but he ignored the problem. Then, in his bedroom in Van Nuys, his ravaged stomach suddenly and violently hemorrhaged blood all over his bed. Michael Robinson remembered:

> This is in 1961, something like that. He rotted his stomach out. He started yelling "Bettie!" from the back bedroom. She'd be sleeping up in the den, and he was yelling and yelling this. Finally she got up and went in there, and he had hemorrhaged all over the bed because he had rotted his stomach out from Tuinals. It ate a hole in his stomach, and he had hemorrhaged, had blown out all this blood all over the place. Of course the ambulance was called. It was like gelatinized blood in that bedroom. I saw it myself after they pulled him out of there. They cut him open, they took his stomach out. His surgeon and doctor was Dr. Starr. He was a good old doctor. They patched him back together, but he lost 75 percent of his stomach. Kind of like having a super lap band done on himself. And he lost weight after that, too.[394]

Merle recovered over the next few months. The plans to move to Nashville were abandoned. He could no longer eat large meals, and digestion was difficult. It did not, however, deter him from drinking as soon as he was able. Speedy West told a grim story: "He'd gulp a glass of whiskey as fast as he could, then he'd run out in the back yard and throw it all up. I asked him what he was doing, he said, 'I'm trying to get my tolerance back up.'"[395] Michael Robinson recalled:

> At that point, he didn't have much food, he was just a snacker. It was a very heavy thing that happened to him there. It wasn't like he was coming out and eating; he was hibernating in the back bedroom. He would come stumbling out and boy, he knows how to stumble. He would come out and raid the refrigerator and get some cheese or some snacks and take off for the bedroom again. I tried to ignore him, and that irked him a little bit too, but he wasn't coherent. I don't know exactly, I stayed away. I learned to have eyes in the back of my head, act like nothing's going on. That bothered him too sometimes. He used to put it like, "Hey you." I couldn't deal with that. I can't deal with a person who is hanging out in a dark bedroom for a month. That's something that an eight-year-old or ten-year-old kid doesn't know what to do with.[396]

Merle's good friend Jack Rogers, who knew Merle back in the WLW days in Cincinnati, bought a house right around the corner from the Travis estate in Van Nuys. Jack and his wife, Margie, were the Travis's closest friends during these days, and provided much moral support to Bettie, Dennis, and Michael while

Merle was incapacitated. Jack didn't drink, so he could be relied upon when all the other musician friends were incapacitated (in several pieces of correspondence Merle wrote over the years, he used the term "Jack Rogers" as a generic term for someone who could be depended on). Margie was a good friend to Bettie and gave her a place to land when things got too rough. Jack Rogers remembered:

> Marge was usually there with Bettie, and I'd go over there and see Merle was passed out. He was passed out for a week sometimes, poor guy. Nothing you could do. Poor Bettie. She'd come, leave the house, come over to stay at our house. They'd finally work out their squabble. I felt sorry for Bettie trying to work with a drunk all the time. Merle would sober up, apologize.[397]

Bettie recalled: "After *Town Hall Party*, if he would go in costume to a restaurant and someone would ask where his horse was, Merle was ready to fight. But he was easy going on the surface. Yet he was never at peace. There was an anger in him, but I could never figure out just exactly, but I think he was angry at himself."[398]

Two other events transpired around the same time as Merle's stomach operation that would greatly affect his revenue stream. One was Gene Autry's decision in 1961 to retire from touring to focus on his businesses at home. His shows had been drawing gradually fewer and fewer people, and the last few years had witnessed a dwindling audience struggling to hear him sing over the whir of amusement park rides. Merle and Autry would remain friends, but now Merle's steady paycheck had ended, as well as his source of emergency money when he needed a big advance (though both Merle and Johnny Cash still sometimes phoned Autry when they got into big trouble and had no one else to turn to; Autry bailed Cash out when he was arrested for smuggling amphetamines over the border in El Paso in 1965).

The second major event affecting Merle in 1961 was that *Town Hall Party*, the popular show where he had been a cast member since the very beginning, ended its run. A great number of the West Coast country musicians who had been united by the show's opportunities began to look elsewhere for work. Some, like Joe and Rose Lee Maphis, moved to Bakersfield, where (unlike in Los Angeles) country music remained popular. Others moved to Nashville, where the country music industry had solidly established itself as "Music City USA." The focus of country music employment on the West Coast turned from Los Angeles dancehalls to Nevada casinos, where jobs were plentiful and paid well.

Merle went into the studio in July 1962 to record an album of guitar duets with his old friend Joe Maphis—his first new instrumental recordings since the sessions that produced *The Merle Travis Guitar* nearly ten years earlier. Joe and his wife, Rose Lee, had recently been signed to Capitol and had released an album of mostly folk-oriented material. It must have seemed like a no-brainer to get Merle and Joe into the studio to re-create some of the old *Town Hall Party* magic. Over three days in mid-July, the two met at the Capitol tower for an informal grab bag of hot guitar performances. Not much, if any, planning went into the album, but they had thousands of performances together under their belt, so getting an album's worth of material wasn't a problem.

In retrospect, the record sounds like Merle and Maphis jamming with a rhythm section behind them. The songs don't seem particularly worked out or arranged. But with their chemistry and experience, it didn't matter—the album was a barn burner. Some of the material dated back to their days in Cincinnati, most notably four Delmore Brothers songs: "When It's Time for the Whippoorwill to Sing," "Midnight Special," "Gonna Lay Down My Old Guitar," and "Don't Let Your Deal Go Down." They also covered the old standard "Corinne, Corinna," which Merle probably knew from Clayton McMichen's popular hillbilly version released in 1929. Other songs, like "Blast Off," were just hot guitar numbers, twelve-bar blues performed at the fastest tempo possible. For some reason, the album's release was delayed for two years, but when *Merle Travis and Joe Maphis—Country Music's Two Guitar Greats* finally came out in 1964, it was well received and sold moderately well. Chet Atkins wrote the liner notes, a favor for his old friend. Merle had recently written the liner notes to Atkins's *Hymns* album, and Atkins had written Merle a letter saying he would be happy to reciprocate for Merle and Maphis.[399]

With Autry no longer on the road and *Town Hall Party* off the air, Merle turned to the folk music circuit for employment. Playing folk festivals, college campus concerts, and the occasional coffeehouse to a younger audience of college students, beatniks, and hippies would prove to be a steady source of income for the rest of his life. In November and December 1962, reprising the lineup that had played the Ash Grove in Los Angeles the year before, he embarked on a short East Coast tour opening for Flatt & Scruggs. It took him to Town Hall in Philadelphia (a few days after Joan Baez appeared there), Shriver Hall at Johns Hopkins University in Baltimore, Jordan Hall in Boston (where he had done the live recording in 1959), and Carnegie Hall in New York, among other prestigious venues. Seeing throngs of young kids getting into folk music and forming their own Kingston Trio–style folk acts must have made an impression. Western swing, hillbilly, and country boogie audiences were creeping into middle age, and it had to have been a bit surreal to realize that he'd gone from playing for two thousand energetic dancers in the 1940s to playing for a hundred graying fans at a club. The youth movement must have seemed strange to him, too, including young

New Englanders in prep clothes learning how to play old songs he had known in his childhood in Kentucky. But he must have seen it as promising in its own way—these kids came from moneyed families.

Certainly Ken Nelson at Capitol Records saw it as well. The Kingston Trio recorded for Capitol and sold millions of albums. Nelson talked to Merle about recording a new album of folk songs. Tennessee Ernie Ford's recording of "Sixteen Tons" had been one of the label's biggest hits. Nelson asked Merle to record an entire album of songs about coal miners and mining.

At some point in 1962, Merle had been committed to a sanitarium. The only details about it come from a 1963 letter written by his lawyer, Jerry Rolston, to Margaret Murray at his song publisher, American Music: "Since speaking with you yesterday, the situation has worsened and it appears likely that Merle will have to go to a sanitarium for a period of time as he did last year. Of necessity, this will increase all of his expenses."[400] But despite this, even in the bad physical and mental shape that he was in, Merle rose to the occasion. Other than the unreleased demos recorded at Gold Star, he hadn't recorded any original songs since 1955, and according to his wife Bettie, his songwriting had all but "dried up."[401] Now he rallied and wrote twelve new original songs about coal mining in a short period of time. Years later, in a studio conversation with Doc Watson used on the Nitty Gritty Dirt Band's 1972 *Will the Circle Be Unbroken* album, he revealed: "Every song on that thing, I made up in two weeks." The March 1963 sessions would result in the album *Songs of the Coal Mines*.

Much in the same vein as Merle's 1946 album *Folk Songs of the Hills*, *Songs of the Coal Mines* starts each song with a spoken-word introduction by Merle. Merle sings and accompanies himself with only solo acoustic guitar. He sounds in good shape; it's difficult to discern from listening alone that he was going through a particularly bad period. Some of the songs are true stories from Merle's childhood that he turned into songs, such as "The Browder Explosion," "The Harlan County Boys," "Preacher Lane," and "Bloody Brethitt County." One of Merle's real-life relatives was immortalized in "The Courtship of Second Cousin Claude" (even though Merle's introduction claims the song is fictional, he did have a cousin, Claude Travis, who decades later would be instrumental in Muhlenberg County's own recognition of Merle Travis). He tried his hand at crafting a new Irish-style folk song with "Dear Old Halifax," sung in an Irish accent. There were funny and lighthearted and realistic songs about miners and their daily lives, including "Miner's Strawberries," "Paw Walked Behind Us with a Carbide Lamp," "Here's to the Operator, Boys," and "The Miner's Wife." "Black Gold" was an attempt at re-creating the somber, working-class mood of "Sixteen Tons." Merle sang in what at the time was called "Negro dialect" on the blues song "Payday Comes Too Slow."

Songs of the Coal Mines was a fine effort. Merle's brother John Melvin wrote the liner notes, which vouched for the authenticity of these songs based on the coal mining life that the Travis family had known growing up. But when the record was released later in the year, it was a critical success but a commercial failure. There are a dozen likely reasons why. Perhaps Merle was too old to appeal to the young folkie crowd, or too many years had passed since the "Sixteen Tons" blue-collar zeitgeist of the postwar 1950s. There was no photo of Merle on the front or back of the album. Whatever the reason, the record failed to find an audience. In an April 1963 letter to song publisher Sylvester Cross, Merle's lawyer Jerry Rolston stated: "Merle must receive some money in the near future or he will be in trouble. As I told Mrs. Murry, some time ago, Merle has been going through a siege of illnesses and for over two weeks… has been at home with a nurse attending him on a 24 hour basis. Bettie considered this cheaper than the sanitarium routine. However, in spite of this his total nursing bill is approximately $1300.00"[402]

Merle's new signature instrument, the long-awaited Guild Merle Travis Solomaster guitar, was finally completed in 1963. Although Guild's Alfred Dronge had originally envisioned it as an instrument that could be mass-produced, the few that Guild did produce were made by hand by a talented Guild luthier named Carlo Greco. Greco had previously worked for Gretsch, and during his time there, he had custom made both a famous rectangular guitar and the wild Jupiter Thunderbird for famed rocker Bo Diddley. At the Guild factory in Hoboken, New Jersey, Greco hand carved all of the fancy details that Merle had asked for using the finest woods, other materials, and finishes. The guitar was a masterpiece.

From a commercial standpoint, though, it was over the top. It was too much, a gilded piece of fine furniture, something that would look incredible in a museum, but not a workingman's guitar. By the time Greco completed a handful of Merle Travis guitars (there were at least four, and possibly five in total), Dronge must have realized that it was too expensive to ever be commercially viable. The company shipped one to Merle for his own personal use. He took promotional photos with it, and Guild made postcards advertising the model and listed it in their catalog. But what Merle and Dronge had originally envisioned as a flagship model that would bring great success to both the artist and the company instead was a boondoggle—one of the flashiest and fanciest guitars ever created, but too difficult to make and too expensive to sell.

Furthermore, despite Merle's input, when he finally received his instrument after the five-year wait, he didn't bond with it, in large part because it was heavy— almost twice as heavy as his Gibson Super 400. Also, Merle preferred smaller necks so he could wrap his left thumb over the top, and the Guild neck was too big. During a visit to Bakersfield in August 1963, he took his new Guild to a young luthier named

Semie Moseley, who built the Mosrite brand of guitar. Semie was no stranger to Merle, as he had built the custom doubleneck guitars for Joe Maphis and Larry Collins that were used on the *Town Hall Party* show. Hoping to have the neck thinned down just a bit, Merle left the new Guild guitar with Semie for modification. When he received it back (an invoice dating to August 1963 shows the work was done at that time), he remarked that Semie had thinned the neck so much that it was now unplayable: "The reason I don't use it more is because the neck was a little too broad, and I took it to a friend and said, 'Make the neck a little smaller.' And he cut it down to where it's like a ukulele neck."[403] Merle also replaced the bridge pickup almost immediately, replacing the original DeArmond Dynasonic with a Guild pickup from a solidbody S-50 inside a hand-carved wooden pickup cover made by Semie Moseley. (There is an invoice showing that Merle shipped the guitar back to Guild in June 1964, for unknown reasons. Evidently after all the work Guild had put into the guitar, Merle still wasn't happy with it.)[404]

Merle also couldn't put his favorite guitar accessory, the Bigsby vibrato, on his new Guild. Guild did not have a formal business agreement with Bigsby vibratos in 1963 and 1964 (although eventually they did, several years later). As a compromise, Merle briefly endorsed an unusual vibrato unit that was meant to work on fixed-tailpiece guitars, the novel Boyd-Vibe made by Solon "Curly" Boyd of El Cajon, California. The Boyd-Vibe was marketed with a box emblazoned: "Merle Travis says... BOYD VIBE is the best!" and Merle was pictured with the Boyd-Vibe installed on his new Guild in the vibrato brochure. "Curly" Boyd's son David remembered that the endorsement of his father's garage-based company came after a night of drinking followed by Merle sleeping on his family's living room couch. (When he woke up in the morning, David asked Merle to teach him how to play "Cannonball Rag.")[405]

Merle must have also felt some disappointment when he learned that Guild would not be putting his signature model into production. He would always return to the Gibson Super 400, though in his later years, he had the Guild reworked with new pickups by his friend Dick "R. C." Allen, and he used it on occasion. But: in the years since that inauspicious unveiling, the Guild Merle Travis Solomaster has achieved near-mythic, legendary status. Among guitar collectors, it is one of the most talked about, yet rarely seen, guitars ever made.

Merle's personal Guild Solomaster remained in his possession until his death. After his passing, his daughter Pat Travis Eatherly inherited the instrument, and currently the Eatherly family has Merle's personal Solomaster on display at the Merle Travis Music Center in Powderly, Kentucky. The second Guild Merle Travis Solomaster wound up at New York's most famous music store, Manny's Music, where it hung high above the counter for many years, ostensibly for sale but priced so high that it was considered a novelty. Then in the late 1960s, Pete Townsend of the Who stormed into the shop and, flush with cash from a royalty check, demanded to see the most expensive guitar in the store. The Merle Travis Solomaster, priced at $1,200, was that instrument, and Townsend took it home. He was photographed several times with it, and it luckily did not meet the same fate as the many other instruments he destroyed on stage. In the 1980s, he sold it to a New York–based collector.

A third Guild Merle Travis Solomaster went to a music store in Louisville, Kentucky. A 1964 newspaper ad by the store touted:

> See the once-in-a-lifetime Hand Made Merle Travis guitar!
>
> The ultimate in finest quality guitars. Completely hand made body and pick-up, required 3 years to build, curly maple throughout, mother of pearl inlays, gold plated tuning machines, tail piece and bridge.
>
> Maybe you can't afford this guitar but at least you can see it at $2000.00.[406]

Two thousand dollars in 1964 would be approximately $17,000 today. The same store still had the guitar as late as 1974, when it was again advertised in the newspaper, still for sale, though the price was now $2,200. At some point thereafter, it disappeared for several decades until it was purchased, in pieces and in need of a total restoration, by guitarist and collector Rick Nielsen of the rock band Cheap Trick. Nielsen had been looking for a Guild Merle Travis for decades. After a painstaking restoration (utilizing some of Guild's original employees), Nielsen now says in interviews that the 1963 Guild Merle Travis model is, in his opinion, "the Holy Grail."[407]

Three of the known Guild Merle Travis Solomasters all feature a sunburst finish. However, a blonde-finish Solomaster appears in a tantalizing photograph that was sent, without explanation, to Dave Stewart of the "Cannonball Rag" newsletter. A photo that Rick Nielsen passed along to this author reveals that the blonde instrument, the fourth Guild Merle Travis model, resides in a private collection of a well-heeled individual. Rumors have persisted for years that there may also be a fifth out in the wild somewhere. The mystery endures, and the Guild Merle Travis Solomaster is today one of the rarest and most desirable electric archtop guitars ever produced in the United States. One might say it paralleled Merle's life and career during this time: it was the greatest in its field, but it appealed only to a small audience and was in various ways unmarketable.

Merle worked sporadically for the rest of 1963. He toured with Johnny Cash's roadshow troupe in May, played a folkie-bluegrass show in the San Fernando Valley at the end of May, and did a stadium *Grand Ole Opry* cavalcade show in Minneapolis in June. In September he appeared as a guest on the *Bill Bailey* television show in Los Angeles. September 1963 also saw him performing at a Capitol Records–sponsored concert at Bakersfield's Civic Auditorium. The cast included most of Merle's circle of California friends, including Joe and Rose Lee Maphis, Johnny Bond, Jean Shepard, Cousin Herb Henson, Rose Maddox, Buck Owens, Tommy Collins, and two rising stars now signed to the Capitol label—Glen Campbell and Roy Clark.

Capitol recorded the concert and released it under the folksploitation title *Country Music Hootenanny*. Most of the stars were hard-core honky-tonk country acts from the previous generation, but it didn't stop Ken Nelson from trying to appeal to the younger folkies with the title. Merle's cut was a cover of the Delmore Brothers' "Midnight Special." In November, Merle played a big "Country Music Spectacular" show at the Great Western Exhibit Center in Los Angeles along with a dozen other big country music stars. It was the day after President John F. Kennedy was assassinated. A week later, Merle turned forty-six years old.

Just after his birthday, he traveled to Kentucky, where the homefolks in Muhlenberg County had planned another "Merle Travis Day" in his honor on November 30. The weather was bad when Merle arrived. Events that were supposed to happen outdoors on the steps of the Muhlenberg County Courthouse were moved indoors. Merle was quoted in the Owensboro newspaper as joking, "I'm happy to be in a Circuit Court room under such pleasant conditions."[408] As he had done in 1956, he once again acted the part of the returning hero. He was given keys to the cities of Central City, Greenville; Evansville, Indiana; and "My Old Kentucky Home" in Bardstown. He also cut the ribbon at a dedication of a new radio station, WKYF. Mose Rager was in attendance, and one can only surmise that given the first opportunity, Merle and Mose sequestered themselves to do some guitar picking. Merle also visited with all three of his siblings, Taylor, John, and Vada.

On return from this visit to Kentucky in late 1963, Merle's timeline becomes murky. Having a near-fatal stomach hemorrhage might have been a rock-bottom incident for most alcoholics, but he had not yet hit rock bottom. His alcoholism followed the standard trajectory. For years as a young man, he had been able to function when he needed to. The next phase found him still having fun, but unable to stop drinking. By the mid-1960s Merle was no longer having fun, and he couldn't stop. His addiction had become full-blown. Blackouts and violent episodes became almost daily occurrences. During this dark period, he put his Martin acoustic guitar with the Bigsby neck in the fireplace at the Ranchito house and was only stopped from setting it on fire by Joe Maphis. Thom Bresh told this author:

> Anybody tell you about Joe Maphis grabbing that Martin and pulling
> it out of the fireplace? Oh yeah, Merle was very upset at the time about

things, and he says, "I'm done pickin', I'm done writin', I'm done with all of it." And Joe Maphis was walking in the house and all, "Merle Travis, you can't think like that." And he says, "I'm done." And Joe said, "I went into the living room there, and there was that Martin." He couldn't even see the head of it. He had it stuffed up the flute of that chimney. Joe said, "Merle, Jesus Christ." He's just talking about "I'm done, I'm getting rid of all the guitars." "Should I pull that thing out?" He said, "I better have that thing over here; I wouldn't give it back to him." Joe said, "Merle, you got a little nuts there sometimes when I had to pull that Martin out of the fireplace. You was going to burn it up."[409]

Merle's memories:

"I go to Camarillo"
"Johnny Cash comes in Camarillo about 5:00"

In early 1964, Merle was committed to Camarillo State Mental Hospital. Michael Robinson notes: "Believe it or not, he ended up doing a little bit of time in Camarillo. I think it was probably a court-ordered type deal."[410] Very little is known about his stay at California's most famous mental hospital (immortalized by saxophone player Charlie Parker's composition "Relaxing at Camarillo," written during his own incarceration there). Camarillo patient records from 1964 are no longer available. We know the hospital treated patients with mental and psychological illnesses, but also had a wing that served as a minimum-security facility for people with alcohol and drug issues to go and "dry out." A handful of letters still exist that were written during Merle's incarceration. Far from psychotic or violent, if anything, Merle just sounds bored:

Dear Sis:

My battle is pretty well over. I'm eating and sleeping well, and have gained a little weight.

I don't remember when I felt better, but still I guess I'll be here until about March 13th... that will be the war's end. I've lost a few battles in my time, but never lost a war—and by gum, this is no exception. I'm here on business—serious business.

I'll probably put this line in every letter, but you can't imagine how glad I am to hear from "folks outside." It's the highlight of any day to get the kind of letters you and ol' John writes—they're read and re-read. I have a habit of doing that....

Love, Merle[411]

Dear Ol' John:

I'm writing this the first day of March. If all goes well I should be getting some action about the 12th of this month—like going home.... I've got my fingers crossed, I don't see no reason why it shouldn't go alright. I know one thing—this 12 days is going to be like 12 years. The hardest by far to put in—wow!

My baby Bettie comes up to visit me on Mondays. Of course you know her, every thing that bugs me she finds fun in. I wish I could have that attitude—maybe I could if my time here was only visits. Well, maybe some day I can look back and laugh—I hope.

Well John, tell all the kinfolks howdy, and you'll be hearing how things come out here. It's about six thirty AM here, so you see I'll have to break back into sleeping a little later when I'm out. Here I'm in bed about 9:30 and usually wake up about six AM. I sleep in a dorm with 3 other guys, my job is to make my own bed, sweep and mop the dorm, clean up my whiskers, etc. then go to breakfast.

Work in the clothing room till 10:30 then go to classes where we read from a science book (7th grade vintage) till 11:30—go to lunch at 12:00—back in the clothing room till 2:30 back in classes till 3:30—eat supper at 5:00—clothing room again until 6:30 then loaf until bed time—so you see, thumb-twiddlin' time is scarace [sic].

You still got time to write if you would—I sure enjoy your letters, I'll try to do better next time.

Yer bro! Merle[412]

The next two years were a mess. Merle got out of Camarillo and played a few shows in 1964. But things in his life remained chaotic. According to Michael Robinson: "He had a Ford Thunderbird around this time. There was a bar he used to go to right down the street from the house, right at the corner of Burbank and Woodman. If you go behind the bar, you'll still see the telephone pole is bent. That's from where he took out the fender on that Thunderbird, backing into the telephone pole behind the bar in a rage."[413] (This author went there and the telephone pole is still bent, as Michael described.)

Convinced that his song publisher, Sylvester Cross at American Music, was cheating him out of royalties, Merle approached his brother John about coming to work for him around this time. John M. Travis notes:

In the sixties, when Merle was so heavily into drugs and alcohol, Merle asked me to move to California and head up a publishing company for

him. He begged and begged. Finally I agreed and turned in my resig-
nation at the gas company in Hopkinsville. On the appointed day when
Merle was supposed to show up—the plan was for him to fly back and we
would drive back in my car because I would need it in California—Merle
never appeared. For another three weeks I never heard a word. Finally,
when Merle called, he did not remember a thing about it.... I went back
to the boss and asked whether my job was still open and went back to
work. I felt humiliated.[414]

Merle saved an arrest record dated November 1, 1964—by all accounts one
of many times he was arrested in that year. Then somewhere around Christmas,
according to Michael Robinson, "He left. He was living down in Hollywood,
that's when he really started getting in trouble with the law. He was just running amok; it was out of control. He set his bed on fire, by probably passing out
while smoking in bed, in some hotel down in Hollywood and ended up in the
hospital."[415]

Merle's memory:

"Set apartment afire almost burned up"

Somehow the incident was kept out of the newspapers. The only documentation that the event actually occurred comes from a get-well card sent to the
hospital when Merle was recovering and a written recollection by Alan Franklin,
one of the first responders on the scene (who happened to be a country-western
fan), found in Ed Kahn's archives:

This story is regarding Merle Travis and an accident that happened to him
in the mid 1960s. The following is the best of my memory as I was there.

During the 1960s I worked for the City of Los Angeles in the capacity of Emergency Ambulance Driver for the Central Receiving Hospital
that handled all of the emergency rescue calls for the city. While I was on
duty, I received a call that a person was involved and injured in a fire in
a motel in Hollywood. This particular motel was located on Hollywood
Blvd. just west of La Brea Avenue.

When I responded to this call, I was so surprised to see that the
injured party was Merle Travis. The fire department responded to a call
of a fire in one of the motel rooms that was occupied by Merle. The
fire department removed Merle from the room and when we arrived, I
noticed that he was suffering from smoke inhalation and minor burns.
Merle was in a semi conscious state. We gave Merle some oxygen and
transported him to Hollywood Receiving Hospital for further treatment.

By coincidence, I knew Merle Travis because I was a big fan of his since 1946 and also I was promoting Dick Curless who had recorded some of Merle's material earlier. During the late 1950s, I met Merle on several occasions at the Town Hall Party T.V. show.

The doctor on duty at Hollywood Receiving Hospital determined that Merle should be hospitalized for further treatment....

At this time, I contacted radio station KFOX in Long Beach, which at the time was the number one country station in the Los Angeles area. I contacted Charlie Williams who was on the air at the time and told him of the injury to Merle....

Charlie told me that he would work on this immediately and get a hold of someone to help Merle. I convinced the doctor to hold off on the transfer of Merle to County Hospital for a couple of hours. I stayed with Merle in the treatment and talked with him and he soon remembered who I was. One of the first things he said was his concern for his hands and if they had been burned.... Charlie Williams succeeded in contacting Merle's private relatives and he soon transferred to a private hospital in the San Fernando Valley....

Some time later, I saw Merle performing at one of the clubs and he recognized me immediately. Merle came on over to me and shook my hand and told me how much he appreciated the help I gave him when he was injured in Hollywood. I remember telling Merle that I was glad to be of help and I really meant it.

Alan M. Franklin, Milo, Maine[416]

In his archives, Merle saved a letter from Sunny Virant (a writer for the *National Hillbilly News* in the 1940s, who had known Merle since 1946) postmarked December 26, 1964. It had been sent to him in care of the Valley Hospital in Van Nuys, which would seem to indicate that Merle spent Christmas of that year in the hospital, recuperating from his burn wounds:

Dear Merle,

. . . Sorry you are in such great discomfort but hope you heal up fast and "purty." It seems the newscast glorifying your achievements and notifying us of being burned is K-F-W-B—but am not sure. The kids were listening to their generations music and I just happened to be at meal with Eddie when the news came on....

Speedy recovery, regards,

Sunny Virant and fam[417]

Merle's memory:

"I go to Saugus"

As a result of the many previous lesser run-ins with the law, the motel fire in late 1964 was the straw that broke the camel's back. Suddenly Merle was facing real jail time. He was able to keep it out of the papers, and to avoid "real" jail by agreeing to serve out a sentence at the Saugus Honor Farm, also known as the Wayside Honor Rancho or the Wayside Drunk Farm (and still operating today as the Pitchess Detention Center). The facility, north of Los Angeles in the Santa Clarita Valley near Saugus and Castaic, existed as a work farm specifically for alcoholics convicted of crimes. It was supposed to allow alcoholic men the opportunity to "dry out" while doing farm chores and gardening. In Michael Robinson's words, "He did some time at the Saugus Honor Farm, which is at Magic Mountain and Bouquet Canyon, let's say. I remember my mom going up there to visit him and me sitting out in the parking lot."[418]

Two years later, again a free man, Merle was served with papers regarding money owed for damages regarding the December 1964 hotel fire. A copy of a letter from Merle to his new lawyer, Jerry Fields, is the only reference we have about Merle's time in the Saugus Honor Farm:

Dear Jerry:

Please find enclosed letter from Mr. George D. Weinberg, Investigator for the County of Los Angeles Bureau of Resources and Collections....

I was under the impression that this matter was settled when my affairs were wholly in your hands. Perhaps I'm mistaken.

I can't help but feel that this affair was an imprisonment instead of a beneficial service. I'm aware, of course, that legally it's otherwise. In reality, it was a useless, expensive incarceration....

My best to you,

Merle Travis[419]

A year after that letter, Merle was served with more legal papers regarding money owed for the hotel fire damages:

Dear Jerry:

Enclosed is the papers served on me concerning the fire incident in Hollywood, California in December, 1964....

I was under the impression that this affair had been settled. I'll await your on future legal steps to be taken.

As ever,

Merle Travis[420]

Merle Travis as a young boy.
(Photo courtesy of Merlene Travis
and Cindy Travis)

Merle's father, William Robert Travis, known as
"Rob" or "Uncle Rob" Travis, early 1900s.
(Photo courtesy of the Eatherly family)

The Travis family, mid-1920s. Standing
(L-R): Merle, Taylor, Vada, and John Melvin.
Seated are Merle's parents, Etta and Rob Travis.

Merle (top left) with his
first professional group,
The Tennessee Tomcats, 1936.

Merle's two greatest guitar mentors,
Ike Everly (left) and Mose Rager (right),
shown here at a 1950s reunion.

Merle (second from right), then known as "Ridgerunner" Travis, with
Clayton McMichen and band. The photo is dated March 28, 1937.

Merle with Red Phillips (far left) and The Drifting
Pioneers in Marion, Indiana, late 1930s.

Merle and his first wife Mary on their
wedding day, April 12, 1937.
(Photo courtesy of the Eatherly family)

Merle (left) is seen on the streets of Cincinnati in
a damaged photo from the late 1930s, across the
street from the boarding house where he lived
with his wife Mary and their daughter Patty.

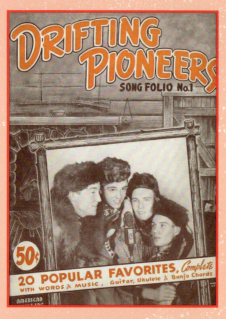

Drifting Pioneers Song Folio, 1940, containing Merle's first published original song, "The Dust on Mother's Old Bible." (Courtesy of Deke Dickerson Photo Archive)

Merle and his lifelong friend, Louis "Grandpa" Jones, shortly after they met in Cincinnati, 1942.

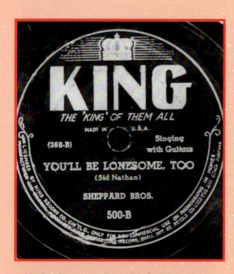

Merle's first recording, with Grandpa Jones, under the pseudonym "The Sheppard Brothers." This label scan comes from the only known copy of the record. (Courtesy of Richard Weize/ Bear Family Records)

Merle's 1943 induction photo for the Marine Corps, a stint that lasted barely six weeks. He was found "unsuitable" for military service and sent home.

One of the first groups Merle worked with in Hollywood, The Trailriders, 1945. (L-R): Wesley Tuttle, Jimmy Dean (Eddie Dean's brother), and Merle.

Jeanne "Jeannie" Jackson Lesher Gehrung, who bore Merle's first out-of-wedlock son, Richard Lesher, in 1945. (Photo courtesy of Sherry Gehrung, Sandra Gehrung, and Gina Lesher)

Merle's first son, Richard Lesher, born in 1945, shown in a musical promo shot in the 1960s. Lesher died in 1979 at the age of 33. (Photo courtesy of Sherry Gehrung, Sandra Gehrung, and Gina Lesher)

Merle and an all-female band (featuring singing partner Carolina Cotton, to Merle's left) in a publicity still for the Soundies Distributing Company, 1945.

Capitol Records promotional photo of Merle and his second wife and singing partner, Tex Ann Nation, 1946.

An inebriated Merle and Tex Ann at Merle's 29th birthday party in November, 1946. Many photos exist from that night—a wild, drunken soiree attended by many of the earliest Capitol Records executives and recording artists.

RAP CHARGES—Radio Musician Merle Travis, who denies he was driving while drunk though policeman says he tore up book and hit him with it. Sidna Kelly, his companion, is also accused by police of being drunk while driving with Travis.

—Los Angeles Examiner photo.

Driver Denies Drunk Charge

VAN NUYS, Sept. 5. — Radio Musician Merle Travis, 29, insisted in Van Nuys court today he was NOT driving while drunk when Motorcycle Officer C. R. Ericson stopped him on Ventura boulevard.

until he has answered the drunk and reckless driving accusations

October 5 Deadline
for R————t R————t
Arm

Merle and Tex Ann make the Los Angeles newspapers on a "drunk charge,"
September 6, 1946. (Los Angeles Examiner newspaper)

One of Merle's earliest published cartoons, from the
Capitol Records country music newspaper Tophand,
1946. (Courtesy of Deke Dickerson Photo Archive)

Merle in the studio in 1947 with his good friend, Capitol Records
A&R man, bassist, and tireless country music promoter Clifford
Snyder, Jr., professionally known as "Cliffie Stone." Both men would
eventually become members of the Country Music Hall of Fame.
(Capitol Records promotional photo, courtesy of Merlene Travis and Cindy Travis)

Merle sings into a microphone at a session in 1947 at Radio Recorders studio in Hollywood, while fellow Capitol recording artist Eddie Kirk plays rhythm guitar. Within a year, Merle would wed Eddie's wife, Judy Hayden.
(Capitol Records promotional photo, courtesy of Merlene Travis and Cindy Travis)

Merle recording at Radio Recorders studio in Hollywood, January 1947.
(Capitol Records promo photo, courtesy of Merlene Travis and Cindy Travis)

Merle juggles guitar cases astride his
Indian Chief motorcycle in front of Wallich's
Music City in Hollywood, 1947.
(Capitol Records promo photo, courtesy
of Merlene Travis and Cindy Travis)

Merle with his Indian Chief motorcycle: "In 1947, I
wouldn't go twenty feet unless I was on my motorcycle."

Merle recorded *Folk Songs of the Hills*, his 78 rpm album of newly-penned and classic folk songs in 1946 and 1947. This is where the song "Sixteen Tons" was heard for the first time.

Virginia "Ginny" Cushman, a child prodigy cornet player from Santa Barbara, California, sent this photo to Merle's attention in a ploy to get a spot in his band. It worked. (Courtesy of Lynn Davis Herrod)

Merle and Ginny Cushman on tour, 1948. She was billed in newspaper advertisements as "Virginia Cushman, hillbillie (sic) trumpet player."

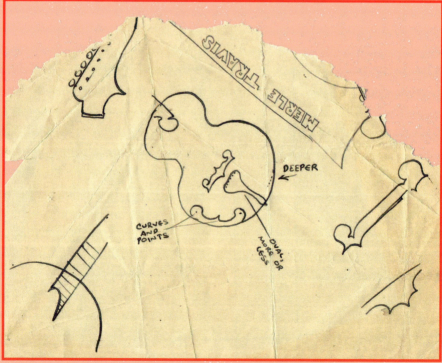

The original drawings Merle created with his groundbreaking idea for a solidbody electric guitar. These were given to Paul Bigsby in early 1948 at KXLA radio station, and were written on the back of *Dinner Bell Round Up* mimeograph paper, the radio show Merle was appearing on at the time.

This KXLA *Dinner Bell Round Up* photo is the only other image to show Merle's 1948 Bigsby solidbody in its original form, with extended headstock, no cutaway, and two knobs. (Courtesy of Karl Anderson Archives)

Merle and Ginny Cushman pose with Merle's brand new Bigsby electric solidbody guitar, in its original incarnation with extended headstock, single cutaway, and two knobs. (Courtesy of Lynn Davis Herrod)

Merle proudly holds his new Bigsby solidbody electric guitar for a promotional photo, 1949.

Merle poses with two of his Bigsby instruments in 1949. Singer Redd Harper holds Merle's Bigsby twelve-string guitar, which was later fitted with a new headstock and given to Hank Thompson, while Merle holds his Bigsby solidbody electric guitar.

Merle holds his Bigsby solidbody guitar in this promo photo from the late 1940s. (Capitol Records promotional photo, courtesy or Merlene Travis and Cindy Travis)

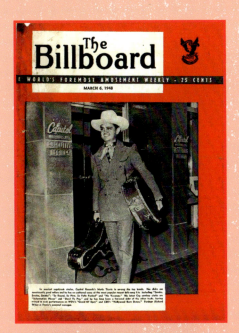

At the height of his commercial success, Merle was featured on the cover of *Billboard* Magazine, March 6, 1948.

A show poster from 1948, advertising Merle as the "King of the Juke Box." (Courtesy of Deke Dickerson Photo Archive)

Merle poses for a group shot while visiting Kentucky on tour in 1947. The extended length DeSoto Surburban car the group toured in was referred to as "the boat." (L-R): Grandpa Jones, Jack Rogers, Mose Rager, Ginny Cushman, and Merle.

The first "Merle Travis Day" celebration in 1947 welcomed Merle and his band home to Drakesboro, Kentucky. The group was met by a huge crowd, which led a parade down Main Street. Merle was presented a key to the city. Those watching him receive the honor include his oldest brother Taylor on the far left (holding Merle's oldest daughter, Patty), Ginny Cushman (behind Merle), and Mose Rager on the far right.

Thom Bresh (left) and Merle, shown here in the early 1960s. Thom and Merle knew one another for two decades before Merle acknowledged that Thom was his biological son. (Courtesy of Thom Bresh)

The only surviving marriage license from one of Merle's many marriages across the border in Mexico (there were at least four "Mexican Marriages," as he called them). Merle and Judy Hayden married in Mexico in December of 1948, and had a second wedding in Fresno a year later in December of 1949.

Merlene Travis, Merle's second daughter, was born in October, 1949. Here Merle holds the new infant, flanked by band members Tex Atchison (left) and Jack Rogers (right).

Wife Chased Him Out, Barefoot Singer Wails

Merle Travis, Complaining Spouse Wielded Pistol, Faces Court Trial on Drunk Charge

Cowboy Singer Merle Travis drawled "Not guilty," when he appeared in the Van Nuys court room yesterday to answer a charge of plain drunk.

Municipal Judge Walter C. Allen released him on $20 bail and set Dec. 15 for a court trial.

Arrested While Barefoot

The Kentucky-born singer was arrested in front of his home, 14927 Victory Blvd., Van Nuys, early yesterday barefoot and clad in pajama tops and dress trousers. He told Officers Pat Murphy and H. E. Cunningham his wife had shot five times in the air with a 38-caliber pistol and she said the next one would be for him.

Travis complained he called for police help seven times before the officers arrived.

Police said they asked Travis if he wanted to go to jail, and the singer mumbled, "Sure," and walked to the police car.

Sings Different Tune

Later, the 32-year-old singer sang a different tune. He said he had been taking sedatives for the past three months under doctor's prescription because he was on the verge of a nervous breakdown. "I don't remember what I told the police," he added.

Meanwhile, Mrs. Travis appeared in court with Song Writer Hal Blair. She burst into tears when the judge asked her if she would provide bail. She went to the bank and obtained money for her husband's release.

Merle made the front page of the Los Angeles Times in December of 1949 with another "drunk charge."

OUT ON BAIL—Cowboy Singer Merle Travis, barefoot and clad in pajama tops and dress trousers, as he was booked on a plain drunk charge at Van Nuys station.
— Times photo

Wife Chased Him Out, Barefoot Singer Wails

Merle Travis, Complaining Spouse Wielded Pistol, Faces Court Trial on Drunk Charge

Shown barefoot and drunk on the front page of the newspaper was devastating for Merle's relationship with Judy Hayden. (Los Angeles Times, December 2, 1949)

In 1950, Merle and Judy Hayden (and their infant daughter Merlene) moved to Richmond, Virginia, to join the cast of the "Old Dominion Barn Dance" on radio station WRVA. The move was to be short-lived.

When Joe and Rose Lee Maphis left Richmond in 1951 to join Merle in California on the Foreman Phillips television show, Merle drew this humorous cartoon to celebrate their cross-country drive. Note details like the "dog house bass" strapped to the top, the "Custom Built by P.A. Bigsby" plaque on the radiator, and the "Marijuana Cigarette Co." box strapped to the running board. (Courtesy of Jody Maphis)

Merle and Joe Maphis perform guitar magic together on stage at the Riverside Rancho in Los Angeles, July 1952. Four-year old Thom Bresh was in attendance that night. (Courtesy of Henry Van Wormer)

Merle and Joe Maphis in a recording studio with
matching Bigsby acoustic guitars, early 1950s.
(Courtesy of Deke Dickerson Photo Archive)

Merle's touring band, 1952. Joe and Rose Lee
Maphis are second and third from left.

Merle holding his first Gibson Super 400 in 1952, shortly before receiving his custom-ordered instrument with his name inlaid on the neck. (Capitol Records promotional photo, courtesy of Merlene Travis and Cindy Travis)

Merle with the finest and most expensive guitar and amplifier one could buy in 1953—a customized Gibson Super 400, and a custom-made Standel 25L15 amplifier. (Courtesy of Deke Dickerson Photo Archive)

Merle with his friend (and employer) Hank Thompson, shown here in the Capitol Recording Studios in Hollywood.

Merle's three daughters, mid-1950s. Clockwise from top left: Patty, Merlene, and Cindy.

Frank Sinatra and Merle on the set of *From Here To Eternity*.
(Columbia Pictures promotional photo)

Merle in a scene with Montgomery Clift in the hit movie *From Here
To Eternity*. Merle played the part of "Hillbilly."
(Columbia Pictures promotional photo)

Merle with one of his greatest friends and
benefactors, cowboy star Gene Autry.

Merle and "Tennessee" Ernie Ford share a hearty laugh after the invigorating
commercial success of Ernie's recording of Merle's song "Sixteen Tons."
(Capitol Records promotional photo)

Merle and Bettie take a promotional photo, cooking in their kitchen in North Hollywood, mid-1950s.

Merle and Bettie stand in their North Hollywood driveway with their Cadillac convertible.

A mid-1950s family portrait with Merle's daughters, Merlene and Cindy, and Bettie's sons, Michael and Dennis. Asked if this was a typical home scenario, Merlene replied: "That was a photo shoot."

April 16, 1955

Mr. Merle Travis
7665 Hollywood Blvd. Apt. #9
Hollywood 46, Calif.

Dear Merle:

THERE IS A BOY AND HIS GUITAR,

HE IS OUR FAVORITE WESTERN STAR.

HE SHOULD PRACTICE DAY AND NIGHT

TO MAKE HIS RECORDS COME OUT RIGHT

     OR

HIS UNCLE KEN IS GOING TO BE REAL UNHAPPY.

Uncle Ken

In 1955, Capitol Records producer Ken Nelson sent Merle a series of letters, encouraging Merle to get his act together and practice his material so the label could have enough songs to release his tour de force album, *The Merle Travis Guitar*.

Merle looks at the newly constructed Capitol Tower in 1955, finished at the time that his song "Sixteen Tons" was the label's biggest record of the year.

The Merle Travis Guitar, also known as "the yellow album," one of the greatest guitar recordings ever released.

HCP010402-1/4/56-VAN NUYS,CALIF: Police, armed, cautiously approach the home
of western songwriter Merle Travis after his wife reported he had threatened
to shoot anyone trying to enter. Earlier he reportedly injured his wife during a drinking spree at home with a friend. Mrs. Travis called police from a
neighbor's home.   UNITED PRESS TELEPHOTO ch/st

On January 4, 1956, Merle's home troubles were blasted on the front pages of newspapers across the country. The media was interested in the story not because it was a hillbilly guitarist who fired off his gun inside the house and struck his wife, but because Merle had written the biggest hit of the previous year, "Sixteen Tons." The headline read, "30 Armed Policemen Seize Barricaded '16 Tons' Writer." (Newspaper clipping from *Valley Times* edition of the *Los Angeles Times*, January 4, 1956)

At Merle's Homecoming show in Ebeneezer, Kentucky, in 1956, Merle and his special guest Gene Autry greet Bunnie Mullins Baugh, who used to host Merle at "Pickin' Parties" at her house in Ebeneezer when Merle was a boy.

Merle and his oldest daughter, Patty, at the dedication of
his monument in Ebeneezer, Kentucky, 1956.

Merle and his home recording studio, 1950s, with his two stepsons, Dennis and Michael.
(Photo courtesy of Michael Robinson)

Merle with Nudie Cohn, the "Rodeo Tailor."
Nudie made a number of expensive, custom
Western suits for Merle, as well as for stars,
such as Elvis Presley and Gram Parsons.

Merle stayed in the public eye during the 1950s
by appearing on numerous television shows.
One of the most popular was *Town Hall Party*,
which ran for three hours live every Saturday
night in Los Angeles. A nationally syndicated
version called *Ranch Party* was shown across the
United States and Canada. In this photo, Merle
shares the Town Hall Party stage with Joe Maphis
(left) and steel guitarist Marian Hall (right).

A surviving Los Angeles County jail receipt from November of 1964.
Merle was arrested numerous times over the years.

Back in the swing of things in 1966, Merle took to the road to try to dig himself out of the hole he had bottomed out in over the previous decade. Judging by the look on his face as he played the ukulele outside his new RV camper truck, it wasn't all smooth sailing. (Courtesy of Merlene Travis and Cindy Travis. Slide scanned and edited by Jim Herrington.)

In 1966, Merle bought a new customized camper truck and took to the highways, often with his wife Bettie (shown here at a scenic overlook) by his side. (Courtesy of Merlene Travis and Cindy Travis. Slide scanned and edited by Jim Herrington.)

Merle and Bettie, shown here with one of their two poodles, got back together in 1966 and began touring the country together. (Courtesy of Merlene Travis and Cindy Travis. Slide scanned and edited by Jim Herrington.)

Newly sober, Merle began writing articles for several magazines and newspapers after moving to Nashville in 1966. Although this is a blurry image, it is the only known photo showing Merle hard at work at the typewriter from this important time in his life. (Courtesy of Merlene Travis and Cindy Travis. Slide scanned and edited by Jim Herrington.)

This color slide shows how Merle's Gibson Super 400 received many evolutionary modifications, by both Shot Jackson and the Gibson Guitar Company. (Courtesy of Merlene Travis and Cindy Travis. Slide scanned and edited by Jim Herrington.)

A humorous cartoon from a 1966 letter to his wife, Bettie, depicting an incident where Merle dropped his Gibson Super 400 and damaged it. (Courtesy Michael Robinson/Deke Dickerson Photo Archive)

Another humorous cartoon from 1966, depicting Merle and Nashville repairman Shot Jackson arguing over whether his Gibson Super 400 is finished with repairs. (Courtesy Michael Robinson/Deke Dickerson Photo Archive)

This cartoon by Merle, saved by guitar maker R.C. "Dick" Allen, shows a guitar player "playing his ass off." (Courtesy R.C. Allen/Deke Dickerson Photo Archive)

Another humorous cartoon from one of Merle's letters to Bettie in 1966, a self-portrait showing Merle's grumpy side. (Courtesy Michael Robinson/Deke Dickerson Photo Archive)

Merle and legendary blues guitarist B.B. King, shown on the set of a PBS television production from 1970 called *American Odyssey: Dark as a Dungeon*, shot on location in Eckley, Pennsylvania.

Merle and Chet Atkins at RCA Studios in Hollywood, recording the tracks that would be released on the 1974 album *The Atkins-Travis Traveling Show*.

In 1977, as a new couple, Merle and Dorothy attended Merle's Country Music Hall of Fame induction ceremony in Nashville.

Merle holding court in a hotel room in Oklahoma, 1981.

Johnny Cash, Marty Stuart, and Merle at a 1981 show at Oral Roberts University in Tulsa, Oklahoma.

Merle and his biological son Thom Bresh performing together on Bresh's Canadian television show in the early 1980s. Merle and Thom became quite close in Merle's later years. (Courtesy of Merlene Travis and Cindy Travis. Slide scanned and edited by Jim Herrington.)

Promotional photo, early 1980s. (Courtesy Merlene Travis and Cindy Travis. Slide scanned and edited by Jim Herrington.)

Merle and Roy Clark trade licks and laughter on the *Hee Haw* television show, early 1980s.

One of the last photos taken of Merle before his death in 1983.

From 1964 to 1965, Merle and Bettie had been unofficially separated for more than a year. When he was on his worst behavior, he stayed away for weeks and months at a time, living in hotel rooms (and sometimes setting them on fire). When he got out of the Saugus Honor Farm, he played some random shows around Los Angeles (including the Ash Grove folk club) and appeared on Gene Autry's television show, *Melody Ranch*. But he did not return to normal home life. Michael Robinson notes: "Yeah, in '65 he ran away from home for a while, and the house was locked. Mom had to sell the house, and there were all these problems going on. It was real bad."[421]

After the stint in Camarillo, followed by the stint at the Saugus Honor Farm, followed by the couple losing the estate on Ranchito due to nonpayment, Bettie finally decided she wanted out of the marriage. Divorce papers were drawn up in March 1965. The Ranchito house was sold, and in addition to receiving half of the profits from the house, Bettie was to receive 25 percent of Merle's songwriting royalties.[422] It took three months for the news to become public, but the story broke in June 1965:

> Songwriter Merle Travis, 47, wrote the lyrical advice his wife followed Monday when she divorced him in Superior Court.
>
> "Get yourself another man," was the way he put it in one of the songs he wrote. Another is titled: "Divorce Me C.O.D."
>
> Travis' wife, Bettie Lou, 41, who lives in the San Fernando Valley, told Commissioner Victor Donatelli that she developed ulcers over the mistreatment she got from her husband.
>
> She said he was so temperamental she dared not have her friends in their home.
>
> Under a property settlement agreement, Mrs. Travis was awarded $250 a month for five years and 25% of Travis' share in the royalties on some 10 songs he either wrote or collaborated on.
>
> Among the best known is "16 Tons."[423]

Bettie moved into an apartment around the corner from the Ranchito house. At this time her son Dennis was serving in the military in Puerto Rico and Michael was enrolled in military school, preparing for a military career of his own. She lived in a small complex that was also home to Pauline Silby, the estranged wife of *Town Hall Party* comedian Leon Silby, aka Quincy Snodgrass. She led a simple life during this time, with a small social circle that included Pauline and Jack Rogers's wife, Marge. She didn't see Merle for nearly a year. She later remembered:

When he was drinking, it was like living in a "Rollie Coaster" [*sic*]. You would start out slow and you'd finally build to the crest where you'd think, "Oh, goodnight, I got to get outa here," you know, and then when he'd finally get to the bottom, then you could pick him up, dust him off, and get him straightened out for a while and he'd be good for a while and then he'd start again, you know. And so that's the way it was. When we separated, I heard that a lot of people tried to help him stop drinking. He finally decided that he really had to do something about it.[424]

When he was released from the Saugus Honor Farm in mid-1965, Merle had lost his house and his family, he had no money, and his career was in shambles. It was time, as Bettie put it, to "pick him up, dust him off, and get him straightened out." When she finally laid eyes on him after a year's separation, she realized they weren't ready to call it quits:

We were divorced and he dropped out of sight. I had moved to a little apartment on Burbank Boulevard.... I heard that Merle was living at the Silver Saddle in Hollywood [Bettie is confusing two similar-sounding establishments here; the Silver Spur was a bar in Hollywood that Merle frequented, but in 1965 he was staying at a Western-themed hotel with attached bar and restaurant in Downey, California, called the Silver Saddle Inn]. Quincy Snodgrass's wife was living across the street from me and said that Quincy was also living at the Silver Saddle. It worked out that the two of them were living together. I took Pauline Snodgrass over there because Pauline needed some money. We found Merle.

We just said "hello" because I wasn't mad at him.... I was disappointed sometimes, but I was never really mad at him. So we got to talking and one thing led to another so we got back together, and hadn't really even been separated a year, you know, so it really, it didn't take. And that's the second time, I guess....

When I ran into him at the Silver Saddle, he wasn't drinking and looked wonderful.

We got divorced and then... during the "interlocutory" we got back together.... We got a camper and Merle went off to Nashville and I stayed with the kids until Mike finished the semester.[425]

Merle was once again convinced that relocating was the only answer to his problems. He wanted to get out of California and away from his string of arrests, incarcerations, and embarrassing incidents. His erratic behavior had alienated many of his friends, chased away his oldest daughter and her husband, and greatly damaged his career opportunities on the West Coast. Moving would mean distancing himself from his three daughters and leaving all the close friends he had remaining from his twenty-two years in California. But despite how much upheaval it would mean, Merle was convinced that he should move to Nashville. Michael Robinson remembered:

> We were living over on the corner of Sunnyslope and Burbank. Travis was coming over there; he straightened his act out. He was squared away again. He was what I liked in him at that point. He was arranging for that move to Tennessee, and they had gone down and bought that Chevy three-quarter-ton pickup truck with the camper on it. He couldn't be drunk and traveling around. He used to try, and he really did a hard sell on getting us back there. I have no problem with it. You know, actually the smartest thing I ever did was leave the San Fernando Valley. I thought the San Fernando Valley was the center of the universe until I left, and then I found out that this is a whole world out there. What was that Tom Waits song? You'd never seen the ocean until you seen it on the East Coast, or something? I love Tom Waits.[426]

Merle on stage at the Grand Ole Opry, 1960s. Although he appeared on the Opry numerous times as a guest, he was never added as a member.

CHAPTER 8

TO NASHVILLE AND BACK, ON THE HILL- BILLY TRAIL OF TEARS

The next few years would represent a huge change in Merle and Bettie's life. Newly sober, Merle hit the road with renewed vigor. The couple moved to Nashville, where they joined a group of Merle's oldest friends in the business. Merle began writing and drawing cartoons on a professional basis, and began writing his autobiography. He also recorded again for Capitol Records, who released several new singles and albums recorded in Nashville, including a new guitar instrumental album, *Strictly Guitar*, and a tribute album with Johnny Bond, called *Great Songs of the Delmore Brothers*. Merle reunited with his friend Johnny Cash, who put him to work on his successful television show, *The Johnny Cash Show*.

After falling off the wagon again, Merle had an addiction-related, stroke-type incident that resulted in a muscle-pulling problem in his face and body that impacted him severely for the rest of his life.

The Nitty Gritty Dirt Band included Merle on their seminal *Will the Circle Be Unbroken* album in 1972, exposing Merle and his most famous songs to a new group of younger-generation fans. Following the *Circle* album, Merle and Bettie returned to Los Angeles, where Merle recorded a small-label EP release with Ray Campi in 1974 and a Grammy-winning collaboration with his old friend Chet Atkins that same year for RCA Records, called *The Atkins-Travis Traveling Show*. Merle and Thom Bresh became musical friends, and finally the secret came out that Thom was Merle's out-of-wedlock son. Eventually Merle's long marriage to Bettie fell apart, and he would find a new flame in Hank Thompson's ex-wife Dorothy.

In late 1965, Merle made preparations to move from Los Angeles to Nashville. He got a new booking agent, "Lucky" Moeller of Moeller Talent Inc., who promised to keep him working steadily. He purchased a new Chevrolet Chinook motor home and had the back and sides emblazoned with the hand-lettered logo "Merle Travis—Country Music Shows." In a 1967 issue of BMI magazine, Merle could barely contain his newfound enthusiasm for traveling:

> I've got the Atlantic Ocean in my back yard, and the Pacific Ocean in my
> front yard. Over one fence is Canada and over the other, Mexico. When
> I take off on those super highways it makes for a year-round vacation,
> not a tour.[427]

Capitol Records executive Joe Allison told historian Ed Kahn: "About Merle and alcohol, it was a Dr. Jekyll and Mr. Hyde situation. He was potentially the greatest talent in the business. When he stopped drinking, he did it better than anyone I know."[428] Merle traveled to Nashville in December 1965 to do his first Capitol recording session there. He was eager to record new material for Capitol, thinking he had a hit single or two left in him. The December session resulted in two songs, "You're a Little Bit Cuter" and "Voo Doo," which were rejected for unknown reasons and remain unissued.

For the moment, Bettie remained in California so her youngest son, Michael, could finish his school semester there. Merle began the long, hard slog of digging himself out of the hole he had dug in the first part of the 1960s. The money he made was garnished to pay off the money he owed. That meant hitting the road, alone, harder than he had since the early 1950s, working one-night stands any place that would have him. Gone were the big Gene Autry paydays. Merle was averaging $200 or $300 a night, just a notch above typical pay for local bands. Bettie Travis recalled: "The period when we moved to Nashville, that was about two, two and a half years of paradise, as far as I was concerned.... Probably about two years, maybe, where he didn't touch anything and we did have wonderful times together."[429] When Bettie passed away, she left behind a stack of letters that Merle sent her from the road in January, February, and March of 1966. After all the years of tragedy and turmoil, these were the items she chose to save from their marriage. The letters were long and came several times a week. In them, Merle detailed his tour and weather details, things that were going wrong or right in the new camper. And in his delicate prose, he poured his heart out. The missives are full of raw emotion from a man who had completely screwed up and was trying to make amends. Some excerpts:

Wed. Nite... Jan. 27
Hello Punkin:
I miss my Bettie, I wish you were here. I'm going to work real hard and make money to get you nice dresses and a nice little suburban house. And I'll always be good to you, and true to you, and think of you constantly, 'cause I love-love-love you...
—Merle

Jan. 31 1966
Dearest Baby: (and ol' Mike)
As I write this I am well, warm and camped out. If I knew a million ways to say I love you, I'd write a million letters telling you so.
I'll always love you with all my heart. If I imagine you're a little unreasonable sometimes, I don't get mad at you—I get hurt. I wouldn't do that if I'd think twice, or if I wasn't so completely wrapped up in you—so completely wrapped up in you, Bettie—
Forgive me for every wrong I do. I wouldn't deliberately cause you one second of unpleasantness for the world. I'll be good and work hard, as soon we'll be together again.
—Merle

Friday, Feb. 4. 1966
Dearest Baby Bet:

I got your letter today, and ummmm—how sweet it is! You're a sweetheart, do it again soon—will y'?

Opportunities are all over the place here [Nashville], and it's an ant's nest of young hopefuls. Some will be stars some day. Others will become bitter because they can [sic] even get in an office. I'm an ol' timer. I knew every big shot here back when, they're ol' friends. So actually, the doors are wide open. Maybe we'll luck into something. Who knows.

My Lindy Pen is giving out, but it still has enough juice to let me set down in writing that I love you. You are the most important thing in the world to me—and will be always. Love me a little, will you? Miss me too if you will, and we'll be together real soon—we'll go touring together—

By by my angel

I love you— ·

—Merle

Feb. 13. '66

Sunday afternoon

Darling:

I hope these letters don't bore you. I just start peckin' away and never know what I'm gonna say. But it's some sort of connection with you, you might say. My mind is completely on you when I'm writing you, in fact it's on you when I ain't writing. I think of you all the time. I love you so very much.

I'm going to work as hard as I can. When we get caught up a little bit I won't have to go at such a pace unless I want to. I believe we could have lots of fun touring together again. It would be different than last time. I feel better and I love you more, if that's possible....

Yours,

—Merle[430]

During 1966, a random meeting occurred on a small highway in California: Merle Travis met Merle Haggard. Haggard had been around for years in Las Vegas and Bakersfield, playing in both Wynn Stewart's and Buck Owens's bands, but recently the "other Merle" had been signed to Capitol and was having hits of his own. He remembered the "meeting of the Merles" in an interview with the author in 2006:

Of course, I had seen Merle Travis before; he played in Bakersfield a lot and had been at that thing at the Municipal Auditorium where they recorded that live album. I was there that night. But I didn't get to meet him until a few years later. He was touring in a camper and had his name on the side of it. I was driving and saw him on the road, so I flagged him down. He stopped, and we had a conversation. I had just started making records for Capitol, and he had been on Capitol for a very long time. This is before I had a bus; he was in a camper, and I was going out doing shows in a station wagon, very early in my career.[431]

By the spring of 1966, Merle, Bettie, and Michael were together in Nashville, living at the home of Grandpa and Ramona Jones. Michael finished his last semester of high school in Nashville, living with the Joneses while Merle and Bettie went out on the road together. Bettie recalled: "I went to Nashville and stayed with Ramona and Grandpa. After summer, we got an apartment, decorated it from the road. We were working lots then. I sold pictures and talked to people, and later on, I also sang with Merle. That was fun, it made it more interesting, you know."[432] Michael notes: "I lived with Grandpa for the rest of that semester up until summer. And this was when he was getting squared back away. Unfortunately, he had done so much damage to his body that it couldn't really be rectified, actually. And it all eventually caught up to him."[433] During this time Merle did some recording with Grandpa for Monument Records, playing guitar (and writing liner notes) for an album titled *Grandpa Jones Makes the Rafters Ring*, as well as singing and playing guitar on an album of gospel quartet numbers released as *Grandpa Jones Remembers the Brown's Ferry Four*.

By August, Merle, Bettie, and Michael were living in a new apartment building called the Imperial House on Bosley Springs Road in Nashville. Merle recorded two new singles for Capitol in March and August 1966—the first singles he had released since 1955: "John Henry, Jr." backed with "That Same Ol' Natural Urge," and "Moon over the Motel" backed with "That Tennessee Beat." Neither made much of a dent, but at least there were new Merle Travis singles being played on the radio and heard on jukeboxes in restaurants and truck stops across the country.

"That Tennessee Beat" was the title song to a 1966 low-budget country-western film shot in Nashville that Merle played a small part in. Like his last two films with Johnny Cash, *That Tennessee Beat* had low production values and was destined to be drive-in fare. Its virtually nonexistent plot revolves around musical performances. Although the film is tedious, it was also oddly enduring. It showed at drive-in movie theaters for years and then found a home on late-night television, where it aired through the mid-1970s.

Now firmly entrenched in Nashville, Merle had his lawyers file a lawsuit against his publisher, Sylvester Cross, and his publishing company, American

Music. Merle had been a client since the beginning of his Capitol Records days in 1946; the songwriting and publishing royalties earned by his songs came through American and were issued to Merle by Cross. Ever since songwriting royalties had become Merle's main source of income, especially since "Sixteen Tons" became a big hit, the relationship between Merle, his lawyer, and Sylvester Cross at American Music had been strange and tense. For more than ten years, to get the money that Merle and his family needed to survive, his lawyer had had to beg for payment, or threaten legal action. Cross always paid, but it was sometimes months or even years late, and there was never any proper accounting to ensure that the payments were fair.

The lawsuit, Travis v. American Music, was ultimately successful. Details have been sealed, but several letters from Merle's new lawyer, Jerry Fields (who took over after Jerry Rolston became ill and retired) tell of the progress and ultimate outcome. Unfortunately for Merle, he had been the perfect entertainer to take advantage of: a Kentucky country boy with little interest in how Beverly Hills lawyers worked, as well as a drug and alcohol addict with an undiagnosed psychiatric problem. Michael Robinson observed: "He was very easygoing and so could be ripped off very easily. Had he not fallen onto the dark side of things, had he had some good business sense, he could've come out a whole lot greater than he did. That's the thing about it: he could've been hugely more successful with a little bit of good guidance and some smart thinking."[434] But even though Merle was victorious in his lawsuit, his legal fees were substantial, and he still owed considerable debts from the last few years when he had been committed at Camarillo and incarcerated at Saugus Honor Farm. Ultimately, in 1967, he received a payout from the lawsuit of just over $10,000 and also received the good news that Hill & Range Publishing (the successor to American Music) was in negotiations to license a parody version of "Sixteen Tons" to a tire company for a guaranteed payout to Merle of $10,000 a year. In the mid-1960s that was big money for a country-western entertainer. When Merle was touring and playing one-night stands, he was lucky to make $2,000 a month.

Merle's newfound sobriety, new surroundings, and influx of publishing money to cover the bills meant that for the first time in a long time, he had the latitude to just be creative. Bettie remembered:

> When [we] were in Nashville, he wrote a lot. Wrote a column for the paper and for a magazine. He didn't write romantic love songs, but little ditties and funny things.... It was when we lived in the apartment on Bosley Springs Road... he was so happy then, and all these things, these "buggyboos" that he had, would begin to fade away. I mean, when we

went back together and we moved from Nashville, you couldn't have found a happier guy, and straighter guy, and friendlier guy, and no fussing and no fighting and everything was fine. I mean, he had really got his act together. He was perfect. You couldn't ask for anybody any nicer, any more generous, more caring in the world. And that's the way that he was. Now that to me, is the real Merle Travis. These other things, these other people, these things that came out in him is like demons or something, and that's not really him, to me, and that's not what I saw when we first started going together, I saw this other [good] side of this man.[435]

Merle's sober creativity during this Nashville period resulted in prose writing, songwriting, cartoons, poems, and a renewed vigor for guitar playing. It was the most creative he had been since the late 1940s. And as Bettie mentions, he began writing a column for the *Nashville Tennessean* in January 1967. Merle noted in the paper: "So it looks like I'll be doin' a little piece for the *Nashville Tennessean*. I'm sure my column will be mediocre at first, but as time goes by it'll not be quite so good."[436] He also wrote autobiographical pieces (chapter 1 of this book came from a piece he wrote called "I Have a Sick Sister in Texas," originally released in a fan publication put out by his booking agent, Lucky Moeller), contributed cartoons to magazines like *Hoedown* and *Country Music Review*, and wrote letters to friends and family at the pace of a man much younger.

The detailed letters he sent Bettie while on the road also offer a window into Merle's guitar situation at the time. In 1966 he was touring with his original Gibson Super 400, his Guild Solomaster, and a custom electric guitar made for him around 1965 by Dick "R. C." Allen. Tragedy struck one night backstage in Phoenix at the beginning of the tour:

Bob drove me back to the Riverside Ballroom where I was to meet scores of fans and pickers, and answer all the usual questions.... I went into the dressing room, layed my guitar on the case which was on a table, and a funny thing happened on the way to the door to take a bow—!

An atom bomb exploded behind me. I glanced around, and alas, my guitar had fallen to the floor and received a nasty busted side and top. I'm sorry to say the old Gibson will be layed [sic] up for a while. I intend to send it back to Gibson, and have them make a new one of it. They will, you know. I used Dick Allen's guitar on the last set.... It don't quite cut the mustard.[437]

There was nothing about the guitar situation in the next letter, but Merle sent an update on the Gibson when he got back to Nashville:

I took the Gibson down to Shot Jackson who makes fine steel guitars, called Sho-Bud. They're really good instruments, and he knows his business.... The side of the Gibson was really messed up....

Well, ol' Shot, like a doctor, looked at the injured box and said, "Good God! We'll have to take the whole back and top off and put a re-enforcement [*sic*] in there. Then we'll put in a piece of wood and sand it down to where you can't tell it." I said, "Shot, just put the pickups in it." He answered, "Then we'll take the finish off the whole thing and put 'er in the spray shop and give it a new finish." I asked him, "Shot, how about just putting the pickups in it." Then he said, "We'll polish the keys and true up the frets. There's a screw missing out of the neck-rod guard... we'll put that in, then we'll oil up the vibrato." I had an idea, so I asked him a favor. I said, "Shot, just put the pick-ups in." "Then we'll put on a new set of my special made strings, at no charge, and adjust the bridge. With a set of Sho-Bud pickups where these have been taken out, it will be helped. Just like a new gittar [*sic*]." "Just put the old pick-ups in, Shot," I replied.

"Then when you play it through one of our great Sho-Bud amplifiers, it'll be the thrill of a lifetime," he said. "JUST PUT THE PICKUPS IN, SHOT!" I pleaded. He said, "That'll take about two weeks." "Two weeks just to change the old original pickups from the Guild over to the Gibson?" I shouted. "Oh no, to repair the guitar like it should be done." Sez he.

Then he had an idea. He said, "Why don't we just put the old pick-ups back in it, and glue the sides together. I can do that in a few minutes. Of course it'll take the glue twelve hours to dry, but it'll work fine then." I warmly embraced him and gave him an affectionate kiss and explained to him that he was a dear and a genius. I wondered how he ever came to think of that.[438]

A follow-up letter about the guitar was penned the following day:

Dearest Bettie:

Well, I went up town to pick up my guitar tonight. I called this morning but Shot wanted to know when I had to have it. I told him I wanted to leave for Cleveland about dark. He said, "Let me keep it 'till seven o'clock.... I want to work on it as long as I can."

So at exactly seven me and Grandpa went in. He was still working on it. I think he'd still be working on it if we'd have stayed. He fixed the sides, the top, polished it, and put new strings on it. It's in very good shape. But not to suit him. I think he wants to engrave a picture of Doye O'Dell on it.

He didn't charge a cent. It's a good thing, of course. I guess you're right. That ol' box is hard to beat. What little I can pick, I can do it best on that ol' gourd.[439]

A few days later, Merle found himself driving past Kalamazoo, Michigan, where the Gibson Guitar factory was located:

I saw a sign that said, KALAMAZOO, NEXT EXIT. My brain started spinning. I pulled over and looked at my map. Kalamazoo, Michigan was forty-one miles north of my route. That's the town where the Gibson guitar factory is. Why not run up there. You don't have to be in Rochester, Minnesota until Thursday, thinks I, so I turned north....

I have no idea what they'll say when I try to crash the Gibson place.... They'd faint if they saw the old box they built back in the early fifties for me. It's been patched over the patches, and glued up over the glued up places. It's been re-finished over the refinished job where they originally finished it, but it's still in good shape. I wish they'd pull a Fender and give me a case.[440]

Two days later, Merle wrote Bettie to tell about his visit to the Gibson factory:

Well, here's the Gibson visit story.... I went in and told the girl at the switchboard that my name was so and so, that I was from California and made records and had been using a Gibson guitar for a hundred years, and that I'd sure like to talk to somebody that might show me around through the place, if I could. "I'm sorry sir, but we've discontinued our tours," she told me.

I started telling her I wasn't necessarily a tourist, but... but... well, I was a... er... you know, a... one of these.... Then out of a door came a business looking sort of a cuss, and said, "Merle Travis, what in the world are you doing here?" He introduced himself as Merrill McCovahie [McConochie], the superintendant [sic] of the joint, and took me to meet the general manager....

What a joint. Ol' Orville started out building things in a little hole in the wall place. Finally they added more and then more, and later even more. Now they've bought a street from the city, and made the factory two blocks long, and two stories high. They order rosewood which is raised in India from Germany. Spruce which is raised in Canada from Maine. Mahogany which is raised in South America from Japan. They get their maple from Vermont.... I don't see why they don't do like Fender and build their boxes out of orange crates and sweet-gum [one of many digs at Fender guitars written by Merle in these letters].

We went by people who was side-shaping, top-matchin' neck-en-forcin' hole-drillin' finger-boardin' dove-tailin' frettin' inlayin' bindin' sprayin' polishin' testin' and what have you. Then we got to the end where the finished product came out. I told ol' Mac they sure were pretty, and that I'd sure like to get a case for mine.

Then we went upstairs. That's where the craftsmen work. The ol' boys that have been with the company a long time and do the particular work.... They also make a solid body one which I guess I'm indirectly responsible for... which they knew. They turn out about 400 finished instruments a day and could sell a thousand a day if they could make 'em.... But the cheaper models are made on an assembly line, where the Birdland [sic], L-5 and Super-400 are whittled out upstairs. It looked so fascinating seeing how delicately the ol' gray-haired fellers was carving and clamping and glueing. I said I'd sure like to have a case for my guitar....

I went with Mac down to his office and we talked a while.... He shook hands and said it was nice of me to go out of my way to come by and see the Gibson factory. He hoped I would come back again. Then he rang a buzzer. A voice said, "Yes?" He said, "Give Mr. Travis a new case for his Super 400." A man brought it in and I left. WHEE! I GOT A NEW BLACK CASE WITH A BRIGHT YELLOW FUZZY INSIDE.[441]

While on tour in California in 1966, Merle returned to the Ash Grove club in Los Angeles. The Ash Grove gig proved a reliable Los Angeles venue for quite a few years in the 1960s. David Lindley, who went on to fame with the psychedelic band Kaleidoscope and a sideman career behind Jackson Browne, Warren Zevon, Curtis Mayfield and Dolly Parton, was a twenty-one-year-old aspiring folkie when he opened for Merle at the Ash Grove a year earlier, in 1965. In Lindley's words:

Are you kidding? Yeah, it scared the shit out of me. Ed Pearl [owner of the Ash Grove] was a real stickler, and he was a guitar player. So him having Merle Travis at the Ash Grove was a huge thing. It was really big, even though he had Mississippi John Hurt and Howlin' Wolf and Muddy Waters and Doc Watson and Lightnin' Hopkins, all of those guys. We went to the Ash Grove as kind of going to church. So what I was doing playing that gig was playing in church. You'd have Travis picking, and the two-finger thing, and we all studied that stuff. We went to the Ash Grove to be able to sit in the front row, and we'd come early to watch those guys play, and that's where I learned how to steal [ideas and guitar licks].[442]

Two old friends were in the audience that night: guitar builders Paul Bigsby and Dick "R. C." Allen. It would be the last time that Merle saw Bigsby, who died two years later. Allen would remain in contact with Merle over the next decade and a half, often working on Merle's guitars when he needed work done.

Allen gave Merle a second custom-built R. C. Allen guitar in 1967 on a visit to Nashville. The newer one was fancier and more elaborately carved. To repay Allen for giving him the guitar, Merle wrote a letter of recommendation and praise, which Allen used for years to promote his instruments:

October 6, 1967
Dear Dick:
I have traveled just about everywhere with my two R. C. Allen Custom Built guitars. All I hear is compliments, which is understandable.
I have never played, or seen a finer instrument. You have combined all the good things in one on your guitars.
The action is unbeatable, the sound is exactly to my liking and the workmanship is that of a craftsman second to none.
The only thing that falls short is my ability to play. I couldn't possibly own a more beautiful and superb guitar.
Your friend,
Merle Travis
Nashville, Tennessee[443]

Just a few years after receiving it, Merle donated the second R. C. Allen guitar to the Country Music Wax Museum, a Nashville-based tourist trap that opened in 1970. Merle was represented in wax form, with his R. C. Allen guitar at his knee. The museum has long been out of business, and the guitar's whereabouts are unknown at this time, along with the Nudie suit and other artifacts Merle donated.

Beginning in 1967, Capitol resumed releasing Travis guitar instrumentals. Michael Robinson remembers Merle at home recording demos:

I used to see him sitting downstairs in the house out on the lake in Hendersonville. I would come down the steps and he would be sitting there looking at me and counting, and I'd just go, "Whoa," and turn around and walk out the door out through the garage and leave that guy alone right then. I'd see him counting, and with his guitar, and then he'd hit one note. So he laid down the first tracks, I believe that's what he was doing right then. But he was going in slow motion. Because when you hear that thing [brought up to normal speed], there's just so much going on, and you go, "Where are all these fingers coming from?"[444]

Nashville producer Kelso Herston took over Merle's recording efforts in January 1967, with the focus on getting a new album of guitar instrumentals on the market. Over the course of four sessions, Merle recorded a batch of new guitar instrumentals that were collected on an album called *Strictly Guitar*. Besides the rerelease of 1940s transcriptions that Capitol released as *Walkin' the Strings* and the duet album with Joe Maphis, *Strictly Guitar* was the first album of guitar instrumentals that Merle had tackled since the mid-1950s. Popular numbers "Cannonball Rag," "I'll See You in My Dreams," "Dance of the Goldenrod," and "Guitar Rag," all recorded for Capitol in the 1950s, were rerecorded. The rest of the album was old standards from the Tin Pan Alley era such as "Way Down Yonder in New Orleans," "Lazy River," "Heart of My Heart," and "Ma, He's Making Eyes at Me" as well as an old Floyd Tillman number, "Gotta Have My Baby Back." "Fisher's Hornpipe," a popular fiddle tune from the eighteenth century, was given a novel treatment with tape-manipulated sped-up guitars using the same technique that Merle had pioneered with "Merle's Boogie Woogie" back in 1947.

Strictly Guitar had limited commercial appeal in the late 1960s. Still, Merle had his die-hard fans, and a certain number of guitar enthusiasts would always buy a Merle Travis instrumental guitar record no matter what. Merle's own opinion of *Strictly Guitar* was quite harsh, however: "I never really got to do the stuff that I wanted to do with the guitar on Capitol. I did one album in Nashville called *Strictly Guitar* that I was very disappointed in. That album's terrible. [For another album], a very brilliant engineer in Hollywood twisted the knobs, and that's called *The Merle Travis Guitar*. That one I'm not too ashamed of. The rest of the stuff sort of embarrasses me. Most people in this business have copies of everything they've ever recorded. I don't have any of mine."[445]

Thom Bresh also remembered Travis's distaste for the guitar sound on *Strictly Guitar*. According to him, Merle would say:

That's what I didn't like about Nashville when I did that guitar album there that they have. I had to run through an amplifier. [They told me] "You can't put that big guitar into the board." And I said, "I did in California on that great album I made out there. Why can't I do it here?" "Oh no, we got that. You just play through that amp. We've got our mics. We know how to do it. We're Nashville." I've never cared for the sound of that album. Well, in the Nashville world, you don't do it that way. In California, Hollywood, you plug it in, those boys turn that, and it's the most beautiful sound. You pick that big echo chamber at Capitol. It makes you pick. You hear what's coming, and you finesse all those things." *Strictly Guitar* sounded little-bitty compared to like they did in Hollywood there.[446]

Capitol's first instrumental release for Merle, before *Strictly Guitar* was released, was a rerecording of "Wildwood Flower," released as a single in 1967. The song (originally performed by Mother Maybelle Carter with the Carter Family in 1928) had been a hit for Hank Thompson, with Merle playing lead guitar, in the mid-1950s. Its perennial appeal with country fans and folkies alike made it a natural choice. Merle's new version was carefully arranged and tightly played. It was snappy, not sloppy. Sadly, the revamp did nothing commercially. In an era of social upheaval and country songs with political messages, Merle's rerecording of the 1920s Carter Family standard was out of place.

In early 1967, Merle and Bettie traveled to the Far East as part of a package tour, playing USO concerts and performing for armed service members. Merle had been a favorite of the AFRS (Armed Forces Recording Service) since the 1940s, recording many live transcription discs that were sent overseas to entertain the troops. This tour, however, was the first time he had personally traveled to a foreign country to play for US troops. It was also around this time that Merle started featuring Bettie as a guest singer. Bettie wasn't a great singer, but she did add feminine flair to Merle's act. The couple was often billed as "Merle Travis and Bettie Lou." Merle recalled in a 1974 interview with Gary Williams: "Bettie was never a professional or anything, but she'd sing around the house, and I said 'that'd go on stage.' She has a lot of gab and charm about her, and she's got a nice smile, and people seem to like her for that."[447] The Far East tour was a long one, beginning in Hawaii in January, then on to Japan, Okinawa, the Philippines, Thailand, Vietnam, and China before returning to Hawaii at the end of April. Merle wrote about it in his weekly column for the *Nashville Tennessean*, detailing humorous experiences and anecdotes about soldiers he met.

Merle was one of several Nashville country stars—the others included Johnny Bond and Hank Thompson—who got together in June 1967 to write the CMA Code of Ethics, a group of suggestions for other country performers to follow. It almost reads like a checklist of rules that the burgeoning "outlaw country" movement was determined to destroy. One can only imagine Willie Nelson or Waylon Jennings looking at such edicts as "At those engagements which are before the public, I shall appear well-groomed, and in the proper costume," or "At no time shall I appear under the obvious influence of drugs, prescribed medication excluded" and laughing maniacally at the now-antiquated prose (spoiler: the CMA Code of Ethics didn't catch on, and the rough-and-rowdy outlaw country musicians would soon overtake the Nashville establishment).

Merle was asked to play the prestigious Newport Folk Festival—the biggest and most popular folk festival in the Northeast—in the summer of 1967. This was the same festival where, two years earlier, Bob Dylan had turned the folk music scene on its head when he arrived and performed his set with electric instruments. Merle, who had been playing electric guitar since 1940, likely wondered what the fuss was about. On Saturday, July 15, Merle participated in the "Country Music and Blues" concert. The lineup was a particularly stellar mixture of legendary musicians. Besides Merle, there were Grandpa Jones, Mother Maybelle Carter, Dave Dudley, Bill Monroe and the Bluegrass Boys, the Chambers Brothers, Sippie Wallace, Muddy Waters, Otis Spann, J. B. Smith, and Robert Pete Williams. Earlier the same day, Merle participated in a guitar workshop, which included a mind-boggling lineup of legends: Mother Maybelle Carter, Muddy Waters, and Sister Rosetta Tharpe. Although Merle took a few candid photos walking around the festival, and newspapers ran a photo of him performing his evening set, there are no known photos or audio from the guitar workshop.

In 1968, Merle was commissioned by Kentucky's governor, Bert Combs, as an official "Kentucky Colonel."

Two "greatest hits" compilation albums were released during this time period. One, *The Best of Merle Travis*, came out on Capitol in 1967 and contained Merle's original recordings of his most popular songs from the 1940s and 1950s, including "Sixteen Tons," "John Henry," "Dark as a Dungeon," and "Nine Pound Hammer," among others. The cover was a striking color photograph of a slim-looking Merle, post-stomach hemorrhage, holding his Guild Solomaster. The second came out on Hilltop Records, a budget label, who licensed the twenty-year-old masters from Capitol Records. Titled *Merle Travis—Our Man from Kentucky*, it also contained original Capitol recordings from the 1940s and 1950s, with several of the same tracks duplicated from Capitol's *The Best of Merle Travis*.

In early 1968, Merle recorded "Country Joe," a novelty song in the "Little" Jimmy Dickens vein. It's a humorous song about a wealthy country-western singing star who wants people to know he's still "common" even though he lives in "a hundred-thousand-dollar home." The single was professionally produced, at least in terms of trying to make a single by a fifty-year-old singer whose personal style had more in common with 1920s Tin Pan Alley and 1940s Western swing than with the pop-tinged country music of the late 1960s. "Country Joe" had all the earworms of a 1968 hit country single—a tight band, background singers, novelty breaks (at one point, the band and background singers break into two measures of "Dang Me" by Roger Miller), and tambourines hitting accents on the choruses. What the song lacked was any connection with the artist known as Merle Travis. It was essentially a "Little" Jimmy Dickens soundalike novelty record. (For those unfamiliar with Dickens, he had a string of successful novelty songs in the 1960s like "May the Bird of Paradise Fly Up Your Nose" and "Who Licked the Red Off Your Candy." Dickens and Travis were friends, at least at this time, and booked by the same booking agency.) "Country Joe" predictably sank without a trace upon release. It couldn't have been more out of touch.

With his finances improved from the settlement of the publishing royalties lawsuit against American Music, Merle began to pay back some of his debts, including to Gene Autry, who had been one of his chief benefactors during the rough times of the early 1960s. Autry sent back a letter that showed how much he valued Merle:

> Dear Merle and Bettie:
> I thank you so much for the checks; but that is not the most important thing. I think I am happiest to know that you are feeling well again and have yourself straightened out. I know very well the problems you have had in the past, and I, too, have had similar problems, so can sympathize with you all the way.
> I am happy that you are doing so well in Nashville, and if I should get back there you can rest assured I will call you two....
> Most sincerely,
> Gene Autry[448]

Merle and Bettie purchased a ranch-style home in 1968 at 576 Indian Lake Road in Hendersonville, outside of Nashville, and moved out of their apartment on Bosley Springs Road. Bettie rcalled: "When we were in Nashville, there was an ad in the paper for a house on Old Hickory Lake, and that afternoon we had bought a house." Those who remember the Hendersonville house describe it as a beautiful lake house that Merle and Bettie were very proud of. And given the setting, it wasn't long before Merle became interested in boats. According to Bettie: "We first had a little tin boat that I called Merle's 'Little Tin Yacht.' Somebody stole it and one afternoon he came in to me and told me, 'I got something I want you to see.'... so we went down there and he had this white... convertible [car] with leather insides, you know, and this was a white boat with leather inside, red, you know, just the same [as the automobile]. And when we were in town, we were up by eight o'clock and out that door and on the lake, and it was great, and we just stayed on the lake all day long."[449]

Merle's good friends Joe and Rose Lee Maphis moved to Nashville with their family in 1968. The Maphises had lived in Bakersfield since *Town Hall Party* ended, but reasoned that if Merle was doing well in Nashville, along with Grandpa and Ramona Jones and several other friends from the old days, they would also be wise to move to Music City. Merle and Joe spent a lot of time together when they were both home in Nashville. At the lake house, Merle and Bettie had a guest book that visitors would sign, and it shows that they were visited by Joe and Rose Lee Maphis, Grandpa and Ramona Jones, Johnny Bond, Jack and Margaret Rogers, Cecil Null, Lightnin' Chance and his family, Connie Smith, "Texas" Bill Strength, Hank Cochran and Jeannie Seely, Gary and Jean Lambert, Sunny and Ned Fairchild—a who's who of late-1960s country music luminaries. The guest book also documents a visit from a California family who had recently relocated to Tennessee—the Mandrells. Barbara Mandrell was a young unknown when she stayed with Merle and Bettie in the summer of 1968. She told this author:

> I was a newlywed, and the reason I came to Nashville was my husband, Ken, was a Navy pilot, and he was sent overseas on a carrier. My father brought me on one of his trips on business, traveling to Nashville. He took us to the *Opry*, and I saw the *Opry* for the first time. And that's where I decided I wanted to get back in the business, and then it was right after that, anyway, that Merle offered for me to stay with them because I had no money to do it any other way. They had a beautiful home. They so graciously and generously offered for me to be able to stay at their house when I first came here and had nothing. [It was a] beautiful home, and big, huge backyard, and there's the lake. This house was just so gorgeous.
>
> And then there was this big, large moose head. And while staying there, I had a cat. My kitty cat. For some reason, I had to go downstairs to do something and while I was down there, I heard this little kind of noise, and I looked over to the side and up on the back of the neck of this moose on Merle's wall was my kitty cat. And she was just scraping those nails, you know how they'll do, just scratching and scratching, as they say, making biscuits. And I saw hair falling to the floor. So I got her down from there, and I picked up all the hair with my hands and got a chair and stood up on it and tried to replace it, laying that hair on the back of that moose's neck and never said a word. I'm such a brave person.
>
> I hadn't been here very long at all when Merle picked up the phone and called his friend Ralph Emery. Merle said he needed to have me on his show; at that time, Ralph's show was on in Nashville at something like four o'clock on weekdays. And so that was the first thing I got to do

when I came to Nashville, and my point is there are no words for me to describe how huge it was.

There was a club called the Black Poodle that had country music, and he was working there, and he had me come and get up on stage and sing a song. Anyway, got me a booking for a week there at the Black Poodle and I got that job. I played the steel guitar, and the sax, and the banjo, and I sang, and whatever. I was doing my thing and I had four different record label offers, but the one with Billy Sherrill at Columbia Records—there was no question that that was a dream come true.

I'm guessing [the houseguest arrangement was] about three months. That's what got me that job there, it was just the kindness and the loving-ness of so many. Merle was such a brilliant man. I mean brilliant. I mean for instance, I'm sitting with him in his den watching TV. He had a nice, large console thing, and don't forget this was like 1968. And we're watch-ing TV and out of the blue, it goes to a commercial or something, he says, "You know, do you ever kind of look at everything that's around you in the house and think of it as antiques? Like, what it's gonna become, or what's gonna replace it in many, many years from now?" And I said, "Well, no. What do you mean? Give me an example." He says, "Well, see that TV there?" He says, "Someday a television's gonna be as big as a wall, and it's gonna be like a screen like at the movies or something." Things like that he'd pick out of the air.

He was also a professional, brilliant cartoonist. And he knew so many facts and smart comments. But he was the most modest person ever. You couldn't give him a compliment—just "Oh, no." I said to him, "You know, you absolutely are a genius. Everything I think about you, you're just a genius." And he kind of laughed and he said, "Okay," he says, "you know you got a circle here, and right here is genius." And he said, "And then you go all the way around and right next to 'genius' is 'idiot.'" Isn't that just wonderful?[450]

Mandrell, of course, went on to country music superstardom with a string of hit records in the 1970s and 1980s. She also hosted a popular network television show in the early 1980s, *Barbara Mandrell and the Mandrell Sisters*, and invited Merle to appear as a guest.

These years in Nashville were a whirlwind of activity. Merle and Bettie stayed on the road much of the time. It would take another entire book to detail all of the varied gigs that "Lucky" Moeller booked for Merle—folk festivals, American Legion halls, country music nightclubs, outdoor country music parks, and as support act on big country music arena shows. Merle was equally at home playing at the Milton High School auditorium in Pensacola, Ike's Blue Room in Indianapolis, or the Ash Grove in Los Angeles. When he was home in Nashville, he worked clubs in Printer's Alley (an area in the lower Broadway part of downtown Nashville, famous for sleazy burlesque clubs and small live music clubs), like the Black Poodle—late-night lounge gigs where he could stretch out and jam or feature sit-in guests like Mandrell. He also appeared on the nationally syndicated *Porter Wagoner Show* in 1968 and several other local country music television shows, like the *National Barn Dance* on WGN in Chicago.

Merle's old roaring buddy Johnny Cash also relocated to Nashville and bought a large house near Merle on Old Hickory Lake in Hendersonville. Cash's popularity had soared thanks to a hugely successful live album recorded at Folsom Prison and released in 1968. The following year, he set his sights on a network television show. *The Johnny Cash Show* debuted in June 1969 and ran for two years on ABC-TV. It was taped on the Ryman Auditorium stage and had a staggering array of A-list guests that included Bob Dylan, Merle Haggard, the Monkees, Glen Campbell, and Ray Charles. It was so popular that it revived careers, as in the case of Doug Kershaw, and gave relative unknowns, such as Buffy Sainte-Marie and José Feliciano, mass exposure to country music audiences for the first time.

Cash brought in his closest circle of friends to help with the production. Carl Perkins, the Statler Brothers, and the late-1960s version of the Carter Family were regular guests. Of course, given Cash's love and respect for Merle, it wasn't long before he found a job for him. The "Ride This Train" segment on *The Johnny Cash Show* was introduced using the format Cash had established on his *Ride This Train* album ten years earlier. It would prove to be one of the most popular segments on the show: using film footage combined with live performance, Cash would narrate a story followed by a song based on an event or character, or a look back at the carefree, quaint life of the old days. Merle was brought in to write the narrations. It would prove to be one of his most lucrative gigs of his career as well as an excellent creative outlet and his steadiest writing job. He recalled in 1974: "Yeah, 'Ride This Train' segment is what I wrote. Ride this train, and it wasn't about trains, it was a way of getting into something, like 'Ride this train into St. Joseph, Missouri, where the Pony Express started,' and you'd go into the Pony Express.... It took a lot of research to do it. But I enjoyed it."[451] It was perfect for someone like Merle, who loved researching history and excelled at writing songs on a deadline. Thom Bresh told this author:

Merle said, "I make things up, 'cause I just tell stories." He said, "That's why I always felt like I was robbing *The Johnny Cash Show* when I did all the train segments. We'd go into a production meeting, and they'd say, 'We need four songs and setups for the B&O Railroad. We want to do this.'" "Alright." He said, "They paid me a lot of money to do that, and I always felt like I was cheating 'em. I'd just go right down to the library, and go in their index and look up the B&O Railroad, and it would tell me where to go and oh, there's five books, I'll take all five of these over here to the table with my yellow pad and go through the contents. Geronimo stops B&O Railroad, well, that'll be good."

He said, "I'd read that little chapter, you can read it and summarize it and make up a song. I'll just make up a verse and I had to keep the melodies real simple so Johnny could sing 'em. But they had his words on cue cards, and I'd write that thing out after I'd read a story. Five, six, seven minutes later, there it is. I only wrote a verse and a chorus, that's it."

He continued, "And then I'd do a setup and they already told me why Geronimo didn't wanna go, and I'd word it so J. R. [Johnny Cash] could just roll off his tongue; that's the way he talks, you know."

He said, "Two, three hours, I'm outta there. I got my week's work done and they paid me all that money. I almost told Johnny, 'They're paying me an awful lot of money for doing nothing.' But Johnny would always just brag on me how I could just go in there, he's a great song-writer himself, but he just thought I was something."[452]

In addition to writing the segments and the accompanying songs for Cash to sing, Merle would also appear on the Cash show as a performer. It was the biggest televised audience he had ever performed for. Some segments were particularly interesting, including a "guitar jam" featuring Merle, Carl Perkins, and Latin singer-guitarist José Feliciano. Merle was featured on the very last episode of *The Johnny Cash Show*, playing "Cannonball Rag," with Cash giving him the lofty introduction as "The greatest of them all—Merle Travis."[453]

Merle repaid the favor when he was extensively quoted in the introduction to Christopher Wren's 1971 book about Cash, *Winners Got Scars Too*:

Johnny Cash is like a virus. You can't help but pay attention to him. He's like the old lady's operation. Out of sight, he's still unforgettable. At the beginning, he had that quality. He's become polished, but even in his early records, things seemed to happen. It's like ink coming out of a homemade basket, it's so obvious this man is different. He's a walking James Whitcomb Riley poem. The more you talk to him, the more you re-read. Nothing goes by him. Nothing gets near him. Nothing is not of interest to Johnny Cash....

John is not a trained singer. He doesn't have a beautiful vibrato. When you hear Johnny Cash sing a song, it sounds like he's saying, "I'm glad I'm singing this song and I want you to listen." It comes out as clear as if he's standing on the courthouse steps, pounding a hammer.[454]

A year after Barbara Mandrell had stayed at their lake house, Merle and Bettie had another houseguest—Merle's youngest daughter, Cindy. Merle had barely seen his daughters Merlene and Cindy over the last ten years, and since he had moved to Nashville, they were completely out of touch. Cindy Travis told this author in a conversation, with interjections from her sister Merlene:

I was dating J Riddle [a famous professional surfer] while he was living in Santa Monica. He and I moved in together when I was probably eighteen. My mom and stepdad were upset about this and disowned me for living in sin. And J's mom, Alice, she kind of took me under her wing.

Anyway, J was trying to teach himself to play the guitar, and I told Alice who my real dad was. She was aware of who he was, his guitar playing and songwriting. One day J and I went over to her house, and she said, "I have some good news for you. I talked to your father, and he wants to see you." Of course, I was thinking she was speaking about my stepdad, John Wesner. You know, he was considered my father.

She said, "Yeah, he's going to send a ticket for you to come out there." I replied, "Well it's just in Westlake Village, what do you mean, what kind of ticket, a plane ticket?" To which she answered, "No, he's living in Nashville." I said, "Merle?" She said, "Yeah, he wants to see you guys." I said, "My God, how did you get a hold of him?" That was before the internet. She just said, "I found him." She was ruthless.

Long story short, we get this ticket, and I said, "This is so weird. I have not seen Merle since—I can't remember when. I hardly know him. I mean, he's my father, and I respect him and appreciate his talents, but I don't know who he is." Anyway, we went there. Everybody was very nice. I just remember the first night because J and I couldn't sleep together in the same room because we weren't married. Which was hysterical. We were living together. J was somewhere in this house and I was in a room somewhere in this house.

We had dinner, black-eyed peas and corn bread, which Dad made. We're all sitting around and talking. I remember Dad was sitting there, kind of strumming the guitar, and I said, "Dad, play something on the guitar for us." I'd never heard him play guitar right in front of me. And he says, "Oh, I can't play that old thing. You can probably play that thing better than I can." I was thinking, "Well, we've come all this way; can't you just strum a few strums for us?"

Then we all went to bed but I couldn't sleep, so I thought, "Alright, he's going to finish the business. If he wanted to kill me, now he can kill all of us. He's in some room drinking himself into a tizzy; he's going to come in here with a gun and shoot me in the head. From what I knew when I was little, which is all that I knew, he'd tried to kill all of us, and mom had to flee. That's all I ever knew. Which is so sad.

[Merlene:] So sad, because I never felt that. I always felt so safe with him.

I thought, okay, I don't know where is the gun. I think I locked the door and I couldn't sleep. I'm like, "Why can't J be with me? I'm scared to death." I couldn't sleep, and I went, "This is going to be the end of me. He's going to take it out, his vengeance out, because Mom left him and here I am."

Anyway, he didn't. The next day, I think we went out on a boat. He said, "Well, let's go out," and he took pictures. We're doing the boat ride on the lake and that was fun, and then we came back, Dad went somewhere and we had dinner at home again. Then, the next day, I think he had to go to work. There were maybe four or five days—

[Merlene:] That's when he would have been working on the Johnny Cash show.

Yeah, possibly. I had no interest in it, really. Now, I would have asked, "Can I go with you?"[455]

After Cindy's visit, Merle reached out to Merlene, who was then living in Simi Valley, near Los Angeles. Merlene recalled their reconnection:

I had just had my daughter Chelene in August of 1970. And he called me at home. My mother answered the phone, and she said, "It's the phone, for you." And she said, "It's funny, he called you Merlene." [After Merle and Judy's divorce, Merlene had been known as Marlene.] So, I got on the phone, and he said, "Is this Merlene?" And I said yes. And he said, "Well, this here's Merle Travis, and I'm kin to you." And then that was always our joke after that, because every time he'd call me he'd go, "This here's Merle Travis, and I'm kin to you," and we'd laugh. But anyway, it was my first time hearing from him since I was a little over ten years old. And he said, "I heard you had a baby. And if you want to talk, I thought maybe we could talk and get to know each other again." And after that we just became really close.[456]

The year 1969 would prove pivotal for Merle. Now sober and settled into Nashville life, he was poised to continue doing positive things for his career. Unfortunately, nothing in Merle's life ever seemed stable for very long. In February he went back into the studio in Nashville, with Kelso Herston producing, to cut another single for Capitol. Thankfully they abandoned the uncomfortably commercial approach of his last single, "Country Joe," and let Merle simply be Merle Travis again. "The Super Highway" and "A World Full of Roses" were both well-executed efforts that sounded like classic Merle. "The Super Highway" was a socially conscious yet humorous song about city people driving past rural hillbillies on the highway and laughing at how they live. It was well written and well produced, and even hinted at the "common folk" lyrical tone of "Sixteen Tons," but lacked a catchy hook to make it click with country music audiences. The flip side, "A World Full of Roses," was a lighthearted song that recalled the best of Merle's Western swing–style records from the 1940s. Unfortunately, it also seemed woefully out of date for 1969. It wasn't a bad single, but it made no dent on the charts and sold poorly. It would be Merle's last single for Capitol.

Merle would make one last album for Capitol, recorded in March 1969. He and Johnny Bond teamed up for a tribute to the Delmore Brothers, released as *Merle Travis and Johnny Bond—Great Songs of the Delmore Brothers*. There was a precedent for it: Labelmate Merle Haggard had been quite successful with a tribute album to Jimmie Rodgers the year before, and was now working on a Bob Wills tribute. Capitol producer and A&R man Ken Nelson reckoned that Merle and Bond doing a tribute to the Delmores was a safe bet. It turned out to be a mixed bag. The two sound like they're having fun (a notion reinforced by the studio photos on the back cover) and harmonize well on the duets. Unfortunately, the production hampered the whole affair. Merle Haggard's Jimmie Rodgers tribute was a success because it felt loose and bluesy, reminding people why they liked Rodgers's music in the first place. Merle and Johnny Bond's Delmore Brothers tribute *should* have felt loose and bluesy, but instead it sounds like an overproduced, 1969-era Nashville country record. The front-cover photo didn't help, either: in an attempt to evoke the 1930s Depression era, Merle and Bond are standing on some railroad tracks, wearing work clothes and looking dirty and roughed up. Unfortunately, Merle also looks old, gaunt, and unhealthy. He later recalled: "When they took the picture for the album cover, they did some sort of trick photography that made us look scrawny. They took the photo by the railroad track near Saugus, California. They said, 'When you get up, don't shave.' I looked awful—Johnny looked pretty good."[457]

Today the record is quite difficult to find—an indication of its nonexistent sales when it was released.

Merle didn't know it at the time, but *Great Songs of the Delmore Brothers* would turn out to be his last record for Capitol. The association had begun with session work in 1944, and he had been signed to the label since 1946. Ken Nelson and other older employees who had been there through the 1940s hits and the million-selling "Sixteen Tons" phenomenon in 1955 respected Merle. And perhaps thanks to this respect, Merle did not get unceremoniously booted like so many of his aging peers did; in the mid-1960s, many of Capitol's early hit makers were let go as younger, hipper artists were signed to the roster. In several interviews thereafter, Merle would claim that Capitol had left the door open to him coming back and making more records, but that opportunity never materialized.

Recall that Merle's primary guitar, his Gibson Super 400, was the world's most expensive guitar when it was made in 1952. By the late 1960s, it was looking ragged. It had been damaged numerous times, including the major damage in 1966. The Super 400 remained Merle's favorite instrument, the one he always returned to. He sent it back to Gibson on occasion to have it repaired or refurbished. Usually the Gibson factory worker would do a fret job, make some adjustments, clean it up, and send it back. After the incident in 1966 it went back to Gibson several times between 1967 and 1969. Photos from this time show Merle with what appears to be a loaner Super 400 with only one volume knob (instead of the usual two volumes and two tones). It's unknown exactly what work Merle was having done on his original Super 400 at this time, but we do know that disaster struck sometime around March 1969 when he received it back from Gibson, having expected the usual simple repair and cleanup, and discovered that they had completely reworked it without asking him first. They'd replaced the original 1952 neck with a new neck. They'd replaced the top, and—to Merle's dismay—changed the position of the neck pickup to sit right where he normally picked. He was furious. He had a local shop put the pickup back where he was used to having it and install a plastic plate over what was now an extra hole in the top. It was nothing short of a tragedy, as Merle recounted in a letter to Gibson's Rendal (Ren) Wall in 1981:

Dear Mr. Wall:

This is one of the first photographs taken of my Gibson Super 400 just after I received it.... I considered it a work of art, absolute perfection....

Mr. Wilbur Marker suggested "I loan it" to the factory in Kalamazoo, in order that they might completely go over it and make it "exactly like new." The company was kind enough to build me a Super 400 to use while they restored my original.

I received the new one at the factory. In examining it, I found the wood it was built of to be something like a first-rate orange crate would be created from.

"Yes, it's just too bad," said Mr. Marker, "there just isn't any more beautiful curly maple." "That's too bad," I said, and thanked my lucky stars that my "Special" guitar had been built when there was fine, beautiful wood.

In time I was called from the Gibson factory that my original guitar was all finished. You will not believe what I found when I examined my "overhauled" instrument.

The neck was no longer a two piece, curly maple neck, but three strips of maple glued together. "Where's my two piece neck?" I inquired. "We don't have the wood to build two piece necks with anymore," said a soulful looking man. "But why did you remove it in the first place?" "To build a solid, non-warpable neck these days," the first sage explained, "we must use three pieces of wood." "But when I left it," I said, "it had a solid, non-warp, two-piece curly maple neck on it!"

The gentlemen saw they were talking to a country hick, teetering on the brink of insanity... so I gave up. (It was never explained)

Then came some questions about the color.... I had the guitar slightly gaudy, but beautifully finished. Around the edges was solid black, fading into a deep red, then into a bright yellow in the center. Gone were my sunburst that drew compliments by the dozens, and covering the body was a slightly bilious brindle of some tasteless hue.... That, too, was unexplainable....

In my little style of playing, I use a thumbpick and fingers. I do my picking between the two pickups you see in this picture. Behold, I found a pickup exactly in the middle of where the two pickups should be. I sweated a while, then asked, "how come?" "I'm no guitar picker, Mister," said a man standing by. "I just install them pickups." "Well, you installed this one in a helluva place," I said, and headed for Nashville where I had Shot Jackson to move it back where it belonged. He camaflodged [*sic*] the hole in the middle with a piece of black plastic, which you'll see in this photograph.

Gone, too, were my cosmetic arm rest and the pickguard to match. That was explained in this way. "We haven't had any of that sort of material for years." Surely they had my pickguard and armrest around someplace, unless somebody at the factory had a strange choice of desserts.[458]

Merle would never forgive Gibson for what they had done to his guitar, but the company did eventually make him two other custom Gibson Super 400s to his specifications. The most expensive guitar ever made, Merle's original 1952 Gibson Super 400, was further altered several times before he donated it to the Country Music Hall of Fame in 1981. The guitar on display there today is barely the original; it may only have the back and sides of the original 1952 body, along with the inlaid overlay on the headstock. The original neck, top, electronics, and accessories have all been changed, and the parts on the guitar in the Hall of Fame Museum are 1970s replacements.

In 1970, Merle was voted into the Songwriters Hall of Fame, the first of several halls of fame he would be inducted into.

The first half of 1970 continued with Merle and Bettie traveling all over the country playing one-nighters. In July, Merle was booked for a television show taping in remote Eckley, Pennsylvania. The program was a PBS network series called *Fanfare* and the episode was titled "American Odyssey: Dark as a Dungeon." The lineup featured Merle, B.B. King, Oscar Brand, Billy "Edd" Wheeler, Tom Paxton, and Jean Ritchie. The setting was the location where the film *The Molly Maguires* had been shot the year before; the musical performances were filmed on sets built to resemble a coal company's "company store." Against this folksy setting, Merle performed "Sixteen Tons," "Dark as a Dungeon," and "Miner's Strawberries" from his *Songs of the Coal Mines* album. Several who were there remember that his guitar broke one or possibly several strings, and he remarked that he didn't have any replacement strings, so B.B. King loaned him his acoustic guitar to finish the taping. "American Odyssey: Dark as a Dungeon" was a big deal at the time, airing nationally on all public stations a year later (and rebroadcast several times throughout the 1970s). Sadly, it is unavailable today—one of a handful of things not easily found on YouTube. A few photos survive that show the meeting of Merle and B.B. King, two giants of the guitar.

On the way home from Eckley, another tragic event happened in Merle's life. According to Bettie:

> They did this thing for PBS or something on the... *Molly Maguires* set. They were there for two or three days and he did an excellent job. We were supposed to go to Toronto to perform a folk festival.... When we got through playing and were going to go over and have lunch before we started... we were driving in the car and he decided that he wanted to have a beer for lunch. And I said, "Oh honey, don't do that, because you know that when you have a beer that it's going to start again, and it's been so nice." And, well, [he said] "I guess I can have a beer if I want

to, now I've gone and done my job." I mean... this same old argument started, you know.

And so he had his beer and then we were driving down the freeway and of course I was upset about the beer and he was upset because I didn't want him to drink it.... I was looking out the window, and he was driving and he said, "Something... something's wrong," and he started pulling and I said, well, get off the freeway, and he didn't know what had happened.... It happened "like that" and that was the beginning of whatever this thing was that he had for the rest of his life. It was a pulling thing through his chest and arms. But when he played the guitar, he didn't pull. He sat and played the guitar most of the time. After that his face became more drawn and he developed lines. No medication would stop it.[459]

Some neurological disturbance had struck, causing a spastic pulling of muscles in Merle's body and face. Michael Robinson recalls:

He called it the Saint Vitus dance, where he would make all these goofy faces and he'd have all this muscle pulling going on. He would make all these very, very strange faces. He couldn't control his nervous system at all. This happened when I was in Vietnam, while they were on tour. But he was never diagnosed. They couldn't find anything wrong, but he said, "I got popping going on inside of my head."

He hurt himself, and he paid a very heavy price for that. After he'd had his stroke, the word that I received was that the doctors don't see anything. Then some old lady from the hills of Kentucky, she sees him for the first time in his life and she says, "Oh, he's had a stroke." That being the type of stroke where you have one side of your face is dead. He was the exact opposite: both sides just did all these weird things and the whole body. Muscle cramps all the time, muscle pulling. From that moment until the end of his life.

The funny thing about it was that he would be having these muscle pulls, but then when he would get on stage and start singing, it went away. And as soon as he stopped singing, it came back. It was a very strange thing.[460]

Whether it was the one beer or the cumulative effect of years of alcohol and pill abuse that caused the neurological damage is impossible to know. But at this point Merle began drinking heavily again. Like most alcoholics, he would clean up for a little while then fall off the wagon again. Both Merle and Johnny Cash would experience similar muscle pulling in their later years, and sometimes referred to their condition as Huntington's chorea, a disease often colloquially called Saint Vitus dance due to the jerky body movements it causes. But the condition is generally inherited. Given the thousands of pills that both men consumed during their roaring years in Los Angeles, it seems a safer assumption that their muscle problems were caused by years of pill abuse.

Larry Collins of the Collins Kids ran into Merle in Nashville in 1970 when Collins was briefly signed to Monument Records:

> I was having breakfast with some of the guys from Monument Records. I had done a deal with Monument. Merle was sitting just a table away from me. He kept looking at me, but he was shaking so bad that he couldn't figure out if it was me or not. Of course, I'd aged, and so had he. He'd been trying to dry out and be the Merle we know and love. So I got up and I went by and I put my hand on his shoulder, and I said, "It's me." He said, "Oh, Larry. I knew it, I knew it."[461]

Merle still kept working. He returned to Kentucky, this time to Madisonville, in Hopkins County, in October 1970 for yet another "Merle Travis Day" celebration. This time the governor of Kentucky made "Merle Travis Day" an official proclamation. He was nominated for the first time that year for a Country Music Association Award. He worked as a session man in late 1970 for an album by Ray Sanders on United Artists called *Judy*. Merle's playing is all over the album, and indeed is spot-on despite the muscle pulling. Throughout 1971 Merle continued to write for and perform on *The Johnny Cash Show*, although it would soon be cancelled. The end of its production was coincident with a broader "rural purge" on the television networks that killed many popular shows that appealed to rural audiences; by the end of 1971, *The Beverly Hillbillies*, *Green Acres*, *Petticoat Junction*, *Mayberry R.F.D.*, and *The Johnny Cash Show* were off the air, even though most of them had high ratings and dedicated audiences.

Although Merle and Bettie loved their ranch home on Old Hickory Lake, when the Cash show paycheck ended, it was only a matter of time before they couldn't afford to live there anymore.

By the early 1970s, Merle's status as a country music legend was cemented. His command of language, endless amusing anecdotes, knowledge of history, and ability to entertain attracted those in the younger generation who looked to learn from their elders. Even so, Merle probably had no idea what he was getting into in August 1971, when he was asked to participate in a recording session with a bunch of young "hippie kids" known as the Nitty Gritty Dirt Band. Although the traditional country establishment was completely unaware of them, the band had a younger following, and they were about to make history with a triple album called *Will the Circle Be Unbroken*. Founding band member John McEuen told this author:

> The Dirt Band had opened for Merle for ten days at the Ash Grove in LA when he was first starting to get back out a little bit. He was a California guy, I believe, at the time, and he just wanted to play somewhere. Songwriter, player, had to go somewhere and play. So I got to know him a little bit there, and I learned a basic finger arpeggio pattern from him that I carry with me to this day, and try to get through "Cannonball Rag."
>
> [Nitty Gritty Dirt Band] album number five, which was *Uncle Charlie and His Dog Teddy*, had three different chart records on it that gave us the appearance of veracity, the appearance of, "they should listen to us," to the record company. So when my brother and I went to the record company and asked, "Can we get some money for this album? Our next project is going to be a two-track acoustic music, bluegrass-based album," Mike Stewart didn't think it would do much, but he gave us the $22,000, which seemed like a lot. It paid for the tape, the people, the music, the hotels, the airfares, pretty much everything. It was done live to two-track and mastered from that, on Scotch 256 [recording tape], I think.
>
> The way it started was I asked Earl Scruggs if he'd record with the Dirt Band for one week in Colorado, and the next week I asked Doc Watson, and they both said yes. And then my brother says, "I want to get Merle Travis." We both highly respected Merle Travis. My brother got Merle Travis—he said, "I'd be glad to be there. I want to meet Doc Watson." So that set that in motion. It was a big deal to us because although most of the people didn't know who Merle Travis was at that time and most of the people west of the Mississippi had never heard of Doc Watson, we thought they should. And we got the meeting of them on tape.[462]

Arthel Lane "Doc" Watson was a highly regarded blind bluegrass musician from North Carolina. He was five years younger than Merle, and both had come up playing a mixture of traditional acoustic country music and electric guitar in Western swing and honky-tonk bands. Watson idolized Merle and his guitar playing, and even named his son Eddy Merle Watson (born in 1949), after Eddy Arnold and Merle Travis. Watson was one of the first guitar stars of the 1960s folk revival. He played both thumb style and flat-picking style, and his fast flat-picking guitar adaptations of fiddle tunes made him a crowd-pleasing hit with folk audiences. Throughout the 1960s he became well known on the folk festival circuit, touring with his son Merle as his accompanist. Yet somehow, Merle and Watson had never met each other before the Nitty Gritty Dirt Band invited them to be guest stars on their new album.

Merle agreed to do the recording with the younger group, but he wanted to feel them out first at a rehearsal at his lake house in Nashville. McEuen remembers:

We got to his house for the rehearsal, and his wife said, "Oh, he's been looking forward to getting that old box out of the closet and tuning it up." She said that three or four times. Then he got out the dustiest guitar case and blew off the dirt or the dust, pulled this relic out of the case and tuned it up, and had to ask his wife, "Which one is out?" And then he tuned it up. "Yeah, I haven't been playing much', been writing on a TV show." And then he said, "I'd like to do 'Cannonball Rag.' How does that start? How does that dad-blamed thing start?" He said "dad-blamed" and "dad-gum."

And then he started to shout through it a bit, and ground it up. I mean, not playing it well. Then he looks it over for fifteen seconds, then he looked up at us and laughed. He played it well. Perfect. He was just drawing us in, being a rascal.

Merle came into the studio first up, first day, and he knocked out his songs in an hour and a half. We had four hours set aside to record his three songs, or three of the ones he was singing lead on and then his instrumentals, and he did them all in an hour and a half. So we sat around and listened to them over and over and over, and that was really cool. Then a day later, Doc Watson was working and he wanted to come by. We'd asked him to be a part of "Circle" ["Will the Circle Be Unbroken," the album's title track] and one of the other songs. And Doc and Merle met, and that's captured on tape, and it's on the album and the reissue as a very important part of it. It was my brother Bill [McEuen], the record producer and manager of the Dirt Band, who thought to record everything on a slow-running machine. It paid off to grab this little piece of country history, and a couple of other little pieces. And his putting that meeting on the album was a very important thing.

Merle Travis and I ran into each other two other times at festivals, and it was really, really neat to think that we had an effect on his career.[463]

Other legends who participated in the recordings included Roy Acuff, Mother Maybelle Carter, Earl Scruggs, Jimmy Martin, Bashful Brother Oswald Kirby, and Norman Blake. The album also featured Nashville session bassist Roy Junior Huskey and well-known bluegrass fiddler Vassar Clements.

Merle's participation in the *Will the Circle Be Unbroken* sessions included him singing and playing "Dark as a Dungeon," "Nine Pound Hammer" and "I Am a Pilgrim" as well as an instrumental showcase of "Cannonball Rag." He also played guitar on several of the group-participation songs, including the title track, "Will the Circle Be Unbroken," "Keep on the Sunny Side," and "I'm Thinking Tonight of My Blue Eyes," all with Mother Maybelle Carter singing lead with the assembled group of young and old musicians. As John McEuen mentions above, an unscripted studio conversation between Merle and Doc Watson that captured their first meeting was caught on tape and put on the album in between songs. Their studio chatter is not particularly profound—just some relaxed, easygoing banter about guitars and music. It is, like the whole album, an unpolished moment of realness in an era where record producers feverishly worked to burnish their product to remove any hint of human frailty or flaw. Its realness made the album believable and appealing.

When Merle left the studio, he had no idea that the record would sell. It was a paycheck, and a chance to meet Doc Watson and pick guitar behind Mother Maybelle Carter. Merle's universe would always revolve around Nudie suits, Cadillacs, flashy guitars, hunting and fishing, drinking, and pretty girls. The college kids with their beards and long hair and fascination with old-time acoustic music were simply not on his radar. It was then a complete surprise to everyone involved when the triple album *Will the Circle Be Unbroken* became a monster hit upon its release in 1972. It appealed to audiences across divides of age and education and region and politics. Much as Tennessee Ernie Ford's "Sixteen Tons" hit at exactly the right time for its message to reverberate, *Will the Circle Be Unbroken* landed in a post-Woodstock, end-of-Vietnam, middle-of-Watergate moment of broken US politics. It was simply a collection of great classic country songs, done well. People were hungry for something like it, and it kept selling, becoming a perennial "catalog" album that is still in print today. It is now certified platinum, and the Nitty Gritty Dirt Band has released a volume 2 (in 1989) and volume 3 (in 2002).

The exposure benefited Merle greatly. It got his name out to young kids who had never heard of Merle Travis, and it reminded the older fans that Merle was still alive, still playing and singing and sounding great. That cameo achieved what the last batch of Capitol singles had failed to accomplish a few years earlier—it gave Merle's career a real shot in the arm. Merle was aware of the album's success but was nonplussed. In a 1979 interview, he told Mark Humphrey: "I've got a gold record over there of *Will the Circle Be Unbroken*. I've got six gold records upstairs. I hope William McEuen doesn't read this, but I've got two copies of the album, and I've never listened to all of it, so I don't know exactly what I said to Doc.... I'll have to dig that out and listen to it sometime."[464]

Michael Robinson, who had returned from tours of Vietnam and the Mediterranean with the Marines, lived with Merle and Bettie in Nashville for a short time, then decided to return to Los Angeles in 1972, leaving them without any children living at home: "My brother, he left for the Air Force, and I was still there doing this thing and traveling with this guy, you know, lugging the amplifiers, doing this, doing that. I could have stayed and kept doing that, but the thing about it is, you end up just being the 'gofer' for the cheeseburgers. And you don't want to be that. I hitchhiked to California from Tennessee. I call Interstate 40 the "Hillbilly Trail of Tears." If I'm on Interstate 40, I always think, 'Am I having an economic problem?' You know, because to me if I'm traveling on 40, something ain't right, somewhere."[465]

Now empty nesters, Merle and Bettie moved into a mobile home and took out a $7,000 loan to purchase a new bus for touring. According to Michael Robinson: "They got rid of the house on the lake and moved into a mobile home over by Old Hickory Boulevard and the Cumberland River. They lived right on the Cumberland River in a mobile home park for a couple of years."[466]

The year 1973 saw more random shows dotted across the country, but two stood out. In May, Merle was invited to participate in a reunion of the *Hometown Jamboree* show in California. It had been twenty years since its heyday, and Merle returned to California to encounter old friends he hadn't seen in years. Tennessee Ernie Ford headlined the show that also featured stalwarts Cliffie Stone, Bucky Tibbs, Wesley and Marilyn Tuttle, Molly Bee, Speedy West, Dallas Frazier, Harold Hensley, Billy Liebert, Sammy Masters, Gene O'Quin, Merrill Moore, and several others. This tight-knit group of West Coast country musicians welcomed Merle back with open arms. The reunion was a big success, and undoubtedly planted the seed in Merle and Bettie's minds of moving back to California.

Another very prestigious gig that happened in July 1973 brought Merle to Washington, DC, to perform at the Smithsonian Festival of American Folklife. He brought along a special guest who had only accepted after much cajoling—his old friend from Drakesboro, Mose Rager—and they had a ball playing together there. Grandpa Jones was also present, joining in musically and interjecting some friendly heckling from the side of the stage. A live recording exists of one of their performances, and the lighthearted fun was clearly infectious and enjoyable for everyone. The only drawback was the festival's proximity to Dulles airport—the noise of airplanes taking off and landing was quite intrusive. Here's a sample of the onstage banter:

Merle: "Ready as a field mose!"

Mose Rager: "Travis said he's ready as a field mouse. Here I go. I'm going to try. Go on Merle. Might get him lost then. Oh man, he's picking the blues now.... I'm going to sing one after he gets through picking."

Merle: "Sing it, Mose!"

Mose Rager: "Now listen, on Merle's part that was good, but brother I never done no worser in my life."

Merle Travis: "I'd hate to hear you when you do good, Mose."

Grandpa Jones: "Hey Mose, can you play that 'Irene' or maybe..."

Mose Rager: "No sir, I don't. I surely don't. I just play what I can get. But Merle... let's let old Merle Travis play one by himself, and I'll just sit and listen, because buddy—he can make one guitar sound like five."[467]

As folk festivals went, this was a prestigious opportunity for Merle. He received much newspaper coverage as well as official recognition from the Smithsonian staff and other government officials involved.

On the financial spectrum, Merle was overextended from advances he'd taken from his publishing royalties. The couple had been living beyond their means, and things in the fall of 1973 seemed quite grim. A letter from his then-publisher, Nashville-based Tree Music International, reads:

Dear Merle:

Your check for this week brings your total due Tree to $5,427.58, and you asked that we keep you advised of your indebtedness.

Merle, we think so much of you and your tremendous talent. However it has been our policy in the past to stop regular weekly advances when the balance reaches a peak such as yours has done. We are enclosing an additional check for $500.00 to carry you through the month of August.

We feel certain that you will be writing those hits again soon, and we most certainly want to continue working with you. I am very sorry that we have found it necessary to take this temporary course of action, but I know now that your health is improving you will be right back on top of things again. When you start sending in good songs again we will be happy to start your checks up again. We hope you understand our position on this....

Kindest personal regards,
Jack Stapp
Tree International[468]

Another game-changing event of late 1973 may have altered Merle and Bettie's view of Nashville. It changed a lot of lives around Nashville. Grandpa Jones's good friend David Akeman, also known as Stringbean, and his wife, Estelle, lived in a small cabin neighboring Grandpa and Ramona Jones. Stringbean was a beloved banjo player and *Grand Ole Opry* star as well as a frequent guest on the popular syndicated TV show *Hee Haw*. He was known to carry around large rolls of cash in the bib of his overalls, due to his distrust of banks. Back in those days, the country music family of musicians, wives, friends, and family trusted each other implicitly. No one ever locked their doors or worried about crime. Several friends, however, had warned Stringbean that flashing big rolls of cash was unwise. Merle was in the close circle of friends who knew Stringbean, along with Grandpa Jones and many *Grand Ole Opry* stars of the same generation. Merle went hunting with Stringbean and Grandpa.

Tragedy occurred on November 10, 1973, when Stringbean and his wife were shot to death at their cabin after an *Opry* performance. The murders brought a shock wave of fear into the formerly carefree country music community. Much as Los Angeles entered a period of fear and distrust after the 1969 Manson family murders, Nashville suffered a similar dark period after Stringbean and Estelle were killed, and it lasted for years.

It was also true that Merle had barely worked in 1973. Once again, California beckoned. In a 1975 interview with Doug Green, Merle went into detail about it:

I moved back and lived here [Nashville] seven years. Seven years, and I enjoyed it, and it's the most wonderful people in the world. Of course, I was born and raised not far from here. But when I was born and raised, there was something I hadn't noticed that I come to find that I had noticed in California. In the summertime, you can just sit still and perspiration will just drip off your face. I'd forgot about that; them hot, dog days of heat and humidity, which don't exist in California. [It] gets hot, but it don't bother you. You just step in the shade. You're cool. Or if a little breeze come by, it's cool, and you don't perspire at all, because the air is completely dry. There's no humidity.

And the wintertime I'd forgot about. You step out the door, it's cold. You say, "It's cold," and that means your car is cold, the ground is cold, the side of the house is cold, the trees are cold, the air is cold. You're at a cold world. I kept saying, well, it's worth it. You're making pretty good money. But, boy, I sure miss that California weather.

And after seven years, why, we got to thinking, "My golly, it sure would be nice to be back out there in that nice weather." So we just said, "Well, we'll pack up and move back to California." I remember, not this last year, the year before, I was out in California, and it was about ninety-five the day I left. It was good and hot, but it was okay. I got back here, it was about eighty-two, and as soon as I walked off the plane, I was covered with sweat. Just the humidity here is awful. But when you lived in it, why, you don't pay much attention to it. But after living twenty-one years in that arid zone, why, I griped about the weather for seven years. So actually, the reason we moved back to California was for the weather.[469]

Upon their return to Los Angeles, initially Merle and Bettie moved in with Jack and Marge Rogers in Van Nuys. Rogers's nephew Jamie Sweet was also living there at the time. Sweet recalled:

When Merle left Nashville and returned to LA, he and Bettie lived with Jack, Margie, and me. I was a junior in high school and a fledgling musician in my own right. One night a few days before Christmas, Merle asked Bettie for the keys to their Cadillac. Merle never drove. Bettie did all the driving, so this was highly unusual. Each day, posthaste, I would come home after school. Merle was usually just starting his day. He routinely would grab his Martin acoustic and start playing. Merle got the keys from Bettie and took off. About thirty minutes later, he returned with a bag containing two fifths of Cutty Sark scotch. I always watched what Merle was doing. He was like my own reality TV show. In this case, when he got home, he took his booty into his room and joined us all in the living room. After about ten minutes, Merle excused himself, went into his room, and then emerged from his room with one of the two fifths of Scotch. He entered the bathroom next to his room, wherein he removed the cap to the bottle of booze and proceeded to drain the entire fifth in one long gulp. Wow, did that look cool.

After killing the fifth, he replaced the cap and placed the empty bottle in the bathroom trash can. Having finished the drink, Merle rejoined us again in the living room. About twenty minutes passed, and again Merle excused himself to his bedroom, reemerged with the other bottle, and discreetly walked into the bathroom, wherein he polished off the second fifth. Once again he did it in one long swig. It was incredible. I had never seen such a display of serious drinking in my life.

The rest of the evening, Merle never faltered or even indicated he was intoxicated. He held it together until he retired to bed for the evening. Later that same night, Merle awoke to use the restroom. When he was returning to bed, he tripped and fell into the dresser. He managed to find his way back into the bed. When he awoke, he realized that he had broken his shoulder in the fall.[470]

Once Merle recovered sufficiently from his injuries, he and Bettie moved into a ranch home at 16606 Osborne Street in Sepulveda, in the middle of the San Fernando Valley.

Merle was now in close proximity to Merlene and Cindy, and he continued to reestablish a relationship with both of them. He also got back in touch with some of his oldest musician friends from the 1940s and 1950s who were still active—Wesley and Marilyn Tuttle, Hank Penny, Nudie the Rodeo Tailor, Cliffie Stone, Harold Hensley, Billy Liebert, and some of the Sons of the Pioneers group, like Rome Johnson and the Pioneers' guitarist—and Merle's old friend—Roy Lanham. These musicians would often gather at Jack Rogers's converted home recording studio in Van Nuys. Merle also became reacquainted with a younger musician named Thom Bresh, who had developed great abilities since Merle had last seen him.

From a young age, Thom Bresh grew up playing guitar and steel guitar around Southern California. His first band was a surf band called Chiyo and the Crescents, who had a regional hit with an instrumental single titled "Pink Dominoes." After the Crescents called it a day, Bresh joined up with Hank Penny's roadshow. Penny hired him when he was underage and technically too young to play in bars, but Penny vouched for him and signed papers to get him working in casinos in Las Vegas and Reno. Bresh worked for Penny for several years, then moved to Seattle to try and get a solo career going. By 1972 he had signed with Kapp Records and was living in Los Angeles again. His thumbpicking guitar abilities had increased to the point where he could sit in and jam with the old-timers on any song and hold his own. In his words:

I was always drawn to guitar players. I was always around great guitar players. I remember being around Roy Lanham, he'd say, "Here's a good lick." I was around Roy Lanham, Thumbs Carllile, Speedy West, Jimmy Bryant—they all tolerated me. Turns out, they all knew I was Travis's kid then. I never had to learn where to put my right hand. I had to learn what to do with the left hand, but never with the right. I remember Travis telling me, "Don't let up with that right hand, don't ever let up."[471]

Up to this time, Bresh knew Merle Travis as a great country guitarist, one who had been in his circle of musician friends. Bresh played Travis style, but he was also adept at Chet Atkins style and Jerry Reed style fingerpicking. He had a suspicion, but didn't know, that Merle was his father:

That was 1974, I think, because I try to remember things by what car I was driving. I had a '74 Porsche at that time. That's when they were having a party over at Rome Johnson's house, same suspects as always, bunch of the [Sons of the] Pioneers. Roy [Lanham], and Harold [Hensley], and Travis supposed to be there. That's why I went over, because they said, "Hey, come to this party, Travis will be here. I know he'd like to see you." Yeah, I'll come by. I got over there.

It was about ten o'clock by the time I got over there and everybody was shitfaced, but they were playing music in different rooms, you know? I went around, said hello to everybody. Then Harold [Hensley] comes up to me, puts his arm around me, and says, "How you doing?" I said, "I'm all right. How about you?" He said, "Oh, you know, Travis wanted to be here tonight so bad. He's sick. He wanted me to apologize to you. Your daddy loves you so much, Bresh. You don't even know." He's looking at me, he says, "Oh, my God. Oh no." I said, "What?" He said, "Oh, you didn't know, did you? I didn't mean to, I'm so sorry."

I figured there was something in there, I just didn't know what it was at this point yet. I said, "Don't worry about it."

Then he calls for Phyllis [Hensley] to get over. What'd he call her, "Sweetie Pie" or something? Sweetie Pie. She said, "What?" Harold said, "I told him about Travis. My God, run my mouth." I said, "Harold, relax. It's fine. It's fine."

Now at least I know something. Now I'm starting to dig it, right? Harold said, "He loves you, though. Oh, God, I don't know if you should tell him I told you. We're all sworn to secrecy. I thought you knew." You know how when you're drunk, you go on and on.

I said, "Forget about it." Then he wanted me to play some songs. I played a couple of things, then said, "I gotta go." By the time I got home, it's about 12:30, I guess. I got over there to the folks' house. I put the coffeepot on. I went in, knocked on my mom's door. She said, "Come in." I opened the door. I said, "I got some cinnamon rolls and coffee's brewing. It'll be ready in about five minutes, about the time you get up." "What time is it?" "It's about quarter to one, looks like." "Well, can't this wait until tomorrow?" "No, it's got to happen right now. Get your buns up. I got you a place set over there with a cinnamon roll, I got one for me, and the coffee will be ready momentarily."

I closed the door, walked back in there. She comes in. She says, "Oh," took a swig of her coffee, "To what do I owe this? Did you go to that party you were going to go to? Did you have a good time?" "Actually, yeah. It was a very informative sort of a party. Interesting, different than the norm." She said, "Did Merle make it there?" "No, Harold came up and told me that he was sick. He couldn't make it. 'Sick,' you know what that means." "Yeah, of course."

"Harold told me 'Your father loves you very much.'" She says, "Oh shit, huh?" "Yeah, kind of. That was kind of my first thought. However, I said it was interesting news and something that I've suspected the last, I don't know, ten years or so, but didn't bother me one way or the other. Now that it's put in my lap, why don't you tell me a story about 1947, if you could go back in your mind?"

She said, "Oh, my God. Well, I was always looking for that right time to tell you. Nothing ever seemed like it was the right time, so I hadn't gotten to it yet. We met and it was not a big thing, but it turned into a big thing after all. Merle came over one night. He says, 'Hell,' when he found out I was pregnant. 'I'll take care of everything. Please, don't make this public. You can't have kids out of wedlock.'"

The next day, when I got up, she said, "What's on your agenda today?" I said, "I want to go pay a visit to Mr. Travis, see what he has to say about all this." She says, "Well, he's fragile, you know? Be easy with him." I'm not pissed off at anybody, you know? This is actually pretty cool, as I've been thinking about it. The last few years, the way he looked at me and the way I looked at him. When I was younger, I really looked a lot like him. People would make comments all the time I'm up on the stage, "You look like a young Travis standing up there." Hank [Penny] said, "Oh yeah, doesn't he, though? He's up there, he's got all those mannerisms. You know how Merle does this, and that? He does that."

I called Merle and I said, "Hey, this is Thom. Can I come by and see you?" "Why do you want to do that? I'm kind of busy today." I said, "You're not busy all day. You got to have ten or fifteen minutes for your son." "Oh, yeah, come on over if you'd like. Harold said he made a little slip-up. I guess I can't say anything, but come right over." Thank you and I hung up, went over there.

Well, I went down there. There's a restaurant. We got in the car, it was a fancy car, and got him a beer. We sat there and drank that thing and told me his story. He said, "You know, I'm just a man. A few drinks and things just got a little out of control with Ruth." He says, "You're pretty great, you know? Are we still friends or do you not want to see me anymore? You want to go have an operation, have your gene taken out or something?" I said, "No, I just want to know, you know? You're my father. Wow. Merle Travis, kind of a big name in guitar playing, my father. That's why I could play guitar." "Yep. Can you draw?" I said, "I can't. No, I draw a stick man and it's out of proportion." "You didn't get the drawing gene, just the picking one? That's the only one you need. Do you make up songs?" I said, "Yeah." "Oh good, I'd like to hear some of them. Do you have an alcohol problem or anything?" "No." "Do you smoke pot?" I said, "Yeah." "Do you have any?" I said, "Yeah." "Just a joint or how do you have it?" "Yeah, roll it up." "Yeah, why don't we seal this relationship with a peace pipe and we use your joint to do that?"

Then he went in the house, and that's where we lit it, in the kitchen. In comes Bettie: "Are you using pot?" He says, "I ain't seen no pot nowhere," and it just reeks. That whole kitchen reeks of pot. He's denying, "No, I haven't seen no pot. We went and had a beer, though." "You're not supposed to have beers." "Well, I'm not supposed to do a lot of things, but I do them. Can I just visit with my son?" "Oh, you finally broke down and told him?" "No, *he* broke down and told *me*." "Oh. Well, welcome to the crazy family. You got a crazy one here, I'll tell you that." And she left the kitchen. He said, "Yeah, she's got to get used to you first and she'll be all right."[472]

The subject of Bresh had been a difficult one for Merle and Bettie to address. In an interview with folklorist Ed Kahn, Bettie remembered when she learned about Thom: "Thom Bresh had come into the picture and I was really hurt that he hadn't told me before. He told me when we were in Vietnam and I think he did it more to hurt me than anything else. I had known Thom since he was a kid. Joe Maphis said it was the biggest secret in town. Everybody knew but me. Harold Hensley was the one who told Thom. I felt sorry for Mr. Bresh. Thom was born before Merle and I were married."[473]

The year 1974 brought about two unrelated recording projects. One of them involved a dedicated fan who recorded in a converted garage; the other was an album with Chet Atkins that would go on to win a Grammy.

Ray Campi was an obscure 1950s rockabilly artist who was in his late thirties, living in Los Angeles, when he began recording throwback rockabilly music in Ronny Weiser's Rollin' Rock Recording Studio—a converted garage in Van

Nuys with some primitive equipment. Campi had grown up in Texas, listening to Merle's music, and had remained a big fan through the years. He had called and interviewed Merle on the phone in August 1973, when Merle and Bettie still lived in Nashville. During the call, Ray pitched the idea of collaborating on a recording, and when Merle moved back to Los Angeles the following year, he worked to make the idea a reality since Merle had no record label deal at the time. Campi later recalled:

> It was after *The Johnny Cash Show* went off the air that Merle Travis returned to California.... I made contact with Merle's daughter, Merlene, and she gave me Merle's new address and phone number and I got in touch with him. After talking with Merle, he agreed to do it, but at the same time he was not too well and it would be a few weeks before he could come to the studio, but he would enjoy doing so....
>
> Finally the big night arrived! I drove my yellow 1966 Cadillac convertible to Merle's house.... When Merle saw my car, he got excited and called his wife to come have a look at it. "Back in 1954 we had a yellow Cadillac convertible!" he exclaimed. "This one is just like it!"
>
> We arrived at Ron Weiser's house in about 15 minutes. I introduced Thom and Merle to Ron, who had the recorder humming, and immediately Merle got out of the case his beautiful Gibson with his name on the neck and soon set himself to work. The first song he played on was "Guitar Rag." We did twelve tunes in total, including a blues instrumental with no vocal.
>
> I always liked the way Merle used the sped-up recording techniques on his version of "Merle's Boogie Woogie"... and I asked Merle to record it for me the same way, which he did.... Ron and I were enthralled that we had just put on tape the great Merle Travis, a hero in our eyes, but in his own, a simple Kentucky boy with some talent and lots of good luck.[474]

Ray also remembered that Merle seemed crestfallen about recording in the small garage studio, recalling that the last time he had made a record in California, it was at the Capitol Tower in Hollywood, home to one of the best studios in the United States. Despite its garage nature, the Rollin' Rock EP has a lot of the primitive charm and authentic feel of Merle's earlier recordings. It was another of Merle's records that bridged the gap into rockabilly music and appealed to rockabilly fans in the United States and Europe, especially during the 1970s, when the genre was in danger of extinction.

The other recording project that happened in 1974 was on the opposite end of the professional spectrum. Merle's old friend and admirer Chet Atkins contacted him with the idea of doing an album together. The idea was the brainchild of Nashville songwriter and raconteur Cecil Null, who was friends with both men. Chet proposed that he fly to Hollywood with Jerry Reed in tow as producer, and record a duets album at RCA's Hollywood Recording Studios on Sunset Boulevard (the same studio where the Rolling Stones had cut "Satisfaction," and Elvis Presley had cut "Burnin' Love," among hundreds of other hits).

They recorded the songs on a multitrack tape recorder, and Chet took the tapes back to Nashville and spent eight months redoing his parts at his home studio. When he was done, he sent Merle a note:

> Merle and Betty,
>   Everyone here is excited about the album. I hope they are right and
> I trust you will like the mixing and editing. It was a labor of love, Merle.
>   —Chet
>   P.S. I'll call in a day or so.[475]

The Atkins-Travis Traveling Show was released in spring 1974. It's a pleasant and listenable jam session between two old friends. Jerry Reed plays rhythm guitar and bass on a few tracks, which, as Hugh Cherry points out in the liner notes, made for a triumvirate of influential guitar heroes on one recording: "A third generation guitarist participated in this memorable session. Producer of the session and rhythm guitarist on a few of the tracks was Jerry Reed. Thus, only three people were visible at the session, the mentor (Travis), the student (Atkins), and the third generation (Reed)."

Shel Silverstein contributed two humorous original songs, "Mutual Admiration" and "Is Anything Better Than This." Silverstein was a true renaissance man. He gained fame as a cartoonist for *Playboy* magazine and an author of children's books, and later wrote many hit songs for the outlaw breed of country artists of the late 1960s and the 1970s. In addition to many hits for artists like Bobby Bare, Tompall Glaser, and Dr. Hook, he wrote "A Boy Named Sue" and "25 Minutes to Go," both recorded by Johnny Cash. The two songs that he wrote for the Atkins-Travis album were humorous insult-comedy routines—lighthearted fun peppered with jibes and jokes, including Merle ribbing Chet that his fingers are so quick that his playing sounds like "someone scared a bunch of chickens."

Of course, the joking worked because the two had a real mutual admiration. Atkins's autobiography, *Country Gentleman* (1974), makes it clear:

> Just when I was feeling my worst, something happened that perked me
> up: Merle Travis visited the station. Homer and Jethro, who were at
> WLW then, invited Merle and me out to dinner. It was a great evening.

Merle was so nice to me, and he even asked me to play the guitar for him. He praised my style for the rest of the evening, putting himself down. He said such things as, "I can't play the guitar. Not like you can, Chester."

Since then, whenever anyone asked him who the greatest guitar player in the country is, he says, "Chester Atkins." I can't understand why because my playing is so much like his. However, he once told a reporter that "most guitar players are like imitation orange juice, but Chester Atkins is the real, fresh-squeezed thing." Imagine—my idol saying something like that about me.[476]

Chet even named his daughter Merle when she was born in 1949, the ultimate proof of how much he idolized Merle.

Merle returned the praise in an interview with Mark Humphrey in 1979: "I don't think that there will ever be a chance for any other guitar player to be as great as Chet. He was born at a time when turn-of-the-century music, the songs of the twenties and big bands, were still around and not laughed at. He knows it all, from the music to commercial stuff to what was recorded this afternoon in Nashville. He is the greatest guitar player that has ever been on this earth, in my opinion.... And that's what I think of Chet Atkins."[477]

The Atkins-Travis Traveling Show abundantly features Travis classics like "Cannonball Rag," "Dance of the Golden Rod," "Nine Pound Hammer," and "I'll See You in My Dreams." It's rounded out by a few old 1920s jazz and pop standards like "If I Had You," "Muskrat Ramble," and "Who's Sorry Now," as well as the obligatory blues song, "Down South Blues," and the obligatory guitar boogie, "Boogie for Cecil" (a nod to Cecil Null, who had sparked the idea for the album). The record was a bit middle-of-the-road for Merle; it could be criticized as too polite and genteel, as lacking the raw hillbilly excitement that "Blue Smoke" or "Sixteen Tons" generated in the 1950s. But it is certainly what a Chet Atkins record from the 1970s sounded like. Chet had by that point established a successful "brand" of polite, polished, semi-easy-listening records that sold by the truckload. *The Atkins-Travis Traveling Show* resembles in particular the other record Atkins released in 1974, *Superpickers*, a collaboration with many of Nashville's most in-demand session musicians.

The album sold reasonably well—much better than Merle's last decade of recordings—and when awards season came around, Merle and Atkins received that year's Grammy for Best Country Instrumental Performance. Thom Bresh remembers of it: "Travis says, 'I won a Grammy award!' I said, 'Well, congratulations!' 'Yeah, ain't that something? It's because Chet told me he always wins a Grammy when he puts out an album and they put him up for it. He always wins it. But he says, 'We'll get a Grammy on this because we're already nominated. People are already reacting to it, and it's a good album.' I said, 'It's a great album! Merle, you be proud of it.' 'Yeah, I'm kind of proud of that, the way it came out.... [Referring to the time it took for Chet to do his guitar overdubs] I don't think Chet played eight months' worth of good, you know?'"[478] Bresh remembers that the album's success brought Atkins out to Hollywood for a meeting with some television executives about a potential special featuring Merle, Atkins, and Jerry Reed, but the idea never went beyond the initial meeting stage.

Merle was also nominated for the first time in 1974 for membership in the Country Music Hall of Fame, which at that time was still relatively new. The Academy of Country Music began the concept in 1961, inducting one to three members per year. The inductees were immortalized on engraved metal plaques installed in the Tennessee State Museum until the Country Music Hall of Fame and Museum building was constructed in 1967, then and expanded and renovated in 1972 (at that point, older country legends like Merle were encouraged to donate or loan instruments and artifacts, and Merle loaned the museum his historic 1948 Bigsby electric solidbody guitar, where it remains to this day). By 1974, many of Merle's friends had been inducted, including Tex Ritter, Gene Autry, the Carter Family, and Chet Atkins. The other 1974 nominees included Minnie Pearl, Owen Bradley, Vernon Dalhart, Pee Wee King, and Kitty Wells. Merle's old friend Pee Wee King was named the 1974 inductee. It would take Merle another three years to get there. However, that same year, the Academy of Country Music in Hollywood gave Merle the Pioneer of Country Music Award, another prestigious honor. Around this time, a young up-and-comer named Marty Stuart got the chance to meet Merle. In an interview with this author, Stuart recalled:

> I met Merle at Grandpa Jones and Ramona's house. Grandpa Jones and Ramona would have these get-togethers, and people'd bring food, and pickin'. Lots of pickin' going on, and you know, cloggin', and just country culture, out at their house in Goodlettsville, Tennessee. For my money, it was the social event of the season; I didn't care anything about Belle Meade society, all that. But when Grandpa and Ramona would have a pickin', it was really something to be invited because the who's who of the old world of country music was usually found out there.
>
> He was the first genius I ever met. He could write a song, he could design a guitar, he could design a costume, he could draw cartoons, he could work on your watch. Everything about him was highly stylized, even the car he drove. Everything about him just reeked of stardom and eccentricity and genius, and he was the first one of those I'd ever

met. It was really, really a big deal to shake Merle Travis's hand. I think everybody regarded him as that [a genius]. And you could tell that everybody understood his frailties, and that was unspoken; but everybody also understood his genius, and that was understood.

There's no doubt in my mind that if he'd decided he wanted to write pop songs, Merle could've hung in there with Johnny Mercer, but I think he understood his audience. And he understood he wrote Johnny Mercer–level songs that he wrote, but kind of more accessible to a country person. To a cowboy, country and western audience.[479]

Thom Bresh has his own thoughts on the "genius" label as applied to Merle:

Geniuses are walking a line between nuts and okay. And he falls on the nut side, and he falls on the okay side. He can be a charmer, and he can be a monster. You don't know which way he's gonna go. But that's part of being a genius. You read up on it. There's a lot of books about geniuses. They walk on a tightrope, and that's why you lose your balance. You fall on the other side.[480]

Merle's memory:

"Rolling Stone gives me write up"

Rolling Stone magazine published an article about Merle in their June 19, 1975, issue that had the potential to boost Merle's career. *Rolling Stone* was, at the time, *the* cutting-edge music magazine in the country. Sadly, Chet Flippo's article, "Merle Travis, Guitar Legend," was mostly an unflattering portrait of an aging former star: "He looked years older than 56… " "He had all but disappeared during the past decade…" "Since then, illness has kept him at home…" "Leo Fender himself was not available, but a company spokesman dismissed Travis's story [that he invented the modern solidbody electric guitar] as 'wishful thinking.'" "Merle Travis has never played a solid body guitar in his life…"[481] Merle was furious with the portrayal, particularly the inaccuracy of the solidbody guitar comments. One can certainly accuse Flippo of lazy research, as Merle could have shown him any number of vintage photographs to prove his assertion. But it was true that Merle looked years older than his age, and that to a young rock music writer he represented an era completely out of touch with the music that was then popular. The *Louisville Courier-Journal* reported sympathetically in 1976:

Now based in California, he's still traveling and playing an active concert schedule… and chafing a lot about a nasty article in *Rolling Stone* magazine last year that depicted him as an ailing, decrepit has-been. Sympathy mail came in from all over the world from fans and acquaintances who said they were sorry to hear he was upon hard times. It was nice to be remembered, Travis said, but he still called the author and told him he would give him a knuckle sandwich next time they met (they haven't met).[482]

Jack Rogers's nephew Jamie Sweet remembered a Christmas spent at Merle and Bettie's house in Sepulveda:

> We spent Christmas with Merle, Bettie, and Bettie's two sons. When we got to Merle and Bettie's home, Merle was in the kitchen smoking a joint with Bettie's son Dennis. I remember thinking what a life Merle had—he could do whatever he wanted. Nobody seemed to care. If I smoked a joint in front of my parents, there would be serious consequences. Whereas when Merle does it, nobody says anything.[483]

Merle and Bettie only lived in their ranch home in Sepulveda for about a year before packing up and moving again. The only explanation ever given for the move was, strangely, that the house had too many roses to maintain, as quoted in the *Santa Clarita Signal*:

> Travis met his wife in California and they settled in a home in Sepulveda. The climate was great, but there was one drawback. "There were roses everywhere," Bettie said. "Big, beautiful roses—red and yellow. Out in front, on the side of the house, and in the backyard. We just got sick of them."
>
> So a friend told them about a home at the Lily of the Valley and they took a look at it and fell in love with it.
>
> The mobile home is decorated with an entire wall devoted to the awards and honors of Merle Travis.[484]

Lily of the Valley trailer park was on Bouquet Canyon Road in Saugus, about an hour northeast of Los Angeles in the Santa Clarita Valley. It was an area where many Western stars had gravitated. Cliffie Stone lived in nearby Canyon Country. Billy Liebert, the Capitol Records accordion and piano player, lived near Cliffie. Tex Williams lived in the area, as well as other Western movie stars from the 1940s era like Montie Montana and Iron Eyes Cody. Merle had done time just down the road at the Saugus Honor Farm ten years earlier. But now, the area offered a relaxed environment with low overhead and plenty of old friends nearby.

Scott Lynch was a young boy who lived in the trailer park during Merle and Bettie's time there. He took care of their poodles when they were out of town, and became very close to the couple. He recalled to this author:

> They came up that canyon to get away from everything. They were looking for peace, and they had found it in our community, and they invited people up. Monte Montana would just ride down and stop by. Iron Eyes Cody would just stop by. Dallas and Tex Williams, and stuff. Santa Clarita was really rich in country music. A lot of it had to do with the guys like Cliffie Stone being right here. [The Travises] had two little white poodles, named Hugo and Gigi. They were two miniature poodles, and they were royal. They got treated very royal. Those two loved each other. He had his-and-hers Cadillacs. They had time out on the porch, and they would just sing.[485]

Merle was nominated again for the Country Music Hall of Fame in 1975, and again he didn't win. That year's recipient was another of his good friends, the country comedienne Minnie Pearl. That same year, Merle had another film role in an MGM Western comedy starring Jeff Bridges and Andy Griffith, *Hearts of the West*. He recalled the experience in a 1975 interview with researcher Doug Green: "The week before I come out here, I'd done some background stuff for a picture starring Andy Griffith... Andy Griffith and him [Jeff Bridges] has made a picture called *Hearts of the West*. I done a bunch of background. I played quite a bit of guitar, and then we had two fiddles. There's all sorts of music."[486]

Michael Robinson points out: "Okay, when you watch the movie *Hearts of the West*, you'll notice that Merle Travis gets billing in this thing, but they never show him up close because they did not understand that he had an affliction [the muscle-pulling] that made it impossible for him to have a close-up. So they always shot at a distance in the movie, which was about the Saugus and Newhall area movie locations back in the 1920s and 1930s."[487] Bettie Travis noted:

> [In Nashville] he had a cataract, and in order to sedate him, they gave him valium and it stopped this [the muscle pulling]. After this, I would give him shots of Valium and he didn't drink, either. By giving him the shots, it controlled his pulling. The doctor trusted me to do this, but when we moved back to California, they would no longer allow me to do this. They gave him the pills, but then he would drink with it. He had already learned years ago that if you take a pill and you get a little drink with it, you get a much higher high and you get well much faster, you know, but you don't really get well, you get sicker, but you don't realize

it. So when we moved back to California, we ran into a lot of problems because of that. It was sad.[488]

During this time in California, it was inevitable that Thom Bresh and Merle's daughters would become acquainted. After a random meeting at one of his performances at a restaurant in the San Fernando Valley, Merlene and Thom became friends. Merlene picks up the story:

> I remember I called Dad and told him I had met Thom, and Dad said, "Yeah, I know the fella." But nothing more than that, you know. And then Thom and I did become really good friends and very close. And then my marriage was going on the rocks, but he was someone to talk to and run things by. Ken [Merlene's first husband] and I were still together, but not really, you know what I mean? It was on its last days. His [Thom's] dad [Bud Bresh] at one point said, "Well, you ought to go after Merlene."
>
> So Dad called and said, "Bettie and I want to know if you want to go and see Thom Bresh at the Portofino Inn." And I said, "Yeah, we'd love to." I was so excited, because he usually didn't invite me out that much. So we went out that night and Jack and Marge Rogers were there, and Ken and me, and Dad and Bettie. And then Thom came over and said hi, but Thom seemed very distant that night, kind of distant and bizarre. I couldn't figure out what was going on.
>
> I remember that night, Bettie staring at me, and Marge staring at me, and it was just weird. I thought maybe they knew that Ken and I were having problems. So anyway, Dad leaned over to me and he said, "Is there anything I could ever say to you, or do, that would make you not love me?" And I said, "Nope, not a thing." And he said, "Thom's as much kin to you as Patty is." And I'm like, "What?"
>
> So he took a break, and Thom and Dad left first—they went out in the alley, I guess probably to say, you know, did you tell her? And so I went into the bathroom, like girls do on breaks. I was with Bettie and Marge. It was the coldest Bettie ever was to me, ever. She said, "What did your dad say to you?" And I said, "He told me that Thom's as much kin to me as Patty is." And she goes, "Yeah, sure." She gave me the feeling she didn't believe it. And then Marge said something to me like, "Be careful about what you believe," or something to the effect that they were pissed off about this information. They weren't happy. But I was in my own head. I was excited. Oh my God, I have a brother. This is the best thing ever. And so we went outside and we all hugged and I said I was excited about it. I was thrilled.[489]

Merle was not yet sixty years old, but he looked much older, and the time Merle and Bettie were living in the Saugus trailer park, he had slipped back into a familiar routine and stayed drunk much of the time. Young neighbor Scott Lynch remembers: "He was feeling really down. The deals that he was getting—Merle felt like he was becoming a nobody. The person that kept Merle going was Cliffie Stone. I'd go over to their house, and it'd be 'Scotty, not right now.' That's what I was told later: 'Scott, he was drunk and he didn't want you to see him.' I said, you know what, I smelled liquor on him, and I told him I didn't like that smell. He fell asleep a couple of times smoking a cigarette. Him and those cigarettes, that was crazy."[490] Yet when Merle was sober and feeling well, his kindness to the people in the neighborhood was unlimited. Lynch also recalls Merle sponsoring a local girl's baseball team that he called the Angels as a humorous tribute to his old friend Gene Autry, who owned the California Angels baseball team.

Thom Bresh remembered another situation from 1976, during a show at the Palomino Club in North Hollywood:

One time we were doing a thing at the Palomino again. It was something else Cliffie called up to do. Travis was drunk when he got there. Cliffie came up and told me. He says, "What the hell's wrong with Travis? I got there, he was on, up there. He was playing and acting half nuts. It didn't seem like him." I went back in that back room there, put my shit down. Cliffie's back there. I said, "What's going on with Travis?"

[Cliffie said] "Oh, you have to go rescue him. Can you get your guitar and just go up there and rescue him, get him off that stage? He's really drunk, and he's missing everything he's trying to play. He's making remarks. Get up there and somehow finesse him off. Could you do that?" He said, "I could do it, but I don't want to. He's liable to try to have words with me because he's pretty shitfaced."

I got my stuff and I walked on up there. He says, "Oh, I guess you want to come up here and pick with me?" I said, "No, I just want to come up and play. I got to do something." Merle said, "Hold on, folks, I want to have a discussion with this young man over the side of the stage. He wants to play with me, pick. I understand I'm Merle Travis, and he wants to play with me because he picks."

You can see the audience is irritated with him. I says, "Let's do a little 'Nine Pound Hammer.' I'll do my songs and we can let this show go on." "I'll play some 'Nine Pound Hammer' with you." Well, it was just obnoxious. I played it and he sang. He couldn't play, of course, couldn't get a chord out of his guitar. Finally, he says, "Ah, you intimidate me too much. I can't pick."

I said, "How about a big round of applause. Merle Travis, everybody? I can't tell you why he's celebrating. I wish I could, but I can't." I said, "Give him a hand." Everybody thought, "Oh, he got shitfaced because something good is happening that he's celebrating." Even Cliffie, he said, "That was nice about saying how he's celebrating. That'd explain why he's drunk, because you can tell he's drunk."

He couldn't talk, he couldn't play, and he was just obnoxious. He'd stop, "Let me start this over again. I can't focus on all these strings on this guitar." He starts, "Let me play something else. I could do this. Everybody, click on your fingers. Well, Sixteen Tons, what do you get?" He couldn't even do the verse. I'm thinking, "Oh boy."

I got him off, but when we got back in that green room I said, "If you ever embarrass me from a stage like that again, I'll never fucking talk to you again." I said, "You're pitiful. You can't play. You're fucking Merle Travis. You play like shit. You sound like shit. You look like shit. You embarrassed the shit out of me, and I'm sick of it."

Cliffie came out and he says, "You were a little harsh." "Fuck him. I'm serious. That's unacceptable." "Well, call him tomorrow. You got to take it easy on him." Anyway, he called me the next day. He said, "I'm Merle Travis. I'm a guitar player." "Yeah. What's up?" "Were you serious when you said you don't want to play with me anymore?" I said, "Yep. You want to drink and get out of hand like you were last night, I don't even want to be seen with you." "Oh. That's good to know. Goodbye, then." He slammed the phone down.

So it was, I don't know, maybe six, eight months later, he called one day and said, "Is this Mot Hserb?" I said, "Yeah." "This is Elrem Sivart. [Merle and Thom had a playful game of referring to each other with their names pronounced backward.] I just wondered if you'd like to have a little jam session. And maybe a T-bone steak or something out here at the house. And I'd like to have a little pickathon with you and see if you can keep up with me or not. Oh, by the way, I ain't been drinking. I've just been picking, and now that I've sobered myself up, I want to see if you're as good as you think you are."

I came out. We played. He was just playing his ass off. Boy, that thumb was right in there. He said, "Yeah, I've got a lot of comments about that night [at the Palomino]. They said I was really obnoxious. You said you didn't want nothing to do with me, and that hurt my feelings because I finally had a son, and then I screwed that up and he don't want nothing to do with me. Like my daughter [Pat] don't want nothing to do with me." He says, "Like Hank [Penny] said, you just get out of hand. You're nuts when you drink. You shouldn't drink because you go nuts. But I love to drink, and I haven't been because I want to prove to you that I can still play, and try to make myself feel better, which I do. I'm just trying to make things right. I've gone a whole lifetime without having a son. Now all of a sudden I got a son, and he's watching out after me, and I'm not used to anybody watching out after me like that. I got a wife that does that. Nags on me when I'm out of sorts. That, being honest with you, that makes me even drink a little more."

He says, "Well, have we buried that hatchet?" I said, "Yeah, as long as you stay straight. I mean, you get as screwed up as you want, but not when we're having to go on stage. It's just embarrassing, and you're Merle Travis."[491]

The two spent a lot of time together while Merle was back in Los Angeles. Bresh recalls one memorable incident that revealed what sort of shape Merle's internal organs were in:

We started coming in through San Fernando on the freeway. He said "Hey Mot! A mile up there, get off there." "That's right in the middle of the Mexican area." "Oh, no. It's fine. They're fine folks. I know a place, and they know me. They make the best, oh, it's the most tasty Mexican food you get."

They brought out some nice big dishes. A dish, little taller than this, full of salsa. Some nice chips, you can see the steam coming off of them. They're fresh chips, big ones, scoopable-looking. I stuck one down in that hot sauce, put it in my mouth, crunched down. Holy shit! I'm telling you, hot! Jesus, my eyes were watering. Merle said, "This is hot? Here. Watch this."

He took the container of hot sauce, put it up, and drank it all the way down. He set it down and it's just red residue in the bottle. And I'm looking at him. "Now, look at my eyes. Are they watering up?" No. "Listen to my voice. La, la, la. Am I losing my voice and everything?" No. "But you say it's hot. And I believe you. I drank that not to be a show-off but to show you what kind of shape my system must be in. That might as well be ketchup for all I care. I don't taste anything hot about it."

He said, "I've had everything in my life. I've drank hair tonic. I've drunk aftershave lotion. I've had peyote with the Indians. I've put some heroin in my veins to see what that was all about. I smoked marijuana and I've had hashish. And I've drunk moonshine, and I've drunk cleaning solution if it says 'alcohol.' I try to drink it. I always had a fantasy of drinking gasoline. When I'm putting gas in a car, I smell it and think, I would give anything in the world to get a big glass of ice and take that nozzle and fill that great, big glass up with gasoline and smell it and be able to drink that. I know that'd kill me sure as could be, but I still have that fantasy. Merlene told me that she has that when she smells gas. She said she'd love to think that she could put ice in a big glass of that and drink it."

He said, "But I haven't had everything. I've had all those things that I told you. But I promise you and I swear to it on my life: I've never, ever touched cocaine." I replied: "What? Cocaine? God, I've done a boxcar load of that shit." "Oh, you don't want to do that. All that other stuff is physically addictive. Cocaine is mentally addictive. You can't feel as good as you can feel if you're sniffing some of that cocaine." He said, "I did a song one time. It says 'Cocaine is for horses and it ain't for men. Doctor said it'd kill you but he didn't say when.' Did you ever hear that?" "I've seen people ruining it. It costs a fortune to get up there again. And you ain't going to get there unless you stay off of it for a month or so." "But you don't want to mess with that." "No," I said.

Merle asked "What is your drug?" I said, "I like margaritas, and I like pot. Those are the two things I like. And I like champagne at times. And that's about it."

I asked, "You said you had heroin?" Merle said, "Yeah, I just wanted to see what the musicians, a lot of musicians put a needle right in their arm, boy. And they go like this. I wanted to see what that was all about because you know I love downers. That's my favorite. Demerol, things like that, the downer pills. Oh, I love that."[492]

When Merle was able to get out and play, some good opportunities came his way. At the beginning of 1976, Cliffie Stone rebooted his *Hometown Jamboree* as a radio show on KLAC, and promoted occasional *Hometown Jamboree* reunion shows. Merle participated in these broadcasts and concerts whenever he felt well enough to do so. The television show *Hee Haw* began in 1969, and continued in syndication starting in 1971. Many of Merle's good friends were regulars, including Grandpa and Ramona Jones and Archie Campbell. Merle was finally brought on as a guest in 1976, performing on his Guild Solomaster (with newly installed R. C. Allen pickups) with Grandpa Jones.

The experience was a great one, and Merle was happy for the opportunity, as *Hee Haw* was one of the few commercially visible outlets for classic country performers at the time. In a letter to his brother John Melvin, he reveals that he was contacted about writing for it: "Sam Louvello [Lovullo], producer of a TV show called *Hee Haw* (I think you get it there) called the house and wondered if I'd like to write for the show. I told him I'd let him know when he got back from Canada, where he was goin'—but again—do I know that many corny gags. We'll see."[493] Merle's archives show that he did write for the show for a period of time in the early 1980s.

In summer 1976, in recognition of the US bicentennial, the Smithsonian put on the largest Folklife Festival it had yet attempted. Merle was brought back to perform on the "Kentucky" stage, and once again he brought his old friend Mose Rager. He traveled to the East Coast and performed first at Lincoln Center in New York in mid-August (the *Louisville Courier-Journal* reported that the audience numbered ten thousand), then headed south to Washington, DC, to perform for a week for the Smithsonian.

The Smithsonian people brought Merle back for a "Country Guitar" concert in October 1976 at the Baird Auditorium inside the museum's Natural History Building. That year Merle was once again nominated for the Country Music Hall of Fame, along with his friends Johnny Cash, Grandpa Jones, Hank Snow, and *Grand Ole Opry* stage manager Vito Pellettieri. Kitty Wells, known as "The Queen of Country Music," was selected as that year's inductee. Merle had been nominated three times at this point without being selected, but he would only have one more year to wait.

In the press, Merle received one of the highest honors a guitarist could achieve when *Guitar Player* magazine (at that time, the only newsstand guitar periodical) put him on the cover of its September 1976 issue, along with a seven-page feature article written by Bob Baxter. It was an excellent feature, Merle's best media exposure in years. Baxter allowed Merle a chance to rebut the *Rolling Stone* piece from the year before, which he was still livid about:

> When *Rolling Stone* came to interview me… I was sitting around in my pajamas by the fireplace, because I had a bad cold. Their article said I hobbled across the room and picked up my guitar. Said I was scrawny-armed, getting very old. After that article, I got more letters sympathizing, "I'm sorry to hear you're in such bad health." If you want to say something that'll please me, say I'm enjoying living out here in California, and that I'm healthy. I just had a physical checkup; there ain't a thing wrong with me.[494]

The *Guitar Player* story certainly boosted the revival of interest in Merle's guitar style that had begun with *Will the Circle Be Unbroken* a few years earlier.

Merle had always had his acolytes since his first recordings in the 1940s. By the mid-1970s, a dedicated group of devotees began communicating with each other. Most of these superfans were finger-style guitarists who loved both the Merle and the Chet styles, although their playing always made it easy to tell which was their favorite.

Some of the first group of "original" Merle and Chet devotees included Eddie Pennington, Royce Morgan, Paul Moseley, Pat Kirtley, Tommy Flint, Frank Hudson, Gene Frances, Charlie Parsons, and Steve Rector from Kentucky; Gary Lambert, Bobby Gibson, Gary Wilson, Michael O'Dorn, and R. C. Allen from the West Coast; Henry Van Wormer in New Jersey; Dave Stewart in Mississippi; and various other thumbpickers from around the country, including Bob Saxton, Bobby Barber (Eddie Pennington remembers Barber as the best Travis picker besides Merle himself), "Moon" Mullins, Dr. Larry Kilgore, Sonny Thomas, Pete Hosey, Mark Hanson, Lee Ridgeway, Maurice Jones, John Matsel, Al Morgan, Tom Owens, and Dr. Bill Lightfoot. Marcel Dadi from France emerged as a European Chet and Merle devotee. Although many of these names are unknown to most readers, and their guitar abilities varied from expert level to amateur, these men preserved Merle Travis's music for future generations when few others cared. *Cannonball Rag* publisher Dave Stewart asserts: "All of these guys played a major role in the rebirth of the 'Travis-style' music."[495]

From this group, Tommy Flint was the first to publish a guitar instructional book: *The Merle Travis Guitar Style* (Mel Bay Publications, 1974). It was a collaboration between Merle—who agreed to take photos of his highly unusual left-hand wraparound technique, as well as show his unique chord shapes and picking techniques—and Flint, who wrote the majority of the instructions and structured the lessons and songs. Merle also contributed a written introduction. Flint's book, sold in music stores all over the country, opened the door to the technique that previously was as much a mystery to the average guitar player as the whereabouts of the Ark of the Covenant or Amelia Earhart. In the era before videotapes, DVDs, or the internet, the only way to learn Merle's unique guitar style was through an instruction book like Flint's and obsessive practicing, either in isolation or in gatherings of like-minded individuals. Complete immersion in the fan lifestyle was the only way to join the club, or even find out about it.

In December 1976, Merle was asked to be a part of a network television *Johnny Cash Christmas Special*. It was the biggest TV exposure he had been offered since the cancellation of Cash's network show five years earlier. Merle videotaped quite a bit for the special, but when the show was broadcast, his participation was edited down to just a few brief shots. Cash sent him a letter after the special aired:

Dear Merle:

Your guitar pickin' was just what the show needed and I didn't know until it was on the air that they cut you as much as they did.

I was disgusted with my own performance, and displeased with my selection of songs, but I was proud to have all the guests I had, especially you.

Thanks for doing the show,

Your friend,

Johnny Cash[496]

The year 1977 began like any other for Merle and Bettie. A *Hee Haw* episode with Tennessee Ernie Ford and Merle as guests revisited the glory days of the mid-1950s. Merle played gigs for Cliffie Stone near their homes in the Santa Clarita Valley, and did acoustic gigs at folkie venues like McCabe's Guitar Shop and Bob Baxter's Guitar Workshop in Los Angeles. There were a few scattered road gigs. In June, at the Fan Fair in Nashville, Merle and Bettie showed up to appear and socialize with their good friends Grandpa and Ramona Jones, Joe and Rose Lee Maphis, and many others. The highlight of the gathering was a jam session featuring Merle, Chet Atkins, Joe Maphis, Billy Strange, and Mose Rager all on stage together. Life rolled on for Merle, but things with Bettie were about to change.

Merle and Bettie had been together for twenty-two years. It was the longest relationship he had ever been in. The pair had seen high times, and extreme lows. Merle had gone into the gutter numerous times, then cleaned up for a while, but the process seemed destined to repeat, over and over. Bettie loved Merle and had stuck by him through situations that would have made most women flee in terror. But even she had reached her limit. With Merle drunk and bedridden most of the time they were at home, she decided to look for work outside of the house. Both were from a generation in which the men were expected to work and pay the bills, and the women were expected to cook and clean and raise the children. But this traditional upbringing was completely at odds with the sexual revolution and women's liberation movements of the 1970s, and their relationship would not survive. Michael Robinson recalled:

It wasn't like he was all bad. He wasn't. You know, whatever happened between them, I don't know. She was going out and working at a carpet store, she just wanted to work. She wanted to get out of the house. Him, I honestly believe that he had some misgivings or some fears about the bequeathments that could happen under California law. He was worried about his wealth or royalties, even though he didn't make any songs after

I was around, and he didn't want to give anything to my mother. I think that his decision was based a lot upon the money. He wanted his blood kin to have that money. That's the way I've always looked at it.[497]

In Bettie Travis's words: "Merle lived his own life in his own way. I think all of the marriages ended because of the drinking. Our first divorce was because of that and then when we got back together it seemed great, and when we moved back to California and the trailer, things got really bad again. I warned Merle that I would leave if he kept drinking."[498]

Merle and Bettie went to Japan for about two weeks in June 1977 to play a few more USO dates. They performed in Shizuoka, Nagoya, Osaka, and Tokyo, and returned to California at the beginning of July. Merle then went to Kerrville, Texas, to play a country and western jubilee with old friends Hank Thompson and Bob Wills's original Texas Playboys over the Fourth of July weekend. When he returned to California, their twenty-two-year relationship was hanging on by a tenuous thread. Bettie had one foot out the door and was preparing her exit.

The couple was paid a visit by their old friend Gary Williams, who arrived at the Saugus trailer park one day just to say hello and wound up staying for several days. He witnessed a messy scene that immediately preceded Bettie's departure, as described in his 1977 book *Girls, Guns, and Guitars*:

> Bettie Travis, who he wed in 1955, a year before the great police drama, is still married to Merle…. Recently, I spent three wild and wooley days with Merle and Bettie Travis at their mobile home, which nestles at the top of a winding desert canyon road near the town of Saugus, not far north of Los Angeles….
>
> It was a nice, sunny afternoon when I pulled up in front of their trailer. As I got out, I took a deep, satisfying breath of pure country air…. I began walking up the stairs to the landing and as I reached the top, Mr. Sixteen Tons, hisself, stepped out of the den door down the patio aways. He was dressed in pajamas, his hair was all mussed and he glared hard at me.
>
> "Hi Merle. What's goin' on?" I asked, sensing that something was amiss.
>
> "More than you might imagine!" was the curt answer. Then he commanded me, "Go next door and tell that guy to come over here!"…
>
> Since I was acquainted with "that guy" next door, whose name is Ivan and whose wife is Eloise, I decided to follow orders. I knocked, and Ivan, a large, red-faced man, greeted me and I entered. In the kitchen to my left stood Bettie Travis, leaning over the sink. When she spotted me,

she exclaimed "Ohhhh, Gary! I was just standing here praying that God would send someone along. And here you are—an answer to prayer!"

Now I was really getting worried.

I muttered something like, "I didn't know you were over here. What's up, Bettie?"

"Merle's next door drinking," she said. "He's got a gun and he shot once and I ran over here because I didn't know if he had shot himself, or was trying to kill me again! Then Ivan went next door and Merle knocked him down!"

I shook my head. "Nothing changes, does it? I thought he had stopped drinking."...

Bettie then came up with this suggestion. "Why don't you go over and try to calm him down.... You're an answer to prayer!" she repeated. "When you two get to playing tapes or singing songs, that will settle him down."

Well, as we have heard, music doth soothe the savage beast, so reluctantly I headed on over to the battlefront. Back over on the Travis porch I carefully slid open the screen, pulled back the curtain a tad and called out musically, "Oh, Merrrrle... are ya there?"

Nothing....

I slowly stepped inside and began moving through the living room. When I got to the back bedroom, where I always sleep when I come a-visitin', I peered around the corner. And there, with his back to me, was Mr. Sixteen Tons. A huge pile of clothing was heaped before him on the bed—and laying on top of it was the gun! I walked up slowly behind him and said, "Hi, there, Trav!" As I put my hand on his shoulder, preparing to mutter some meaningless platitudes, he grunted something I didn't catch and reached for that shootin' iron!

Instinctively I leaped from behind and succeeded in wrestling the gun out of his hand. Mumbling something else unintelligible, he turned and walked briskly out of the room. Was he going after another gun, I wondered? I examined the gun—a Smith & Wesson of .38 caliber—and saw that it was fully loaded and ready for business....

Then I heard what I considered at that moment to be an incredible sound. It was the familiar strains of the famous Merle Travis thumbpicking guitar style, a-comin' through the gloom. And it was not a recording, it was he, live and in person, in the living room, going, "Plunk, plunk, a-plunka..." Since he had both hands on a guitar, I figured he couldn't very well shoot me, so I went on in to join him.

Looking up at me, disheveled and bleary-eyed, pajama-clad Trav calmly suggested, "Let's pick.".…

Now here's the thing about Merle Travis. It seems most everyone these days claims to be a guitar player, and it's true that many can play with speed and skill. But unlike the multitude of pickers, Merle's style is unique and also he does everything in good taste. Also, I can't imagine that anyone could know more songs than he does.… So, each time I come-a-visiting, I get the benefit of valuable music lessons, too. That is, if I survive.…

Bettie decided to send a scout over to see if all was now quiet on the western front. Eloise peeked in through the curtains and asked, "How are you fellows doing?"

To which Merle pleasantly answered, "Oh, me 'n' Gary's just pickin' away."

Then, Bettie, too, showed her face.… Merle suddenly stopped playing and announced, "Bettie, here, sings that one."

"Oh?" I muttered, being caught up in the excitement of this news.

"Bettie," he then commanded, "show Gary how you sing this one."

I doubted very much if she was in the mood for vocalizing right then, but her beloved spouse insisted. "Go on! Sing it!"

So, she began to comply. "Ev'rywhere you go, sunshine fol—"

"NO!" Merle stopped her. "Sell it! Throw your arms out wide and sell it to the audience!"

So, with arms outstretched and gyrating to the beat, Mrs. Sixteen Tons, who shortly before had been terrified out of her gourd after being chased out of the house by gunfire, stood there in the doorway and gave it her all…

It was full showbiz.

And, at least temporarily, all was peaceful in Gunsmoke Canyon.…

For the next three days I worried about that gun in the bedroom drawer, but every time I asked her what I should do about it, Bettie insisted that I not tell her where it was, so that she wouldn't have to lie to him about it (religious convictions, I guess). She also strongly admonished me not to take it out of the house. "He gets violent without his gun," she explained.

Uh huh. That made sense.

I kept telling Bettie that I wanted to leave, but she insisted I was an answer to prayer and that I stay the night. And so I did.…

WHAM! A garbage can hit the house and I woke up for the last time. Since the sun was now out, I crawled outta bed and staggered into the front room, feeling much refreshed from this good night's sleep. Merle was already up and his greeting this groggy morn was, "Let's pick."

So, away we went, "plunk, plunk a-plunka..."

In recent times, Merle has developed yet another problem. He suffers from a nerve disease called Chorea. At times it causes him to groan and grimace and thrash awkwardly about. I looked up Chorea in a medical book, and it says that this affliction can be caused by burning the candle at both ends and abusing your body over a long period of time—something Merle has been known to do. It also stated that one thing that could cause the disease to be fatal is the consumption of alcohol—something Merle has also been known to do. Needless to say, I'm a mite worried about my music teacher....

Back at the Travis trailer I was ready for beddy bye, but when I suggested it, Merle insisted, "Let's pick!" So we did, for hours and hours, until almost dawn. Between pickin's, he related that recently some Optimist representatives had been out to his house to see if he also qualified to join the very exclusive Masons. He said, "One of them asked me, 'Do you believe in God?'" And I answered, "Hell yes, I believe in God!" Then they asked me, "Have you ever been arrested?" And I told 'em, "Why don't you go to the police and have 'em run a make on me?" And they said, "We never do it that way. We'd just like to ask you if you've ever been arrested. Have you?" And I said, "As a matter of fact, I have." "What for?" they asked. And I said, "What would you like to hear about first?"... "Just tell us," they said. "Well, there was seventeen drunk driving arrests.... I've got a record as long as your arm."

To my knowledge, the Masons have not yet taken Merle to their bosom as one of their very own.

While I was there, long-suffering Bettie fixed us several very fine repasts, chicken and dumplings, etc.—which she and I ate. Merle didn't eat anything, but just continued to swill Heineken Dark and munch handfuls of Valium pills.

After another fitful night, I awoke to hear a car leaving the drive. Peeking out the window, I saw it was Bettie. When I went into the den and asked Merle where she was going, pajama-clad Trav expounded, "To the beauty parlor, where she goes every week. Keeping herself beautiful is the main thing in life to her."

Planning to leave as soon as feasible, I asked him when she was likely to return. "She'll be gone till about four." Pretty soon he produced two cans of lima beans.

"How much of a hobo are you?" he asked.

"What do you have in mind?"

"How would you like to join me in some cold lima beans outta the can?"...

Accepting one of the cans, I went into the kitchen and heated it. "I'll warm yours up, if you like," I offered.

"No! I'm used to eatin' 'em like this," he insisted. Besides, that would have spoiled his moment of martyrdom. The round den table must have been fallen on at some time because everything that we placed on either outer edge slid off onto the deeply carpeted floor, including several beers and part of a can of cold lima beans....

"Come on, let's pick," said he. And so we did, on into the afternoon. While we were flailing away on our guitars, the trailer park's lady manager came to the door and firmly stated, "Mister Travis, your guest has had his camper parked in front of your trailer overnight and that is against the park's rules. He will have to move it over to the guest parking area."

On a previous visit I had been similarly chastened for walking my dog and for stepping over a low retaining wall, rather than walking around the far end of it. The management, needless to say, runs a very tight ship. They insist on having everything orderly and proper and do not tolerate any deviation from the norm—let alone any serious untoward incidents. And they have living among them Mr. Sixteen Tons, alias the Kentucky Wonder....

When Merle ran out of beer, he asked me, "Would you go to the store and get me a six-pack of Heineken Dark Beer? Two would be better."

There is only one store in the area. It's a 24-hour, 7-11 store, located about a mile down the curving canyon road. They carry Heineken Dark Beer and Merle trades there quite regularly. Although I didn't want to contribute to the problems at hand, I knew that if I didn't go, he'd go himself—and he was certainly in no condition to get behind the wheel of a car. So, reluctantly, I agreed to go after his groceries. The store had several six-packs of Heineken Dark, but I bought only one. When I returned, all six bottles were forthwith consumed by him. All except those that slid off the den table onto the carpet.

Finally Bettie came home and again I started making graceful exit remarks, "Sure has been swell visitin' you folks. Wouldn't have missed it fer nuthin'."

"You might as well stay the night," answered Bettie. Then Merle spoke up.

"Gary, come on and ride down to the store with me and get some beer."

"Well, I'd sure like to, but..."

"Okay, I'll go myself." he snapped testily, and out the back door he went.

"Merle has no driver's license," said Bettie, with pleading eyes.

I really wasn't surprised to hear this. And even if he had, I doubted very much if he could manage to drive all the way down that winding mountain road in his condition. So I headed out the back door, and I see that he's already in his car.

Now, here's where the real fun begins...

I have a dog that means a great deal to me. In fact, I'm afraid that my emotional well being depends too much on the health of my springer spaniel, Mickey. As soon as Merle got the car door open, Mickey leaped inside with him. I ran up to the open door and implored Merle to let me do the driving.

"No, I'm drivin'!" he declared.

Let me explain that there is only a narrow space between the trailer's wall and the driver's door, and overhead is a vast metal canopy that covers not only the car, but the entire length of the trailer home. It is no simple "canopy," but a long, wide metal extension of the trailer, and it is supported at the outer edges by several metal posts.

By now, Bettie is out on the porch, directly in front of the car (a Cadillac, naturally, which bears the personalized license plate: "16 TONS"). And me? I'm wedged in between the car and trailer, playing a tug o' war with the open driver's door, begging Merle to let me drive. Suddenly, he shoves it in reverse, guns the motor and goes flying backwards. Realizing that I'm in eminent danger of being crushed between the door and wall, I start back-pedaling in a hurry. It was a hair-raising moment. But, I am saved when the car door is jammed up hard against the trailer wall and the car is brought to a jarring halt.

"Merle!" I pled, "Please! I'm begging you to let me do the driving!"

"I'm driving!" he firmly repeated. Now he shoved it into "drive," cut the wheel sharply to the left, tromped down on the accelerator and drove headlong through two garbage cans and right into the house! And when I say "into" I mean into.

Several large sections at the bottom of the trailer caved in and went flying away and the car came to a crashing halt under the house—just to the left of the porch and Bettie.

I ran forward then to jerk his door open, but he hit the button and I was locked out. With mounting hysteria I pleaded for my dog. "Please let Mickey out of the car!"

But, instead, he hits reverse again, cuts the wheel in the opposite direction and guns 'er. Just in time, I jumped out of the way of this 16 Tons of killer car. He missed me, but this time he takes out the post pillars that are holding up the overhead porch and the whole works come crashing down with a thunderous BANG!

This didn't stop the out-of-control death wagon, though. He keeps on backing out and screeches onto the community driveway....

The driveway now looked like the aftermath of a blitzkrieg strike by a German Messerschmitt in World War Two.

I'd lost it all by now. Blindly ignoring the danger, I ran out in front of the Juggernaut and hollered, "I WANT MICKEY! PLEASE LET MY DOG OUT!" And now I'm at the passenger's door, yelling my head off. Surprisingly, he did stop the car and he tried to hit the door lock, which works automatically off a single button. But he hits every button except the right one. The windows are going up and down, the windshield wipers are flopping wildly. Everything's moving but the door button. Then, he finally hits the right one. I jerk the door open, the dog jumps out and the 16 Ton car careens off down the driveway on a mad zig-zag course. I stand there with mouth agape, watching it disappear out of sight.

Staggering back into the house, I mumble to Bettie, "He can't make it down the hill and back. He just can't!"

Calmly, as if she had long ago resigned herself, she only said, "I just hope he doesn't kill someone else, too."

When I sat down in the den and looked at my hands, I noticed they were visibly trembling. "Shall I go after him?" I asked.

"No, just pray," she answered. Sometimes in life, religious conviction is the only help for the troubled.

"How long can this go on?" I asked her.

"Until one day, when I walk out the door, and on my way out I'll say, 'Okay, you just go ahead and sit there and drink.' And I'll be gone."...

Then we heard a car pull up. Cops? No, it was him! He had actually made it all the way down the hill and back in one piece. Walking in the back door, carrying a six pack of Heineken Dark, Merle Travis looked at me and congenially said, "Let's pick."

"Huh?" I probably gasped.

He grabbed up a guitar and started flailing away, and pretty soon I joined him. And I learned new and various ways to play diminished and demolished chords, by the most knowledgeable music teacher a guy ever had—and all for free.

"Gary, you've only got three choices of diminished positions and also it's much mellower to play your augmented position like this (demonstrating) rather than on just the first four strings."

It crossed my mind that right now he might be more concerned about other matters, such as extensive damages to the house, a possible if not probable eviction notice, a bent "16 TONS" license plate—to say nothing of a sprung car door and smashed front end, and of the very possible arrival of the police and perhaps another barricaded standoff, or even a shootout.

But no… "Ya see… when you find the third harmony note, which is the tonic chord…"

But, all good things have to come to an end. So, despite Bettie's urging that I spend another night, I made a rather awkward exit at long last. My very sincere parting words were, "GOD BLESS YOU BOTH!"

And I still haven't caught up on my rest.

But I've learned a lot on the guitar.

—Aftermath—

The day following my departure from Bedlam, Bettie did likewise. And on that same afternoon a neighbor finally called the police after seeing Merle running up and down the community driveway without any clothes on (I never heard if he was waving his Smith & Wesson, as well). Soon, a police car and an ambulance pulled up. The cops took away his guns and the ambulance hauled Merle away to the hospital, where they pumped out his stomach—an "overdose," his neighbor told me.

By now you'd think that I, too, would have had an overdose—of Merle Travis. But not having a lick of sense myself, I find it impossible to write off ol' Trav. And so, I have just spent several more days with my music teacher, helping to fill in Bettie's place as his house pal. Merle has high hopes for her return sometime in the near future, and I'm happy to report that he is currently on the wagon, and he vows that he has taken his last drink—ever.

Uh huh.

Well, miracles do sometimes happen.[499]

Merle was alone in the trailer. Bettie was gone, staying with Jack and Marge Rogers, and it appeared that this time she was not coming back. This time was different than all the other hundreds of times in their twenty-two-year relationship.

Merle, being of the old school, was virtually helpless without a female companion to take care of him. Merlene notes:

I got divorced in '76. And dad would always come visit, and then Bettie left him. He was a mess. If I'm remembering it correctly, she was gone and bank accounts were cleared out and all that.

Now, I don't know, he didn't really ever talk finances with me, and he wasn't good at that stuff anyway. But he was living in the mobile home, and I worried about him being alone, 'cause he's never—my mother said he could never be without a woman, ever. And she was right. I was worried about him. So, I'd check on him.

And then one time I said, "I'm gonna come out and visit you." "Well, honey, I don't know if today's good." I said, "Why? Where are you goin'?" "Oh, the place is a mess." I said, "I'm coming out. Maybe we can go get some dinner or something." And I went out there, and he was a mess. He wasn't drunk, but he was just depressed, and sad. I always worried because he didn't eat. And he was like a child. If he was concentrating on this, and then he'd go, "I'm gonna write this let—that's a nice looking pen, let me see what that pen is like." And then he'd pick up that pen and maybe use it and he'd go, "You got that blue in there, maybe I'll just see what that—What's this box of cookies? Well, I'm not hungry. What is this thing?" He was all over the place.

He conducted his life like that. He would open a can of beans—the man would live on beans—'cause he was hungry. Then he'd eat a couple bites. His hunger pains would go away, and then he'd be distracted. Then he'd go do whatever he's gonna do and come back and he'd be hungry again, but he'd go get another can of beans. I must've picked up twenty-five cans of half-eaten beans through that whole house.

He loved Mexican food. He'd go out and he'd order, "I'm gonna have me some enchiladas, and maybe a tamale, and that's what I want." He'd order the meals where you get the enchilada and the tamale and the rice and beans. He'd look at me and smile and go, "Gonna eat this now."

Then he'd take his fork and start mixing it all together, and then eat it like it was a chore. He never just enjoyed food. He *talked* about enjoying food. He could make you want to eat ham when he sang that "Hominy Grits" song. You want hominy grits. "That was a fine meal," he'd say. You could always get him to eat Mexican food.

So anyway, he was kind of a mess there. I said, "You gotta get outta here, Dad. You're just getting depressed, and this isn't good. Why don't you go see Cliffie, or your friends?" He said, "Well, maybe I'll take a…" He said, "I've got a friend in Oklahoma, and she's been after me to come take a visit and I think I will." I said, "Okay."

Then the next thing I knew, he said, "Honey, I'm gonna take a little time off and I'm gonna go visit my friend Dorothy Jean Thompson in Oklahoma. She's Hank Thompson's ex-wife and we used to hunt together. She's a little gal, but she can take down a bear the same size I can." And he was bragging on her, and all this stuff. And I said, "Good, good, you'll have a good time." And off he went.

He came home, and he was happier. And then a little while later, he says, "I'm gonna go visit my friend Dorothy Jean again." And he'd come back. And then he called me and said, "Can you pick me up at the airport?" and I said, "Yeah." He says, "Well, I'm bringing Dorothy Jean home with me. I think it's about time you meet." I was kinda like, "Hmmm?"

I'd say, "Do you like her, Dad?" He goes, "Oh, she's a friend. I've liked her for a long time." Dorothy was so nervous to meet me, I guess. But I loved her immediately.[500]

Merle had known Dorothy since she and Hank Thompson began dating in the late 1940s, and the two had remained close friends through her divorce from Thompson, which became final in 1970. She lived in a big, isolated home on Lake Tenkiller, thirty miles outside Tahlequah, Oklahoma. It was a deluxe ranch home that Hank had built for the two of them with his music royalties in the mid-1950s. It was made for entertaining: it had a swimming pool, a large bar area, a small elevator for loading musical equipment, even a recording studio. It had fireplaces, a pink bathroom with a Cinderella tub and asymmetrical his-and-hers pink sinks, and a walk-in closet built for hanging heavy rhinestone-laden Nudie suits. There was a boat dock, from the time in the late 1950s when Hank and Dorothy had owned matching Chris-Craft speedboats.

Since her divorce she had lived there alone—the couple never had children—and welcomed visitors. Merle and Bettie stayed with her many times over the years when they were driving through Oklahoma. Merle and Dorothy had had a mutual attraction even when they were married to other people—Hank Thompson had even joked about it, decades earlier. Now that they were both single, their attraction blossomed into a full-blown romance over the space of a few months.

Dorothy saved many of her letters from Merle. The ones he wrote her in July, after Bettie left, show him pouring on the honey as thick as he could muster:

July 21, 1977

My darling Dorothy:

Even though I have just spent a week in heaven with an angel, I still feel like an hour-old ghost starring at eternity... and you say you're in shock!

Last night after talking with you, the happiest heart on earth spent a night beating through night I never knew to be so black, but so filled with beautiful dreams—of you, my love.

When I was finally awake, only you were on my mind....

There'll be no bolts of lightning, no thundering in our love—let God do those things with his elements. We can laugh together at it all, and walk in the rain holding hands.

And I'll say to you, Dorothy, I love you more and more.

—Merle—

July 23, 1977

Dorothy my own very angel:

Do you mind if I dream? Dream that in our very hearts we hold what makes dreams a reality.

Let's dream together—let each of us realize that the bitter years were nothing more than a bad yesterday, that, even though we're not children, we can look forward to a tomorrow of laughs and loves with youth's very potentiality of loves and all it has to offer.

I'll hold you close—close—and you can teach my yearning flesh so much!

Tonight, my angel (Dorothy), sang to me of years to come that makes me want to go out and flaunt a banner and shout to the world—"She Loves Me"—

Then go to bed thinking of the many days ahead that shine like a jewel in the "belly button" of the only girl (you, Dorothy, darling) that I ever really loved.

—Merle—[501]

Dorothy received a dozen letters like these in July and August 1977, and Merle succeeded in igniting a prairie fire of country romance between the two old friends. Having spent less than a month as a single man, he had found his next life partner.

Merle found himself in divorce court in August, where he wrote his notes on the proceedings by hand in a small notebook:

> The deputy yawned. He sat against the wall in a chair at Superior Court in Van Nuys. He'd been there since 9:00 in the morning, and it was 20 till 11:00...
>
> The mating call of the hippo Hurricane Doreen had left the streets wet at the unlikely time of August 17, 1977. As Californians say, it's most unusual.
>
> My spouse's attorney just walked in, avoiding my eye, as did my former wife who sat against the wall behind me.
>
> The judge, a balding man, just came in, and is questioning a young Mexican construction worker.
>
> Lee Perkal, my attorney just came in an whispered good news to me. My alimony was cut from an asked 1700 dollars a month to 500.
>
> All the time my thoughts were on my darling Dorothy, and my light heart sang.
>
> We'll make it, because we'll love our way down thru the years, and laugh at discordant bygones.
>
> I've needed a girl like Dorothy, oh so long—and alas, I wind up with the real live doll that I've admired so long, and now love so very much.[502]

Merle was living in Oklahoma with Dorothy by September, where he received warm letters from his closest friends, including Nudie the Rodeo Tailor and Jack Rogers, wishing him well in his new situation. In October 1977, Merle was once again nominated for the Country Music Hall of Fame. As a three-time nominee and a three-time loser, he must have wondered if he'd be passed over yet again. Merle and Dorothy showed up at the Hall of Fame ceremony, and this time, Merle was inducted into the Country Music Hall of Fame. The country music community, who had known Merle and Bettie Travis as a married couple for decades, was abuzz: Merle Travis had showed up to the ceremony with Hank Thompson's ex-wife, Dorothy. The gossip kept the phone lines busy for days. It was as much of a scandal as this group of mostly sixty-year-old, polyester-clad, highly religious, mid-1970s Nashville country music stars could absorb.

The next phase of Merle's life had begun. He was Oklahoma bound.

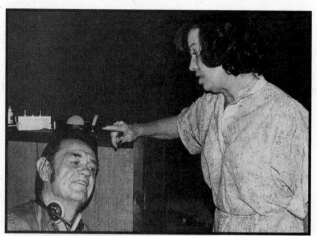
Merle and Dorothy at one of Merle's CMH recording sessions in
Albuquerque, early 1980s.

CHAPTER 9

RAINBOW'S END

Merle moved to Oklahoma to be with Dorothy Thompson in the fall of 1977, and
he would live there with her until he passed away in 1983. In many ways, these
were the best years of his life, as he felt he had found his soul mate. His legacy
and reputation had been cemented with his induction into the Country Music
Hall of Fame and other honors that he would receive in these last years. In other
ways, these were the most difficult years of his life, as his health suffered from the
decades of self-abuse. He found renewed interest in recording thanks to a new
deal with CMH Records and made more recordings in those last few years than
he had since the 1940s. Merle's last years were those of a man living on borrowed
time—he made the most of them, but eventually the decades of hard living caught
up with him. This chapter tells the story of these final years.

Merle and Dorothy's appearance in Nashville at the Country Music Hall of Fame induction ceremony on October 10, 1977, was their first public outing together. Merle received the highest honor in his field. That year he was the only awardee, and at that moment only the thirtieth inductee (as of this writing there are 139, so it is still a rare honor). Many of Merle's good friends were present—indeed, the elite group of beloved Hall of Famers included many of his close friends. Through all the trials and tribulations of the last twenty years, he could finally hang his hat on an achievement that age and ailments could not take away from him.

The spotlight was on the sixty-year-old star and his new fifty-year-old sweetheart, and even though many were unaware of the problems he and Bettie had faced over the years, his friends were pleased to see him with a new lady friend, grinning from ear to ear. Interviewed by WSM personality Ralph Emery as the ceremony ended, Merle was eager to let everyone know about Dorothy Thompson:

Ralph Emery: "Do you mind if I talk to you a moment? Merle, how are you?"

Merle: "Fine, Ralph, how are you?"

Ralph: "I was just talking to Roy Clark, who won the instrumentalist of the year award, and he had some misgivings about accepting it in front of you and Chet Atkins."

Merle: "Well, he deserved his, I didn't deserve mine."

Ralph: "Well, I know people used to say something to you about writing '16 Tons' and you would always say, 'Oh, that old thing.' Merle Travis tonight became the newest member of the Country Music Hall of Fame, and I imagine they're jumping up and down back in Muhlenberg County."

Merle: "Well, I hope so. That's home to me. That is, I was born and raised there.... At this time, I'm living in Oklahoma."

Ralph: "Merle, I thought you lived in California..."

Merle: "No, since July I've been living in Oklahoma..."

Ralph: "Merle, I want to join everybody who offers their congratulations to you. I think it is a most deserved honor."

Merle: "Thank you, Ralph. And it's good to see you again. You all be well."

Ralph: "Thank you, same to you. Now, you said you live in Oklahoma City?"

Merle: "No, I live in Tahlequah. That is the capital of the Cherokee Nation down on Lake Tenkiller."

Ralph: "Why do you happen to live down there?"

Merle: "Well, I went through divorce some… quite a while ago, and this young lady named Dorothy Thompson, who I've known for thirty years, and me and her got to runnin' around together and fell in love… and so we just decided by golly, we'd just go down… and she owns a place down there, so I ended up down in Oklahoma."

Ralph: "Wow. I again congratulate you. Come back and see us here in Nashville."

Merle: "I sure will, Ralph."[503]

Merlene Travis-Maggini recalls:

I remember when I met Dolly Parton, the year Dad won the Hall of Fame. She was just adorable. She came out and said, "Uncle Merle!" She's sitting on his lap and he said, "Dolly, if I'd known you were going to be so famous, then I'd been nicer to you on the way up." She giggled. Then he introduced me to her. She said, "It's so nice to meet you." She asked, "Do you sing?" I said, "No, I don't sing." She asked, "Do you pick?" I said, "No, no, I don't pick at all." She asked, "Do you write?" I said, "No, I don't really write." Then she said, "How can you be Merle's daughter?" My dad said, "Dolly, don't you know? Talent skips a generation." I've never forgotten that.[504]

Merle's bronze bas-relief plaque has hung in the Country Music Hall of Fame and Museum since 1977, both in its initial location and now in the prestigious Rotunda at the Hall of Fame's new location, built in 2001. The inscription reads:

A man of seemingly limitless talents, Merle Travis of Rosewood, Kentucky, is known for his innovative guitar style, his distinctive singing, his songwriting—both humorous and serious—and for acting, and even his skill as a cartoonist. His varied talents gave him great popularity on radio, record, stage, film and television in a career of over forty years, and he stands as one of the most influential guitarists in the history of American Music.

Like a cat on his tenth life, Merle had been given another chance when many in the business had written him off, and he began working on a reboot of his recording career. During his last year or two in California, he had advertised himself as a recording artist for Shasta Records, the label run by his old friend Jimmy Wakely. Shasta released *Merle Travis—The Guitar Player, Singer and Composer*, an album of vintage radio broadcasts with one new recording. Merle also contributed one song to a Shasta compilation, *Saturday's Heroes*, along with Wakely, Gene Autry, and Johnny Bond—Merle's peers from the 1940s and 1950s. But he wanted to start recording new music again.

CMH (Country Music Heritage) was a Los Angeles–based record label that was producing a lot of classic country and bluegrass albums. Joe and Rose Lee Maphis had just released an album of acoustic bluegrass on the label, and Grandpa Jones, Mac Wiseman, and other friends were also CMH artists. Unlike many other labels producing this type of music, owner Martin Haerle gave advances to the artists, paid for recording sessions and hotels, took out substantial advertising in the press, promoted the releases on commercial radio, and stocked the records in truck stops and other places where fans of traditional country music would find them. Merle's initial pitch to Haerle was for an album featuring him and Joe Maphis recorded live at McCabe's folk club in Los Angeles. In early October, a week before the Hall of Fame ceremony, Haerle responded with a rejection letter, but one that hinted at something happening in the future:

Oct. 3, 1977

Dear Merle:

As per your request, I have contacted Ms. Margaret Rogers in regard to the proposed live recording at McCabe's. Ms. Rogers quoted a $2000 talent payment for your services in connection with the recording.

After careful consideration, I contacted Ms. Rogers today and advised her that we will pass up this opportunity to record you and Joe at this time.... Our total recording budget for 1977 is already depleted by prior commitments.

I hope that we will be able to work out something at some other time. In my book, you are still the greatest and I sincerely hope that your nomination for the "Country Music Hall of Fame" award will result in your election—an honor which you have long deserved.

Sincerely,

Martin Haerle

C.M.H. Records[505]

In late October, Merle and Dorothy went to Los Angeles, where Merle played the McCabe's show with Joe and Rose Lee Maphis, and also performed at a coffee shop at the University of California at Riverside, which advertised their upcoming guest as "The Newly Inducted 30th Member of the Country Music Hall of Fame." Somewhere around this time, Merle also borrowed a thousand dollars to help with his move to Oklahoma from his friend Nudie the Rodeo Tailor and left his Gibson Super 400 as collateral. Merle took his time repaying the thousand dollars—long enough that Nudie offered to sell the guitar to a few interested parties—but Merle eventually got it back.[506]

The couple settled in to life together in Oklahoma and began a loving relationship that would endure for the rest of Merle's life. Merle was a difficult and complicated man, in poor health and still drinking, but Dorothy seemed to understand him. More than any of his other significant others, she didn't try to change him; she just let him be Merle. Merlene confirmed to Ed Kahn: "Dorothy really loved him and he was everything to her. He was her husband, lover, child that she never had, friend. She was younger than him. He required forty-eight hours of every day and she was happy to give that. In a restaurant, she would put the cream and the sugar in his coffee."[507] The little notes, cards, and letters the two exchanged—dozens of which they saved—demonstrate their bond, a schoolboy-schoolgirl crush between two older country music showpeople:

Darling Dorothy:
I'm still in love with you—
"Hot Dang, Yea Boy!"
Regards,
Merle Travis

Hi Sweetheart—
Open those beautiful eyes
And read this:
I LOVE YOU!!!
—Dorothy

Dearest Dorothy:
Being very much in love with you (only forever, however), I feel compelled to inform you of this.
With my highest esteem,
Merle Travis

Merle, my love:
Have a fun day, and know that every minute I'll be loving and missing
you...
Love of my life, you are all things to me.
I love you!
—Dorothy[508]

Dorothy Thompson was a tough, petite Texas woman. She had a stern yet
beautiful face, her mouth usually dangling a lit cigarette. She had been taking care
of the Oklahoma lake house and property by herself for years, which was a full-
time job. Dorothy had also spent twenty years married to Hank Thompson, and
she knew intimately the exhaustion, excitement, demands, and disappointments
of the country music road-warrior lifestyle (Hank had also taught Dorothy to
hunt and shoot). She was exactly the sort of no-nonsense, take-charge woman
Merle needed.

By now Merle had revived his relationship with Merlene and Cindy, but his
relationship with his first daughter, Pat Travis Eatherly, was still broken down;
they had not seen or spoken to each other in years. Merle called Pat in December
1977, as recounted in Pat's book *In Search of My Father*:

Unofficial rumors led me to learn that the marriage between Dad and
Bettie had ended. He was now in the company of a longtime friend,
Dorothy Thompson. I was told she'd accompanied him on October 10,
1977, when he was inducted into the Country Music Hall of Fame. I'd
learned he was now living in Tahlequah, Oklahoma.

He had once again become a stranger to us. Then, unexpectedly one
cold December evening, he called.

"Patty, this here's your ol' Pappy." It wasn't hard to guess Dad had
been drinking. After a confusing time of trying to make sense out of his
conversation, he spoke these poetic and philosophical words. His thick
speech slurred:

Know me as I am,
Love me if you will,
Hate me if you must.

What did he mean by this? Was he asking me if I hated him? "Dad,"
I answered his unspoken question, "I don't hate you. There have been
times where I've been disappointed. There have been lots of times when
I didn't understand, but I don't hate you."

His conversation continued, and he began making ugly accusations about Mother. It had been over ten years since her death.... He'd avoided speaking of her through the years. Now, all of a sudden, he unfairly badgered her memory. When we finally hung up I tried to rationalize that once again alcohol was speaking and not Merle Travis.[509]

In December 1977, Merle slipped going down the lake house stairs and broke his knee. He was admitted to the Tahlequah City Hospital and released a day later. A letter he wrote to a family member, now in his archives, details the experience and introduces a local ex-deputy named Paul Center, who would later figure heavily in his life story:

We closed in Jackpot, Nevada, Christmas Day, 1977. We'd flew home and on the night of December 27th while Dorothy was talking on the phone to her folks in Waco, Texas, I was out in the "clubroom" trying to find out why my sterio [sic] outfit was playing through only one speaker. I thought I saw the mistake, and went out in the garage to get a screwdriver. Comin' back into the clubroom, which is set down three steps, I was hurrying along with only the firelight to see by. I hit the first two steps, but forgot about the third one, and stepped out into open air. I hit the floor on my left knee.

It really didn't hurt much, but I figured something was wrong when I felt down and my knee cap was about six inches up my thigh. I hollered for Dorothy, who came running. I told her my problem, and she sailed back to the phone to call Deputy Paul Center. I pushed the knee-cap back down and walked into the room where she was.

In a short time Paul come down the road, throwed me in his vehicle and took off for the hospital in Tahlequah....

The knee kept swelling up, because the doc took the cast off shortly after I was out of the hospital. Dorothy would run me in to Tahlequah and Doctor Masters would say, "Just a little fluid that needs draining. Nothing to worry about." He'd stick a needle in there and draw out about a half pint of red, murky fluid.

Dr. Masters told me I didn't need the crutches in an amazingly short time. I was walking around with a cane. There was only one drawback. When I'd bend my leg the least bit it would have no more strength than a paper leg would have. I'd forget about it, put a little weight on it, and fall flat. I done this falling in some of the most embarassing [sic] places. One night, out in the clubroom I was walking by a little fountain with a blowfish cured in archenich [arsenic]. I put some weight on the leg and down I went right on top of the blowfish. Dorothy was pretty concerned, because she was afraid the blowfish stickers would poison my arm. I was a little more concerned when I told her that I believed my wrist was broken....

Time kept going by, and the knee wasn't getting a bit better. Dorothy was more concerned than I was.... She insted [sic] we go to Tulsa and see a specialist. We did, and they throwed me in the St. John Hospital in Tulsa April 24th.

Doctor Roundsaville operated. I came out of it and was greeted by the jolly news that just a little longer and he'd have to have took the leg off at the knee!...

They had to knock me out and operate, you might say, to take off the cast and the wiring. I didn't feel a bit of pain after they took the rod and wires out. I walked up and down the hall on crutches. Doctor Roundsaville told Dorothy, "Take him home."

What Doctor Masters had done was just dig in there and get the busted up knee cap, and sew it up. He forgot to tie the ligaments and leaders, which caused it to be limber. What's more, they told me, he must have forgotten to wash his hands and tools.

It's close to a hundred miles from here to Tulsa, but little Dorothy drove up to spend time with me every day but about three. How she stood it I don't know. She's not all that strong. But she was raised on a ranch in Texas with a pretty big family. She knows all about hard work and hot sunshine and zero winters....

I am going up and down steps and walking around the house here. Dorothy says I don't have a limp. I believe I do when I sit for a while then get up....

This has not been the bright and shining year I'd like it to have been, but thanks to Dorothy I have not been lonesome and I still have a leg.[510]

While Merle was laid up with problems from his broken knee and wrist, in March 1978 he saw the broadcast of the episode of PBS's *Austin City Limits* that he and Chet Atkins had taped the previous year. It would be shown throughout 1978 and rebroadcast all over the United States for the next two years. Also in early 1978, Thom Bresh (then known by his given name, Tom Bresh) released his own version of Merle's "Smoke! Smoke! Smoke!" as the first single of his new record deal with ABC-Dot Records. The ABC deal was probably Bresh's best shot at the big time (he had had some records with MGM in 1975 and 1976). An article promoting the new release noted that Merle had "known Tom since he was a baby" and "expressed hope for a million-seller by Tom."[511] In March, Merle was honored on a television special called *Country Night of Stars*. The show, taped at Constitution Hall in the nation's capital, also honored other Country Music Hall of Fame members "Uncle" Dave Macon, Tex Ritter, and Red Foley. Tennessee Ernie Ford appeared as one of fourteen special guests for the nationally broadcast special.

Back in California, Merle's divorce with Bettie was under way. Bettie's lawyer was fighting for alimony; Merle was fighting to retain rights to all the songs he had written, since California law dictated that anything written during their marriage was joint property. The only thing going for Merle was the fact that he had written very few songs during their long marriage; he'd penned his biggest hits years before they ever met. Bettie revealed that she waited until Merle moved to Oklahoma to move back into the trailer at Lily of the Valley in an interview with researcher Ed Kahn: "I told him that we would part as friends but I couldn't handle the drinking.... I left but always thought that we would get back together again. I left, he stayed and then went to Oklahoma and I moved back in [to the mobile home in Saugus]. Until he married Dorothy, I thought he would come back home."[512] Scott Lynch, the neighbor boy at the Saugus trailer park, notes: "When Merle left, it broke our hearts. Bettie stayed in that mobile home for twenty [more] years."[513]

Bettie had kept Merle's 1962 Cadillac convertible as part of the divorce settlement. Merle loved the car and missed it more than anything else he had lost in the relationship. Merle arranged to buy it back from Bettie. Merlene notes:

Bettie had it, and he wanted it. He wanted to buy it back from her. So he gave me the money, all in cash. I don't remember how much now, but it was a lot of money at the time. He said, "I made an arrangement to buy it back from Bettie." He asked me, "Do you think you could pick it up for me?" I said, "Sure." I went out there, she was out in Saugus, and got it. I think that's the last time I saw Bettie. Knowing Dorothy, I think she arranged it and probably paid for it. I don't know that for a fact. But she's the one who encouraged him to get it back: "That's your car, Merle."

So he gave me the money, and Alan and I drove there and got it. Poor Alan had to drive. It's like a huge boat with these huge fins in the back, about as long as this room. It was white with red interior. He loved red, that was his favorite color. We got in the car, and it needed some work. We're driving home and it would periodically honk. And the lights would go off and on, on the freeway all the way from Saugus. We got him back the Cadillac.

And then he said, "I'm gonna take it over to Casa De Cadillac and have 'em fix it up for me." And I told him, "Ooh, that's gonna cost a lot." He said, "They've been good to me for years." So he got that car back, he loved that car, and they took it back to Oklahoma with them. He called me one day and he said, "The Cadillac's doin' great." And then he said, "I went and had it painted." I replied, "Oh nice, what color did you have it painted?" He said, "Yeller." A yellow car with red interior? Wow, that's a nice combination—not. And then he told me, "Yeah," he says, "it looks pretty, it's a bright yeller." He said, "I was drivin' down the street and a car full of black fellas pulled up next to me, and they said, 'Nice wheels!'" Then he said, "I knew I was in style." Can you imagine what he looked like driving around in that car?[514]

Merle loved his new surroundings in rural Oklahoma. He made friends with the local politicians, the surrounding Native Americans of the Cherokee Nation, and the local police (one interview subject who asked to remain anonymous revealed that the local deputies would give Merle marijuana they'd confiscated in drug busts). One friend whom Merle and Dorothy began calling on in times of need was an ex-deputy named Paul Center, who lived nearby. They thought he was a deputy and referred to him as such; they may not have known that Center had been relieved of his job and charged with a crime for lying to a grand jury about tipping off a local strip club that was about to be raided. During the subsequent state investigation and corruption scandal, Center was fired, and the local sheriff and undersheriff resigned.

Since Merle had left California somewhat abruptly, a lot of people were unaware that he had moved, including Thom Bresh, until he received a phone call out of the blue:

It was always a guessing game with him. He called me, asked me, "Where do you think I am now?" I had no idea. "I can smell the beans, I can smell the cornbread about ready to come out of that oven, honey sitting right in front of me. And, sitting right next to me, by the way. Beans, cornbread, ham hocks, some of my favorite stuff. I'm sitting here with Dorothy Jean Thompson. I'm right here with Dorothy Jean. And I don't know how much happier a fellow can get. I'm at Hank Thompson's house, it *was* Hank's house, it's Dorothy's house now. It's got a big bar, a nice bar that overlooks the lake, and if you pull the string, so to speak, this big picture comes up and there's double glass and a control room looks into the bar, and those Canon plugs (for connecting studio cables) are all over the place in the walls. So this doubles as a recording studio! I guess I can say it's my recording studio, it was Hank Thompson's, but..." So anyway, he was so thrilled that he had gotten together with Dorothy Jean.[515]

In 1977 Bresh began cohosting (with Myrna Lorrie) a country music television show out of Toronto called *Nashville Swing*. The show featured Bresh and Lorrie along with a variety of country music superstars. Merle would appear a total of six times over the show's run.

After Merle's knee and wrist recuperated, Merle and Dorothy began touring together. Now that he was a Country Music Hall of Fame inductee, Merle found he could get booked almost anywhere, and so he and Dorothy climbed into their Cadillac, Dorothy at the wheel, and got to work. They traveled to the West Coast in August, playing at the Great American Music Hall in San Francisco and the Zen Crook Music Festival in San Bernardino with Joe and Rose Lee Maphis, among other gigs. The following month found them in Nashville, celebrating the tenth anniversary of *Hee Haw*, hobnobbing backstage with Chet Atkins, Grandpa Jones, and Roy Clark. Merlene recalled:

> His favorite color was red. Out at the house in Oklahoma, they were having company over for dinner. Dorothy had to prepare all the food, and do all this stuff. And you know how far out they were from town. So, one afternoon Merle comes walking in the kitchen and he says, "Dorothy Jean, let's go to town. I've got a hankerin' for some red boots." She said, "Merle, we can't go into town. We've got company comin', I've gotta prepare all this food." Then he said, "Well, it won't take but a little bit of time to get some red boots." She said he was just like a little kid. "Well, we can go into town tomorrow and get you some red boots, but we can't now..." You know, explaining all the things.
>
> He said, "Alright, I'll wait 'til tomorrow." And so, time goes on, company comes, and he's upstairs, and then she says, "Merle, the company's here." They come down, and they're all sittin' around. Everybody is thinking, "It smells like paint in here." Dorothy said that Dad was just having this iced tea and smiling at everybody. She says, "Merle, it smells like paint. Do you smell paint?" He said, "No." She said, "I do." The guests said, "We do too." He says, "Oh, well, it might be my boots. I painted my boots red." He had spray painted his boots red. That's how he was.[516]

Cindy Travis remembers the new lease on life that Merle seemed to undergo after getting together with Dorothy: "I really loved when I would get to see them. Dorothy, she was so good for Dad, as well as just being a wonderful person.... He started sending us Christmas gifts (with his drawings on the outside brown mailing paper). We always knew it was Dorothy's doing, but for the first time in my life, it felt like we had Dad back."[517]

In 1978 Merle was contacted by the marketing team at Gibson Guitars, then based in Nashville, about nominating him for their new Gibson Hall of Fame. Merle was inducted in 1979, and he later spoke about it with pride on a television show interview with Archie Campbell.

Merle did some recording in Nashville in 1978 with his old friend Shot Jackson. But he was displeased with the results, and sent a stern letter to the owner of tiny Vetco Records:

Dear Lou:

If you were to record Shot Jackson when he had no finger-picks, or perhaps a couple of strings gone from his dobro, I'm sure you could understand if he asked you to not release the recordings.

If Mac Wiseman should wheeze through a few songs just after having his tonsils removed, just trying to be gallant and keep a promise, you'd understand why he'd object to having the songs released.

All my life I've depended on the fingernail of my right index finger as a must for whatever sort of guitar playing I've ever done. When I recorded for you, it was broken off completely, as I showed you. Shot gave me a metal pick, but it takes years to develop a touch playing in that manner.

It wouldn't help either of us to release what you have. I couldn't go around selling the albums saying that I played a few choruses on six of the tunes, and you couldn't really say that you were selling a Shot Jackson–Merle Travis album.

You're a likeable gentleman, and Shot's an old friend. I want both of you to understand. Just don't release the tapes we made and use my name.

I'm returning the $100.00 you advanced me. I hope that soon we can do some recording that we'll both not be ashamed of.

Your friend,

Merle Travis[518]

The album, which originally was to be released as a joint Shot Jackson and Merle Travis album, was released as *Shot Jackson and Friends*. Merle's photo was used on the cover as one of four "special guests." He couldn't have been happy. Listening to the album today, the recorded parts sound fine. There is some uncorroborated speculation that Bobby Barber, a world-class Travis picker from Georgia, overdubbed Merle-style parts on the album, replacing Merle's parts note for note, but played correctly. From this embarrassing moment forward, Merle would use a metal fingerpick on his index finger, and he quickly became adept with it.

Later in 1978, Merle worked out a deal with Martin Haerle and signed with CMH Records for an exclusive, multi-album contract. For a sixty-year-old country music veteran, it was a great opportunity: Merle would have complete control over the song choices and recordings, and Haerle was a devoted classic country music fan intent on sinking his own money into radio airplay, distribution, and promotion. Haerle, did, however, want the recording sessions, which he was paying for, done somewhere cheaper than Los Angeles or Nashville, but still at a studio he trusted to deliver a professional product—namely, John Wagner's recording studio in Albuquerque. Wagner told this author:

> Haerle was working in Nashville, Tennessee, with Starday-King Records and some of those types of labels. I had been doing some productions for those labels. Starday-King, I produced Wayne Cochran and the C.C. Riders for them. What happened, Martin decided at some point that he wanted to start a record label, and he decided that he would relocate in Los Angeles and work out of Los Angeles. Basically his whole idea was to pick up all the old classic music artists, and record and distribute them again. Because a lot of these people, the record companies had kind of brushed aside. They didn't care about them that much.
>
> Then, a friend of mine who knew Martin real well had told him, "You can do this a lot more economically in New Mexico than you can do it in Los Angeles." So Martin said, "Well, we'll try that."
>
> Joe Maphis said, after we did one, he told Martin Haerle: "We ought to get Merle Travis to come out here to New Mexico." Because he said that Merle was really burned out on the way Nashville had treated him, kind of like he was a has-been. He was not real up about trying to record or do anything. I mean, he was just kind of living his life in Oklahoma. Joe called him and said, "Merle, you need to drive down here and let's do an album together and just sell this." Talked him into it.[519]

Albuquerque may seem like an odd location for a studio, but it was on Interstate 40, the city had a major airport, and the studio was professionally equipped. Merle and Joe Maphis met there to record over three sessions on April 4, 5, and 6, 1979. Joining them were Billy Linneman on electric bass and Murrey "Buddy" Harman Jr. on drums—the rhythm section for the *Grand Ole Opry* at the time. Haerle obviously wanted all the firepower he could get behind Merle and Joe. The assembled group knocked out thirty tracks in those three days, just as seasoned professionals used to do it in Merle's younger days—performed live in the room with no overdubs. Merle told Mark Humphrey at the time: "Working with Martin Haerle at CMH has been enjoyable, because we were able to take our time. Human nature what it is, when they told us 'Take all the time in the world and do it the way you want it done,' me and Joe Maphis cut thirty tunes in about two and a half days, which is unheard of. But that's the way we wanted them to sound."[520] And John Wagner told this author: "We would just set them up and we didn't do hardly any, ever do any overdubbing or anything. That way we could just go through them as fast as they liked it: set it up, get the best isolation we could, and cut."[521]

Released in fall 1979 as *Merle Travis and Joe Maphis—Country Guitar Giants*, the album showcased the two musicians' broad repertoire. There were the obligatory guitar barn burners like "Alabama Jubilee," "Wildwood Flower," and "Cannonball Rag." There were classic country standards done instrumentally, like Grandpa Jones's "Eight More Miles to Louisville," Bob Wills's "San Antonio Rose," and Hank Williams's "I Saw The Light." There were Tin Pan Alley songs and big-band-era standards ("Somebody Stole My Gal," "Lover," "Say 'Si Si'"), blues songs ("Mose Rager Blues," "Memphis Blues,"), bluegrass numbers ("Free Little Bird," "Black Mountain Rag"), and Western ballads ("High Noon," "Back in the Saddle Again"). It was a showcase of what these two old masters could pull off, drawn from the thousands of times they had shared a stage on tour, or on television shows like *Town Hall Party*.

The recordings were intended to be commercial-sounding, modern recordings of vintage-style music. Listening to the CMH catalog today, the production style Wagner used gives the albums a somewhat dated sound—meaning, they sound very much like commercial recordings made in the late 1970s and early 1980s. Today, it is doubtful anyone would favor the 1979 rerecording of "Cannonball Rag" over the 1952 original, but when it was released, the CMH album was a breath of fresh air—real country music played by real country musicians.

Best of all, the double-vinyl LP format allowed a large physical space on the inside gatefold cover for Merle to write extensive liner notes. It was some of Merle's best writing, with detailed history and explanations of why each song was selected. Just one paragraph allows us a glimpse inside his head:

> Upon hearing this album, some well-meaning person will surely say: "Joe Maphis and Merle Travis are playing some tunes that are not country music. They're playing some modern, popular music." They will be right, partly, and wrong, mostly. "San Antonio Rose" is more modern than "Lover"; "I Saw the Light" is more modern than "Somebody Stole My Gal"; "Alabama Jubilee" was a popular vaudeville song before the writer of "Eight More Miles from Louisville" was born. With the coming of

country music shows on radio, we took many of the uptown, Tin-Pan Alley songs as our own, sped them up, changed a chord or two, forgot the introductory verses, sang them in our rural accents and were happy when years later friends would say: "I like the real country songs. The ones like 'Bury Me Beneath the Willow' and 'Li'l Liza Jane.'"

The front and back cover photos show Merle and Joe, clad in 1970s country denim fashion with their revamped 1970s-era instruments, standing in the New Mexico desert. John Wagner recalls: "Martin Haerle flew out a photographer to take that [cover photo]—a guy that had done some of his other album covers. They went down by the river, the Rio Grande, where you can kind of see the Sandia Mountains in the background."[522] The symbolism of the two distinguished-looking older men looming large in the foreground with a barren landscape behind them reinforced the album's concept of two giants in their chosen field. And indeed, *Country Guitar Giants* proves that Merle and Joe Maphis still had it. Their playing has the fire and passion of men half their age. The album sold well, at least above expectations, and has remained in print to this day through a CD release in 2003 and now an available digital download (as is the case for the rest of the CMH back catalog).

Without pause, Merle went back to Albuquerque in late May to record his next album project for CMH. The idea now was to rerecord definitive presentations of his greatest and best-loved songs, most of which were out of print and not commercially available in the late 1970s, for a double album called *The Merle Travis Story*. Once again the rhythm section of Billy Linneman and Buddy Harman was flown out to Albuquerque, where they were augmented by three veteran members of Bob Wills's Texas Playboys: Alex Brashear on trumpet, Herb Remington (whom Merle had worked with in 1944 in Los Angeles with Ray Whitley's band) on steel guitar, and Johnny Gimble on fiddle and electric mandolin. Gimble's friend Curly Hollingsworth, an excellent Western swing piano player, also joined the group of seasoned musicians.

In a mere two days of marathon recording, the group managed to get twenty-four songs committed to tape, destined to be another double-vinyl LP with a gatefold cover. *The Merle Travis Story* was ambitious. It includes, of course, Merle's biggest hits, "Sixteen Tons," "Dark as a Dungeon," and "Smoke! Smoke! Smoke!" as well as all of his chart records for Capitol: "Fat Gal," "I Like My Chicken Fryin' Size," "So Round, So Firm, So Fully Packed," "Divorce Me, C.O.D.," "Sweet Temptation," "Steel Guitar Rag," "Cincinnati Lou," "When My Baby Double Talks to Me," "Kentucky Means Paradise," "I'm a Natural Born Gamblin' Man," and "Bayou Baby." There were songs Merle had recorded for the *Folk Songs of the*

Hills album, "I Am a Pilgrim," "John Henry," "That's All," and "Nine Pound Hammer," and a smattering of his best-known instrumentals, including "I'll See You In My Dreams," "(Goodbye My) Blue Bell," "Dance of the Goldenrod," and "Up a Lazy River." Even "Re-Enlistment Blues" from *From Here to Eternity* got a reworking. There was one new composition, "Start Even," a humorous talking blues with acoustic accompaniment.

The *Merle Travis Story* covered a huge swath of Merle's professional career. The detailed liner notes were written this time by folklorist Archie Green, who had met Merle in 1960 with fellow researcher Ed Kahn. As with *Country Guitar Giants*, Merle's most diehard fans would probably never favor the 1979 rerecordings over the original Capitol records from the 1940s and 1950s, but they weren't CMH's target audience. This album was made for people who bought albums in truck stops and department stores, who still remembered the name Merle Travis but couldn't find his old, out-of-print material. By that measure, *The Merle Travis Story* was a success. It was a current product that Merle could promote and CMH could sell.

Martin Haerle was excited, and his excitement rubbed off on Merle. Throughout Merle's life—from his days at WLW radio with the Drifting Pioneers, to his period of high output at Capitol in the 1940s, to his brief but productive period of sobriety in Nashville in late 1960s—he always worked best when he had a project on which to focus his creative energy. And Haerle at CMH gave Merle almost unlimited opportunity to devise new artistic ideas.

Merle's next CMH project was an album of mostly new material, *Light Singin' and Heavy Pickin'*, recorded in September 1979, again at John Wagner's studio in Albuquerque. The backing group was nearly the same as *The Merle Travis Story*, but with Texas steel guitar legend (and namesake of the MSA pedal steel brand) Maurice Anderson taking the place of Herb Remington. The group tackled a batch of new and old original songs that Merle had assembled. A few were songs he had recorded for Capitol in the late 1960s: "Voo Doo" was one such from 1965 that Capitol hadn't issued, and "Moon over the Motel" and "That Same Ol' Natural Urge" were both songs that Capitol had issued as singles, with little promotion, in 1966. There were a few older numbers that got a redo, including "Knee Deep in Trouble," "Green Cheese," and "Kinfolks in Carolina," which Merle had cut for Capitol in the early 1950s. "Dorothy" was a new original that Merle had written about his sweetheart. Among the other new originals on the album, "Dorothy" stands out from the rest, for the simple reason that you can hear him pouring out his heart with every line, complete with references to his own fragile health:

"I had a test, made of my chest
And best they could tell,
I'd certainly fell... for Dorothy
I had a chart, made of my heart
And the cardiogram
Proved that I am
In love with Dorothy"[523]

Even as Merle and the assembled Western swing band were recording *Light Singin' and Heavy Pickin'*, Haerle wrote Merle a letter, excitedly revealing his plans for the next batch of albums he wanted to release, which included ideas as varied as Charlie Daniels–type hit singles, a Merle Travis history album, and a new album of Brown's Ferry Four–styled gospel songs with Grandpa Jones and Sonny and Bobby Osborne.[524]

Having a record label president express this much excitement and personal interest was foreign to Merle, who had sputtered at Capitol since the mid-1950s. He felt revitalized and grateful for the new opportunities. Merle and Dorothy took to the highway, bringing his renewed vigor to shows all over the nation. Throughout 1979 they traveled to places like the Turah Pines Bar in Missoula, Montana; the DuQuoin Farm and Folk Festival in southern Illinois; a Western music festival with the Sons of the Pioneers in Claremont, California; and Club Lorelei in New York City. They traveled to Indiana for the Bean Blossom bluegrass festival (where Merle saw his old friend, harmonica legend Lonnie Glosson from the Cincinnati days), the Champlain Valley Fair in Vermont with Minnie Pearl, Stages Music Hall in Chicago with Jethro Burns of Homer and Jethro, and the Crossroads Theater in Nixa, Missouri, where Merle jammed on stage with father-and-son Travis pickers Jerry and Randy Buckner, who called themselves the Springfield Coonhunters.

The year 1979 also saw the inauguration of the Merle Travis Fingerpicking Contest at the Ozark Folk Center in Mountain View, Arkansas. Merle's old friends Grandpa Jones and Ramona had recently moved to Arkansas and were behind the new music festival. The contest became a yearly event, and still takes place today. When it first started, Merle would show up and serve as judge, along with other luminaries in attendance, and perform a concert.

In the midst of all this activity, including some of the busiest touring he had ever done, Merle was back on the bottle. As it had throughout his life, his alcoholism had various manifestations: drinking but able to play, drunk and unable to play, sobered up for a short while, passed-out drunk and in bed for days. Dorothy dealt with it as best she could. She understood it, but it made life difficult. Merlene Travis-Maggini recalled:

One time, when he was with Dorothy, he was visiting my little "doll-house" place I had after I got divorced. He was standing at the sink, and he got one of those great big Looney Tunes glasses, a big tall glass, and he put a bunch of Scotch in there, maybe two-thirds full, and then he put Kahlua in on top of the Scotch, and then he put milk on top of that. The milk was for his stomach. He said he had learned about this from the local Cherokee Indians out there in Oklahoma, he said they called it a "Wahoo."

I just stood there. He said, "You may not want to watch me drink this." I said, "Why?" He said, "Well, sometimes I have a hard time keeping it down, but I need it for my nerves." I told him, "If you can drink it, I can watch." I thought I could discourage him, silly me. So he drank that whole glass straight down, and then stood there at the sink holding on, and literally—you know when you're going to throw up, but you try to hold it back? That's what he was doing. Just gagging and just forcing it to stay down. And then finally it stopped—that kind of gagging, not opening his mouth type of gagging, but that type of gagging to fight to keep it in. Finally, it stayed down. He was a bit sweaty, and his hairs were a little bit messed. He looked over at me with that big dimpled grin and he said, "That was a 'Wahoo.'"[525]

Merle had somehow made it into his sixth decade. His muscle pulling, bad knee, and other ailments contributed to the visage of a man who walked a tight-rope between life and death, but the music and his new surroundings kept him going. According to Michael Robinson: "By God, '77 to '83—he did pretty good lasting that long in as bad a shape as he was in."[526]

Merle returned to Albuquerque in 1980 to record one of the most ambitious guitar projects he had ever undertaken: a double album of instrumental guitar music, *Merle Travis Guitar Standards*. The backing band featured Billy Linneman on bass; Nashville A-team rhythm guitar man Ray Edenton; Elvis Presley's former drummer, D.J. Fontana; and Billy Liebert, Merle's old pal from the 1940s, on keyboards. Thom Bresh came out to New Mexico for the sessions as coproducer with John Wagner. Bresh recalls: "He called me one day and said he had this thing from CMH, and said everything was on top of each other, you can't hear the guitar, and the piano ain't up enough. John Wagner is a nice guy, but can you mix that again somehow? I remixed it for him. He said, 'Absolutely that's what I want to hear, now I can hear everything.'"[527]

The album's theme—guitar standards—was a curious one for that moment. The music was impressively unhip but performed with the reverence and love it deserved. The release failed to find an audience, but it was a stellar album none-theless. It included the music Merle (and Billy Liebert) had grown up with: Tin Pan Alley and jazz standards ("After You're Gone," "Don't Get Around Much Anymore," "Hot Toddy," "Bye Bye Blues," "Sweet and Lovely," "Tea for Two"), Mexican marches ("La Marcha de los Mexicanos"), gospel songs ("On the Jericho Road"), and other American popular music ("Roaring Twenties Medley," "Trib-ute to Ted Lewis," "Mack the Knife"). Again Merle took the opportunity to write his own liner notes for the gatefold. They are splendid, but space constraints pre-vent reproducing them in their entirety, so a few paragraphs will have to suffice:

> I have a fantastic collection of things that are not worth a penny, yet I wouldn't sell them for a million dollars. They're called memories. Here's a few tunes that connect with a lot of them in a Hollywood movie sort of way. When I hear these old melodies my memory-projector starts turning. A bright light shines through the stored up footage and they're projected right there on the silver screen of my mind in glorious color.
>
> Once again I can see that skinny kid sitting on top of an L&N boxcar riding through the green countryside of western Kentucky. The kid is me and I'm heading for the southern Indiana town of Evansville. I have two brothers living there. My older brother, Taylor, works in a machine shop. I'll force him and my sister-in-law, May, to put up with me. The other brother, John, we called him by his middle name then, which was Melvin. He works when he can find something that pays a dollar or two.
>
> The year is 1935. The United States of America wears shoes with holes in the soles. There's a number of patches on Uncle Sam's trousers and he eats what he can get. Years later these times will be called the Great Depression. Once, John, who's a little more than two years my senior, helped load some barrels of vinegar into trucks one day and came out of it all with a possible seventy-five cents. He took me to a movie. I can see this husky young vinegar-loader walk up to the ticket booth at Loews Theatre and order two tickets. With our fifteen cent admissions, we go into the cool darkness of the theatre. We're all set to see the film version of the famous Broadway production, *Showboat*. We're watching a young Alan Jones sing to the beautiful leading lady, Irene Dunn. The song is MAKE BELIEVE. The movie crew in my mind yelled, "It's a take. Print it!" Print it they did. Forty-six years later I recorded it for this album.

Merle kept busy and creatively engaged with liner notes and other writing projects when he was at home in Oklahoma. He wrote liner notes for other CMH projects besides his own, including for his old friend Mac Wiseman's double album *Songs That Made the Jukebox Play*. Another guitar magazine, *Guitar World*, began publishing in 1980, and the very first issue featured Merle's in-depth piece "Merle Travis Remembers: The Fingerpickers of Muhlenberg County." The piece was well written, humorous, and educational, and thereafter the magazine retained him as a contributing editor. Over the course of the next year, Merle wrote many informative articles about his old friends Chet Atkins, Roy Lanham, Joe Maphis, and Paul Bigsby.

Merle and Dorothy had been living together for three years now. Merle was firmly of the old school and wanted to get married, but Dorothy was still receiving alimony from Hank Thompson, and would continue to do so as long as she stayed unmarried. Thompson, who remained friends with Merle, humorously referred to Merle as his "husband-in-law."[528] Merlene told this author: "He told me he wanted to marry Dorothy, but Dorothy didn't want to get married because she got alimony until she remarried or died. And she had a big place to take care of out there, and she did it by herself. He kept after her until, I guess, she said she would. I guess that was good for them, but I don't know how good it was for Dorothy financially."[529] The ceremony took place in California on May 24, 1980, at the San Fernando Valley home of their old friend Nudie the Rodeo Tailor. Wesley Tuttle was the best man and remarked that he had been present for all of Merle's marriages except his first (it's likely that Tuttle didn't know Merle and Ginny Cushman had been "Mexican married for one day," as Merle put it in his "Merle's Memories" list of life notes). Indeed, Tuttle had been present when Merle married Tex Ann Nation, Judy Hayden, Bettie Robinson, and now Dorothy Jean Thompson. In attendance were many of Merle's old friends, including Harold Hensley, Tex Williams, Rex Allen, Eddie Dean, Jimmy Wakely, and Thom Bresh. Merlene remembered the occasion:

> Nudie and Bobbie [Nudie's wife] walked Dorothy down the aisle. I think Nudie and Bobbie were more excited about Dad getting married than Dad and Dorothy were. They had an outdoor party area set up. Dorothy told me, "They each latched an arm around my arms, almost carrying me. You'd think I was gonna run away!" You would have been in heaven because every old country star from California was in attendance.[530]

In late 1980, Merle's old friend Dolly Parton, whom he had known since her earliest days in Nashville as a member of Porter Wagoner's road show, released her album *9 to 5 and Other Odd Jobs*. It included a version of Merle's "Dark as a Dungeon," which brought about a welcome cash infusion after the album spent ten weeks at number one on the charts, was licensed for release in almost every country on the planet, and was certified gold ("Dark as a Dungeon" has proved especially resilient through the years—it has been recorded by Johnny Cash, Willie Nelson, Rose Maddox, the Country Gentlemen, Harry Belafonte, The Weavers, John Cougar Mellencamp, Wall of Voodoo, the Seldom Scene, Queens of the Stone Age, Charlie Louvin, Amy Grant, and Bob Dylan, to name a few).

Since the 1940s, Merle had used his old Martin acoustic guitar with the Bigsby neck exclusively. But in the late 1970s, through Doc Watson's recommendation, he began playing a Mossman acoustic. Mossman guitars were made in small quantities by Stuart Mossman of Winfield, Kansas, and the company began prominently featuring Merle in their advertising in 1980, 1981, and 1982. He was quoted in the ads saying: "These guitars sound better than any of the new Martins I've played."[531] Another guitar that Merle began playing in the early 1980s was a Japanese-made Alvarez-Yairi acoustic that he found at a music store in Oklahoma. Although they never had a formal endorsement deal, Alvarez began using Merle in their advertising, touting: "Merle walked into a music store down in Oklahoma, and walked out with an Alvarez-Yairi DY-90."[532]

Also, now that Gibson Guitars had put him in their Hall of Fame, Merle got in touch with Rendal "Ren" Wall at Gibson Guitars headquarters in Kalamazoo, Michigan. Merle was still fuming that Gibson had replaced the top and neck on his original 1952 custom Gibson Super 400 without asking him. He wrote a letter to Wall and asked him to take a 1950s Super 400 he had purchased and combine it with the original pieces from his altered Super 400 to make one guitar as close to his original one as possible:

> Dear Mr. Wall
>
> One day Shot Jackson called saying he had an old Super 400, and wondered if I'd like to buy it. I went down to his music store and there was an ol' timer with good wood. I bought it. It had been tinkered with and the strings didn't go straight over the screws in the pickups, which ruins the presence of sound, as you know. I never used it.
>
> Now that you have the two guitars [speaking of his original Super 400 and the one from Shot Jackson], here's what I wish you would do. I'll ask only one thing (maybe a dozen!). If possible, put the fancy (?) head, plus the fingerboard on the two piece neck... and use the old back (the one the airlines hasn't got to yet) with the nicer maple. If you could only find some material similar to the stuff the original armrest and pickguard was built of... I'll dance at your weddin'....
>
> Call me anytime, your friend,
> Merle Travis[533]

Instead of hacking apart two vintage Super 400 guitars to make one instrument, Gibson came up with an idea: Merle could donate his original Gibson Super 400 (at this point a mishmash of original and replacement wood and parts) to the Country Music Hall of Fame and Museum in Nashville, and in exchange, Gibson would make him a new Super 400 to take its place, using the instrument Merle had bought from Shot Jackson. Ren Wall remembers:

At that particular time I was in artist relations, and so they made me kind of the head of that project. Then I delivered actually two of them to Merle. The first one, there were some things about it that he didn't like, so we wound up building another one. The first he didn't like, there was a couple of letters that were leaning. One of the inlays on the fingerboard wasn't quite where you could see it just right. Real particular on what looked unprofessional, as he put it: How come this letter is tilted? And honest to goodness, you had to really look, the letter was maybe angled just enough to worry after you looked at it a while. "Yeah, I guess you're right." It was one of those things, it was so miniscule that I don't know if he had a bad day going or what, but anyway, I just shook my head. "Yeah, I see what you mean." There was a couple of things. The fingerboard inlay and the headstock where it says "Special." It wasn't the same font as the original, of course; that's what he was concerned with. He wanted to flare the binding in the f-holes a certain way. Make sure it had an ebony bridge, Gibson medium strings. At that particular time his sound was P-90s. That gave him the thump on the bottom end that you couldn't get with a humbucker. Of course the top two-piece tiger-striped carved top is what was the big change. He wanted to change the volume pots and also to put a "dead" switch [an on/off switch] on the bass side, I remember that. Also, the first one that we built only had one bracket holding the finger rest. He wanted two brackets holding it instead of one because, he said, everybody knows that it's going to work loose after a little bit of time. And also the truss rod cover only had one screw, and he said, "Well, that's going to work loose and it needs two screws." And so it just went on and on. And when I went back to the factory, they were really surprised.[534]

The second guitar that Gibson built for Merle was visually based on his original 1952 Super 400, but with one important difference: Merle wanted the arched top to be solid, uncarved from the back side, and made out of figured quilted maple. The solid top hidden in what looked like a hollowbody instrument was a similar concept to the 1951 Bigsby electric he owned for a short time, as well as the

Guild Solomaster. Ren Wall remembered building the second one and delivering it to Merle in Oklahoma:

> The company decided, well, we'll try it one more time. When we built the second one, he was happier than a skunk. He was just really happy with it. I flew it out, and he picked me up at the airport in his yellow Cadillac convertible with the bull horns on front. His wife was all dressed up in her Indian garb and he was sitting in the back seat. You're talking about a *memory*, when he picked me up the airport and the top was down on that yellow Cadillac convertible. Both of them fully dressed in their turquoise jewelry and their Western wear, and Merle singing "Sixteen Tons." "You load Sixteen Tons, what do you get?" He was singing that in my ear when we were driving back to Tenkiller Lake. He was all dressed up, too, in his Western outfit, and they let me drive with the top down. We drove back up to Tenkiller Lake, up there where he lived, and I spent the day with him, and had lunch with him, and got a lot of pictures. We went down to the Indian reservation and he bought me some moccasins, and I had him sign the inside. But anyway, we spent time together and I never will forget, we went down to the Indian reservation and there was a place to eat. We stopped in, and while we were in there, he drew a cartoon character of me with a cowboy hat on and the "Everlasting hills of Oklahoma." I don't know if you know that song, but he wrote that on there and wrote a little kind of a cartoon character. He was really good at that character drawing and stuff like that.
>
> What was funny to me was that at his home, he had bars just like a prison on all of his windows. And so it was pretty well fortified. And when we were there, went up to his bedroom and was getting ready to dress for something and he took out that old Guild guitar that was made that kind of looked like a circus guitar and it had so many colors and binding. And then what amazed me too was that in his bedroom he had grocery sacks, paper grocery sacks, full of pictures. Just all around the perimeter of the wall, a lifetime of pictures. We got along pretty good, and we thought a lot of each other.[535]

The new Super 400 was finished in 1981. It was a shiny, revamped, modern version of Merle's signature instrument. It had modern features found on other Gibson instruments of the early 1980s (including tuners with built-in, fold-out string winders that Merle apparently didn't discover for some time after receiving the guitar), but Merle insisted on old-style single-coil P-90 pickups even though Gibson hadn't used them for years. Merle knew his tone, and he loved P-90s.

In October 1982, Merle donated his original Gibson Super 400 to the Country Music Hall of Fame, where it remains to this day. Eddie Pennington remembers that Merle removed the pickups and the tailpiece before donating it and replaced them with stock units from another guitar because he valued the original ones too much.[536] Of course, as previously mentioned in this book, by this point Merle's "original" Super 400 only contained the original back and sides of the body and the headstock overlay. The top on the body, neck, pickups, and hardware had all been changed out over the years. At the dedication ceremony, Merle remarked: "This guitar has been around the world with me. I have one daughter, 30 and another 33 [years old], and this is my other child who falls somewhere in between the two. It's a truly fine instrument." Ren Wall was quoted in the same article regarding the new Super 400: "We spent over a year on this guitar. It is not only one of the most expensive models, but it's one-of-a-kind and the only one we'll ever build."[537]

Merle played the new Super 400 on the majority of his shows for the remainder of his life. Today it resides at the Kentucky Music Hall of Fame and Museum in Renfro Valley, Kentucky. (Merle is a member of the Kentucky Hall of Fame there, inducted posthumously when it opened in 2002.)

Merlene was dating a musician named Alan Maggini in the early 1980s, and the couple set a date to get married in July 1981 in California. Merlene asked her father to come with Dorothy, and to play at the wedding. Merle was excited about the idea, but he ran into a snag in early 1981. Merlene recalls:

He wound up in the hospital with phlebitis [an inflammation due to blood clots in the legs]. I think it was January 1981. They put him in the hospital, and the doctor said to him, "Well, you've got to stop drinking." And he said, "I can't." And the doctor goes, "No, this is not a joke." He said, "I've heard that your daughter is getting married in July." And he said, "Yes. I'm going to be at her wedding, and she's even asked me to play at her wedding." And so, the doctor said to him, "Well, if you want to see your daughter get married, you need to stop drinking now, or you won't live that long." He said, "If you start drinking again, you won't last; you'll be dead in three months."

And so he stopped completely. So when we started planning the wedding, I said to Dorothy, "We just won't have any alcohol at all, so Dad's not tempted." She said, "Don't do that to your father. That would be so humiliating to him." She said, "You go on and live your life. And he's not drinking at all. And he's doing just great with it. And so, you go ahead and you serve whatever you want to serve." And I said, "Okay, I never thought about it like that."[538]

It may have been more than the phlebitis that finally jolted him into reality. Sometime in the spring of 1981, he injured himself and broke some ribs, which also caused him to curtail his drinking, as detailed in a letter from Dorothy to Merle's brother John Melvin in May 1981:

Dear John M.:

Miracles come in small packages—or broken ribs as in our good fortune. For some unknown reason, the bottle is being ignored, not entirely, but what a change! Merle is like the Merle that we both know and love so well, and I am happier than I've ever been. He doesn't get out of bed and go down for "a little taste" as he calls it, but he does have a drink before supper, or at times, one before lunch as we don't eat breakfast....

I almost feel ashamed to thank the good Lord for those broken ribs, but I've prayed long enough for something to happen, or at least I feel that way. He is overweight from drinking, not eating as he blames it on. He weighed 188 at the doctor's office last Monday. Now, he wants to get out of that size 42 as he has some beautiful new suits in both 36 and 38. He is the kindest, most thoughtful, considerate, loving man in the whole world![539]

The California wedding brought Merle and Judy Hayden, mother of Merlene and Cindy, into the same room for the first time in more than twenty-five years. Merlene recalled:

Prior to the wedding, they knew they were going to have to see each other. I don't know the date this happened. My mom used to watch my little girls—my daughters were little girls at the time—and she used to always say, "Taking care of my grandbabies saved my life." She was just enjoying—it gave her purpose to get up and get over there.

When Alan and I were going to get married, of course she knew Dad was back in my life and everything. And things had calmed down. She'd ask about him now and then, and once in a while tell a story. She wasn't so angry anymore. As I used to say, it comes with old age. My mother was sixty-one when she died, by the way. But at the time, I thought that was old.

One day she said, "Merle and Dorothy are going to come visit me today." I said, "What?" She responded, "Yeah, is it okay if they come here?" I said, "Yeah." So, they did, and everybody was there. John [Wesner] and my mom, and Dorothy and Dad. Dorothy is the one who told me about it. Because I asked Mom, "How'd it go?" She told me, "It was nice." She added, "Your dad did a little picking; I did a little singing." Then she said, "Dorothy is just delightful."

But I remember when Dorothy told me that it was a little awkward and a little quiet when they first got together. But at one point, because Dad had his guitar with him, he said, "Do you still sing like an angel?" And she said, "Are you still the best picker around?" He replied, "Well, I don't know about that." Then she said, "Well, I don't either, but if you want to pull out your guitar, let's give it a try." And apparently Dad played and Mom sang. Dorothy said, "Merlene, it was just beautiful. It was like the hatchet was buried."

They were both there at the wedding. Not a lot of interaction, because it was hotter than hell that day, and it was an outdoor wedding. It was a day for the records.[540]

On that same trip to California, Merle did an interview with Judy Raphael for *Country Rhythms* magazine. Most of the interview covers the same subjects Merle spoke of on dozens of occasions, but a few paragraphs reveal something about Merle's own view of himself, the kind of music he played, and his place in history:

Judy Raphael: "You have said somewhere that you never considered yourself a country musician. What do you mean?"

Merle: "I never considered myself a 'real' country musician. I think of people like Grandpa Jones, or maybe somebody like that; I can play 'Sweet and Lovely' and a few classics, and I can have a calling contest with your grandmother about the top tunes of the 30's—I knew all of those. But never in my life did I think, 'I'm a country musician.' Oh, I'm not trying to dodge the fact that I booked myself that way, and I followed the music. But never did I think of myself that way. But we, you see, we have pigeon-holed music so! Put this over there under 'C' for cornball [country] or that into Rock 'n' Roll. You get it all messed up! What's pleasing to the ear is music. A female crow listens to the male crow and he sounds very good."

Judy Raphael: "Do fans that type you one way or another annoy you?"

Merle: "Well look, if you're talking about my style of playing I'll give you an example of how hard it is to classify music. We held a little jam here last night and we made a tape of it. Quincy Snodgrass would get off a snappy jazz rhythm intro, and Harold Hensley would take off on the fiddle and it sounded like Stephane Grappelli or Joe Venuti. Ten minutes later, we'd get some harmonies going, singing Bob Nolan's 'This Ain't the Same Old Range'—then we'd end up doing some negro spirituals. Now what would YOU call that tape? A blues tape? A jazz tape? A negro spiritual tape? Now, in my career, they've come up to me and said, 'Oh, you're the guy that wrote "Smoke, Smoke, Smoke." I'd say, 'Yup, and I wrote three or four more, too.'"[541]

A month after the wedding, Merle and Dorothy were in Mountain View, Arkansas, for the annual Merle Travis Thumbpicking Contest. One of the other judges that year was Marty Stuart, who by that time was a member of Johnny Cash's touring band. Stuart recalls that weekend in his book *Pilgrims: Sinners, Saints, and Prophets*:

Merle Travis was a genius. He was a guitar great, prolific song-writer, journalist, teller of tall tales, actor, cartoonist, watch repairman, inventor, jack of all trades, and one of country music's pioneer statesmen.

I hung out with him for a weekend in the summer of 1981. We were in Mountain View, Arkansas, to judge the Annual Merle Travis Thumbpicking Contest. Guitar players who imitated Merle's style had come from all over the world to compete for the prize and to be in the presence of Travis himself.

We decided before we'd heard any of the contestants that regardless of how good or bad they were, we were going to declare all of them the first place winner. Merle's theory was that anybody who survived the winding mountain drive to where the contest was held should win for just making it up the hill. And we both thought that the main judge should be the bad guy to the ones who didn't place. Not us.

Outside of the contest, it was mainly a weekend of roaring, playing music, telling stories, and playing cards. On Saturday night after the guitar show had ended and the true winner was finally determined, Travis and me struck up a serious poker game back at the hotel. After a couple of hours, I had played down to my last ten dollars. I had what I thought was a winning hand with three kings. He edged me with three aces. When I lost my last ten dollars, he said, "Well, let's yak a while. I hear you're thinking about leaving J. R.'s [Johnny Cash's] band to go out on your own to be a country music singing star." I told him that I was.

He said, "Do you sing better than you play cards? If you're really going to do it, you're gonna be in for plenty of ups and downs. When the bad times come, that's when you'll see what you're made of on the inside. Hard times will come, and they usually get around to passing, if you don't pass out first."

With that, he poured himself another shot of booze, then pointed to his glass and said, "Sometimes bad luck has a way of following a feller around his whole life. If you ever go through a streak of this kind of sour luck and you finally find the strength to fight back, you'll need a little inspiration to get you back on track." He held up my ten dollar bill and said, "I'll sell you ten dollars' worth of advice. What you do is:

1. Go buy yourself a new Cadillac.
2. Go to Nudie's and get some new cowboy clothes.
3. Find you a beautiful girl.
4. Find your guitar, dream up a new song, and start singing it.

Then, watch the future start brightening up.

Sometimes, you just have to start brightening it up one little day at a time. What I'm trying to tell you is to never let show business break your heart. It ain't worth it. But regardless of all of that, always give them a good show."

He was the best at it. He was from the old line of hillbilly royalty. They knew how to shine on the outside even when they were crying on the inside. He had the act mastered.

Not long afterwards, I saw him for the last time. He was at a stoplight at the intersection of Gallatin Road and Due West in Madison, Tennessee. He was riding in a canary yellow Cadillac convertible. The license plates bore the name of his most popular song, "16 Tons." His new wife, Dorothy, was chauffeuring him about. The aviator sunglasses and his turquoise bolo tie were the perfect accessories to complement his forest green suit that Nudie had made for him and fully embroidered with deer and acorns all over it. He was a vision.

While we were waiting for the light to change, I said, "Hey Trav, how're you doing?"

He lowered his shades and winked. That told me all I needed to know.

When he pulled away, the sun caught the reflection of the rhinestones on his suit. It looked like a million crystals had shattered into a mirror and were bouncing back up into heaven. As he faded out of sight, I started thinking about the words to one of his songs:

"I am a Pilgrim and a stranger,
Traveling through this wearisome land.
I've got a home in that yonder city, good lord
And it's not, not made by hand."[542]

The year 1981 again brought Merle back to Albuquerque to record—this time a solo guitar album featuring only Merle, and no band. The idea was to showcase his unique style of thumbpicking, unaccompanied. Thom Bresh came along to coproduce. Bresh notes:

He wanted me to come to Albuquerque and produce a record with him, just him and the guitar. But he had to go to Wagner's studio in Albuquerque. Got me a plane ticket, and I came in. If I had DATs [digital audio tapes], I'd have the damnedest album on Travis. He'd sit in the hotel room and just play the shit out of this thing. There's nothing wrong with him now. He sounds like the old Travis, but fine aged. The thumb was right on; the songs were cool. If I had a couple mics and a DAT machine, I would record him right there in the room, I'd-a been done. They were so perfect, so cool, he was drinking iced tea, puffing on the cigarette, leaning on that Martin.[543]

John Wagner recalls of those sessions:

There's an interesting story behind that. Merle wanted to do that album that came out as *Travis Pickin'*. I think I did it with him, and it was just me and him. Maybe Bresh was there; I can't remember. But we did the album, and we finished it. Then, a few weeks later, or a month later, Merle called me and he said, "I don't like the way I played on that. I want to do it again." So I said, "Okay." Well, Martin approved it and I said, "Okay, let's do it again." So he got in the car and he and Dorothy drove out.

He had that guitar, that Martin with the Bigsby neck on it. That's what he used. So he got there, and Thom, I know Thom was there for the remaking; he came too. We set up and we were all ready to go and Merle's already there to do it. He went in the studio and he was doing something and he dropped that guitar. It broke the neck off of it. The neck came off. So he was really bummed and really frustrated about that. We kind of stood around for a little while, trying to figure out what we're going to do. He kind of said, "Well, I don't have to get my guitar picks and all that." I mean, it was just one of these downer things, and he left and they left.

The album that he didn't like came out. It was *Travis Pickin'* and it got nominated for a Grammy.[544]

Despite Merle's unhappiness with the first recording session, *Travis Pickin'* is a tour de force, one of the best guitar records he ever made. His picking is in fine form, and he moves with breakneck speed through fast numbers like "Rose Time," "Too Tight Rag," "White Heat," and "The World Is Waiting for the Sunrise." There are masterful thumbpicking performances of old pop and Tin Pan Alley songs, of course: "There'll Be Some Changes Made," "You're Nobody 'Til Somebody Loves You," and "Love Letters in the Sand." Bob Wills and Cindy Walker's "Sugar Moon" gets a thumbpicking workout. Ballads and blues round out the album, with dynamic versions of "Born to Lose," "Night Sounds," and "Drifting and Dreaming."

The album's greatest achievement concerns something that producers often went astray with when recording Merle—namely, as was the case with the Nashville guitar album *Strictly Guitar* in 1968, a tendency to overproduce Merle's guitar. *Travis Pickin'* succeeds because it sounds like Merle playing by himself on a front porch, unencumbered by commercial demands. It is the Muhlenberg County style in its natural element. Listening closely, we can hear some of the reasons why Merle wanted to re-record the record. There are times where his playing is ragged. There are many passages where you can hear his fingers dragging on the low strings, making squeaks. There are undoubtedly songs that Merle felt he could play faster and cleaner. But throughout, the playing is incredibly soulful. As Mark Humphrey noted in a review for the *Los Angeles Reader*, "It has a relaxed informality and warmth that's satisfying in a different way: Like white lightnin' matured to become fine sippin' whiskey."[545]

The album's realness may have accounted for *Travis Pickin'* being nominated for a Grammy in 1981 in the Best Country Instrumental Performance category. It didn't win, but the mere fact that an acoustic album with little commercial appeal was nominated was a big achievement. Thom Bresh sent a letter of congratulations after *Travis Pickin'* came out:

> Travis,
>
> Your album *Travis Pickin'* is playing on the turntable right this minute as I write this note. In listening to it, I was compelled to write to you and just say how great I think it is. I'm so proud of you!
>
> Your guitar "speaks" with such character—there is but only one Merle Travis, and you're very lucky to be him. I shall always admire what you are to the world, and be forever thankful for what you are to me.
>
> All my love,
> Thom '81[546]

Merle also participated in a few other CMH recording sessions during this time. Joe Maphis cut a double album called the *Joe Maphis Flat-Picking Spectacular* to showcase his own mighty talents, and Merle appeared as a guest on five songs (the album also featured Arthur "Guitar Boogie" Smith and Zen Crook as special guests). Merle and Grandpa Jones teamed up on a CMH double album—an ambitious effort called *Merle and Grandpa's Farm and Home Hour*. The idea was to replicate a 1940s-era live radio broadcast, complete with a script (written by Merle) and a variety-show atmosphere that included songs by Merle, Grandpa, Ramona Jones, Alisha and Marsha Jones, and Joe and Rose Lee Maphis, and numbers featuring the entire cast singing with a large group of musicians backing them up. It was a wonderful concept, beautifully executed. It's not the type of album that one plays on a daily basis, but it's an inspired idea from a seasoned group of veterans who came of age in the golden era of live radio.

Grandpa was not entirely on board with Haerle and CMH, stating in a 1981 interview, "This last album, we don't think it's near as good as the other one that we did here [Nashville]. What he did, was took us out there and worked us, day and night, in Albuquerque, and he's got some kind of deal out there where he can do it a lot cheaper than he can here. But he did us… I don't know how many songs, fifty or sixty songs, I've come to the conclusion that he's just trying to get up a whole lot of songs, and then sell 'em, like Starday did."[547]

Merle did not live to see the release of the *Farm and Home Hour*. It came out in 1985, two years after he passed. On the interior, a banner across the top reads: "This album is dedicated to the late and great Merle Travis, an American Country Music legend." In addition, Merle participated in the recording of another album that did not see release until after his death, *The Clayton McMichen Story*. The tribute album was done in conjunction with CMH artist Mac Wiseman and was not released until 1988, the last album of Merle's on the label. Like the other CMH projects, *The Clayton McMichen Story* was an ambitious project, a double album covering McMichen's extensive repertoire. Merle and Joe Maphis also made a guest appearance on a CMH album by the group Badlands, featuring Zen Crook and producer John Wagner, which was as close to a modern Top 40 "urban cowboy" country act as CMH ever got. Although Badlands were not traditional bluegrass or country, Merle and Joe contributed solos on a cover of the Bob Wills Western swing classic "Big Ball's in Cowtown."

Merle and Dorothy continued to tour, playing almost every weekend at different locales across the country. While touring through Texas, they stopped to see Pat Travis Eatherly and spend some time with her children. Their relationship was still strained, but both parties tried to make the best of it, as Pat recalled in *In Search of My Father*:

Then on February 21, 1982, it happened. Dad came to visit in our Fort Worth home. I recorded the date in my Bible with the notation, "A long overdue visit with my 'earthly' father." Later I learned that he too recorded this date on his calendar with the notation beside it: "Feudin' Over!"

It started with a phone call on Valentine's Day. During the course of the conversation Dad proposed, "Pat, let's forget yesterday and start a new tomorrow." He eagerly accepted our invitation to visit this time.

I'll always remember that late afternoon when my family watched the big black Lincoln Continental pull into our driveway. Dorothy was behind the wheel, and she quickly made her way around the car to help Dad gather his pipe, glasses, and other paraphernalia. I smiled to myself as I caught a glimpse of the clothes, guitars, and record albums filling the backseat. The slowness of Dad's movements and a few added wrinkles reminded me of the time that had passed.

"Hi there Pat, how 'bout a big hug for your ol' Pappy?" When our arms wrapped around each other, I was grateful for this "new tomorrow."

Then he turned his attention to his granddaughters. During the last twenty years I'd focused my attention on being a mother to three daughters. Dad hardly knew them. The girls were nineteen, seventeen, and ten years old.

Tricia, our youngest, was taking violin lessons in school. She could play one little ditty that sounded kind of country. She placed a chair on the wide fireplace hearth, turned on an overhead spotlight, and stole her grandfather's heart when she announced, "Grandpa, your stage is ready."

Dad's eyes lit up when he saw Tricia taking her violin out of the case. "I want to play with you," she announced.

"Dorothy," Dad asked his wife, "would you get my Baby Martin out of the car?" Soon Dad and Tricia were playing away to the tune of "Bile Them Cabbage Down." Tricia giggled as Dad sang the lyrics. "Who-o-o whew, play it, Little Tricia," Dad would inject like he had done on *The Atkins-Travis Travelin' Show*, a Grammy Award–winning album. Tricia didn't show tremendous promise of inheriting that Travis style, but to me it was the most beautiful music I'd ever heard. Our hearts were finally in harmony.

Afterwards, Tricia looked at Dad and noted, "Grandpa, you sure do play your instrument well." Dad gave the Travis chuckle I was familiar with on his talk record.

There were a few more visits like this one. Sometimes Dad came to our town, Fort Worth, to play on the Johnny High Country Music Revue at Will Rogers Memorial Center... my pounding heart nearly leaped out when Dad introduced me from the stage....

"I'd like you to meet the most beautiful girl in the world, my daughter Pat and her ugly (ha) husband, Gene Eatherly." He added, "And I want to tell you I have three wonderful granddaughters, Dawn, Tricia, and..." He went blank. He couldn't remember our middle daughter's name. I squirmed. I felt embarrassed for him, but my heart was so full of love there was no room for anger. [Merle was prone to such brain-synapse lapses, especially after his pill and alcohol-related neurological damage. Dorothy Travis insisted to Eddie Pennington in later years that Merle hadn't forgotten Pat's daughter's name, but rather his brain merely got "stuck."[548]] After what seemed like an eternity, a fan and friend of ours, who regularly attended the show, yelled out, "Paige!"

"That's it, Paige," Dad flashed one of his big smiles. "Did you ever get stage fright?" he added, cleverly covering his blunder.

I breathed easier and found myself enjoying his show as much as any of his fans. After his performance, the crowd cheered him with a standing ovation. "That's my Dad," I responded proudly.

Finally, I thought, the past is forgiven. I was thankful I, too, could agree, "Feudin' Over!"[549]

Merle also managed to see his grandchildren in California, on a trip that he and Dorothy made to play at Knott's Berry Farm in Orange County. He hadn't spent much time with them as they grew up but related his pleasure at seeing his extended family in a letter he wrote to his brother, John Melvin:

How'do, John M. & Ev:

It never appeared to be much of a trip when my gal Dorothy and me set out for California to do two Tuesday nights in a row at Knott's Berry Farm, which is a place out in Orange County, pretty close, and in competition with Disneland [sic]. Just a lotta rides whirling around, kids runnin' in every direction and tourists with funny lookin' hats on throwin' balls at wooden milk bottles tryin' to win a fuzzy green frog with pop-eyes.

When we drove up to Merlene's house her new husband was puttin' in a new faucet combination over the sink. The old one had gone haywire and he was sweatin' and had plumber-like tools scattered all over the place. He broke off some pipes and couldn't get the broke off parts out of the wall, seein' as how they were an inch back in a hole.... Alan, Merlene's hubby managed to put the new rig on, turned on the water and it was working pretty well. Merlene looked at the mess and with her hands waving in the air, and with a side-ways sort of grin shouted, "So, who needs water!"

Our other daughter [Cindy] was in town, we learned. They had promised to bring the kids out to Knott's Berry Farm Tuesday night "to see Grandpa perform." Which they did. That was all we got to see of them for Merlene and her man was going on vacation the next day... but we at least got to see her eyes sparkle, like mom's used to, we were amazed at how the grandkids had grown, and Cindy, completely different from Merlene walked around about looking composed and beautiful.

Cindy has a semi-sad expression, but behind the expression is a keen sense of humor, and when she laughs her honey-blonde hair bounces about her shoulders as her head tosses. You'd like her... the quiet one... as a baby we called her ol' Stone Face.[550]

Cindy Travis remembers that night as well, with a twist Merle didn't put in the letter to his brother:

I moved to Aspen in 1976... and came back to visit Merlene in the summer of 1977. He was playing at Knott's Berry Farm, and Merlene said Dad was playing there, and let's go surprise him since I was in town and hadn't seen him in so long. We watched his set standing in the audience—it was outdoors, and really hot—and after he finished, we went up some side stairs to the backstage. Merlene went up to him, said something like, "Hi, Dad, that was great, and we're here to surprise you," and they gave each other a great big hug and kiss, and then Merlene stepped aside, and I was standing there with a smile. Then he looked at me, and said, "Well, hello there! And, who are you?" To which I replied, "I'm your daughter, Cindy." I felt very embarrassed, not only for myself, but also for him, as I'm sure he must have felt awful.[551]

Although Merle had been a guest on the *Grand Ole Opry* many times, now that he was in closer proximity to Nashville and a Country Music Hall of Fame inductee, he made a last-ditch effort to become a regular member. In a letter to *Opry* general manager Hal Durham in late 1981, he wrote about his jinxed effort in 1961 to join the *Opry* cast (using his oft-repeated story that he forgot to show up). Then he launched into a renewed effort, with gusto:

I renewed (heaven knows how) an old acquaintanceship with a mild, charming little lady whom I had first met in 1948. She was married to one of my best friends... and is still a friend. Cupid has his ways... and so it came to pass... we fell in love and were married.

Mr. Durham, you have allowed me to be on the *Grand Ole Opry* twice as of late. There's no way to tell you how much I appreciate it. My wife Dorothy enjoyed the trips (if possible) more than I did.

Once again I spun stories with Roy Acuff, brought to mind times of old when I first met "Oswald" and Jimmy Riddle. "Howdy" Forrester played fiddle at my wife's first wedding over 25 years ago... Grandpa Jones kept the likes of Billy Grammer in stitches with his stories... Hank Snow, a dear friend of yesterday beamed, as he introduced his beautiful singing partner to me... Marty Robbins sang one of my songs to me (without my request) in his dressing room... How wonderful to visit with Kirk McGee, Bill Carlisle, Vic Willis, Bill Monroe and so many of the older men... but then I got a hug and a kiss from the likes of Connie Smith, Jean Shepard, Jan Howard... and others who'd bow so low.... I love 'em....

I looked around, knowing I wouldn't see them, but their spirits said a silent hello to me.

Stoney Cooper, tall, silent and smiling... Patsy Cline, with her quips and vigor... Lester Flatt had a joke to tell in his slightly nasal voice... Skeeter Willis, tuning his guitar looked happy... Cousin Jody, with his nose touching his chin was all set to make people a little happier... Stringbean had a dandy of a fish story... Tex Ritter snorted as he laughed... Hawkshaw Hawkins towered above the rest, waiting for his turn... Jack Anglin and George Morgan were swapping stories... Jim Reeves, had a beautiful ballad in mind... Cowboy Copas, with his throaty voice was telling some funny story about Lazy Jim Day... Ira Louvin... tuning his mandolin...

They left the *Opry*... every act will follow sooner or later... It's nothing to be morbid about, and going is just as natural as coming... wherever they went, I want to go with them. And I want to leave from the *GRAND OLE OPRY.*

I'm as healthy as I've ever been in my life. I've spent 47 years of my life trying to entertain folks. I've never asked for a job, so let me put it this way.

If you can ever see fit to make me an *Opry* member, I'll be there. If you see a spot where you can squeeze me in, just holler... I'll be there.

—Merle Travis[552]

Sadly, this was one dream that Merle would never realize. Durham responded with a professional, polite, yet disappointing reply:

Dear Merle:

. . . The makeup of the *Opry* roster is a matter that concerns us daily, and while the changes take more time than we would like, we haven't found an appropriate shortcut. I am pleased that you are willing to continue to occasionally guest on our show until such time as we can logically consider a different arrangement.

I hope you enjoy a prosperous and happy holiday season, and please be aware that some of your most enduring fans are right here at the *Opry*.

Yours truly,

Hal Durham[553]

In December 1981, Merle was profiled in a Waco, Texas, newspaper and summed up his current mental state and plans for the future: "Just 'cause a fellow ages a little is no reason to stop. Fishermen don't stop fishing when they get old. I just love to play music. Lots of fellows older'n me are still playing, still going strong. I did decide it was time for a new career. So next year I'll be a regular on *Hee Haw* as well."[554]

Merle also appeared on the NBC television show *Barbara Mandrell and the Mandrell Sisters*. Barbara had come a long way since she was a houseguest of Merle and Bettie's back in 1968. She was now one of the biggest superstars in country music, and wanted to film an episode where she paid tribute to those who helped start her career. She told this author: "I had a television variety series on NBC with my sisters, Louise and Irlene Mandrell. One of the desires of my heart was to have on the show one week Joe Maphis, Merle Travis, Gordon Terry, and Norman Hamlet, who taught me how to play steel guitar. So I did. I had them all as guests, and it was amazing. It was wonderful to have them on there. That's when I last saw Merle."[555]

Merle was as busy as he had ever been in 1982. He began the year with a taping of *Down Home Country Music* on KLRU in Austin. He did shows in Fort Worth in February. New episodes of *Hee Haw* began airing in February featuring Merle as a guest. He also appeared on a television special among a stellar lineup of guest stars for a salute to Roy Acuff titled *50 Years, King of Country Music*. In May he returned to Fort Worth for another concert, then went to Mountain View, Arkansas, for the annual Merle Travis Thumbpicking Contest. In June he appeared at Fan Fair in Nashville, followed by taping thirteen weeks of *Hee Haw* over a couple of weeks in late June. In early August, Merle went to Memphis for their Memphis Film Festival, where he reunited with his old Western movie buddy Charles Starrett as well as dozens of film stars from previous decades. Dorothy wrote about the event in a newsletter called "Travis Travelins": "August 4th through 7th we'll be at the Memphis Film Festival, Holiday Inn Rivermont. This is the first year Merle has been invited, and we are so excited. They will show old Cowboy movies 24 hours a day in several rooms at once, they post the movies and time they will be shown in each room, and they will be running some that Merle made years ago. It will be so much fun to see Merle's eyes light up among old friends."[556]

Dorothy also wrote about another movie opportunity that came Merle's way in the summer of 1982: "BIG NEWS! July 20th brought a call from California with a request. Seems as how they want Merle to be in a movie with CLINT EASTWOOD! If the scheduled filming goes as planned, Merle will be through by (August 20), so I'll probably start hookin' it down the old super-slab for Oklahoma and meet Merle in Tulsa. Oh yes, the working title of the movie is *HONKY TONK MAN*. Again, he will be among friends of many years, and be making new friends of the others. Gee, I'm all goose bumps."[557] *Honky Tonk Man* was a Clint Eastwood vehicle loosely based on the life of Jimmie Rodgers, the "Singing Brakeman." The bulk of the film has Eastwood's character dealing with tuberculosis, as Rodgers did, and covers his recording sessions right before his death. Merle joined several of his old friends, including Texas Playboy Johnny Gimble, who played Bob Wills; singer Ray Price, who played Tommy Duncan (Bob Wills's most famous vocalist); and latter-day Texas Playboy and Buddy Holly sideman Tommy Allsup. Merle played the guitar with the "Texas Playboys" group portrayed in the film. His time on screen is brief, but memorable.

In 1982, Dorothy began having serious health problems of her own. She eventually was hospitalized and had to have heart surgery. Merlene recalled: "She did smoke a lot. They both did. But she smoked all the time. She was one of those, get up in the morning and make the coffee with a cigarette in her mouth. She eventually had to have triple-bypass surgery."[558] When Dorothy was hospitalized and during her long period of recovery, their local ex-deputy friend Paul Center stepped in to drive Merle to his appearances. Center began referring to himself as Merle's "road manager" and inserted himself into Merle and Dorothy's lives.

Merle returned to Albuquerque in late 1982 to record a project he had wanted to do for a long time. He had always loved blues, and he especially loved the dialects, stories, and African American ethnic flavor of real, down-home acoustic blues. His next project was to be a blues album sung in African American dialect, with spoken-word introductions before each song also in authentic Southern black dialect (Merle had already done this once, on a song called "Payday Come Too

Slow" on his album *Songs of the Coal Mines*). The idea was to demonstrate his influences as he remembered them. He wanted to call the album *N****r Blues* because that was what the music was called in Kentucky when he heard it as a youngster—he defined it as a style of music, not a racial slur—but Haerle wisely objected. The working title was still undetermined when Merle went to Albuquerque to record. Thom Bresh confirms:

> Merle wanted to cut an album called *Black and Blues* and tell the stories of how the black men would talk and then sing the songs the way they did it. He pitched it to the CMH guy, and the guy didn't want to do it. He was messing with Lane's [Lane Brody, Thom's girlfriend at the time] twelve-string and recorded demos in Travis's home studio. He would tell the story, and then he would play it. He was doing all the dialects. CMH took all the intros out and just used the songs. Travis said, "It's called 'n****r blues,' is what it is. I'm not trying to sound nasty, but that's what it's called. It's a style of music."[559]

Merle and Haerle never resolved the conflict about the concept or title. Bresh remembered: "He showed up here in Nashville and said he had something he was 'extremely un-proud of,' it was retitled *Black 'n' Blues,* and 'all the stories were taken off, and the dialects, and now I just sound like a drunk old fool!'"[560] It is true that without knowing the concept behind the concept album, Merle's singing sounds like no other recording of his—strange, high, and affected. It takes some getting used to, and Merle's adaptation of a black man's singing style and vernacular would hardly be politically correct today, but he does a good job of interpreting the material as he felt it. His bluesy guitar playing is on point, and the song choices are excellent, from blues standards "Stack O'Lee" and "Key to the Highway" to "Merry Christmas, Pretty Baby" to "(I'm Gonna Move Way Out) To the Outskirts of Town." Some hillbilly blues fit right in the mix, including "Dry Bread," "Cocaine Blues," and "Step It Up and Go."

The album contains not one but two songs about cocaine. Besides "Cocaine Blues," Merle also covered "Take a Whiff on Me," a pro-cocaine anthem originally released as "Cocaine Habit Blues" by the Memphis Jug Band. Lead Belly recorded a version with the "Take a Whiff on Me" title in 1934, probably the one that Merle was most familiar with. The song has also been performed by a variety of white performers, including North Carolina fiddler Charlie Poole (as "Take a Drink On Me"), Woody Guthrie, and more recently Old Crow Medicine Show. The origin of the song goes much further back, to the turn of the century, where it derived from a popular number called "Hop Joint," which had similar lyrics with many regional variations. On his version of "Take a Whiff on Me" (as well as the rest of the album), Merle played a twelve-string acoustic guitar as an homage to Lead Belly's instrument of choice. The guitar was a cheap Takamine twelve-string that Merle bought en route to Albuquerque, and only used for this project (it is now on display at the Duncan Center in Greenville, Kentucky).

The promotional literature for the album noted how Merle's covers of cocaine songs from the 1920s and 1930s were timely in the 1980s gilded age, when the drug was popular again. Despite Merle's protestations that he never did cocaine, the two pro-cocaine songs and the song "Whiskey," sung from the perspective of a highly inebriated sot, were true-life tales from a man who had spent much of his life pursuing an elusive high. The photos on the album cover show him posing as an old itinerant musician—worn-out blue jeans, gingham shirt, floppy hat, and 1930s-era bluebird arm tattoos exposed (he normally kept them covered up, especially for professional purposes). Once again Merle was dressing the part of a character, but the end result made him look like a beat-up legend, down on his luck.

Despite Merle's best intentions, and some unique musical performances, the album that was eventually released as *Rough, Rowdy and Blue* came out as an afterthought in 1986, three years after Merle's passing. One of the few reviews upon release said, "The package has the earmarks of a collector's item; it was recorded in '82. Travis died the following year.... The *Rough, Rowdy and Blue* collection spotlights Travis more as a soul-flavored blues singer than as a traditional country balladeer."[561]

Merle kept touring. For the most part, he performed to adoring crowds who were happy to be in the presence of a legendary Hall of Fame guitarist, singer, and songwriter. Still, it was impossible to ignore how aged and frail Merle looked. He was working a lot of dates in Texas around this time since Dorothy, who was from Waco, had hooked him up with a booking agent from her hometown. Always a hotbed of country music, Texas offered many opportunities for work, but not all of them were glory gigs. Some were just work. A November 1982 letter to the editor in the *Bee-Picayune* of Beeville, Texas, detailed what must have been one of the most humiliating gigs of Merle's career:

> Travis appeared, free, with public invited, on Sunday night, Oct. 31, at the Crow's Nest, Enlisted Men's Club at NAS [Naval Air Station] Chase Field. His performance was fantastic. The only complaint from this country music lover was some undesirables in the audience making derogatory remarks, some of which I am quite sure were audible to Travis, such as "Hurry and get your autographs before he drops dead." Travis will celebrate his 65th birthday this month and God grant him the right to celebrate many, many more.... Sunday night's audience was NOT a true picture of Texans.... Thank you for hearing me out. I was

rather ashamed of Beeville for not turning out and embarrassed for some
of those who did with their loud foul mouths.

—L. Ruth Haggerty[562]

Merle was sixty-five years old in the spring of 1983, when two career high-
lights came his way. Merle and Dorothy were invited to a special honoring of
country music stars by then-president Ronald Reagan at the White House. They
attended but were lost in the shuffle of 450 other country stars and industry people,
and Merle did not get a picture taken with the president. Also that spring, Merle
and Dorothy were invited to be special guests at the Kentucky Derby Breakfast at
the governor's mansion in Louisville. It was an excuse to get dressed to the nines
and hobnob with political and entertainment luminaries as well as Kentucky's
richest citizens. Former president and first lady Jimmy Carter and Rosalynn Carter
were there, as well as future president and first lady George H. W. and Barbara
Bush. Celebrities Foster Brooks, Connie Stephens, Lena Horne, Tom T. Hall,
Hank Williams Jr., Bill Monroe, and O.J. Simpson were in attendance. Merle
was given star treatment and took photos with Governor John Young Brown Jr.
(whose big claim to fame before he became a politician was making Kentucky
Fried Chicken into a successful national franchise). In the photo he kept of himself
with the governor, Merle is beaming with pride.

In the mix of nightclub shows, country music fairs, and folk festivals was one
show on Labor Day weekend in 1983, when Merle appeared at the Delaware Bluegrass Festival and a young writer and musician named Kenny Mullins approached
him to do an interview. Mullins told this author:

In '83, Merle was gonna play, and I was doing some writing for a local
magazine, and I talked them into letting me go up there and do an
interview. I knew everybody at that festival because I went there all the
time. This particular year, Merle Travis was supposed to play, and I was
real eager 'cause I never met him before, and all my life he was the guy
who got me started playing guitar. Him and Chet Atkins.

I went there to see Merle at the festival and do the story, and you
know, I was pretty nervous. I just got my nerve up, and I knocked on
the back door. He said, "Come in," and I opened the door and there he
was sitting there with his wife. He looked at me and said, "You must be
the feller from the magazine." I said, "Yes sir, I sure am." He picked up
that Gibson Super 400 and handed it to me and he said, "I hear you're a
picker; pick me somethin'."

That's not what I was expecting. Merle gave me his guitar and I'm
like, "Oh Lord, what am I gonna do." All I could do was stare at it. So I

took the guitar and I sat down. He offered me a thumb pick and I tried it on and it didn't feel right, but he told me I could keep it, so I kept it. He had grooves cut on the inside of the thumb pick, I guess to keep it from sliding off his thumb.

So, I pulled out one of my own and I sat down and I made sort of a half-assed attempt at playing "Cannonball Rag." I kinda got through it. He smiled and said, "Well, let me show you somethin'." He came around behind me and he said, "Now, you do the pickin' and let me make the chords here." He got behind me and started making a chord, 'cause I wasn't playing the right chords, see. He made the chords, and I did the pickin'. That was so nice; that was just great.

He was real nice to me, his wife was real nice to me, and we talked for a long time. I ended up not doing the story, though, because he was not in good health. He was obviously in a lot of pain 'cause we went outside the trailer to sit on the steps, and in order for him to sit on the step, he had to just lower himself so easy, and he grimaced the whole time, just to sit down. He was real skinny, but his stomach was really distended. I was pretty shocked, actually, at how sick he was. That's one of the reasons I didn't write the story, because I didn't want to go into any of that. It just kind of shocked me.

We talked about Joe Maphis. I asked him about that record he made with Joe Maphis back in the early sixties. He said, "They made that in two hours." I said, "Really?" and he said, "Oh yeah, we just came in, we just sat down, we had a six pack, I drank three, he drank three, and we were done." Like, wow, they didn't even have tunes; they just made it up on the spot.

We did talk about the blues, Merle and I did, and he liked Blind Blake a lot. That was a big influence on him. Lonnie Johnson, of course everybody liked Lonnie Johnson. He mentioned Blind Blake and Reverend Gary Davis. He met some of these folks. Merle played the Newport Folk Festival back in the sixties. He met a lot of those guys, Mississippi John Hurt. He didn't call him an influence, but he knew him and he liked the way he picked. He called Blind Blake an influence.

We were talkin', and I asked him, well, who did you learn from. He brought up Ike Everly and Mose Rager. Then I asked him, "I hear there's a real bluesy thing in your sound, where'd you get that from?" He said, "Well, everybody worked in the mines had the blues." He said, music back where he come from, "Everybody picked together, black folks and white folks, and everybody had the blues together." I do remember that line was I think a direct quote.

He gave me a business card and he said, "If you're comin' out that way, you give me a call and come out and see me and we'll put on a pot of coffee and pick some music."[563]

In the fall of 1983, Paul Center took over the reins as Merle's driver, as Dorothy was too sick to travel. Dorothy gave Center strict instructions not to let Merle drink, but Merle's old habit got the best of him, and he began drinking heavily again. Merlene notes: "All of a sudden, this Paul Center was his road manager. And he had me fooled, too. I thought he really cared. And maybe he did. I can't blame him—Dad is the one that drank—but he didn't stop him. He said one time, 'He's a grown man; if he wants to drink he can drink.' Dorothy was really upset about that."[564]

Eddie Pennington spoke extensively to Dorothy in later years, and she revealed how fragile Merle was. The years with Bettie had left Merle feeling worthless, and without a permanent home in the world. When Merle began drinking again, he was afraid that Dorothy would divorce him. Dorothy revealed to Eddie a tender moment between the married couple at their Oklahoma house:

Dorothy told me that a long time after Merle had lived there he had went upstairs, and she went up there and he was sitting on the floor at the foot of the bed crying. He said he had messed up and was drinking and crying terrible. She said he was crying and rocking. He said "I'll have to leave here now, and I'm happier here more than I've ever been in my life." She said she assured him again, "This is your home and you will never have to leave," and after that he quit drinking... until that guy came around and got him back to drinking.[565]

When Merle began drinking again, his muscle-pulling returned stronger than before, and he scheduled a visit to the Mayo Clinic in Minnesota for early November 1983. He would not live to make the appointment. Sadly, just as his doctor had predicted two years earlier, once he began drinking again, it only took three months to do him in. On October 20, 1983, Merle Travis, the great man of thumbpicking guitar, writer of beloved American songs, and Country Music Hall of Famer, quietly passed away. Dorothy wrote about the events of Merle's death in a letter to Merle's sister Vada:

Vada,
I've been in such a state of absolute shock that I really don't know what all has been going on. There are so many questions I need answered, so many things I want to know about.

I wish I knew what caused Merle's attack. He saw our Doctor the week before I did for a regular check-up as I always insisted. Everything was fine. He knew I was doing okay, we came home Saturday and all was well. I thought he was tired as he said he was. The day this happened (Wed.) he went for a long walk in the rain as he wanted to do so bad. Then he came home, ate bacon and eggs, then we went upstairs for me to read and him to listen to records. I got up to fix supper, Paul came in about 5:15 and woke him up as he was asleep on the floor. Paul left and Merle came in the kitchen and opened a Coke, went to club room and poured it in a glass and I watched him drink it.

Then he came back into the kitchen and we were standing by the dining table. He was going to change pants before supper as the jeans were down in the kitchen. He reached into his pockets with both hands and pulled out his pocket knife and thumb picks in one hand, and his keys in the other. As he placed them on the table he just slid across it and that was it. I thought he had fainted. I tried to roll him over, I called his name over and over and told him how much I needed him—I got help on the way from the nearby phone, and the Sheriff Deputy had just completed his life-saving course....

They wouldn't let me be with Merle 'till they got him to intensive care. They had to use the electric paddle three times to get a heartbeat, but he never had a brain wave from the time it happened. I went into the room with Merle and talked to him and told him how desperately I loved and needed him. Two people in there watching me said his right eye moved as I told him the same thing I told him every night—"Goodnight, precious man, I love you, and sweet dreams." I talked to him just like he knew everything I said.

They told me to leave and get some rest, so I stayed in town with Phyllis. Hospital called at 7 and said he was worse, and by the time we got there they had pronounced him dead at 7:20. The Doctor finally convinced me that if he'd been standing by his side instead of me the night before at 6 pm, that he couldn't have done a thing for him because he was actually dead and never knew a pain or anything at all. If it had to be, I thank God that he didn't suffer any.

Vada, when we come [sic] home from the hospital, we snuggled every night and talked of our bright future. We were going to move to Nashville, Merle was offered a job as staff-writer for Acuff-Rose Music, *Country Music* magazine had just called a few weeks before and wanted him to write an article each month and draw 2 cartoons too per month.

We were so happy that things were going our way for a change. One thing in particular that I want you to know, we held hands and thanked God for saving me, for his blessings he had sent, for our health and happiness, and we prayed out loud together. For the first time, I remember asking Merle if he prayed, and he said oh yes, I do, all the time. I thanked him for giving me Merle to love and for all the love he'd given me. We were so close, but somehow praying together made us even closer in a spiritual way. I am so thankful for that special night of prayer because I knew then that Merle had made his peace with God.

There was never a moment that I didn't love Merle, there was never a moment that I didn't want to be right by his side, right or wrong. I loved him just for what he was. He never knew how great a man he was.

One thing is for certain, I may have been his 4th wife, but nobody could have loved him more than I did. Somehow, someway, I'll make it without him, but right now I just don't know how I'll do it. I still can't write or talk about him without tears streaming, but they say time will help.

I love you Vada,

—Dorothy[566]

When Merle collapsed at the table, he was still alive, but barely. The paramedics and hospital staff kept him alive with machines in the hopes that the family could make it there before he passed. Merlene flew to Dallas and met Pat and Gene, and they raced to Tulsa to try and see Merle before he expired. Unfortunately, they arrived too late, and he was gone. The news spread quickly among Merle's family, friends, and the extended network of country music people and guitar fans. Several days after Merle's death, Cary Ginell hosted a special "Tribute to Travis" on his *Cary's Country Store* show on radio station KCSN-FM in Los Angeles. Many of Merle's closest friends called in to the program, but the best summation of emotion and facts came from his close friend Hank Penny:

I wasn't shocked when I got the phone call that he had passed away, because Travis had sort of harmed himself in the last ten years. He was an unhappy man, I don't think he ever really found happiness on this plane. We grew up together, on WLW in Cincinnati, on the *Midwestern Hayride* and the *Boone County Jamboree*. When I say grew up together, we were very young men, watching one another get ready for our profession and prepare to go out and do our thing, so to speak. I think that Travis has millions of friends, everywhere, but not too many people really knew him. I don't think there's but two people who really knew Merle Travis.

One of them is Joe Maphis, and the other is myself. We spent a lot of time with him, we were with him when there was troubles, and trials and tribulations, and we tried to help, and sometimes it was kind of tough.

But Trav was a genius. He was a great authority on Abraham Lincoln, he was capable of writing some of the finest literary pieces, he had not too much education, but he pulled himself up by the bootstraps and made it all come about. He was also a very fine cartoonist. He would draw a caricature of you in about five minutes—a caricature that would speak loud and strong of your personality. Travis represents one of the finest careers that our profession has ever known. He'll be sorely missed. There is no replacement. There is a tremendous void. Merle Travis was one of the truly greats, and I am proud to say that he was my buddy, my friend, my pal. We'll miss him.[567]

Plans were set in motion for a memorial service in Muhlenberg County. Dorothy arranged to have a viewing at a funeral home in Tallequah. Merlene (joined later by her husband, Alan), Pat Travis Eatherly and her husband Gene, and Thom Bresh and his girlfriend Lane Brody all traveled to Oklahoma and met at Dorothy's house for the viewing before driving to Kentucky for the memorial service. Dorothy asked Merlene to pick out the suit for Merle to wear, and she selected a pinstriped Nudie suit with a red scarf, red being Merle's favorite color. Merlene told this author: "When we went in to view Dad, it was one of the hardest moments in my life. Patty [Pat Travis Eatherly] was a wreck, but she made it and so did I."[568]

Eddie Pennington recalled a later phone conversation with Dorothy: "Dorothy told me that after they viewed Merle's body before his cremation, they had the funeral home change Merle's clothes. Paul Center went and got those clothes and also had Merle's new recorder he had bought to record on, and wouldn't give them back. Dorothy said she had to talk pretty rough to him to get most of the stuff back."[569] Paul Center drove the car that carried Merlene, Alan, Pat, and Gene to Kentucky for the memorial service. Cindy flew to Nashville and stayed with Marty Stuart and his then-wife Cindy Cash before joining with Merlene and Pat and the rest of the group driving to Kentucky. Gene Eatherly had a heart attack en route from Nashville to Ebenezer and had to be hospitalized in Bowling Green, Kentucky. Pat stayed there with him, missing the memorial service.

A crowd gathered at Ebenezer Baptist Church underneath a tent on Sunday morning, October 23, 1983. Besides Merle's family members, which included his brother John Melvin and his sister Vada, some of his closest friends were in attendance, including Grandpa and Ramona Jones, Joe and Rose Lee Maphis, Chet

Atkins and his wife Leona, Mose Rager and his wife Laverda, country star Charlie Walker, and Marty Stuart and Cindy Cash. Many other well-known guitarists were in attendance, including Tommy Flint, Billy Grammer, Odell Martin, and Eddie Pennington. Paul Center took on master of ceremony duties for the service, though no one in the immediate family was pleased to have him there. In their eyes, Merle would have still been alive if Paul had stopped him from drinking, as Dorothy had instructed.

A detailed description of the event was published in the *Owensboro Messenger-Inquirer* the next day:

> They came by the hundreds Sunday to stand on a soggy Muhlenberg County hilltop beneath somber skies to say goodbye to a friend and former neighbor.
>
> Merle Travis, the country music legend who died Thursday in Oklahoma at age 65, didn't come home to lie in the churchyard in this crossroads community where he grew up.
>
> Travis didn't believe in funerals. At his instructions, his body was cremated and returned to his home in Cherokee County, Oklahoma.
>
> But friends gathered anyway to say goodbye behind the limestone and bronze monument they erected in 1956 in Travis' honor. Ironically, the monument is on the edge of the cemetery at Ebenezer Baptist Church.
>
> Muhlenberg Sheriff Harold "Roadblock" McElvain, one of a dozen police officers on hand to direct traffic, estimated the crowd at nearly 1,200.
>
> Standing in the crowd by the monument were some of the greats of country music, dozens of those who grew up with Travis and many of the curious.
>
> Across the road and behind the trees, a giant coal shovel stood at attention, as if it were saluting the man who set the Muhlenberg mines to music with songs like "Sixteen Tons" and "Dark as a Dungeon."
>
> Among those from Nashville were Chet Atkins, the guitar great who was widely influenced by Travis; Louis Marshall "Grandpa" Jones, who worked with Travis as a member of the Browns Ferry Four; Joe Maphis; and Charlie Walker.
>
> Johnny Cash had been on his way from Virginia, but he became ill and returned home.
>
> There were flowers from Hank Thompson and Don and Phil Everly.
>
> Travis' gold-plated Gibson guitar sat on a stand as friends took turns at the microphone to reminisce about the man they had loved.

Paul Center, who had worked with Travis for the past six years, told the gathering, "Some of his last wishes were not to have a big ceremony or any big, drawn-out performance. He just wanted his friends to speak, informal and simple."

Musician Thom Bresh said, "He wanted no preacher here. And I'm no preacher."

Bresh bowed his head and prayed, "Heavenly Father, Merle is sitting up there in your waiting room. I think if you'll listen to all his friends, you'll let him in."

Singer Lane Brody, representing Travis' wife Dorothy, who is recovering from surgery, said, "The emptiness he leaves will never again be filled. He touched us as a common man of deep sincerity as well as a pioneer in country music."

Mrs. Travis, she said, plans to devote the rest of her life to her husband's memory. Plans are already underway for a Merle Travis scholarship and museum, Ms. Brody said.

Maphis said, "One of the greatest days of my life was when I met Merle. I loved him like a brother. It's a sad day, but let's be happy for Merle. We know he's gone to the right place."

Jones added, "We know Merle had a lot of friends because of the crowd here today. I don't think he ever realized just how big he was in this business. So many copied his style but there will never be another Merle Travis."

The crowd broke into spontaneous applause for the first time.

Center told about Travis sitting beside the Illinois River in Oklahoma, listening to whippoorwills. "He was always looking for his rainbow's end," Center said. "Two nights before he died, he said he had found his rainbow's end in Cherokee County, Okla. 'I feel free here. I don't have to worry about anything here,' he said."

Center added, "He did not fear death. He was ready."

Then Ms. Brody stepped back to the microphone to lead 1,200 voices in singing "Amazing Grace."

Bresh brought out a 1937 guitar that Travis used when composing most of his hits. "This guitar was Merle's best friend. It watched him laugh and watched him cry," Bresh said. "It's only right that it be here today."

With that, he picked "I'll See You in My Dreams" as several in the crowd wept silently.

[Chet] Atkins, with tears running down his face, was unable to approach the microphone.

For more than an hour, they talked and sang. And then they drifted back to their cars and went away, taking their memories of Travis with them.[570]

The *Louisville Courier-Journal* gave additional details regarding Chet Atkins's composure during the service: "Guitar virtuoso Chet Atkins, called on to speak during the informal memorial service, came forward from where he had been standing in the crowd but was unable to speak. He told master of ceremonies Paul Center, 'I just can't.' Then he laid his head on his wife's shoulder and sobbed."[571]

Merlene remembers: "Many of Dad's boyhood friends spoke and that was amazing to hear. Of his humbleness, his love of nature, and his curious nature. One lady said that she would remember 'hearing' Dad long before you'd see him. She said the most beautiful whistling could be heard and then out of the woods would walk a barefoot, smiling Merle. I loved that visual."[572] As the crowd dispersed, the family visited and shared funny stories and hugs.

It was a tragedy that the great Merle Travis was gone. His family and friends wished that he could have lived a longer life, made more music, told more stories, made them laugh again. On the other hand, it was nothing short of a miracle that Merle's ravaged body had made it to sixty-five. Through that lens, it was an achievement that he lived long enough to see his musical legacy firmly cemented. In his later years he realized what an influence he had been, what a huge pillar of country music history and guitar playing he represented, and he had enjoyed well-deserved glory and adulation. A quote from a jam session later in his life reveals what it had all meant to him:

> I don't figure I've ever been paid a penny for playing on stage. That ain't the way I look at it. I pay them…. I always feel like that when I come off, how much do I owe you. I enjoy playing, I enjoy getting up there and picking. Getting that applause, and the lights, and the hard work is all that other stuff. [You get paid for] getting there… and getting back… and getting rested up.[573]

Merle's body was cremated at a funeral home in Tulsa, and his ashes remained at the funeral home for several years while Dorothy and the family tried to figure out what they wanted to do with them. Merlene related to Ed Kahn in 1988:

> Toward the end of his life, he [Merle] knew that he wanted to be cremated. He wanted his ashes to be spread over the LA area that had meant something to him…. He wanted ashes spread over the San Fernando

Valley and Capitol Records as he thought of this as his home. He didn't want ashes spread over the water, as he had a real fear of deep water. He liked fishing and such, but when he thought about the depth of water, he was frightened. His old friend Gene Autry told him, if you have any trouble with this, just let me know and I'll distribute the ashes from my plane for you. When the time came, I tried, at Dorothy's request, to get in touch with Gene. The secretaries demanded to know what it was about and I finally had to tell one. She called back and said that there was nothing they could do—Gene didn't have a plane. I was never able to get in touch with him directly.[574]

Guitarist Eddie Pennington, who worked professionally as a mortician and funeral director, was in touch with Dorothy regularly. Pennington suggested that Merle's ashes should come back to Kentucky. Pennington told this author:

Me and Dorothy got to be real close. I met her in '87 out in Mountain View [Arkansas]. And so we got to be very close. We talked on the phone all the time. They never had buried Merle—his ashes or anything with him. And so I kept talking to her, and I told her, I said, "Over at the monument you could have a place." She said she didn't feel right taking him out to California where he wanted to be scattered. She said, "Things had changed so much; he wouldn't be happy with the all the changes out there."

I'd have dreams about Merle, and man, he was just—traveling. It was like he was tormented. He hadn't been getting any rest or anything.

So anyhow, she had the ashes. This was five years after he died, and so she shipped the ashes. I was working at the funeral home at the time, and the box, I put him [the urn containing Merle's ashes] in a Wilbert Vault. And then her and Kay came up, Mr. John [John Melvin Travis] came down, and Miss Vada and them came. I dug the grave and put him right in front of that monument. So there's where he's buried at. John Madsen, Mr. John Travis's preacher, he had a few words. Then they went on down to Vada's house. I stayed and finished the gravel [covering the box containing the ashes] after they left.

After Merle died, I would often have the dream of him, and he was just traveling and so worn out. I had that dream many times. But after his ashes were buried at his monument, I never had it again, and I think he's at peace now.[575]

Merle's new monument at Ebenezer Baptist Church in
Ebenezer, Kentucky. Merle's ashes were placed at the
base of the monument several years after his death.
(Courtesy of Deke Dickerson.)

CONCLUSION

THE LEGACY OF MERLE TRAVIS

In the decades since Merle Travis's death in 1983, his stature as a music legend
has grown, not diminished. During his lifetime, Merle's fame was tied to his
fragile and often incapacitated physical self. Since his death, his contributions

have survived, thrived, and expanded in influence beyond anything he could have imagined. It is possible to argue that there has never been a comparable figure in country music history.

After Merle's death, a group of dedicated fans, in conjunction with Merle's family members, worked to keep his memory alive. *Cannonball Rag* (subtitled "A Newsletter Dedicated to the Life and Music of Merle Travis") was published for many years by Dave Stewart of Corinth, Mississippi. The newsletter united fans in the pre-internet era, spreading news of thumbpickers' clubs and associations and their respective guitar contests and events. Merle's children and other relatives often attended these events. During the 1980s and 1990s, it was a small, close-knit community of players and fans.

Bobby Anderson, who brought Merle to Ebenezer for the monument dedication in 1956, published a newsletter called *That Muhlenberg Sound*, which was also the title of his 1993 book about the area's musical history.

In 1994, Bear Family Records compiled a five-disc box set that made all of Merle's recordings from 1943 to 1955 available for the first time in decades. The accompanying booklet was the first attempt to document Merle's life story, albeit only up to 1955. The box set brought Merle's music into the homes of a whole new generation of listeners—ones who played compact discs instead of scratchy old 78 rpm records.

Merle's home area in Muhlenberg County, Kentucky, has hosted music fans and encouraged interest regarding Merle's history in the region, as well as the broader legacy of Kentucky guitar players and playing styles. Every Saturday night for as long as anybody can remember, the Drakesboro Community Center has hosted a picking party and jam session for local thumbpickers and other musical artists. The Drakesboro City Hall building stands on the site where Mose Rager had his barbershop for decades, across the street from where he lived. In 1992, Drakesboro erected the "Home of the Legends" fountain across the street from the Community Center, honoring Merle, Mose Rager, Ike Everly, and Kennedy Jones. Various local streets are named after these and other musicians.

Merle's cousin Claude Travis worked tirelessly for years to bring attention to Muhlenberg County's native son, including petitioning the state to rename Highway 246 between Beechmont and Ebenezer the "Merle Travis Highway." He was interviewed for this book before he passed away in 2019.

Another major Kentucky site is the Merle Travis Music Center in Powderly, adjacent to Paradise Park, where Merle's birth home has been relocated from its original spot in Rosewood. The Music Center is the home of an annual thumb-picking contest, the National Thumbpickers Hall of Fame, and a museum housing many artifacts that belonged to Merle (including his personal Guild Solomaster

guitar) and other notable Muhlenberg County musicians. The complex in Powderly took years to materialize. It started in 1996, when Eddie Pennington was
performing at the Smithsonian Folklife Festival (the same festival where Merle
and Mose Rager performed in 1973 and 1976) and was seen by a high-powered
Washington, DC, lobbyist named Ted Jones. Jones struck up a friendship with
Pennington and asked if he could help the people back home in Kentucky in any
way. Pennington responded that a live music building of some sort would be a
great help. Jones introduced Pennington to Senator Ted Stevens of Alaska, and
Stevens arranged for Pennington's son Alonzo and Rodney Kirtley to perform at
some functions for senators to arrange for some funding. Kentucky Senator Mitch
McConnell vetoed the request, balking at putting money toward a music center
in such a small rural community, but Stevens followed up with a funding request
for just under one million dollars, a threshold with a much lower bar of scrutiny,
which was subsequently approved. Muhlenberg County added some money of
their own, and the building, parking lot, and Paradise Park with its music pavilion
were built for around $1.4 million. The Merle Travis Music Center opened in
December 2007 and has served the area ever since. Community members have
worked at the building and maintained the building and park.

Merle's legacy is honored at other museums in the area. The Muhlenberg
County Music and History Museum in Central City pays tribute to Merle and
other Muhlenberg County artists, with many artifacts on display. The Duncan
Cultural Center in Greenville has a display dedicated to Merle that contains one
of his Western suits and two of his later guitars.

The original limestone rock used for the Merle Travis marker in 1956 eroded
over the years, so in 1991 it was replaced with a larger, more substantial marble
monument. Merle's ashes are buried there, so the site now serves as his gravestone
and a memorial that fans can visit. The attached Ebenezer Baptist Church Cemetery is also the final resting place of his parents, Rob and Etta, his sister Vada, and
Mose Rager (Ike Everly is buried in nearby Central City, Merle's oldest brother
Taylor Travis is buried in Evansville, Indiana, and Merle's other brother John
Melvin Travis is buried just outside Princeton, Kentucky).

On the other side of the state, the Kentucky Music Hall of Fame in Renfro
Valley pays tribute to Merle (who was posthumously inducted into the Kentucky
Music Hall of Fame when it first opened in 2002). The museum there has one of
Merle's suits and his 1981 Gibson Super 400 on display.

The Country Music Hall of Fame and Museum in Nashville still displays Merle's two most notable instruments, his 1948 Bigsby solidbody electric guitar and his
oft-reworked 1952 Gibson Super 400. Every day the museum welcomes thousands
of visitors, some of whom learn about Merle for the first time by seeing his famous

guitars. Nashville also hosts occasional concerts in honor of Merle. In 2017, an all-star concert at the City Winery celebrated his one hundredth birthday, with headliners Tommy Emmanuel, Thom Bresh, John Jorgenson, Eddie Pennington, Doyle Dykes, and many more engaging in a remembrance of Merle's music.

Gibson Guitars has occasionally rallied to pay tribute to one of the company's most famous players. In addition to a few "Merle Travis style" customized Super 400s they've made over the years, in 1998 the Gibson custom shop in Nashville commissioned a Merle Travis Commemorative Super 400 for its NAMM show display, to join similar artistic "presentation" guitars done for Chet Atkins, Les Paul, and B.B. King. The idea for the guitar was suggested to Gibson by Paul Yandell and built by custom shop senior design engineer Jim Hutchins (better known as Hutch). The highly elaborate and painted guitar is an incredible artistic tribute to Merle, adorned front and back with scenes from his life and career.

The Martin Guitar Company also honored Merle with a tribute guitar in 2009. It was an authentic reproduction of Merle's famous Martin D-28 acoustic with the Bigsby neck—the first time Martin had ever built a Bigsby-style neck. One hundred "Merle Travis Signature Model" D-28s were made, and today they are highly coveted collectors' items.

Merle's Bigsby solidbody guitar has been duplicated many times, on a custom-order basis. The Bigsby company made a limited run of Bigsby solidbodies loosely based on Merle's guitar, though technically not a reissue, in the mid-2000s. Dick "R. C." Allen made several copies over his lifetime for customers (Allen passed away in 2014). Allen's friend Eric Galletta built faithful copies of Bigsby guitar number two (a guitar owned by R. C. Allen) on a limited production basis, the closest to a legitimate copy of the Merle Travis Bigsby that has been manufactured at the time of this writing.

Players who want to learn the Merle Travis thumbpicking style now have a variety of instructional manuals and videos to consult. In addition to the original Mel Bay *Merle Travis Guitar Style* book written by Tommy Flint (still in print, nearly five decades later), there is an instructional video made by French guitarist Marcel Dadi for Stefan Grossman Guitar Workshop, still available. Michael O'Dorn, a California guitarist who knew Merle well in the 1970s, penned a Mel Bay–published book, *Getting into Travis Picking*. Mark Hanson published *The Art of Contemporary Travis Picking* in the 1980s, still in print after thirty years. Bruce Emery published a book called *Travis-Style Guitar from Scratch*. Thom Bresh released an instructional video, *The Real Merle Travis Guitar—Like Father, Like Son*, through Homespun Videos. And there are hundreds of instructional videos on YouTube, by amateur and professional players alike, all attempting to decode the difficult and seductive Travis-picking style.

The passing decades have spawned a whole new generation of younger musicians learning the style. Musicians of a younger era carrying the torch include J. T. Oglesby, Sean Mencher, Alonzo Pennington, Joel Paterson, Caleb Coots, Evan Twitty [who was sadly killed in an automobile accident before this book was finished], Katelyn Prieboy, Bella Speelman, Parker Hastings, Dan Bankhurst, Tanner Duckworth, Saxon and Jarvis Whittaker, Shane Hennessy, Elias Bartholomeo, and a crop of other enthusiastic young finger-style and thumb-style players.

Merle's children have worked to ensure that he is not forgotten. Pat Travis Eatherly wrote two books in her lifetime. The first, *In Search of My Father* (1987), was a story about her personal religious journey and her troubled relationship with Merle. Pat later said that she regretted writing the book and followed it up in later years with a much more heartfelt book about Merle's life, *A Scrapbook of My Daddy, Merle Travis* (2000). Pat and her husband, Gene Eatherly, participated in many of the Merle Travis–related concerts and get-togethers over the years, and she loaned or donated many items relating to her father to museums in Kentucky, where they can still be seen today. Pat Travis Eatherly passed away in 2006.

Merlene and Cindy, Merle's two younger daughters, both live in California. Merlene Travis-Maggini enjoyed a career in music publishing and as a successful music executive, retiring as Vice President of Music Affairs for Sony Pictures. Merlene and Cindy take care of the publishing concern called Merle's Girls Music and manage the Merle Travis Legacy.

Thom Bresh continues to play the music of Merle Travis at concerts and guitar clinics throughout the country, and no one has worked more tirelessly to promote Merle's iconic guitar style. One late-breaking bit of news that occurred just before this book went to print: after decades of not knowing for sure, Thom submitted a DNA swab to 23andMe, and was matched to both the Travis family and Richard Lee Lesher's family (the son Merle had out of wedlock in 1945). Just as he (and Merle) had always suspected, Thom Bresh is now confirmed as the biological son of Merle Travis.

Some of the aforementioned events and museums are small and regional, but they add up to a lot. Merle's musical appreciation persists, from the hollers of rural Kentucky where his life began to the four corners of the globe. But what to make of this man's life on this planet? To simply lump Merle Travis in with other deceased country music stars of the twentieth century would be to overlook the massive influence of his specific legacy.

For instance: enter any guitar store, anywhere on the planet, and you'll see hundreds if not thousands of solidbody electric guitars. Every single one of those instruments can trace its lineage to the solidbody electric guitar that Merle designed with Paul Bigsby in 1948.

In those same stores, you will see dozens of guitar vibratos, from the Fender Stratocaster, to modern designs like the Floyd Rose and the Kahler, to the old but still ubiquitous Bigsby vibrato. These vibratos all trace their lineage to Merle's request that Paul Bigsby invent a guitar vibrato that would stay in tune. Since Merle put the first Bigsby vibrato on his Gibson Super 400 in 1952, the guitar vibrato has been popularized across the globe.

Rock music would be very different without Merle Travis's guitar style—a style that was adapted by Scotty Moore when he played with Elvis Presley, and by Carl Perkins, Duane Eddy, Eddie Cochran, and even George Harrison of The Beatles. Although Merle never considered himself a rock 'n' roll guitarist, his Travis-picking style was a major cornerstone of the genre. The echoes can still be heard today, even in the music of modern acts who don't realize that their influences were influenced by Merle Travis. A good example would be Lindsey Buckingham of Fleetwood Mac, who plays in a finger style that would not be possible were it not for Merle's groundwork.

Folk music would be very different today if that 1960s generation of folkies hadn't grown up on a steady diet of Merle's *Folk Songs of the Hills* album, the success of "Sixteen Tons" in the mid-1950s, and Merle's many appearances on *Town Hall Party* and other television shows. His compositions influenced innumerable folk acts, from early clean-cut college groups like the Kingston Trio through the long-haired folk-rockers of the late 1960s and early 1970s. In an interview conducted for this book, Chris Hillman of the Byrds, the Flying Burrito Brothers, and the Desert Rose Band revealed that he watched Merle and Joe Maphis on *Town Hall Party* every week when he was young. Many other rockers of the psychedelic generation that came of age in Los Angeles shared similar sentiments, including guitarist David Lindley and rock critic Robert Hilburn. Merle's participation on the Nitty Gritty Dirt Band's landmark album *Will the Circle Be Unbroken* endeared him to an entire generation of folk-oriented youths with acoustic instruments.

Country-western music would be a completely different genre today without Merle Travis, since the incredibly influential Nashville guitarist and record producer Chet Atkins took his style from Merle and considered him his greatest influence. What would country music have been without Chet Atkins? And would young Chester Burton Atkins have become the great Chet Atkins without a burning desire to emulate his hero, Merle Travis?

Capitol Records still does business at the Capitol Tower in Hollywood today. Likely most of the rappers and pop stars who pass through its hallways (and the people who buy their records) have no idea that Capitol wouldn't be in business today if Merle hadn't saved them from insolvency in 1947 when he wrote the blockbuster hit "Smoke! Smoke! Smoke! (That Cigarette)," or that earnings from

Tennessee Ernie Ford's 1955 hit version of "Sixteen Tons" paid for much of the construction of the now-iconic Capitol Tower, which opened in 1956.

When I agreed to write Merle's life story, I decided to immerse myself in this complex subject. I knew that to fully understand his journey, I had to see it with my own eyes, understand it from firsthand knowledge. I hit the road on several trips spanning three years.

During a week in Muhlenberg County, Kentucky, with my host, Bill Harlan, I visited the lonesome farm in tiny, unincorporated Rosewood where Merle was born. The air was thick and still, and it didn't seem like much had changed since 1917, except for the cars. Farm families still live in Rosewood in hundred-year-old houses and sit on their porches to watch the world go by. On Saturday night, pickers gather in nearby Drakesboro to play thumb-style guitar. It's more of a social gathering than a performance, much the way music in the area has always been. My host took me to one of his own performances with a local country-western band. The elderly audience danced, some with the aid of walkers and canes, and supper was served. At the end of the evening, the entire audience gathered in a circle, holding hands with the band and myself, and prayed. Harlan took me to his church in Greenville, where I was introduced to the entire congregation. Afterward, we went out to a fancy after-church supper. One evening Harlan and I visited with his long-term music partner, Royce Morgan, and his wife, Theda, along with cousin Claude Travis, and reminisced about sixty-five years of music in Muhlenberg County. Later, at his home, Claude Travis showed me his collection of Kentucky Coal Company "flickers" and "scrip." I visited Eddie Pennington in nearby Princeton, where he expertly showcased the proper way of Travis picking as a fleet of Gibson Super 400 guitars and newer replicas rested on their own separate couch nearby. Harlan, who had grown up with the Everly Brothers as childhood friends, pointed out the place where Cleaton Crossing had once been, the site where "Cannonball Rag" got its name. As Harlan and I drove around Muhlenberg County, a dozen times we passed Ebenezer Baptist Church and Merle's stone marker and ashes. One night, late, I had a particularly memorable glimpse of the marble monument in shadow, standing silent sentry over the rural county's famous guitar player and songwriter.

I visited Cincinnati, where Merle first found fame performing on WLW in the late 1930s. Local historian Brian Powers showed me around the various locations where Merle and his first wife, Mary, lived, and the former WLW studios in the Crosley Building, now abandoned. Black and white culture, Northern and Southern culture, the wealthy and the poor, mix in Cincinnati, neighborhood by neighborhood, as they did when Merle lived there. The Albee Theater, where Smiley Burnette first enlightened Merle about the allure of California, as well as

Syd Nathan's original record shop, are long gone, victims of urban renewal. When entering the Queen City and again as I was leaving, I saw riverboats heading up and down the Ohio River and imagined a ragged, barefoot Kentucky kid with a cheap Gretsch archtop guitar bumming rides and playing on the streets for pennies and dimes—and the occasional quarter when he got lucky.

In tiny Hillsboro, Ohio, I visited ninety-five-year-old Jack Rogers, the only surviving close associate of Merle's from the 1940s. When I called to ask if Rogers was home before visiting, he replied, "Yeah, what's left of him." We spent the day looking through ancient photographs, laughing, and reliving stories from the old days. Toward the end of the visit, Jack remarked: "Merle was my best friend," and burst into tears. Rogers passed away as this book was going to print, just a few days shy of his ninety-seventh birthday.

On a side trip to Arkansas to visit with Ginny Cushman's daughter Lynne Davis Herrod, I passed by Mountain View, where Grandpa Jones and his wife Ramona had settled and where the Merle Travis Annual Thumbpicking Contest is held every year. It was a beautiful, peaceful setting. Lynne dug out old photo albums of her mother and even showed me the cornet she had played on recordings with Merle.

In Nashville, the city where Merle and Bettie lived for seven years, I found much of the old country music capital gone, obliterated by young hipsters hell-bent on making names for themselves. Although the demographics have changed, the city serves the same purpose now as in the previous decades—it is a place for musicians to hustle and try to make their music-business dreams happen. Visiting the Country Music Hall of Fame and Museum and seeing Merle's plaque in the Rotunda and his two most famous guitars on display, I felt his professional legacy was secure, even though most of the visiting busloads of tourists were more interested in the displays full of sparkly things owned by the current crop of country artists. Nudie's Bar is a new tourist watering hole on lower Broadway, directly across from where Shot Jackson's Sho-Bud guitar shop was in the 1960s. Inside, I found several of Merle's outfits and one of his later Super 400 guitars on display behind a band playing Pat Benatar songs at top volume at noon. There couldn't have been a more jarring juxtaposition of history and reality, but that's the new Nashville.

On the outskirts of Nashville, ninety-six-year-old Rose Lee Maphis and her son Jody welcomed me into their home and regaled me with stories about Merle and a much different Nashville than exists today. Merle's running buddies and musical partners Joe Maphis and Johnny Cash are buried nearby, both interred in the Carter Family cemetery plot in Hendersonville. Jody's memories made the old Nashville sound like a wide-open town full of hustlers, crackpots, incredible musicians, record business thieves, and Printer's Alley strippers. It was quite the vivid picture of the late-1960s and early-1970s era when Merle lived there, with its dark taverns full of thick cigarette smoke and the aroma of stale, cheap beer. However real versus imagined, it sounded like a lot more fun than today's shiny condos. Rose Lee Maphis passed away just as this book was going to print, a few months shy of her ninety-ninth birthday.

Back home in Los Angeles, I wandered the many Merle-related landmarks, trying to imagine what Hollywood must have looked like to a country boy newly arrived at the end of World War II. Most of the apartment buildings and small houses where he lived in his first decade on the West Coast are now gone, but the Ranchito house in Van Nuys, the one he purchased with the "Sixteen Tons" money, was vacant and for sale—on the real estate market for the first time since Bettie had to abandon it in 1965. Walking through the house, I imagined Merle in the back bedroom, suffering the awful stomach hemorrhage that almost killed him in 1961. I pictured Bob Wills cooking stew in the kitchen at eight o'clock in the morning, and Webb Pierce wearing his Nudie suit, slipping and falling into the pink bathtub. I squinted my eyes and saw Merle and Johnny Cash in the middle of a pill bender, shooting their guns at the back wall in the yard, then realizing the wall was made of hollow stones. The Ranchito house was full of country music ghosts.

The San Fernando Valley has changed drastically since the days of orange groves and sagebrush, horse trails and cowboys. Suburban houses and apartment buildings now occupy every square inch of what used to be farmland. Unbelievably, ninety-five-year-old Marilyn Tuttle still scoots around like a spry twentysomething in the house that she and Wesley purchased in the 1950s. A night owl, Marilyn sends me Facebook messages at midnight. Just up the freeway at a cemetery in Newhall, her husband Wesley is buried, along with Cliffie Stone, Tex Williams, and other stars of the 1940s and 1950s who were part of Merle's circle of cowboy friends.

The Capitol Tower still stands in Hollywood, but shortsighted city management has recently allowed giant condos to be constructed on either side of it, obscuring its view and the landscape of Hollywood in general. Much of the old Hollywood, like the old Nashville, is being torn down and replaced with new buildings where young people want to live. It is hard to imagine the era when hillbillies drove convertible Cadillacs down these same boulevards en route to barn-dance television shows.

North of Los Angeles, the Lily of the Valley trailer court in Saugus exists much as it did in the 1970s, when Merle and Bettie spent the final years of their marriage there. The trailer they lived in still occupies the same spot, the damage from Merle sideswiping it with his car long since repaired. Down the road, the Saugus Honor Farm where Merle once went to dry out sits with the silent memories of men like Merle who, at times, let alcohol ruin their lives. The surrounding hillsides still brim with the history of all the Western movies shot there, and the nearby city of Newhall has a Cowboy Walk of Fame. All the great men and women who once rode those horses and picked those guitars and commissioned all those fabulous custom Nudie suits have passed on, replaced by a different, more casual generation. Film crews still show up occasionally, but the era of the Western movie has ridden off into the sunset.

Up the coast from Los Angeles, Merlene and Cindy, Merle's two living daughters, keep the memory of their famous father close by at all times. Various personal items and guitars that belonged to him are on display in their homes, and at a small storage unit in an undisclosed location, all of the items Merle possessed when he died are safely under lock and key. Anyone coming to California these days looking to pan for gold might be sadly disappointed, but anyone looking for the secrets, facts, and photographic documentation of Merle Travis's life would certainly call that stash of artifacts, photographs, letters, Nudie Suits, and memorabilia a gold mine. Merlene speaks of her famous father:

> When I dream about him, I always feel good and safe. He's young, like when I was a little girl, and he's always happy to see me, and we laugh because he's just told me a story and makes those funny faces he would make to get me to crack up. I loved his Stan Laurel imitation, and that's the one he usually does in my dream, and I just totally crack up. It's never about music, or fame, or sad or depressing. He's Dad and he's available and he's giving me his complete attention in whatever we're doing. He's got the big ol' deep dimpled grin that I love so much. When I wake up, I truly feel he came to visit me and that, wherever he is, he's letting me know he is okay.[576]

Fifty miles outside Las Vegas in the hot Nevada desert, Michael Robinson, Bettie's son and Merle's stepson for twenty-two years, was more than happy to talk to me about the man he once called his father. We spent hour upon hour recalling good times and bad, looking through old photographs and letters. It seemed cathartic for Robinson to speak about a large swath of his life that no one had ever asked him about. He spoke of a recent dream:

> He came to me in a dream not too long ago, but it wasn't like it was a dream; it was him. He came to me and showed me something. I don't know if I told you this, but it was like I was watching him on stage and

he was looking to my right, and it was him on his best day. Because I was getting worried about dying. He used to have these pinstriped cowboy pants with this red-and-black checkered shirt and a gray Stetson hat. And it was him on his best day, before he met me, back in 1947 or something like that, the year before I was born, and that was him on his best day. And he was showing me that after this whole thing is over, you can be your best on your best day. It was a very strange dream. It was like him coming to show me something—just him paying a visit. It was really him. So we're still friends.[577]

The whole time I was there talking to Michael, Bettie Travis was there in the room with us, her ashes in an urn on the coffee table.

On a trip through the Midwest, I pointed my rental car toward Oklahoma because I heard that Dorothy Travis's house on Lake Tenkiller was for sale. Somehow, after she died, the property had been opened to the elements and subsequently invaded by vandals and varmints. Although the once-grand estate lay in ruins, I still wanted to see the house where Hank Thompson lived and where Merle Travis died. Miles outside Tallequah, I saw the "16 Tons" rock on the side of the road (painted by ex-deputy Paul Center and his son after Merle died) and turned down the gravel two-lane that had once been called Hank Thompson Road. The road ended at the lake, with a chained-up driveway and a "For Sale" sign hung gamely for no one to see. I walked up the driveway in waist-high weeds to see what was left of the house Hank Thompson had built in 1955.

The once-sparkling lakefront estate was merely a shell. There was graffiti, and the pool was empty and cracked. The doors were off the frames and the windows were broken. I went inside. It was difficult to imagine how anyone could have let this happen to a place that had been home to two Country Music Hall of Fame artists. It was in ruins, but I could tell how opulent and well constructed it had once been. I stood in the bar area, littered with broken glass but still vaguely intact, and thought about all the visitors who had spent hours celebrating here, the music that once rang through the rafters. I stood in the large room that used to be the kitchen and dining area and pictured Merle, frail from years of abuse and touring, emptying his pockets and peacefully collapsing on the table. I thought about how unendingly quiet the house must have been for Dorothy after Merle passed away.

In some ways, I knew my obsession with retracing Merle's steps was unnecessary and frivolous, a fan boy's fool's errand. I could have written this book without spending quite so much time traveling down small roads and wandering through abandoned houses. But it felt important and necessary, if only from a purely selfish standpoint. I enjoyed every minute of it. By the end of my travels, I could feel Merle's presence in every sentence that I wrote in this book, and I was so much better able to evoke the landscapes of his life from having seen all those locations for myself. I could sense him flinching over details of his drunkenness and epic failures, but at the same time I knew he'd insist those stories stay in the book. I knew he would be glad that the documentation of his amazing inventions, songs, guitar styles, jokes, drawings, stories, and many other talents were finally gathered in one place for the world to read about and appreciate. It was hard to comprehend: One man did all that? Yes, he did. And he did it naturally, as easy as falling off a log. People like that come along only once in a great while, and I felt like justice had been done in finally telling Merle Travis's life story. It was an important thing to do.

I flew across the ocean to play at a music festival in Spain in early 2020. At least two musicians there had custom-made guitars built to resemble the Bigsby guitars Merle designed in the 1940s. There were Italian and Spanish and French and Dutch and British and Finnish guitarists, all playing various derivatives of the Travis-picking style. A guitarist from Chicago named Joel Paterson played an afternoon concert on the beach overlooking the Mediterranean with his band, the Modern Sounds. As Paterson deftly played Merle's showcase guitar piece, "Cannonball Rag," a crowd of guitar acolytes gathered, watching every move his hands made. When played expertly, as Paterson is capable of, Travis-style thumbpicking hypnotizes an audience; they simply can't believe that what they are hearing is real. That moment I witnessed in Spain confirmed that no one need worry about Merle Travis's legacy. The music is too good; it'll never die. Merle Travis will never be forgotten.

A ♪ from Merle Travis

CORN BREAD

1 CUP CORN MEAL

½ t S SALT

⅛ t S SODA

1½ TBL S BAKN PDR

¼ CUP FLOUR STIR HERE

1 EGG — ~~¼ CUP~~

} 1⅓ BTR MLK CUPS

3 TBLS OIL

450 - OVEN HEAT

EXTRA GREASE IN SKILLET, GET HOT IN OVEN

Merle's recipe for his famous cornbread. For those who need extra coaching, the small "t" before the S means teaspoon, and the large "T" before the S means tablespoon. "BTR MLK" is buttermilk. Use a cast iron skillet and get it very hot in the oven before coating the inside with a thin layer of bacon grease or vegetable oil applied with a paper towel. Pour in the batter. If your skillet is hot enough, it should take between 11 and 14 minutes to fully cook. Test with a toothpick stuck in the top. If it pulls out with batter sticking to the toothpick, it needs more time. If it pulls out clean, it's done.

RESEARCH

The following is a selection of resources consulted in the writing of this book. For specific quote sources, see the notes.

BOOKS

Anderson, Bobby. *That Muhlenberg Sound*. Beechmont, KY: Muhlbut, 1993.

Atkins, Chet, with Russ Cochran. *Chet Atkins: Me and My Guitars*. Milwaukee, MN: Hal Leonard, 2001.

Atkins, Chet, with William Neely. *Country Gentleman*. Chicago: Henry Regnery, 1974.

Autry, Gene, with Mickey Herskowitz. *Back in the Saddle Again*. New York: Doubleday, 1978.

Babiuk, Andy. *The Story of Paul A. Bigsby*. Milwaukee: Hal Leonard Corporation, 2008.

Bryant Epps, Lorene. *Jimmy Bryant: Fastest Guitar in the Country!*. Self-published, 2001.

Buckner Ford, Jeffrey. *River of No Return: Tennessee Ernie Ford and the Woman He Loved*. Nashville: Cumberland House, 2008.

Camplin, Paul. *A New History of Muhlenberg County*. Nashville: Williams Printing, 1984.

Causey, Warren B. *The Stringbean Murders*. Nashville: Quest, 1975.

Clark, Cottonseed. *Cottonseed Clark's Brushwood Poetry and Philosophy*. Self-published booklet, 1945.

Clements, Sidna J. [aka "Tex Ann" Nation], *Cobwebs, Memories and Miracles*. Self-published, 1988

Delmore, Alton, with Charles K. Wolfe. *Truth Is Stranger Than Publicity*. Nashville: Country Music Foundation and Vanderbilt University Press, 1995. Originally published 1977.

Drifting Pioneers Song Folio No. 1. Portland, OR: American Music, 1939.

Favorite Songs of the WLW Boone County Jamboree. Chicago: M. M. Cole, 1941.

Fratallone, Stephen. *Eddie Dean: The Golden Cowboy*. Albany, GA: BearManor Media, 2014.

Gentry, Linnell. *A History and Encyclopedia of Country, Western, and Gospel Music*. Nashville: McQuiddy, 1961.

George-Warren, Holly. *Public Cowboy #1: The Life and Times of Gene Autry*. Oxford: Oxford University Press, 2007.

Green, Douglas B. *Singing in the Saddle: History of the Singing Cowboy*. Nashville: Nashville: Country Music Foundation and Vanderbilt University Press, 2002.

Grein, Paul. *Capitol Records 1942–1992, 50th Anniversary*. Los Angeles: Capitol Records, 1992.

Griffis, Ken. *Hear My Song: The Story of the Celebrated Sons of the Pioneers*. Northglenn, CO: Norken, 1994.

Hilburn, Robert. *Johnny Cash: The Life*. New York: Little, Brown, 2013.

Hoskyns, Barney, et al. *75 Years of Capitol Records*. Los Angeles: Taschen, 2016.

Jackson, Carlton, and Nancy Richey. *Mose Rager: Kentucky's Incomparable Guitar Master*. Morley, MO: Acclaim, 2016.

Jones, Grandpa, with Charles K. Wolfe. *Everybody's Grandpa*. Knoxville, TN: University of Tennessee Press, 1984.

Kice, Warren. *Hank Thompson: My Side of Life*. Fort Worth, TX: Branch-Smith Printing, 2007.

Kienzle, Rich. *Southwest Shuffle: Pioneers of Honky-Tonk, Western Swing, and Country Jazz*. New York: Routledge, 2003.

Kingsbury, Kent, et al. *Who's Who in Country Music*. Culver City, CA: Black Stallion Country, 1981.

Lomax, Alan. *The Folk Songs of North America*. New York: Doubleday, 1960.

Mandrell, Barbara, with George Vecsey. *Get to the Heart*. New York: Bantam, 1990.

Merle Travis Hit Parade Folio No. 1. Hollywood, CA: American Music, Inc., 1956.

Moust, Hans. *The Guild Guitar Book*. Milwaukee, MN: Hal Leonard Corporation, 1995.

Nelson, Ken. *My First 90 Years Plus 3*. Pittsburgh: Dorrance, 2007.

Nudie, Jamie Lee, and Mary Lynn Cabrall. *Nudie the Rodeo Tailor.* Layton, UT: Gibbs Smith, 2004.

Port, Ian S. *The Birth of Loud: Leo Fender, Les Paul, and the Guitar-Pioneering Rivalry That Shaped Rock 'n' Roll.* New York: Simon & Schuster, 2019.

Shaughnessy, Mary Alice. *Les Paul: American Original.* New York: William Morrow, 1992.

Stone, Cliffie, with Joan Carol Stone. *You Gotta Be Bad Before You Can Be Good!.* Woodstock, NY: Beekman, 2000.

Stuart, Marty. *Pilgrims: Sinners, Saints, and Prophets.* New York: Rutledge Hill, 1999.

Travis Eatherly, Pat. *In Search of My Father.* Nashville: Broadman, 1987.

Travis Eatherly, Pat. *A Scrapbook of My Daddy.* Self-published, 2000.

Van Maastricht, Norm. *Paul Yandell, Second to the Best: A Sideman's Chronicle.* Atglen, PA: Schiffer Books, 2016.

Williams, Gary, *Girls, Guns and Guitars.* Self-published, 1977.

Wolfe, Charles K. *In Close Harmony: The Story of the Louvin Brothers.* Jackson, MI: University Press of Mississippi, 1995.

Wolfe, Charles K., and Kip Lornell. *The Life and Legend of Lead Belly.* New York: HarperCollins, 1992.

Wren, Christopher, with an introduction by Merle Travis. *Johnny Cash: Winners Have Scars Too.* New York: Dial, 1973.

NEWSPAPERS

[No author]. "Muhlenberg Countians Know Merle Travis as Local Success." *Owensboro Messenger,* May 19, 1946, 8A.

Ladd, Bill. "The Home Town Smokes Travis Out." *Louisville Courier-Journal,* November 16, 1947, 81–83.

Loffer, Lee. "Blondie, Dagwood Cavort from Van Nuys Artist's Pen." *North Hollywood Valley Times,* April 15, 1948, 5.

Ames, Walter. "Television, Radio, News and Programs." *Los Angeles Times,* March 29, 1951, 22.

Curtiss, Lou. "Memories of Merle," part 1. *San Diego Troubadour,* August 2019, https://sandiegotroubadour.com/memories-of-merle/.

Curtiss, Lou. "Memories of Merle," part 2. *San Diego Troubadour,* September 2019, https://sandiegotroubadour.com/memories-of-merle-2/.

MAGAZINES

Baxter, Bob. "Merle Travis: The Man, the Music." *Guitar Player*, September 1976, 20–36.

Flippo, Chet. "Merle Travis, Guitar Legend." *Rolling Stone*, June 19, 1975, 24.

Flippo, Chet. "Chet Atkins: The Rolling Stone Interview." *Rolling Stone*, February 12, 1976, 30.

Humphrey, Mark. "Merle Travis talking to Mark Humphrey," parts 1–4. *Old Time Music* nos. 36/37/38/39 (1981–82).

Lightfoot, William E. "Mose Rager from Muhlenberg County: 'Hey, C'mon, Buddy, Play Me a Good Rag!.'" *Adena* 4, no. 2 (Fall 1979): 3–41.

Raphael, Judy. "Merle Travis Remembered—The Last Interview." *Country Rhythms*, April 1984, 28, 59.

Travis, Merle. "Chet Atkins with His Guitar Down." *Guitar World*, November 1980, 34–37.

Travis, Merle. "Merle Travis Remembers: The Fingerpickers of Muhlenberg County, Ky." *Guitar World*, July 1980, 16-20.

Travis, Merle. "Merle Travis on Crazy Joe Maphis." *Guitar World*, January 1981, 54–59.

Travis, Merle. "Merle Travis Remembers Paul A. Bigsby… The Man Who Could Make Any Damn Thing!." *Guitar World*, September 1980, 54–57.

Travis, Merle. "Remembrances of Merle Travis," parts 1 and 2. *JEMF Quarterly*, Volume XV, Nos. 54/56 (Issue #54: Summer, 1979. Issue #56: Winter, 1979).

Travis, Merle. "Roy Lanham—I Saw By His Outfit That He Was a Cowboy." *Guitar World*, July 1981.

Travis, Merle. "The Life Story of Merle Travis." *The Capitol*, Volume 4, No. 5, May 1946, 10.

West, Hedy. "Merle Travis on Homeground." *Sing Out Magazine* 25, no. 1 (May–June 1976): 20–28.

Wolfe, Charles K. "Off The Record: The Sheppard Brothers." *Journal of the Academy for the Preservation of Old-Time Country Music*, no. 16 (August 1993): 24–25.

LINER NOTES

[No author]. Merle Travis, *The Merle Travis Guitar*. Capitol LP T 650, issued 1956.

[No author]. Merle Travis, *Back Home*. Capitol LP T 891, issued 1957.

[No author]. Merle Travis, *Merle Travis—Our Man from Kentucky*. Hilltop JM-6040, issued ca. 1965.

[No author]. Merle Travis, *The Best of Merle Travis*. Capitol LP T 2662, issued 1967.

[No author]. Merle Travis, *Strictly Guitar*. Capitol LP ST 2938, issued 1968.

Atkins, Chet. *Merle Travis and Joe Maphis—Country Music's Two Guitar Greats*. Capitol LP T 2102, issued 1964.

Cherry, Hugh. Chet Atkins and Merle Travis, *The Atkins-Travis Traveling Show*. RCA APL 1–0479, issued 1974.

Green, Archie. Merle Travis, *Folk Songs of the Hills*. Bear Family reissue BCD15636.

Kahn, Ed. Merle Travis, *TRAVIS!*. Capitol LP T 1664, issued 1962.

Kienzle, Rich. Merle Travis, *Guitar Rags and a Too Fast Past*. Bear Family box set BCD 15637. Used by permission of Bear Family Records.

Smith, Packy. Wesley Tuttle, *Detour*. Bear Family box set BCD 16416.

Smith, Packy. Tex Ritter, *Blood on the Saddle*. Bear Family box set BCD 16260.

Smith, Packy. Gene Autry, *That Silver Haired Daddy of Mine*. Bear Family box set BCD 15944.

Stone, Cliffie. Merle Travis, *Walkin' the Strings*. Capitol LP T 1391, issued 1960.

Travis, John Melvin. Merle Travis, *Songs from the Coal Mines*. Capitol LP T 1956, issued 1963.

Travis, Merle. Merle Travis and Johnny Bond, *Great Songs of the Delmore Brothers*. Capitol LP ST 249, issued 1969.

Travis, Merle. *Merle Travis and Joe Maphis—Country Guitar Giants*. CMH Records CMH-9017, issued 1979.

Travis, Merle. Merle Travis, *The Merle Travis Story*. CMH Records CMH-9018, issued 1979.

Travis, Merle. Merle Travis, *Merle Travis Guitar Standards*. CMH Records CMH-9024, issued 1980.

Wakely, Jimmy. Merle Travis, *Merle Travis—The Guitar Player, Singer and Composer*. Shasta LP 523, issued ca. 1976.

AUTHOR INTERVIEWS

Bobby Anderson, October 13, 2018, Nashville, Tennessee

David Boyd, 2010, San Diego, California

Thom Bresh, October 13–14, 2018, Nashville, Tennessee

Sandra Burinda, August 27, 2018, Ridgeland, Wisconsin

Ray Campi, April 8, 2019, Eagle Rock, California

Jimmy Capps, May 5, 2019, telephone

Larry Collins, May 4, 2020, telephone

Lynne Davis Herrod, October 2–3, 2018, Yellville, Arkansas

Gene Eatherly, July 15, 2018, telephone

Betsy Gay, March 30, 2019, telephone

Betsy Gay, October 29, 2019, Saugus, California

Merle Haggard, December 28, 2006, telephone

Chris Hillman, April 14, 2020, telephone

David Lindley, May 14, 2020, telephone

Scott Lynch, March 3, 2019, telephone

Barbara Mandrell, October 17, 2018, telephone

Rose Lee Maphis and Jody Maphis, October 17–18, 2018, Nashville, Tennessee

John McEuen, October 22, 2019, telephone

Royce Morgan, Claude Travis, and Bill Harlan, October 6, 2018, Beechmont, Kentucky

Kenny Mullins, March 28, 2019, telephone

Michael O'Dorn, April 4, 2019, telephone

Eddie Pennington, October 6, 2018, Princeton, Kentucky

Helen "Tillie" Peters, July 27, 2018, telephone

Brian Powers, October 10, 2018, Cincinnati, Ohio

Herb Remington, August 5, 2018, telephone

Michael Robinson, July 12–13, 2018, telephone

Michael Robinson, July 16–17, 2018, Indian Springs, Nevada

Michael Robinson, May 4, 2020, telephone

Jack Rogers, July 29, 2018, telephone

Jack Rogers, October 11, 2018, Hillsboro, Ohio

Dave Stewart, October 15, 2018, Corinth, Mississippi

Marty Stuart, September 24, 2019, telephone

Jamie Sweet, April 28, 2020, text

Merlene Travis-Maggini, March 26, 2020, telephone

Merlene Travis-Maggini and Cindy Travis, numerous conversations via email and text, 2017–20, and in person on September 25, 2018, Santa Barbara, California

Marilyn Tuttle, July 13, 2018, San Fernando, California

Marilyn Tuttle, October 8, 2019, telephone

John Wagner, March 27, 2020, telephone

Rendal Wall, April 29, 2020, telephone

Lynn Wells, October 7, 2018, Greenville, Kentucky

Johnny Western, July 22, 2018, telephone

INTERVIEWS NOT CITED ELSEWHERE

Johnny Bond with Douglas B. Green, July 1, 1974, CMF Oral History Project

Leo Fender with Tom Wheeler in *American Guitars*, 58–67. New York: Harper & Row, 1982.

Joe and Rose Lee Maphis with Douglas B. Green, January 7 and 15, 1975, CMF Oral History Project

Hank Penny cassette interview with Greg Drust, parts 1–2, date unknown, courtesy Virginia Curtiss

Hank Penny with Cary Ginell, *Roots and Branches*, KCSN, June 29, 1987, courtesy Cary Ginell

Hank Penny cassette tape with Foxy John and Melvin Wilson, July 10, 1985, International Hotel, Calgary, courtesy Virginia Curtiss

Cliffie Stone with Lou Curtiss and Tom Sims cassette tape, parts 1–2, February 26, 1984, courtesy Virginia Curtiss

Billy Wilson with Gary Wilson cassette tape, date unknown, courtesy Dave Stewart

ARCHIVES

Archie Green Archives and Ed Kahn Collection, Southern Folklife Center, Wilson Library, University of North Carolina, Chapel Hill (special thanks to Steven Weiss, Tim Hogdgon, and Aaron Smithers)

Charles K. Wolfe Archives, Center for Popular Music, Middle Tennessee State University (special thanks to Rachel K. Morris):

WOLFE-01048—1982 Travis Jam ¾

WOLFE-02010—Merle Travis 5/6 10–19–82

WOLFE -01022—Merle Travis 10–19–82

WOLFE-02036—Grandpa and Ramona Jones talk about Merle Travis

WOLFE-00938—Grandpa Jones 11 663

WOLFE-00772—77 CMA int 625

WOLFE-02025—Grandpa Jones Int 6–22–81

WOLFE-02028—Grandpa Jones 10–9–82 side 3

WOLFE-00030—289 Bob Wills INT-78s

WOLFE-01138—Mose Rager

WOLFE-00391—Red Jones Interview

WOLFE-00830—Clyde and Marie Dilleha, Springfield, May 2, 1980

WOLFE-01015—Fred Foster interview 9/27/96

WOLFE-01084—Mose Rager interview, Joy Heimgarner, ca. 1979

RESEARCH TRIPS

Merle and Dorothy Travis home, Hank Thompson Road, Park Hill, Oklahoma, 2016

Merle and Bettie Travis Home, 348 Lily-of-the-Valley Trailer court, Saugus, California, July 14, 2018

Merle and Bettie Travis home, 5731 Ranchito, Van Nuys, California, July 19, 2018

Sandra Burinda home, Ridgeland, Wisconsin, August 27, 2018

Lynne Davis Herrod home, Yellville, Arkansas, October 2–3, 2018

Cincinnati, Ohio: Brian Powers; Cincinnati Public Library (WLW former site); Travis Cincinnati home sites; downtown, October 10, 2018

Jack Rogers home, Hillsboro, Ohio, October 11, 2018

Bobby Anderson, Mother Maybelle Carter Nursing Home, Madison, Tennessee, October 13, 2018

Muhlenberg County sites: Merle Travis Music Center (Powderly); Paradise Park (Powderly); Merle Travis birth site (Rosewood); Ebenezer burial site; homes of Bill Harlan (Greenville), Royce Morgan (Beech Creek), and Claude Travis (Beechmont); Drakesboro City Hall thumbpickers gathering; Cleaton Crossing, October 4–9, 2018

Eddie Pennington home, Princeton, Kentucky, October 6, 2018

Kentucky Music Hall of Fame / Renfro Valley Barn Dance, Kentucky, October 9, 2018

Thom Bresh home, Nashville, Tennessee, October 13–14, 2018

Dave Stewart home, Corinth, Mississippi, October 15, 2018

Rose Lee and Jody Maphis home, Nashville, TN Tennessee October 17, 2018

Cindy Travis's home, Santa Barbara, California, September 25, 2018

Ray Campi home, Eagle Rock, California, April 8, 2019

Virginia Curtiss home, El Cajon, California, October 11, 2019

Betsy Gay home, Saugus, California, October 29, 2019

SPECIAL THANKS TO:

Merlene Travis-Maggini, Cindy Travis, Thom Bresh, Lindsey Westbrook, Claude Travis, Eddie and Penny Pennington, Bill and Ann Harlan, Dave and Becky Stewart, Michael Robinson, Dawn Eatherly, Dave Travis, Kenny Mullins, Lynne and Ronnie Herrod, Brian Powers, Jack Rogers, Jamie Sweet and family, Marilyn Tuttle, Rose Lee Maphis, Jody Maphis, Barbara Mandrell, Herb Remington, Bobby Anderson, Gary Williams, Kevin Coffey, Richard Weize, Patrick Milligan, Laurence J. Zwisohn, Dave Sax, Charles K. Wolfe, Ed Kahn, Bill Lightfoot, Archie Green, Mark Humphrey, Marty Stuart, Johnny Western, Ken Campanile, Damian Fanelli and the staff of *Guitar World* magazine, Ray Campi, Cary Ginell, Avery Bradshaw, Brenda Colladay, Chris Richards, Jim Herrington, my girlfriend Sally Jo Burns, my daughter Evelyn Dickerson, and Scott B. Bomar at BMG Books for believing in the project and making it a reality.

ENDNOTES

1 Marty Stuart, *Pilgrims: Sinners, Saints, and Prophets* (New York: Rutledge Hill, 1999), 113.

2 Author interview, September 25, 2018.

3 Author interview, October 13, 2018.

4 The passages of Merle's writings have been edited for concision. The writing in this chapter comes from "I Have a Sick Sister in Texas," a text Merle produced in 1966 for an (unknown) Lucky Moeller fan magazine and also distributed to friends. Merlene and Cindy Travis archives.

5 Undated but 1980s, Merlene and Cindy Travis archives.

6 Earl T. Dukes interview cassette, courtesy Dave Stewart.

7 Ed Kahn interview with Merle Travis, July 10, 1961, audio recording, Ed Kahn Collection, box 3, folder 18, FT-20360/12553, Southern Folklife Collection, Wilson Library, University of North Carolina, Chapel Hill (hereafter "Ed Kahn interview with Merle Travis, July 10, 1961").

8 Merle Travis jam session cassette tape with John Hartford no. 3, Charles K. Wolfe Audio Library, WOLFE-01048–1, Center for Popular Music, Middle Tennessee State University, Murfreesboro.

9 Ed Kahn interview with Merle Travis, July 10, 1961.

10 Letter to Pat Travis Eatherly, undated but 1980s, Merlene and Cindy Travis archives.

11 Ed Kahn interview with Merle Travis, July 10, 1961.

12 Bobby Anderson, *That Muhlenberg Sound* (Beechmont, KY: Muhlbut, 1993), viiii.

13 Eddie Pennington interview with John Melvin Travis, 1987, cassette tape courtesy Eddie Pennington.

14 Mark Humphrey interview with Merle Travis, June 21, 1979, courtesy Mark Humphrey.

15 Douglas B. Green interview with Merle Travis, October 17, 1975, CMF Oral History Project.

16 Eddie Pennington interview with John Melvin Travis, 1987, cassette tape courtesy Eddie Pennington.

17 Author interview, October 6, 2018.

18 Eddie Pennington interview with John Melvin Travis, 1987, cassette tape courtesy Eddie Pennington.

19 Eddie Pennington interview with John Melvin Travis, 1987, cassette tape courtesy Eddie Pennington.

20 Mark Humphrey interview with Merle Travis, June 21, 1979, courtesy Mark Humphrey.

21 Ed Kahn interview with Merle Travis, July 10, 1961.

22 Bill Lightfoot interview with Kennedy Jones, 1977, cassette tape courtesy Dave Stewart.

23 Bill Lightfoot interview with Kennedy Jones, 1977.

24 Author interview, October 13–14, 2018.

25 Bill Lightfoot interview with Mose Rager, 1977, "Mose Rager from Muhlenberg County: 'Hey, C'mon, Buddy, Play Me a Good Rag!.'" *Adena* 4, no. 2 (Fall 1979): 3-41

26 Ed Kahn interview with Merle Travis, July 10, 1961.

27 Ed Kahn interview with Merle Travis, July 10, 1961.

28 Art Kaul, "Mose Rager: Legend With A Thumbpick," *Owensboro Messenger-Inquirer*, September 11, 1977, 25.

29 Carlton Jackson and Nancy Richey, *Mose Rager: Kentucky's Incomparable Guitar Master* (Morley (MO): Acclaim, 2016), 31.

30 Merle Travis, "Foreword," hand-typed document for unknown publication, Merlene and Cindy Travis archives.

31 Joseph Wilson, liner notes for Smithsonian Folkways Eddie Pennington album, quoted in Jackson and Richey, *Mose Rager: Kentucky's Incomparable Guitar Master*, 73.

32 Letter dated May 25, 1979, reproduced in Jackson and Richey, *Mose Rager: Kentucky's Incomparable Guitar Master*, 88.

33 Quoted in Anderson, *That Muhlenberg Sound*, 31.

34 Bill Lightfoot interview with Mose Rager, 1977.

35 Art Kaul, "Mose Rager: Legend With A Thumbpick," *Owensboro Messenger-Inquirer*, 25.

36 Earl Talmadge Dukes cassette interview, date unknown, courtesy Dave Stewart.

37 Mark Humphrey interview with Merle Travis, June 21, 1979, courtesy Mark Humphrey.

38 Ed Kahn interview with Merle Travis, July 10, 1961.

39 Mark Humphrey interview with Merle Travis, June 21, 1979, courtesy Mark Humphrey.

40 Lou Curtiss, "Memories of Merle," part 1, *San Diego Troubadour*, August 2019, https://sandiegotroubadour.com/memories-of-merle/.

41 Ed Kahn interview with Merle Travis, July 10, 1961.

42 Mark Humphrey interview with Merle Travis, June 21, 1979, courtesy Mark Humphrey.

43 Curtiss, "Memories of Merle," part 1.

44 Bill Ladd, "The Home Town Smokes Travis Out," *Louisville Courier-Journal*, November 16, 1947, 81–83.

45 Earl Talmadge Dukes cassette interview, courtesy Dave Stewart.

46 Earl Talmadge Dukes cassette interview, courtesy Dave Stewart.

47 Ed Kahn interview with Merle Travis, July 10, 1961.

48 Charles K. Wolfe interview with Louis "Grandpa" Jones and Ramona Jones, July 5, 1993, WOLFE-02036–1, Charles K. Wolfe Audio Library, Center for Popular Music, Middle Tennessee State University, Murfreesboro.

49 Douglas B. Green interview with Merle Travis, October 17, 1975, CMF Oral History Project.

50 Ed Kahn interview with Merle Travis, July 10, 1961.

51 Ed Kahn interview with Merle Travis, July 10, 1961.

52 Earl Talmadge Dukes cassette interview, courtesy Dave Stewart.

53 Dave Stewart interview with Sleepy Marlin, April 29, 2002, cassette courtesy Dave Stewart.

54 Merle Travis Military Records 1943–44, obtained through National Personnel Records Center, National Archives, St. Louis.

55 Ed Kahn interview with Merle Travis, July 10, 1961.

56 Ed Kahn interview with Merle Travis, July 10, 1961.

57 Dave Stewart interview with Sleepy Marlin, April 29, 2002, cassette courtesy Dave Stewart.

58 Douglas B. Green interview with Merle Travis, October 17, 1975, CMF Oral History Project.

59 Mark Humphrey interview with Merle Travis, June 21, 1979, courtesy Mark Humphrey.

60 Douglas B. Green interview with Merle Travis, October 17, 1975, CMF Oral History Project.

61 Merle Travis jam session cassette tape with John Hartford no. 2, Charles K. Wolfe Audio Library, WOLFE-01022–2, Center for Popular Music, Middle Tennessee State University, Murfreesboro.

62 Mark Humphrey interview with Merle Travis, June 21, 1979, courtesy Mark Humphrey.

63 Hugh Cherry interview with Merle Travis, 1982, courtesy Dave Stewart.

64 Curtiss, "Memories of Merle," part 1.

65 Hugh Cherry interview with Merle Travis, 1982, courtesy Dave Stewart.

66 Author interview, September 25, 2018.

67 Pat Travis Eatherly, *A Scrapbook of My Daddy* (Self-published, 2000), 26, 30–31.

68 Alton Delmore with Charles K. Wolfe, *Truth Is Stranger Than Publicity* (1977; repr., Nashville: Country Music Foundation and Vanderbilt University Press, 1995), 173.

69 Dave Stewart interview with Sleepy Marlin, April 29, 2002, cassette courtesy Dave Stewart.

70 Curtiss, "Memories of Merle," part 1.

71 Douglas B. Green interview with Merle Travis, October 17, 1975, CMF Oral History Project.

72 Ed Kahn interview with Merle Travis, July 10, 1961.

73 [No author], "Pity Daniel Boone," unknown newspaper [clipping], September 26, 1937, Merlene and Cindy Travis archives.

74 Curtiss, "Memories of Merle," part 1.

75 Charles K. Wolfe interview cassette tape with Louis "Grandpa" Jones and Ramona Jones, July 5, 1993, WOLFE-02036–1, Charles K. Wolfe Audio Library, Center for Popular Music, Middle Tennessee State University, Murfreesboro.

76 Mark Humphrey interview with Merle Travis, June 21, 1979, courtesy Mark Humphrey.

77 Gene Bear interview with Wesley Tuttle on *Bear Country* public access television show, date unknown but early 1990s, courtesy Marilyn Tuttle.

78 Gary Williams interview with Merle Travis, March 20, 1974, used with permission of Gary Williams.

79 Charles K. Wolfe interview cassette tape with Louis "Grandpa" Jones, June 22, 1981, Charles K. Wolfe Audio Library, WOLFE-02025–1, Center for Popular Music, Middle Tennessee State University, Murfreesboro.

80 Merlene Travis, text to the author, May 13, 2020.

81 Douglas B. Green interview with Merle Travis, October 17, 1975, CMF Oral History Project.

82 Letter undated but 1939, Eatherly Family archives.

83 Mark Humphrey interview with Merle Travis, June 21, 1979, courtesy Mark Humphrey.

84 Newspaper clipping, date and newspaper unknown, Merlene and Cindy Travis archives.

85 Earl Talmadge Dukes cassette interview, courtesy Dave Stewart.

86 Merlene and Cindy Travis archives.

87 Grandpa Jones with Charles K. Wolfe, *Everybody's Grandpa* (Knoxville: University of Tennessee Press, 1984), 80.

88 Merle Travis, "Ramblin' Roy Lanham," *Guitar World*, July 1981, 73-74, 76.

89 Curtiss, "Memories of Merle," part 1.

90 Merle Travis, "Ol' Crazy Joe or the Joe Maphis I Know," *Guitar World*, January 1981, 55.

91 Author interview, September 25, 2018.

92 Jones with Wolfe, *Everybody's Grandpa*, 80–81.

93 Chet Flippo, "Chet Atkins: The Rolling Stone Interview," *Rolling Stone*, February 12, 1976, 30.

94 Arkie Kinkade, "Merle Travis: Radio, Stage, Screen and Recording Star," *Hillbilly News*, May–June 1947, 2.

95 Jones with Wolfe, *Everybody's Grandpa*, 82–83.

96 Mark Humphrey interview with Merle Travis, June 21, 1979, courtesy Mark Humphrey.

97 Jones with Wolfe, *Everybody's Grandpa*, 99.

98 Mark Humphrey interview with Merle Travis, June 21, 1979, courtesy Mark Humphrey.

99 Delmore with Wolfe, *Truth Is Stranger Than Publicity*, 274–75.

100 Mark Humphrey interview with Merle Travis, June 21, 1979, courtesy Mark Humphrey.

101 Delmore with Wolfe, *Truth Is Stranger Than Publicity*, 276-279.

102 Ed Kahn interview with Merle Travis, July 10, 1961.

103 Curtiss, "Memories of Merle," part 1.

104 Ed Kahn interview with Merle Travis, July 10, 1961.

105 Jones with Wolfe, *Everybody's Grandpa*, 96–97.

106 Mark Humphrey interview with Merle Travis, June 21, 1979, courtesy Mark Humphrey.

107 Ed Kahn interview with Merle Travis, July 10, 1961.

108 Jones with Wolfe, *Everybody's Grandpa*, 97–98.

109 Ed Kahn interview with Merle Travis, July 10, 1961.

110 Douglas B. Green interview with Merle Travis, October 17, 1975, CMF Oral History Project.

111 Jones with Wolfe, *Everybody's Grandpa*, 98.

112 Curtiss, "Memories of Merle," part 1.

113 Mark Humphrey interview with Merle Travis, June 21, 1979, courtesy Mark Humphrey.

114 Letter dated December 25, 1964, Ed Kahn collection, box 3, folder 15, #20360 p. 8, Southern Folklife Collection, Wilson Library, University of North Carolina, Chapel Hill.

115 Report of Aptitude Board, January 28, 1944, Merle Travis military records 1943–44, obtained through National Personnel Records Center, National Archives, St. Louis.

[116] Author interview, July 12, 2018.

[117] Dave Stewart interview cassette tape with Sleepy Marlin, April 29, 2002, courtesy Dave Stewart.

[118] Letter to Jane Allen, February 9, 1944, Ed Kahn Collection, box 3, folder 17, #23060, Southern Folklife Collection, Wilson Library, University of North Carolina, Chapel Hill.

[119] Report of Aptitude Board, January 28, 1944, Merle Travis military records 1943–44, obtained through National Personnel Records Center, National Archives, St. Louis.

[120] Ed Kahn interview with Wesley Tuttle, March 3, 1995, Ed Kahn collection, box 3, folder 18, pp. 146–47, #20360, Southern Folklife Collection, Wilson Library, University of North Carolina, Chapel Hill.

[121] Charles K. Wolfe interview cassette tape with Louis "Grandpa" Jones and Ramona Jones, July 5, 1993, WOLFE-02036–1, Charles K. Wolfe Audio Library, Center for Popular Music, Middle Tennessee State University, Murfreesboro.

[122] Charles K. Wolfe interview cassette tape with Louis "Grandpa" Jones and Ramona Jones, July 5, 1993, WOLFE-02036–1, Charles K. Wolfe Audio Library, Center for Popular Music, Middle Tennessee State University, Murfreesboro.

[123] Ed Kahn interview with Merle Travis, July 10, 1961, pp. 34–35.

[124] Curtiss, "Memories of Merle," part 1.

[125] Dave Stewart interview cassette tape with Sleepy Marlin, April 29, 2002, courtesy Dave Stewart.

[126] Ed Kahn interview with Wesley Tuttle, March 3, 1995, p. 148, Ed Kahn collection, box 3, folder 18, pp. 146–47, #20360, Southern Folklife Collection, Wilson Library, University of North Carolina, Chapel Hill.

[127] Ed Kahn interview with Wesley Tuttle, March 3, 1995, p. 147, Ed Kahn collection, box 3, folder 18, pp. 146–47, #20360, Southern Folklife Collection, Wilson Library, University of North Carolina, Chapel Hill.

[128] Ed Kahn interview with Merle Travis, July 10, 1961, p. 36.

[129] Author interview, March 30, 2019.

[130] Letter undated but mid-1980s following Merle's death, Merlene and Cindy Travis archives.

[131] Ed Kahn collection, box 3, folder 17, #20360, pp. 8–9, Southern Folklife Collection, Wilson Library, University of North Carolina, Chapel Hill.

[132] Press release dated June 2, 1947, Merle Travis letterhead, Merlene and Cindy Travis archives.

[133] Ed Kahn interview with Wesley Tuttle, March 3, 1995, p. 6, Ed Kahn collection, box 3, folder 18, pp. 146–47, #20360, Southern Folklife Collection, Wilson Library, University of North Carolina, Chapel Hill.

[134] Lou Curtiss, "Memories of Merle," part 2, *San Diego Troubadour*, September 2019, https://sandiegotroubadour.com/memories-of-merle-2/.

[135] Author interview, August 5, 2018.

[136] Possibly unpublished, Merlene and Cindy Travis archives.

[137] Author interview, July 22, 2018.

[138] Letter dated May 5, 1944, Ed Kahn Collection, box 3, folder 17, #20360, Southern Folklife Collection, Wilson Library, University of North Carolina, Chapel Hill.

[139] Letter dated August 29, 1944, Ed Kahn Collection, box 3, folder 17, #20360, Southern Folklife Collection, Wilson Library, University of North Carolina, Chapel Hill.

[140] Cottonseed Clark, *Cottonseed Clark's Brushwood Poetry and Philosophy* (self-published booklet, 1945), 55.

[141] Author interview, October 8, 2019.

[142] Archie Campbell interview with Cliffie Stone, *Yesteryear in Nashville*, TNN, date unknown but 1990s, author's collection, courtesy Virginia Curtiss.

[143] Archie Campbell interview with Cliffie Stone, *Yesteryear in Nashville*, TNN, date unknown but 1990s, author's collection, courtesy Virginia Curtiss.

[144] Walter Ames, "Television, Radio, News and Programs," *Los Angeles Times*, March 29, 1951, 22.

[145] Curtiss, "Memories of Merle," part 2.

[146] Wesley Tuttle on Cary Ginell, *Cary's Country Store—Tribute to Travis Part Two*, KCSN, October 26, 1983, courtesy Cary Ginell.

[147] Curtiss, "Memories of Merle," part 2.

148 Letter dated March 27, 1945, Ed Kahn Collection, box 3, folder 17, #20360, Southern Folklife Collection, Wilson Library, University of North Carolina, Chapel Hill.

149 Douglas B. Green interview with Merle Travis, October 17, 1975, CMF Oral History Project.

150 Possibly unpublished, Merlene and Cindy Travis archives.

151 Mark Humphrey interview with Merle Travis, June 21, 1979, courtesy Mark Humphrey.

152 Ed Kahn interview with John Melvin Travis, May 19, 1986, additional notes p. 2, Ed Kahn Collection, box 3, folder 18, #20360, Southern Folklife Collection, Wilson Library, University of North Carolina, Chapel Hill.

153 Ed Kahn interview with John Melvin Travis, May 19, 1986, p. 24, Ed Kahn Collection, box 3, folder 18, #20360, Southern Folklife Collection, Wilson Library, University of North Carolina, Chapel Hill.

154 Ed Kahn Collection, box 3, folder 17, #20360, Southern Folklife Collection, University of North Carolina, Chapel Hill.

155 John W. Rumble interview with Cliffie Stone, 1992, CMF Oral History Project.

156 Ed Kahn interview with Merle Travis, July 10, 1961.

157 Curtiss, "Memories of Merle," part 2.

158 *Austin City Limits*, date unknown but late 1970s, author's collection.

159 Ed Kahn interview with Merle Travis, July 10, 1961.

160 Hank Penny quoted by Rich Kienzle, liner notes to Bear Family's *Merle Travis: Guitar Rags and a Too Fast Past* box set, BCD 15637, p. 22. Used by permission of Bear Family Records.

161 Douglas B. Green interview with Merle Travis, October 17, 1975, CMF Oral History Project.

162 Jones with Wolfe, *Everybody's Grandpa*, 100–102.

163 Mark Humphrey interview with Merle Travis, June 21, 1979, courtesy Mark Humphrey.

164 John W. Rumble interview with Cliffie Stone, 1992, CMF Oral History Project.

165 Curtiss, "Memories of Merle," part 2.

166 Cliffie Stone quoted by Rich Kienzle, liner notes to Bear Family's *Merle Travis: Guitar Rags and a Too Fast Past* box set, BCD 15637, p. 22. Used by permission of Bear Family Records.

167 Ed Kahn interview with Merle Travis, July 10, 1961.

168 Letter to Paul May, March 15, 1980, Merlene and Cindy Travis archives.

169 Cliffie Stone, "With Only 2 Records, Merle Travis Leaps to Fame in Billboard Poll," *Capitol News* 5, no. 2 (February 1947): 8.

170 Charles K. Wolfe and Kip Lornell, *The Life and Legend of Lead Belly* (New York: HarperCollins, 1992), 230.

171 Douglas B. Green interview with Merle Travis, October 17, 1975, CMF Oral History Project.

172 Ed Kahn miscellaneous papers, p. 189, box 3, folder 16, #20360, Ed Kahn Collection, Southern Folklife Collection, Wilson Library, University of North Carolina, Chapel Hill.

173 Merle Travis jam session cassette tape with John Hartford no. 4, Charles K. Wolfe Audio Library, WOLFE-01048–2, Center For Popular Music, Middle Tennessee State University, Murfreesboro.

174 Mark Humphrey interview with Merle Travis, June 21, 1979, courtesy Mark Humphrey.

175 Mark Humphrey interview with Merle Travis, June 21, 1979, courtesy Mark Humphrey.

176 Author interview, October 13–14, 2018.

177 Dorothy Horstman, *Sing Your Heart Out, Country Boy* (Nashville: Country Music Foundation Press, 1975), 48.

178 Curtiss, "Memories of Merle," part 2.

179 Merlene and Cindy Travis archives.

180 Letter dated 1980, Merlene and Cindy Travis archives.

181 Letter dated December 1987, Eatherly Family archives.

182 Tex Ann Nation [aka Sidna J. Clements], *Cobwebs, Memories and Miracles* (self-published, 1988), 69.

183 Ed Kahn phone interview notes with Joe Allison, 1994, Ed Kahn Collection, box 3, folder 18, #20360, Southern Folklife Collection, Wilson Library, University of North Carolina, Chapel Hill.

184 [No author], "Driver Denies Drunk Charges," *Los Angeles Examiner*, September 6, 1946, 1.

[185] Author interview, July 13, 2018.

[186] Email to the author, December 6, 2019.

[187] Author interview, October 13–14, 2018.

[188] Author interview, July 16–17, 2018.

[189] Author interview, October 13–14, 2018.

[190] Letter to Mark Pritcher, Chet Atkins Appreciation Society, August 16, 1995, courtesy Dave Stewart.

[191] Letter to Dave Stewart, May 20, 1996, courtesy Dave Stewart.

[192] Letter to Mark Pritcher, Chet Atkins Appreciation Society, August 16, 1995, courtesy Dave Stewart.

[193] Mark Humphrey interview with Merle Travis, June 21, 1979, courtesy Mark Humphrey.

[194] Letter to Dave Stewart, May 20, 1996, courtesy Dave Stewart.

[195] Billy Liebert quoted by Rich Kienzle, liner notes to Bear Family's *Merle Travis: Guitar Rags and a Too Fast Past* box set, BCD 15637, p. 33. Used by permission of Bear Family Records.

[196] Clipping from unknown publication, dated August 4, 1947, Merlene and Cindy Travis archives.

[197] Bob Baxter, "Merle Travis: The Man, the Music," *Guitar Player*, September 1976, 32.

[198] Mark Humphrey interview with Merle Travis, June 21, 1979, courtesy Mark Humphrey.

[199] Mark Humphrey interview with Merle Travis, June 21, 1979, courtesy Mark Humphrey.

[200] Merle Travis, liner notes to *Merle Travis and Joe Maphis—Country Guitar Giants* (CMH Records, 1979).

[201] Mark Humphrey interview with Merle Travis, June 21, 1979, courtesy Mark Humphrey.

[202] Dave Stewart, interview with Ginny Cushman, *Cannonball Rag*, no. 20 (April 1997): 3. *Cannonball Rag* was a self-published fan publication that ran for several years. It is unknown if a complete run is in any library or research facility.

[203] Author interview, October 11, 2018.

[204] Author interview, October 11, 2018.

[205] Dave Stewart, interview with Ginny Cushman, *Cannonball Rag*, no. 20 (April 1997): 3.

[206] Letter to Dave Stewart, May 18, 1996, courtesy Dave Stewart.

[207] Stewart interview with Cushman, 3.

[208] Stewart interview with Cushman, 3.

[209] Stewart, interview with Cushman, 4.

[210] Wesley Tuttle quoted by Rich Kienzle, liner notes to Bear Family's *Merle Travis: Guitar Rags and a Too Fast Past* box set, BCD 15637, p. 38. Used by permission of Bear Family Records.

[211] Merle Travis, "Merle Travis Remembers Paul A. Bigsby... The Man Who Could Make Any Damn Thing!." *Guitar World*, September 1980, 54–57.

[212] Wesley Tuttle quoted by Rich Kienzle, liner notes to Bear Family's *Merle Travis: Guitar Rags and a Too Fast Past* box set, BCD 15637, p. 38. Used by permission of Bear Family Records.

[213] Author interview, July 13, 2019.

[214] Snake River Jack, "Adlib on Merle Travis" exact date unknown, but article references 1947, self-published fanzine, clipping in Merlene and Cindy Travis archives.

[215] Judy Raphael, "Merle Travis Remembered—The Last Interview," *Country Rhythms Magazine*, April 1984, 59.

[216] Letter undated but 1940s, Merlene and Cindy Travis archives.

[217] Ed Kahn interview with John Melvin Travis, May 19, 1986, pp. 24–25, Ed Kahn Collection, box 3, folder 18, #20360, Southern Folklife Collection, Wilson Library, University of North Carolina, Chapel Hill.

[218] Lee Loffer, "Blondie, Dagwood Cavort From Van Nuys Artist's Pen," *North Hollywood Valley Times*, April 15, 1948, 5.

[219] Douglas B. Green interview with Merle Travis, October 17, 1975, CMF Oral History Project.

[220] Author interview, October 13–14, 2018.

[221] Author interview, October 13–14, 2018.

[222] Hank Thompson quoted by Rich Kienzle, liner notes to Bear Family's *Merle Travis: Guitar Rags and a Too Fast Past* box set, BCD 15637, p. 39. Used by permission of Bear Family Records.

[223] Author interview, July 22, 2018.

[224] Glen Claussen, "Merle Travis—His Dream Came True," *Folk Hillbilly Jamboree*, October 1949, 15, author's collection.

[225] Bigsby ad, *Jamboree*, May 1949, 2, author's collection.

[226] Bigsby flyer, ca. 1951, author's collection.

[227] Tom Wheeler, *American Guitars: An Illustrated History* (New York: Harper and Row,1982), 67.

[228] Author interview, 2002.

[229] Letter to Paul May, March 15, 1980, Merlene and Cindy Travis archives.

[230] Author interview, July 16–17, 2018.

[231] Author interview, October 17, 2018.

[232] Author interview, July 22, 2018.

[233] Mark Humphrey interview with Merle Travis, June 21, 1979, courtesy Mark Humphrey.

[234] Harold Hensley quoted by Rich Kienzle, liner notes to Bear Family's *Merle Travis: Guitar Rags and a Too Fast Past* box set, BCD 15637, p. 40. Used by permission of Bear Family Records.

[235] Hank Penny quoted by Rich Kienzle, liner notes to Bear Family's *Merle Travis: Guitar Rags and a Too Fast Past* box set, BCD 15637, p. 42. Used by permission of Bear Family Records.

[236] Joe Maphis quoted by Rich Kienzle, liner notes to Bear Family's *Merle Travis: Guitar Rags and a Too Fast Past* box set, BCD 15637, p. 42. Used by permission of Bear Family Records.

[237] Wesley Tuttle quoted by Rich Kienzle, liner notes to Bear Family's *Merle Travis: Guitar Rags and a Too Fast Past* box set, BCD 15637, p. 42. Used by permission of Bear Family Records.

[238] *Jamboree*, December 1948, 11, author's collection.

[239] Letter to Dave Stewart, May 18, 1996, courtesy Dave Stewart.

[240] *Ballad of the West* promotional literature, courtesy Dave Stewart.

[241] Author interview, September 25, 2018.

[242] *Jamboree*, December 1948, 26, author's collection.

[243] Author interview, October 11, 2018.

[244] Author interview, September 25, 2018.

[245] Sunny Ciesla, "On The Sunny Side," *Record Roundup*, February 15, 1949, 13, Merlene and Cindy Travis archives.

[246] Author interview, September 25, 2018.

[247] Author interview, September 25, 2018.

[248] [No author], "Wife Chased Him Out, Barefoot Singer Wails," *Los Angeles Times*, December 2, 1949, Section 2, p. 1.

[249] [No author], "Cowboy Crooner Changes Mind On Drunk Charge," *Los Angeles Times*, December 14, 1949, 16.

[250] Rich Kienzle, *Southwest Shuffle: Pioneers of Honky-Tonk, Western Swing, and Country Jazz* (New York: Routledge, 2003), 103.

[251] Gene Bear interview with Wesley Tuttle on *Bear Country* public access television show, date unknown but early 1990s, courtesy Marilyn Tuttle.

[252] Author interview, July 22, 2018.

[253] Joe Maphis quoted by Rich Kienzle, liner notes to Bear Family's *Merle Travis: Guitar Rags and a Too Fast Past* box set, BCD 15637, p. 43. Used by permission of Bear Family Records.

[254] Johnny Sippel, "Folk Talent and Tunes," *Billboard*, September 2, 1950, 101.

[255] Merle Travis, "Good Morning Hollywood," unpublished, ca. 1950, Merlene and Cindy Travis archives.

[256] Merlene and Cindy Travis archives.

[257] Charles K. Wolfe interview cassette tape with Louis "Grandpa" Jones and Ramona Jones, July 5, 1993, WOLFE-02036–1, Charles K. Wolfe Audio Library, Center for Popular Music, Middle Tennessee State University, Murfreesboro.

[258] Letter undated but 1950, Merlene and Cindy Travis archives.

[259] Author interview, September 25, 2018.

[260] Curtiss, "Memories of Merle," part 2.

[261] Author interview, October 17, 2018.

[262] Charles K. Wolfe interview cassette tape with Louis "Grandpa" Jones, October 9, 1982, Charles K. Wolfe Audio Library, WOLFE-02028–1, Center for Popular Music, Middle Tennessee State University, Murfreesboro.

[263] Author interview, October 17, 2018.

[264] Author interview, October 17, 2018.

[265] Hank Thompson quoted by Rich Kienzle, liner notes to Bear Family's *Merle Travis: Guitar Rags and a Too Fast Past* box set, BCD 15637, p. 55. Used by permission of Bear Family Records.

[266] Author interview, September 25, 2018.

[267] Author interview, September 25, 2018.

[268] Travis Eatherly, *A Scrapbook of My Daddy*, 68.

[269] Mark Humphrey interview with Merle Travis, June 21, 1979, courtesy Mark Humphrey.

[270] Unknown source (possibly *Downbeat* magazine), hand-dated 1952, reprinted in the liner notes to Bear Family's *Merle Travis: Guitar Rags and a Too Fast Past* box set, BCD 15637, p. 54. Used by permission of Bear Family Records.

[271] Letter to Paul May, March 15, 1980, Merlene and Cindy Travis archives.

[272] Curtiss, "Memories of Merle," part 2.

[273] Tom E. Danson, "TV-Radiologic" column, *Glendale News Press*, June 8, 1953, n.p., Merlene and Cindy Travis archives.

[274] "Video-Radio Briefs," *Los Angeles Times*, September 4, 1953, 24.

[275] Card dated "Christmas 1980," Merlene and Cindy Travis archives.

[276] Author interview, May 4, 2020.

[277] Letter dated March 17, 1953, Merlene and Cindy Travis archives.

[278] Letter undated but ca. late 1953 or early 1954, Merlene and Cindy Travis archives.

[279] Letter undated but late 1953 or early 1954, Merlene and Cindy Travis archives.

[280] Hank Thompson quoted by Rich Kienzle, liner notes to Bear Family's *Hank Thompson and his Brazos Valley Boys* box set, BCD 15904, p. 31. Used by permission of Bear Family Records.

[281] Letter dated November 17, 1953, Merlene and Cindy Travis archives.

[282] Email to the author, December 6, 2019.

[283] Merlene and Cindy Travis archives.

[284] Email to the author, December 10, 2019.

[285] Author interview, September 25, 2018.

[286] Author interview, September 25, 2018.

287 Author interview, September 25, 2018.

288 Author interview, September 25, 2018.

289 [No author], "TV Actress Turns Down Reconciliation," *Los Angeles Times*, July 23, 1954, 24.

290 Email to the author, December 26, 2019.

291 Author interview, September 25, 2018.

292 Author interview, September 25, 2018.

293 Email to the author, December 26, 2019.

294 Note dated 1983, following Merle's death, gifted by Michael Robinson to the author.

295 Author interview, July 22, 2018.

296 Ed Kahn interview with Bettie Travis, January 30, 1995, p. 4, Ed Kahn Collection, #20360, box 3, folder 18, Southern Folklife Collection, Wilson Library, University of North Carolina, Chapel Hill (hereafter "Ed Kahn interview with Bettie Travis, January 30, 1995").

297 Author interview, July 16–17, 2018.

298 Author interview, July 12, 2018.

299 Ken Nelson, *My First 90 Years Plus 3* (Pittsburgh: Dorrance, 2007), 111.

300 Ken Nelson quoted by Rich Kienzle, liner notes to Bear Family's *Merle Travis: Guitar Rags and a Too Fast Past* box set, BCD 15637, p. 42. Used by permission of Bear Family Records.

301 Letter to George Marlo, BMI, Merlene and Cindy Travis archives.

302 Merle Travis jam session cassette tape with John Hartford no. 5, Charles K. Wolfe Audio Library, WOLFE-02010–1, Center for Popular Music, Middle Tennessee State University, Murfreesboro.

303 Author interview, July 22, 2018.

304 Author interview, July 22, 2018.

305 Merlene and Cindy Travis archives.

306 Ed Kahn interview with Bettie Travis, January 30, 1995, pp. 7–8.

307 Author interview, July 16–17, 2018.

308 Ed Kahn interview with Bettie Travis, January 30, 1995, p. 4.

309 Author interview, July 12, 2018.

310 Travis Eatherly, *A Scrapbook of My Daddy*, 79.

311 Author interview, September 25, 2018.

312 Ed Kahn interview with Bettie Travis, January 30, 1995, pp. 4–5.

313 Email to the author, April 6, 2020.

314 Author interview, October 11, 2018.

315 Jeffrey Buckner Ford, *River of No Return: Tennessee Ernie Ford and the Woman He Loved* (Nashville: Cumberland House, 2008), 109.

316 Jack Fascinato on Cary Ginell, *Cary's Country Store—Tribute to Travis Part One*, KCSN, October 24, 1983, courtesy Cary Ginell.

317 Quoted in Ted Olsen, liner notes to Bear Family's *Tennessee Ernie Ford: Portrait of an American Singer, 1949–60* box set, BCD 17332, p. 39.

318 Ford, *River of No Return*, 109–10.

319 Quoted in Ted Olsen, liner notes to Bear Family's *Tennessee Ernie Ford: Portrait of an American Singer, 1949–60* box set, BCD 17332, p. 39.

320 Ford, *River of No Return*, 110–11.

321 Author interview, July 22, 2018.

322 [No author], "Gene Autry Launches New Christmas Song," *Clarke County Tribune* (Quitman, MS), November 25, 1955, 8.

323 Ed Kahn interview with Bettie Travis, January 30, 1995, p. 6.

324 Merlene and Cindy Travis archives.

325 Ed Kahn interview with Bettie Travis, January 30, 1995, pp. 8–9.

326 Author interview, July 16–17, 2018.

327 Author interview, October 17, 2018.

328 United Press Telephoto HCPO10402, January 4, 1956, courtesy Tom Fallon.

329 United Press Telephoto HCPO10403, January 4, 1956, courtesy Tom Fallon.

330 [No author], "'16 Tons' Writer Amok," *Los Angeles Mirror-News*, January 4, 1956, 1.

331 Author interview, May 4, 2020.

332 Author interview, October 17, 2018.

333 [No author], "30 Armed Policemen Seize Barricaded '16 Tons' Writer," *Los Angeles Times*, January 5, 1956, 2.

334 [No author], "30 Armed Policemen Seize Barricaded '16 Tons' Writer," *Los Angeles Times*, January 5, 1956, 2.

335 Author interview with Michael Robinson, May 4, 2020.

336 Author interview, September 25, 2018.

337 Author interview, May 4, 2020.

338 Gary Williams, *Girls, Guns and Guitars* (self-published, 1977), 81–82.

339 Author interview, October 17, 2018.

340 Postcard dated May 25, 1956, Eatherly Family archives.

341 Clipping from *Johannesburg Star*, May 28, 1956, Merlene and Cindy Travis archives.

342 Oliver Walker, "Audience of 3,000 for Hollywood Show," *Johannesburg Star*, May 29, 1956, 11, Merlene and Cindy Travis archives.

343 [No author], "Hollywood Parade at Olympia Ice Rink," unknown newspaper, May 29, 1956, Merlene and Cindy Travis archives.

344 Clipping, early June 1956, Merlene and Cindy Travis archives.

345 Clipping, early June 1956, Merlene and Cindy Travis archives.

346 Postcard, undated, Merlene and Cindy Travis archives.

347 Author interview, October 13, 2018.

348 Author interview, October 13, 2018.

349 Author interview, October 13, 2018.

350 Author interview, October 7, 2018.

351 Travis Eatherly, *A Scrapbook of My Daddy*, 83.

352 [No Author], "Friends Pay Tribute To Composer Travis," *Owensboro Messenger-Inquirer*, July 1, 1956, 23.

353 Letter dated March 14, 1956, Merlene and Cindy Travis archives.

354 Williams, *Girls, Guns and Guitars*, 82–83.

355 Author interview, July 16–17, 2018.

356 Author interview, October 17, 2018.

357 Author interview, May 4, 2020.

358 Author interview, July 16–17, 2018.

359 Ray Campi telephone interview with Merle Travis, August 4, 1973, courtesy Ray Campi.

³⁶⁰ Robert Hilburn, *Johnny Cash: The Life* (New York: Little, Brown, 2013), 117–18.

³⁶¹ Hilburn, *Johnny Cash: The Life*, 124.

³⁶² Author interview, July 12, 2018.

³⁶³ [No author], "Pills Hospitalize Cowboy Singer's Wife," *Los Angeles Times*, August 19, 1956, 59.

³⁶⁴ [No author], "Wife of Singer Fights Ex-Mate to Keep Sons," *Los Angeles Times*, October 25, 1956, 2.

³⁶⁵ [No author], "Singer Merle Travis Weds Wife Again," *Sacramento Bee*, November 9, 1956, 17.

³⁶⁶ Author interview, July 22, 2018.

³⁶⁷ [No author], "Merle Travis and Wife Win Custody of 2 Boys," *Los Angeles Times*, December 6, 1956, 69.

³⁶⁸ Author interview, July 13, 2018.

³⁶⁹ Author interview, July 22, 2018.

³⁷⁰ Williams, *Girls, Guns, and Guitars*, 149.

³⁷¹ Author interview, July 12, 2018.

³⁷² Author interview, July 13, 2018.

³⁷³ Author interview, July 13, 2018.

³⁷⁴ Author interview, July 13, 2018.

³⁷⁵ Mark Humphrey interview with Merle Travis, June 21, 1979, courtesy Mark Humphrey.

³⁷⁶ Letter to Merle Travis c/o Pacific Music Supply, dated March 17, 1959, courtesy Thomas Sims Archives.

³⁷⁷ Mitch Greenhill, "15 Years Old: Divided Loyalties with Merle Travis," from the forthcoming book *Running with the Herd*, quoted in the CD liner notes for *Merle Travis—Live in Boston* (Rounder Records, 2003), used with permission from Mitch Greenhill.

³⁷⁸ Mark Humphrey interview with Merle Travis, June 21, 1979, courtesy Mark Humphrey.

³⁷⁹ Mark Humphrey interview with Merle Travis, June 21, 1979, courtesy Mark Humphrey.

³⁸⁰ Introduction to James Burton, "Cannonball Rag," audio from CD, *Town Hall Party 1958–1961* (Country Routes RFDCD 15).

[381] Author interview, July 22, 2018.

[382] Author interview, July 22, 2018.

[383] Author interview, July 16–17, 2018.

[384] Merlene and Cindy Travis archives.

[385] Author interview, July 12, 2018.

[386] Author interview, July 22, 2018.

[387] From Charles Wolfe's liner notes for *The Louvin Brothers—Close Harmony* box set, Bear Family BCD 15561. Used by permission of Bear Family Records.

[388] Author interview, May 5, 2019.

[389] Charles K. Wolfe interview with Louis "Grandpa" Jones and Ramona Jones, July 5, 1993, WOLFE-02036–1, Charles K. Wolfe Audio Library, Center for Popular Music, Middle Tennessee State University, Murfreesboro.

[390] Ed Kahn interview with Merle Travis, July 10, 1961.

[391] Author interview, July 12, 2018.

[392] Pat Travis Eatherly, *In Search of My Father* (Nashville: Broadman, 1987), 83–85.

[393] Douglas B. Green interview with Merle Travis, October 17, 1975, CMF Oral History Project.

[394] Author interview, July 12, 2018.

[395] Lee Jeffriess oral interview with Speedy West, 1992, Speedy West's home, Broken Arrow, Oklahoma, recounted to the author, 2018.

[396] Author interview, July 13, 2018.

[397] Author interview, October 11, 2018.

[398] Ed Kahn interview with Bettie Travis, January 30, 1995, pp. 6–7.

[399] Letter dated October 4, 1962, Merlene and Cindy Travis archives.

[400] Letter dated February 7, 1963, Merlene and Cindy Travis archives.

[401] Ed Kahn interview with Bettie Travis, January 30, 1995, pp. 4–5.

[402] Letter dated April 22, 1963, Merlene and Cindy Travis archives.

[403] Mark Humphrey interview with Merle Travis, June 21, 1979, courtesy Mark Humphrey.

[404] Shipping invoice dated June 17, 1964, Merlene and Cindy Travis archives.

405 Author interview, 2010.

406 Music Center ad, *Louisville Courier-Journal*, December 13, 1964, 34.

407 Rick Nielsen, "1963 Guild Merle Travis," *Guitar Aficionado* No. 1 (Summer 2009): 98.

408 Herb Parker, "Muhlenberg County Honors Merle Travis," *Owensboro Messenger-Inquirer*, December 1, 1963, 15.

409 Author interview, October 13–14, 2018.

410 Author interview, July 12, 2018.

411 Letter to Vada Adler dated January 13, 1964, Merlene and Cindy Travis archives.

412 Letter dated March 1, 1964, Merlene and Cindy Travis archives.

413 Author interview, July 16–17, 2018.

414 Ed Kahn interview with John Melvin Travis, May 19, 1986, Ed Kahn Collection, box 3, folder 18, #20360, Southern Folklife Collection, Wilson Library, University of North Carolina, Chapel Hill.

415 Author interview, July 12, 2018.

416 Letter to Ed Kahn, undated but probably 1980s, Ed Kahn Collection, box 3, folder 18, collection 20360, Southern Folklife Collection, Wilson Library, University of North Carolina, Chapel Hill.

417 Letter dated December 26, 1964, Merlene and Cindy Travis archives.

418 Author interview, July 16–17, 2018.

419 Letter dated August 18, 1966, given to the author by Michael Robinson.

420 Letter dated September 20, 1967, given to the author by Michael Robinson.

421 Author interview, July 16–17, 2018.

422 Divorce agreement from Rolston, Duchowny & Fields to Bettie Travis, March 15, 1965, given to the author by Michael Robinson.

423 [No author], "Writer's Wife Takes 'Advice'—Gets Divorce," *Los Angeles Times*, June 8, 1965, 98.

424 Ed Kahn interview with Bettie Travis, January 30, 1995, p. 3.

425 Ed Kahn interview with Bettie Travis, January 30, 1995, pp. 1–2.

426 Author interview, July 12, 2018.

427 William T. Anderson, "Merle Travis," *BMI (The Many Worlds of Music)*, November, 1967, 12.

[428] Ed Kahn interview notes with Joe Allison, April 4, 1994, Ed Kahn Collection, box 3, folder 18, #20360, Southern Folklife Collection, University of North Carolina, Chapel Hill.

[429] Ed Kahn interview with Bettie Travis, January 30, 1995, p. 3.

[430] Letters given by Michael Robinson to the author.

[431] Author interview, December 28, 2006.

[432] Ed Kahn interview with Bettie Travis, January 30, 1995, p. 2.

[433] Author interview, July 16–17, 2018.

[434] Author interview, May 4, 2020.

[435] Ed Kahn interview with Bettie Travis, January 30, 1995, p. 7.

[436] Merle Travis, "Music Star Adds Pencil to Guitar," *Nashville Tennessean*, January 22, 1967, 3.

[437] Letter dated January 29, 1966, given by Michael Robinson to the author.

[438] Letter dated February 9, 1966, given by Michael Robinson to the author.

[439] Letter dated February 11, 1966, given by Michael Robinson to the author.

[440] Letter dated February 13, 1966, given by Michael Robinson to the author.

[441] Letter dated February 15, 1966, given from Michael Robinson to the author.

[442] Author interview, May 14, 2020.

[443] Author's collection.

[444] Author interview, May 4, 2020.

[445] Mark Humphrey interview with Merle Travis, June 21, 1979, courtesy Mark Humphrey.

[446] Author interview, October 13–14, 2018.

[447] Gary Williams interview with Merle Travis, March 20, 1974, used with permission of Gary Williams.

[448] Letter dated September 16, 1966, courtesy Merlene and Cindy Travis archives.

[449] Ed Kahn interview with Bettie Travis, January 30, 1995.

[450] Author interview, October 17, 2018.

[451] Gary Williams interview with Merle Travis, March 20, 1974, used with permission of Gary Williams.

452 Author interview, October 13–14, 2018.

453 *The Johnny Cash Show*, season 2, episode 26.

454 Introduction to Christopher Wren, *Winners Got Scars Too* (New York: Dial, 1973), 2–3.

455 Author interview, September 25, 2018.

456 Author interview, March 26, 2020.

457 Mark Humphrey interview with Merle Travis, June 21, 1979, courtesy Mark Humphrey.

458 Letter dated May 11, 1981, courtesy Dave Stewart.

459 Ed Kahn interview with Bettie Travis, January 30, 1995, p. 5.

460 Author interviews, July 12 and July 16–17, 2018.

461 Author interview, May 4, 2020.

462 Author interview, October 22, 2019.

463 Author interview, October 22, 2019.

464 Mark Humphrey interview with Merle Travis, June 21, 1979, courtesy Mark Humphrey.

465 Author interview, July 12, 2018.

466 Author interview, July 12, 2018.

467 Cassette tape courtesy Eddie Pennington.

468 Letter dated August 13, 1973, Merlene and Cindy Travis archive.

469 Douglas B. Green interview with Merle Travis, October 17, 1975, CMF Oral History Project.

470 Text to the author, April 29, 2020.

471 Author interview, October 13–14, 2018.

472 Author interview, October 13–14, 2018.

473 Ed Kahn interview with Bettie Travis, January 30, 1995, p. 10.

474 Ray Campi, "Merle Travis Remembered, Part Three" *Now Dig This*, Issue 140, November 1994, 29-30, used with permission of Ray Campi.

475 Letter dated July 1974, Merlene and Cindy Travis archives.

476 Chet Atkins with William Neely, *Country Gentleman* (Chicago: Henry Regnery, 1974), 105.

[477] Mark Humphrey interview with Merle Travis, June 21, 1979, courtesy Mark Humphrey.

[478] Author interview, October 13–14, 2018.

[479] Author interview, September 24, 2019.

[480] Author interview, October 13–14, 2018.

[481] Chet Flippo, "Merle Travis, Guitar Legend," *Rolling Stone*, June 19, 1975, 24.

[482] Ward Sinclair, "Travis and Rager Get Together to Play the Music They Invented," *Louisville Courier-Journal*, August 28, 1976, 6.

[483] Text to the author, April 28, 2020.

[484] Bob Carlsen, "Singer Finds Happiness," *Santa Clarita Signal*, July 9, 1976, 1, 3.

[485] Author interview, March 3, 2019.

[486] Douglas B. Green interview with Merle Travis, October 17, 1975, CMF Oral History Project.

[487] Author interview, July 12, 2018.

[488] Ed Kahn interview with Bettie Travis, January 30, 1995, p. 6.

[489] Author interview, March 26, 2020.

[490] Author interview, March 3, 2019.

[491] Author interview, October 13–14, 2018.

[492] Author interview, October 13–14, 2018.

[493] Letter dated April 1976, Merlene and Cindy Travis archives.

[494] Baxter, "Merle Travis: The Man, the Music," 34.

[495] Note to the author, 2018.

[496] Letter dated December 9, 1976, Merlene and Cindy Travis archives.

[497] Author interview, July 12, 2018.

[498] Ed Kahn interview with Bettie Travis, January 30, 1995, p. 10.

[499] Williams, *Girls, Guns, and Guitars*, 320–29.

[500] Author interview, September 25, 2018.

[501] Merlene and Cindy Travis archives.

[502] Notes dated August 17, 1977, Merlene and Cindy Travis archives.

[503] Ralph Emery interview cassette tape with Merle Travis, Country Music Hall of Fame induction ceremony, October 10, 1977, Charles K. Wolfe Audio Library, WOLFE-00772–1, Center for Popular Music, Middle Tennessee State University, Murfreesboro.

[504] Author interview, September 25, 2018.

[505] Merlene and Cindy Travis archives.

[506] Eddie Pennington, email to the author, April 12, 2020.

[507] Ed Kahn interview with Merlene Travis, April 18, 1988, Ed Kahn Collection, box 3, folder 18, collection 20360, Southern Folklife Collection, Wilson Library, University of North Carolina, Chapel Hill.

[508] Notes dated 1977–81, Merlene and Cindy Travis archives.

[509] Travis Eatherly, *In Search of My Father*, 173–74.

[510] Letter undated but mid-1978, Merlene and Cindy Travis archives.

[511] Vern Nelson, "Country Music and Stage Review," *South Pasadena Review*, February 1, 1978, 10.

[512] Ed Kahn interview with Bettie Travis, January 30, 1995, p. 10.

[513] Author interview, March 3, 2019.

[514] Author interviews, September 25, 2018, and March 27, 2020.

[515] Author interview, October 13–14, 2018.

[516] Author interview, September 25, 2018.

[517] Email to the author, May 11, 2020.

[518] Letter from Merle Travis to Lou Ukleson, February 28, 1979, Merlene and Cindy Travis archives.

[519] Author interview, March 27, 2020.

[520] Mark Humphrey interview with Merle Travis, June 21, 1979, courtesy Mark Humphrey.

[521] Author interview, March 27, 2020.

[522] Author interview, March 27, 2020.

[523] Merle Travis, "Dorothy," Silverhill Music BMI.

[524] Letter dated September 18, 1979, Merlene and Cindy Travis archives.

[525] Author interview, March 26, 2020.

[526] Author interview, July 12, 2018.

[527] Author interview, October 13–14, 2018.

[528] Warren Kice, *Hank Thompson: My Side of Life* (Fort Worth: Branch-Smith Printing, 2007), 242.

[529] Author interview, September 25, 2018.

[530] Author interview, September 25, 2018.

[531] Mossman ad, 1981, Merlene and Cindy Travis archives.

[532] Alvarez-Yairi ad, 1980, Merlene and Cindy Travis archives.

[533] Letter dated May 11, 1981, courtesy Dave Stewart.

[534] Author interview, April 29, 2020.

[535] Author interview, April 29, 2020.

[536] Email to author, April 10, 2020.

[537] [No author], "Merle Travis Donates Guitar to Hall of Fame," *Nashville Tennessean*, October 20, 1982, 19.

[538] Author interview, March 27, 2020.

[539] Letter dated May 14, 1981, Merlene and Cindy Travis archives.

[540] Author interview, March 27, 2020.

[541] Raphael, "Merle Travis Remembered—The Last Interview," 28.

[542] Stuart, *Pilgrims*, 125–27. Lyrics to "I Am A Pilgrim," words and music by Merle Travis. Copyright 1941, 1969 Universal-Duchess Music Corporation, a Divison of Universal Studios, Inc. Copyright renewed. International Copyright secured. All rights reserved.

[543] Author interview, October 13–14, 2018.

[544] Author interview, March 27, 2020.

[545] Mark Humphrey, "Record Mix," *Los Angeles Reader*, December 1981, unknown page (taken from press clipping), Merlene and Cindy Travis archives.

[546] Letter dated July 31, 1981, Merlene and Cindy Travis archives.

[547] Charles K. Wolfe interview cassette tape with Louis "Grandpa" Jones, June 22, 1981, Charles K. Wolfe Audio Library, WOLFE-02025–1, Center for Popular Music, Middle Tennessee State University, Murfreesboro.

[548] Eddie Pennington, email to the author, April 13, 2020.

[549] Travis Eatherly, *In Search of My Father*, 187–90.

[550] Letter dated September 16, 1981, Merlene and Cindy Travis archives.

551 Email to the author, May 11, 2020.

552 Letter dated November 3, 1981, Merlene and Cindy Travis archives.

553 Letter dated November 16, 1981, Merlene and Cindy Travis archives.

554 [No author], "Merle Travis Here Christmas Day," *Waco Tribune-Herald*, December 18, 1981, 6, Merlene and Cindy Travis archives.

555 Author interview, October 17, 2018.

556 "Travis Travelins," undated but 1982, Merlene and Cindy Travis archives.

557 "Travis Travelins," undated but 1982, Merlene and Cindy Travis archives.

558 Author interview, March 27, 2020.

559 Author interview, October 13–14, 2018.

560 Author interview, October 13–14, 2018.

561 Norman Rowe, "Merle Travis Disc Spotlights Blues," *Richmond Times-Dispatch*, January 4, 1987, 4.

562 Letters to the Editor, *Bee-Picayune* (Beeville, TX), November 4, 1982, unknown page (taken from press clipping), Merlene and Cindy Travis archives.

563 Author interview, March 28, 2019.

564 Author interview, March 27, 2020.

565 Email to the author, April 12, 2020.

566 Letter dated December 27, 1983, Eatherly Family Archives.

567 Hank Penny on Cary Ginell, *Cary's Country Store—Tribute to Travis Part One*, featuring Hank Penny, Tex Williams, and Inez Wakely, KCSN, October 24, 1983, courtesy Cary Ginell.

568 Email to the author, April 1, 2020.

569 Email to the author, April 12, 2020.

570 Keith Lawrence, "Merle Travis 'Found His Rainbow's End,'" *Owensboro Messenger-Inquirer*, October 24, 1983, 15.

571 Bill Powell, "Songwriter's Pals, Admirers Share Stories of a Fine Man," *Louisville Courier-Journal*, October 24, 1983, 11.

572 Email to author, April 1, 2020.

573 Merle Travis jam session cassette tape with John Hartford no. 3, Charles K. Wolfe Audio Library, WOLFE-01048–1, Center for Popular Music, Middle Tennessee State University, Murfreesboro.

574 Ed Kahn interview with Merlene Travis, April 18, 1988, Ed Kahn Collection, box 3, folder 18, collection 20360, Southern Folklife Collection, Wilson Library, University of North Carolina, Chapel Hill.

575 Author interview, October 6, 2018.

576 Email to the author, May 11, 2020.

577 Author interview, May 4, 2020.